lonely planet

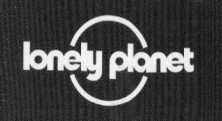

Etain O'Carroll, Aaron Anderson,
Marc Di Duca

Cycling
BRITAIN

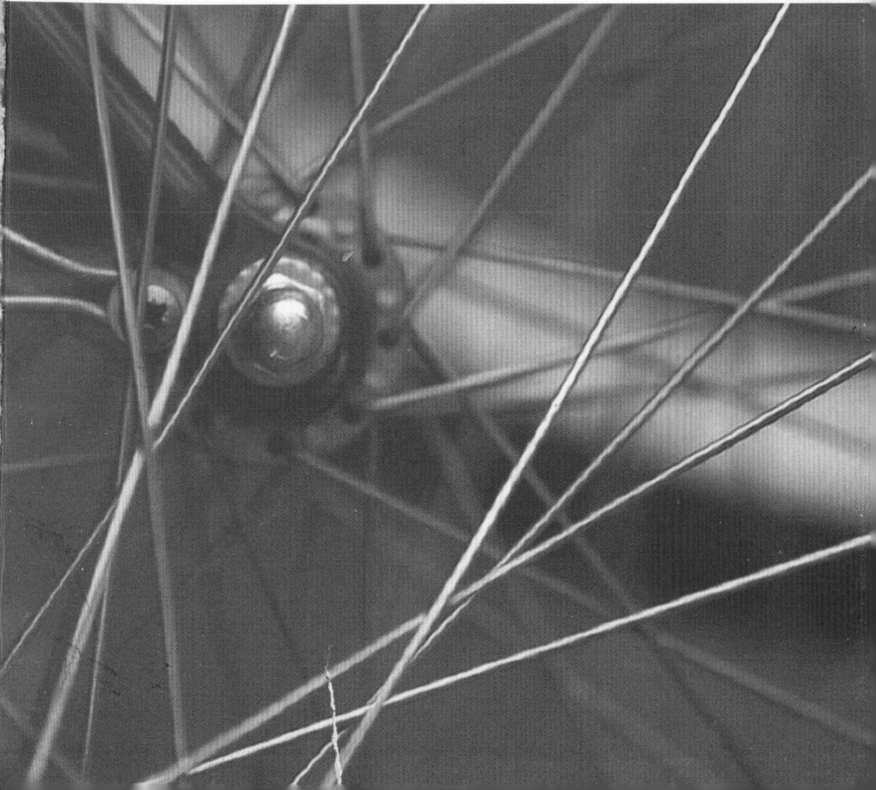

LONDON

 LONDON EYE

Spy down on London's most famous landmarks and get a fix on the city's winding streets with a bird's eye view of the metropolis from the stunning London Eye (p44). Perched on the bank of the Thames, this is the world's largest sightseeing wheel and the perfect place to plan your trips across the city.

2 CHANGING OF THE GUARDS, BUCKINGHAM PALACE

Join the throng of tourists waiting for that quintessential London attraction, the changing of the guards at Buckingham Palace (p41). Arrive early if you're hoping to snap a picture of the bright red uniforms and the famous bearskin hats, otherwise wait for the crowds to disperse and snap one of Her Majesty's humble abode instead.

3 HAMPTON COURT PALACE

Follow the quiet, leafy lanes southwest of the city to the 16th-century Hampton Court Palace (p50), a grandiose vestige of Tudor England. Let costumed historians lead you around the lavish State Apartments, the Great Hall and the Tudor kitchens before losing yourself in the 60 acres of riverside gardens.

4 WEST END

Get a glimpse of London's soul as you wander the streets of the infamous West End (p44) from Soho to the Strand. A heady mixture of consumerism and culture, you'll find museums, galleries and historic buildings fighting for space with plush hotels, famous theatres and tacky tourist traps.

Contents

Land's End to John O'Groats 305

Cyclists Directory 348

Transport 360

Your Bicycle 369

Health & Safety 389

Glossary 397

Behind the Scenes 400

Index 405

CYCLING REGIONS - INDEX MAP

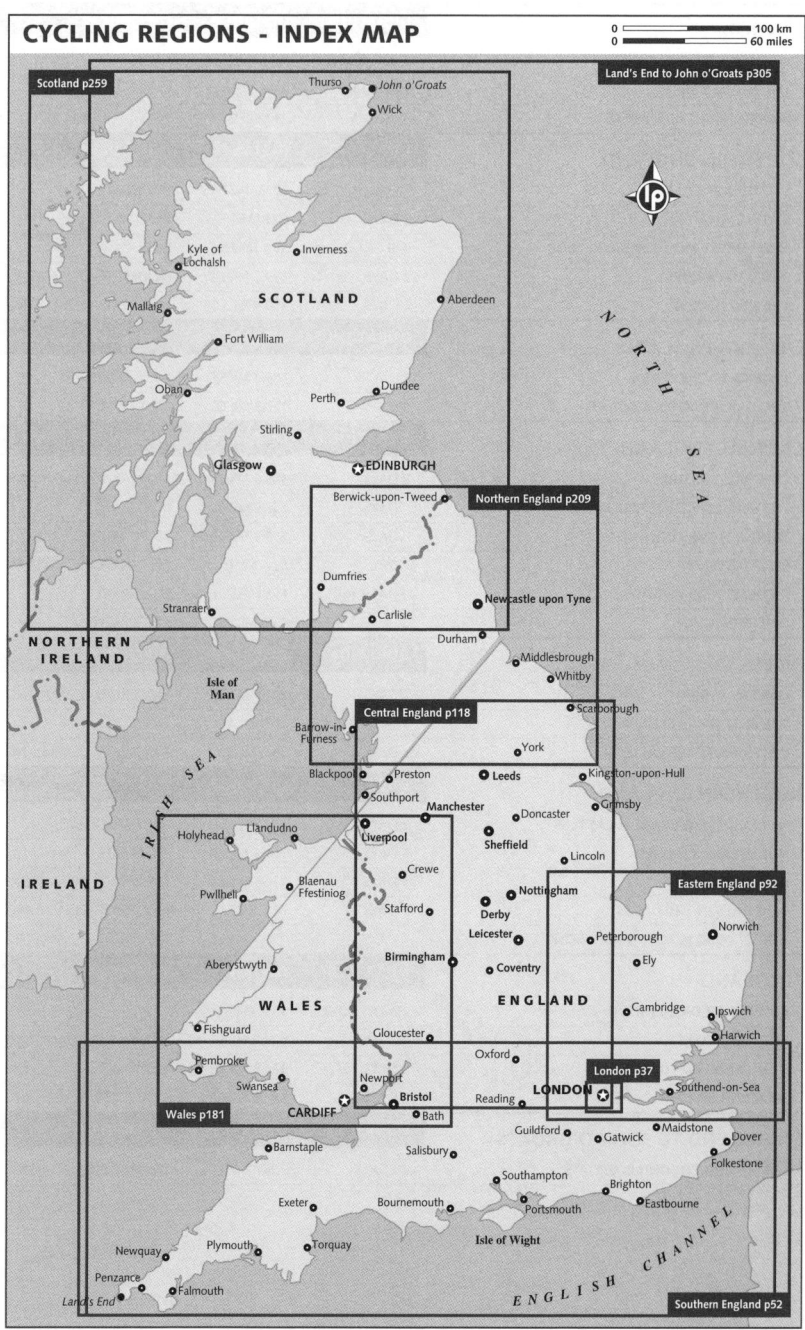

0   100 km
0   60 miles

Scotland p259

Land's End to John o'Groats p305

Thurso
John o'Groats
Wick

Kyle of
Lochalsh
Inverness

Mallaig

SCOTLAND
Aberdeen

Fort William

Oban
Dundee
Perth

Stirling

Glasgow
EDINBURGH

Berwick-upon-Tweed
Northern England p209

Dumfries
Newcastle upon Tyne
Carlisle
Durham

NORTHERN
IRELAND
Middlesbrough
Whitby

Stranraer

Isle of
Man
Scarborough

Barrow-in-
Furness
Central England p118

York

Blackpool
Preston
Leeds
Kingston-upon-Hull

Southport
Manchester
Doncaster
Grimsby

IRISH SEA

Holyhead
Llandudno
Liverpool
Sheffield
Lincoln

Pwllheli
Blaenau
Ffestiniog
Crewe
Nottingham
Eastern England p92

Stafford
Derby
Leicester
Peterborough
Norwich

Aberystwyth
Birmingham
Ely

Coventry
Cambridge

WALES
ENGLAND
Ipswich

Fishguard
Gloucester
Harwich

Pembroke
Oxford
London p37

Newport
Southend-on-Sea
Swansea
Bristol
LONDON

Wales p181
CARDIFF
Bath
Reading

Barnstaple
Guildford
Gatwick
Maidstone
Dover

Salisbury
Folkestone

Southampton
Brighton

Exeter
Bournemouth
Portsmouth
Eastbourne

Newquay
Plymouth
Torquay
Isle of Wight

Penzance
Land's End
Falmouth
ENGLISH CHANNEL
Southern England p52

NORTH SEA

IRELAND

Table of Rides

LONDON	DURATION	DISTANCE	DIFFICULTY
WESTMINSTER & THE CITY	1–3½ HOURS	8.5 MILES	EASY
THE THAMES EAST	2–5 HOURS	9.5 MILES	EASY
RICHMOND & THE THAMES	3–4 HOURS	24 MILES	EASY

SOUTHERN ENGLAND	DURATION	DISTANCE	DIFFICULTY
SOUTHEAST COAST	4 DAYS	193.8 MILES	MODERATE
RYDING WIGHT	2 DAYS	53 MILES	EASY–MODERATE
NEW FOREST MOUNTAIN BIKE RIDE	4–6 HOURS	39.2 MILES	EASY
AVON TO THAMES	3 DAYS	139.6 MILES	MODERATE–DEMANDING
THE SOUTHWEST	7 DAYS	350.4 MILES	MODERATE–DEMANDING

EASTERN ENGLAND	DURATION	DISTANCE	DIFFICULTY
THAMES TO THE WASH	3 DAYS	158.3 MILES	EASY–MODERATE
SUFFOLK & NORFOLK COAST	4 DAYS	175.3 MILES	EASY–MODERATE

CENTRAL ENGLAND	DURATION	DISTANCE	DIFFICULTY
CENTRAL EXPLORER	8 DAYS	385.6 MILES	MODERATE–DEMANDING
THE MARCHES, CHESHIRE & LANCASHIRE	5 DAYS	258.9 MILES	MODERATE
THROUGH THE MIDLANDS	3 DAYS	152.1 MILES	MODERATE
PEAK DISTRICT	2 DAYS	83.4 MILES	MODERATE–DEMANDING
A COTSWOLDS TRIANGLE	4 DAYS	195 MILES	MODERATE
CHILTERN RIDGE	3–4½ HOURS	45.2 MILES	MODERATE

WALES	DURATION	DISTANCE	DIFFICULTY
LÔN LAS CYMRU	7 DAYS	261.7 MILES	MODERATE–DEMANDING
THE BEST OF ANGLESEY	1½–2½ HOURS	16.9 MILES	EASY
VIEWS FROM THE VALLEY	2 DAYS	36.2 MILES	MODERATE–DEMANDING

NORTHERN ENGLAND	DURATION	DISTANCE	DIFFICULTY
NORTHUMBRIA COAST & CASTLES	2 DAYS	107 MILES	EASY–MODERATE
NORTHERN EXPLORER	5 DAYS	201.5 MILES	MODERATE
SEA TO SEA (C2C)	4 DAYS	130.6 MILES	MODERATE–DEMANDING
TWO DAYS IN THE DALES	2 DAYS	66.8 MILES	MODERATE–DEMANDING
NORTH YORK MOORS & MANSIONS	4 DAYS	139.7 MILES	MODERATE–DEMANDING

SCOTLAND	DURATION	DISTANCE	DIFFICULTY
EDINBURGH ORIENTATION	1½–2½ HOURS	15.7 MILES	EASY
THE WEST COAST	10 DAYS	424.7 MILES	MODERATE–DEMANDING
HIGHLANDS CIRCUIT	3 DAYS	126.8 MILES	MODERATE
SCOTTISH BORDERS	3 DAYS	125.6 MILES	MODERATE

LAND'S END TO JOHN O'GROATS	DURATION	DISTANCE	DIFFICULTY
LAND'S END TO JOHN O'GROATS	20 DAYS	1051.2 MILES	DEMANDING

The Authors

ETAIN O'CARROLL

Travel writer and photographer Etain O'Carroll grew up in small-town Ireland and regular childhood trips to England were tinged with the excitement of eating gammon and pineapple in motorway service stations and meeting all those cousins with funny accents. In between were the trips to the chocolate-box villages, stately homes, massive castles and ruined abbeys. Now living in Oxford, Etain's childish awe has become a long-term appreciation for the fine architecture, bucolic countryside and rich heritage of her adopted home. Etain has worked on the last three editions of Lonely Planet's *England* and *Great Britain* and cycles on a daily basis.

LONELY PLANET AUTHORS

Why is our travel information the best in the world? It's simple: our authors are passionate, dedicated travellers. They don't take freebies in exchange for positive coverage so you can be sure the advice you're given is impartial. They travel widely to all the popular spots, and off the beaten track. They don't research using just the internet or phone. They discover new places not included in any other guidebook. They personally visit thousands of hotels, restaurants, palaces, trails, galleries, temples and more. They speak with dozens of locals every day to make sure you get the kind of insider knowledge only a local could tell you. They take pride in getting all the details right, and in telling it how it is. Think you can do it? Find out how at **lonelyplanet.com**.

AARON ANDERSON

Aaron has been messing around with bikes since he was a kid – one of his first jobs was in a bicycle shop. Although he later made the switch to professional micro-brewer and then Lonely Planet travel writer, he never gave up his passion for riding. *Cycling Britain* was Aaron's 8th Lonely Planet title. He has also worked on the first edition of *Grand Canyon, Arizona & New Mexico Trips* (writing all the cycling content) as well as *Madagascar & Comoros, Washington DC City Guide* and *Thailand*. When not on the road, he lives in Boulder, Colorado with his wife, Becca Blond, their bulldog Duke and, of course, his two bikes.

MY FAVORITE RIDE

When it comes to riding bikes, I like fat tyres best. There is just something about cycling off-road - bombing fast down rocky single-track or pushing my physical limits on steep leg-buster climbs - that really appeals to me. That said, my favorite ride is the Brecon Beacons Gap (p203) mountain bike ride in Wales. This 24.1 mile romp starts and ends in the attractive town of Brecon, and includes fantastic views - at one point you fee like you're cycling through a Norwegian fjords with fantastic views of pine-covered hill-sides rising from the edge of the Brecon Canal's shimmering edge.

MARC DI DUCA

No sooner had seven-year-old Marc's stabilis-ers come off than he was pedalling frantically alongside his parents on a cycling holiday through the heather-clad hills of North Yorkshire, tackling monster gradients on little fat wheels. Three decades, several countries and many bikes later, Marc can still find no better way to escape life's hectic pace than to take to the hills on two wheels. He has cycled his way through several countries including Austria, Germany, and the Czech Republic where he helped plot out new cycle routes for the country's national cycle network. But for Marc there's no better cycling destination than the dales and dunes of his native northern England with its big skies and desolate hills. Always on the lookout for thrilling places to ride, his latest biking dream is to ride across the ice of Siberia's Lake Baikal.

Route Descriptions, Maps & Charts

CYCLING ROUTES

This guide covers the best areas for cycle touring in Britain. The rides do not traverse the country from north to south or east to west, but have been selected because they are scenic, pass through interesting towns or historic areas, are lightly used by cars and easy to reach by public transport. Rides vary from one to 20 days, catering to both the novice and the experienced cyclist, and link easily with one another, offering continuity for extended trips. Various transport options for getting to and from the rides are suggested.

In most cases, the rides have been designed to make carrying camping gear and food optional. Each ride is broken into a set number of days, with accommodation and food options available at each day's destination. In some cases alternative destinations are offered.

Cyclists can use this book as an introduction and planning tool, as well as an on-the-road guide. We hope that once cyclists become familiar with local circumstances they will start planning their own routes, too.

Times & Distances

Each ride is divided into stages, and we suggest a day be spent on each stage. In some cases the distance for a particular stage is relatively short, but attractions en route, or nearby, warrant spending extra time – distance junkies may decide to condense two stages into one day.

The directions for each day's ride are given in terms of distance (in miles) from the starting point (specified on the cue sheets).

A suggested riding time has been given for each day's riding. Because individual riding speed varies widely, these should be used as a guide. They only take into account actual riding time – not time taken for rest stops, taking photographs, eating or visiting a museum – and are generally based on an average riding speed of between 6mph and 12mph.

Ride Difficulty

Each ride is graded according to its difficulty in terms of distance, terrain, road surface and navigation. The grade appears in the Table of Rides at the beginning of the book and at the start of each ride.

Grading is unavoidably subjective and is intended as a guide only; the degree of difficulty of a particular ride may vary according to the weather, the weight in your panniers, whether children are cycling, pre-trip training or how tired and hungry you are. It's also worth keeping in mind that Britain has an intricate network of roads, and 'easy' navigation here might be considered quite complex in, say, Australia or New Zealand.

Easy These rides involve no more than a few hours riding each day, over mostly flat terrain with good, sealed surfaces. They are navigationally straightforward.

Moderate These rides present a moderate challenge to someone of average fitness; they are likely to include some hills, three to five hours of riding, and may involve some unsealed roads and/or complex navigation.

Demanding These are for fit riders who want a challenge, and involve long daily distances and/or challenging climbs, may negotiate rough and remote roads, and present navigational challenges.

MAPS & PROFILES

Most rides in this book have an accompanying map that shows the route, services provided in towns en route, attractions and possible alternative routes and side trips, depending on the map scale. The maps are based on the best available references, sometimes combined with GPS data collected in the field. They are intended to show the general routes only of the rides we describe and are not detailed enough in themselves for route finding or navigation. For greater detail, we also recommend the most suitable commercial map available in the 'Maps' section of each ride.

Most chapters also have a regional map showing the gateway towns or cities, principal transport routes and other major features. Map symbols are interpreted in the legend on the inside front cover of this book.

CUE SHEETS

Route directions are given in a series of brief 'cues', which point out features en route and tell you at what mileage point to change direction. These pages could be photocopied or cut out for on-the-road reference and used with a recommended map. The only other thing you need is a cycle computer.

To make the cue sheets as brief and simple to understand as possible, we've developed a series of symbols (see the Map Legend on the cover flap) and laid down the following rule:

Once your route is following a particular road, continue on that road until the cue sheet tells you otherwise.

Follow the road first mentioned in the cues even though it may cross a highway, shrink to a lane, change name (we generally only include the first name, and sometimes the last), wind, duck and climb its way across the country. Rely on us to tell you when to turn off from it.

Because the cue sheets rely on an accurate odometer reading we suggest you disconnect your cycle computer (pop it out of the housing or turn the magnet away from the fork-mounted sensor) whenever you deviate from the main route.

Planning

Cycling in Britain is immensely rewarding: there's a huge variety of terrain with plenty of challenges for serious cyclists and yet stunning scenery accessible even to novices. Best of all it's pretty hassle free. You won't have to negotiate large distances between destinations, so there's no need to struggle with huge bags of supplies, no fear of running out of inner tubes half-way up a mountainside, and no need to rough it (unless, of course, you really want to). Despite Britain's dense population, there are also plenty of quiet country roads and over 10,000 miles of marked cycle trails. You'll find villages with cosy hotels and B&Bs, friendly bike shops and well-stocked supermarkets everywhere you go, so even if you forget your whole kit, you can buy it on arrival.

Although Britain is by no means a cheap destination, you can easily keep costs down by planning carefully, doing some camping and being willing to cook for yourself. Cycling is a much-loved and well-supported sport in Britain, so you've little to worry about except deciding where to go and enjoying the ride.

This book focuses specifically on cycling related information and destinations. You'll find more general travel information in Lonely Planet's *Great Britain* guide, which gives in-depth coverage of travel in Britain, as well as information on a huge variety of destinations and attractions across the country.

WHEN TO CYCLE

The weather is a constant topic of conversation in Britain. It's not so much that it's in any way extreme but it is always changing. You'll go from beautiful sunny skies to downpours, hail and thunder in the blink of an eye and just as you get out all your wet weather gear the sun will come back out again. Despite its unpredictable nature, there are seasonal patterns to the weather. Temperatures are higher in summer (June to August), and there's normally more sunshine, though July and August, along with the winter months, are often the rainiest of the year. Conversely, winter (November to February) may enjoy fantastic clear spells between bouts of rain or snow, while spring (March to May) or autumn (September to October) can often produce the finest weather of the year. There are also north-south variations: southern England might be chilly, while northern Scotland enjoys a heat wave. Or vice versa. Be prepared for anything and you won't get a surprise.

For cycling, April to October is the best period to visit Britain. You'll get the pick of the weather, long, long days and plenty of cycling events and festivals happening around the country. However, July and August are school summer holidays and you'll find attractions and accommodation very busy and peak season prices in force. Roads also get very busy during this season. For the best all round experience, plan to visit from between April and late June, or from early September to mid-October. Although April and October are less busy you'll have to take your chances with the weather.

Overall, the least hospitable months for cyclists are November to February. It's cold in the south, very cold in the north, and daylight is short. In Scotland, north Wales and the hills of northern England, roads can sometimes be closed by snow. Reaching the islands off the Scottish mainland can also be a problem as high winds disrupt ferry services.

WHAT TO BRING

Maximum flexibility on the road comes from carrying everything – including camping gear – on the bike. But you'll need to choose lightweight clothing and equipment if this is what you decide to do. Fortunately the short distance between towns and villages reduces your need to carry food; generally you'll only need a day's supply at most.

For more weather fact and figures see the Climate Charts (p535).

The great choice of accommodation in Britain also makes touring without camping equipment an easy option. You'll need to be slightly more organised when planning a route and – if touring in midsummer – need to book accommodation in advance, but riding without a tent and sleeping bag is a great weight saver.

If you choose to join a supported tour you'll probably have to carry little more than water, snacks and wet-weather gear. It's hardly independent travel, but it sure feels good on long uphill climbs.

EQUIPMENT CHECKLIST

This list is a general guide to the things that might be useful on a bike tour. Don't forget to take on board enough water and food to see you safely between towns.

Bike Clothing

- cycling gloves
- cycling shoes and socks
- helmet and visor
- long-sleeved shirt or cycling top
- padded cycling shorts (knicks)
- sunglasses
- T-shirt or short-sleeved cycling top
- high-vis vest
- waterproof jacket and pants

Off-Bike Clothing

- change of clothing
- sandals
- swimming gear
- sunhat
- underwear and socks

Equipment

- bike lights (rear and front) with spare batteries
- elastic cord
- camera and spare film/memory cards
- cycle computer
- day-pack
- medical kit* and toiletries
- mosquito repellent
- padlock
- panniers and waterproof liners
- pocket knife
- sewing kit
- sleeping sheet
- small handlebar bag and/or map case
- small towel
- sunscreen
- tool kit, pump and spares*
- torch (flashlight) with spare batteries and globe
- water containers
- water purification tablets, iodine or filter

*see the boxed texts First-Aid Kit p389 and Spares & Tool Kit p375 for more information on what to bring.

MOUNTAIN BIKING

Britain hosts a lively mountain bike scene, with tens of thousands of recreational riders and more than 100,000 miles of paths, unsealed tracks and lanes. The bridleway network, which accounts for 90% of the off-road trails around Britain, is open to cyclists and clearly marked on OS Landranger maps.

Mountain bikers can also use two minority types of track – Roads Used as Public Paths (RUPPs), and Byways Open to All Traffic (BOATs). These occur only in certain parts of the country and are also marked on OS maps. Unclassified Country Roads (UCRs) are also legal for mountain bike riding. Country parks will often have dedicated tracks and signboards showing where you can ride.

In Scotland you can ride on legally recognised rights of way and in open country there is generally open access that assumes you will ride responsibly and observe seasonal restrictions regarding hunting, game and wildlife.

There are an increasing number of trails across the country and a good place to go for information is the UK website of the **International Mountain Biking Association** (www.imba .org.uk). The **CTC** (www.ctc.org.uk) also has information on trails and events and **British Cycling** (www.britishcycling.org.uk) is the place to go for competition news.

Clothing

For maximum comfort you're always best off using cycling-specific clothing, waterproofs and footwear. Wear padded Lycra bike shorts ('knicks') and lightweight, breathable cycling tops for the most comfort. For cool or very sunny conditions long-sleeved tops are best. Waterproofs are essential when cycling in Britain, even in mid-summer. Breathable, waterproof overpants are a good idea but in the summer many cyclists prefer to wear only a waterproof top and let their knicks get wet. For touring in cooler months lycra tights or padded thermal 'longs' can keep the cold at bay. To make yourself more visible to motorists choose bright colours for all your cycling gear.

Fingerless cycling gloves reduce jarring on your hands, stop sunburn and protect your palms if you fall. Full-finger gloves are a sensible addition for cycling in Britain, even in summertime. You can also get thin polypropylene 'inner' gloves – best worn under regular fingerless gloves – or longer wind- and/or rain-resistant models.

Helmets aren't compulsory in Britain but it's still a good idea to wear one. A cloth cover with a peak to help keep sun and rain off your face, and a legionnaire-style back flap to protect your neck from sunburn can also be helpful. Sunglasses or eye wear with clear protective lenses are essential. They protect your eyes from UV radiation, insects, and from drying out in the wind.

Stiff-soled cycling shoes transfer power more efficiently from pedal stroke to pedal. Soft-soled training shoes lack the same 'drive' and using them can leave you with sore feet. Thermal socks and neoprene booties are useful for cold and/or wet days.

Off the bike, pack as little additional clothing as you can reasonably get away with. Choose colours that will look acceptable without washing, and that will endure a bit of flapping around on your panniers – the unofficial (and very effective) on-the-road clothes-drying rack. Campers need to place greater emphasis on warm clothing. Thermal underwear is warm and compact, and a synthetic fleece jacket is great for warmth. Take only lightweight cotton trousers – you can wear your thermals underneath on a cold night. And don't forget to take a spare pair of shoes.

Bicycle

Obviously the type of bike you'll need depends on the type of riding you intend to do. Jack-of-all-trade hybrid bikes are a good starting point for beginners. The flat handlebars and a saddle position that allows you to sit almost upright make them great for the school run or a trip to the shops. For long-distance cycling however, you'll be much better off with a proper touring bike.

Touring bikes give you all the practical elements you'll need for a long-distance ride combined with the performance of a racing bike. The frame is stiffer than a racing bike and the back wheel stronger in order to carry the extra weight of luggage but you'll also get mudguards, a rear carrier, a lightweight frame, a wide range of gears, powerful brakes and dropped handlebars. Dropped handlebars make it easier for you to work harder on climbs and give a choice of hand positions to relieve fatigue.

If you're planning some serious mountain biking then you'll need a bike specifically designed for this style of riding. Mountain bikes are the biggest sellers in UK bike shops although few are ever used for their real purpose. If you're planning a lot of off-roading you will need the fat knobbly tyres, low gears, straight handlebars, and front suspension of a proper mountain bike. If you're just thinking about the odd tow path and disused railway line, stick to a hybrid or touring bike.

Read up on the types of bicycle and necessary additional equipment for touring in the Your Bicycle chapter (p309) before arriving and go in with a good idea of what you're after. For more information see the Buying or Hiring Locally section, below.

Buying & Hiring Locally

Cycling is steadily gaining in popularity in Britain and you'll find bike shops in almost every town. The range and quality of the goods they stock however can vary enormously. In major centres you'll find bike shops with a good range of bicycles and accessories for all types of cycling, including specialist touring bikes. Smaller towns may only have the essentials, but at least you'll be able to get standard-sized tyre tubes and puncture repair kits.

GUIDED & GROUP RIDES

If you'd like to take the hassle out of planning a cycle tour, have the comfort of a support team to carry your bags or simply fancy joining a group of other cyclists, an organised tour might be for you. There are loads of companies that offer cycling tours in Britain. National operators are listed below; you'll find information on regional cycle tour options in the destination chapters. For more information on cycling organisations see the Cyclist's Directory p348.

Beics Eryri Cycle Tours (www.beics.co.uk) Specialises in Welsh cycle tours, with good coverage of Snowdonia and the Lôn Las Cymru trail.
Bicycle Beano (www.bicycle-beano.co.uk) Offers tours in the South Downs, Welsh borders, Snowdonia, Pembrokeshire and Oxfordshire.
Cotswold Country Cycles (www.cotswoldcountrycycles.com) Organises cycle tours across the Cotswolds.
Country Lanes (www.countrylanes.co.uk) Offers both supported and self-guided tours in the New Forest and the Lake District.
CTC Cycling Holidays (www.cyclingholidays.org) The most comprehensive range of cycling holidays in the UK.
Scottish Cycle Safaris (www.cyclescotland.co.uk) Organises four to seven day tours of Scotland.
Scottish Cycling Holidays (www.scotcycle.co.uk) Self-led, group and tailor-made cycle tours of Scotland.
Wildcat Bike Tours (www.wildcat-bike-tours.co.uk) Coast to coast and mountain tours across Scotland.

A decent bike will cost you about £250 to £400, but for a quality frame and components expect to pay £500 or more, and for a top class touring bike, at least £1000. Some shops sell second-hand equipment or you could try the small ads in the cycling magazines for private sellers.

It's also possible to hire a bike, though most shops cater for short-term hire and offer a range of hybrid and mountain bikes rather than tourers. Rental bikes also vary in age and quality so take your time when choosing. Look for the basics – frame and wheels – to be in good shape, a comfortable saddle (if you haven't brought your own) and quality alloy components. Rates vary according to the type of bike and hire period. Weekly rates are about £35 to £50 with prices reducing for each subsequent week. If you're hiring for an extended period, don't be afraid to haggle. You'll find a list of cycle hire shops on www.cycleweb.co.uk, and details of local outfitters in the destination chapters of this book.

COSTS & MONEY

If you're a global traveller, whatever your budget you'll know that Britain is expensive compared with many other countries. But don't let that put you off. If funds are tight you'll still have a great trip with some forward planning, a bit of shopping around and a modicum of common sense. A lot of stuff is cheap or good value, and some is completely free.

For midrange travellers, basic hotels cost around £50 to £120 for a double room, except in London, where doubles in midrange hotels start at around £80. When it comes to eating, a decent three-course meal with wine in a smart restaurant will set you back by about £25 to £35 per person.

Backpackers on a tight budget need £36 a day for bare survival in London, with dorm beds from £18, basic sustenance £12, and transport around £6 unless you prefer to bike it. Out of London, costs drop. Shoestringers need around £30 per day for hostels and food. Midrangers will be fine on £60 to £85 per day, allowing £25 to £35 per person for B&B accommodation, £12 to £18 for lunch, snacks and drinks, £15 to £25 for an evening meal. Admission fees are the same for everyone – work on £10 per day.

Travel costs depend on transport choice. Trains can cost anything from £10 to £50 per 100 miles, depending when you buy your ticket. Long-distance buses (called coaches in Britain) cost about half the train fare for an equivalent journey. Car drivers should allow £12 per 100 miles for fuel, plus around £5 per day for parking. Rental costs £25 to £60 per day, depending on model and duration.

HOW MUCH?

See also Lonely Planet Index, inside front cover.

YHA Hostel £15

Pub lunch £9

Bicycle tube £4

Large latte £2.30

Brooks saddle £70

BACKGROUND READING

Slow Coast Home by Josie Drew is a cross between journal of miscellany and chatty letter to a friend, as the globetrotting cyclist completes a 5000-mile tour of England and Wales.

The Full English by Mike Carden is a warm and witty account of a cycle tour through England as the author struggles with the weather, mid-life crises, man-flu and a bike with an attitude problem.

Two Wheels by Matt Seaton is a compilation based on two years' worth of columns from the *Guardian* newspaper.

Heroes, Villains and Velodromes by Richard Moore gets inside the mind of Chris Hoy, Britain's champion track cyclist and offers an insight into the gruelling regime that revolutionised the British cycling team.

Notes from a Small Island by Bill Bryson, although based on travels in the 1970s, is still incisive.

The English: A Portrait of a People by Jeremy Paxman examines the evolution of English national identity in recent years.

TOP FIVE HISTORICAL TRAILS

The following routes take you through some of the most historic parts of the country:

Northern Explorer Crammed with sites connected with border warfare, this ride takes you past Hadrian's Wall, Roman remains, Lanercost Priory and Carlisle Castle (p217).

Central Explorer Evidence of Roman and Viking occupation is obvious on this ride through the glorious stone towns and villages of central England where castles are two-a-penny and the Brontë sisters found inspiration (p120).

Southeast Coast This ride kicks off in high gear at England's ecclesiastical centre, Canterbury, and passes through a string of historic towns and villages en route to Portsmouth (p53).

The Best of Anglesey Historical earth forts stand testament to Wales' earliest settlers (p198).

Kilmartin Glen Known as the 'cradle of modern Scotland', this stretch on the West Coast ride is where the Scotti tribe first came to Scotland from Ireland (p265).

TOP FIVE ADRENALINE PUMPERS

Looking for something more adventurous? These gruelling climbs and mind-blowing descents will challenge your fitness and reward you with superb views and well-earned pride.

Grampian Mountains Not for the faint-hearted, the Scottish Highlands section of the Land's End to John O'Groats ride serves up a nightmarish climb with a reward of 10 glorious miles, dropping in altitude from 626.7m (2089ft) to 324.6m (1082ft) (p331).

Glen Lyon This long, gradual ascent through Scotland's longest and loneliest glen is a gloriously scenic ride with mountains unfolding all around (p285).

The Gap This challenging, long, gradual (from 180m/590ft to 600m1965ft) climb offers fine views across the Brecon Beacons and a superb, lengthy descent (p203).

Penrith to Allenheads This tough ride offers testing climbs up into the northern Pennines followed by a breakneck descent into Nenthead, one of England's highest villages (p233).

Buxton to Langsett The Strine's Moor road is beloved of cyclists for its challenging ascents and eerily beautiful surroundings (p151).

INTERNET RESOURCES

There are loads of online resources for cyclists in Britain with plenty of advice and ideas for planning a trip..

Backpax (www.backpaxmag.com) Cheerful info on cheap travel, visas, activities and work.

British Cycling Federation (BCF; www.britishcycling.org.uk) The governing body of cycling with event calendar, competition results and news.

CTC (Cyclists' Touring Club; www.ctc.org.uk) One stop shop for cycling news, events listings, route information, maps, advice and more.

Cyclehub (www.cyclehub.co.uk) A portal site with a directory of links to everything from bike manufacturers and shops to product reviews, nutrition and fitness.

Lonely Planet (www.lonelyplanet.com) Travel news, information and advice, as well as a dedicated 'On Your Bike' section on the Thorn Tree bulletin board.

Met Office (www.met-office.gov.uk) Weather information and forecasts for Britain.

National Byway (www.thenationalbyway.org) Information on the 4,000-mile signposted leisure route around the UK.

Ordnance Survey (www.ordnancesurvey.co.uk) All the maps of Britain you could ever need.

Sustrans (www.sustrans.org.uk) Information and route maps for the National Cycling Network.

Visit Britain (www.visitbritain.com) The official travel and tourism site.

Environment

The island of Britain sits on the eastern edge of the North Atlantic and consists of three nations: England in the south and centre, Scotland to the north and Wales to the west – together making up the state of Great Britain.

THE LAND

Britain is not a place of geographical extremes – there are no Himalayas or Lake Baikals – but even a relatively short journey can take you through a surprising mix of landscapes. Southern England's countryside is gently undulating, with a few hilly areas like the Cotswolds, and farmland between the towns and cities. East Anglia is mainly low and flat, while the Southwest Peninsula has wild moors and rich pastures with a rugged coast and sheltered beaches that make it a favourite holiday destination.

Ever wondered about the origin of the names Oundle or Merthyr Tydfil? The *Oxford Dictionary of British Place Names* by AD Mills is a fascinating study of the geographical roots of Britain's town and village titles.

In northern England, farmland remains interspersed with towns and cities, but the landscape is bumpier. A line of large hills called the Pennines (fondly tagged 'the backbone of England') runs from Derbyshire to the Scottish border, and includes the peaty plateaus of the Peak District, the delightful valleys of the Yorkshire Dales and the frequently windswept but ruggedly beautiful hills of Northumberland. Perhaps England's best-known landscape is the Lake District, a small but spectacular cluster of hills and mountains in the northwest, where Scafell Pike (a towering… 978m) is England's highest peak.

In Wales the Black Mountains and Brecon Beacons lie to the south and Snowdonia, site of 1113m (3650ft) Snowdon, the highest peak in Wales, is in the north. In between lie the wild Cambrian Mountains, rolling down to the spectacular cliffs and shimmering river estuaries of the west coast.

For real mountains, though, you've got to go to Scotland, especially the wild, remote and thinly populated northwest Highlands – separated from the rest of the country by a diagonal gash in the earth's crust called the Boundary Fault. Ben Nevis (1343m/4406ft) is Scotland's – and Britain's – highest mountain, but there are many more to choose from. The Highlands are further enhanced by the vast cluster of beautiful islands that lie off the loch-indented west coast.

TOP FIVE SCENIC CYCLES

o Enjoy some of Scotland's finest views as you ride through the **Isle of Skye's Cuillin Range,** which weaves from the smooth and rounded 'Red Cuillins' to dark and towering jagged peaks (p265).

o Lush countryside, craggy cliffs, sandy beaches and charming seaside towns greet you along the **Cornish Coastline** in the Southwest ride (p72).

o For compact and accessible mountain scenery it's hard to beat the **Brecon Beacons & Snowdonia Regions** on the Lôn Las Cymru ride (p184).

o Placid sea lochs, white sandy beaches and picturesque harbour towns are backed by dramatic peaks in the **Isle of Mull** (p275).

o Challenge your legs in some of Britain's wildest and most beautiful uplands where the undulating roads take you past the pretty stone villages of the **Peak District** (p141).

South of the Scottish Highlands is a relatively flat area called the Central Lowlands, home to the bulk of Scotland's population. Further south, down to the border with England, things get hillier again; this is the Southern Uplands, a fertile farming area.

WILDLIFE

Despite a dense population and intense farming, Britain still boasts a great diversity of plants and animals – a reflection of the range of natural habitats found here. On a short tour you're likely to see examples of several different habitats in a matter of days, if not hours.

Some of the best examples of Britain's habitats are protected in national parks and other designated areas. Rides covered in the main route descriptions pass through some of the areas including lowland woods carpeted in shimmering bluebells and high moors where stately herds of deer roam. Many of these natural treasures are hidden away however, and you'll need to get off the bike in order to enjoy them properly.

Animals

In farmland areas, rabbits are everywhere, but if you're cycling through the countryside be on the look out for brown hares, an increasingly rare species. They're related to rabbits but much larger. Although hare numbers are on the decline, down on the riverbank the once-rare otter is making a comeback, while in farmland the black-and-white striped badger is under threat from farmers who believe they transmit bovine tuberculosis to cattle. Conservationists say the case is far from proven, and seem to have won the argument; mooted badger culls were abandoned by the government in July 2008.

Common birds of farmland and similar countryside (and urban gardens) include the robin, with its instantly recognisable red breast and cheerful whistle, the wren, whose loud trilling song belies its tiny size, and the yellowhammer, with a song that sounds (if you use your imagination) like 'a-little-bit-of-bread-and-no-cheese'. In open fields, the warbling cry of a skylark is another classic, but now threatened, sound of the English outdoors. A larger bird is the pheasant, originally introduced from Russia to the nobility's shooting estates, but now considered naturalised and commonly seen in farmland and moorland.

In woodland areas, mammals include the small white-spotted fallow deer and the even smaller roe deer. Woodland is full of birds too, but you'll hear them more than see them. Listen out for willow warblers (which have a warbling song with a descending cadence) and chiffchaffs (which, also not surprisingly, make a repetitive 'chiff chaff' noise).

If you hear rustling among the fallen leaves it might be a hedgehog – a cute-looking, spiny-backed insect-eater– but it's an increasingly rare sound these days; conservationists say they'll be extinct in Britain by 2025.

In contrast, foxes are widespread and well adapted to a scavenging life in rural towns, and even city suburbs. Grey squirrels (introduced from North America) have also proved very adaptable, to the extent that native red squirrels are severely endangered because the greys eat all the food. Much larger than squirrels are pine martens, which are seen in some forested regions, especially in Scotland. With beautiful brown coats, they were once hunted for their fur, but are now fully protected.

Perhaps unexpectedly, Britain is home to herds of 'wild' ponies, notably in the New Forest, Exmoor and Dartmoor, but although these animals roam free they are privately owned and regularly managed. There's even a pocket of wild goats near Lynmouth in Devon, where they've apparently

For a quick guide of where to go and what to do try www.visitbritain.co.uk and click on Things to See & Do and Cycling Itineraries.

Collins Complete Guide to British Wildlife by Paul Sterry is portable and highly recommended, covering mammals, birds, fish, plants, snakes, insects and even fungi with brief descriptions and excellent photos.

Britain's Best Wildlife by Mike Dilger is a 'Top 40' countdown of favourites compiled by experts and the public, with details on when and where to see the country's finest wildlife spectaculars.

If feathered friends are enough, the *Collins Complete Guide to British Birds* by Paul Sterry combines clear photos and descriptions, plus when and where each species may be seen.

gambolled merrily for almost 1000 years. Wild goats can also be seen on the Great Orme peninsula in North Wales, but were introduced here only a century ago.

The most visible moorland mammal is the red deer. Herds survive on Exmoor and Dartmoor, in the Lake District, and in larger numbers in Scotland. The males are most spectacular after June, when their antlers have grown ready for the rutting season. The stags keep their antlers through the winter and then shed them again in February.

Also on the high ground, well-known and easily recognised birds include the red grouse, which often hides in the heather until almost stepped on, the curlew, with it's stately long-legs and elegant curved bill, and the lapwing with its spectacular aerial displays. Mountain birds include red kites, while on the high peaks of Scotland you may see the grouse's northern cousin, the ptarmigan, or golden eagles, Britain's largest birds of prey.

Down by the sea, mammals include two types of seal, the larger grey seal and the common seal, which is actually less common than the grey. You can take boat trips to see their colonies in Norfolk and Northumberland. Dolphins, porpoises, minke whales and basking sharks can all be seen off the west coast, particularly off Scotland, and especially from May to September. Whale-watching trips are available from several Scottish harbour towns. Estuaries and mudflats are feeding grounds for numerous migrant wading birds; easily spotted are black-and-white oystercatchers with their long red bill, while flocks of small ringed plovers skitter along the sand.

On the coastal cliffs in early summer, particularly in Cornwall, Yorkshire and northwest Scotland, countless thousands of guillemots, razorbills, kittiwakes and other breeding sea birds fight for space on crowded rock ledges, and the air is thick with their sound. Even if you're not into bird-spotting, this is one of Britain's finest wildlife spectacles.

> Adders are Britain's only venomous snake but are not aggressive and will only attack if threatened or harassed. Bites are very painful and require urgent medical treatment but pose little danger to a healthy adult.

Plants

In any part of Britain, the best places to see wildflowers are in areas that evade large-scale farming. The chalky hill country of southern England and the limestone areas further north (eg Peak District and Yorkshire Dales) erupt with great profusions of cowslips and primroses in April and May.

For woodland flowers, the best time is also April and May, before the leaf canopy is fully developed so sunlight can reach plants such as bluebells – a beautiful and internationally rare species.

Another classic English plant is gorse: you can't miss the swaths of this spiky bush in heath areas like the New Forest. Legend says it's kissing time when the gorse is in bloom. Luckily its vivid yellow flowers show year-round.

In contrast, the blooming season for heather is quite short, but no less dramatic. On the Scottish mountains, the Pennine moors of northern England, and Dartmoor in the south, the wild hill-country is covered in a riot of purple in August and September. In the Scottish highlands you'll find true alpine species as well as the more common peat moss, heather and bilberry.

> For more in-depth information on the nation's flora and fauna, www.wildaboutbritain .co.uk is an award-winning site that is comprehensive, accessible and interactive.

Britain's natural deciduous trees include oak, ash, hazel and rowan, with seeds and leaves supporting a vast range of insects and birds. The New Forest in southern England is a good example of this type of habitat. In some parts of Scotland, stands of indigenous Caledonian pine can still be seen. As you travel through Britain you're also likely to see non-native pines, standing in plantations empty of wildlife –

although an increasing number of deciduous trees are also planted these days.

NATIONAL PARKS

Way back in 1810, poet and outdoors-lover William Wordsworth suggested that the Lake District should be 'a sort of national property, in which every man has a right'. More than a century later, the Lake District became a national park (although quite different from Wordsworth's vision), along with the Brecon Beacons, Cairngorms, Dartmoor, Exmoor, Loch Lomond & The Trossachs, New Forest, Norfolk & Suffolk Broads, Northumberland, North York Moors, Peak District, Pembrokeshire Coast, Snowdonia and Yorkshire Dales. A new park, the South Downs in southern England, is in the process of being created.

Combined, Britain's national parks now cover over 10% of the country. It's an impressive total, but the term 'national park' can cause confusion. These areas are not state owned, nearly all land is private, and they are not total wilderness areas. In Britain's national parks you'll see roads, railways, villages and even towns. Development is strictly controlled, but about 250,000 people live and work inside national-park boundaries.

Despite these apparent anomalies, national parks still contain vast tracts of mountain and moorland, with rolling downs, river valleys and other areas of quiet countryside, all ideal for cyclists.

In addition to the national parks you'll also find various other designated areas of protection in Britain, including Areas of Outstanding Natural Beauty (AONBs), National Scenic Areas (NSAs), Sites of Special Scientific Interest (SSSIs), Forest Nature Reserves (FNRs) and Countryside Stewardship Schemes (CSSs).

Bicycle tourers will generally have no access problems in any conservation area provided that they stick to the roads. If you plan to ride off-road you should always check before proceeding; in parts of Britain thoughtless off-road riding has resulted in considerable damage to trails. For more information on rules for off-road riding see the Permits & Fees section in the Cyclist's Directory p358.

It's worth noting also that there are many beautiful parts of Britain that are not national parks (such as mid-Wales, the North Pennines in England, and many parts of Scotland). These can be just as good for cycling and are often less crowded than the popular national parks.

ENVIRONMENTAL ISSUES

With Britain's long history of human occupation, it's not surprising that the country's appearance is almost totally the result of people's interaction with the environment. Since the earliest times people have been chopping down trees and creating fields for crops or animals, but the most dramatic changes in rural areas came after WWII in the late 1940s, continuing into the '50s and '60s, when a drive to be self-reliant in food meant new – intensive and large-scale – farming methods. The visible result: an ancient patchwork of small meadows changed to a landscape of vast prairies, as walls were demolished, woodlands felled, ponds filled, wetlands drained and – most notably – hedgerows ripped out.

For many centuries, these hedgerows had formed a network of dense bushes, shrubs and trees that stretched across the countryside protecting fields from erosion, supporting a varied range of flowers, and providing shelter for numerous insects, birds and small mammals. But in the rush to improve farm yields, thousands of miles of hedgerows were destroyed.

The Gem series includes handy little books on wildlife topics, such as Birds, Trees, Fish and Wild Flowers.

To explore Britain's national parks from your computer, before gearing up your bike and getting out there, an excellent portal site is www.nationalparks.gov.uk

Britain's right-of-way network has existed for centuries so single trails slicing through wilderness such as those in Australia or the USA don't exist. Even famous long-distance routes simply link many shorter paths.

Hedgerows have come to symbolise many other environmental issues in rural areas, and in recent years the destruction has abated, partly because farmers recognise the anti-erosion qualities, partly because they don't need to remove any more, and partly because they're encouraged to 'set aside' such areas as wildlife havens – although in 2008 set-aside land was under threat as farmers sought to take advantage of soaring grain prices. Nonetheless, subsidies from government or European agencies are now available to replant hedgerows.

Environmental issues are not exclusive to rural areas. In Britain's towns and cities, topics such as air and light pollution, levels of car use, public-transport provision and household-waste recycling are never far from the political agenda, although some might say they're not near enough to the top of the list.

Perhaps the politicians are only representing public opinion. While numerous surveys show high proportions of respondents saying they care about sustainability, a poll in mid-2008 revealed that only 1% of holidaymakers considered the environmental impact of flying as a priority when booking their trip.

Meanwhile, back in the country, in addition to hedgerow clearance, other farming techniques remain hot environmental issues: the use of

> Britain's new 'hedgerows' are the long strips of grass and bushes alongside motorways and major roads. Rarely trod by humans, they support rare flowers, thousands of insect species plus mice, shrews and other small mammals – so kestrels are often seen hovering nearby.

RESPONSIBLE CYCLING

Cycling responsibly means looking out for other trail users as well as the trail itself. It's all common sense – we all enjoy the countryside and want to keep it at its best – but in Britain, the dense population and wet weather make it worth remembering the following points:

Cycling Basics

- Give way to pedestrians, wheelchair users and horse-riders, leaving them plenty of room.
- Fit a bell: let people and horses know you're coming.
- Make sure you've got working lights; they're required by law after dark.
- Go through puddles; if you go round them they just get bigger.
- Stay off soft areas if there's been a lot of rain.
- Try not to skid on trails as it wrecks the path.

Rubbish

- If you've carried it in, you can carry it back out – that means everything from empty packaging, to citrus peel, cigarette butts, tampons and condoms.
- Make an effort to pick up rubbish left by others.
- Don't burn or bury rubbish, it disturbs soil and encourages erosion and weed growth. Buried rubbish takes years todecompose and will probably be dug up by wild animals who may be injured or poisoned by it.

Human Waste Disposal

- If a toilet is provided at a campsite, please use it.
- Where there isn't one, bury your waste. Dig a small hole 6in deep and at least 100ft from any stream, 165ft from paths and 650ft from any buildings. Take a lightweight trowel or a large tent peg for the purpose. Cover the waste with a good layer of soil. Toilet paper should be burnt, although this is not recommended in a foret, above the tree line or in dry grassland; otherwise, carry it out – burying it is a last resort. Ideally, use biodegradable paper.

pesticides, monocropping, intensive irrigation, and the 'battery' rearing of cows, sheep and other stock. The results of these unsustainable methods, say environmentalists, are rivers running dry, fish poisoned by runoff, and fields with only grass and not another plant to be seen. These 'green deserts' support no insects, so in turn some wild bird populations have dropped by an incredible 70%. This is not a case of wizened old peasants recalling the idyllic days of their forbears; you only have to be over about 30 in Britain to remember a countryside where birds such as skylarks or lapwings were visibly much more numerous.

But all is not lost. In the face of apparently overwhelming odds, Britain still boasts great biodiversity, and some of the best wildlife habitats are protected (to a greater or lesser extent) by the creation of national parks and similar areas, or private reserves owned by conservation campaign groups such as:

Wildlife Trusts (www.wildlifetrusts.org)
Woodland Trust (www.woodland-trust.org)
National Trust (www.nationaltrust.org.uk)
Royal Society for the Protection of Birds (www.rspb.org.uk).

Many of these areas are open to the public – ideal spots for walking, bird-watching or simply enjoying the peace and beauty of the countryside.

The Environment Agency is responsible for everything from clean air and flood warnings to boat permits and fishing licenses. Find lots more at www.environmentagency.gov.uk

---

o Contamination of water sources by human faeces can lead to the transmission of giardia, a human bacterial parasite.

Camping

o In remote areas, use a recognised site rather than create a new one. Keep at least 100ft from watercourses and paths. Move on after a night or two.

o Pitch your tent away from hollows where water is likely to accumulate.

o Leave your site as you found it – with minimal or no trace of your use.

Washing

o Don't use detergents or toothpaste in or near streams or lakes; even it they are biodegradable they can harm fish and wildlife.

o To wash yourself, use biodegradable soap and a water container at least 165ft from the watercourse. Disperse the waste water widely so it filters through the soil before returning ot the stream.

o Wash cooking utensils 165ft from watercourses using a scourer or gritty sand instead of detergent.

Fires

o Use a safe existing fireplace rather than making a new one. Don't surround it with rocks – they're just another visual scar – but clear away all flammable material for at least 7ft. Keep the fire small (under 10 sq ft) and use a minimum of dead, fallen wood.

o Be absolutely certain the fire is extinguished. Spread the embers and drown them with water. Turn the embers over to check the fire is extinguished throughout. Scatter the charcoal and cover the fire site with soil and leaves.

Access

o Many of the rides in this book pass through private property, although it may not be obvious at the time, along recognised routes where access is freely permitted. If there seems to be some doubt about this, ask someone nearby if it's OK to ride through.

History of Cycling

Britain has a unique place in the history of cycling with home-grown inventors playing a crucial role in pioneering new ideas and technology that led to the introduction of pedal and chain drives and pneumatic tyres.

EVOLUTION OF THE BICYCLE

The first attempts at creating two-wheeled, rider-propelled machines appeared in Europe in the early 19th century. Entirely made of wood, these crude but steerable 'swiftwalkers' were popular with Victorian early-adopters but they never became a practical means of transportation.

See boneshakers, penny-farthings and over 250 historic bikes at the National Cycle Collection (☎ 01597 825531; www.cyclemuseum.org .uk; Llandrindod Wells, Wales)

It was in Scotland that the first pedal cycle was invented in 1839. Blacksmith Kirkpatrick Macmillan created a system of treadles, rods and cranks that powered the rear wheel of a swiftwalker and by 1942 he had mastered the art of cycling and managed to ride the 140 miles to Glasgow and back, averaging 8mph.

In 1861 Pierre Michaux and his son Ernest unveiled their own version of the pedal bike in Paris. The velocipede had two cranks that were rotated by the rider's feet and its design swiftly caught on. The Michaux family made 142 velocipedes in 1862 and by 1865 they were cranking out 400 a year. Despite its popularity it was an uncomfortable beast and was commonly known as the 'boneshaker'.

In Britain the Coventry Sewing Machine Company, spurred on by their young foreman James Starley, invented a bicycle with a large front wheel and a small rear wheel in 1870. The 'high-wheeler' or 'ordinary' had a gear that allowed the wheel to be turned twice for each pedal revolution making it far more efficient to ride. Using metal construction rather than wood, Starley lightened the bike and added solid rubber tyres for comfort. The 'penny-farthing' as it came to be known, was a huge success but notoriously prone to accidents.

In response HJ Lawson developed a new revolution in cycling, a chain-driven bike. He launched his first 'safety bicycle' in 1874. The bike was more stable and easier to stop than the high-wheeler but owners complained that pedalling so near to the ground left their feet muddy.

For a fascinating look at the evolution of the bicycle try *Bicycling Science* by DG Wilson, which combines scientific and engineering information with human physiology to chart the past, present and future of cycling.

By 1885 James Starley's nephew, John K Starley, had adapted the design and launched the Rover Safety bike with its revolutionary diamond-pattern frame. The strong, compact frame was lighter and more efficient and it soon dominated the market. In 1888 JB Dunlop, a Belfast veterinarian, went one step further and fitted the first pneumatic tyres to bicycle wheels making cycling significantly faster and more comfortable.

Thanks to these advances cycling became a functional means of transport rather than just a gentleman's leisurely pursuit and soon manufacturers were clamouring to build inexpensive bikes for the masses.

By 1893 bikes could freewheel, had efficient, easy-to-use brakes and had greatly increased worker's mobility. The new bikes also revolutionised women's dress, ushering in an era of 'common sense' dressing for women – bustles and corsets were highly impractical as cycling-wear.

Since then bicycles have come a long way but specialised off-road bikes didn't emerge until the 1970s, when the first BMX and mountain bikes were developed in California. Despite increasing interest in cross-country biking, it was the late 1980s before mountain bikes became readily available in Britain.

THE PERFECT CYCLING SOUVENIR

One piece of British-designed cycling equipment that has largely survived the technological onslaught is the Brooks saddle. Proudly handmade in Nottingham for over 140 years, few pieces of cycling kit enjoy such a loyal following. The Brooks remains the saddle of choice of many touring cyclists despite changing little over the intervening years. Achieving saddle nirvana on a Brooks can require some effort though. During the 'breaking in' process the leather, like a good pair of shoes, moulds to fit the contours of your rear. People have come up with all sorts of ways to speed up the process, but neither bashing the seat with a rolling pin nor soaking it in the bathtub is endorsed by the manufacturer. In reality there's no real substitute for time on the road. Happy owners speak of the all-leather, copper-riveted Brookes with missionary zeal however. If you're looking for a perfect British cycling souvenir you could do far worse than a visit to www.brookssaddles.com.

COMPETITIVE CYCLING

Although cycling remained a gentleman's pastime (a penny-farthing cost an average man six months wages) until the 1890s, organised cycling was quick to catch on among those who were lucky enough to own the latest models.

The first recorded cycling race was held in June 1868 at Hendon, Middlesex; the first world championship was in 1893 and cycling became part of the Olympic Games in 1896. Meanwhile competitors were beginning to get organised and the National Cyclists Union (NCU), now the British Cycling Federation (BCF), was founded in 1878, as was the Bicycle Touring Club (now the Cyclists' Touring Club, CTC). Britain's first off-road cycling club, the Roughstuff Fellowship was established in 1955.

In the early 20th century British cycle racing declined, car use rose and road racing was banned by the NCU. In its place time-trial racing took off and it was 1942 before Britain had its next mass-started road race. The Tour of Britain began in 1951 but professional cycling – long a feature of the cycling scene in Europe – wasn't introduced until 1965. By then British riders were already making a mark on the professional racing scene. Sixties cycling legend Tom Simpson competed in the Tour de France throughout the decade and tragically died on Mont Ventoux in 1967, and Barry Hoban won eight Tour stages between 1967 and 1975.

Sustained financial support for the Great Britain Cycling Team only became a reality in 1997 but in its wake performance by British cyclists immediately began to improve. In recent years the team has enjoyed unprecedented levels of success in international competition with medals at every World Senior Track Championships since 1999. In 2004 an Under-23 Olympic Academy programme was established and a Junior Development programme was launched the following year.

The investment paid off and at the Beijing Olympics in 2008 Britain dominated the cycling events winning a record-breaking 14 (eight gold, four silver, two bronze) medals in cycling events. Britain's boy wonder Chris Hoy won three gold medals.

The Cyclists' Touring Club is the oldest cycling organisation in Britain. It was founded in 1878, when the bike of choice was the penny-farthing, and the national scandal of the day was 'lady bicyclists' wearing trousers.

Roule Britannia: A History of Britons in the Tour De France by William Fotheringham is a fascinating insight into the tragedy and triumphs of the British riders who took cycling's greatest challenge.

RECREATIONAL CYCLING

Recreational cycling also declined in the early 20th century, making a comeback in the inter-war years. Increased interest in cycling caused manufacturers to apply lightweight technologies previously reserved for racing cycles to touring bikes in the 1920s, and in the '30s cycling boomed as the Great Depression meant cars became unaffordable.

SUSTRANS & THE NCN

The sustainable transport charity Sustrans was set up in 1977 in response to the energy crisis and has become one of Britain's biggest success stories. When it first announced its objective of creating a network of cycle paths and quiet roads throughout Britain it was barely taken seriously, but by 2000 the National Cycle Network (NCN) was launched with 5000 miles of routes.

Today, the bike-friendly tentacles of the network reach into every corner of Britain, with 10,000 miles of trails passing through major cities, villages and across national parks. Over 230 million journeys are made on the NCN each year and 75% of the UK's population live within a couple of miles of the network. The growth of cycling, coupled with near-terminal car congestion, has earned the scheme lots of attention – not to mention serious millions from government, regional authorities and the national lottery.

Strands of the network in busy cities are aimed at commuters or school kids, while other sections follow the most remote roads in the country and are perfect for touring. Among these, the Bristol & Bath Railway Path, Lôn Las Cymru (the Welsh National Cycle Route) and Sea to Sea (C2C) route appear in this book. Along many stretches of the NCN you'll find a great selection of artworks to admire earning the network a billing as the country's largest outdoor-sculpture gallery.

The whole scheme is a resounding success and a credit to the visionaries who persevered against inertia all those years ago. For more details see www.sustrans.org.uk.

Manchester Velodrome (www.manchester velodrome.com) is Britain's foremost indoor cycling track, home to the Great Britain Cycling Team and available for one-hour track 'taster' sessions.

The International Mountain Biking Association UK (www .imba.org.uk) is a one-stop shop for all your mountain biking needs with information on everything from trails and access to maps and guides.

Cycling's popularity remained relatively constant again until the 1950s, when the British public, cautious with their money through years of wartime austerity, went on a consumer-goods spending spree. Their primary interest was the motor car, and the number of cars on British roads tripled between 1945 and 1955. In broad terms the bicycle slump continued until the early 1970s, when the oil-price crisis led to another cycling surge, which has been sustained more or less until the present day.

In the mid-80s mountain bikes first appeared on Britain's streets and by the early '90s a new wave of young, adventurous cyclists had taken to the hills and forests, enthused by the prospect of an adrenaline-fuelled sport that was open to all. From 1995 to 1997 there was a huge increase in popularity of downhill mountain biking in Britain with new tracks and clubs springing up all over the country.

Today increasing oil prices, congested roads, concerns about the environment and interest in a healthy lifestyle have caused a boom in cycling. The numbers of commuters using the National Cycling Network has doubled in recent years and increasing pressure from cycling campaign groups is beginning to pay off. Although only 2% of journeys in Britain are made by bicycle (compared to 27% in the Netherlands), several cities are planning the introduction of bike hire schemes and Transport for London claims there has been a 91% increase in number of cyclists on the capital's roads since 2000. Campaigners however, warn that the cycling revolution desperately needs increased government funding; currently Britain spends just £1 per capita per annum on cycling infrastructure and training, a measly fifth of the European average.

London

London became sexy way back in the swinging '60s and nearly half a century later the UK's biggest city is still one groovy gal. Despite heavy grey skies and an endless drizzle, London remains an upbeat city with an energetic vibe found nowhere else in the country. Sophisticated yet edgy, London is a cultural icon that's always up for a good party. And so she should be, this is the city that introduced the world to pop music, trashy tabloids and Hugh Grant, after all. From stone faced guards outside the Queen's residence at Buckingham Palace to cherry red double-decker buses meandering past Westminster Abbey and Big Ben, London is filled with trademark images.

Seeing London on a bike may seem intimidating at first, but there is no better introduction to her sights, sounds and smells than from the saddle of your titanium horse. Get off the clogged main arteries and explore the narrow side streets, where the air reeks of pigeon poop and curry and the chic martini bar sits just around the corner from the city's red light sleaze, and you'll get a picture for what makes this multi-cultural metropolis really tick.

Even if big city road biking isn't your idea of fun, give this chapter a shot. The Thames East trip combines mostly traffic-free cycling with riverside pub-hopping. Or try the Westminster & the City ride on a Sunday, when two of the city's major roads are shut to cars and you cruise past palatial parks and royal gardens in peace. To really experience London's wild side peddle around the park-heavy southwest, where our Richmond & the Thames route offers 15 miles of traffic-free biking.

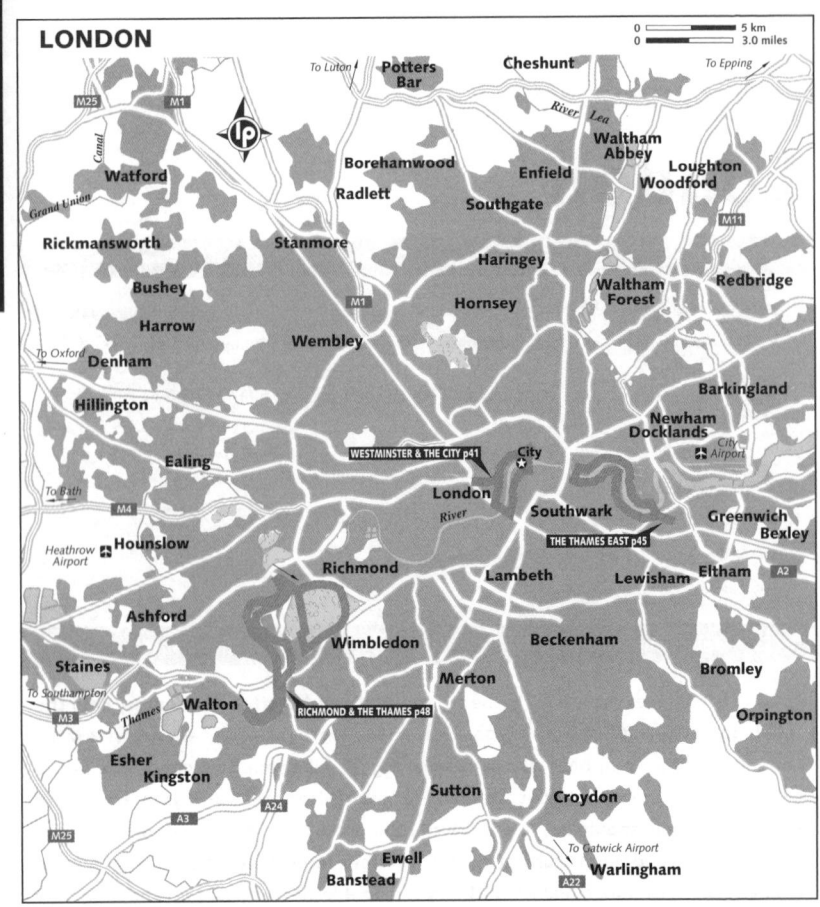

LONDON

(Map showing Greater London and surrounding areas)

Key locations labelled on map include: To Luton, Potters Bar, Cheshunt, To Epping, River Lea, Waltham Abbey, Borehamwood, Enfield, Loughton, Woodford, Watford, Radlett, Southgate, Rickmansworth, Stanmore, Haringey, Waltham Forest, Redbridge, Bushey, Hornsey, Harrow, Wembley, To Oxford, Denham, Barkingland, Hillington, Newham, Docklands, City Airport, Ealing, WESTMINSTER & THE CITY p41, City, London, To Bath, Heathrow Airport, Hounslow, River, Southwark, Greenwich, Bexley, THE THAMES EAST p45, Richmond, Lambeth, Lewisham, Eltham, Ashford, Wimbledon, Beckenham, Bromley, Staines, Merton, To Southampton, Walton, RICHMOND & THE THAMES p48, Orpington, Thames, Esher, Kingston, Sutton, Croydon, Ewell, To Gatwick Airport, Banstead, Warlingham

HISTORY

The Romans, London's first developers, built a wooden bridge across the Thames in about AD 43 and, some 200 years later, a defensive wall enclosing the square mile now known as the City of London. The Romans left in approximately 410, and little is known of London between then and the last years of Edward the Confessor's reign, when Westminster Abbey and Palace were first established.

After 1066, the Normans chose Westminster as their place of residence and government, while the City remained the centre of commerce and trade.

By the 14th century, London had grown into a vibrant city of about 80,000 people –

its food-supply arteries extended up to 60 miles into the surrounding countryside and air pollution was becoming a problem. The Black Death, which struck 1348–49, slowed the City's development – for a time.

The maze of streets that characterises much of central London – and proves such a navigational challenge to visiting cyclists – began to grow beyond the immediate surrounds of the City and Westminster in the 16th century, during Elizabeth I's reign. Another outbreak of the plague in 1664–65 killed about 70,000 and was immediately followed by the 1666 Great Fire, which burnt about 80% of the City. Development continued unevenly until the 19th century, during which time London acquired many of the characteristics of a modern city including public transport (first buses, in the late 1820s, then railways).

The 20th century saw a gradual rise in the use of private transport and increasing congestion on London's streets, which even the greater emphasis on planning that followed WWII has largely failed to quell. Today, Greater London is home to between 7 and 12 million people (depending on where you draw the boundary).

The City is in the midst of a reconstruction frenzy in preparation for the **2012 summer Olympic games**. The infrastructure legacy of the Games will include the usual stadia and pools but also roads, bridges and even a future-proof upgrade to the sewage system.

ENVIRONMENT

London's climate is about as good as Britain gets, although it still seems to rain more often than it's sunny. Summer temperatures range from an average low of 12°C to a top of 21°C during the day, while winter averages hover below 10°C (but usually above 0°C).

PLANNING

For more-detailed information on London, check out Lonely Planet's London city and encounter guides. *Time Out* magazine, published weekly, is a staggeringly detailed listing of London entertainment, attractions, art and much besides. There are tourist offices at Heathrow, Gatwick, Luton and Stansted airports, at Waterloo International Terminal, Victoria Station and Liverpool Street Underground station. The **London Cycling Campaign** (LCC; ☎ 020 7928 7220; www.lcc.org.uk; 30 Guildford St, MC1N) is the premier cycling organisation in London and produces 14 cycle-route maps to Greater London. These show sign posted London Cycle Network (LCN) routes, as well as traffic-free paths, places you should walk your bike, and each includes a map of Central London on one side.

Cycle Hire

Following is a list of London bike shops on or near the rides described in this chapter.

WESTMINSTER & THE CITY
Bikepark (☎ 020 7430 0083; Stukeley St, WC2)
Covent Garden Cycles (☎ 020 7836 1752; 2 Nottingham Court, Shorts Gardens, WC2)

THE THAMES EAST

The Magic Bicycle Company (☎ 020 7375 2993; 187 Whitechapel Rd, E1)

Robinsons Cycles (☎ 020 7237 4679; 172 Jamaica Rd, SE16)

Witcomb Cycles (☎ 020 8692 1734; 25 Tanners Hill, SE8)

RICHMOND & THE THAMES

Action Bikes (☎ 020 8547 0775; 22 Eden St, Kingston)

Moore Bros (☎ 020 8744 0175; 61 London Rd, Twickenham)

Richmond Cycles (☎ 020 8892 4372; 425 Richmond Rd, East Twickenham)

PLACE NAMES

If you're riding to a street address, make sure you're clear on the postcode as there's a lot of duplication of names. Greater London has 18 High Roads and about 50 High Streets.

INFORMATION SOURCES

British Travel Centre ☎ 020 8846 9000
London Tourist Board www.londontown .com
Victoria Tourist Information Centre ☎ 020 7730 3488

GETTING THERE & AROUND

London is serviced by both over-ground and underground railways, an extensive bus network, taxis and mini-cabs. Generally, bikes are not accepted on London buses.

Black cabs can certainly fit a bike – sometimes two – and most mini-cab companies have larger vehicles that you may be able to pre-book for transporting cycles.

Bikes are allowed – it would be stretching it to say they're welcome – on all London over-ground and some Underground rail services. The **Underground's** 'shallow' routes – Circle, District, Hammersmith & City, and Metropolitan lines – allow bikes on all sections outside of peak hours (7.30-10am & 4-7pm, Mon-Fri & all day Sat & Sun). Bikes can't be taken on the Victoria line or the 'deep' sections of the Bakerloo, Central, Jubilee, Northern and Piccadilly lines, which account for most central London Underground stations. Bikes travel free on the Underground – for information call ☎ 020 7222 1234. Several different companies control London's overground railway lines, some of which don't permit bikes during peak hours. Bikes usually travel free, but check with the train operating company. Bicycles are carried free on train services from Heathrow and Gatwick airports to central London.

On the **Heathrow Express** (☎ 020 8745 0578; www.heathrowexpress.co.uk), which runs between Heathrow and London (Paddington), there's a limit of three bikes per train at busy times.

All **Gatwick Express** (☎ 0870 530 1530; www.gatwickexpress.co.uk) services from Gatwick to London (Victoria) have a roomy luggage van.

BIKING TO LONDON FROM HEATHROW AIRPORT

If you're one of those hard core cyclists wanting to jump on your bike as soon as the plane touches down, then follow this 11-mile route from Heathrow Airport, via East Hammersmith, about 5 miles west of Central London, where there are connections for the Underground lines.

Leaving Heathrow terminals one, two and three, head north on the vehicle tunnel. Take the west ramp at 0.5 miles, before looping around onto the Northern Perimeter Rd. Leaving terminal four, go southeast on Swinton Rd, then turn right onto Snowdon Rd (0.1 miles). At 0.2 miles, turn left at the roundabout onto Shrewsby-Swansea Rd. The bikepath (right at 0.5 miles) leads to Cain's Lane. The routes join at the intersection of Bath, Great West and Great South-West Rds, then continue, by traffic-free path, beside the Great West Rd. In the Great West Rd/M4 overpass section there's some twisting and road-crossing before the route veers left onto Chiswick High Rd and joins the traffic. Chiswick High Rd becomes King St at Goldhawk Rd and continues direct to Hammersmith. The last section requires some walking – King St becomes one-way against you, and there are usually far too many people around for footpath riding.

This cycle route is also a good option if you are only using London as a landing pad and want to avoid the chaos of the city by joining up with one of the cross-country cycle routes. The entire ride takes around 1½ hours.

WESTMINSTER & THE CITY

Duration 1–3½ hours
Distance 8.5 miles
Difficulty easy
Start/Finish Duke of Wellington Place

Summary Experience London's most revered attractions on this easy urban bicycle tour best undertaken on a Sunday when two of the city's major roads are closed to cars, creating a long, congestion free, green corridor to cruise.

From the twin towers of **Westminster Abbey** to the entrance gates of **Buckingham Palace**, this city cycle tour makes a long lazy loop around London's iconic attractions. And even though you pause to reflect at some of the city's most popular gathering places such as **Covent Garden**, **Trafalgar Square** and **St Paul's Cathedral**, this route also takes in the best of London's big green parks and follows the river banks of the silvery blue **River Thames**. Ride on a Sunday, when two of the main roads are closed to cars, and you're in for a truly blissful cycling experience.

PLANNING

This ride is tailored to Sunday, when Constitution Hill and The Mall, near Buckingham Palace, are closed to vehicle traffic and the City, are quiet. Expect dense pedestrian crowds, however, especially in summer. Cleated shoes are not recommended on this route as it takes in packed tourist precincts and one-way streets. Expect to be regularly dismounting and walking.

When to Cycle

It's best to savour this ride for a Sunday, when usually congested Constitution Hill and The Mall are closed to cars, and you get to cycle past some of London's most iconic real estate in blissful silence – no honking horns, engine exhaust or screeching breaks mar your experience.

THE RIDE

Begin at **Hyde Park Corner** on the western edge of 19-hecare **Green Park**. Peddle east on **Constitution Hill** passing velvet meadows, blanketed with daffodils in spring, and big old trees and keep an eye out for

Buckingham Palace (☎ 020 7766 7302; www .royalcollection.org.uk; The Mall, SW1; adult/child £16/8.75; 9.45am-6pm, late Jul-late Sep) on the right. Lock up the bike, and take a quick stroll over to the Queen's house. Built in 1803 for the Duke of Buckingham, it replaced St James's Palace as the monarch's London home in 1837. If you've got the urge to drop in for a cup of tea, a handy way of telling whether she's home is to check whether the yellow, red and blue royal standard is flying. If you've never seen it before, the **Changing of the Guards** ceremony makes the ultimate cheesy London photograph. Dressed in bright uniforms and bearskin hats, the regiment of guards outside the palace changes over at 11.30am (daily from May to July and on alternate days for the rest of the year, weather permitting) in one of the world's most famous displays of pageantry. When you've had your fill (it gets dull pretty quick) hop on the bike, circle around the **Queen Victoria Memorial** and into another long green traffic-free cruise through **St James's Park**, an aristocratic enclave of palaces, manicured flowerbeds, exclusive gentlemen's clubs, ornamental lakes, famous hotels, historic shops and elegant buildings and you'll be ready to declare this bit of pavement the best cycling in London town.

Sadly your traffic-free ride ends when you leave **Horse Guards Road** and head up Storey's Gate towards **Westminster Abbey** (1.5 miles; ☎ 020 7222 5152; www .westminster-abbey.org; 20 Dean's Yard, SW1; adult/child £12/9, tours £5, audio-guides £4; 9.15am-4.30pm Mon, Tue, Thu & Fri, 9.15am-6pm Wed, 9.15am-2.30pm Sat). Dismount to cross **The Sanctuary**, then take your time walking past the Abbey, where all but two English monarchs since 1066 have been crowned. Resist the temptation to visit on this occasion. Cycle parking is banned in this area – your bike will be removed if you lock it and leave it. The neogothic-style **Houses of Parliament** (☎ 0870 906 3773; www.parliament.uk; Parliament Sq, SW1) face you as you exit the Abbey precinct next to the **Palace of Westminster** (☎ 020 7222 5152). The palace's most famous feature is another iconic London landmark – find the clock tower, aka **Big Ben**. The 13-ton bell, named after Benjamin Hall, who was commissioner of works when the tower was

LONDON

WESTMINSTER & THE CITY

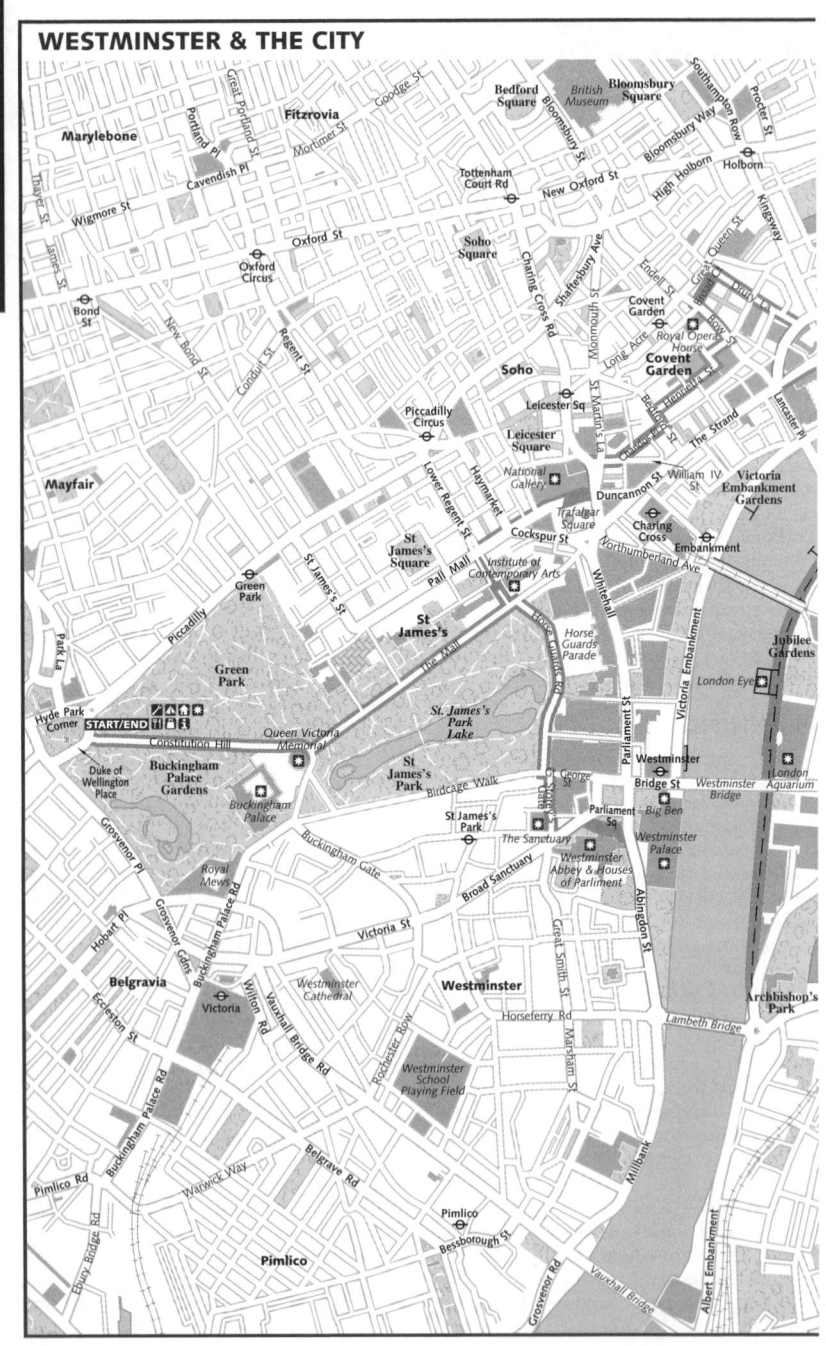

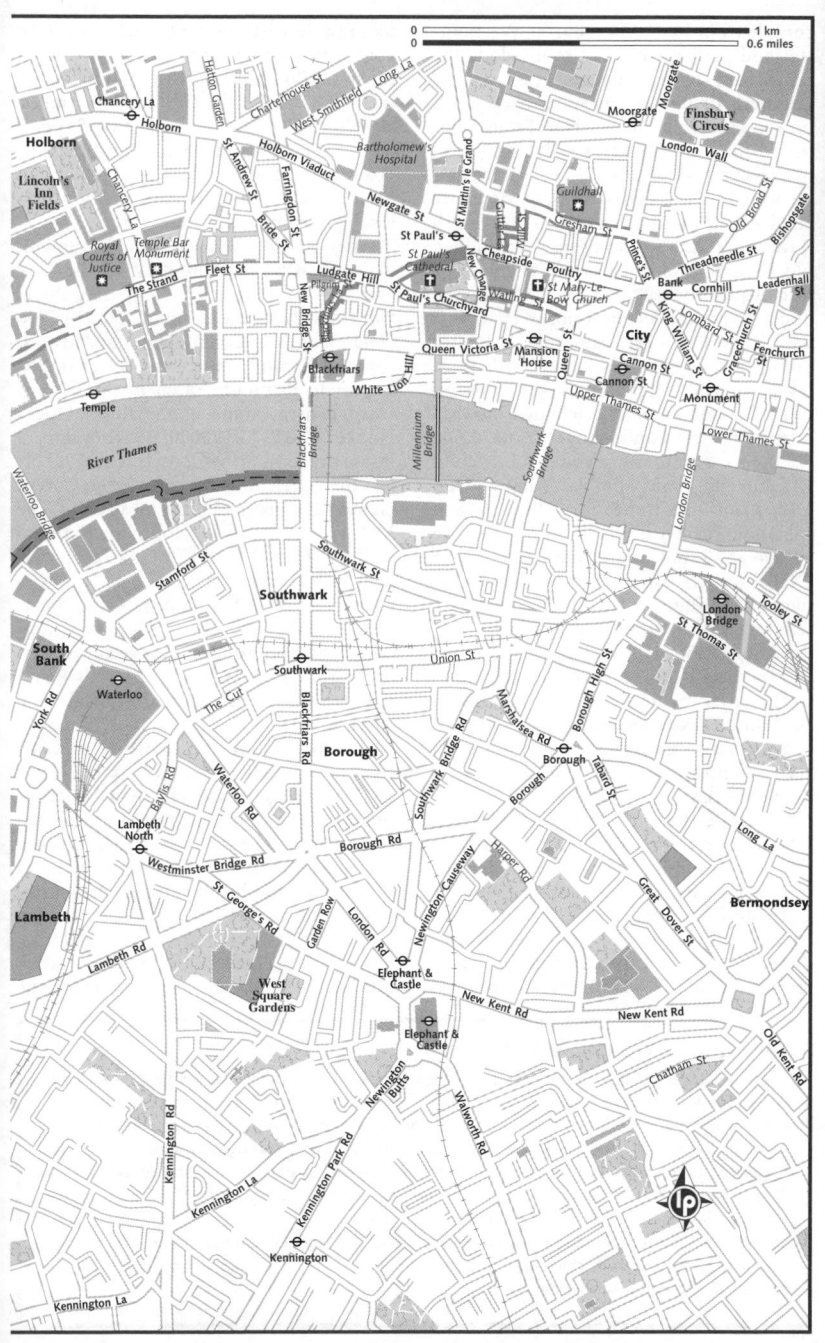

completed in 1858. After touring Westminster and Parliament, head south along the north bank of the Thames, crossing over **Lambeth Bridge** and heading back north on the other side of the river. From Lambeth Bridge to **Blackfriars Bridge** you're in a shared pedestrian-and-cycle precinct – be watchful for pedestrians, particularly children. Along this section of the **South Bank** you pass a wealth of sights including: old County Hall, now home to the **London Aquarium** (☎ 020 7967 8000; www .londonaquarium.co.uk; County Hall, SE1; adult/child £14/9.75; 10am-6pm, last entry 5pm), one of Europe's largest with three levels of fish! Afterwards take a ride on one of London's most celebrated 'newish' attractions, the **London Eye** (☎ 0870 500 0600; www.londoneye.com; adult/child £15.50/7.75; 10am-8pm Jan-May & Oct-Dec, 10am-9pm Jun & Sep, 10am-9.30pm Jul-Aug). The Eye doesn't actually resemble an eye at all, but in a city where there's a CCTV camera on every other corner the name is fitting. Originally designed as a temporary structure to celebrate the year 2000, the 135m-tall (443ft), slow-moving Ferris wheel is now a permanent addition to the cityscape and largest of its kind in the world. Passengers ride in an enclosed egg-shaped pod, which takes 30 minutes to rotate completely and offers a 25-mile view on a clear day.

Cross the River Thames for the second time at Blackfriars Bridge and the Sunday crowds diminish. Now you're in heart of the old City, and apart from **St Paul's Cathedral** (4.4 miles; ☎ 020 7236 4128; www .stpauls.co.uk; adult/child £10/3.50; 8.30am-4pm Mon-Sat), Christopher Wren's masterpiece built 1675–1710, there's not a lot

to draw tourists here at weekends. Take your time peddling the streets around **St Mary-Le-Bow church**, also built by Wren, in 1680. Look for the **Guildhall** (5.1 miles; ☎ 020 7606 3030; www.cityoflondon .gov.uk; Gresham St, EC2; admission free; 10am-5pm Mon-Sun May-Sep, 10am-5pm Mon-Sat Oct-Apr), the seat of the City's local government for 800 years.

After passing **Temple Bar Monument**, which marks the boundary of the City and Westminster, and the imposing **Royal Courts of Justice** (6.1 miles; ☎ 020 7936 6000), take care veering right into **Aldwych** from the Strand – there is a lot of traffic. Expect to dismount often in the **Covent Garden** area, home of the **Royal Opera House** (☎ 020 7304 4000; www.royalopera house.org; Bow St, WC2; tickets £5-190) offers free lunch-time concerts. From Covent Garden it's just a short haul back to The Mall, but along the way stop at the **National Gallery** (7.2 miles; ☎ 020 7747 2885; www .nationalgallery.org.uk; Trafalgar Sq, WC2; admission free; 10am-6pm Sat-Thu, 10am-9pm Fri) and the heart of visitor's London, **Trafalgar Square**. This section is best done on foot, crossing St Martin's Place, then walking on the footpath to Pall Mall. After a bump down the stairs (7.5 miles), it's worth visiting the **Institute of Contemporary Arts** (7.5 miles; ☎ 020 7930 3647; www.ica.org.uk; The Mall, SW1; admission Mon-Sun £2/3; noon-11pm Mon, noon-1am Tue-Sat, noon-10.30pm Sun). The one-stop modern art shop includes film, photography, theatre, installations, talks, performance art, DJs, digital art and book readings. Stroll around the galleries, watch a film, browse the bookshop then head to the bar for a beer. End your trip the

---

TAKE A WALK ON THE WEST END

We told you part of the joy of exploring London happens off the bike, and the City's **West End** is a good place to do it. Synonymous with big budget musicals and frenzied flocks of shoppers, the West End is a strident mix of culture and consumerism. More a concept than a fixed geographical area it none-the-less takes in **Piccadilly Circus** and **Trafalgar Square** to the south, **Regent St** to the west, **Oxford St** to the north and **Covent Garden** and the **Strand** to the east. Elegant **Regent St** and frantic **Oxford St** are the city's main shopping strips. At the heart of the West End lies Soho, a grid of narrow streets and squares hiding gay bars, strip clubs, cafes and advertising agencies. **Carnaby St** was the epicentre of the swinging London of the '60s, but is now largely given over to chain fashion stores, although some interesting independent boutiques still lurk in the surrounding streets.

way you began: zipping past manicured lawns, mirrored lakes and royal gardens, partaking in a lazy Sunday in the City, traffic-free and altogether Zen cycling experience.

THE THAMES EAST

Duration 2–5 hours
Distance 9.5 miles
Difficulty easy
Start Tower Bridge
Finish Tower of London
Summary This mostly flat River Thames route visits three of the most popular sights in London – Tower Bridge, the Tower of London and Greenwich – with multiple stops at riverside pubs.

Get to know both banks of the Thames intimately on this meandering route that not only takes you to storied attractions such as the Tower of London, but also stops for pints (and perhaps a plate of fish and chips) at many a fine pub along the snaking silvery blue river. Best of all, it's mostly traffic-free!

PLANNING

The route mostly follows quiet roads, but midweek is probably best for cycling as tourist crowds at either end of the route – in the Tower Bridge area, and at Greenwich – can be intense, especially during summer. However, the Greenwich markets are at their busiest and most interesting Friday to Sunday. Dress warmly during winter, when cold winds off the Thames can make this route particularly hard on exposed fingers – long gloves are recommended.

GETTING TO/FROM THE RIDE

Tower Bridge is the most easterly of the Thames bridges. The nearest Underground station is Tower Hill (Circle and District lines) – the nearest over-ground stations are Fenchurch St and London Bridge. If you're riding, approach on the south side of the Thames.

THE RIDE

Discover some of London's most interesting pubs on this leisurely, mostly flat and traffic-free bike loop along both banks of the River

Thames. You won't need to consult your map much while on this route – its very well marked and follows either the Thames path or an LCN route the entire way.

William Curtis Park is the starting point for this trail, which passes first through old docklands. Cobblestones on Shad Thames and overhead walkways above lend a flavour of the area's mercantile past, but rather expensive-looking shops and eateries now predominate. Just before St Saviour's Dock, featured in Dicken's *Oliver Twist*, you'll pass the **Design Museum** (0.2 miles; ☎ 020 7403 6933), which shows the fascinating evolution of product design. Many of the old riverside warehouses along the Bermondsey Wall have been re-kitted as groovy apartments, but look between the modern for charming examples of old London hidden in the shadows.

Also keep an eye out for **The Angel** (0.8 miles; ☎ 020 7237 3608; 101 Bermondsey Wall East, SE16), the first in a promised series of fantastic riverside pubs to stop for a pint, a plate of traditional English food and a history lesson. On Bermondsey Wall East, The Angel has survived the changing city and hosted a few of the famous names – James Cook reputedly among them. Opposite The Angel is all that's left of Edward III's moated manor house, built in the mid-14th century. Further east, The **Mayflower Pub** (☎ 020 7237 4088; 117 Rotherhithe St, SE16) was named for the Pilgrim Fathers' vessel, which moored near this site before the voyage to America in 1620.

Stay off the bike and walk through the Bonding Yard Walk area. A little further along on the **Dockside Heritage Walk**, interpretive signs remind you that the Thames was busy with trading vessels as little as 40 to 50 years ago. Until the rise last century of public road and rail transport, the Thames was also London's main passenger artery, with about 20 million people each year travelling on paddle steamers. The riverfront here is inextricably linked to the Royal Navy, and fighting ships were built, repaired and supplied at the historic **Deptford Victualling Yards** for five centuries.

Be careful of pedestrians in the **Greenwich Pier** area (4.9 miles), in fact it's safer to dismount on busy days. This is the site of the magnificently restored **Cutty Sark** (the world's only surviving tea clipper,

THE THAMES EAST

Houndsditch
Aldgate East
Aldgate
Aldgate High St
Braham St
Leadenhall St
Fenchurch St
Alie St
Leman St
Mansell St
Prescot St
Fenchurch St. Station
Tower Hill
Tower Gateway DLR
Dock St
East Smithfield
Tower Bridge

Whitechapel

Commercial Rd

Shadwell

Cannon St Rd

Cable St

The Highway

Whitehorse Rd

Limehouse DLR
Commercial Rd
Limehouse
Limehouse Basin
Narrow St

King Edward Memorial Park
Free Trade Wharf
Prospect of Whitby

River Thames

Wapping Way

Salter Rd

Tower of London
END
START
William Curtis Park

St Katherine Dock Way

St Katherine's Dock

Wapping

Wapping (Closed until 2010)

Wapping High St

Rotherhithe-Rotherhithe Tunnel

Nature Reserve

Tooley St
Tower Bridge Rd
Druid St
Design Museum
Bermondsey Wall West
Mayflower Pub
The Angel
Bermondsey Wall East
Mill St
George Row
Chambers St

Brunel Rd

Rotherhithe (Closed until 2010)

Bermondsey St
Long La
Abbey St
Jamaica Rd
Bermondsey
Grange Rd

Bermondsey

Canada Water

Lower Rd

Redriff Rd
Surrey Dock Rd
Finland St

Surrey Quays (Closed until 2010)

Greenland Docks

Southwark Park

Rotherhithe

Clifton Rd

Old Kent Rd
Rolls Rd
Albany Rd
Trafalgar Ave

Rotherhithe New Rd

South Bermondsey

Evelyn Rd

Trundleys Rd

Deptford Park

Old Kent Rd

New Cross Gate
New Cross Rd

Queens Rd (Peckham)

Peckham Rd

Peckham

New Cross

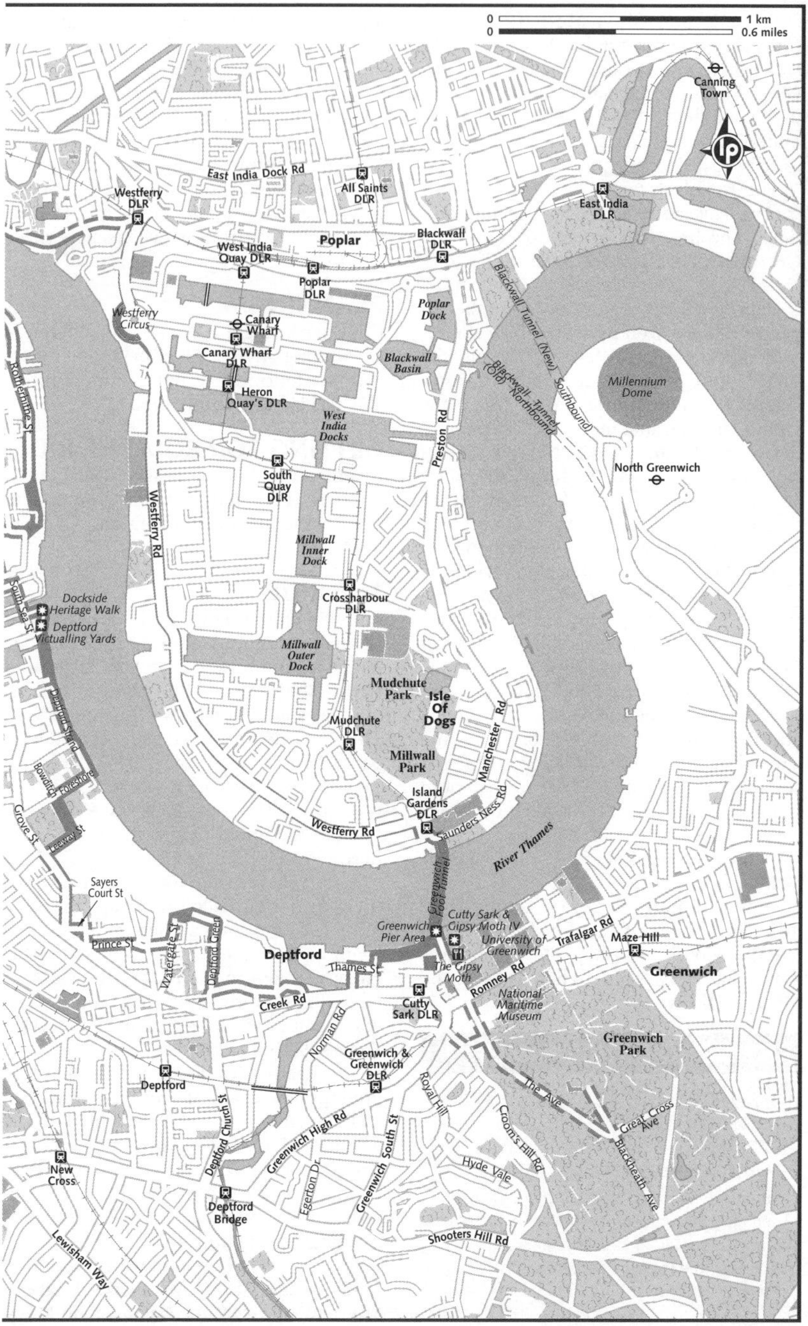
0 1 km
0 0.6 miles
Canning Town
East India Dock Rd
All Saints DLR
Westferry DLR
East India DLR
Poplar
Blackwall DLR
West India Quay DLR
Poplar DLR
Poplar Dock
Westferry Circus
Canary Wharf
Canary Wharf DLR
Blackwall Basin
Heron Quay's DLR
Blackwall Tunnel (New) Southbound
Blackwall Tunnel (Old) Northbound
Millennium Dome
West India Docks
Preston Rd
Rotherhithe St
South Quay DLR
North Greenwich
Westferry Rd
Millwall Inner Dock
Crossharbour DLR
Dockside Heritage Walk
Deptford Victualling Yards
South Sea St
Millwall Outer Dock
Mudchute Park
Isle Of Dogs
Mudchute DLR
Manchester Rd
Deptford Strand
Millwall Park
Bowditch
Foreshore
Island Gardens DLR
Saunders Ness Rd
Grove St
Leeway St
Westferry Rd
River Thames
Greenwich Foot Tunnel
Sayers Court St
Cutty Sark &
Gipsy Moth IV
Greenwich Pier Area
University of Greenwich
Trafalgar Rd
Maze Hill
Prince St
Watergate St
Deptford Green
Deptford
Thames St
The Gipsy Moth
Romney Rd
Greenwich
National Maritime Museum
Creek Rd
Cutty Sark DLR
Norman Rd
Greenwich Park
Greenwich & Greenwich DLR
Deptford
Royal Hill
The Ave
Crooms Hill Rd
Great Cross Ave
Deptford Church St
Greenwich High Rd
Greenwich South St
Blackheath Ave
New Cross
Hyde Vale
Egerton Dr
Deptford Bridge
Shooters Hill Rd
Lewisham Way

built 1869) and **Gipsy Moth IV**, Francis Chichester's vessel for his 1966–67 world circumnavigation. Have lunch at the **The Gipsy Moth** (☎ 020 8858 0786, 60 Greenwich Church St, SE16). Not only is it at the midpoint of the ride, it's another fantastically British riverside pub.

The route's second half includes some trickier navigating and a few walking sections. The first walk is the 400-yard long **Greenwich Foot Tunnel** under the Thames (5 miles), where cycling is prohibited (although you'll invariably see a number of people riding as you push your bike along).

Traffic is busy at Westferry Circus (6.9 miles) – take particular care here. It's worth stopping at **Limehouse Basin**, where the Grand Union Canal meets the Thames.

Go straight ahead where Narrow St veers right up to the busy Highway, dismount and follow the Thames Path past Stone Stairs and Free Trade Wharf to King Edward Memorial Park. Once you remount on Glamis Rd, it's an easy ride along relatively quiet streets. Reward yourself for navigating the maze with a pint at our favourite north bank pub, the venerable **Prospect of Whitby** (☎ 020 7481 1095; 57 Wapping Wall, E1). From here you'll continue west through Wapping, following cobblestoned streets where fashionable pubs, cafes and shops line the waterfront. Keep an eye out for foot traffic. You'll want to dismount upon reaching the **St Katherine's Dock** area. Weave around St Katherine's Dock, past the Tower Hotel and under **Tower Bridge** to the Tower of London. It's worth spending some time here – dating from 1078, the **Tower of London** (☎ 020 7709 0765) is a World Heritage site, famous as a prison for the likes of Sir Thomas More and Henry VIII's wives.

RICHMOND & THE THAMES

Duration 3–4 hours
Distance 24 miles
Difficulty easy
Start/Finish Richmond tourist office

Summary Nearly 15 miles of traffic-free peddling through London's wild southwest, home to numerous peaceful green havens, including the largest of London's Royal Parks, Richmond Park.

This pleasant roll takes you through Richmond Park, largest of London's Royal Parks, and past the Thames' tidal limit to magnificent Hampton Court Palace. Nearly 15 miles of the route is traffic-free. Public open space accounts for large areas in London's southwest, and this route winds past or through the best of these peaceful green havens. Sections along the Thames pass grand riverfront mansions, boat sheds and pubs.

PLANNING

Consider hiring a mountain bike if you're not touring on one. All of the route is rideable on a touring bike, but is more comfortably tackled by mountain bike.

GETTING TO/FROM THE RIDE

Richmond is 9 miles southwest of Central London. The nearest Underground and overground station is Richmond (District line).

THE RIDE

From Richmond Town Hall, site of the **Museum of Richmond** (☎ 020 8332 1141), the moderate climb to 955-hectare **Richmond Park** (☎ 020 8948 3209) takes in charming views east from posh Richmond Hill. The 7-mile long 'leisure path', shared with pedestrians, around the park's perimeter can be busy, especially at weekends, so limit your speed. The route goes past **Pembroke Lodge**, childhood home of philosopher Bertrand Russell, now a cafe.

After a short section of sealed road and a tricky turn (right, into River Lane) the route turns left onto the path along the Thames south bank. From here to Teddington the going is rough in places, but the views of life around the river are charming. Several grand homes grace the area, including **Ham House** (9.3 miles; ☎ 020 8940 1950). The restored early 17th-century mansion sits in grounds little changed over three centuries.

Teddington Lock, the limit of the tidal Thames, is passed about 2 miles before Kingston upon Thames. These mostly residential areas have long histories, largely because the Thames was fordable hereabouts. Teddington (Tudinton in earlier times) dates to 969. **Kingston**, which tradition holds as the coronation place of several 9th- and 10th-century Anglo-Saxon kings,

RICHMOND & THE THAMES

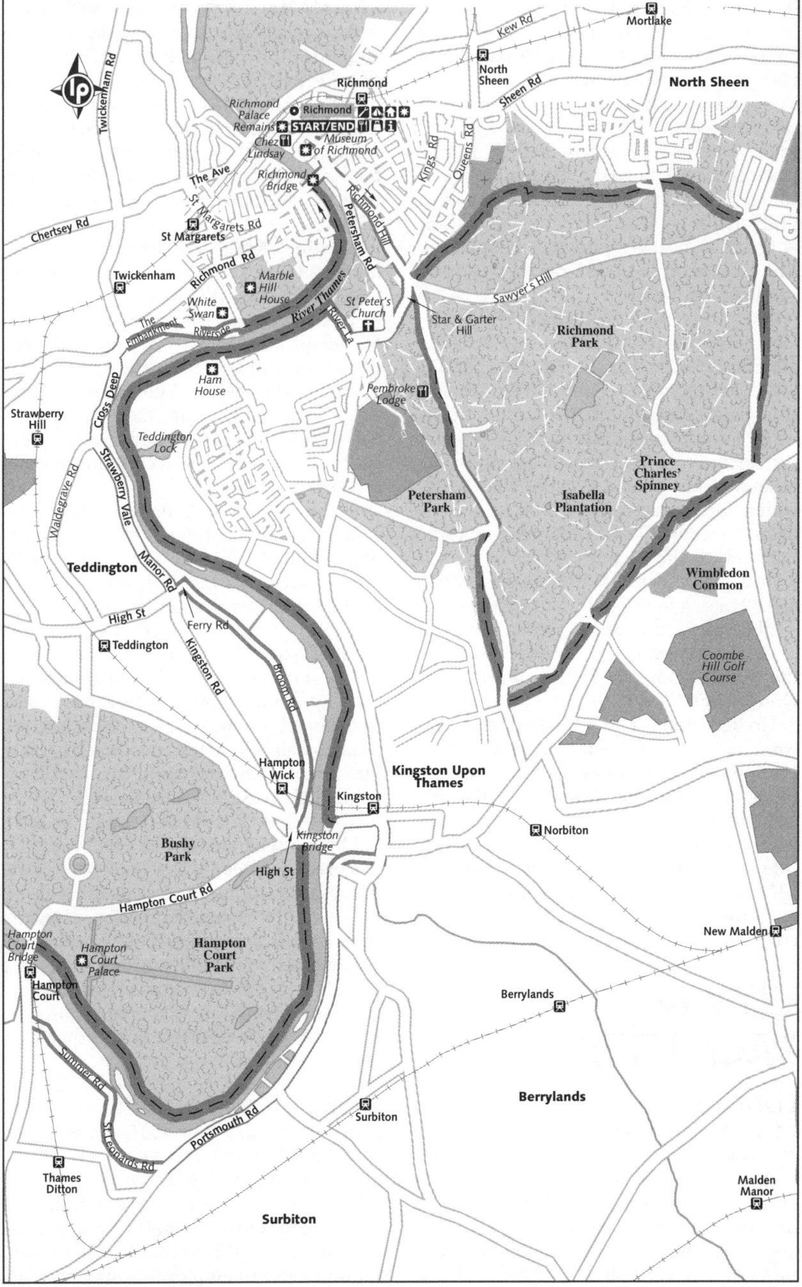

| 0 | 1 km |
| 0 | 0.5 miles |

Mortlake

Kew Rd

North Sheen

North Sheen

Twickenham Rd

Richmond

Sheen Rd

Richmond
Palace
Remains

Richmond
START/END

Chez
Lindsay

Museum
of Richmond

Kings Rd

Queens Rd

The Ave

St Margarets Rd

Richmond
Bridge

Chertsey Rd

St Margarets

Richmond Rd

Marble
Hill
House

Richmond Hill

Petersham Rd

Savyer's Hill

Twickenham

White
Swan

The Embankment

Riverside

St Peter's
Church

Star & Garter
Hill

**Richmond
Park**

River Thames

Riverside

Strawberry
Hill

Ham
House

Pembroke
Lodge

Cross Deep

Teddington
Lock

Waldegrave Rd

Strawberry Vale

**Petersham
Park**

**Isabella
Plantation**

**Prince
Charles'
Spinney**

Teddington

Manor Rd

High St

Teddington

Ferry Rd

Broom Rd

Kingston Rd

**Wimbledon
Common**

*Coombe
Hill Golf
Course*

Hampton
Wick

**Kingston Upon
Thames**

Kingston

Norbiton

**Bushy
Park**

Kingston
Bridge

High St

Hampton Court Rd

Hampton
Court
Bridge

Hampton
Court Palace

**Hampton
Court
Park**

Berrylands

New Malden

Hampton
Court

Summer Rd

Portsmouth Rd

Surbiton

Berrylands

St Leonards Rd

Thames
Ditton

Surbiton

Malden
Manor

was recorded as early as 838, as Cyninges-tun (King's Estate). Today Kingston is one of outer London's main retail centres, and crowds of shoppers can make navigation tricky through the town centre. Follow the 'All Routes' LCN signs and you can't go wrong – you'll know you're on the right track when you pass the Guildhall, resting place of the Anglo-Saxon kings' coronation stone. Traffic is bearable along the short Portsmouth Rd (A307) section, and it thins after the right turn onto St Leonard's Rd. The section on the A309 can be busy, and caution is required.

The return route to Richmond first follows Barge Walk path, which passes splendid **Hampton Court Palace** (16.5 miles; ☎ 020 8781 9500), built by Cardinal Wolsey and enlarged by Henry VIII in the 16th century, with renovations and additions by Wren in the 1690s. From Kingston Bridge, the route follows roads – including the busy A310, which fortunately has fine cycle lanes – back to pleasant Twickenham before turning back to the Thames. Reward yourself with a break at the **White Swan** (☎ 020 8892 2166), a lovely pub right on the river.

The ride's final section passes several beckoning riverside pubs and, north of the Warren Footpath, historic **Marble Hill House** (☎ 020 8892 5115) and its verdant encircling park. The Palladian villa was whacked up for Henrietta Howard, George II's mistress, and was later home to Mrs Fitzherbert, George IV's secret wife. It's been beautifully restored and is adorned with Georgian furniture. Celebrate your ride with dinner at **Chez Lindsay** (☎ 8948 7473; 11 Hill Rise, Richmond, TW10). This once royal attraction is still home of fine crepes, and a nice place to linger.

CITY & FACILITIES

LONDON
☎ 020 / Pop 7.51 million

The UK's vibrant capital is filled with the best sleeping, eating and entertainment options on the island, and maybe all of Europe. From bustling markets to ancient history to world-class nightclubs and theatres, London has it all.

Sleeping

Brown's Hotel (☎ 020 7493 6020; www .brownshotel.com; 30 Albemarle St, W1; d £325-615; tube Green Park) Splash out at swanky Brown's, where Rudyard Kipling penned many of his works, Kate Moss has frequented the spa and both Queen Victoria and Winston Churchill dropped in for tea. There's a lovely old-world feel to Browns which manages to not come across snooty.

Hoxton (☎ 020 7550 1000; www.hoxton hotels.com; 81 Great Eastern St, EC1V; d/ tw £59-189; tube Old St) A novel approach to pricing means that while all the rooms are identical, the first ones on any given day are offered at £59: an absolute steal for a hotel of this calibre. Rooms are a decent size, scrupulously clean, have comfy beds with quality linen and a well designed desk space where you can access the internet through the TV.

St Christopher's Village (☎ 020 7407 1856; www.st-christophers.co.uk; 163 Borough High St, SE1; dm £16-24, d/tw £52; tube London Bridge) With three locations on the same street sharing a main reception, there's quite a range of experiences on offer here. The main hub is the Village, a huge amp-up party hostel, with a club that stays open until 4am at the weekends and a spa pool on the roof terrace. The others are much smaller, quieter and, frankly, more pleasant. **St Christopher's Inn** (121 Borough High St, SE1) is situated above a very nice pub. The **Orient** (59 Borough High St, SE1) has a separate women's floor.

Threadneedles (☎ 020 7657 8080; www .theetoncollection.com; 5 Threadneedle St, EC2; d £370-499; tube Bank) The incredible stained-glass dome in the lobby of this city centre hotel points to its former status as a bank HQ. Today the bar and restaurant are still popular with 'suits', but the atmosphere is chic. At weekends the top-end spot is an absolute bargain.

Eating

Fifteen (☎ 0871 330 1515; www.fifteen .net; 15 Westland Pl, N1; breakfast £2-8.50, trattoria £9-18, restaurant £22-24; tube Old St) It can only be a matter of time before Jamie Oliver becomes Sir Jamie. His culinary philanthropy started at Fifteen, set up to give unemployed young people a shot at a career. The Italian food is beyond excellent and, surprisingly, even those on limited budgets can afford a visit. In the trattoria a croissant and coffee will only set you back £3.50, while a £9 pasta makes for a delicious lunch.

Nobu (☎ 020 7447 4747; www.nobu restaurants.com; Metropolitan Hotel, 19 Old Park Ln, W1; dishes £10-26; tube Hyde Park Corner) One of London's most famous eateries, Nobu's dining room is surprisingly unremarkable but it does have nice views over Hyde Park. It's nonetheless out-of-this-world when it comes to exquisitely prepared and presented Japanese dishes. Ordering the sublime lunchtime bento box (£28) is a sensible way of limiting the financial pain, especially compared to the £50 to £90 chef's choices.

Sacred (☎ 020 7734 1415; 13 Ganton St, W1; mains £3.60-5.30; 7.30am-8.30pm Mon-Fri, 9.30am-8pm Sat, 10am-7pm Sun; tube Oxford Circus) The spiritual paraphernalia and blatant Kiwiana don't seem to deter the smart Carnaby St set from lounging around this eclectic cafe. It must be something to do with the excellent coffee, appealing counter food and deliciously filling cooked breakfasts (try the scrambled eggs with salmon and goat's cheese).

Sketch (☎ 0870 777 4488; 9 Conduit St, W1; Parlour mains £4-14; Gallery mains £11-27, Lecture Room two-course lunch/ eight-course dinner £30/90; tube Oxford Circus) A design enthusiast's wet dream, with shimmering white rooms, video projections, designer Louis XIV chairs and toilet cubicles shaped like eggs. And that's just the Gallery, which becomes a buzzy restaurant and bar at night. The ground-floor Parlour has decadent cakes and decor, and is surprisingly affordable.

Song Que (☎ 020 7613 3222; 134 Kingsland Rd, E2; mains £4.70-6.90; tube Old St) If you arrive after 7.30pm expect to queue as this humble eatery has already had its cover blown as one of the best Vietnamese in London.

Southern England

SOUTHERN ENGLAND

HIGHLIGHTS

- Stand on the edge of the landmass and contemplate the sea at **Land's End** (p83)
- See ancient Roman baths and take a dip at a spa in **Bath** (p67)
- Be king (or queen) for a day at majestic **Windsor Castle** (p67)
- Indulge your artistic side at the **Glastonbury Music Festival** (p74)
- Take part in the UK's largest **charity bike ride** (27,000 riders) (p3) along the scenic route between London and the trendy seaside resort town of Brighton
- Celebrate all things two-wheeled with hundreds of cycling events at the annual **National Bike Week** (p354)
- See amazing performances by talented musicians and bop to a variety of music from retro to rock at **Isle of Wight Festival** (p61)

CYCLING EVENTS

London to Brighton Bike Ride (June)

TERRAIN

This region is fun to bike, with mostly undulating hills, including some big roller coasters around Cornwall and Exmoor National Park – in Kent, Sussex and Somerset you'll find mostly flat riding through low-lying areas.

Telephone Code: ☎ 0117   **www.visitsoutheastengland.com**

Cycling in Southern England, past rows of mossy green hedges and sheer grey cliffs, is an epic adventure through the country's most storybook countryside. Whether you're on the beach at Lyme Regis or exploring the Roman legacy in historic, photogenic Bath, you can be sure that not only are the timeless ruins and picture perfect castles as charming as their evocative names predict, they are among the warmest, sunniest bits of England!

History buffs will love this corner of the country, which is scattered with the remnants of ancient civilisations and battlegrounds, including the impressive secret war tunnels through Dover Castle.

From the raw, ethereal beauty of Land's End to the Bohemian rhapsody of Londoners favourite weekend beach retreat, Brighton, England has a lot of good beachfront property, and Cornwall is where to head for the warmest, clearest water, and best surfing. In the middle of it all is Canterbury, England's spiritual heart, where you should lock the bike and pause to check out the magnificent cathedral before cruising the ancient winding streets and grabbing a pick-me-up espresso.

PLANNING

Biking is in Southwest England these days, especially around Bath, Bristol and Somerset where the number of cycling visitors has increased by 24 percent since 2003 (well above the national trend). Bristol has even been named the UK's first official 'cycling city', with £11.4 million in government funds awarded to transform it into a cycling mecca. Expect bicycle traffic to increase in the coming years – especially since the southwest also boasts the warmest and sunniest weather in Britain (the brave can even surf near Cornwall).

The following websites have great info and maps:

o www.bristol.gov.uk/cycling
o www.cywest.com.uk
o www.travelbristol.org
o www.sustrans.org.uk

GATEWAYS

See London (p37) and Bristol (p84).

SOUTHEAST COAST

Duration 4 days
Distance 193.8 miles
Difficulty moderate
Start Canterbury
Finish Portsmouth

Summary Rolling downs and winding lanes mixed with breathtaking natural scenery balances nicely against a backdrop of rich historical and cultural attractions. The only downer is the traffic.

From the ecclesiastical centre of Canterbury to the chalky white cliffs and dark blue sea near Dover, this route takes in the counties of Kent, East and West Sussex and Hampshire, and traverses some of England's most bucolic and historical countryside. The proximity of the ride to central London – no portion of the route is more than 65 miles away – makes it a popular weekend road-trip, and is both a blessing and a curse. If you don't mind sharing the road with a stream of honking cars and lorries, you'll love the easy access to Britain's principal gateway city. But if you like more space on the road, this may not be the trip for you. Get past the traffic, however, and you'll be one happy rider –

there are plenty of pubs to grab meals, lovely B&Bs to rest your head and attractive, friendly and easily navigated towns to explore along the way.

PLANNING

Late spring to early summer, or early autumn, is best – avoid summer school holidays.

Maps

The ride is covered by OS Travelmaster Map No 9 1:250,000 *South East England*. The OS Cycle Tours: *Kent, Surrey & Sussex* could be useful if you plan to explore off the route.

Cycle Hire

Canterbury Cycle Mart (☎ 01227 761488; Lower Bridge St, Canterbury)
Rock 'n' Road Cycles (☎ 023 9229 4770; 10 Lord Montgomery Way, Portsmouth)

GETTING TO/FROM THE RIDE
Canterbury (start)
BUS

Eurolines (www.eurolines.com) connects Canterbury with London (£22, four hours).

TRAIN

The **National Rail Service** (☎ 08457 48 49 50; www.nationalrail.co.uk) runs services from London Victoria station to Canterbury (£25, two hours). The train trip from Dover Priory (ferry port to/from France) to Canterbury is less than 30 minutes (£6).

Portsmouth (finish)
BUS

National Express Bus service from London to Portsmouth (£8, three hours)

TRAIN

The **National Rail Service** (☎ 08457 48 49 50) offers services from Portsmouth Harbour to London (£35, two hours) among other destinations.

THE RIDE
Day 1: Canterbury to Hythe
5–7 hours, 44.4 miles

Wide open spaces, coastal towns and castles are the highlights of this meandering day. Your cycling odyssey begins in beautiful **Canterbury**, a city that has drawn crowds of

SOUTHERN ENGLAND

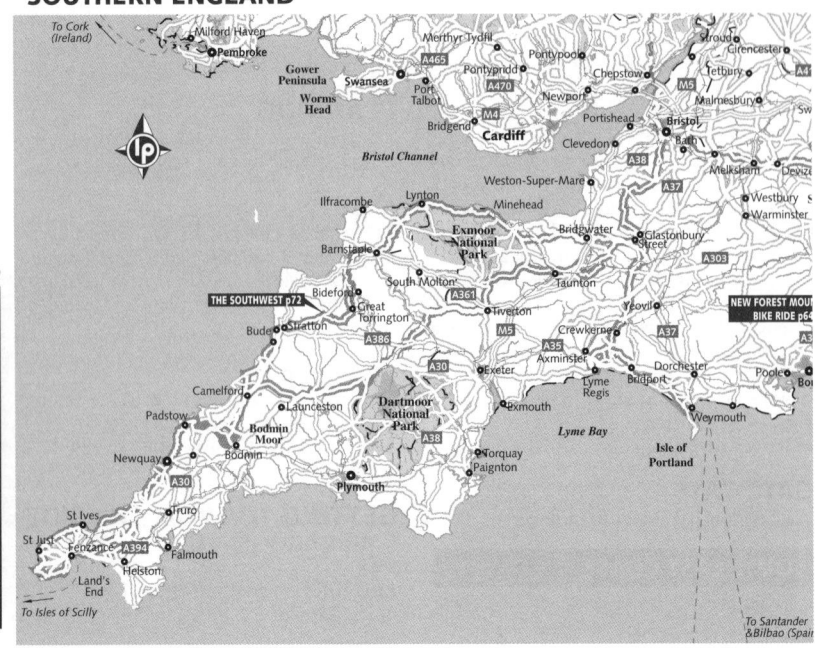

SOUTHEAST COAST – DAY 1

CUE			GPS COORDINATES	
start		Canterbury TIC	15 16'47"N	1 04'52"E
0 miles		go NE on St Margaret's St		
	⌐	(50yd) High St/St George's St		
0.2	⌐	Lower Chantry Lane		
0.3	⌐ ◎	Longport/A257		
	▲	0.5 miles moderate climb		
3.8		Littlebourne	51 16'32"N	1 10'08"E
6.6	⌐	B2046, Wingham	51 16'24"N	1 12'54"E
6.7	⌐	Staple Rd		
6.8	↘	'to Staple'		
8.6	↘	School Lane, Staple	51 15'46"N	1 15'17"E
8.7	⌐	Lower Rd/Fleming Rd		
10.6	⌐	'to Sandwich'		
12.6	⌐	Sandwich	51°16'29.32"N	1°20'20.03"E
12.9	↘	Cattle Market/Harnet St		
13.1	⌐	Strand St		
13.2	↘	The Quay/bikepath		
17.5	⌐	unsigned road		
17.7	⌐	Ethelbert Rd		
	⌐	(50yd) Godwyn Rd		
17.8	⌐	The Marina/Beach St		
19.0	★	Deal	51°13'18.85"N	1°24'9.62"E
	⌐	Deal Castle Rd		
19.1	⌐	The Strand/A258		

CUE CONTINUED			GPS COORDINATES	
19.9	↘	'to Kingsdown'		
20.4	★	Walmer Castle		
21.6	↗	unsigned road		
22.0	⌐	Chalk Hill Rd, Kingsdown	51°11'1.94"N	1°23'42.19"E
23.0	⌐	A258		
23.1	⌐	Front St		
23.4	⌐	'to Martin Mill'		
24.9	⌐	'to Martin Mill'		
25.2	⌐	'to St Margaret's'		
25.7	⌐	A258		
	⌐	(50yd) 'to St Margaret's'		
26.9	⌐	'to Dover', St Margaret's	51° 9'11.03"N	1°22'21.95"E
29.3	★	White Cliffs Historic Site		
30.3	★	Dover	51° 7'52.09"N	1°19'6.86"E
	⌐	A258		
30.4	⌐	Connaught Rd		
31.0	⌐	Frith Rd/Eaton Rd		
32.2	⌐	College Row		
32.3	⌐	B2011		
	▲	3.4 miles moderate climb		
35.7	⌐	Old Dover Rd		
36.8	⌐	B2011		

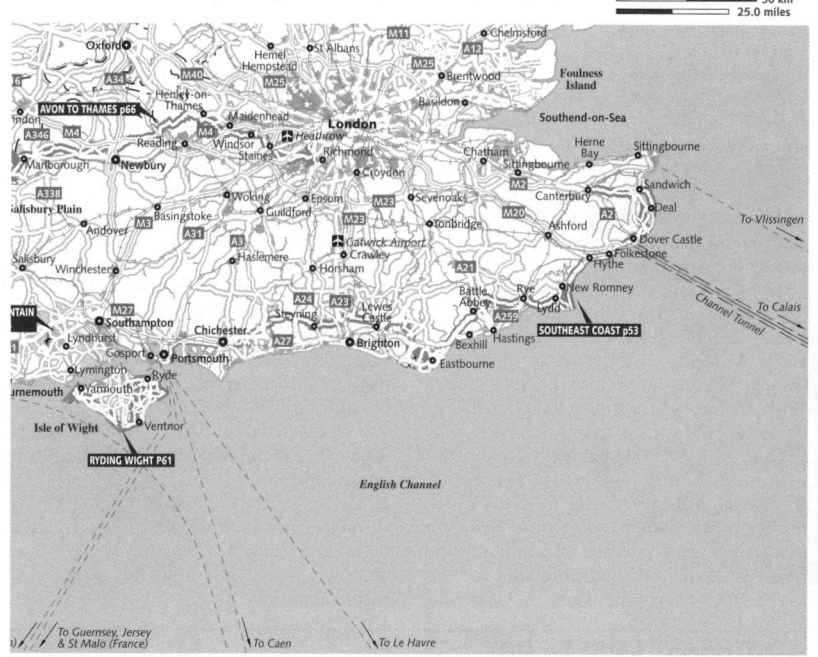

pilgrims and tourists since the 12th century martyrdom of Archbishop Becket. These days it's a market town and service centre, with over two million visitors annually but, remarkably, manages to retain its character. Its primary attraction, **Canterbury Cathedral**, has been England's ecclesiastical cornerstone since the early 7th century. The cathedral, **St Augustine's Abbey** and

St Martin's Church were inscribed on the Unesco World Heritage list in 1988. Check it out before getting on your bike and following the A257 out of Canterbury and into the charming Kent countryside. If you're riding on the weekends or during rush hour, this is the stretch of pavement that sees a lot of road traffic, so be careful. Once you reach the rolling hills east of Canterbury heading to pretty Sandwich, the traffic thins and the ride becomes a lot more relaxing. **Sandwich** is reputedly one of England's most complete medieval towns. Until the 17th-century, English Channel tides came far enough up the River Stour estuary to make Sandwich a Cinque Port. You'll leave Sandwich on the bikepath beside the Stour, which joins St George's Rd. Cyclists pay no toll at the entrance to **Sandwich Bay Private Estate**. On the Ancient Highway, which crosses the estate, you'll be entertained by birdsong and the sight of golfers duffing their shots on the area's famous links courses.

The route is flat from Sandwich all the way to Kingsdown. En route, you'll pass Deal (where, it's claimed, Julius Caesar

CUE CONTINUED		GPS COORDINATES	
36.9	★	Battle of Britain Memorial	
37.8	↰	Dover Rd	
38.4	↖⊙	Morrison Rd/Tram Rd	
39.0	★	Folkestone	51° 4'49.06"N 1°11'6.93"E
	↰	Harbour St	
39.1	↱	Lower Sandgate Rd	
39.2	↰	Harbour Approach	
39.3	↱	Marine Pde/Castle Rd	
40.6	↰	High St/A259	
41.8	↘	Prince's Parade	
43.5	↱	Twiss Rd	
43.8	↰	East St/A259	
	★	Royal Military Canal	
43.9	↖⊙	A259	
44.4		Hythe TIC	51° 4'16.73"N 1° 4'21.11"E

landed in 55 BC) and Walmer, both of which have fine castles – built by Henry VIII as protection against possible French invasion. From Kingsdown, short climbs and descents punctuate the few miles to Dover. There's no charge for cyclists to enter the **White Cliffs historic site** (29.3 miles), where you'll get the best views of Dover's bustling, 600-acre port. The route passes near **Dover Castle**, standing a proud 114m (375ft) above the sea, and avoids the town centre.

The day's longest climb leads you out of town on the B2011. It's steady rather than steep, and the **Battle of Britain Memorial** at its top is a good place to catch your breath. The evocative monument – under skies that, in 1940, witnessed the most hectic aerial battles in Britain's defence – was opened in 1993. Head downhill from the memorial through Folkestone and across the **Royal Military Canal**, built as a defensive moat when Napoleon was Europe's main man, and into the pleasant seaside resort of Hythe. Your resting spot for the night is an engaging place, with period

houses lining the old streets and lanes that tumble down Quarry Hill to High St.

Day 2: Hythe to Eastbourne
6–8 hours, 59.1 miles

The day starts 2.8 miles from the Hythe tourist office on the **seafront promenade**. The first 5.5 miles are a glorious off-road section to **Littlestone-on-Sea**. From here it's a long, pancake flat ride (pump up the tunes and spin) all the way to Dungeness on the Coast Drive. Consider visiting the 43.5m (143ft) **Old Lighthouse at Dungeness** – with good weather you'll get spectacular views north to the white cliffs and east to France. The road to Lydd-on-Sea has fast-moving traffic and can be trying, but the bird life in the **Royal Society for the Protection of Birds (RSPB) Denge Reserve** and its watchers will keep you entertained.

The rest of the journey to Rye twists through fairly stark terrain broken by such delights as quarries and electricity stanchions. Distant hills hold the promise of nicer surrounds.

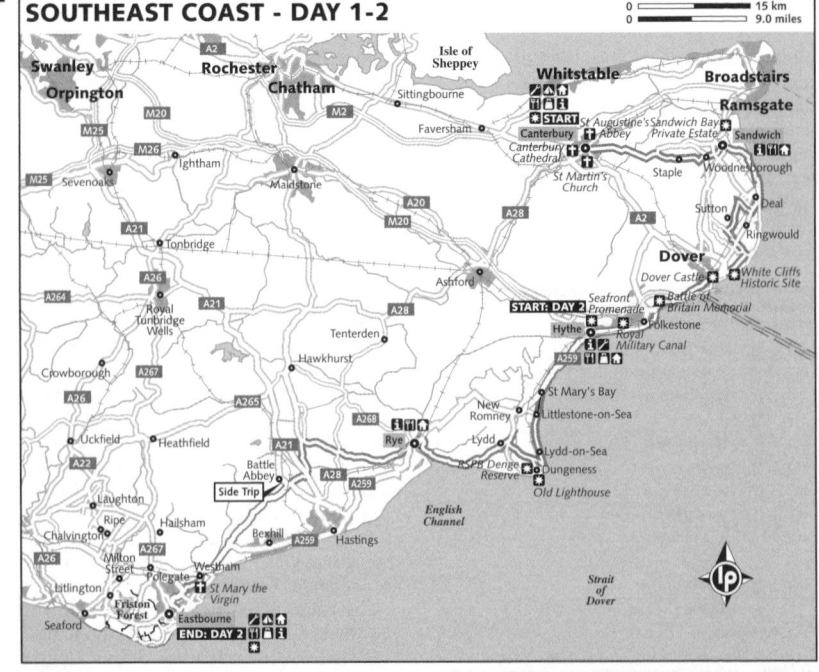

SOUTHEAST COAST - DAY 1-2

SOUTHEAST COAST – DAY 2

CUE		GPS COORDINATES
start	Hythe TIC	51° 4'16.73"N 1° 4'21.11"E
0 miles	go SW on A259	
2.8	onto seafront esplanade	
5.3	Dymchurch	51° 1'29.19"N 0°59'46.59"E
8.3	Marine Parade,	50°58'52.25"N 0°58'4.68"E
	Littlestone-on-Sea	
9.3	Greatstone-on-Sea	50°58'5.98"N 0°57'44.78"E
12.1	Lydd-on-Sea	50°56'55.45"N 0°57'58.72"E
12.3	Battery Rd	
	Old Dungeness Lighthouse	
14.2	Denge Reserve	
15.5	'to Rye', Lydd	50°57'7.75"N 0°54'27.82"E
16.0	Tourney Rd	
21.0	Camber	50°56'1.32"N 0°47'45.76"E
24.7	New Rd/A259	
25.3	Rye	50°57'8.57"N 0°44'1.87"E
25.7	A259	
26.1	Wish St/Cinque Ports St	
26.2	B2089	
31.8	Broad Oak	50°58'3.38"N 0°38'14.70"E
36.1	B2165, Cripps Corner	50°57'45.43"N 0°31'49.34"E
36.2	B2244	
38.2	Sedlescombe	50°56'5.76"N 0°31'57.42"E
39.0	A21	

CUE CONTINUED		GPS COORDINATES
39.5	Marley Lane	
41.6	A2100, Battle	50°54'55.15"N 0°29'9.28"E
●●	Battle Abbey 1 mile	
41.7	B2095	
43.8	'to Catsfield'	
44.0	Catsfield	50°53'49.25"N 0°26'54.76"E
45.3	Ninfield	50°53'11.22"N 0°25'31.14"E
45.5	A269	
45.6	B2095	
49.3	A259	
52.2	Castle Rd/High St	
	Pevensey Castle	
52.6	Westham	50°48'59.47"N 0°19'27.59"E
52.8	Eastbourne Rd/Hide Hollow	
54.2	'to Town Centre'	
55.0	Highfield Link/Cross Levels Way	
56.4	Kings Drive/Bedfordwell Rd	
57.8	Upper Ave	
58.0	(2nd exit) Upper Ave/The Avenue	
58.4	Station Parade	
58.5	Grove Rd (left fork)	
58.7	South St	
58.9	Gilredge Rd	
59.0	Hyde Gardens (4th right)	
59.1	Eastbourne TIC	50°46'4.88"N 0°17'1.93"E

Lovely **Rye** is so Olde English it's almost twee and, not surprisingly, tourists crowd its cream-tea and antique shoppes. The B2089 out of Rye can get busy with traffic, but for the next 20-or-so miles it provides a taste of Weald woodlands. Forest tracts, rolling farmlands and attractive villages make it a memorable section. There's a short stretch on the A21 just after Sedlescombe, then more quiet pedalling up to the short side trip to **Battle Abbey tourist office** (☎ 01424 773721), site of William of Normandy's clash with King Harold II in 1066 (go right at 46.1 miles).

Apart from the turns around Catsfield and Ninfield (the signs can confuse) it's a fairly straightforward run to Eastbourne. The route passes Ninfield and Pevensey Castle, William's first stronghold on English soil – parts of the old Roman fort walls still stand. **St Mary the Virgin church** in nearby Westham was the first Norman church in England, built in 1080. While it may lack Brighton's mad sparkle, **Eastbourne** is a quintessentially, do-like-to-be-beside-the-seaside English coastal resort. Beyond the inevitable fun pier and legion fish and chip joints, it's a dignified

place, renowned for its gardens, theatres and grass court tennis centre, site of the annual women's tournament that's a traditional Wimbledon lead-up.

Day 3: Eastbourne to Steyning
5–7 hours, 45.9 miles

With fair weather, this day is likely to be the tour's highlight. Mostly, the route skirts north of the beautiful **South Downs** on quiet, sealed roads, passing through charming villages and towns.

The route out of Eastbourne on the A259 includes one of the day's longer climbs and is usually busy with traffic, which evaporates once you've turned right towards Litlington (6.6 miles). From here, the going is easy and undulating all the way to Lewes. There are some tricky turns around the villages of Chalvington and beautiful Ripe – keep following the signs to Ripe and Laughton and you won't go wrong.

Lewes, roughly the halfway mark, is a fascinating place to explore. The remains of **Lewes Castle** date back to Norman times and the adjacent museum puts the region's various masters in perspective. The narrow

SOUTHERN ENGLAND

SOUTHEAST COAST - DAY 3-4

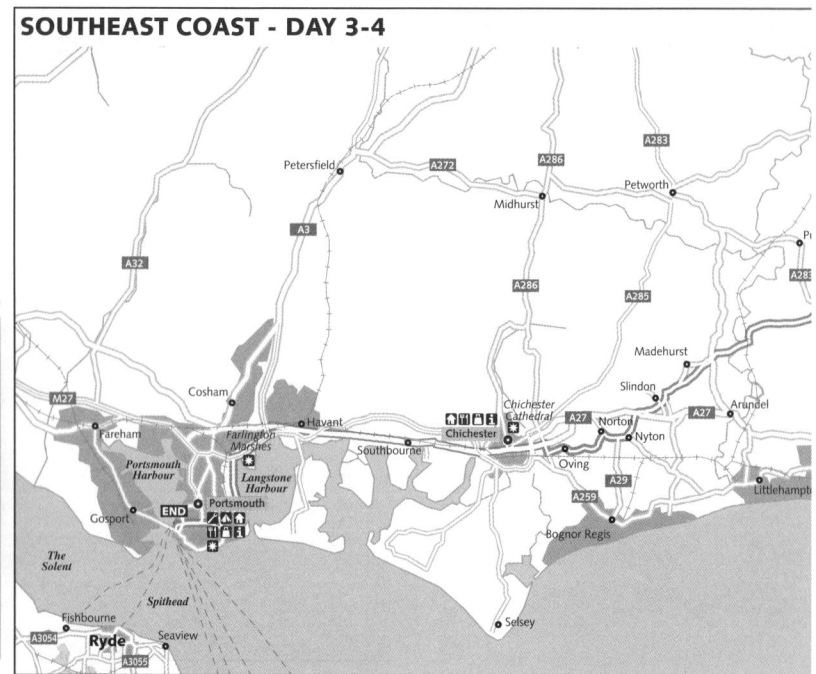

SOUTHEAST COAST – DAY 3

CUE			GPS COORDINATES	
start		Eastbourne TIC	50°46'4.88"N	0°17'1.93"E
0 miles		go N on Cornfield Rd		
0.0	↰	(50yd) Terminus Rd/Upperton Rd		
0.5	↖	The Goffs/East Dean Rd		
	▲	1.5 miles hard climb		
3.6		East Dean	50°45'25.73"N	0°12'23.49"E
	▲	0.7 miles hard climb		
6.6	↱	'to Litlington'		
8.2		Litlington	50°47'48.83"N	0° 9'37.53"E
9.0	↰	'to Alfriston'		
9.6	↖	'to Alfriston'		
9.9	↱	'to Berwick Stn'		
12.7	↰	'to Chalvington'		
13.6	↗	'to Chalvington/Ripe'		
14.4	↰	'to Ripe'		
15.2	↰	'to Laughton/Lewes', Ripe	50°53'54.91"N	0° 8'4.18"E
15.3	↱	'to Laughton'		
16.1	↱	'to Laughton'		
16.8	↰	'to Laughton'		
17.9	↰	B2124 'to Ringmer', Laughton	50°53'43.41"N	0° 5'19.66"E
20.8	↰ ⊙	B2192 'to Lewes', Ringmer	50°53'31.91"N	0° 3'14.59"E
22.2	●● ↰	Glyndebourne Opera House 2 miles ↺		

CUE CONTINUED			GPS COORDINATES	
23.4	↰	Malling Down/A26		
24.4	↖	Eastgate St		
24.5	★	Lewes	50°52'32.32"N	0° 1'3.23"E
	↱	High St/Western Rd		
	▲	1.5 miles hard climb		
25.3	↗	Spital Rd		
25.4	↱	Nevill Rd/A275		
27.1	↰	B2116		
29.6		Plumpton	50°54'10.61"N	0° 4'4.75"W
32.8	↰	B2112, Ditchling	50°56'19.37"N	0° 6'22.05"W
	↗	(60yd) B2112		
34.7	↖	A273, Clayton	50°55'40.38"N	0° 8'58.99"W
	▲	0.5 miles steep climb		
35.8	↱	'to Pyecombe/London A23'		
36.2	↱	over bridge 'to London A23'		
37.7	↰	'to Newtimber Hill'		
38.0	↖	Saddlescombe Rd		
38.3	↗	'to Poynings'		
38.5	↰	'to Fulking/Edburton', Poynings	50°53'39.89"N	0°12'12.75"W
39.5		Fulking	50°53'22.32"N	0°13'32.95"W
41.6	↰	A2037		
43.2		Upper Beeding	50°52'48.58"N	0°18'1.37"W
44.0	↰ ⊙	'to Steyning'		

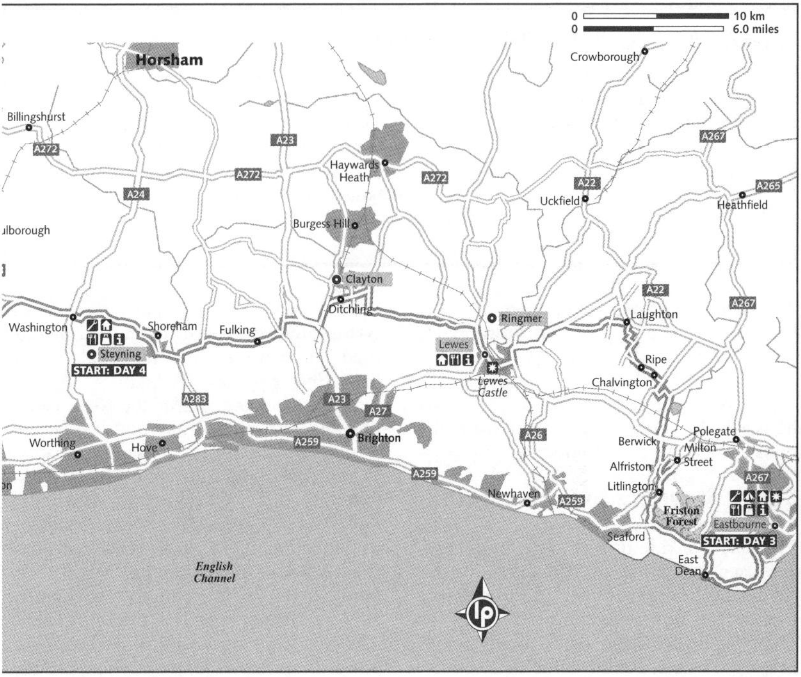

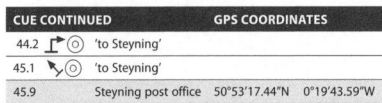

SOUTHERN ENGLAND

CUE CONTINUED		GPS COORDINATES	
44.2	⬡⊙	'to Steyning'	
45.1	⬡⊙	'to Steyning'	
45.9		Steyning post office	50°53'17.44"N 0°19'43.59"W

lanes (known locally as 'twittens') that drop steeply south from High St are worth a look – Walwers Lane and Church Twitten are probably the most arresting. Lewes is also known for it's impressive festivities on Bonfire Night (5 November). The first part of the climb up High St is very steep and you may find it easier to walk, if your bike is heavily laden.

After a short run on the A275 comes a magical section in the lee of the South Downs. The route winds through lovely tracts of woodland, broken by broad views north over Sussex countryside. **Ditchling** (32.8 miles) is a nice spot for a break. From here catch speed up on steep descent because it's a stiff climb up past Ditchling Beacon.

The route takes another steep climb, but then a relieving descent en route to Pyecombe, near which a bikepath lets you avoid the roaring A23 traffic. The next section includes the quiet, pretty villages of Poynings, Fulking and Edburton. Expect a few miles of heavier traffic on the A2037

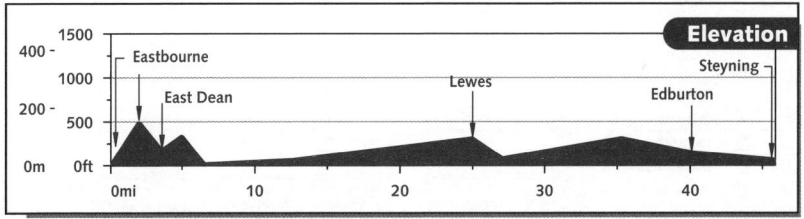

THE SACRED AND THE PROFANE

Chichester Cathedral has been an inspiration across the ages and and has a few unique distinctions to prove it. Described by architectural historian Nikolaus Pevsner as 'the most typical English cathedral', Chichester is the only English cathedral visible from the sea, and despite its age features works by several modern artists including a stained glass window by Marc Chagall.

The beautiful building inspired Leonard Bernstein to write the Chichester Psalms, considered among the composer's finest work, but it has also hosted a performance by rock band Pink Floyd, who played at the funeral of their manager, Steve O'Rourke.

and A283, but things quiet down after the turn to Serene and pretty **Steyning**, your home for night three. A thriving market and port town in the Middle Ages, today it's a quiet place where many Tudor and Stuart houses still stand. It boasts several friendly pubs and good eating joints.

Day 4: Steyning to Portsmouth
5–7 hours, 44.4 miles

This day is a ride in two parts, both characterised by some of the tour's busier roads and heaviest traffic. The undulating first part of the route continues along the picturesque northern flank of the South Downs. There's a solid climb of 1.5 miles over the downs after Houghton village, followed by a howling fast two miles of straight downhill.

The route's second part, from about Nyton onwards, is mostly on level, straight roads, broken only by a mid-route visit to busy Chichester at 29A South St. It's easy navigating in and out of the town centre, but take care in surrounding traffic. Dismount in the busy shopping precinct. While here, you must pay a visit to the 900-year-old **Chichester Cathedral** (☎ 01243 782595; www.chichester cathedral.org.uk; West St; requested donation £5; open 7.15am-7pm Jun-Aug, 7.15am-6pm Sep-May). The church was begun in 1075 and largely rebuilt in the 13th century. Three storeys of beautiful arches sweep upwards, and Romanesque carvings are dotted around. The freestanding church tower was built in the 15th century, and the spire is 19th century. Take a break on its grassy lawn.

SOUTHEAST COAST – DAY 4

CUE		GPS COORDINATES
start		Steyning post office 50°53'17.44"N 0°19'43.59"W
0 miles		go NW on High St/Horsham Rd
0.9	⬏	A283
7.0	⬏	B2139, Storrington 50°55'4.42"N 0°27'5.66"W
10.3	★	Amberley Museum
11.7		Houghton 50°53'40.23"N 0°33'10.74"W
	▲	1.5 miles moderate climb
17.4	↘/⊙	A29
18.5	⬏/⊙	A29
18.8	↗	B2233
19.6	⬏	minor unsigned road
21.5		Oving 50°50'13.53"N 0°43'15.65"W
22.5	⬏	B2144
23.0	⬏	B2144
24.2	⬏	The Hornet
24.4	↘	The Hornet/East St
24.7	★	Chichester 50°50'11.39"N 0°46'45.19"W
	⬏	South St/Southgate
25.0	⚠	walk on footpath (RHS)
25.1	⬏	Ave de Chartres
25.2	↘/⊙	A259

CUE CONTINUED		GPS COORDINATES
26.0	↙/⊙	A259
26.3		Fishbourne 50°50'9.29"N 0°48'55.98"W
26.9	●●⬏	Roman ruins & museum 1 mile ↺
30.9		Southbourne 50°51'12.54"N 0°54'33.13"W
33.6	↑/⊙	Emsworth Rd 'to Havant'
35.1	↘	Bedhampton Rd/B2149
35.6	↘/⊙	Bedhampton Hill/B2177
36.0	⬏/⊙	'to Portsmouth'
36.3	⬏	'to rejoin A27'
37.7	↘	'to Southsea A2030'
38.0	⬏/⊙	A2030 (use bikepath)
	★	Farlington Marshes Reserve
40.5	↑	rejoin Eastern Rd/Velder Ave
41.0	⬏/⊙	Milton Rd/Eastney Rd
41.4	⬏	Goldsmith Ave/W Churchill Ave
43.2	↘	Lord Montgomery Way
43.4	⬏	St Michael's Rd/Anglesea Rd
43.7	⬏	Queen St
44.3	⬏	The Hard
44.4		Portsmouth 50°48'49.61"N 1° 6'4.99"W Harbour tourist information centre

From Chichester to Portsmouth the route is flat and – easy cycling aside – the outlook somewhat drab after a few days in the Sussex countryside. The A259 traffic isn't so noticeable – the road only occasionally narrows, and you can opt for roadside bikepaths here and there. The final miles into Portsmouth are surprisingly pleasant (apart from a few moments close to, but not endangered by, fast-moving traffic). More than half of the route's last 6 miles are on bikepaths or roadside cycle lanes, and there are fine views of the **Farlington Marshes**, a bird reserve, and **Langstone Harbour**. Trashed in parts by WWII bombing, **Portsmouth** isn't the prettiest place at first glance, but its long association with the Royal Navy lends it a certain gritty aura. But it will do as a sleeping spot for the night.

GET OFF THE PATH: CYCLING THE SOUTH DOWNS WAY

The 100-mile off-road South Downs Way (SDW) national trail is the only one of England's classic long-distance walks that's also a bridleway for its entire length, and therefore open to cyclists. And biking it is a true pleasure.

Cycling the SDW takes as long or as short as you like. It's been done in two days, but such haste robs you of the chance to enjoy some of southern Britain's finest vistas and prettiest villages. If you aim to cover 20 miles to 30 miles a day you'll complete the route in four days and have energy for off-track detours. Be prepared for regular dismounts to open and close gates – there are more than 80 along the route.

You could tackle the SDW on a touring bike, but a lot of the terrain really merits a mountain bike. Tracks, particularly up on the ridge line, are often strewn with flints and sharp stones – the rough going makes for some challenging climbs and descents. Make sure your touring toolkit is up to scratch before departure, and carry spare brake blocks and a couple of inner tubes in addition to your puncture repair kit. As with any off-road cycling, you shouldn't ride alone. The path passes within a few miles of Eastbourne.

RYDING WIGHT

Duration 2 days
Distance 53 miles
Difficulty easy–moderate
Start Ryde
Finish Yarmouth
Summary Warm, quiet and compact, the Isle of Wight is a cyclist's paradise, with easy access via ferry, pretty and welcoming towns and short days in the saddle.

Often referred to as 'England in miniature', the Isle of Wight is a cyclist paradise that's home to some of the UK's most varied terrain. From lush velvet hills rolling into the sea to narrow lanes through tidy hedge row arches, this route has something for everyone: Beginners get a beautiful introduction to the sport on quiet country roads where traffic is rarely an issue – experts have the chance to kick back and really enjoy the stupendous ocean views and deep and mysterious green gullies. Although cyclists have been tasting the island's addictive outdoor pleasures for decades now, it's only been since the turn of the century that Wight has started to attract the young and trendy Londoner looking for a romantic country weekend on the beach – with a buzz. Which White's gastro oriented pubs, slick hotels and festivals dedicated to everything from cycling to garlic to rock star bands now provide (with pride).

ENVIRONMENT

The island's most striking feature is the chalk white ridge stretching from its most westerly point, The Needles, to Culver Cliff, near its most easterly tip. Remarkably, considering how much smaller it is than the North and South Downs (p57), this is actually Britain's deepest chalk bed.

PLANNING

The best times to ride are during the late spring or early summer, or during the short autumn season. Temperatures are warmer here than in other parts of Britain, so you can get away with riding later in the season. Avoid summer school holidays – the Isle of Wight is a very popular spot with British families on short breaks, and the place becomes crowded and uncomfortable to cycle around. Plus hotels fill up and prices rise.

If you are planning on sleeping here during July and August, book ahead.

Our Ryding Wight trip is based substantially on the great 62-mile Round-the-Island (RTI) cycle route, but our two-day version skips two of Wight's largest (and least cycle friendly) towns, Cowes and Newport. We travel clockwise around the island, but for a bigger challenge, ride this route in reverse and do the entire loop – the biggest hills come going counter-clockwise in the rugged southern section.

Maps

OS Travelmaster Map No 9 1:250,000 *South East England* or Landranger 196 *The Solent & Isle of Wight* are the best maps for this area. The Isle of Wight council's excellent *Round-the-Island Cycle Route* map (free at the island's tourist office) is very useful – the council also publishes four guides to off-road cycling on the island. For further explorations use Ron Crick's *A Cyclist's Guide to the Isle of Wight* and *Cycling Wight*, by John Goodwin and Ian Williams, in two parts.

GETTING TO/FROM THE RIDE

Unless you can perform miracles and cycle across the sea, there's no way to directly ride to the start in Ryde. You can take your bike on the passenger ferry in Portsmouth (the ending point for our **Southeast Coast ride** on p53) and motor south on open ocean for about 15 minutes to the Isle of Wight.

Ryde (start)
BUS

Southern Vectis (☎ 0870 532 373; www .islandbuses.info) runs busses to Ryde from points around the island (only the remote southwest corner between Blangang Chine and Brook does not receive regular services). Buses run around every 15 minutes. Check the schedule online.

FERRY

Wightlink (☎ 0870 582 7744; www.wight link.co.uk) passenger ferries sail from Portsmouth to Ryde pier – it costs £11 for the 15-minute crossing (bikes free). Ferries leave from the western end of Portsmouth Harbour train station. The ferry runs every half-hour.

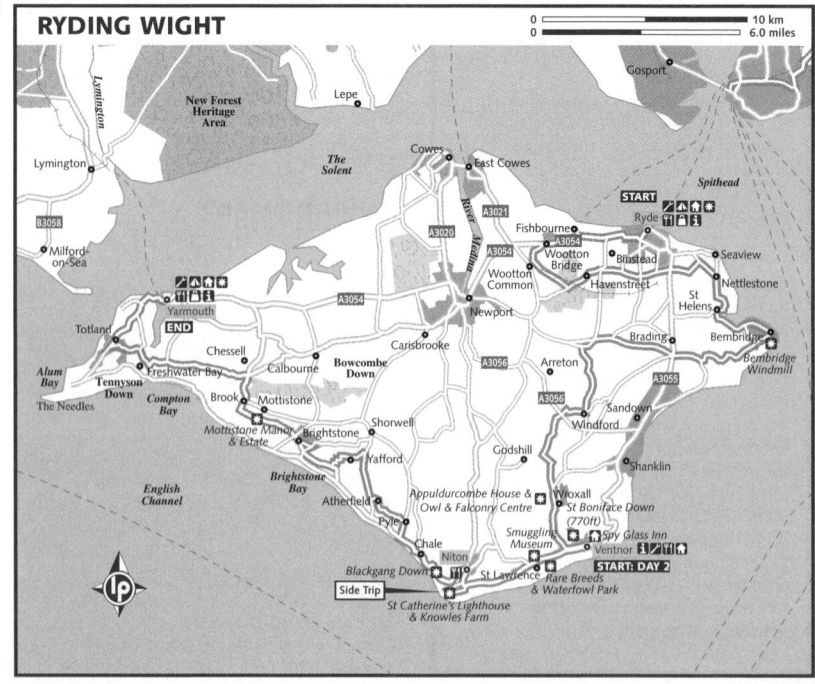

Yarmouth (finish)

TRAIN
South West Trains (☎ 023 8021 3600) has regular services from Lymington station to Southampton, Southampton airport and London Waterloo station.

FERRY
Wightlink car and passenger ferries sail from Yarmouth to Lymington – tickets cost £11 for the 35-minute journey.

THE RIDE
Day 1: Ryde to Ventor
3–4 hours, 27.1 miles

Our ride begins in **Ryde**, the Isle of Wight's largest town, and where the ferry from the British mainland alights. There's no need to linger. The city is crowded with a work-day atmosphere, too much traffic and a tacky seafront. You'll have to grin and bear it (try to avoid the morning rush, maybe grab a coffee in one of the Georgian or Victorian buildings lining the downtown – it's not that bad) and ride the A3054 motorway about 3 miles south to the junction with B3330, where you'll get off the highway and onto the cycling route's quiet country lanes through thick hedgerow arches that cut north for 12.3

miles to Wight's last surviving windmill. The **Bembridge**, which comes with creaky-looking ancient wooden machinery, is well worth a pause if you're cycling between March and October, when the National Trust monument is open. Wannabe falconers and bird lovers should follow the signs to the **Owl and Falconry Centre** another 11 miles north at mile marker 23.3. Down a half-mile long manicured drive, the centre is part of the historic **Appuldurcombe House**, and features three acres of falcon, hawk, owl, vulture and kite aviaries open from 10am to at least 4pm. The British sport of royals has been practiced here since Henry the VIII first visited in 1539. Aside from flying displays, the centre offers visitors a number of courses allowing them to experience the thrill of falconry (vegetarians beware, this involves your falcon hunting, and killing, rabbits and ducks).

After you've gotten your falcon fix, continue east along the coast and then to the islands northern most tip, **Ventnor**, where you'll crash for the night. You will wind down the southern face of the National Trust-managed Ventnor Downs, which rises abruptly from the seaside to one of the island's highest points, 231m (770ft) **St Boniface Down**.

RYDING WIGHT – DAY 1

CUE			GPS COORDINATES
start		Ryde TIC	50°43'47.92"N 1° 9'47.18"W
0 miles		go S on Union St	
0.2	↙	High St	
0.3	↱	Garfield Rd	
0.4	↰	Victoria St	
0.5	↱	John St/Queens Rd	
0.8	↱	Binstead Rd/A3054	
{2.2	★	Quarr Abbey ruins}	
3.1	↰	Firestone Copse Rd	
4.6	↰	Newnham Rd	
4.8	↱	Stroudwood Rd/Carters Rd	
6.8	⚠	narrow railway bridge	
7.2	↙	Preston Rd (at give way signs)	
8.2	↱	Gregory Ave	
8.5	↱	B3330	
10.4	↘	pass left of St Helens Green	
10.5	↰	Latimer Rd	
10.8	↰	B3395 'to Bembridge'	
12.2	↱	'to Bembridge Windmill'	
{12.3	★	Bembridge Windmill}	
14.1	↰	B3395	
16.3	↘	Lower Adgestone Rd	

CUE CONTINUED			GPS COORDINATES
16.8	↱	unsigned minor road	
16.9	↰	unsigned road (opp vineyard)	
17.9	↱	'to Alverstone'	
19.1	↘	'to Apse Heath'	
19.5	↱	Forest Way	
20.0	↱	unsigned minor road	
	↰	(10yd) 'to Newport'	
20.2	↰	'to Newport' Bathingbourne Lane	
22.1	↱	A3020	
	↰	(40yd) Redhill Lane	
23.3	↰	Appuldurcombe Rd	
{	★	Appuldurcombe House & Owl Centre}	
23.4	↱	B3327	
23.8	↱	West St/Rew Lane	
25.2	↱	B3327	
25.7	↰	Ocean View Rd/Mitchell Ave	
26.4	↱	Spring Hill	
26.6	↰	High St	
26.7	↱	Victoria St	
26.8	↱	Albert St	
26.9	↱	Pier St	
27.0	↱	High St	
27.1		Ventnor TIC	50°35'41.93"N 1°12'21.10"W

Once you arrive in town, look for the **Spy Glass Inn** (p91) on the seafront esplanade. It's your crash-pad for the night, and also where to grab a few pints and grub before heading to bed.

Day 2: Ventnor to Yarmouth

3–4 hours, 26 miles

The second day follows the RTI cycle route past wonderful ocean views for most of the ride – crank up your MP3 player and just roll – you're guaranteed to get a smile on your face well before you get tired. Expect some traffic along the day's first portion of the ride – which follows the A3055 – but it's worth putting up with, because once you lose it expect a series of roller coaster hills past lovely arch-typical English country-

RYDING WIGHT – DAY 2

CUE			GPS COORDINATES	
start		Ventnor TIC	50°35'38"N	1°12'9"W
0 miles		go W on High St		
0.0	↗	(50yd) Church St/A3055		
0.1	↗	Alpine Rd/Zig Zag Rd/A3055		
1.8	★	St Lawrence	50°35'14"N	1°14'23"W
3.6	↰	St Catherine's Rd		
3.9	↱	Sandrock Rd		
	●●↑	lighthouse & farm 0.5 miles ↻		
	▲	0.4 miles moderate climb		
4.2	↰	A3055		
4.6		Niton	50°35'15"N	1°17'5"W
	▲	1.1 miles moderate climb		
7.4	↱	'to Atherfield Green'		
7.9	↰	Atherfield Rd		
10.3	↰	'to Yafford'		
10.9	↱	'to Brighstone'		
11.1	↰	'to Brighstone'		
11.4	↰	'to Thorncross'		
12.0	↱	Mill Lane 'to Brighstone'		
12.7	↱	New Rd		
13.1	↰	B3399		
13.3		Brighstone	50°38'33"N	1°23'41"W
15.1	★	Mottistone Manor & Estate		
15.7	↰	'to Brook'		
	↰	(40yd) unsigned road		
16.0	★	Brook	50°39'6"N	1°27'2"W
16.3	↱	A3055		
21.8	↱	Alum Bay New Rd/B3322		
	●●↰	Needles Old Battery 2.6 miles ↻		
25.6	↱◎	River Rd		
25.7	↰	St James St		
25.9	↰	Quay St		
	↰	(30yd) The Quay		
26.0		Yarmouth TIC	50°42'21"N	1°30'2"W

side homes and lush woodland stands. The ocean stretches south from the shoreline, where steep emerald hills meet dark, deep ocean water blue stretches of open ocean.

Just two miles into the ride you'll stumble across both the **Smuggling Museum**, open daily from April to September; and the **Rare Breeds & Waterfowl Park**, open year-round. After another 1.9 miles park your bike and follow the signs to the 1840s St **Catherine's Lighthouse** and National Trust-listed **Knowles Farm**. Both are reached via a short climb from the bike route – the later features fields divided by stone walls rather than hedges. Guglielmo Marconi, inventor of the first successful wire telegraph, lived at Knowles for a time and conducted some of his earliest experiments in wireless here.

There are several places to grab a bite in **Niton** before completing the climb up **Blackgang Down**, from which you'll get what's probably the island's best outlook, including awesome sweeping views northwest towards the chalk cliffs of West Wight.

Mottistone Manor & Estate (☎ 01983 741020) at 15.1 miles, has a magnificent garden. From here continue north to **Yarmouth**, the busy ferry port where this cycling route ends.

NEW FOREST MOUNTAIN BIKE RIDE

Duration 4–6 hours
Distance 39.2 miles
Difficulty easy
Start/Finish Lyndhurst

Summary Get a taste for mountain biking on this off-road trail through Europe's largest surviving ancient pasture woodland; the trip is perfect for novice fat tire cyclists – the path is wide and level.

This trail can be ridden on a touring or mountain bike, but it's so much more fun on the later. Mostly flat, wide and easy to navigate the off-road trail is fun for novice and experienced riders alike (if you know what you are doing, go fast). The 148 sq mile **New Forest** is Europe's largest surviving area of ancient pasture woodland. It's not a national park – day-to-day management is mainly in the hands of the Forestry Commission (FC), but New Forest lands are

NEW FOREST MOUNTAIN BIKE RIDE

CUE		GPS COORDINATES
Start	Lyndhurst TIC, main car park	50°52'19"N 1°34'30"W
0 miles	go north to High St	
0.0	(50yd) Gosport Lane (A35)	
0.4	A35/Chapel Lane	
1.0	A35	
1.2	'to Emery Down'	
1.3	livestock grid	
1.6	'to Bolderwood'	
2.8	2.2 miles dirt section begins	
3.7		
4.0		
5.0	(20yd) unsigned rd	
6.0	livestock grid	
6.9	3.4 miles dirt section begins	
7.4	follow FC cycle track sign	
7.9	follow FC track No 3 sign	
9.2	follow FC track No 4 sign	
11.1	2.8 miles dirt section begins	
13.9	unsigned rd, 3.7 miles dirt section begins	
14.6	'to Burley'	
15.3	livestock grid	
18.3	Lyndhurst Rd	
19.1	2.2 miles dirt section begins	
19.3	follow FC cycle track sign	
21.3	Lyndhurst Rd	
22.1	A35, livestock grid	
22.5	Rhinefield Ornamental Drive	

CUE CONTINUED		GPS COORDINATES
22.8	1.4 miles dirt section begins	
24.0	follow FC cycle track sign	
24.2	Rhinefield Ornamental Drive	
24.6	dirt section begins (1.9 miles)	
25.5	unsigned track	
26.9	follow FC track No 26 sign	
27.8	'to Brockenhurst'	
29.2	Rhinefield Rd	
	(70yd) North Weirs	
	0.8 miles dirt section begins	
30.0	Burley Rd	
30.4	The Rise	
30.6	Sway Rd (B3055)	
31.0	Lyndhurst Rd (A337)	
31.4	Balmer Lawn Rd (B3055)	
31.6	'to Beaulieu'	
	6.6 miles dirt section begins	
32.1	'to cottage'	
32.2	'to Beaulieu'	
33.6	follow FC track No 39 sign	
35.0	follow FC cycle track sign	
36.8	'to Lyndhurst'	
37.3	follow FC track No 36 sign	
38.2	Beechen Lane	
38.4	Clay Hill (A337)	
39.0	High St (A337)	
39.1	Church Lane	
39.2	Lyndhurst TIC	50°52'19"N 1°34'30"W

actually governed by arcane (and charming) traditions and laws that date back to William the Conqueror's time.

HISTORY

William named the New Forest when setting it aside as a royal deer-hunting preserve in 1079. He introduced Forest Law, which allowed commoners (land users) to graze livestock but not to fence. The early, fairly draconian, laws were replaced by the more relaxed *Charter of the Forest* in 1217. This 'Forest Magna Carta' established the Court of the Verderers, which still sits today in Lyndhurst. The New Forest's traditional 'police' – the Agisters – still oversee the drift, or round-up, of commoners' livestock prior to branding, tail-marking and worming.

ENVIRONMENT

Free-roaming, grazing animals nibbled new tree shoots keeping the forest as mostly heath, grass and moor lands from William's time

until the late-15th century. The increased demand for boat-building timber saw the first *Inclosure Act* passed in 1482. New Forest timber was first recorded as being used for naval ships in 1611. A 1698 Act allowed the Crown to use of a maximum of 6000 acres of woodland, and the navy needed it – a large wooden warship consumed up to 60 acres of timber. The New Forest's biggest threat today is tourists (some 25 million annually) and the FC is kept busy with forest track maintenance and erosion repairs, removal of alien and pest plant species, and the restoration of the forest's rare lowland valley mires (75% of Europe's remaining lowland valley mires are in the New Forest).

PLANNING

It's possible to ride all year. The forest is beautiful in the greenery of spring and summer but the crowds are intense. The forest in winter can appear stark but there are fewer people about.

Maps & Books

The Forestry Commission's *Cycling in the New Forest: The Network Map* is basic but does the job. The OS Outdoor Leisure Map 1:25,000 *New Forest* is best for detail, or the OS Landranger series 1:50,000 has two maps that cover the area – No 195, *Bournemouth & Purbeck*, and No 196, *The Solent & Isle of Wight*. Hancock & Tom's *MTB Guide to Hampshire and New Forest* is useful if you're planning an extended stay.

GETTING TO/FROM THE RIDE
Lyndhurst (start/finish)
TRAIN

Don't even think of driving a car here, especially in summer. Train stations at Ashurst, Brockenhurst and Beaulieu Rd provide immediate access to the forest and are a short ride (less than five miles) from the New Forest's main centre, Lyndhurst. Trains to/from London Waterloo run regularly with **Connex South Central, South West** and **Virgin tourist office** (☎ 0845 748 4950) for timetable and fare information. Outside peak times you should find a service on which bikes are free – otherwise, a £3 reservation fee may apply. Lyndhurst is also on the train line to Weymouth, which is the start of the Southwest Coast ride (see p53).

THE RIDE

Cycling in the New Forest provides a wonderful break from the road, and the best part of this route is that its 25 miles of off-road tracks are well-signposted, invariably smooth and mostly very flat. A mountain bike is best for the ride, but you'll manage it easily on a touring bike. There's something of interest at just about every stage. Most noticeable are the ubiquitous ponies for which the New Forest is renowned (remember: no feeding), but expect to see all manner of livestock. The changing habitats are also fascinating. You'll pass through moorland, heath and magnificent, whispering oak and pine forest and, remarkably in this part of the England, enjoy spells of genuinely peaceful solitude.

If you tackle the route in spring, the **Rhinefield Ornamental Drive** section (22-24 miles) will be ablaze with rhododendron blossoms. Unfortunately, these densely flowering evergreens are a pest, and they're eradicated when they spread into the surrounding forest. The only thing a cyclist may find tiresome are gates – there are 21 on the route, plus several cattle grids. Be especially careful around Lyndhurst if you're touring on a summer weekend – the traffic can be intense.

From **Lyndhurst** tourist office, go north to High St then circle around with the town-centre one-way traffic flow on Gosport Lane and Chapel Lane to the A35 (at 1 mile). On leaving the A35 (1.2 miles), the change of tempo is almost immediate: deciduous trees soar overhead, casting cool shadows, and cows wander freely. In Brockenhurst, go right at **The Rise** (30.4 miles) on Burley Rd, then left at **Sway Rd** (the B3055; 30.6 miles) and left again onto Lyndhurst Rd (the A337, 31 miles). After just 400 yards on the A-road, go right at **Balmer Lawn Rd** (the B3055) then veer left ('to Beaulieu') at 31.6 miles – the route is back on dirt for the last time, for the day's longest off-road section (6.6 miles).

AVON TO THAMES

Duration 3 days
Distance 139.6 miles
Difficulty moderate–demanding
Start Bristol
Finish Richmond (London)

Summary Travel from Britain's cycling city, Bristol, to her capital city, London, on this three-day jaunt that includes traffic-free riding along the country's most famous railway track and sightseeing in picture-perfect Bath.

Southwest England's largest city, Bristol, has exploded on the cycling scene in recent years, and is now the hub of Britain's bike movement – and named the first 'cycling city' in a government scheme. As a result, the cycle paths around here are some of the best in the country. This 140-mile jaunt takes you from Bristol's heart, along the famed **Bristol & Bath Railway Path** (B&BRP), Sustrans' flagship traffic-free path, past the Roman splendor of Bath, the region's most impressive city, across Wiltshire Downs around Marlborough, Avebury and Royal Windsor before popping you into leafy Richmond, a quiet suburb in southwestern London.

HISTORY

The historical sites in this part of England cover almost the entire period of documented history. West Kennett Long Barrow dates from about 3500 BC and the prehistoric complex around Avebury was established from about 2600 to 2100 BC. Bath was first developed by the Romans as a spa town but it wasn't until the Georgian era that the city's distinctive appearance was established. Windsor Castle's association with British royalty extends back 900 years.

PLANNING

Summer is more pleasant although crowds can slow progress in busy centres such as Bristol, Bath and Windsor. Winter riding is fine – the route's high point is about 240m (720ft).

Maps

The route is entirely covered by two OS Travelmaster maps 1:250,000: No 8, *South West England & South Wales*, and No 9, *South East England*. Parts of the route follow NCN 4, and Sustrans' *Severn & Thames* route map 1:100,000 is useful, especially for the B&BRP section.

GETTING TO/FROM THE RIDE
Bristol (start)
BUS

National Express (www.nationalexpress .com) runs regular coach service to multiple points in London (from £8, 2.5 hours), including Heathrow Airport.

TRAIN

Bristol is the southwest's major rail hub, and trains leave regularly for London, the Midlands and Somerset/Devon/Cornwall.

BICYCLE

Bristol is passed through on day five of the Land's End to John O'Groats ride (p306), in the chapter of the same name.

Richmond (finish)

Richmond is 9 miles southwest of central London.

TRAIN

Richmond has an Underground station on the District line and an above ground station.

BIKE

If you're continuing into central London by bike, take the wonderful riverside bikepath, which will keep you out of the traffic as far as Putney Bridge.

THE RIDE
Day 1: Bristol to Marlborough
5–7 hours, 51.3 miles

There is a new sense of swagger and self-belief around Bristol these days – while the once-great trades of shipbuilding, manufacturing and the railways have long since sailed upriver, the city has steadily reclaimed its rightful place as an economic powerhouse, gastronomic centre and a cultural force to be reckoned with. The crumbling docks have been gentrified into an almost glamorous waterfront filled with sidewalk cafes and pubs. The streets are packed with cutting-edge restaurants, designer bars and quality museums. Bristol is still home to one of the most notoriously dangerous streets in Britain, and there's a definite raw, rough around the collar feel to this working class city, but there's also optimism in the air. After getting a feel for Bristol's edge, hop on your bike and hit the prettiest cycle-way in the region, the B&BRP. The 16-mile ride east to Bath is nothing short of delightful. Even the swarm of cyclists, walkers, runners and lets not forget the doggies, does little to dissuade us from riding. In the early sections, especially, there are a lot of feeder paths joining the route, so stay alert.

Bath (16.1 miles) defies superlatives – except if you're discussing the number of tourists gadding about the place in summer – it's history stretches back to Roman times and its wonderful Georgian architecture has seen it described on the World Heritage List. Outside of central London, this is about as intensely busy as it gets. The visiting hordes and maze of streets make Bath city centre a sensible place to walk the bike, and – to encourage a meandering course hereabouts – the route is intentionally not prescribed in the section between Green Park Rd and George St (roughly half a mile).

From around 28.1 miles, near Melksham, to Horton (39.2 miles), the route wanders onto some A-roads and you should be careful of traffic. The remaining section to Marlborough, across the downlands of

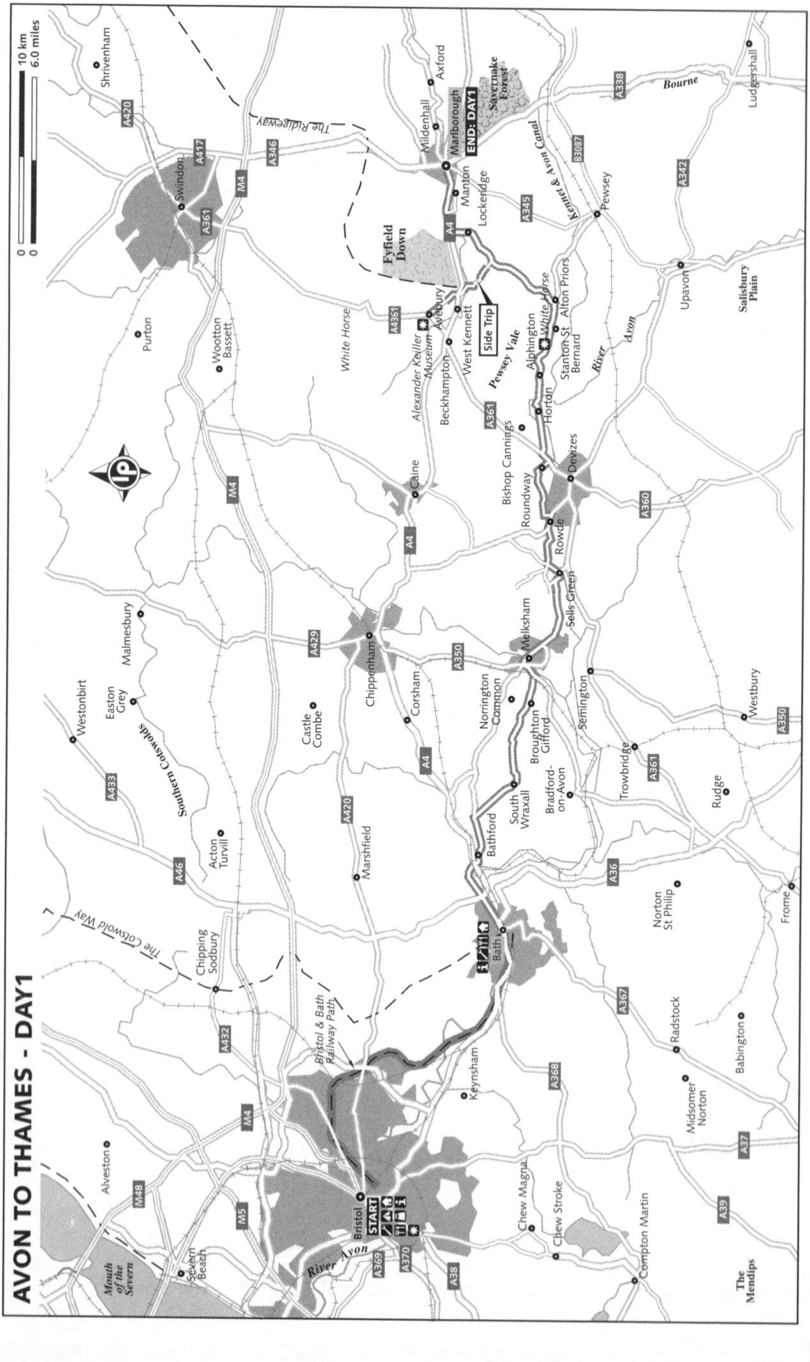

AVON TO THAMES – DAY1

10 km
6.0 miles

Shrivenham

A420

The Ridgeway

A346

Axford

Marlborough

Savernake Forest

A338

Bourne

Ludgershall

Swindon

A361

M4

A4

Mildenhall

Manton

Lockeridge

Kennet & Avon Canal

Pewsey

B3087

A342

A345

Wootton Bassett

Purton

White Horse

Fyfield Down

A4361

Avebury

West Kennett

Alexander Keiller Museum

Beckhampton

Side Trip

Pewsey Vale

White Horse

Alphington

Stanton St Bernard

Alton Priors

Horton

River Avon

Upavon

Salisbury Plain

A361

Calne

Bishop Cannings

Roundway

Rowde

Devizes

A360

Sells Green

A4

Southern Cotswolds

Malmesbury

Westonbirt

Easton Grey

M4

A429

Chippenham

Corsham

Castle Combe

A4

Norrington Common

Melksham

Broughton Gifford

Sterlington

A350

Westbury

Trowbridge

A361

Rudge

A46

Acton Turville

A420

Marshfield

South Wraxall

Bathford

Bradford-on-Avon

A36

Chipping Sodbury

The Cotswold Way

M432

Bath

Bristol & Bath Railway Path

Norton St Philip

Frome

A367

Radstock

Babington

Alveston

M48

M5

M4

Bristol

Keynsham

A368

Midsomer Norton

A37

Severn Beach

Mouth of the Severn

River Avon

A369

A370

A38

Chew Magna

Chew Stoke

Compton Martin

A39

The Mendips

START

END: DAY1

AVON TO THAMES – DAY 1

CUE		GPS COORDINATES
start	Bristol TIC	51°27'23"N 2°35'26"W
0 miles	go N on High St	
0.0	(40 yd) cross to Castle Park	
0.3	follow 'to B&BRP' signs	
1.0	B&BRP bikepath	
5.8	0.5 miles dirt path	
14.0	Brassmill Lane	
14.4	River Avon bikepath	
16.1	Bath	51°22'54"N 2°21'32"W
	Green Park Rd	
16.6	George St/London Rd/A4	
18.9	Batheaston	51°24'24"N 2°18'38"W
19.8	Bathford Hill/Upper Kingsdown Rd	
	1.7 miles moderate climb	
21.5	unsigned road (opp golf course)	
23.5	South Wraxall	51°22'54"N 2°14'32"W
25.1	'to Broughton Gifford'	
27.7	B3107 'to Melksham'	
28.1	(3rd exit) A350	

CUE CONTINUED		GPS COORDINATES
29.0	A365 'to Devizes'	
32.5	'to Bromham', Sells Green	51°21'25"N 2° 4'13"W
33.0	'to Rowde'	
34.4	A342, Rowde	51°21'49"N 2° 1'59"W
34.9	'to Roundway'	
37.7	A361	
38.2	'to Horton'	
43.0	White Horse	
43.8	'to Marlborough'	
	1.1 miles moderate climb	
46.9	Avebury 6 miles	
48.1	'to Manton'	
49.9	Manton	51°24'56"N 1°45'12"W
50.0	unsigned rd (past Oddfellows Arms)	
50.5	thru St John's Church yard	
50.6	A4 'to tourist information centre'	
51.1	George Lane	
51.2	Figgins Lane	
51.3	Marlborough TIC	51°25'7"N 1°44'0"W

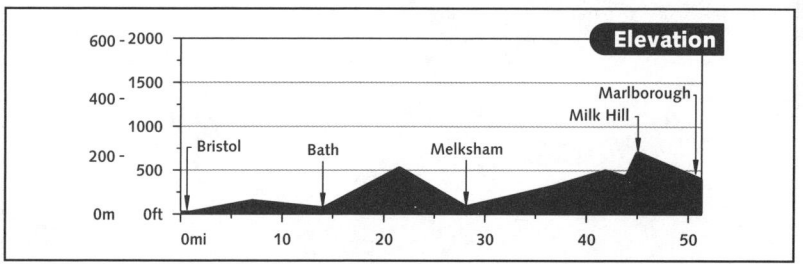

central Wiltshire, is quiet and the scenery beautiful. Look for mysterious 'crop circles' in the fields (try to imagine how pleased the farmers are to see tourists trampling paths through perfectly good grain crops to reach the circles). Near Stanton St Bernard, you'll pass a striking **White Horse** just before commencing the climb up Pewsey Down. Once up, it's a pleasant roll to Marlborough. The former market town dates back to the Saxon times, and is where you'll spend the night.

SIDE TRIP: AVEBURY
1–1½ hours, 6 miles
A left (signposted to East Kennett and West Overton) at 46.9 miles will take you towards fascinating Avebury and nearby Silbury Hill (one of the largest artificial hills in Europe built from 2500 BC) and West Kennett Long Barrow (a burial ground dating from 3500

BC). Along with Stonehenge, these are the best-known sites of prehistoric Britain. The **Avebury tourist office** (☎ 01672 539425) is the place to begin inquiries. Relics from the Avebury stone circle are displayed at the **Alexander Keiller Museum** (☎ 01672 539250), named for the philanthropic marmalade magnate who bought most of Avebury to preserve its archaeological treasures.

Day 2: Marlborough to Henley-on-Thames
5–6 hours, 45.2 miles
After a gentle enough start surrounded by more sights, sounds and smells of rural England, this is the day that you begin to feel London's inexorable pull. For most of the morning the route winds through the rolling hills between the two great roads that lead west from the capital, the M4

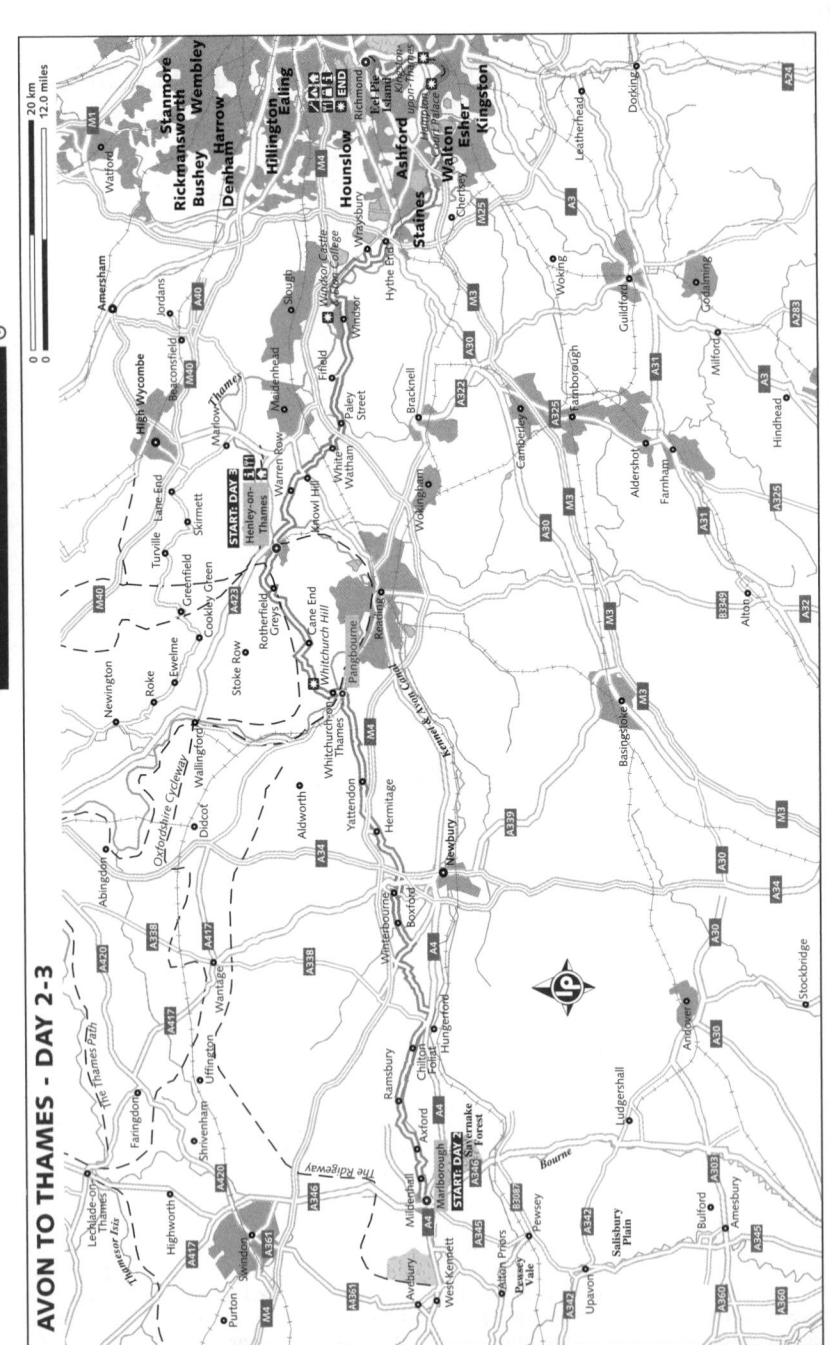

SOUTHERN ENGLAND

AVON TO THAMES – DAY 2-3

AVON TO THAMES – DAY 2

CUE			GPS COORDINATES	
start		Marlborough TIC	51°25'7"N	1°44'0"W
0 miles		go N on Hilliers Yard		
0.1	⌐	High St		
0.3	↘	Kingsbury St		
	⌐	(50yd) Silverless St		
4.6	↙	'to Ramsbury'		
6.3		Ramsbury	51°26'33"N	1°36'17"W
6.6	⌐	'to Hungerford'		
7.8	⌐	B4192		
9.5		Chilton Foliat	51°25'55"N	1°32'23"W
9.8	⌐	'to Leverton'		
14.0	⌐	unsigned road		
14.6	⌐	Church Hill		
15.5	⌐	B4000		
16.8	⌐	'to Boxford'		
17.8	⌐	unsigned road (opp The Bell), Boxford	51°26'29"N	1°23'2"W
	⌐	(20yd) 'to Winterbourne'		
18.3	⌐	'to Winterbourne'		
20.1	⌐	'to Newbury', Winterbourne	51°26'51"N	1°20'42"W
20.3	⌐	unsigned road		
21.1	⌐	B4494		

CUE CONTINUED			GPS COORDINATES	
21.2	⌐	Arlington Lane		
21.8	⌐	A34 access ramp		
	⌐	(30yd) A34 overpass 'to Curridge'		
23.5	⌐	'to Hermitage'		
24.0	⌐	B4009		
24.3		Hermitage	51°27'17"N	1°16'7"W
24.9	⌐	'to Yattendon'		
27.9		Yattendon	51°28'1"N	1°12'23"W
30.3	⌐	'to Pangbourne'		
33.6	⌐	A340, Pangbourne	51°28'56"N	1° 5'14"W
	⌐ ◉	(40yd) A329		
33.7	↘	B471		
34.2	▲	0.5 miles steep climb		
34.8		Whitchurch Hill	51°30'24"N	1° 4'30"W
35.0	⌐	'to Goring Heath'		
36.4	⌐	'to Goring'		
36.6	⌐	B4526		
37.6	⌐	A4074		
38.5	⌐	'to Gallowstree Common'		
40.7	⌐	'to Henley'		
41.6	⌐	'to Henley'		
45.2		Henley-on-Thames TIC	51°32'19"N	0°54'24"W

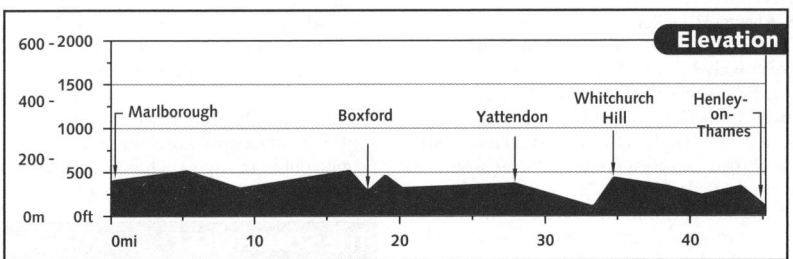

Elevation

Marlborough — Boxford — Yattendon — Whitchurch Hill — Henley-on-Thames

and A4, but you'll only occasionally catch glimpses of these fume-oozing monstrosities. You finally cross the M4 – mercifully, on an overpass – at about 26 miles. From Yattendon to Pangbourne you need to watch the navigation – it's quite a maze of minor roads and there are some tricky twists.

After crossing the River Thames at the toll bridge (bikes are free) outside Pangbourne, you face the day's only real climb, up **Whitchurch Hill** (34.2 miles). It's a solid incline, but fortunately only short. Navigating becomes trickier in the following section, through Rotherfield Peppard and Rotherfield Greys. Be particularly careful on the steep uphill pinch around 40.8 miles

to 40.9 miles – if you're heavily laden and slow it may be better to dismount and walk on the footpath on the left-hand side of the road.

By now you'll have a sense of the greater level of traffic about (Henley is only 40 miles from London) and you need to be watchful on the hill into Henley. Dismount when you reach the one-way town centre road system (pull over into the car parking spaces outside **The Victoria pub**) and walk the last few yards to the tourist office. Henley lies on a beautiful bend in the Thames, and the perfect way to end your day in the saddle involves sitting on your butt at a riverside pub, watching the sunset and sipping a pint.

AVON TO THAMES – DAY 3

CUE			GPS COORDINATES
start		Henley-on-Thames TIC	51°32'19"N 0°54'24"W
0 miles		go E on Falaise Square/Hart St	
0.3	⌐	Wargrave Rd/A321	
2.0	⌐	'to Warren Row'	
2.4	↗	unsigned road	
3.0	⌐	'to Warren Row'	
5.3	⌐	A4	
5.4	⌐	'to Shottesbrook'	
7.8	⌐	'to Waltham St Lawrence'	
8.0	⌐	unsigned road	
8.1	⌐	B3024	
9.3		Paley Street	51°29'0"N 0°45'4"W
10.1	⌐	A330	
10.6	⌐	B3024	
13.6	⌐	B3024	
16.3	⌐	Sheet St, Windsor	51°28'47"N 0°36'21"W
16.4	↘	High St/Thames St	
16.5	★	Windsor Castle	
16.7	⌂	across River Thames	
16.8	↑	High St (Eton)/Slough Rd (B0322)	

CUE CONTINUED			GPS COORDINATES
17.0	★	Eton College	
17.6	⌐⊙	B3026 'to Datchet'	
18.4		Datchet	51°29'2"N 0°34'47"W
18.8	⌐⊙	B376 'to Staines'	
19.2	↗⊙	B376 'to Staines'	
20.5	⌐⊙	B376 'to Staines'	
22.0		Staines Rd/B376	
24.6	↗⌂	Staines Rd, Staines	51°26'49"N 0°32'49"W
24.7	⌐	Clarence St/High St	
25.0	⌐⌂	South St/B376	
25.3	⌐	B376 'to Laleham'	
27.1	⌐⊙	B376 'to Shepperton', Laleham	51°24'34"N 0°29'21"W
29.8	⌐⊙	A244	
30.2	⌐⊙	Fordbridge Rd/B375	
33.4	⌐	A308	
35.2	⌐⌂	A309	
35.3	⌐	onto Thames Path	
	★	Hampton Court Palace	
		(follow Richmond & the Thames route)	
43.1		Richmond TIC	51°27'32"N 0°18'23"W

Day 3: Henley-on-Thames to Richmond
5–6 hours, 43.1 miles

This ride moves from pockets of what could reasonably be described as 'country', to what is inescapably city. The A321, which takes you away from Henley, can be busy, but it's followed by a longish stretch of rural and semi-rural roads. However, once the B3024 takes a right towards Windsor (13.6 miles) you'll be in and out of traffic for the rest of the day.

Try to go through Windsor on a weekday. **Windsor Castle** (☎ 01753 831118) is fascinating and well worth a visit, but it's one of the most popular attractions in Britain and practically sinks under the weight of tourists on summer weekends. Just across the river, snobbish **Eton College** (☎ 01753 671171), school of umpteen British prime ministers, is open from Easter to the end of summer (afternoons only during school terms). It's an interesting place with several historic buildings – the seemingly endless green, green playing fields are a revelation.

From Eton the going is flat and fast and you need to be on the watch for traffic, especially through busy Staines. At **Hampton Court Palace** (☎ 020 8781 9500) you leave the road for a glorious riverside path for a few miles. The Guildhall in **Kingston-upon-Thames** contains the resting place of the Anglo-Saxon kings' Coronation Stone – from Kingston, the route follows London Cycle Network bicycle routes or lanes past Teddington, where the Teddington Lock marks the limit of the tidal Thames, to Twickenham. From there, you hug the river on the Warren Footpath into Richmond, which is nine miles southwest of Central London. You can hook up with public transport or follow the bikepath into the city. See the London chapter (p37).

THE SOUTHWEST

Duration 7 days
Distance 350.4 miles
Difficulty moderate–hard
Start Weymouth
Finish Falmouth

Summary This week-long tour of England's southwest takes you from the North Dorset Downs through southern Dartmoor along the coast. This longer tour for fit riders features plenty of ups and downs as it follows mainly back country lanes through the counties of Dorset, Somerset, Devon and Cornwall.

Southwest England offers up, on one diverse, sea-fringed platter, the pick of Britain's cities, coast and countryside. Stretching west from Hampshire to the soaring cliffs and golden sands of Cornwall, the ride takes in Dorset's chocolate box-pretty villages, Wiltshire's prehistoric sites, Bath's exquisite Georgian cityscape, Bristol's buzzing nightlife, hippy-chic Somerset and Devon's beguiling blend of moors and shores. There are even stops for surfing, and reflection at the end of the earth (or at least island).

HISTORY

Like much of the south, the west contains abundant evidence of past cultures and kingdoms. Cornwall, in particular, retains a flavour of its Celtic past. Along with tangible history, throw in a tangy dash of legend and mysticism. Glastonbury Abbey, reached on the route's second day, is said to be the burial place of King Arthur – Tintagel, off-route on day five, is supposedly where Arthur was born. In more recent times, Dorset has become indelibly associated with writer Thomas Hardy, who was born and died in the county and based many of his novels in it.

PLANNING

This is one of the warmest parts of Britain and the route can be tackled year-round, but April to June and September to November are best. In midsummer, seaside resorts (and the roads leading to them) get particularly crowded, especially in Cornwall. In midwinter, the higher parts of the route in Exmoor can be gloomy and disheartening in poor weather.

Maps

The route is entirely covered by OS Travelmaster Map No 8 1:250,000 *South West England & South Wales*. Parts of the route follow NCN 3 and Sustrans' 1:100,000) *West Country Way* route map, which is very useful, especially for the Tarka and Camel trail sections. The OS's Cycle Tours books *Dorset, Hampshire and Isle of Wight*; *Avon, Somerset and Wiltshire*; and *Cornwall and Devon* (all £10) are useful for planning day rides off the route.

GETTING TO/FROM THE RIDE
Weymouth (start)
BUS

National Express (www.nationalexpress .com) runs busstes between Weymouth and London (£20, 4.5 hours).

TRAIN

Weymouth is linked by rail to Bristol, Southampton and London. All trains carry a 'limited' number of cycles except those arriving in or leaving London during peak times. The journey from London takes around three hours and the standard one-way fare is £60 – bikes travel free.

BICYCLE

Weymouth is about 50 miles from Lyndhurst, where the New Forest ride starts/ends.

Falmouth (finish)
BUS

National Express (www.nationalexpress .com) runs buses between Falmouth and London (£39, eight hours).

TRAIN

Trains run from Falmouth through Plymouth and Exeter to Bristol and London. The journey to London takes 5½ to 6 hours and the standard one-way fare is £15.

THE RIDE
Day 1: Weymouth to Lyme Regis
4-5 hours, 37.6 miles

Primarily a sweep through rolling Dorset farm country, this is an up-and-down ride kind of day that includes some intense short climbs. The day begins on the sometimes busy B3157, slowly moving inland from the sweep of 10 mile-long Chesil Beach and the seabird haven of Fleet Lagoon.

The day's first difficult climb, up Black Down, is a beauty: a 0.8-mile rise at an average gradient of 17%. It's worth the strain. From **Hardy Monument** (side trip at 8.7 miles) you'll get grand views – weather permitting – of Weymouth, the Dorset countryside, Chesil Beach and Fleet Lagoon and, of course, of the moody English Channel. The run from here to Bridport starts with the roller-coaster downhill to the village of Littlebredy and passes through charming Long Bredy and Litton Cheney.

There's evidence of Bridport's past as a rope-making centre in the town's narrow rope walks – the **tourist office** (☎ 01308 424901, 32 South St) can tell you more. Consider dropping in to **Wheels N' Deals Cycle Warehouse** (☎ 01308 420586; 37 St Michaels

THE SOUTHWEST – DAY 1

CUE		GPS COORDINATES	
start	Weymouth TIC	50°36'33.07"N	2°27'9.26"W
0 miles	go W on Esplanade		
0.1	King St		
0.3	Swannery Bridge/Abbotsbury Rd		
1.3	Chickerell Rd/B3157		
7.3	Portesham	50°40'10.40"N	2°33'52.83"W
7.5	'to Hardy Monument'		
	0.8 miles steep climb		
8.7	Hardy Monument 1.5 miles ↻		
9.1	'to Littlebredy'		
10.0	'to Littlebredy'		
10.5	Littlebredy	50°41'57.27"N	2°34'58.39"W
12.0	Long Bredy	50°42'29.61"N	2°36'42.24"W
12.1	'to Litton Cheney'		
13.5	Litton Cheney	50°42'48.75"N	2°38'16.76"W

CUE CONTINUED		GPS COORDINATES	
17.9	B3157		
18.1	Burton Bradstock	50°42'11.14"N	2°43'39.29"W
20.1	Bridport	50°43'58.51"N	2°45'6.76"W
21.5	West St		
21.7	Dottery Rd/B3162		
23.2	'to Broadoak'		
24.3	Broadoak	50°45'54.27"N	2°48'1.34"W
27.5	'to Marshwood'		
	1.5 miles hard climb		
29.2	B3165, Marshwood	50°47'35.64"N	2°52'39.81"W
34.0	A35		
	(20yd) Lyme Rd/B3165		
35.7	Uplyme	50°44'7.23"N	2°57'27.08"W
37.4	Broad St/Church St		
37.6	Lyme Regis TIC	50°43'30.94"N	2°55'55.54"W

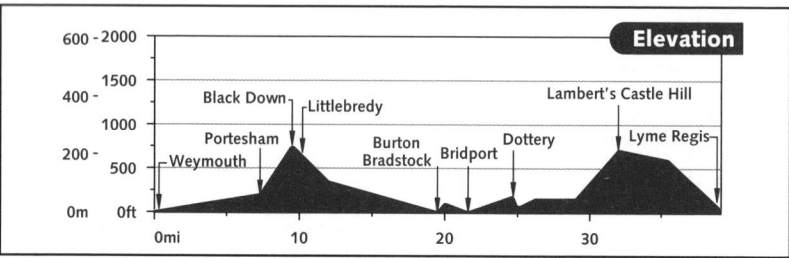

Trading Estate) as it's the last proper bike shop you'll pass for more than a day.

The winding lanes in Marshwood Vale, between the B3162 and B3165, lead through classic rural Dorset (remember, cowpat bespattered roads are very slippery in the wet) and the views make up for the steep climb into Marshwood village. From here you go 5 miles to the lovely seaside town of **Lyme Regis**, your stopping point for the evening. East and west of Lyme is heritage coastline with the limestone cliffs that yielded Britain's first dinosaur fossils.

Day 2: Lyme Regis to Glastonbury
4–5 hours, 39.8 miles

There is some solid up-hill-and-down-dale action to open the day. The climb out of Lyme is followed by a plunging downhill to the village of Wootton Fitzpaine, which is followed by a grinding climb back up to the B3165. On the way, stop for a walk around **Coney's Castle**, a hill fort of the Dumnonii people. Around 500 BC, this was the frontier country between the Dumno-

nii, from which 'Devon' was derived, and the Durotriges people, who were based at Maiden Castle, near Dorchester.

Once you're on the B3165, follow ridge tops, rising and descending all the way to Crewkerne, a fair place to stop

THE OTHER GLASTONBURY

To many people, the village of Glastonbury is practically synonymous with the **Glastonbury Festival of Contemporary Performing Arts** (www.glastonburyfestivals .co.uk), an often mud-soaked extravaganza of music, street theatre, dance, cabaret, carnival, ecology, spirituality and general all-round weirdness that's been held on and around Piltdown Farm, near Glastonbury, for the last 30 years. The festival has become the longest-running performing arts festival in the world, attracting some of the world's biggest acts and crowds of more than 120,000 festival-goers.

THE SOUTHWEST – DAY 2

CUE		GPS COORDINATES
start	Lyme Regis TIC	50°43'30.94"N 2°55'55.54"W
0 miles	go N on Church St/Charmouth Rd	
0.0	▲ 1.3 miles hard climb	
1.6	↘ 'to Axminster'	
1.8	↘ 'to Axminster'	
2.3	⌐ A35	
2.6	↘ 'to Wootton Fitzpaine'	
	⚠ 1 mile steep narrow descent	
3.9	↰ 'to Whitchurch'	
4.0	↗ 'to Whitchurch'	
4.8	↰ 'to Fishponds'	
	▲ 1.3 miles hard climb	
6.0	★ Coney's Castle	
6.3	↑ 'to Axminster'	
7.0	⌐ B3165	
8.5	Marshwood	50°47'35.39"N 2°52'39.27"W
16.0	Crewkerne	50°52'59.14"N 2°47'44.94"W
16.8	↰ A356	

CUE CONTINUED		GPS COORDINATES
22.3	↰ B3165 'to Bower Hinton'	
23.5	★ Martock	50°58'14.24"N 2°45'58.91"W
24.0	↘ North St	
26.9	⚠ single-lane bridge	
27.6	Long Sutton	51° 1'31.93"N 2°45'31.05"W
28.2	⌐ A372	
28.5	↰ B3165 'to Somerton'	
30.1	★ Somerton	51° 3'13.09"N 2°43'50.17"W
30.7	⌐ B3165 'to Glastonbury'	
31.0	⌐◎ 'to Glastonbury'	
31.3	↰ 'to Glastonbury'	
31.5	⌐ B3153	
33.6	↰ 'to Glastonbury'	
34.6	⌐ 'to Butleigh'	
35.6	Butleigh	51° 6'4.72"N 2°41'19.55"W
37.5	⌐ 'to Glastonbury'	
39.8	⌐ High St	
39.1	Glastonbury TIC	51° 8'50.09"N 2°43'4.84"W

for morning tea. The A356, which leads from Crewkerne, is busier than anything encountered earlier but it has a similarly rural feel – hedges come right to the roadside and the views of encircling farmlands are wonderful. In Martock, a solid, stony looking place, the **old school** (c.1660) and **All Saints Church** catch the eye. Blotches of lichen on weathered grey stone lend the small church a feeling of permanence and belonging, like some grand old tree in a forest.

By the time you're back on the B3165 bound for Somerton, the Dorset Downs are well behind you and the countryside is a flat patchwork of hedges. Somerton, like Martock, is a town built solid with stone. The Market Place is particularly striking, with shops, a church, several pubs and a castellated rotunda all in uniform grey stone. After a descent and a climb, the remaining miles into **Glastonbury** are mostly flat,

with striking Glastonbury Tor looming. The town is England's 'New Age capital' and is your sleeping spot for the night. Like any place that attracts people from all points on the spiritual compass, Glastonbury is a mixture of those who've 'found' themselves (as much as anyone ever does) and those who are probably destined to spend the rest of their lives looking.

Day 3: Glastonbury to Lynton & Lynmouth
6–8 hours, 60.4 miles
This big day starts in traffic on the A39 and A361, which is fortunately soon behind you. After this comes an interlude on the strange, almost eerie Somerset moorlands. The low-lying farmlands here are sometimes divided by canals, not hedges – if you're cycling through here on a wet day it feels like the entire precinct is about to go under.

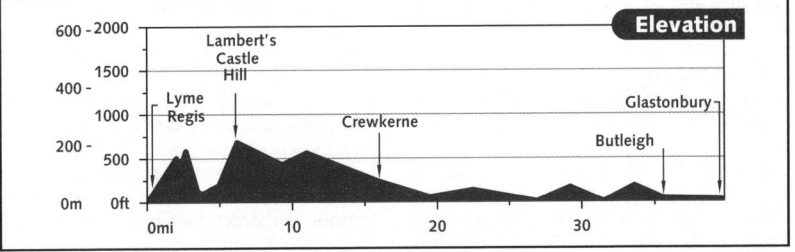

THE SOUTHWEST - DAY 1-4

Getting through Bridgwater can be a bit of a trial, but by once you reach the big roundabouts near Cannington the worst is past. You'll have pedalled towards the Quantock Hills throughout the morning. At about the 22 miles mark, veer off the A39 and shortly after climb up the hills' steep eastern face to **Dead Woman's Ditch** (25.3 miles). The Quantocks' shallow acid soils and the practice of 'swaling' (burning off heather to encourage green shoots for livestock feed) discourages forest growth, so the hills have a stark appearance.

The next 10 miles are very up and down and care is needed on some steep descents. Cleeve Abbey (35 miles) contains some interesting relics, including 13th-century pave-ment tiles. It was founded in the 12th century and dissolved in 1536. There are good views of Dunster from the route – pretty **Dunster village** is just off the route and a nice place for a tea stop. Further on, the route leaves the A39 at Allerford and winds into Porlock, two more charming villages.

The longest climb of the day – and the chapter – follows: the 4.3-mile spin up the toll road through Porlock Manor Estate. It's a gradual climb through woodland groves and fields with stunning views most of the way – definitely a highlight. The return to the A39 brings some more traffic but the stretch into Lynmouth is fast and the outlook – the Bristol Channel and Wales to the north and Exmoor's stark plateaus

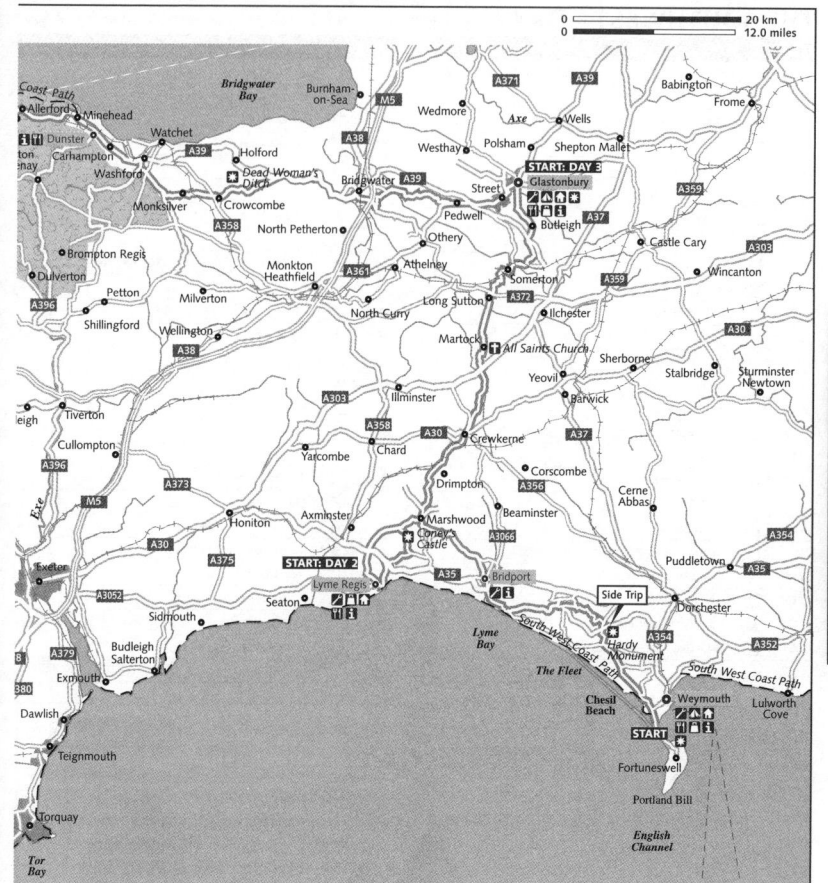

and plunging valleys to the south – is engrossing. The day ends with the screaming ride down Countisbury Hill into **Lynmouth** – road signs suggest you consider walking and the soaring cliffs to the right certainly give cause to keep a firm grip on the brakes.

Day 4: Lynton & Lynmouth to Bude

6–8 hours, 60.8 miles

Morning traffic and some steady climbs persist only as far as Blackmoor Gate, where you return to quiet lanes for the run to the village of Loxhore. The last section into Loxhore features a narrow, twisting downhill where care is needed. From here,

the road runs near the lovely River Yeo for much of the way into Barnstaple.

A largish and lively place, Barnstaple has some decent bike shops if you're in need of spares or repairs – **Cyril Webber** (☎ 01271 343277; Bear St) and the **Bike Shed** (☎ 01271 328628; The Square) are both close to the route. The somewhat fiddly navigating to get through Barnstaple is rewarded when you join the **Tarka Trail** (19.6 miles) – for the next 18 miles the going is traffic-free and mostly flat, with wonderful views over the Rivers Taw and Torridge. The trail surface is mostly dirt or fine gravel but it's well kept and presents no problem for touring bikes. As tempting as it is to really wind up some speed,

THE SOUTHWEST – DAY 3

CUE		GPS COORDINATES
start	Glastonbury TIC	51° 8'50.09"N 2°43'4.84"W
0 miles	go W on High St	
0.0	(50yd) Magdalene St	
0.2	Street Rd/A39	
0.8	A39	
4.7	A361 'to Taunton'	
6.6	'to Moorlinch'	
6.8	'to Moorlinch'	
7.4	'to Bridgwater'	
7.7	'to Sutton Mallet'	
9.0	unsigned road	
9.3	'to Bridgwater'	
11.6	Chedzoy	51° 8'1.47"N 2°56'37.72"W
11.9	'to Bridgwater'	
13.4	'to Bridgwater'	
13.7	Bridgwater	51° 7'42.02"N 3° 0'13.25"W
14.7	'to Minehead'	
15.7	'to Minehead'	
16.4	'to Minehead'	
18.5	'to Minehead'	
19.2	'to Minehead'	
21.9	unsigned road	
23.9	'to Crowcombe'	
	1.2 miles hard climb	
26.4	0.7 miles steep descent	

CUE CONTINUED		GPS COORDINATES
27.1	'to Stogumber'	
28.5	0.6 miles steep winding descent	
30.1	'to Monksilver'	
30.3	'to Monksilver'	
31.7	'to Monksilver'	
32.2	B3188 'to Minehead'	
35.0	Cleeve Abbey	
35.2	A39	
38.0	Carhampton	51°10'22.95"N 3°25'5.12"W
38.2	2.3 miles bikepath	
39.4	subway under A39	
40.5	rejoin road	
40.9	'to Porlock'	
44.7	Selworthy 2 miles	
45.6	'to Allerford'	
46.3	'to Porlock'	
47.2	'to Porlock'	
47.6	A39 'to Lynmouth'	
	(30yd) Toll Road	
	Porlock Manor Estate	
	4.3 miles moderate climb	
51.9	A39 'to Lynmouth'	
58.9	1.1 miles steep descent	
60.0	Lynmouth	51°13'54.51"N 3°49'52.97"W
60.1	Seafront Rd	
60.4	Exmoor NP TIC	51°13'48.90"N 3°50'10.72"W

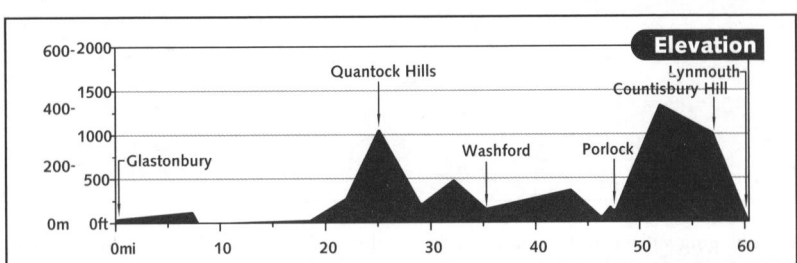

remember that walkers have right of way on the trail. The **Bideford Tarka Trail Centre** (28.9 miles), at the old Bideford train station, is a great place to stop for information and refreshments.

The day's last third will take you from Devon into Cornwall. The roads are mostly very quiet (with the exception of a short section on the A388 around the 48 miles mark) although navigating is confusing at times. You'll certainly learn (if you didn't already know) that back-road cycling in this part of England provides an interconnected series of climbs and descents. You'll

also notice that the road surfaces are generally in a poorer state as you get further west (although there are none so terrible that they must be avoided).

After the tricky descent into Stratton, there's a short climb and a few more turns before a sweeping downhill into **Bude.** One of Cornwall's seemingly innumerable coastal resort towns, Bude has pleasant beaches and a relaxed family air, especially on Summerleaze Beach, the sandpatch nearest town. It's also very popular with surfers, lending a fun, roguish vibe to the pub scene.

THE SOUTHWEST – DAY 4

CUE			GPS COORDINATES	
start		Lynton TIC	51°13'48.90"N	3°50'10.72"W
0 miles		go W on Lee Rd		
0.2	↰	'to Barnstaple'		
1.2	↙	'to Barnstaple' (at give way signs)		
1.6		Barbrook	51°12'48.48"N	3°50'32.21"W
1.7	↱	A39		
	▲	1.3 miles moderate climb		
6.2	▲	1.7 miles gradual climb		
8.2	↰	A399		
8.5	↱	'to Loxhore'		
11.5	⚠	1.1 miles narrow winding descent		
12.0		Loxhore	51° 7'52.73"N	3°58'42.44"W
13.9	↱	'to Barnstaple'		
18.5		Barnstaple	51° 4'50.22"N	4° 3'29.88"W
18.6	↑	Bear St (walk)		
18.7	↱	Boutport St		
	↰	(20yd) Joy St		
18.8	↱	High St		
19.0	↰ ⊙	North Walk/Castle St		
19.4	↱	Long Bridge		
19.6	↑	bikepath/Tarka Trail (TT)		
20.1	⚠	17.3 miles dirt trail		
28.9	★	Bideford TT Centre		

CUE CONTINUED			GPS COORDINATES	
37.4	↱	unsigned road		
38.3	↘	stay on larger road		
38.4	↗	stay on larger road		
38.6	↰	'to Peters Marland'		
39.4	↱	'to Shebbear'		
39.8	↘	stay on larger road		
40.3	↱	'to Shebbear'		
42.3	↱	'to Shebbear'		
43.1	↱	'to Shebbear'		
43.2		Shebbear	50°51'42.13"N	4°13'9.59"W
43.9	↱	'to Thornbury'		
44.0	↰	'to Thornbury'		
46.2	↱	'to Milton Damerel'		
46.8	↰	'to Milton Town'		
48.5	↰	A388		
49.4	↱	'to Sutcombe'		
57.9	⚠	0.7 miles narrow winding descent		
58.6		Stratton	50°49'51.81"N	4°31'8.67"W
59.0	↰	unsigned road (opp post office)		
	↱	(30yd) A3072		
59.3	↰	A39		
59.6	↱	A3072		
60.8		Bude TIC	50°49'39.02"N	4°32'44.31"W

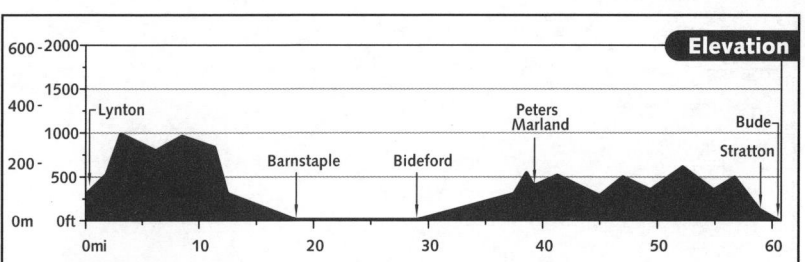

Elevation

Lynton — Barnstaple — Bideford — Peters Marland — Stratton — Bude

Day 5: Bude to Newquay
6–8 hours, 60.9 miles

This tour's longest day (by a whisker) includes some fascinatingly steep – although fortunately short – climbs and descents, magnificent coastal and rural scenery and another extended stretch on a traffic-free path.

The best of the hills keep your eyes on the road during the first 6 miles out of Bude. The sandy beaches and craggy cliffs along here are stunning but you'll work hard for the view – gradients near Millook reach 30%, unrideable uphill and requiring extreme caution on descents (you may prefer to dismount for some downhills). Thankfully, things level out approaching Wainhouse Corner, and the hills into and out of

interesting Boscastle are long and gradual rather than plunging and rearing.

About 5 miles past Boscastle, the **British Cycling Museum** (☎ 01840 212811) has more than 400 bikes as well as books and exhibits covering cycling since the early 19th century – it's open Sunday to Thursday year-round.

The first section of the **Camel Trail**, from 32.3 miles to 40.4 miles, is a bit rougher under the tyres than the Tarka Trail (p78), but is still quite manageable on a touring bike. Through Dunmere Wood the trail hugs the River Camel and the shady outlook with burbling water nearby is particularly pleasant. There's a bit of traffic to contend with through Wadebridge but the

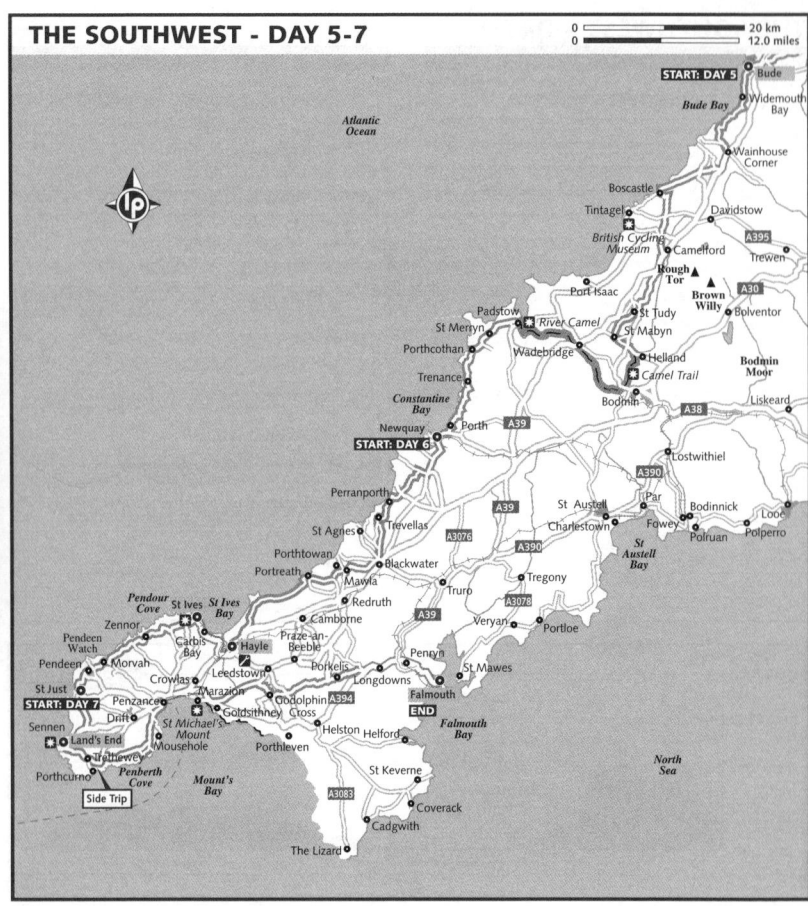

THE SOUTHWEST - DAY 5-7

THE PADSTOW 'OBBY 'ORSE

Every year on 1 May the residents of Padstow re-enact a curious ritual with its origins in medieval fertility rites. A man dressed up as a horse in a tentlike costume parades through town preceded by a masked 'teaser'. Women are occasionally dragged under the horse costume and pinched. Eventually the 'obby 'orse is ritually killed, only to spring to life again the next year – a reminder of days when the village leader may have been killed and his blood sprinkled on the ground to ensure fertility for another year.

cycle lanes are well signposted and navigation isn't a problem. The final miles on the trail to Padstow feature magnificent views across the wide, tidal part of the River Camel.

The day's last section is classic up-and-down Cornwall coastal terrain and the final few hills are tiresome, but again the views are a good distraction. You end in **Newquay**, Britain's surfing capital. Perched on the cliffs above a cluster of white-sand beaches and packed with enough pubs, bars and dodgy clubs to give Ibiza a run for its money, it's the capital of Cornish surfing, and if you're looking to learn how to brave the waves, this is the place to get off the bike and do it.

THE SOUTHWEST – DAY 5

CUE			GPS COORDINATES	
start		Bude TIC	50°49'39.02"N	4°32'44.31"W
0 miles		go E on The Crescent		
3.4		Widemouth Bay	50°47'21.20"N	4°33'27.63"W
3.6	↑	'to Millook'		
5.0	▲	0.6 miles very steep climb		
7.6	↰	'to Wainhouse Corner'		
8.3	↰	'to Wainhouse Corner'		
9.1	↱	A39		
10.5	↱	B3263		
15.5		Boscastle	50°41'23.49"N	4°41'34.11"W
	▲	2.1 miles moderate climb		
16.2	↰	B3266		
20.1	★	British Cycling Museum		
22.0	↱	A39		
22.2	↰	B3266		
26.2	↱	'to Wadebridge'		
26.7	↰	'to St Tudy'		
27.4	↘	Wadebridge Rd		
27.5	↱	'to St Mabyn'		
27.9	↱	'to St Mabyn'		
30.2		St Mabyn	50°31'34.65"N	4°45'49.98"W
30.3	↰	'to Bodmin'		

CUE CONTINUED			GPS COORDINATES	
30.5	↱	'to Bodmin'		
31.5	↱	B3266		
31.6	↰	'to Helland'		
32.3	↱	join Camel Trail (CT)		
	⚠	8.1 miles dirt trail		
40.4	↑	Guineaport Rd, Wadebridge	50°30'47.16"N	4°49'51.86"W
40.7	↱ ⊙	The Platt/Eddystone Rd		
41.0	↑	rejoin Camel Trail		
41.6	⚠	4.5 miles dirt trail		
46.1	↑	thru riverfront car park		
46.4	↘	Station Rd/School Hill		
46.8	↱	A389		
47.5	↰	B3276		
51.5		Porthcothan	50°30'29.13"N	5° 1'19.64"W
55.9	↱	'to Newquay'		
56.9	↱	B3276		
59.4	↱ ⊙	Henver Rd/Cliff Rd		
60.6	↰	Berry Rd		
60.7	↙	Mount Wise		
60.8	↱	Marcus Hill		
60.9		Newquay TIC	50°24'47.93"N	5° 4'54.49"W

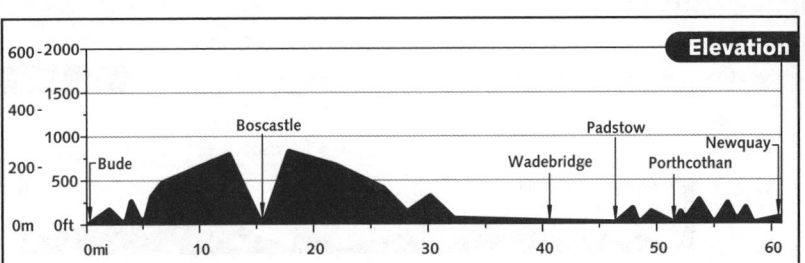

Elevation chart showing elevation in metres (0–600) and feet (0ft–2000), with distance 0mi to 60. Labelled points: Bude, Boscastle, Wadebridge, Padstow, Porthcothan, Newquay.

Day 6: Newquay to St Just
5–7 hours, 47.5 miles

This (mercifully) shorter day features some striking coastal terrain, especially past St Ives on the stretch towards St Just and Land's End. It's another day with quite a few climbs and descents – fortunately, none as steep as those encountered out of Bude – but the wild end of the world scenery makes up for it (as does flying down, down, down).

The A3075 out of Newquay can be busy with traffic, but you're soon off it and following back roads to Perranporth, which you enter after a pacey downhill, and exit climbing. There is some tricky navigation after you turn off the B3285, with a particularly high number of unsigned roads.

After Mawla there's a pleasant flat stretch of around 3 miles on the old **Portreath**

FROM BIKE TO BOARD: SURF'S UP, NEWQUAY

Dig out the board shorts, slip on the shades and prepare to dangle your toes off the nose – Newquay is one of England's best places to learn to surf and is awash with schools, offering everything from half-day taster lessons (£25-30) to full-blown, multiday 'surfaris' (from £130). Head to Tolcarne Beach to take a lesson with the **Animal Surf Academy** (☎ 01637 850808; www.animalsurfacademy.co.uk; Tolcarne Beach, Newquay).

THE SOUTHWEST – DAY 6

CUE			GPS COORDINATES	
start		Newquay TIC	50°24'47.93"N	5° 4'54.49"W
0 miles		go N on Marcus Hill		
0.0	⌐	(30yd) East St		
0.2	⌐	Berry Rd/Trenance Rd		
0.6	⌐⊙	Trevemper Rd		
0.8	⌐⊙	A392		
1.4	⌐⊙	A3075		
3.5	⌐	'to Cubert'		
4.2	⌐	'to Trebellan'		
5.2	⌐	unsigned road		
6.6	⌐	B3285		
7.6	⌐⊙	'to Perranporth', Perranporth	50°20'36.88"N	5° 9'17.16"W
7.9	⌐	B3285 'to St Agnes'		
	▲	1 mile moderate climb		
10.6	⌐	'to Redruth' (on descent)		
11.0	⌐	unsigned road		
11.7	⌐	unsigned road		
12.3	⌐	unsigned road		
13.0	⌐	B3277		
	⌐	(30yd) 'to Mount Hawke'		
13.1	⌐	'to Mount Hawke'		
13.4	⌐	unsigned road		

CUE CONTINUED			GPS COORDINATES	
15.1	⌐	unsigned road		
15.3	⌐	'to Mawla'		
16.1	⌐	unsigned road		
16.4	★	Portreath Tramroad		
16.5	⌐	follow Tramroad		
17.4	⌐	B3300		
18.8		Portreath	50°15'41.19"N	5°17'17.50"W
22.5	★	Hell's Gates		
25.1	★	Gwithian	50°13'15.65"N	5°23'8.22"W
27.3	⌐⊙	B3301		
28.8	⌐⊙	'to St Ives'		
30.0	⌐⊙	A3074		
30.3	⌐⊙	A3074		
32.0		Carbis Bay	50°11'52.67"N	5°27'56.61"W
33.7	⌐	'to town centre'		
33.9	★	St Ives	50°12'46.24"N	5°28'46.59"W
34.0	⌐	B3306		
	▲	2.1 miles moderate climb		
38.9		Zennor	50°11'29.78"N	5°34'3.57"W
44.7	★	Pendeen	50° 9'3.04"N	5°40'1.32"W
45.6	★	Levant mine & steam engine		
46.5		Botallack	50° 8'8.47"N	5°41'1.44"W
47.5		St Just war memorial clock	50° 7'29.02"N	5°40'49.56"W

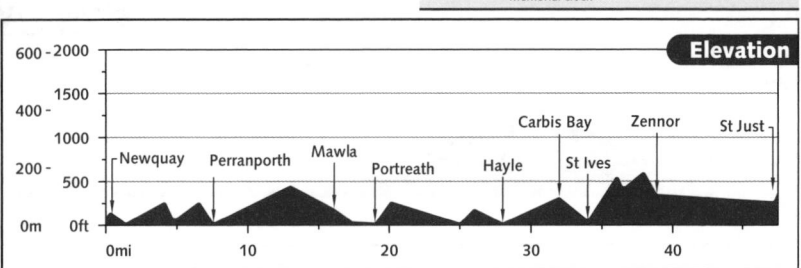

Tramroad. Built in the early 19th century, this tram ran between Portreath Harbour and copper mines inland.

After the climb out of Portreath the ocean and cliff views are spectacular, especially from lookouts around the 22.5-mile mark, from which you'll see the craggy coastal formations known as **Hell's Gates**. A few miles further down the road, **Hayle Cycles** (☎ 01736 753825; Penpol Tce) in Hayle, is the last bike shop for quite a few miles.

Beautiful **St Ives** (33.9 miles) is the day's highlight town. If you're short of time, taking in the view of the town centre and harbour from **Malakoff Gardens** will suffice, but if possible, take a break and visit the wonderful **St Ives Tate Gallery** (☎ 01736

796226), which overlooks Porthmeor Beach.

The day's longest hill – the 2.1-mile grind out of St Ives on the B3306 – follows, rewarded by stunning views northeast across St Ives Bay. The next section is a joy, winding along the coastal hills and passing through several isolated settlements including Zennor, where DH Lawrence wrote part of *Women in Love*. In Pendeen, the **Levant Beam Engine** (☎ 01736 786156) is Cornwall's oldest steam beam engine, and has been restored to working order. Although the day 'officially' ends at **St Just**, there's accommodation spread from here to Sennen, an easy 4 mile ride south and the nearest village to Land's End.

Day 7: St Just to Falmouth
5–6 hours, 43.4 mles

With all the hard work done on the tour, today is a simple spin around Cornwall's – and England's – extreme southwest. There are no major traffic worries, no big hills and plenty of time to take in some lovely and very recognisable sights.

Land's End is the day's best-known waypoint, and although locals will tell you it fails to live up to its end-of-island reputation, seeing it for this first time, this cyclist thought the windswept cliffside views were wild. Stand at the point and look to the right for surfers riding another smashing coastal break. There is a cheesy **theme park** (☎ 01736 871501) and the **Land's End Hotel** sully the cliff above an otherwise rugged coast – but sadly the famed signpost (6.2 miles) is a let-down, with the resident photographic concession extracting £5 for a picture.

The section from Land's End to Penzance is more pleasant, the roads are generally quiet and the views of rural West Cornwall are refreshing. There are several prehistoric sites hereabouts – one, the **Tregithian stone circle**, is on the route and easily accessible (and free). The run downhill to Penzance is a pleasure, bringing with it the first sight of Mount's Bay.

There's some traffic to contend with as you make your way through and beyond Penzance, but the reward is worth it. **St Michael's Mount** (☎ 01736 710265), a 14th-century castle, rises above a rocky island just offshore from pretty Marazion – you can walk across a causeway (at 21.2 miles) at low tide (there's a ferry for high-

SOUTHERN ENGLAND

THE SOUTHWEST – DAY 7

CUE		GPS COORDINATES
start	St Just war memorial clock	50° 7'29.02"N 5°40'49.56"W
0 miles	go S on A3071	
0.4	B3306	
3.3	A30	
4.1	Sennen	50° 4'13.05"N 5°41'43.42"W
6.0	Land's End car park	
	past hotel & attractions	
6.2	Land's End signpost	
	(retrace outward route to BB315)	
6.9	B3315	
8.9	Trethewey	50° 3'20.63"N 5°39'29.65"W
{9.2	Minack Theatre 2 miles ↺}	
10.9	B3315	
13.3	Tregithian stone circle	
17.9	Penzance	50° 7'7.32"N 5°32'13.92"W
18.9	'to Redruth'	
	(50yd) Jew St	
19.5	A30	
20.1	'to Long Rock	
20.6	Long Rock	50° 7'43.86"N 5°30'11.90"W

CUE CONTINUED		GPS COORDINATES
20.8	'to Marazion'	
21.2	St Michael's Mount walk	
21.8	Marazion	50° 7'24.19"N 5°28'26.89"W
23.6	Goldsithney	50° 7'30.95"N 5°26'11.18"W
27.1	'to Godolphin'	
28.0	Godolphin House	
28.6	Godolphin Cross	50° 8'1.11"N 5°20'50.72"W
28.7	'to Nancegollan'	
34.4	Porkellis	50° 9'19.95"N 5°13'54.58"W
34.7	unsigned road (at Star Inn)	
35.3	'to Falmouth'	
37.1	'to Penryn'	
37.4	A394	
38.0	Longdowns	50° 9'50.64"N 5° 9'33.31"W
38.3	unsigned road (100yd past Texaco)	
40.6	'to Penryn town centre'	
40.8	'to Penryn town centre'	
41.6	Falmouth Rd	
42.5	North Parade/Greenbank	
43.3	The Moor/Killigrew St	
43.4	Falmouth TIC	50° 9'22.96"N 5° 4'12.96"W

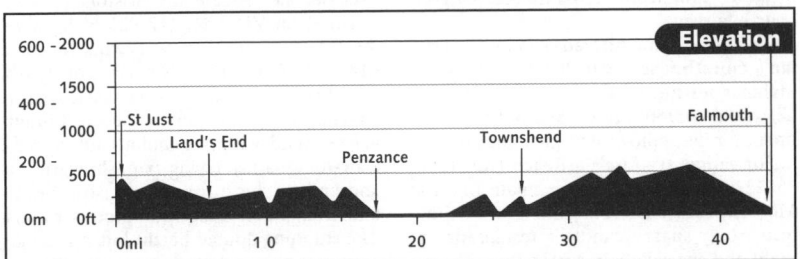

tide access) to the mount, which is open from April to October.

Most of the remaining miles to Falmouth pass through quiet Cornwall countryside. **Historic Godolphin House** (28 miles; ☎ 01736 762409), a grand 15th-century home, is worth a look. It's open limited hours – Thursday in May and June, and Tuesday and Thursday in July and August.

Expect some heavier traffic after the left turn onto the A394 (37.4 miles) – the final run through Penryn and into Falmouth is mostly downhill, with delightful views of Carrick Roads and Falmouth Bay. While it's not Cornwall's most vibrant town, **Falmouth** has the advantage of a more historically authentic ambience than a tourist hot-spot like Newquay. The town and beaches are easy on the eye and some of the nearby villages on the Lizard Peninsula are quite charming.

TOWNS & FACILITIES

BUDE
☎ 01288 / pop 9200

Tucked in at the end of the River Neet and a 19th-century canal, Bude is both a popular family getaway and surfing hangout, thanks to its fantastic nearby beaches. It can have quite a groovy-tanned-and-tattoos feeling some places such as **Crooklets** and a more classic bucket-and-spade affair nearest town on **Summerleaze** beach. For spares and repairs go to **Tracks** (☎ 01288 240297; 20 Queen St).

The **Camelot Hotel** (☎ 0800 781 2536; www.camelot-hotel.co.uk; Downs View; s/d £49/98) is the pick of Bude's B&Bs. Simple rooms dot a garden-wrapped facade and pleasant views from across the nearby golf course fairway.

The fresh, uncluttered rooms at **Dylan's Guesthouse** (☎ 01288 354705; www .dylansguesthouseinbude.co.uk; Downs View; s/d £45/60) are decked out in white linen, throws, pillows and pleasant pine.

For eating, try **Life's a Beach** (☎ 01288 355222; Summerleaze Beach; mains £11-16; Mon-Sat). It transforms from a lunch time bistro to a snazzy candlelit restaurant by night and specialises in seafood.

The owner catches the skate and monkfish at **Scrummies** (☎ 01288 359522; Lansdown Rd; mains from £7; 8am-10pm), a fab fish cafe.

BRISTOL
☎ 0117 / pop 410,000

Boom-town Bristol may not be as pretty as her older sister Bath (and really, she isn't) but she's just as interesting. After being in the doldrums for decades, this former hub of shipbuilding, manufacturing and the railways has undergone a transformative regeneration. It's also a good place to cycle – perhaps not surprising given that Sustrans is headquartered here – with well signposted routes around town and the B&BRP leading the way. Bike shops nearest the town centre include **Bristol Bicycle Workshop** (☎ 0117 926 8961; 84 Colston St) and **Bike-Tech** (☎ 0117 929 7368; 12-14 Park St).

Sleeping
Arches House (☎ 0117 924 7398; www .arches-hotel.co.uk; 132 Cotham Brow; s £29-45, d £52-65) vegetarians will love this Victorian guesthouse – breakfasts are meat-free and packed with organic, fair trade treats. The rooms are traditional but the thinking is very modern: electricity comes from renewable sources, cleaning products are eco-friendly and the owners could run classes in recycling and composting.

Berkeley Square Hotel (☎ 0117 925 4000; www.cliftonhotels.com; 15 Berkeley Sq; s £69-137 d £115-180) in the midst of the kind of leafy square a nightingale would sing in, this hip hotel brings baroque imagination to a Georgian townhouse. Painted gazelle heads, day-glo settees and rococo mirrors dot the lobby, while the bedrooms mix decanters of gratis sherry with views over Berkeley Square and Bristol.

Hotel du Vin (☎ 0117 925 5577; www .hotelduvin.com; Narrow Lewins Mead; d £145-160, £195-215) this enclave of stylish, sexy luxury is housed in converted sugar warehouses, neatly signally the sweet indulgence found within. Fabulous futon beds, claw-foot baths, frying-pan showerheads and a mix of chic furniture, industrial beams and iron pillars grace sumptuous rooms. The stunning double-height loft suites may make you weep when you have to leave.

Eating

Bordeaux Quay (☎ 0117 943 1200; Canons Way; brasserie mains £10; restaurant mains £17-21; lunch & dinner) funky, friendly, Bordeaux Quay, neatly fulfils all your food needs in one: it's a restaurant, brasserie, bar, deli, bakery and cookery school. Their efforts to shrink the food-miles map have produced a menu bursting with organic, seasonal, regionally sourced ingredients, and proves 'sustainable' can equal 'delectable'. Settle down at a sanded wooden table in the cool, calm light interior and try the squash and rocket linguini or the roast seabass with *buerre rouge*. Great, green, guilt-free food.

Cafe Maitreya (☎ 0117 951 0100; 89 St Marks Rd; 3 courses £20.95; dinner Tue-Sat) voted the UK's top vegetarian restaurant two years running, the Maitreya has firmly established itself as one of the city's most inventive eateries. The seasonal menu is renowned for its culinary creativity, and dabbles in everything from red onion tartelette to cashew nut roulade.

Obento (☎ 0117 929 7392; 69 Baldwin St; mains £4-10; lunch & dinner Tue-Sun) somewhere to satisfy those wasabi cravings, this minimalist Japanese restaurant finds diners tucking into teriyaki chicken, fresh sushi and hot noodles at sleek bench tables. Their neatly packaged, three-course, bento lunch boxes are practically works of art.

Rocotillo's (☎ 0117 929 7207; 1 Queens Row; mains from £4; breakfast & lunch) Bristol's version of a traditional American diner, complete with bar stools, leather booths and an open grill kitchen, serves gourmet burgers and the best milkshakes in town.

CANTERBURY

☎ 01227 / pop 42,000

Beautiful Canterbury has drawn crowds of pilgrims and tourists since the 12th century martyrdom of Archbishop Becket. These days the city, a market town and service centre, has about two million visitors annually but, remarkably, manages to retain its character. Its primary attraction, Canterbury Cathedral, has been England's primary ecclesiastical centre since the early 7th century. The cathedral, St Augustine's Abbey and St Martin's Church were inscribed on the Unesco World Heritage list in 1988.

Sleeping

Cathedral Gate Hotel (☎ 01227 464381; www.cathgate.co.uk; 36 Burgate; s/d without bathroom from £42/72, with bathroom from £67/101) this much-photographed 15th-century hotel adjoins the spectacular cathedral gate, which it predates: a fact that becomes evident upon exploring its labyrinthine passageways where few rooms escape an angled floor, low door or curvy walls. Rooms are simple, but worth it for the fantastic position.

Yew Tree Park (☎ 01227 700306; www .yewtreepark.com; Stone St, Petham; tent & 2 adults £12-17) set in gentle rolling countryside 5 miles south of the city, this lovely family-run campsite has plenty of soft grass to pitch a tent on and a heated swimming pool from around May through to September.. Call for directions and transportation information.

Eating

Goods Shed (☎ 01227 459153; Station Rd West; lunch £8-12, dinner £10-16; lunch & dinner) farmers market, food hall and fabulous restaurant all rolled into one, this converted station warehouse by the railway is a hit with everyone from self-caterers to sit-down gourmets. The chunky wooden tables sit slightly above the market hubbub but in full view of its appetite-whetting stalls, and country-style daily specials exploit the freshest farm goodies available.

Karl's (☎ 01227 764380; 43 St Peter's St; snacks £3-7; 9am-6pm Mon-Sat) the walls of this bright little deli are crammed with fine cheeses, artisan breads and pastries, coffee beans and food friendly wines. The deli is run by a husband and wife team, and you can sample their delicious wares (including fantastic deli sandwiches and cheeseboards) in a comfy dining space at the back of the shop or in their small garden.

Old Brewery Tavern (☎ 01227 826682; High St) trendy boozer (part of a small chain of 'gastro-cool' pubs) in a large open space adorned with back and white prints of brewery workers of old, and a white brick courtyard with a huge curved wood and soft leather sofa. The choice of beers is plentiful, and there's a good wine list as well as a solid menu of English pub classic such as fish pie and gammon, egg and chips – albeit a swanky version.

EASTBOURNE
☎ 01323 / pop 94,000

While it may lack Brighton's mad sparkle, Eastbourne is a quintessentially, do-like-to-be-beside-the-seaside English coastal resort. Beyond the inevitable fun pier and legion fish and chip joints, it's a dignified place, renowned for its gardens, theatres and grass court tennis centre, site of the annual women's tournament that's a traditional Wimbledon lead-up.

Sleeping & Eating

Da Vinci Hotel (☎ 01323 727173; www .davinci.uk.com; 10 Howard Sq; d from £69) Pegged as an 'art hotel', each room in this boutique B&B is named after a famous artist and prints are hung accordingly, with bold, bright colours to match. There's a space in the reception dedicated to displaying the work of local artists.

Beach House (☎ 01323 738228; www .thegreenhousebar.com; lunch & dinner) the nicest of Eastbourne's beachfront cafes is a laid back space with a large wooden deck on the beach outside. It serves great big breakfasts, homemade burgers, as well as wines and beer on tap.

FALMOUTH
☎ 01326 / pop 21,500

Falmouth has the advantage of a more historically authentic ambience than a tourist hot-spot such as Newquay and is a pleasing blend of bustling port, holiday resort and mildly-alternative student town. The town and beaches are easy on the eye and some of the nearby villages on the Lizard Peninsula are charming in an isolated kind of way.

Sleeping & Eating

Dolvean Hotel (☎ 01326 313658; www .dolvean.co.uk; 50 Melvill Rd; s £41, d £70-92; wi-fi) there's hardly a piece of fabric in this plush five star B&B that isn't ruched, swaged and draped. The bigger rooms sport brass bedsteads and antique mirrors.

Hawthorne Dene Hotel (☎ 01326 311427; 12 Pennance Rd; s/d £40/80) Edwardian elegance rules the roost at this family-run hotel with its ranks of old photos and booklined gentleman's lounge. The antique-themed bedrooms feature springy beds, polished woods and teddy bears – most also have a sea view.

Boathouse (☎ 01326 315425; Trevethan Hill; mains £6-10; lunch & dinner) this fantastic gastropub is so laid-back it's almost horizontal. It's especially popular with Falmouth's creative crowd, who come for the generous plates of food, cold beer and chilled-out vibe.

Hunky Dory (☎ 01326 212997; 46 Arwenack St; mains £13-25; dinner only) fisherman often ferry their just-caught catch past diners at this stylish restaurant – the seafood is that fresh. The design blends pale wood and rough whitewashed walls; while the menu mixes European and Asian flavours with classic Cornish produce – try the crispy skinned sea bass or the Newlyn cod wrapped in prosciutto.

GLASTONBURY
☎ 01458 / pop 9000

Realign those chakras and open that third eye – you've just touched down in England's hippy-central. A bohemian haven and centre for New Age culture since the days of the 'Summer of Love'. Glastonbury is still a favourite hang-out for festival-goers, mystics and counter-cultural types of all descriptions.

Sleeping & Eating

Chalice Hill (☎ 01458 830828; www .chalicehill.co.uk; Dod La; s/d £70/90) this grandly luxurious, utterly delightful B&B is the place to stay in Glastonbury. Set in a rambling Georgian house, it's dripping with quirky charm – stripped wooden floors combine with a sweeping staircase, ornate mirrors and stylish modern art. The effect is deeply elegant, but also wonderfully easy-going – that it's a five-minute walk into town, but is surrounded by soothing, tree-shaded grounds, adds to the appeal.

Parsnips (☎ 01458 835599; www.pars nips-glastonbury.co.uk; 99 Bere La; s/d £50/65) swimming against the tie-die and crystal tide, this stylish B&B has opted instead for a fresh design topped off by gingham flourishes and plumped up quilts. There's a comfy guest lounge, a bright conservatory and a refreshing lack of spiritual guidance.

Mocha Berry (☎ 01458 832149; 14 Market Pl; mains £5-8) this ever-popular cafe is the top spot in Glastonbury for a frothy latte, a fresh milkshake or a stack of breakfast pancakes.

HENLEY-ON-THAMES
☎ 01491 / pop 10,500

Henley lies in a splendid setting alongside the River Thames – it's hard to imagine a nicer way to spend an afternoon than sitting and sipping at one of the riverside pubs. Henley's best known for its rowing regatta, a long-standing annual opportunity for grown men to wear boaters.

Sleeping & Eating

Hotel du Vin (☎ 01491 848400; www .hotelduvin.com; New St; d £145-295; mains £15-21) set in the former Brakspears Brewery, this upmarket hotel chain scores highly for its blend of industrial chic and top-of-the-line designer sophistication. The spacious rooms and opulent suites are slick and stylish and are matched by a walk-in humidor, incredible billiards rooms, huge wine cellar and a popular bistro.

    The Old School House (☎ 01491 573929; www.oldschoolhousehenley.co.uk; 42 Hart St; d £75-85) this small, quiet guesthouse in the town centre is a 19th-century school house in a walled garden and has a choice of two pretty guest rooms decked out in simple but comfortable style. Exposed timber beams and rustic furniture give it plenty of character while the central location can't be beaten at this price.

    Green Olive (☎ 01491 412220; 28 Market Pl; meze £4-10) a popular Henley haunt, Green Olive dishes up piled plates of traditional Greek meze in a bright and airy building with a lovely garden to the rear. Choose from over 50 dishes including spannakopitta, souvlaki, mussels with feta, stifado and moussaka.

HYTHE
☎ 01303 / pop 14,000

The ancient Cinque Port of Hythe is a pleasant seaside resort these days. It's an engaging place, with period houses lining the old streets and lanes that tumble down Quarry Hill to High St. The Norman tower on St Leonard's Church, which dates from 1080, is the dominant feature.

Information

Visit the **Hythe Tourist Information Centre** (☎ 01303 267799; Red Lion Sq) and the regional tourism website www.visitkent .co.uk for sleeping and eating options.

LYNTON & LYNMOUTH
☎ 01598 / Lynmouth pop 1500

Only the particularly hard-hearted would find nothing to like about the twin villages of Lynmouth, at the mouth of the River West Lyn, and Lynton, perched about 210m (689ft) above. It's the perfect place to get off the bike and explore the Exmoor coastline on foot for a few days.

Sleeping & Eating

St Vincent House (☎ 01598 752244; www .st-vincent-hotel.co.uk; Castle Hill; d £74) Run by an Anglo-Belgian couple and named 'Hotel of the Year' by Les Routiers no less, this elegant establishment brings a dollop of class to the quiet streets of Lynton. The house once belonged to a comrade of Nelson's, and all the delightful, pared-back rooms are named after battleships from Horatio's fleet. There's a relaxed, old-world atmosphere and a spiral staircase so sweeping, that you'll feel like a film star.

    Greenhouse (☎ 01598 753358; 6 Lee Rd; mains £9; 9am-9.30pm) Cole Porter tunes, a log-burning stove and conservatory-style dining create a cafe-cum-restaurant of gently eccentric charm. Evenings see a smooth segue from gourmet baguettes, cinnamon-scented toast and superb cream-teas, to supper-time comfort food like pan-fried salmon with hollandaise, and crab with new potatoes.

LYNDHURST
☎ 023 / pop 3000

New Forest's 'capital' is a good base from which to explore the national park or simply stop off for a pint, a cuppa or a map. The quaint country village of Lyndhurst is one of the larger settlements, has an excellent information centre, as well as several cosy pubs and restaurants.

Sleeping & Eating

Waterloo Arms (☎ 023 8028 2113; Pikes Hill; mains £7-15; lunch & dinner) this cosy 17th-century thatched pub serves good-value meals in a snug wood-beamed interior. On the town's northern edge, it's signposted off the A337 to Cadnam.

    Whitley Ridge (☎ 01590 622354; www .whitleyridge.com; Beaulieu Rd; Brockenhurst; rooms £95) if you hanker after a country house atmosphere, head here. Set in 14 acres of dappled grounds, this ivy-clad Georgian pile pampers guests amid elegant period-style rooms finished with contemporary twists (think flat-screen TVs and gilt mirrors). The classy restaurant conjures up organic, seasonal, locally sourced creations finished with dashes of Anglo-French flair, and it's all tucked away 4 miles south of Lyndhurst at Brockenhurst.

LYME REGIS

☎ 01297 / pop 4500

It would take a lot to dull the appeal of this lovely seaside town, its harbour and historic stone jetty, **The Cobb**. There's a calm assurance about the place and its people; the streets and lanes lead steeply down to a town centre delightfully free of modern development.

Sleeping & Eating

Broad Street (☎ 01297 445792; 57 Broad St; three courses £27; dinner Thu-Sat, plus Tue, Wed & Sun in high season) whitewashed walls, crisp white linen and old chapel chairs dot the interior of this innovative restaurant. The food has flair too: confit of duck, roast tomato and beetroot puree sits alongside pot roast pollack with spinach and leeks. Impeccably sourced ingredients, their local credentials are outlined on the menu, include wild garlic gathered from the woods. Bookings are essential.

Old Lyme Guest House (☎ 01297 442929; www.oldlymeguesthouse.co.uk; 29 Coombe St; s from £40, d £70) once home to Lyme's old post office, this stone-fronted house is now an award-winning B&B, with several frilly rooms finished in pale creams and soft hues, topped off by patterned curtains and china trinkets.

MARLBOROUGH

☎ 01672 / pop 8000

This former market town dates back to Saxon times. The town's name is derived from 'Merle Barrow', a mound now in the grounds of Marlborough College that was said to be the burial place of Merlin, King Arthur's legendary magician.

Information

Higher Rew (☎ 01672 842681; www.high errew.co.uk; sites £12; Apr-Oct) A fabulous, tranquil campsite (there's no pool) with good, clean facilities. Tucked away high in the fields around Salcombe, it's a mile's walk to South Sands.

Visit the **Marlborough Tourist Information Centre** (☎ 01672 513989; The Library, High Street) and regional tourism website www.visitwiltshire.co.uk and www .marlboroughwilts.co.ukfor further information on the region.

NEWQUAY

☎ 01673 / pop 19,500

Hordes of hard-core surfers, party-animals and wannabe-board riders all make a bee-line for bright, breezy, brash Newquay. Perched on the cliffs above a cluster of white-sand beaches and packed with enough pubs, bars and dodgy clubs to give Ibiza a run for its money, it's the capital of Cornish surfing.

Sleeping & Eating

Base Surf Lodge (☎ 01637 874852; www .basesurflodge.com; 20 Tower Rd; dm £15-20) a superior surf lodge – slatted blinds, tiled floors and big sunset murals brighten up the lounge-bar, while pine bunk beds and off-white walls characterise the upstairs dorms.

Carlton Hotel (☎ 01637 872658; www .carltonhotelnewquay.co.uk; 6 Dane Rd; s £45, d £68-94) swanky rooms, frilly edged beds, DVD players and country-cream furnishings run throughout this upmarket B&B, on a quiet terrace just off Headland Rd.

New Harbour Restaurant (☎ 01637 874062; South Quay Hill; mains £10-15; lunch & dinner) in a lovely spot beside the old harbour, this relaxed restaurant is a fine place to escape the crowds along Newquay's main drag. Fish and seafood are the menu's staple – think crab claws, homemade fishcakes and skate wing.

Beach Hut (☎ 01637 860877; Watergate Bay; mains £13-17; breakfast, lunch & dinner) surf boards on the walls, panoramic views of the waves and floorboards patterned by sandy footprints, help make this beach-side bistro the perfect hangout. The menu re-defines surf'n'turf: miso blackened mackerel, Fowey mussels with Cornish cider and homemade burgers with smoked Tintagel cheese. In the winter they tend to close at dusk.

PORTSMOUTH

☎ 023 / pop 196,500

Trashed in parts by WWII bombing, Portsmouth isn't the prettiest place at first glance, but its long association with the Royal Navy lends it a certain gritty aura. The city's points of interest, not surprisingly, are mostly associated with maritime and coastal defences.

Sleeping

Southsea Backpackers Lodge (☎ 023 9283 2495; www.portsmouthbackpackers.co.uk; 4 Florence Rd, Southsea; dm £15, d £33-38) This old-fashioned backpackers hostel is a warren of four- to eight-bed dorms. The shower-to-people ratio isn't that high, but there are other extras like a pool table, patio and BBQ.

Fortitude Cottage (☎ 023 9282 3748; www.fortitudecottage.co.uk; 51 Broad St, The Point; s from £45, d £70-80) The ferry-port views from this fresh and airy B&B are interesting, if industrial. The lovely bay-windowed breakfast area is ideal for munching a sausage as the ships come in.

Sally Port Inn (☎ 023-9282 1860; High St, Old Portsmouth; s/d/f £45/70/80) The slightly worn bedrooms in this 16th-century inn are showing their age; they also share bathrooms. But history buffs might enjoy the slanting floors, beams scavenged from shipwrecks and a Georgian cantilever staircase built with a ship's mast.

Florence House Hotel (☎ 023 9275 1666; www.florencehousehotel.co.uk; 2 Malvern Rd, Southsea; d £70-140; wi-fi) Edwardian elegance combines beautifully with modern flourishes at this superstylish oasis of boutique bliss. It's a winning combination of plush furnishings, sleek bathrooms, open fireplaces and the odd chaise longue – the suite, complete with spa bath, is top-notch, and they'll even prepare you a picnic basket for day-tripping jaunts down the coast.

Somerset House (☎ 023 9275 3555; www.somersethousehotel.co.uk; 10 Florence Rd, Southsea; d £110-190) At this late-Victorian sister to Florence House (opposite), the same team has created another achingly tasteful haven of designer calm. Here, stained glass, dark woods and polished floors cosy up to Balinese figurines and the very latest word in luxury bathrooms.

Eating

Sallyport Tea Rooms (☎ 023 9281 6265; 35 Broad St, The Point; breakfast £3.75-5.25, lunch £3-5; 10am-5pm Tue-Sun) Just as a traditional teashop should be: civilised, filled with fussy collectibles and serving up loose-leaf speciality teas and other old-fashioned delights to the strains of 1940s jazz.

Custom House (☎ 023 9283 2333; Gunwharf Quays; mains £8; lunch & dinner) The Old Customs House was until 1986 the shore establishment of HMS Vernon, and for over 110 years was a centre of naval innovation and invention. The best of Gunwharf Quays' numerous swanky eateries. Custom House is in the 1790 Vernon Building, now a traditional-style pub with better-than-average bar food.

al forno (☎ 023 9282 0515; 39 Osborne Rd; mains £8; noon-10pm) This cool little Italian brings a touch of la dolce vita to not-terribly Continental Southsea. The decor may not be traditional (think burgundy candy stripes and elegant chairs), but the chef still rustles up all the old pasta and pizza favourites.

Agora Restaurant (☎ 023 9282 2617; 9 Clarendon Rd, Southsea; mains £8.50-10.50; dinner) Festooned with fake beams, this familial little Turkish hookah bar serves up tasty Mediterranean food, washed down with ouzo and raki. Watch out for its occasional belly-dancing nights.

Lemon Sole (☎ 023 9281 1303; 123 High St, Old Portsmouth; mains £9.50-18; lunch & dinner) A colourful little pick-your-own seafood restaurant, Lemon Sole lets you size up freshly netted critters at a counter, then choose how you want them cooked. Try the seafood and shellfish chowder, the devilled mackerel or the stunning fish platters (£39 for two). The menu includes vegie and meat options, too. It's all tucked away in a lemon-yellow, gold and blue interior with a whole wall full of wine bottles at the end.

Bistro Montparnasse (☎ 023 9281 6754; 103 Palmerston Rd, Southsea; lunch mains £11-22, two-/three-course dinner £27/32; lunch & dinner Tue-Sat) Along with polished wooden floors and chic decor, this classy, cosy bistro serves up French classics with an English twist. Wild mushroom and spinach Wellington, and local sea bass with crab ravioli are among the treats.

RYDE
☎ 01983 / pop 26,000

The Isle of Wight's largest town, Ryde offers pleasant beaches, a range of services and proximity to the mainland.

Sleeping & Eating

Kasbah (☎ 01983 810088; www.kas-bah .co.uk; 76 Union St; s/d £50/80; mains £7; lunch & dinner) this funky B&B-cum-bar brings a hot blast of the Mediterranean to Ryde. Intricate lanterns, stripy throws and furniture fresh from Marrakesh dot the smoothly-comfy rooms. Falafel, tapas and paella are on offer in the chilled bar downstairs.

STEYNING
☎ 01903 / pop 6000

Serene and pretty, Steyning was a thriving market and port town in the Middle Ages (the River Adur was then navigable to Steyning). It's a quiet place where many Tudor and Stuart houses survive to the present, enlivened by interesting historical footnotes, several friendly pubs and some good places to eat.

Sleeping & Eating

There's basic camping available (no showers) at **White House Caravan Site** (☎ 01903 813737; Newham Lane; sites for two £6). **Springwells Hotel** (☎ 01903 812446; www.springwells.co.uk; 9 High St; s £41-62, d £69-117) is an attractive building on the main street, offering a choice of en suite rooms or cheaper rooms with shared bathrooms.

Further along, **Chequer Inn** (☎ 01903 814437; www.chequerinnsteyning.co.uk; 41 High St; s/d/tr £45/70/80, mains £6-11; breakfast, lunch & dinner) has rooms above an atmospheric, woodbeamed, 500-year-old pub, which serves food.

On the southern outskirts of town, technically in Bramber village, there are more rooms at the **Castle Inn Hotel** (☎ 01903 812102; www.castleinnhotel.co.uk; The Street, Bramber; s/d £50/70, mains £6-11; lunch daily, dinner Mon-Sat).

For a break from pub food, and a magnificent one at that, the misleadingly named **Saxons** (☎ 01903 813533; 76 High St; mains £6-15; lunch & dinner), serves the best Indian food this side of Brick Lane.

ST JUST
☎ 01736 / pop 4500

Inland from Cape Cornwall, isolated St Just-in-Penwith is a friendly village, the community of artists and writers hereabouts lending the place a pleasant, easy-going air.

Sleeping & Eating

For sleeping try the **Land's End YHA Hostel** (☎ 0870 770 5906; Letcha Vean; dm £10; Easter–Oct) in an isolated spot half a mile south of the village. This no-frills affair has smallish dorms and a basic kitchen, but is ideal if you're hiking the coast path.

Cookbook (☎ 01736 787266; 4 Cape Cornwall St; lunch £4-8, dinner from £8; 10am-5pm, plus from 7pm Sat) Another bohemian hangout, where wonderful home-cooked food rubs shoulders with a huge range of secondhand books. The soups, cakes and sarnies are super, and the coffee's served in mugs made by a local potter.

Kegen Teg (☎ 01736 788562; 12 Market Sq; mains £6-10; 9am-4.30pm Mon-Sat) St Just's artsy types flock to this wholefood cafe for its handmade smoothies, fair trade coffee and sticky cakes. There's always a daily-changing soup on the menu, and the sandwiches, chillis, curries and stews are all prepared with loving care.

A number of pubs in St Just offer bar meals in the £5 to £10 range. The **Wellington Hotel** (☎ 01736 787319; Market Sq) is a good choice and there's also a popular fish and chip shop (Market Sq).

The **Star Inn** (☎ 01736 788767; Fore St) is a great pub that often has folk music sessions and does good bar meals.

VENTNOR
☎ 01983 / pop 6000

A pretty town with an often-mentioned 'Mediterranean feel', Ventnor enjoys a sheltered southerly aspect and is reputedly one of the sunniest spots on the island. This quiet, Victorian-era spa town has a lovely Botanic Gardens with a diverse range of plants from around the world and some nice pubs overlooking the sea. The town is compact and, given the hills, it's a fair idea to walk around rather than ride once you've settled into accommodation.

Information

Ventnor tourist office (☎ 01983 853625; 34 High St) has all the tourist info you need.

Sleeping & Eating

Up the hill from the tourist office, at the boutique hotel **Hambrough** (☎ 01983 856333; www.thehambrough.com; Hambrough Rd, Ventnor; d £150-187, £210), it's hard to say which are the better views: the 180 degree vistas out to sea or ones into rooms full of subtle colours, clean lines and satiny furnishings. Espresso machines, dressing gowns and heated floors keep the luxury gauge set to high; one room overlooks the hills behind.

Back in Ventnor, the busy bar at the beach-side **Spy Glass Inn** (☎ 01983 855338; The Esplanade, Ventnor; mains £8) is festooned with nautical knick-knacks and dishes up crowd-pleasing grub.

The staid, self-contained flats at **Spy Glass Inn** (☎ 01983-855338; www.thespyglass.com; The Esplanade; apt £70) have swirling carpets and creaky cane furniture, but also rudimentary balconies overlooking the sea. The busy bar below is festooned with nautical knick-knacks and serves up crowd-pleasing grub (mains £8).

WEYMOUTH

☎ 01305 / pop 52,000

In spite of its slightly worn appearance, Weymouth is a lively place and a pleasant starting point for a longer tour. George III's dip in Weymouth waters in 1789 sealed the town's destiny as a tourist drawcard; a somewhat cross-eyed statue of 'Farmer George' on Royal Terrace proclaims his affection in the hearts of Weymouth people.

Sleeping & Eating

Chatsworth (☎ 01305 785012; www.thechatsworth.co.uk; 14 The Esplanade; s £35-45, d £80-108) watery views are everywhere at this super-trendy B&B – the terrace is just a yard-arm from yacht berths, while bedrooms overlook the seafront or the harbour. The views inside are of purple satins, vanilla candles and worn wood.

Perry's (☎ 01305 785799; 4 Trinity Rd; mains £12-18; lunch Tue-Fri, dinner Tue-Sat) effortlessly stylish, but also relaxed, this Georgian townhouse is a study of snowy white tablecloths and flashes of pink. Just try and resist the Lyme Bay scallops, twice baked Dorset Blue Vinny cheese soufflé or the crab soup. Weymouth's cognoscenti book the window table on the first floor (it has a fabulous harbour-view) for a two-course lunch (a bargain at £15).

YARMOUTH

☎ 01983 / pop 1000

Compact Yarmouth is a busy ferry port and it's also worth a look around. The west Wight towns – Yarmouth, Totland and Freshwater – are close to one another (a couple of miles at most), opening up accommodation options beyond Yarmouth. **Yarmouth tourist office** (☎ 01983 760015) is on The Quay.

Information

Visit the **Yarmouth Tourist Information Centre** (☎ 01983 813818; The Quay) and the regional tourism website www.isleofwight.com to sleeping and eating facilities.

Eastern England

- Join freewheeling students, professors and scientists on the cycle lanes of **Cambridge**, one of Britain's most cycle-friendly cities (p98)
- Savour big-sky views of the reclaimed **Fens** around the **Wash** from the comfort of your saddle (p93)
- Get sand in your spokes on the wide beaches at **Sheringham** and **Hunstanton** (p111)
- Indulge in some paparazzi-style royal spotting as you pedal across the Queen's estate at **Sandringham** (p112)

TERRAIN

Low-lying lands throughout with pancake-flat fenlands to the north around the Wash. A lot of the region is at sea level and therefore vulnerable to flooding.

Telephone Code: ☎ 01223	www.visiteastofengland.com

EASTERN ENGLAND

Of all the counties of England, the flatlands of Essex, Cambridgeshire, Suffolk and Norfolk offer some of the least taxing cycling along rambling country lanes through mostly smooth landscapes. These lead the cyclist leisurely through sleepy communities, which have changed little in 200 years and still retain their bucolic personalities unaffected by the passage of time. They wind past some of the largest private estates in England, including Sandringham, belonging to the Queen herself, to the sandy coastline where some of the UK's best kept holiday secrets are kept, as well as through the fens, a huge area drained in the 17th century and now a haven for wildlife and an important agricultural area. It's hard to imagine that this backwater of rural bliss is just an hour or two by car from London.

Of course the east is not all empty landscapes, flint farmhouses and creaking windmills. The routes described here will plunge you two-wheeled into Cambridge, a city at the leading edge of international science and technology, and pretty cycle-friendly to boot. The busy port of Felixstowe is not a place many arrivals to these shores might see, unless they're wrapped in cardboard and have come from China that is, and bustling Colchester is a place built on Roman ruins.

So if hills are not your scene, look no further than East Anglia's level landscape, where a church steeple or a windmill's blades can be seen for miles around and where your arrival in the saddle may still arouse genuine curiosity. But also remember in this realm of flatness, where there are no lung-busting ups to be suffered, there are no freewheeling downs to be enjoyed.

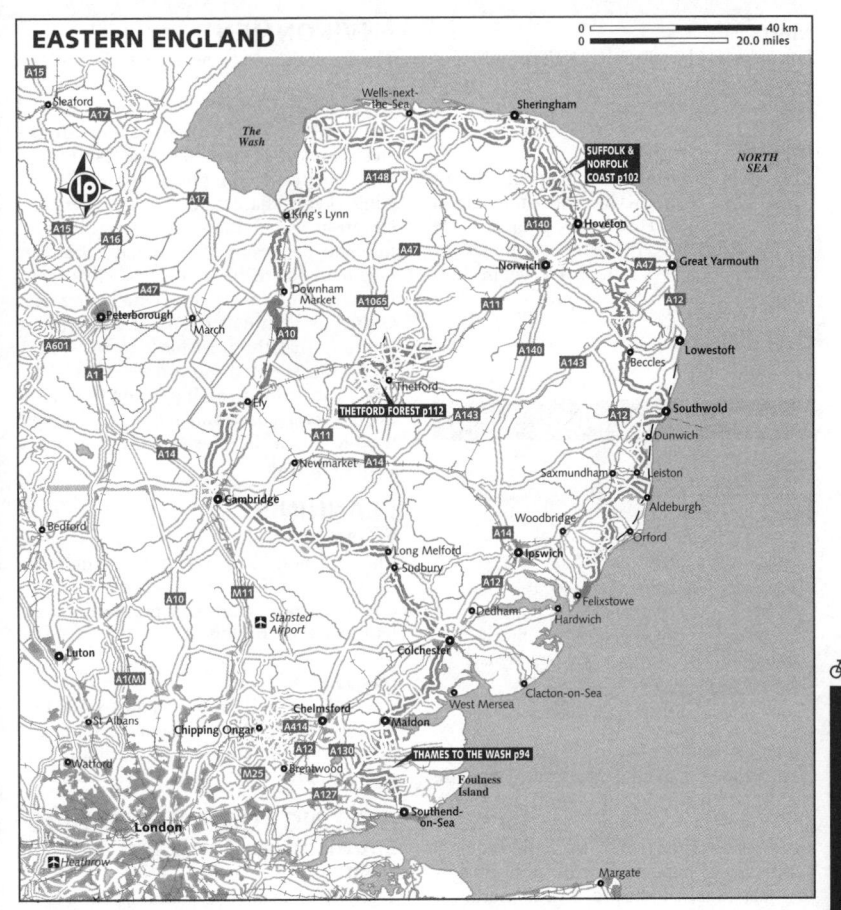

EASTERN ENGLAND

SUFFOLK & NORFOLK COAST p102

THETFORD FOREST p112

THAMES TO THE WASH p94

EASTERN ENGLAND

ENVIRONMENT

A lot of Eastern England is at sea level or, in the case of the sinking fens (reclaimed marshlands), below it, which makes the entire region especially vulnerable to flooding from inland waters, rising sea levels and the largest of spring tidal storm surges. Livestock farming is abundant, as are bird and small-mammal populations. Over the centuries the lack of good stone in the north promoted flint to building material number one.

CLIMATE

Very little rain falls in East Anglia making it one of the driest parts of the country. The area can suffer drought in isolation from

the rest of the UK as much of the prevailing rains that blow in from the Atlantic fall on Wales and the Midlands before they reach the eastern shores. Balancing that, however, is the region's exposure to the colder North Sea and to chilly northeasterlies from the Continent and Siberia.

PLANNING
When to Cycle

April to September is the period when cyc-ling is most pleasant in East Anglia. Roads can get busy with a regular influx of sightseeing and tourist traffic on summer weekends, but as the routes described here stick mostly to country lanes, this shouldn't be a problem.

Maps

For general planning the OS Travel Map – Road 1:25,000 *East Midlands & East Anglia* covers the entire region.

Information Sources

The **East of England Tourist Board** (☎ 01473 822922; www.visiteastofengland .com Dettingen House, Dettingen Way, Bury St Edmunds, IP33 3TU) compiles information on every aspect of travel in England's six easternmost counties.

GATEWAY

See London (p37).

THAMES TO THE WASH

Duration 3 days
Distance 158.3 miles
Difficulty easy–moderate
Start Southend-on-Sea
Finish King's Lynn

Summary A relaxing cycle along the traffic-free country lanes and across the level landscapes of East Anglia, calling at medieval cathedrals, watery nature reserves and creaking windmills as you go.

Cutting a route between two of England's best known coastal features, this gentle ride links the historically significant towns of Colchester, Cambridge, Ely and King's Lynn, passing en route through timeless countryside peppered with old villages of pink-washed houses and medieval churches. Your camera is bound to get a workout here. The route allows riders to combine visits to wildlife reserves, windmills, flood defences and the urban delights of Cambridge, sampling the full flavour of East Anglia from the saddle without having to change gear too much.

From a lazy cyclist's point of view this ride can hardly be beaten. Few if any hills can be found in this part of the country, though Cambridgeshire is perhaps more rolling than you might expect. Each day ends in a large town meaning accommodation is easy to find and villages with shops and pubs come every few miles. If you only have two days to spare, ride from Colchester to King's Lynn to explore the more picturesque parts of the region.

ENVIRONMENT

The Rivers Crouch (near South Woodham Ferrers) and Blackwater (near Maldon) cut wide estuaries into the South Essex coastal plain. Higher farmland can be found to the west between Colchester and Cambridge. The Fenlands to the north around Ely and King's Lynn, characterised by their very low elevation and flatness are historically significant; the result of impressive drainage begun in the 17th century to create vast farming lands – by the Dutch engineer Cornelius Vermuyden. So accurate was his thinking that the final piece in his watery jigsaw was adopted and completed as late as 1968. King's Lynn, an important port serving the east coast and mainland Europe, used to be on the Wash itself but now lies 5 miles inland.

PLANNING
When to Cycle

The best months to cycle in East Anglia are from May to September, when the southerly farmlands are at their prettiest and the fens lose their bleakness.

Maps

The OS Travel Map – Tour 1:100,000 *Norfolk* (sheet 20) and *Suffolk* (sheet 21) between them cover East Anglia in its entirety.

GETTING TO/FROM THE RIDE
Southend-on-Sea (start)
TRAIN

Trains run from two London stations to two Southend stations: London Fenchurch St to Southend Central (£12.50, one hour, every 15 minutes), and London Liverpool St to Southend Victoria (£12.90, one hour, twice hourly). Bikes can travel at off-peak times only (free).

BICYCLE

Don't attempt to ride to Southend from London – the 40 miles of dual carriageway and grim landscape is only for 'die-hards'.

King's Lynn (finish)
TRAIN

Trains start at King's Lynn for London Kings Cross (£26, 1¾ hours, hourly). Bikes travel free, but can only be carried on trains arriving in London at off-peak times.

BICYCLE

King's Lynn is the starting point of the Suffolk & Norfolk Coast ride (p102) later in this chapter. The town also lies on the 369-mile Eastern Heritage Cycle Route (NCN 1) from Hull to Felixstowe, a Sustrans route. To pick up the Central Explorer ride (see p120) and travel north, follow the NCN 1 westwards for 50 miles to Boston – turn off at Holbeach for Spalding to travel south.

THE RIDE
Day 1: Southend-on-Sea to Colchester

3–5 hours, 44.8 miles

After leaving Southend on some hectic roads and having cleared the uninteresting satellite settlements of Rochford and Ashingdon, the route soon plunges into true East Anglian countryside with its many river estuaries, almost traffic-free back roads and distinctive plasterwork houses.

The first interesting place to apply the brakes is Battlesbridge on an inlet of the tidal River Crouch. **Old Battlesbridge Mill** (13.3 miles) in a picturesque spot on an inlet of the river has been converted into one of the country's biggest antiques centres housing over 80 dealers. So having strapped a 200-year-old Welsh dresser to your rear rack you'll be ready to push on.

Beyond the small town of South Woodham Ferrers, the traffic thins even more and the lanes turn decidedly pastoral on the approach to Maldon. You should reach this pleasant historic town after around two hours, and it's an appealing place to halt. Wheeling your bike, explore the well preserved **quayside** on the River Blackwater where distinctive whitewashed timber sail lofts and beautiful Thames barges, now used for leisure cruises on the wide sea inlet to the east, can still be seen. Sea salt has been produced here for 2000 years and **Maldon salt** is sold all over the world. Once a thriving industry, today only one company (the Maldon Crystal Salt Company) still produces this once priceless commodity in the traditional way.

THAMES TO THE WASH – DAY 1

CUE			GPS COORDINATES	
start		Southend central station	51°32'13"N	0°42'55"E
0 miles		go E on unnamed station alleyway		
0.1	⌐►	High St (walk)		
0.4	◄⌐	Pier Hill (walk)		
0.5	◄⌐	Marine Parade		
0.9	◄⌐ ⊙	Southchurch Ave		
2.5	◄⌐	Southchurch Rd 'to Chelmsford'		
2.7	⌐► ⊙	'to Rochford'		
4.7	⌐►	'to town centre'		
5.1	⌐►	'to town centre'		
5.3	↑	past The Rose & Crown pub		
5.9	⌐► ⊙	unsigned road (5th roundabout)		
7.8	◄⌐	'to Hullbridge'		
10.2	⌐►	Lower Rd 'to Hullbridge'		
11.4	⌐►	Watery Lane 'to Chelmsford'		
13.0	⌐►	'to Chelmsford', Battlesbridge	51°37'22"N	0°34'13"E
{13.3	★	Battlesbridge Mill		
13.8	⌐► ⊙	(4th exit) B1012		
16.0	◄⌐	onto dual carriageway		
16.1	◄⌐ ⊙	'to East Hanningfield'		
16.8	⌐►	'to Woodham Ferrers'		
17.4	↑	Edwins Hall Rd		
19.1	◄⌐	Howe Green Rd		
20.8	◄⌐	'to Purleigh (not 'Cock Clarks')		
22.0	⌐►	'to Maldon', Purleigh	51°41'14"N	0°39'31"E
22.3	⌐►	Church Hill (on left bend)		
23.2	◄⌐	unsigned road (at railed bridge)		
23.6	⌐►	B1010		
23.6	↑	Blind Lane (cross B1018)		
24.4	◄⌐	unsigned road (at T-junction)		
26.1	⌐► ⊙	'to Promenade Park'		
26.7	⌐►	into Promenade Park		
26.8	↑	thru car parks to quayside		
26.9	★	Maldon	51°43'52"N	0°40'28"E
	◄⌐	along quayside		
27.1	↑	unsigned road		
27.2	↑	Queens Head		
27.3	⌐►	High St		
27.5	⌐► ⊙	B1018 'to Colchester'		
28.3	⌐► ⊙	B1022 'to Tolleshunt D'Arcy'		
28.6	◄⌐	B1022 'to Colchester'		
29.0	⌐►	'to Tolleshunt Major'		
31.6	◄⌐	'to Tolleshunt Major'		
31.7	⌐►	'to Tolleshunt Major'		
32.6		Tolleshunt Major	51°46'6"N	0°45'13"E
34.2	◄⌐	B1026 'to Colchester', T D'Arcy	51°46'17"N	0°47'42"E
37.2	◄⌐	B1026 'to Colchester'		
{40.5	★	Abberton Reservoir reserve)		
43.7	⌐►	'to long stay car park'		
44.3	↑	Headgate/Head St		
44.5	⌐►	High St		
44.8		Colchester tourist office	51°53'21"N	0°54'16"E

EASTERN ENGLAND

THAMES TO THE WASH - DAY 1-2

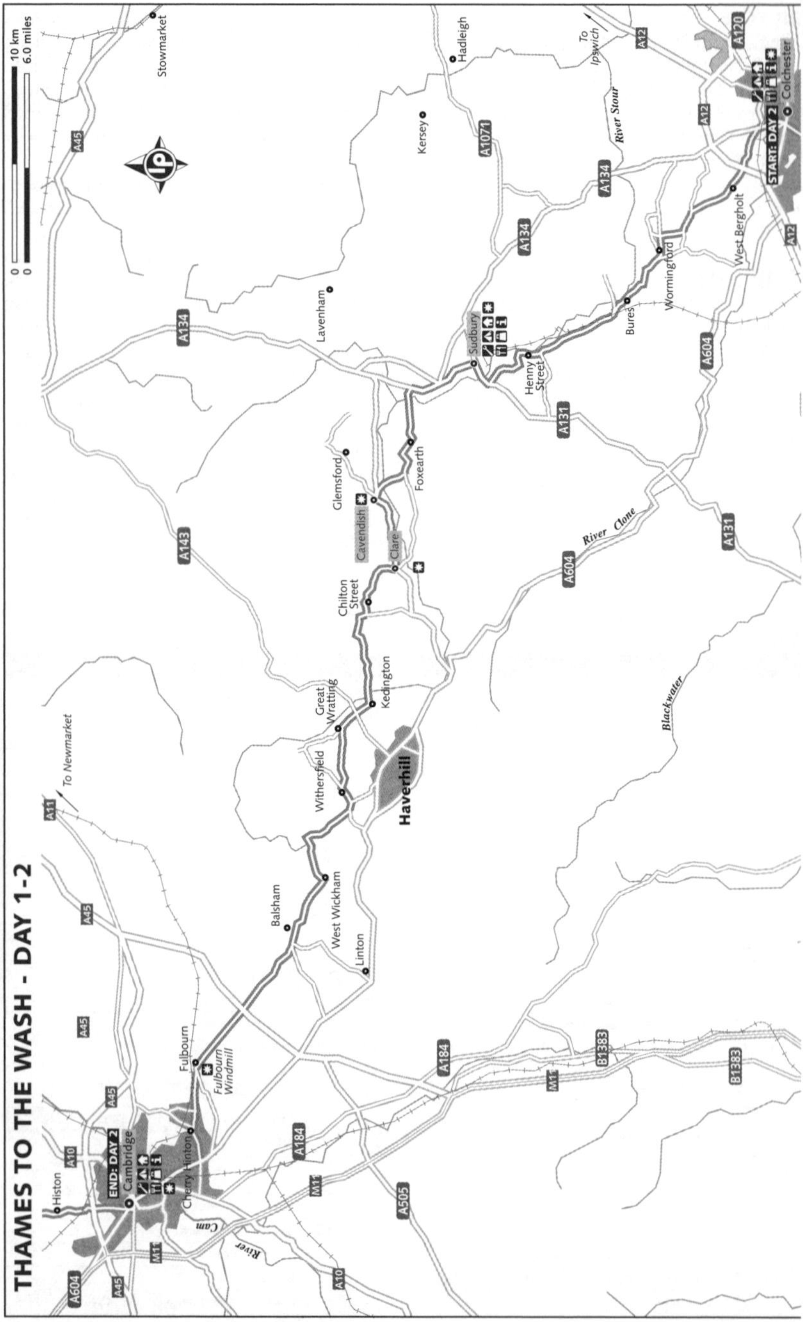

10 km
6.0 miles

Stowmarket

Hadleigh

To Ipswich

A120

Colchester

START DAY 2

West Bergholt

A72

A12

A12

Kersey

A1071

A134

River Stour

A134

Wormingford

A604

A131

Bures

Lavenham

A134

Sudbury

Henny Street

A131

Glemsford

Foxearth

Cavendish

Clare

River Colne

A604

A131

Chilton Street

A143

Kedington

Great Wratting

Blackwater

Withersfield

Haverhill

To Newmarket

A11

Balsham

West Wickham

Linton

A45

A505

A184

B1383

B1383

M11

Fulbourn

Fulbourn Windmill

A45

A11

A10

Histon

A604

M11

A45

END: DAY 2

Cambridge

Cherry Hinton

River Cam

A10

M11

A184

A505

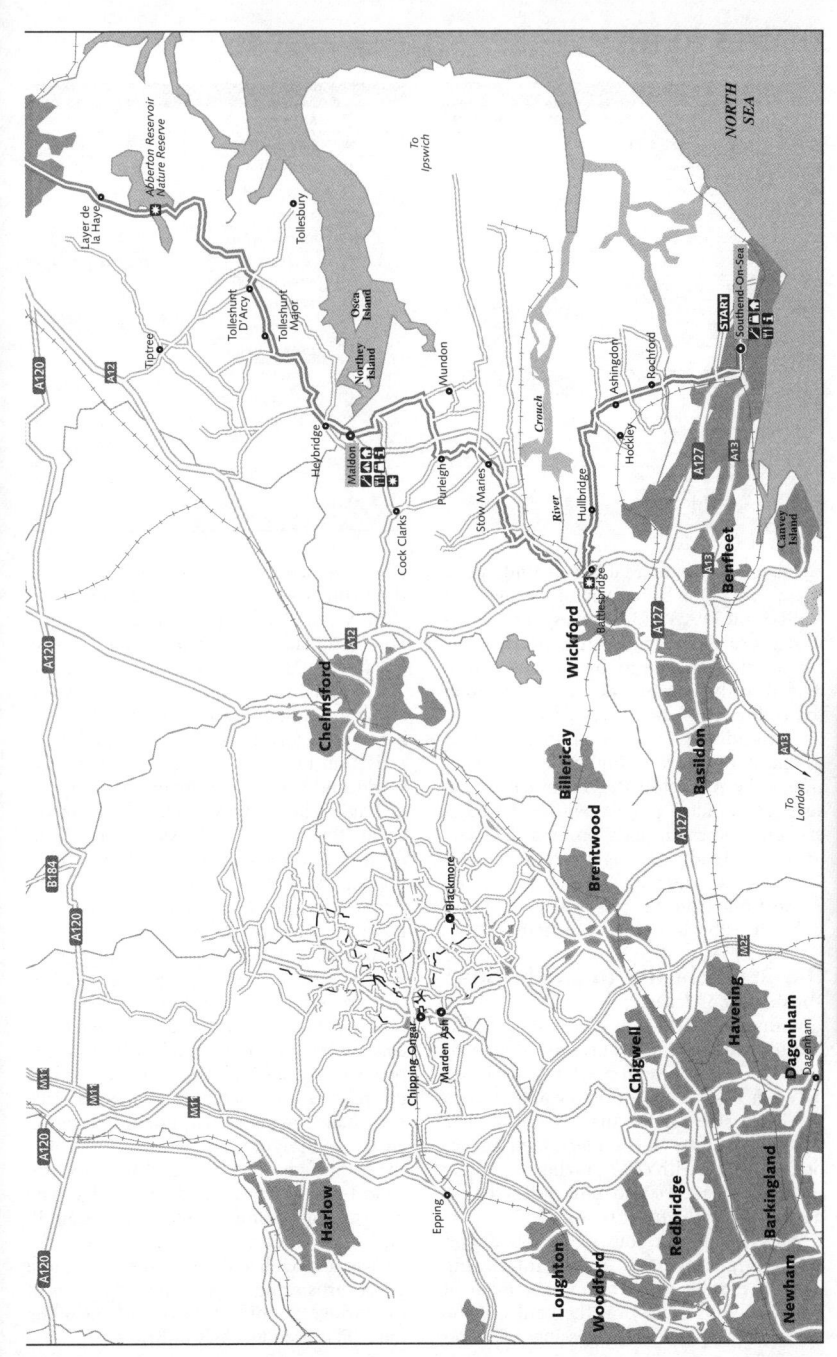

THAMES TO THE WASH – DAY 2

CUE		GPS COORDINATES	
start	Colchester tourist office	51°53'21"N	0°54'16"E
0 miles	go W along High St		
0.3	⌐ North Hill		
0.5	⌐⌐ Middleborough		
0.6	⌐⌐ ⊙ 'Garrison Traffic'		
0.9	⌐⌐ ⊙ 'to Sudbury'		
1.2	⌐ A134 'to Sudbury'		
1.4	⌐⌐ ⊙ (1st exit) B1508 'to Bures'		
3.3	West Bergholt	51°54'44"N	0°50'59"E
9.3	⌐⌐ 'to Lamarsh', Bures	51°58'20"N	0°46'29"E
14.9	⌐ A131		
15.5	★ Sudbury	52°2'31"N	0°43'42"E
	⌐⌐ 'to Stowmarket'		
15.8	↘ 'to A134 Bury'		
16.7	⌐⌐ ⊙ 'to Foxearth'		
17.4	⌐⌐ B1064 'to Foxearth'		
19.2	Foxearth	52°4'10"N	0°40'31"E
21.4	★ Cavendish	52° 5'14"N	0°38'3"E

CUE		GPS COORDINATES	
	⌐⌐ A1092		
24.2	★ Clare	52° 4'38"N	0°34'51"E
	⌐ B1063 'to Newmarket'		
25.9	⌐⌐ 'to Kedington', Chilton Street	52°5'33"N	0°33'52"E
28.2	⌐⌐ 'to Kedington'		
29.8	⌐ B1061, Kedington	52° 5'40"N	0°29'25"E
31.3	⌐⌐ 'to Withersfield', Great Wratting	52°6'23"N	0°27'47"E
33.1	⌐⌐ 'to Haverhill'		
33.5	⌐ 'to Cambridge', Withersfield	52°6'26"N	0°25'8"E
33.8	⌐ 'to West Wratting'		
39.0	⌐⌐ 'to West Wickham' (at T-junction)		
40.6	⌐ 'to Fulbourn', West Wickham	52°7'1"N	0°21'15"E
42.5	⌐⌐ B1052 'to Fulbourn', Balsham	52°7'53"N	0°19'12"E
47.9	Fulbourn	52°10'59"N	0°13'19"E
53.5	⌐⌐ Downing St		
53.6	⌐ Corn Exchange		
53.7	Cambridge tourist office	52°12'15"N	0° 7'9"E

Leaving pleasant Maldon behind, some tricky navigation brings you to the village of **Tolleshunt D'Arcy** (34.2 miles). The Tolles were a local Saxon tribe that came under attack in the 12th century by the Arcyes who landed in the nearby estuary. It's said that the Tolles' cry of 'die Arcyes' gave the village it's misleadingly French sounding name.

The nature-lovers' highlight of today's ride is the **Abberton Reservoir nature reserve** (40.5 miles), popular with bird-watchers and another fine location for a chocolate break. The road passes right across the water providing eye-catching views on both sides. A short ride from the reservoir you'll begin to hit the suburbs of busy Colchester.

Day 2: Colchester to Cambridge

3½–5½ hours, 53.7 miles

Country lanes take you swiftly out of Colchester and into the picturesque Stour Valley with the River Stour marking the border between Essex and Suffolk (you'll stay on the Essex side for the first 14 miles). The valley is a pretty and undervisited corner of East Anglia with cows grazing peacefully in water meadows and pink-washed flint houses lining the quiet roads.

After around an hour or so you should reach arguably the most interesting halt on today's ride, the market town of **Sudbury** (15.5 miles) on the banks of the River Stour. Apart from possessing a wide and

attractive market square, it's best known as the birthplace of Thomas Gainsborough, the 18th-century landscape and portrait painter. His birthplace is **Gainsborough's House** (☎ 01787 372958; www.gainsborough .org; 46 Gainsborough St), the town's top attraction containing a museum and art gallery. The permanent exhibition is the largest collection of Gainsborough's works in the world and a must for anyone with a love of English landscapes. Back on the market square the painter's statue stands proudly in front of St Peter's Church. Sudbury's other popular association is with the BBC TV series *Lovejoy*, which cast Sudbury and nearby Long Melford in starring roles.

Around 6 miles out of Sudbury you'll trundle into the pretty village of **Cavendish** (21.4 miles) which, along with **Clare** (24.2 miles) a few miles further on, is a centre for collectibles. Cavendish also boasts some impressive thatched buildings and a huge village green lined with mature trees, a good place for a halt. Having skirted around Haverhill an arrow-straight road takes you from Balsham through open farmland to Fulbourn, almost on the outskirts of Cambridge. The painstakingly restored **Fulbourn windmill**, one of the finest in the area, overlooks the village from a hill to the west. Just a few more pedal turns brings you to the cycle lanes of Cambridge, a tourist hotspot and one of the most bike-friendly cities in Britain.

Day 3: Cambridge to King's Lynn
4–6 hours, 59.8 miles

This potentially long day offers heaps to see as the route leaves Cambridge for the flat and atmospheric fenlands. The traffic evaporates after Cottenham (5.9 miles) where you should look out for the **All Saints Church** with its oriental-style tower. From here the fens stretch out towards another tower, that of Ely Cathedral.

Quaint **Ely** (16.6 miles; pronounced 'ee-lee') is worthy of a lengthy stop and you should allow at least a couple of hours to see everything. Once an island surrounded by gooey marshland, it takes its name from the eels that swam around it. In fact eel stew and eel pie are still local staples found on menus in the town's restaurants. Ely's historical centrepiece is the magnificent Norman Roman-esque **cathedral**, one of England's finest, with a sublime view of the clean cut interior. The octagon and lantern towers were constructed in 1322 after the original central tower collapsed. The town was also home to Oliver Cromwell, the Protestant military leader of the victorious parliamentarian forces in the Civil War, who subsequently made himself lord protector of the country. He resided for ten years at what is today called **Oliver Cromwell's House**, is home to the tourist office (near the cathedral). Down the hill from the Georgian town is the lively waterfront of the River Great Ouse (pronounced 'ooze').

After Ely, the ride re-enters the weird and wonderful landscape of the Fens. This area is drained into The Wash by the Great Ouse and the route follows the huge embankment, which holds back the river and stops it re-flooding Norfolk's low-lying farmland. From Ten Mile Bank, unsurfaced roads lead to **Denver Sluice** (36.6 miles; see boxed text p102), one of the main gates in the vast drainage system and flood defences. **Denver Mill** (☎ 01366 384009; www.denvermill .co.uk) a little further on has been restored to its former glory and is the only working windmill in all East Anglia. Take a look round the mill then grab a drink and bite to eat in the cafe before hitting the road again. More single track roads, not always with the smoothest surfaces, roughly follow the river into King's Lynn and the end of the ride.

SIDE TRIP: WELNEY WILDFOWL & WETLANDS TRUST BIRD RESERVE

At Ten Mile Bank (34 miles) you can veer off the main route and take a side trip to **Welney Wildfowl & Wetlands Trust bird reserve**

THAMES TO THE WASH – DAY 3

CUE			GPS COORDINATES
start		Cambridge tourist office	52°12′15″N	0° 7′9″E
0 miles		go W on Wheeler/Benet St		
0.1	⌐►	King's Parade/Trinity St		
0.4	◄⌐	Bridge St/Magdalene St		
0.9	⌐►🏠	'to Histon'		
	◄⌐	(33yd) B1049 'to Histon'		
3.4		Histon	52°15′12″N	0° 6′15″E
5.9		Cottenham	52°17′6″N	0° 7′30″E
9.6	⌐►	'to Witchford'		
11.2	◄⌐	'to Witchford'		
14.6	⌐►	'to Ely', Witchford	52°23′11″N	0°12′5″E
14.8	⌐►	A142 'to Ely'		
16.1	◄⌐	'to City Centre'		
16.4	⌐►	unsigned road (at tourist office)		
16.4	◄⌐	(55yd) Palace Green, Ely	52°23′56″N	0°15′42″E
	★	cathedral		
	⌐►	(55yd) The Gallery/Station Rd		
17.1	◄⌐	A142 'to station'		
17.7	◄⌐	Adelaide Rd 'to District Centre'		
23.6	◄⌐ ⊙	'to London'		
23.6	⌐►	'to Black Horse Drove'		
33.4	↑	'to Ten Mile Bank'		
	●●⌐►	Welney bird reserve 10 miles ↻		
34.0		Ten Mile Bank	52°32′49″N	0°21′48″E
36.6	★	Denver Sluice & Mill		
38.8	◄⌐	Downham Rd, Denverr	52°35′25″N	0°22′51″E
39.1	◄⌐ ⌐►	'to town centre' (dogleg)		
39.6	◄⌐	Priory Rd		
40.0	⌐►	Bridge St, Downham Markett	52°36′14″N	0°22′47″E
40.2	◄⌐	High St		
	↑	(220yd) 'to swimming pool'		
41.4	◄⌐	'to Stowbridge'		
43.8	⌐►	'to St Mary Magdalen', Stowbridge	52°38′13″N	0°21′59″E
46.8	⌐►	unsigned road, Wiggenhall St Mary M	52°41′57″N	0°20′42″E
48.7		Wiggenhall St Germans	52°42′4″N	0°21′42″E
59.2	◄⌐ ⊙	'to town centre' (thru gate)		
59.4	◄⌐	Millfleet 'to South Quay'		
59.5	◄⌐	Boal St 'to South Quay'		
59.7	⌐►	along South Quay		
59.8	⌐►	Purfleet Place		
59.8		King's Lynn tourist office	52°45′14″N	0°23′34″E

EASTERN ENGLAND

THAMES TO THE WASH - DAY 3

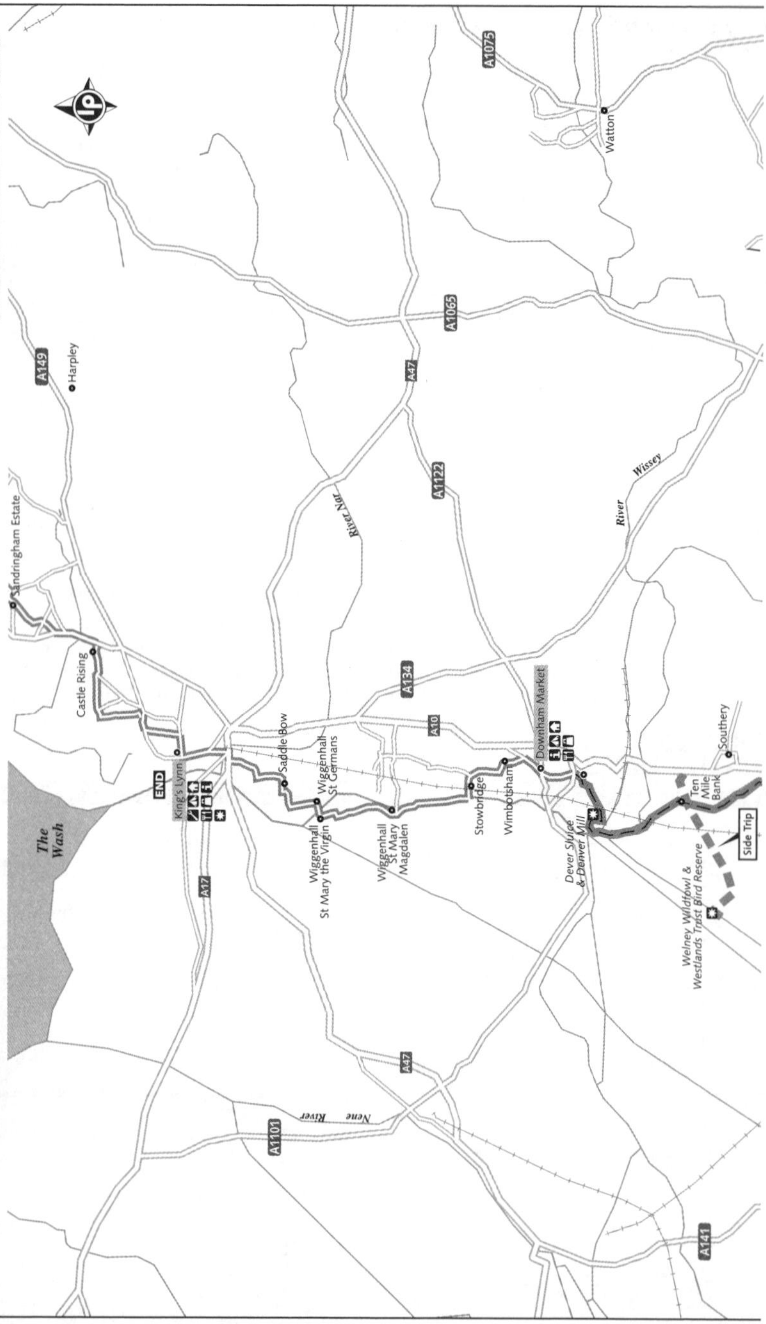

Watton

A1075

A149
Harpley

A1065

A47

Sandringham Estate

A1122

Castle Rising

River Nar

River Wissey

A134

The Wash

Saddle Bow

A10

Downham Market

Southery

King's Lynn
END

Wiggenhall
St Mary the Virgin

Wiggenhall
St Germans

Wiggenhall
St Mary
Magdalen

Stowbridge

Wimbotsham

Denver Sluice
& Denver Mill

Ten
Mile
Bank

A47

Welney Wildfowl &
Westlands Trust Bird Reserve

Side Trip

A47

A1101

Nene River

A141

0   10 km
0   6.0 miles

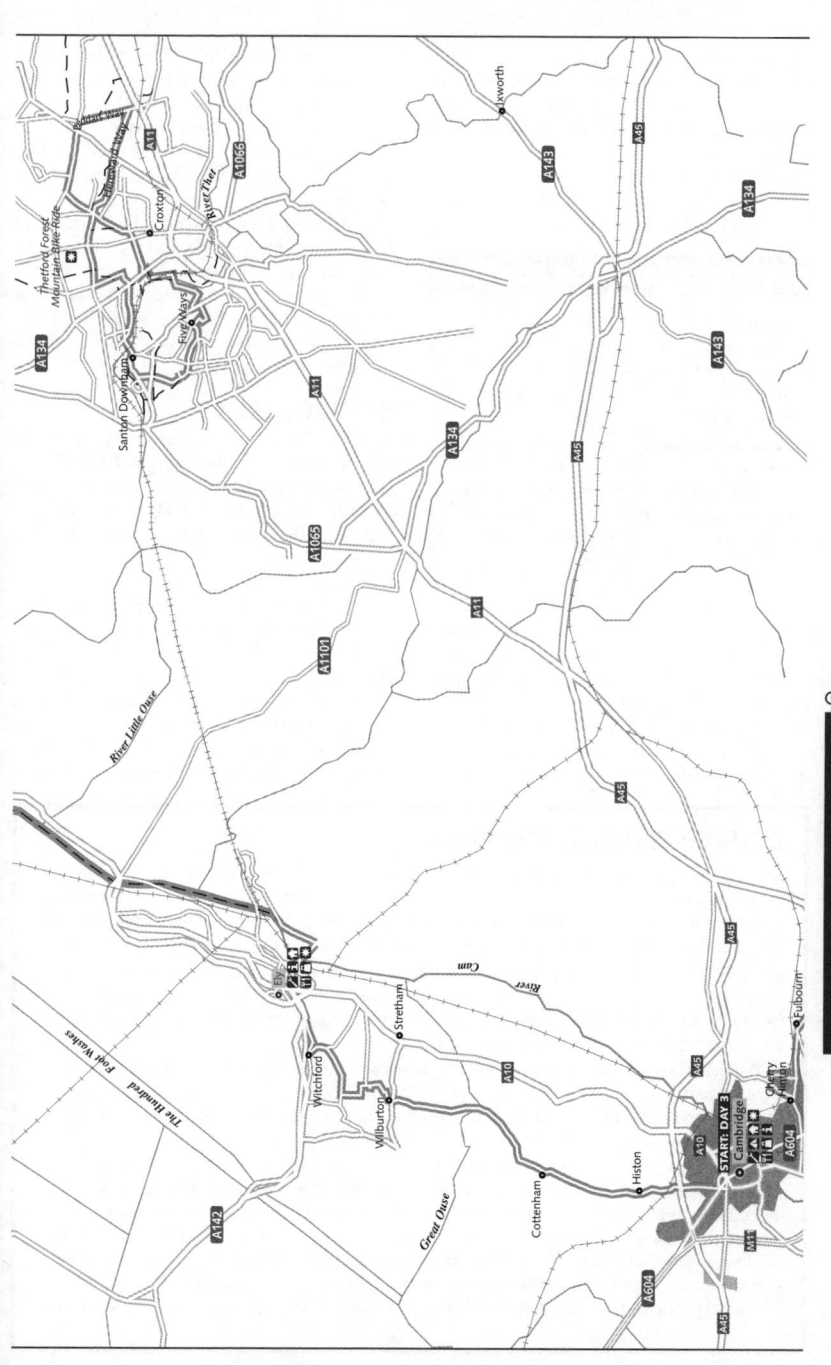

(☎ 01353 860711) about 4 miles west. This treasure-trove of migrating and roosting fowl is observable from hides, and in the summer months special walks are marked out which are otherwise flooded during the rest of the year. Thousands of swans winter here from October to February, their numbers peaking during January.

SUFFOLK & NORFOLK COAST

Duration 4 days
Distance 175.3 miles
Difficulty easy–moderate
Start Felixstowe
Finish King's Lynn
Summary Chopping and changing between the inland Broads and sandy shore, this fascinating ride takes cyclists onto river ferries, past noble abbeys, into pretty seaside towns and even past the Queen's own country pad at Sandringham.

The East Anglian coastline from Felixstowe to the Wash is ideal country for relaxed cycle touring. The going is steady, the views are wide and the sights and pretty villages a constant diversion. Both the Suffolk and Norfolk shores are infused with a fine quality of light and a strange sense of remoteness, despite existing less than 100 miles from one of the world's great cities. Perhaps this is because these regions remain a secret to the majority of Britons whose common belief is that they are flat, ergo dull, though the image has no basis in fact.

This is not a trip concerned with dodging traffic-plagued A-roads, but a country-lane tour through a well-to-do region with a traditionally-minded population. The route both dips its toes in the chilly North Sea and heads in land to explore some of the lumpier bits of Norfolk.

ENVIRONMENT

The low shoreline of East Anglia is made up of dunes, marshes and cliffs with nature reserves rich in flora and fauna. These include the reserves at Minsmere in Suffolk and Blakeney Point in Norfolk, with its 400-strong seal colony. Coastal erosion has virtually eradicated the old cliff top town of Dunwich in Suffolk, while settlements along the North Norfolk shore such as Wells-next-the-Sea lie inland of brackish marshes, once covered by the North Sea.

Inland, the scene is rural, with reclaimed lands around the Norfolk Broads. The old water-filled peat-diggings form an important protected habitat for bird and water life,

DENVER SLUICE & THE FENS

Flat and fertile, the Fenland Plain lies in a massive arc around the Wash and makes up nearly all the prime farming land in England. The region was hard-won and remains under constant threat from flooding and rising sea levels. The relationship between water and land is so finely balanced here that it is constantly measured in inches, with a great percentage of the area below sea level.

Although the Fens are bleak and inhospitable in grim weather, things are much more secure than 400 years ago, when upland rivers and gale-driven tides pushed and pulled the water freely over large areas. Much of the land was little more than marsh and summertime pastures were often drowned during the winter.

The great drainage works, a series of cuts, drains and sluices, of which the Denver Sluice is a critical part, were begun in the 16th century. The work continues today as engineers attempt to predict and control the effect of global warming and rising sea levels, which complicate the effects of wind, rain and tide.

The original Denver sluice (the first the route passes over) was built by Dutch engineer Sir Cornelius Vermuyden, the key engineer in the vast project. It was rebuilt in 1835 and enlarged in 1923. The second sluice the route crosses, the AG Wright sluice, was constructed after the disastrous flooding of 1947 when almost 40,000 acres of fenland went under water after unusually heavy winter snowfalls melted. It was one of the last pieces in Vermuyden's watery jigsaw and provided the area with a little dry security. But with global warming now a virtually unstoppable reality, the balance between man and water could soon swing back the other way.

and are one of Britain's most popular destinations for boating holidays. North Norfolk disproves the popular conception that East Anglia is all flat, with hills that rise to nearly 100m (330ft) a few miles in from the sea.

PLANNING
When to Cycle
East Anglia is good for cycling from Easter to October when Suffolk and Norfolk are in full bloom and the resorts are crammed with the English at play. At this time accommodation should be booked well ahead. Out of season, the charm of the little towns is just as evident, if not more so, though things can be grim inland. East Anglia is one of the driest parts of the country, but during the winter it can bear the full force of cold Continental winds.

The ferry at Bawdsey runs only on occasional weekends in the winter (call Felixstowe tourist office for details, see p114), and the detour is long. The ferry at Walberswick (Southwold tourist office, see p116) runs in the summertime and school holidays, but the road route detour is fine, if busy.

What to Bring
Campsites line the route so loading a tent and other camping gear is a good idea if you're on a tight budget. Major towns have bike shops, but the smaller ones don't always have specialist stockists. Food and accommodation are never far away.

Maps
The OS Travel Map – Tour 1:100,000 *Norfolk* (sheet 20) and *Suffolk* (sheet 21) cover the entire route in sufficient detail.

GETTING TO/FROM THE RIDE
Felixstowe (start)
TRAIN
Felixstowe is accessible by train from London Liverpool Street via Ipswich (£31.50, two hours, hourly). Bikes go free of charge on both legs of the journey but cannot be carried on services departing London at peak times.

King's Lynn (finish)
For details on how to get to and from King's Lynn see the Getting to/from the ride section (p94) of the Thames to the Wash ride earlier in this chapter.

THE RIDE
Day 1: Felixstowe to Southwold
2½–4½ hours, 41.4 miles
The beautiful Suffolk coast is indented with tidal river estuaries and speckled with other-worldy towns with lots to explore. Allow plenty of time to savour this day, which starts and finishes with ferry crossings and features three side trips. If the ferries aren't running some busy road detours, which can eat away time.

Leaving Felixstowe behind, the roads become rural beyond the **Bawdsey ferry** (Old Felixstowe) across the River Deben. Wave the bat, and the harbourmaster in a white cap fetches you and your bike for £3.50 (daily from April-October, some weekends only from November-March).

ALTERNATIVE ROUTE: VIA WOODBRIDGE
If the Felixstowe Ferry is not running for any reason, you're in for a long detour involving a retreat to Felixstowe. Luckily the diversion follows the Suffolk Coastal Cycle Path for the first few miles – just follow the signs back from the ferry and continue to the town of Woodbridge, the site of a historic tidal mill, and **Sutton Hoo,** the fabulous 7th-century Anglo-Saxon royal burial ground from which a complete longship has been excavated. Digging continues at this enormous site. From there turn southeast onto the B1083, which will bring you to Alderton and back to the route.

From Alderton the route continues to trace the coast then cuts inland to Butley.

SIDE TRIP: ORFORD
At the town of Butley, an 8-mile side trip south (13.2 miles) will bring you to the town of Orford, home to a fine 12th-century **Norman castle** built by Henry II to defend the shore from invaders. Across the River Alde is National Trust protected **Orford Ness,** the largest shingle spit in Europe and used as a military test site. Orford has a pleasant seashore, a superb setting for a picnic lunch.

Back on the route the ride through peaceful lanes brings you to **Snape Maltings** (☎ 01728 688303) on the picturesque River Alde. The old buildings have been converted into cafes, shops and a concert venue that every June plays host to the **Aldeburgh**

SUFFOLK & NORFOLK COAST - DAY 3

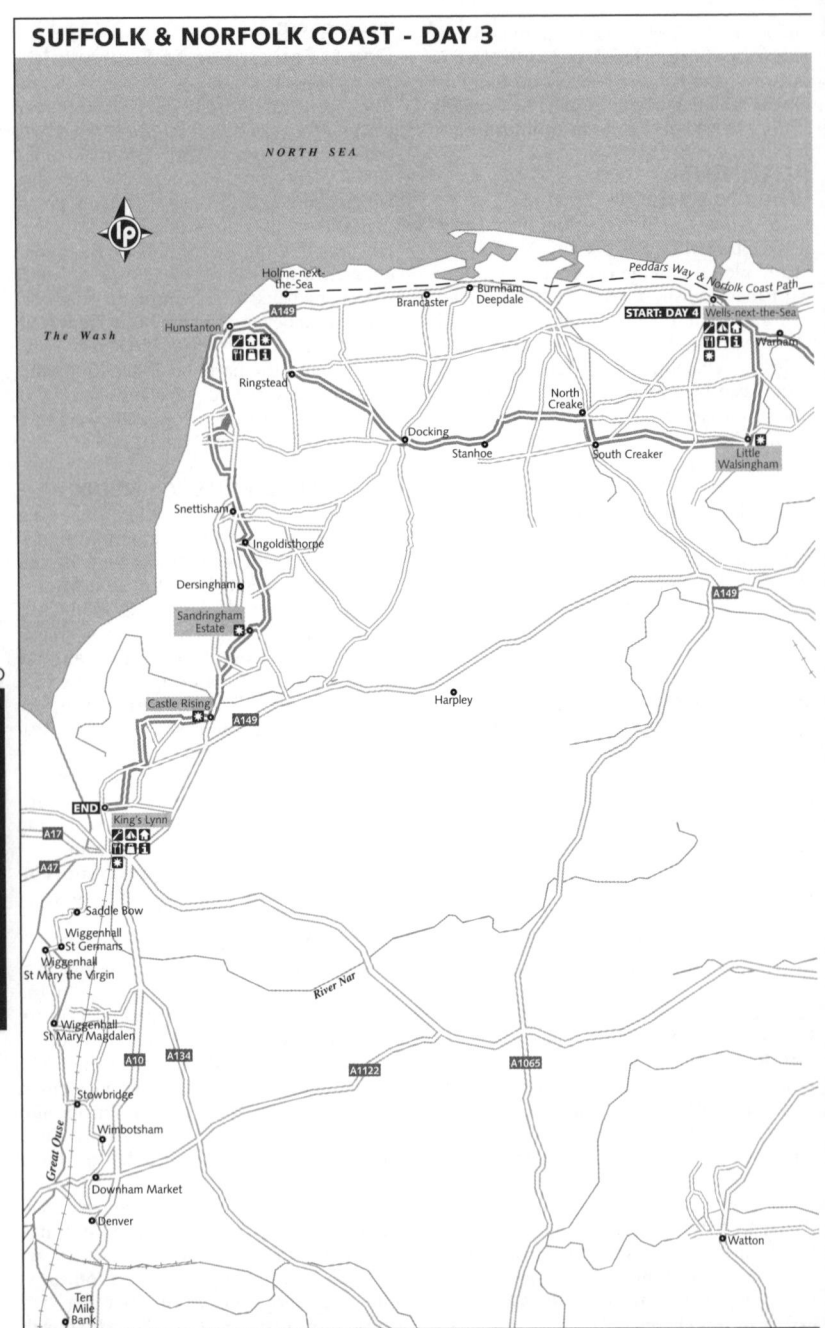

EASTERN ENGLAND

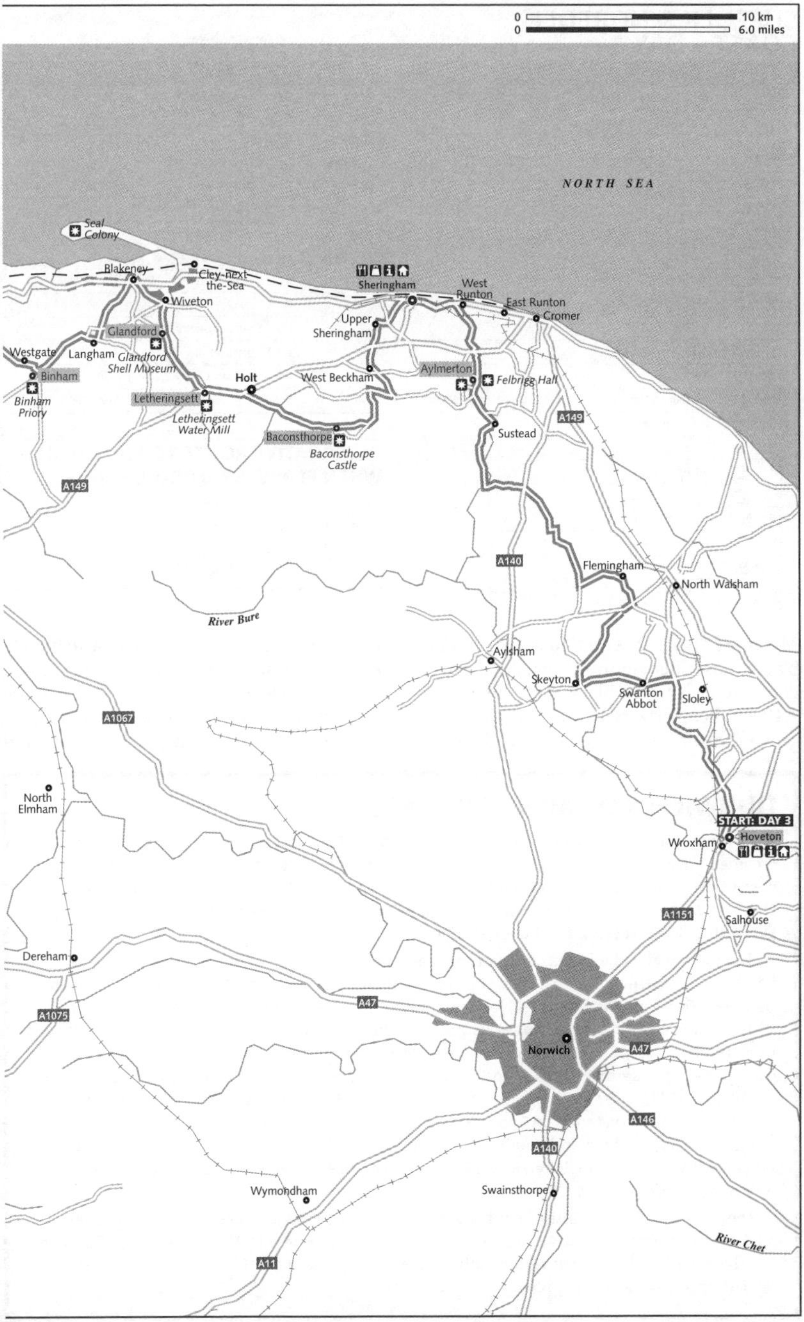

NORTH SEA

Seal
Colony

Blakeney
Cley-next-
the-Sea
Wiveton
Sheringham
West
Runton
East Runton
Cromer

Upper
Sheringham

Westgate
Langham *Glandford*
Glandford *Shell Museum*

Aylmerton
Felbrigg Hall

Binham
*Binham
Priory*

Holt
West Beckham

Letheringsett
*Letheringsett
Water Mill*

Sustead

Baconsthorpe
*Baconsthorpe
Castle*

A149

A140

Flemingham

North Walsham

River Bure

Aylsham

Skeyton
Swanton
Abbot
Sloley

A1067

North
Elmham

START: DAY 3
Hoveton
Wroxham

EASTERN ENGLAND

A1151

Salhouse

Dereham

A47

A1075

Norwich

A47

A146

A140

Wymondham

Swainsthorpe

River Chet

A11

0 ————— 10 km
0 ————— 6.0 miles

SUFFOLK & NORFOLK COAST – DAY 1

CUE			GPS COORDINATES	
start		Felixstowe train station	51°58'1"N	1°21'2"E
0 miles		go E on High Rd West		
0.8	↑	Cliff Rd		
2.6		Old Felixstowe	51°58'36"N	1°22'48"E
		catch ferry over River Deben		
2.6	↰	unsigned road		
5.7	↱	unsigned road (at stores), Alderton	52° 1'28"N	1°24'52"E
	●●↑	Woodbridge 12 miles ↻		
12.9	↱	B1084, Butley		
13.2	↰	'to Snape'		
	●●↑	Orford 8 miles ↻		
15.5	↰	'to Tunstall'		
15.6	↱	'to Snape', Tunstall	52° 8'37"N	1°26'47"E
16.2	↱	B1069 'to Snape'		
17.9	★	Snape	52°10'8"N	1°29'58"E
18.4	↱	'By Road'		
19.5	↱	A1094		
23.5	↑⊙	'to town centre'		
23.9	↰	'to Thorpeness'		
	●●↱	Aldeburgh 1 mile ↻		
25.7		Thorpeness	52°10'44"N	1°36'51"E

CUE CONTINUED			GPS COORDINATES	
27.6	↱	B1122 'to Leiston', Aldringham	52°11'35"N	1°34'40"E
28.6		Leiston	52°12'20"N	1°34'28"E
	●●↱	Sizewell nuclear plant 3 miles ↻		
28.8	↱	B1122 'to Yoxford'		
29.8	★	Leiston Abbey		
30.8	↱	B1125 'to Blythburgh'		
33.7	●●↱	Dunwich 5 miles ↻		
37.1	↱	B1387 'to Walberswick'		
39.6		Walberswick	52°18'56"N	1°40'1"E
40.1		River Blyth ferry point		
		catch ferry over River Blyth		
40.1	↱	unsigned road/Ferry Rd (along river)		
41.4		Southwold tourist office	52°19'34"N	1°40'42"E

ALTERNATIVE ROUTE TO SOUTHWOLD WHEN FERRY IS NOT RUNNING

37.1	↑	'to Blythburgh Village'		
37.8	↱	A12 'to Lowestoft		
38.4	↱	A1095 'to Southwold'		
42.5		Southwold tourist office	52°19'34"N	1°40'42"E

🚲 **Music Festival**, an event founded in 1948 by composer Benjamin Britten. After Snape comes today's traffic black spot, the narrow A1094 where drivers like to put their foot down. This brings you quickly to the coast where a quick detour to arty **Aldeburgh**, one of the finest towns on the Suffolk coast, is a must. Here fresh-from-the-net fish are sold from ramshackle huts, handsome pastel-coloured houses, independent shops and

DUNWICH'S DISAPPEARING ACT

The purpose of going to Dunwich is to marvel at something you can't see any more. The first recorded advance by the sea was made in the 11th century, and since the 13th century the waves have swallowed up six of the former town's eight churches and its town walls (entirely). Only the western fringes of what was once an important harbour settlement remain reducing Dunwich to a hamlet of a few hundred souls.

The town had its heyday as a gated town and port in the time of King John, but the sea had been encroaching for centuries even before then. The Domesday Book of 1086 records that between 1066 and 1086 the local Norman manor lost 120 acres of land to the waves. In the 13th century, when the town was at its peak, St Felix's was the first church to succumb, followed by St Leonard's around 1300. In 1328 violent storms choked the harbour with shingle and the river jumped course several miles northwards to Walberswick. St Bartholomew's and St Michael's tumbled in 1331, followed shortly by St Martin's and St Nicholas' – St John's was dismantled in time to save the materials. In 1350, 400 houses, shops and windmills disappeared under the briny, in 1570 the Gilden and South Gates were both swallowed and St Peter's was saved the same fate by human demolition. It would have been under the sea by the time the town's first history was written in 1754.

The ocean's progress persisted in the 20th century when the last medieval parish church, All Saints, was eaten up and the town's western gate disappeared in 1968. These days Dunwich is a shadow of its former self with a 19th-century church and the old leper hospital the only reminders of a once thriving town.

art galleries line the High St, and a sweeping shingle beach stretches along the shore offering tranquil big-sky views. After a short stretch along the shoreline to Thorpeness, it's back inland to Aldringham. Then follow the signs around Leiston (28.6 miles) past the ruins of **Leiston Abbey** from where it's possible to make a side trip to the **Sizewell nuclear power plant**. Sadly the visitors centre closed in 2001 due to fears of a terrorist attack and has been demolished.

At Westleton turn right (33.7 miles) for a side trip back to the coast and the half-village of **Dunwich** (see boxed text p106), which for the last millennium has been busy disappearing under the waves of the North Sea. The main route runs to Walberswick (39.6 miles) for the rowboat ferry (cyclists 80p), which takes you across the narrow River Blyth to Southwold. If the ferry is not operating, take the busy A12 and A1095 into Southwold.

Day 2: Southwold to Hoveton

2½–4½ hours, 41 miles

Turning inland to avoid remoter reaches of the coastline as well as the big coastal towns of Lowestoft and Great Yarmouth, this day begins by exploring the farmland that extends to the charming and historic market town of Beccles (14.7 miles) on the River Waveney. Follow the brown tourist signs north from the town centre for a taste of tranquillity and refreshments on the quayside.

With Beccles firmly behind you, the route heads over the marshes to the Reedham ferry (operates year round; cyclists 80p), a contender for the shortest car ferry trip in the country. The service is reliable enough but is occasionally interrupted by a very low tide. Quite incredibly this is the only place vehicles and bikes can cross the River Yare between Norwich and Great Yarmouth. If the ferry's not running, the road detour via Great Yarmouth is long and you'll encounter some very heavy traffic en route. The **Reedham Ferry** (☎ 01493 700429) is also the name of the inviting pub on the other side, a very convenient place to stop and refuel and to watch the life of the river gently roll by. The pub has a reputation locally for excellent food and a warm welcome for visitors.

If you've diverted around the ferry, you'll rejoin the route at Acle, in Saxon times a fishing community next to the sea but today a village 8 miles from the coast. Acle lies on the edge of the **Norfolk Broads** (see boxed text p110), famous for its 125 milesof safe navigable lakes and waterways. The prettiest cycling miles lie between South Walsham and Wroxham but the only time you'll actually enter the virtually roadless Broads, and then only briefly, is at **Malthouse Broad** at Ranworth (34.7 miles). The day concludes as you cross the humpbacked bridge dividing the twin towns of Wroxham and Hoveton on the River Bure, often described as the gateway to the Broads.

SUFFOLK & NORFOLK COAST – DAY 2

CUE		GPS COORDINATES	
start	Southwold tourist office	52°19'34"N	1°40'42"E
0 miles	go NW on High St		
0.6	↱ B1127 'to Wrentham'		
3.4	↰ 'to Stoven'		
4.6	↰ ↱ A12/'to Brampton' (dogleg)		
10.2	↱ 'to Ringsfield', Redisham		
14.5	↑ Ballygate 'to town centre'		
14.7	Beccles	52°27'13"N	1°33'49"E
14.8	↰ 'to Quay, Gillingham'		
15.2	↰ 'to Gillingham'		
	●●↑ quayside 0.5 miles ↺		
15.9	Gillingham	52°28'12"N	1°33'0"E
16.0	↰ A146 'to Norwich'		
16.5	↱ ⊙ A143		
16.6	↰ 'to Raveningham Rd'		
	follow signs 'to Reedham Ferry'		

CUE		GPS COORDINATES	
19.7	↱ ↰ B1136/'to Reedham F' (dogleg)		
23.8	River Yare ferry point		
	catch ferry over River Yare		
23.8	↑ B1140		
30.4	↱ Norwich Rd		
30.5	↰ 'to South Walsham', Acle	52°38'21"N	1°32'53"E
30.7	↰ South Walsham Rd		
33.6	↱ 'to Ranworth', South Walsham	52°39'52"N	1°29'41"E
34.7	★ Ranworth		
36.5	↑ 'to Wroxham'		
38.8	↱ 'to Light Traffic Only', Salhouse	52°40'15"N	1°23'47"E
38.9	↱ B1140 'to Wroxham'		
39.9	↱ A1151 'to Hoveton'		
40.9	↰ 'to tourist centre'		
41.0	Hoveton tourist office	52°42'49"N	1°24'33"E

EASTERN ENGLAND

SUFFOLK & NORFOLK COAST - DAY 1-2

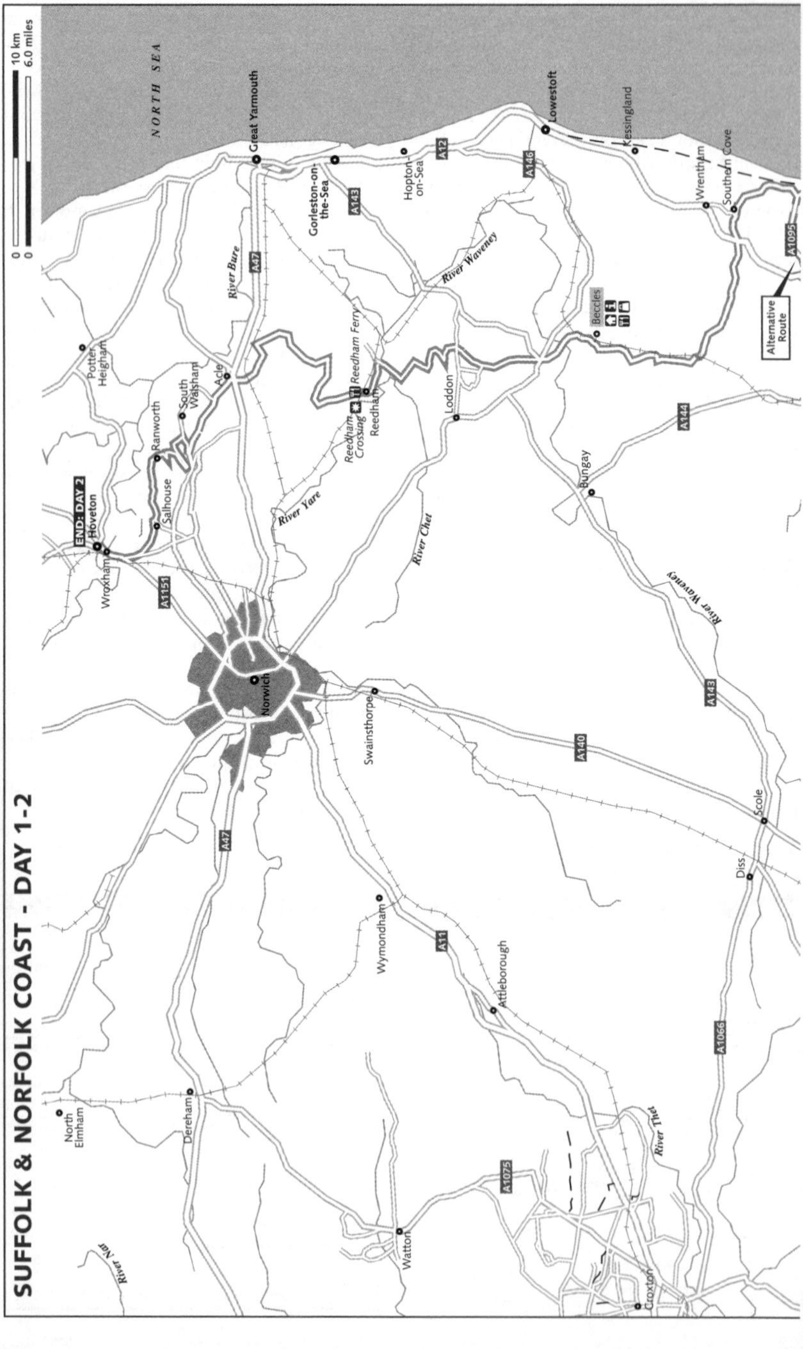

NORTH SEA

10 km
6.0 miles

Great Yarmouth

Gorleston-on-the-Sea

Hopton-on-Sea

A47

A143

Lowestoft

Kessingland

A12

A146

Wrentham

Southam Cove

A1095

River Bure

River Waveney

Potter Heigham

Beccles

Alternative Route

South Walsham

Acle

Reedham Ferry

Reedham Crossing

Reedham

Loddon

A144

Ranworth

Salhouse

River Yare

River Chet

Bungay

END: DAY 2
Hoveton

Wroxham

A1151

River Waveney

Norwich

A47

Swainsthorpe

A140

A143

A11

Wymondham

Attleborough

Scole

Diss

A1066

North Elmham

Dereham

River Wensum

River Thet

A1075

Watton

Hoxton

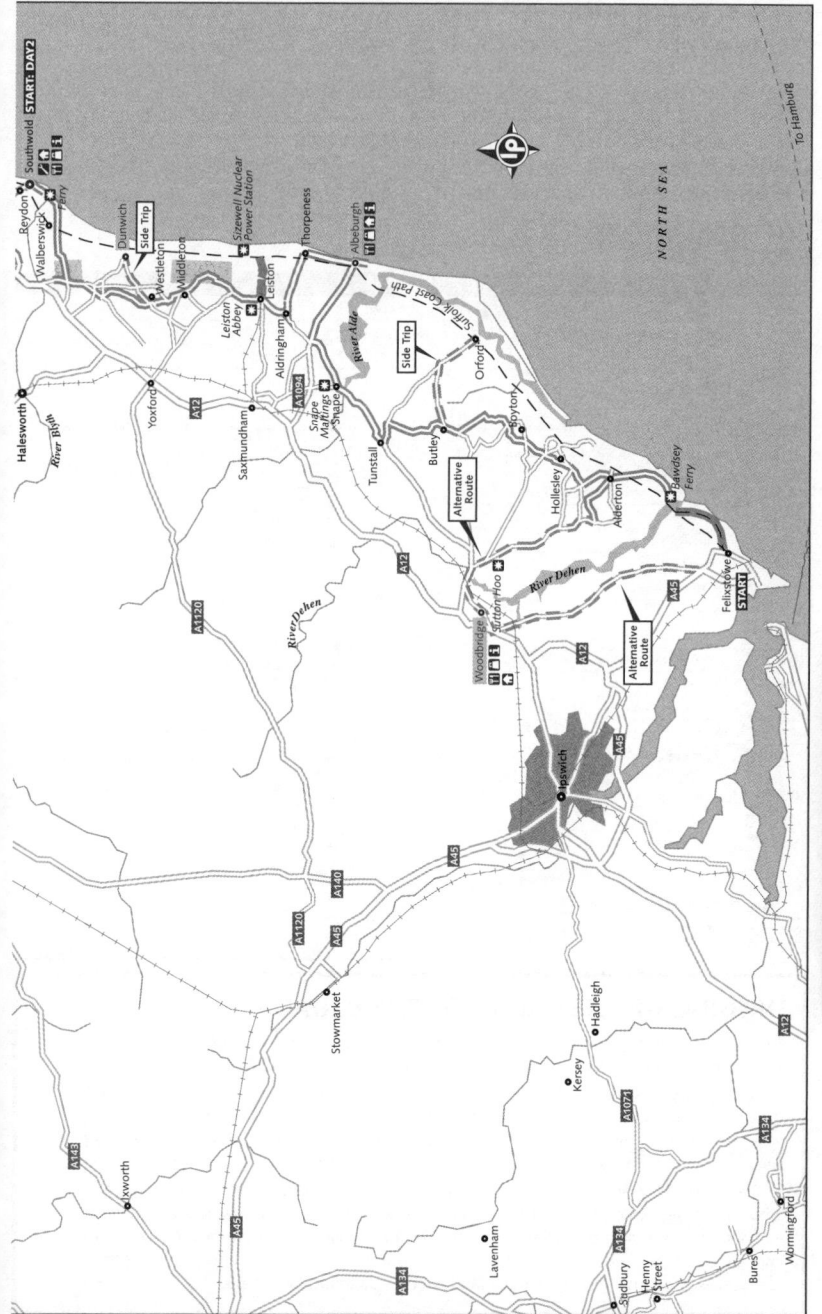

Day 3: Hoveton to Wells-next-the-Sea

3–5 hours, 48.2 miles

Today's stretch takes you on to the North Norfolk coast through rural countryside and handsome estates. For the first 20 miles of today's ride make sure you have your map head on as you'll have to negotiate a mesh of narrow weaving country lanes. The houses and villages lining the way are mostly built of flint and the majority are at least a couple of hundred years old. In this out-of-the-way bit of Britain church spires and towers, many also of flint, dot the horizon in between fields of sugar beet.

SUFFOLK & NORFOLK COAST – DAY 3

CUE			GPS COORDINATES
start		Hoveton tourist office	52°42'49"N 1°24'33"E
0 miles		go W on Station Rd	
0.1	⌐►	'to Horning'	
0.2	⌐►	'to Scottow'	
6.9	⌐►	'to North Walsham'	
7.0	⌐►	'to Felmingham', Swanton Abbot	52°46'40"N 1°21'32"E
8.0	⌐►	'to Felmingham'	
10.3	⌐►	B1145, Felmingham	52°48'52"N 1°20'19"E
10.4	⌐►	'to Suffield'	
11.5	⌐►	unsigned road	
13.4	⌐►	'to Aldborough'	
15.5	⌐►	A140 'to Cromer'	
15.9	⌐►	'to Hanworth'	
18.1	⌐►	'to Sustead'	
18.4	⌐►	unsigned road, Sustead	52°53'8"N 1°14'59"E
19.3	⌐►	'to Aylesmerton'	
19.6	⌐►	'to Aylesmerton'	
20.1	⌐►	'to Aylesmerton'	
21.0	⌐►	'to West Runton', Aylmerton	52°54'37"N 1°14'32"E
21.5	⌐►	A148/unsigned road (dogleg)	
21.8	⌐►	'to West Runton'	
22.9	⌐►	'to Sheringham', West Runton	52°56'15"N 1°14'38"E
24.6		Sheringham	52°56'40"N 1°12'43"E
	●●⌐►	Sheringham beach 1 mile ↺	
24.8	⌐►	B1157 'to Upper Sheringham'	

CUE			GPS COORDINATES
27.3		West Beckham	52°54'41"N 1°10'41"E
27.3	⌐►⌐►	'to Baconsthorpe' (dogleg)	
28.1	⌐►	'to Baconsthorpe'	
29.3	⌐►	unsigned road	
29.4	⌐►	unsigned road	
29.9	★	Baconsthorpe	52°53'22"N 1°9'11"E
32.6	⌐►⌐►	A148/'to town centre' (dogleg)	
32.8	★	Holt	52°54'21"N 1°5'25"E
	⌐►	High St	
33.0	⌐►	A148 'to King's Lynn'	
34.0	★	Letheringsett	52°54'26"N 1° 3'45"E
34.3	⌐►	'to Glandford'	
36.0	★	Glandford	52°55'55"N 1° 2'16"E
37.1		Wiveton	52°56'37"N 1° 2'20"E
	●●⌐►	Cley-next-the-Sea 2 miles ↺	
38.1	↑	'to Blakeney Quay' (cross A149)	
38.4		Blakeney	52°57'6"N 1°1'20"E
	⌐►	along quayside	
38.8	●●⌐►	Morston Quay 2 miles ↺	
40.6	⌐►	B1156 'to Binham', Langham	52°55'52"N 0°59'6"E
42.9	★	Binham	52°55'3.62"N 0°56'54"E
	⌐►	'to Warham'	
46.2	⌐►	'to Wells'	
47.6	⌐►⌐►	A149/'to town centre' (dogleg)	
47.9	⌐►	'to town centre'	
48.0	⌐►	Staithe St	
48.2		Wells tourist office	52°57'22"N 0°51'7"E

DIGGING UP THE ORIGIN OF THE BROADS

For centuries the origin of the Norfolk Broads was unclear – the rivers were undoubtedly natural and many thought the lakes were too, but no one could explain how they had formed.

The mystery was solved when records were discovered in the remains of St Brenet's Abbey on the River Bure. They showed that from the 12th century certain parts of land in Hoveton Parish were used for peat digging. The area had little woodland and the only source of fuel was peat. Since East Anglia was well populated and prosperous, peat digging became a major industry.

Over a period of around 200 years, approximately 25,000 acres were dug up. However, water gradually seeped in, causing marshes and then lakes to develop. The first broad to be mentioned in records is Ranworth Broad in 1275. Eventually the amount of water made it almost impossible for the diggers and the peat-cutting industry died out. In no other area of Britain has human effort changed the natural landscape so dramatically as here.

SUFFOLK & NORFOLK COAST – DAY 4

CUE			GPS COORDINATES
start		Wells tourist office	52°57'22"N	0°51'7"E
0 miles		go W on The Quay		
0.1	↰	The Glebe		
0.2	↰	Clubbs Lane		
0.4	↰	Station Rd		
0.5	↱	High St/Church Plain		
0.8	↰	A149		
0.9	↱	'to Walsingham'		
5.4	★	Little Walsingham	52°53'39"N	0°52'25"E
5.5	↰	'to S & N Creake'		
10.5	↱	B1355, South Creake	52°53'7"N	0°45'54"E
11.3	↰	'to Stanhoe', North Creake	52°54'31"N	0°45'20"E
14.0	↰	'to Docking'		
16.8	↱	B1454 'to Hunstanton', Docking	52°54'6"N	0°37'24"E
17.4	↱	'to Ringstead'		
21.6	↱	'to Hunstanton', Ringstead	52°55'58"N	0°32'18"E
22.1	↰	'to Hunstanton'		
23.4	↰	A149 'to Heacham'		
24.2	↱	'to seafront'		
25.2	↱	unsigned road, Hunstanton	52°56'11"N	0°29'4"E
25.4	↱	Westgate		
25.7	↰⊙	B1161		
26.2	↱⊙	A149		
26.6	↱	'to Heacham'		

CUE CONTINUED			GPS COORDINATES
27.6	↱	'to beaches'		
28.0	↰	'to South Beach'		
28.1	↰	Staithe Rd		
29.0	↱	A149		
30.2	↰⊙	'to Snettisham'		
30.6	↱	Church Rd 'to Bircham'		
30.9	↱	'to Bircham'		
31.3	↱	NCN 1 bikepath		
32.2	↰	Sherborne Rd		
33.6	↑	NCN 1 bikepath		
34.8	↱	NCN 1 bikepath		
35.0		into Sandringham estate		
35.8	↘	NCN 1 bikepath		
36.3	↑	NCN 1 bikepath		
36.9	↰	A149		
38.3	↱	'to Castle Rising'		
38.8	★	Castle Rising castle		
39.5	↱	Ling Common Rd 'to N Wootton'		
41.3	↱	A1078		
41.9	↱	A148 'to King's Lynn'		
42.7	↰	NCN 1 bikepath (by Hamburg Way)		
44.2	↱	unsigned bikepath (at T-junction)		
44.3	↰	unsigned road (over railway crossing)		
44.3	↱	NCN 1 bikepath		
44.7		King's Lynn train station	52°45'13"N	0°24'11"E

Huge estates are common in these parts and after around an hour the route passes through the grounds of **Felbrigg Hall** (☎ 01263 837444). Nearby Aylmerton has a fine example of a typical **Norfolk round-towered church**, built in flint over seven centuries ago.

Your tyres hit the coast at West Runton, a village between the semi-large coastal towns of Cromer and Sheringham (24.6 miles). The latter has a fine sandy **beach** and if you've packed lunch, this is a good a place as any to unfurl the picnic blanket.

Hopefully you've made it to Sheringham in good time as the remainder of the route is packed with attractions worth chaining the bike to a lamppost for. First up is **Baconsthorpe Castle** (29.9 miles), a 15th-century part-fortified house now in ruins and looked after by English Heritage. A little over 3 miles on browse the antique and art shops of Holt (32.8 miles) before heading to Letheringsett to see Norfolk's only working **water mill** (☎ 01263 713153) and part-time tourist attraction. Buy a loaf

of bread or a cake from a baker's shop within a 20-mile radius of Letheringsett and chances are the flour will have come from between the grindstones of this mill. **Glandford Shell Museum**, 2 miles further on, is a private collection built up over 60 years and well worth a brief stop. After that comes Blakeney, a fascinating town on marshland that was once part of the sea. Regular boat trips to the **seal colony on Blakeney Point** leave from the seafront (Bishops Boats; ☎ 01263 740753; £10; 1-1½ hours).

Turning back inland, the ruins of 12th-century **Binham Priory** (40.6 miles) with its gravestone-littered grounds warrant a short halt before trundling into Wells-next-the-Sea just in time for a fish supper and a well-deserved pint.

Day 4: Wells-next-the-Sea to King's Lynn
3–5 hours, 44.7 miles
Inshore hills debunk the myth that Norfolk is completely flat everywhere and can come as a bit of a shock for the legs. Coming out

MOUNTAIN BIKING: THETFORD FOREST

Thetford Forest is East Anglia's most mountain bike-friendly area with a dense network of tracks and trails weaving between the pine trees. You can ride wherever you like as long as you don't stray onto army land, and the sandy soil drains readily after rain, making this all-weather biking terrain. The area is covered by the excellent OS Explorer 1:25,000 *Thetford Forest in the Brecks* map, which shows all paths, tracks and military areas in mindboggling detail.

A recommended sample route begins at the Squirrel Maze near the High Lodge Forest Centre to the west of Thetford town. From there head towards the village of Santon Downham, to the north of which you can join the Hereward Way cycle route. Stay on this past the Devil's Punchbowl (a glacial ice hollow in which the water mysteriously rises and falls) until you reach the junction with the Peddars Way. Cross Roudham Heath, following the long distance path for 1.5 miles to the road, then turn left, cross back over the A1075, and keep going past the military camp. From Thorpe Great Heath head south towards Croxton then loop round on rough tracks back to the Forest Centre. This figure of eight measures around 25 miles and you'll certainly need a good map to navigate your way round.

Cycles can be hired from **Bike Art** (☎ 01842 810090; all day hire £16) next to the High Lodge Forest Centre.

---

of Wells, the gradient steepens past **Little Walsingham** (5.4 miles), an erstwhile religious centre and place of pilgrimage. Here you shouldn't miss the Anglican Shrine of Our Lady of Walsingham built in 1061, nor the village's grade one listed public loos on medieval High St!

Gentle hills emerge as the route crosses through higher farmland to a whopping elevation of 88m (288ft) above sea level (don't forget your altitude sickness pills). You can then freewheel all the way to the coast and the popular Norfolk resort of **Hunstanton** (25.2 miles), overlooking the Wash to Lincolnshire. Hunstanton lacks quaint charm, but makes up for it in facilities and is a perfect place to eat. Heacham, to the south, is much smaller but continues the theme of less-than-attractive sand flats and caravan parks.

NCN 1 points the way through the little villages on the eastern side of A149, and bisects the Queen's estate at **Sandringham** (35 miles), which has extensive off-road riding. **Castle Rising** (☎ 01553 631330) on the northern outskirts of King's Lynn has one of the best preserved 12th-century keeps in the country and was used as a location for the BBC *Blackadder* series starring Rowan Atkinson, aka Mr Bean. It's open for the public to explore. This final day, the toughest on the ride, finishes on a rail trail leading to the train station in bustling King's Lynn.

TOWNS & FACILITIES

CAMBRIDGE
☎ 01223 / pop 108,863

Cambridge, home to one of the world's leading universities and dozens of beautiful historical buildings, is also a city of bicycles with pedal power responsible for around 25% of all commuter journeys. The train station's bike parking facility is a sea of used and abused pushbikes and the morning rush hour in some parts of the city is a crush of spokes and handlebars.

In 2008 the city announced it intended to spend 7.2 million to improve already good cycle infrastructure, confirming its commitment to a sustainable transport future.

The city is a busy place, packed for much of the year with students, tourists and the odd resident. However, its human scale, water-meadows and breathtaking colleges earn Cambridge top marks from most visitors.

Information

The large and often bustling **tourist office** (☎ 0871 226 8006; The Old Library, Wheeler St) can help with maps, accommodation, tours, tickets and cycle-related queries, and is open year round.

Supplies & Equipment

In a city where cycling is one of the most popular ways of getting from A to B, there is, understandably, a corresponding number of bicycle repair shops to service this mode of transport. By all accounts, Cambridge's best bike shop is **University Cycles** (☎ 01223 355517; 9 Victoria Ave) where you can stock up on spares, buy a secondhand bike or get your derailleur rerailluered, though you're advised to call ahead due to the shop's popularity. Nor does the city lack outdoor stockists with nationwide chains **Field & Trek** (☎ 01223 307156; 32 Fitzroy St), **Blacks** (☎ 01223 351904; 19 Fitzroy St) and **Millets** (☎ 01223 307406; 18-19 Sydney St) all vying for trade.

Sleeping & Eating

Highfield Farm Touring Park (☎ 01223 262308; www.highfieldfarmtouringpark .co.uk; Long Rd, Comberton; sites £9-11) is 4 miles southwest of the city centre. No credit or debit cards are accepted here.

Cambridge YHA (☎ 0845 371 9728; 97 Tenison Rd; dm £13.95) is located just a block away from the railway station. This large Victorian house contains dorms sleeping up to eight people and there's secure cycle storage on the premises. This is one of the UK's busiest youth hostels outside of London so booking ahead is recommended at all times of year.

Harry's Bed & Breakfast (☎ 01223 503866; 39 Milton Rd; s/d £65/75) originally an Edwardian nursing home, this lively four-room B&B is a real gem. The perennially cheerful host bends over backwards for guests and the en suite rooms are tastefully fitted out. Rates include free wi-fi, secure cycle storage and, joy of joys, free local and national calls! Now there's an offer you can't refuse.

Cambridge Garden House (☎ 01223 259988; www.cambridgegardenhouse.com; Granta Pl, Mill Lane; s/tw from £115/125) with an enviable riverside city centre spot, the interior of this top-end hotel surpasses expectations formed by its ugly modern shell. Design-mag perfect rooms decorated in suede, leather, dark wood and boldly striped carpets, river-facing pool and waterside gardens from which to watch punters glide past add a bit of luxury to a cycling trip.

Rainbow Vegetarian Bistro (☎ 01223 321551; www.rainbowcafe.co.uk; 9a King's Pde; mains £8.45) first-rate vegie fare and a pious glow emanate from this snug subterranean gem, accessed down a narrow passageway off King's Parade. The menu features exotic dishes made with organic ingredients such as scrumptious Latvian potato bake and Indonesian gado gado.

The Eagle Pub (☎ 01223 505020; 8 Bene't St) Cambridge's most famous pub has loosened the tongues and pickled the grey cells of many an illustrious academic, among them Nobel Prize-winning scientists Crick and Watson who are thought to have discovered the form of DNA. It's a traditional 16th-century tavern with five cluttered rooms and a pub grub with everything well under a tenner.

Michaelhouse (☎ 01223 309167; Trinity St; mains £4-7) supplies fair trade coffee and focaccia among soaring Gothic arches, or take a pew within reach of the altar at this stylishly converted church which still has a working chancel. The simple lunch menu is mostly vegetarian but also offers wine and beer for when God's back is turned.

COLCHESTER

☎ 01206 / pop 104,390

As Britain's oldest recorded town it can come as no surprise that Colchester has a rich and sometimes colourful history. Before London's rise to prominence, it was the capital of Roman Britain and these days it's home to a handful of significant sites including a fine castle.

Information

Colchester's centrally located **tourist information office** (☎ 01206 282920; www.visitcolchester.com) opposite the Castle Museum, offers internet access, and staff are capable of fielding any Colchester-related query you care to bowl at them.

Supplies & Equipment

It's not difficult to guess what goes on at **Colchester Cycle Stores** (☎ 01206 563890; 50 St Johns St) where they've been patching up broken bikes for over 30 years. **Cycle King** (☎ 01206 867756; 48a East St) has the advantage of being open seven days a week. The high street outdoor retail duo of **Blacks** (☎ 01206 369428; 27 St Johns Wlk) and

Millets (☎ 01206 574615; 17-18 High St) both have stores in this corner of Essex.

Sleeping & Eating

Colchester Camping & Caravan Park (☎ 01206 545551; www.colchester camping.co.uk; Cymbeline Way, Lexden; sites £7 plus £5 per adult) about 1.5 miles west along the Lexden Rd bikepath, this is the closest campsite to Colchester.

Old Manse (☎ 01206 545154; www .theoldmanse.uk.com; 15 Roman Rd; s/d £35/60) a lovely Victorian home with a chunk of Roman wall in its garden, the small Old Manse is just a few minutes' walk from the centre and is run by a motherly hostess. The three rooms are tastefully done out and the breakfast is a sociable communal affair.

Rose & Crown Hotel (☎ 01206 866677; www.rose-and-crown.com; East St; s/d from £90/100) This endearingly lopsided 14th-century posting inn with leaded windows and exposed timber frame is the town's oldest hotel but features a modern wing. The bar is the most atmospheric in Colchester and the restaurant serves an interesting fusion of French and Indian cuisines.

Garden Cafe @ the Minories Art Gallery (☎ 01206 500169, 74 High St; mains £5-7) an eccentric little neo-Gothic folly graces the sprawling garden behind this artsy cafe housed in a town house art gallery of big repute. Portions are large.

Lemon Tree (☎ 01206 767337, 48 St Johns St; mains £9-14) this zesty little eatery is graced by a knobbly Roman wall and cavern in the corner and imaginative British and continental cooking on the menu. A blackboard of specials, gourmet nights and occasional live jazz make this one of Colchester's liveliest places to eat.

Strada (☎ 01206 542854; 19-20 North Hill; pizzas £9, other mains £11-16). The Colchester branch of Strada, a chain with mock Italian eateries across the south of England, serves up respectable portions of pasta, pizza and meat dishes, perfect fuel for a day on two wheels.

FELIXSTOWE

☎ 01394 / pop 29,349

If you've ever bought a cheap Chinese import in the UK, chances are it came to you via Felixstowe on the mouth of the River Orwell, which handles a third of Britain's freight. In fact your bike may already have been here! Around the corner and seemingly oblivious to its trading raison d'être, the pleasant, flower-bedecked Edwardian town faces the open sea and is a moderately popular holiday resort with pier, promenade and pavilion.

Information

Felixstowe's **tourist office** (☎ 01394 276770; 91 Undercliff Rd West) is next to the pier on the seafront.

Supplies & Equipment

Cycle repairs are handled by **Flynn Star Bicycles** (☎ 01394 274701; 25b Cobbold Rd) in the town centre where you can also hire bikes for around £10 a day. Replace battered camping gear and buy much needed waterproofs at **Millets** (☎ 01394 672203; 52 Hamilton Rd). If you're cooking your own en route to The Wash there's a convenient if small **Tesco Metro** (88 Hamilton Rd) in the town centre.

Sleeping & Eating

Peewit Caravan Park (☎ 01394 284511; Walton Avenue; sites £13) is a small friendly campsite to the south of the town centre, just a short walk from the beach. It's open from Easter through to October.

Waverley Hotel (☎ 01394 282811; www .waverleyhotel.net; Wolsey Gdns; s/d from £60/70, mains £7.50-13.50) be sure to ask for a room with a sea view at this large hotel just back from the seafront. Hopefully this will distract you from the sometimes kitschy furnishings in the otherwise decent enough rooms. The restaurant downstairs does a bog-standard line in international dishes, which satisfy the belly if nothing else.

Norfolk Guesthouse (☎ 01394 283160; www.thenorfolk.com; 1-3 Holland Rd; s/d from £40/60) possibly Felixstowe's best B&B sporting four stars from www.enjoyEng land.com. This cosy guesthouse is amazing value for money with well-appointed rooms, lots of thoughtful extras and always a warm Suffolk welcome. You'll have to dig a bit deeper for a sea view though.

Undercliff Fish & Chip Restaurant (55 Undercliff Rd West) cod and chips doused in salt and vinegar washed down with milky tea from a pot-for-one – that's what keeps

EASTERN ENGLAND

the British going during holidays by the sea, and it's what you'll find here.

The Alex (☎ 01394 282958; 123 Undercliff Rd West, mains £8.25-18) touted as the best sea view restaurant in Suffolk, the Alex is a glossy cafe/bar, which may look like a cappuccino-culture product of the 'naughties' but has in fact been serving food here since the late 1920s. Recipes from around the world have been gathered together to create a bar menu of imaginative light meals and an evening selection of more substantial mains.

KING'S LYNN
☎ 01553 / pop 34,565

Once sited on the Wash itself, King's Lynn now lies marooned 5 miles inland with the fishing industry operating from new docks. The town centre and old quayside still contain an ample number of historical buildings, merchants' houses and port and civic buildings despite the intrusion of one of the UK's ugliest town centre shopping precincts. A local seaweed delicacy called samphire and locally caught seafood can be bought from the Tuesday market, should you pitch up in town that day.

Information

King's Lynn **tourist office** (☎ 01553 763044; www.visitwestnorfolk.com; Customs House, Purfleet Quay) is housed in the imposing Customs House dating from 1683 and is open year round. Staff organise guided summer walks of historic Kings Lynn as well as providing all the usual services.

Supplies & Equipment

Anglian Motor Cycles (☎ 01553 763572; 19 Tower Pl) actually does most of its trade in pushbike parts and repairs, despite the name. Almost opposite is **Cycle Life** (☎ 01553 660363; 6 Tower Pl) stocking a wide range of accessories and new bikes. **Millets** (☎ 01553 776169; SU17a, Vancouver Centre) keeps this corner of Norfolk supplied with tents and sleeping bags.

Sleeping & Eating

Kings Lynn Caravan & Camping Park (☎ 01553 840004; New Rd, North Runcton; sites £15) the nearest campsite to the town 3 miles southeast on the A47 (Norwich Rd).

Fairlight Lodge (☎ 01553 762234; www.fairlightlodge.co.uk; 79 Goodwins Rd; s/d £35/52) there are seven tastefully furnished country-style rooms, four en suite and some overlooking the pretty garden at this charming Victorian guesthouse, a short ride from the town centre.

Bank House (☎ 01553 660492; www.thebankhouse.co.uk; Kings Staithe Sq; s/d £80/100) this outstanding B&B has ticks in all the right boxes – history, location, atmosphere, comfort and welcome. On the waterfront near the tourist office, it's housed in an elegant 18th-century former bank with five-star hotel standard rooms mixing original features and modern furnishings.

Crofters Coffee House (☎ 01553 773134; 27 King St; meals £4.50-7) this long brick-vaulted undercroft, once used as a civil-war gunpowder store and now a low-lit cafe, scores top marks for atmosphere and serves light lunches, hot drinks and cakes and is situated in the Guildhall Arts Centre.

Riverside Rooms (☎ 01553 773134; 27 King St; mains £12-19) overlooking the water from a converted 15th-century warehouse, with crisscrossing beams overhead and elegant white-linen tables below, this place serves a confident but slightly uninspired menu of classic dishes.

Bradley's (☎ 01553 819888; www.bradleysbytheriver.co.uk; 10 South Quay; mains £13-19) eat in the elegant Georgian dining room at this riverside restaurant, or relax at the bar with some lighter snacks (£8), either way you're bound to be pleased as this is probably the finest food the city has to offer.

SOUTHEND-ON-SEA
☎ 01702 / pop 610,257

Southend works hard to give London daytrippers a good time beside the seaside. Screeching funfairs and amusements line the beachfront opposite a glassy expanse of Thames Estuary and an encampment of kiosks and greasy spoon cafes keep the holidaying masses fed. Low tide exposes a vast area of mud flats, best seen from the 100-year-old, 1.33-mile-long pier, allegedly the longest in the world. Southenders may look enviously at you and your bicycle – you have a ready means of escape, they don't.

Information

Southend's **tourist office** (☎ 01702 215120; www.visitsouthend.co.uk; Southend Pier, Western Esplanade) is located at the entrance to the pier.

Supplies & Equipment

Bike Doctors (☎ 01702 600069; www.bike doctorsltd.co.uk; 102a Southchurch Ave) will have your two-wheeler back on the road in no time and stock an Alladin's cave of bike bits, clothes and alike. There's also a well-stocked branch of **Cycles UK** (☎ 01702 471367; www.cyclesuk.com; 995-1003 London Rd) a short ride east along London Rd. Outdoor supplies are available at a branch of **Millets** (☎ 01702 463316; 4-19 York Rd).

Sleeping & Eating

Gleneagles (☎ 01702 333635; 5 Clifftown Parade; s from £35.50, d from £55) a handsome mid-19th-century terraced building facing out into the estuary, the Gleneagles has crisply maintained rooms with period style and a few thoughtful extras. Rates include a full-on English breakfast.

Westcliff Hotel (☎ 01702 345247; Westcliff Pde, Westcliff-on-Sea; s/d £69/85) the late Victorian building of this three-star hotel enjoys an eye-catching cliff top setting a short distance to the west of the town centre. Rooms are stylishly fitted out and there's a list of facilities and services as long as Southend pier.

Arosa Guesthouse (☎ 01702 585416; www.arosaguesthouse.co.uk; 184 Eastern Esp; s/d from £35/55) the highly rated Arosa is one of the town's better B&Bs where stylishly furnished rooms come with en suite facilities and flat screen TVs.

Spaghetti Junction (☎ 01702 473388; 767 London Rd, Westcliff-on-Sea; pasta & pizzas £6) you'll need spadeloads of carbs to get you through East Anglia, so start building them up with a plate of pasta at this cosy Italian place in Westcliff.

Fisherman's Wharf (☎ 01702 346773; Western Esp; mains £6.50-21) think of a fish, add chips and you've basically got the menu at this seafront temple to British seafood. If you're weary of fish and chips, there's an ocean of lobsters, crabs and fish species to try as well as beef steaks, chicken and sausages. You'll find the restaurant's low white building near the pier.

SOUTHWOLD

☎ 01502 / pop 3858

Southwold is a genteel seaside resort where beach huts cost more than a northern semi and the visitors are very well-to-do. Its reputation as a well-heeled holiday getaway has earned it the nickname 'Kensington-on-Sea' after the upmarket London borough, and its lovely sandy beach, pebble-walled cottages, cannon-dotted cliff top and rows of beachfront bathing huts are all undeniably picturesque. Over the years the town has attracted many artists including Turner, Charles Rennie Mackintosh, Lucian Freud and a young Damien Hirst.

Information

The **tourist office** (☎ 01502 724729; www .visit-southwold.co.uk; 69 High St) is adept at helping with accommodation and general information.

Supplies & Equipment

For bike repairs and spares try **Southwold Cycles & Auto Accessories** (☎ 01502 725400; Blyth Rd). For snacks and self catering supplies head for **Somerfields** (2 Market Pl) near the tourist office, or the **Co-op** (2 Queen St).

Sleeping & Eating

Gorse House (☎ 01502 725468; www .gorsehouse.com; 19B Halesworth Rd; Reydon; d from £55) a 10-minute walk from the seafront but well worth the effort, this lovely B&B is one of the best in the area. The two rooms here are newly decorated in simple, contemporary style with subtle-patterned wallpapers, silky throws and flat-screen TVs.

Home @ 21 (☎ 01502 722573; www .northparade.southwold.info; rooms £65-85) this friendly place has rooms with four-poster or half-tester beds that are slightly out of keeping with their surroundings but comfortable none the less.

Sutherland House (☎ 01502 724544; www.sutherlandhouse.co.uk; 56 High St; d £140-200) set in a beautiful 15th-century house dripping with character and period features this small hotel has just three rooms featuring pargetted ceilings, exposed beams and elm floorboards but decked out in sleek, modern style. The top-notch restaurant (mains £10-20) specialises in local food with the menu showing how many miles the principal ingredient in each dish has travelled.

The Crown (☎ 01502 722275; www.adnams.co.uk; 90 High St; mains £12-17) this special old posting inn has a superb restaurant that changes its meaty seasonal menu daily. It also has a wine bar, wood-panelled snugs and serves real ales. It also has a few plush rooms (doubles from £132).

WELLS-NEXT-THE-SEA
☎ 01328 / pop 2451

The little town of Wells-next-the-Sea, as Blakeney, is nowadays protected from the North Sea by marshes and creeks. An impressive tide brings in new crabs for holidaying children to catch on the quayside, the focal point of the town. It is easily distinguished in postcards by the soaring, dodgy-looking overhang of its grain store building.

A little further along, the marina is full of boats and their owners going about their business. The town was once dependent on fishing for its livelihood, but alas no more.

Information
The small **tourist office** (☎ 0871 200 3071; www.visitnorthnorfolk.com; Staithe St) can help with all inquiries but is open from March until October only.

Sleeping & Eating
Wells YHA Hostel (☎ 0845 371 9544; Church Plain; dm £11.95) is superb little 32-bed hostel with mostly family-sized rooms and housed in an ornately gabled early-20th-century church hall.

Fern Cottage (☎ 01328 710306; www.ferncottage.co.uk; Standard Rd; s/d £60/80) set in a beautiful Georgian house the rooms here retain some period character with open fireplaces and cast-iron beds.

Globe Inn (☎ 01328 710206; www.globeatwells.co.uk; mains £8-14) is a good bet. It's on the green and also has a selection of bright, spacious rooms with contemporary style (£65-110).

WROXHAM & HOVETON
☎ 01603 / pop 2451

Wroxham and Hoveton on the south and north banks of the River Bure are known collectively as 'the Gateway to the Broads'. More than a dozen boatyards line the banks of the river and in summer the little place teems with people embarking on barge trips. The two towns are linked by a Mostar-style bridge, one of the most humpbacked on any main road in the UK.

You'll soon notice the local retail scene is dominated by Roys of Wroxham, a local family business that began at the turn of the century when two capitalist-minded brothers first brought groceries in from London to supply the new holiday trade.

Information
The excellent **Broads Information Centre** (☎ 01603 782281; Station Rd, Hoveton) stocks heaps of free information on local walks, cycles routes, nature and attractions as well as accommodation and restaurant lists and maps.

Sleeping & Eating
Sloley Farm Campsite (☎ 01692 536281; Sloley; sites £8) is a small camping ground around 5 miles north of Hoveton.

King's Head (☎ 01603 782429; Station Rd; d £44, mains £8-16, sandwiches £5) this classically British small-town 'pub with rooms' charges a hefty £7.50 extra for breakfast. The wide-ranging menu downstairs in the pub is a tasty mix of best-of-British and foreign intruders.

Hotel Wroxham (☎ 01603 782061; The Bridge; s/d £70/100) to keep visitors on their toes, the Wroxham contrives to be on the Hoveton side of the river. Disowned by the town, some say the balconies affording attractive river views are the best observation points in town as it's the only place you can't see the hotel itself. Despite its lack of charm, rooms are very comfortable, well kept and cheaper without a balcony.

The Bridge (☎ 01603 783509; Wroxham Bridge, Norwich Rd; mains £8.50-15, sandwiches £5) located on the right as you cross the bridge from Hoveton to Wroxham, the town's top eatery specialises in superb East Anglian seafood as well as serving generous plateloads of meat, pasta and curry. Sit inside or out by the river to watch the boats glide by.

Ken's Traditional Fish & Chips (Norwich Rd) locals claim Ken fries the best fish supper in town. Housed in a makeshift-looking shack by the main road on the Hoveton side of the bridge.

Central England

HIGHLIGHTS

- Pedal to the top of Mam Tor for wide-sky northern views across the popular **Peak District** (p146)
- Check out the bike-friendly city of **York** with its magnificent minster and preserved Roman and Viking heritage (p127)
- Roll into **Stratford-upon-Avon** in time to catch a comedy or tragedy in the very town where Shakespeare was born (p160)
- Load your bike onto the ferry across the **Mersey** for a visit to one of Britain's once great trading ports (p134)
- Marvel from the saddle at the hills and valleys of the **Long Mynd**, one of Britain's top mountain biking escapes (p135)

TERRAIN
Undulating, green and divided by the Pennine hills, which provide the region's high point towards the north

Telephone Code: ☎ 0161	www.discovereastmidlands.com

From the Welsh border in the west to the pancake-flat Fens in the east, and from the well-to-do outskirts of the capital to beyond the gritty northern cities, central England (as defined by this guide) is a large and diverse area offering endless possibilities for the cyclist with wanderlust. With regions of desolate beauty nestling against grim northern cityscapes and ridge-top getaway routes rising just beyond the ends of the London Underground, this huge chunk of Great Britain allows you to achieve a sense of escape while never very far away from Britain's population hotspots.

Hills are the name of the game the further north and west you pedal with the Cotswolds, the Pennines, the Peak District and the Chilterns all providing differing but always quintessentially British upland beauty. Wedged in between are evocative names such as Oxford, Stratford-upon-Avon, Shrewsbury and Chester, as well as lesser-known gems such as Oundle and Cirencester. The flatter east is easier on the legs while the eye is drawn to the architecture of Lincoln, Stamford and York, and to the long views across England's black-soil agricultural heartland.

Most of the routes tactfully skirt around the mega-cities of the midlands and the north but with ever-improving and now well-funded cycle infrastructure, don't be too afraid to mingle with the gas-guzzlers for a bit of urban excitement. York is kindest on the cyclist, but Oxford, Liverpool and even parts of Manchester are becoming increasingly cycle friendly.

CENTRAL ENGLAND

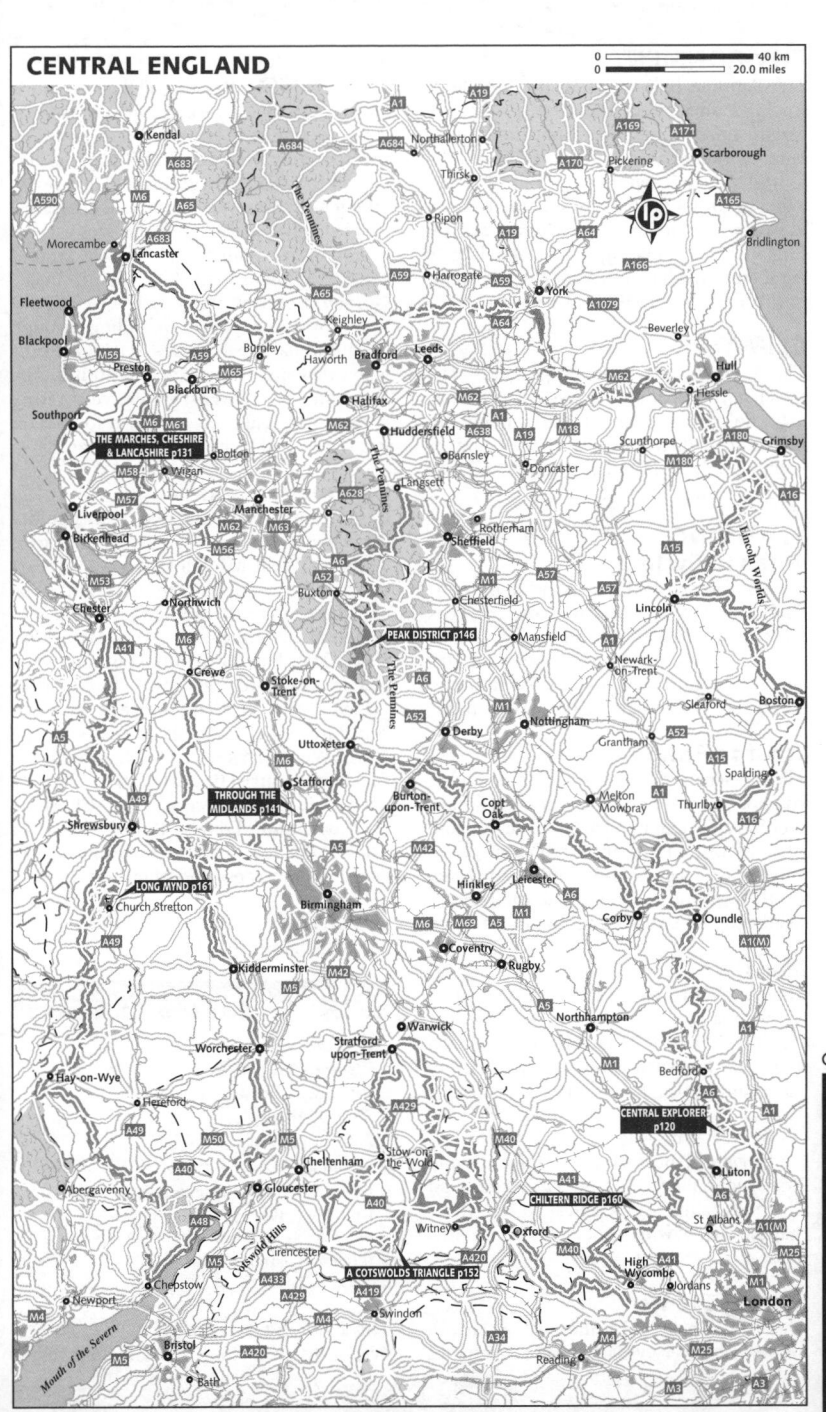

ENVIRONMENT

The Pennine hills begin in the middle of England and bisect the country as they extend northwards, providing the highest land in the region. Out in the west, the foothills of the Marches rise out of fertile valleys without the harshness of their Welsh mountain cousins. Elsewhere, central England is undulating, green and largely rural from the Thames Valley in the south to the Yorkshire Dales in the north.

CLIMATE

The temperature drops slightly as you travel northward, and things get considerably cooler as soon as you start climbing to higher ground. The weather in the Pennines is changeable and can be very cold and wet, so always ride prepared.

PLANNING

When to Cycle

Unless you're planning to head into the Pennines in mid winter or cross the Peak District in February, the weather is mostly pretty benign in England's heartlands. Inland temperatures tend to fall lower in winter than at the sea and are higher in summer.

What to Bring

The further north you travel and the higher you go, the more warm clothes and waterproofs you'll require. Towns in the upland areas of Britain are an outdoor kit geek's paradise with a gear shop seemingly on every street, so if you underestimate the region's weather, extra layers are always easy to buy.

Maps

You'd be hard-pressed to find a single map of the area covered here, well not one that didn't have all the other bits of Britain on it as well. For such a substantial chunk of the country you'll need several maps for general planning, the best choice being the OS Travel Map – Road 1:250,000 *Northern England* (sheet 4), *East Midland's and East Anglia* (sheet 5) and *Wales and West Midlands* (sheet 6). Needless to say, these maps overlap with other regions in this guide.

Cycling Events

The **CTC York Cycle Show** (www.ctc.org .uk) is held every year in June at the city's Knavesmire Racecourse. The event is made up of a trade fair attracting all the top brands and thousands of bike companies, special rides, auctions and entertainment, as well as incorporating the **York Cycle Rally**, the biggest in the country with over 40,000 riders taking part. **Bike Week** (www.bikeweek.org .uk) held around the same time sees various events big and small taking place around central England. The CTC South Bucks **Golden Beeches Rally** (www.ctc.org.uk) is comprised of three days' riding through the autumnal beech forests of the Chilterns when they are at their most beautiful. The **Lancaster Cycle Fest** (www.celebrating cycling.org) held every even year focuses on innovative and technical cycle design.

Information Sources

Central England (as defined by this guide) is covered by several regional tourist boards. **Tourism West Midlands** (www.visitheart ofengland.com) deals with information for anywhere along the border with Wales to Birmingham, Stratford-upon-Avon and Shropshire. **East Midlands Tourism** (www .discovereastmidlands.com) looks after things from Northamptonshire to Lincolnshire as well as the Peak District – the North West is covered by the **Lancashire & Blackpool Tourist Board** (☎ 01257 226600; www.visitlancashire.com), the **Cheshire & Warrington Tourist Board** (☎ 01244 346543; www.visitchester.com) and smaller boards in Liverpool and Manchester.

GATEWAY

See Manchester (p174).

> **CENTRAL EXPLORER**
>
> **Duration** 8 days
> **Distance** 385.6 miles
> **Difficulty** moderate–demanding
> **Start** St Albans
> **Finish** Lancaster
>
> **Summary** From the flat fens of Lincolnshire to the challenging Pennine uplands of Lancashire, this epic tour is an adventure on two wheels with heaps of Britain's heritage thrown in along the way.

This blockbuster, eight-day cycle marathon over a distance most ordinary folk might think you were mad or just overambitious to attempt, will see your wheels grip tarmac (and occasionally other surfaces) for a mammoth 385.6 miles. Surprisingly the eight days are not all about hard slogs and racking up the miles, but give ample opportunity to explore cathedral cities such as St Albans, Lincoln and York and fascinating old rural market towns such as Oundle, Stamford and Boston as you go. The ride crosses Britain's north-south divide and if you think the landscapes change en route, just wait till you hear the accents.

You'll need to have a reasonable level of fitness to keep pedalling for over a week, especially towards the end when the lung-busting ups (and the wind-through-your-helmet downs) get bigger and scarier. Of course, you can stay as long as you want in between sections, with Stamford, Lincoln and York all worth of a few days of sightseeing.

Three days of the trip from Boston to the Humber follow the NCN 1 route whose signposting makes navigation child's play. Every mile of this cycle path has been carefully chosen for its peacefulness, beauty and safety.

ENVIRONMENT

England's geography changes markedly as the ride progresses, from the softer southern landscapes to the harsher northern slopes – with their rich mineral deposits, unforgiving climate and an economic history of heavy industry and mining.

PLANNING
When to Cycle

Bad weather in the Pennines is a serious matter, and many high roads are closed by snowfall in the winter. May and September present the best riding weather though even late September can see the temperature deteriorate.

What to Bring

In this well-populated part of England you are never far from shops and pubs, but carry a minimum of fluid, snacks and bike repair items just in case. Bike shops feature in virtually all the starting and finishing towns. Campsites are thin on the ground so you'll have to seek out conventional accommodation every other night.

Maps

As this ride extends a very large distance almost from the outer limits of London to Morecambe Bay, it would be impractical to carry the number of detailed maps (such as the OS Landranger or OS Explorer series) needed. Stick to the larger scale maps listed above (see Central England/Planning/Maps p120), which cover the route in just a couple of sheets.

GETTING TO/FROM THE RIDE
St Albans (start)
TRAIN

Regular **First Capital Connect** (Thameslink; www.firstcapitalconnect.co.uk) runs services to St Albans from London St Pancras (£9; 20-30 minutes, several per hour). Bikes go free, but cannot be carried weekday evenings from 4pm to 7pm.

BICYCLE

The route from central London to St Albans amounts to little more than 20 miles of unedifying urban sprawl and is only for purists. Take the A5 Edgware Rd from Marble Arch in the centre as far as the M1 motorway, then the A5083.

Lancaster (finish)
TRAIN

Express **Virgin Trains** (☎ 08457 222 333; www.virgintrains.co.uk) services run southwards to London Euston (£68.30 return, 3 hours, up to twice hourly) and northwards to Glasgow (£23, 2½ hours, hourly). In both directions bikes go free but you must make a reservation before travelling. York can also be reached via Preston (£44.50, three hours, up to twice hourly). The first section of the journey is by Virgin Trains so same rules as above apply before switching to the more easy-going Northern Trains in Preston.

BICYCLE

Lancaster is on the End-to-End ride (see the Land's End to John O'Groats chapter p306) and is the final destination for the Marches, Cheshire and Lancashire ride later in this chapter (p131).

THE RIDE
Day 1: St Albans to Bedford
2½–4 hours, 39.1 miles

This peaceful first day's ride, through exquisite villages and rolling farmland, leads

CENTRAL EXPLORER – DAY 1

CUE		GPS COORDINATES
start	St Albans main train station	51°45'1"N 0°19'37"W
0 miles	go W on Victoria St	
0.3	St Peters St	
1.2	B651 'to Sandridge'	
5.5	Wheathampstead	51°48'42"N 0°17'38"W
6.9	B651 Ballslough Hill 'to K'ton'	
8.2	B651/'to Hitchin' (dogleg), Kimpton	51°51'3"N 0°17'44"W
10.3	'to Hitchin', Whitwell	51°52'35"N 0°16'59"W
10.7	B651 'to Hitchin'	
13.4	B656 'to Hitchin'	
16.0	(3rd exit) 'to town centre'	
16.5	unsigned road (past church), Hitchin	51°56'52"N 0°16'56"W
16.6	at church yard	
[	Market Place town square]	
16.7	go N thru arcade & car park	
16.8	A505	
16.9	A505/U Tilehouse St, 'to Barton'	
17.0	B655 'to Barton'	
18.1	'to Pirton/Shillington'	

CUE CONTINUED		GPS COORDINATES
19.8	Walnut Tree Rd, 'to Shillington'	
20.0	unsigned road (at Fox pub), Pirton	51°58'11"N 0°20'3"W
20.3	'to Shillington'	
22.0	'to Gravenhurst', Shillington	51°59'36"N 0°21'36"W
22.5	'to Gravenhurst'	
22.7	'to Lower Gravenhurst'	
23.6	'to Upper Gravenhurst'	
26.0	A507, 'to Shefford'	
26.9	'to Clophill'	
28.1	'to Haynes', Clophill	52° 1'35"N 0°25'29"W
30.3	'to Haynes West End'	
31.0	A6/'to Haynes West End' (dogleg)	
31.2	unsigned road uphill	
33.0	'to Bedford', Houghton Conquest	52°3'47"N 0°28'28"W
34.0	B530 'to Bedford'	
36.7	A421 'to Bedford'	
37.2	A6 'to Bedford'	
37.3	follow signs 'to town centre'	
39.1	Bedford tourist office (LHS)	52°8'9"N 0°28'1"W

through the counties of Hertfordshire and Bedfordshire to the hustle and bustle of multicultural Bedford. The climbs and descents along the way afford views over handsome landscapes despite the region's high population density.

The first stretch of the route takes you along the relatively quiet B651 to Wheathampstead, which has a pretty flint church. Otherwise just keep rolling along until you hit the market town of **Hitchin** (16.5 miles), a superb place for a breather but probably too early for lunch. Hitchin has been described as one of England's most visually satisfying towns, and you can judge for yourself as you explore the cafe-sprinkled streets and cobbled Market Place, which date back to Saxon times.

The next stretch sees you cross the county line just after Pirton, before more country lanes take you to the busy A507 where care should be taken on the approach to Clophill. From the high land before Houghton Conquest (31.7 miles) stop to take in the view across the Great Stour Valley, to the chimney stacks of Stewartby brickworks to the west and the gargantuan airship hangars to the east, about 2.5 miles east of Cardington. These defunct hangars were built in the 1920s to house the historic airships R100 and R101. Protracted discussions have been going on for years about installing an airship and balloon museum in one of them.

Day 2: Bedford to Oundle
2½–4 hours, 38 miles
Today's short ride is a truly beautiful affair, particularly in the summer months when the hedgerows are in full bloom. The traffic is mostly light, though crossing the A6 (14 miles) near Sharnbrook needs care. Sorry gradient lovers – no hills yet.

The first sight of the day is the **Stevington Windmill** just before the village of the same name. It's one of the few surviving post mills (a mill whose whole upper timber body revolves on a post depending on wind direction) left in the country. After around 45 minutes you should reach the old bridge crossing of the River Great Ouse water meadows at Odell.

At Denford the route links up with another river, this time the Nene, which will accompany you to the conclusion of the day's ride. Around 4 miles beyond Thrapston take a short detour to the particularly well-preserved old village of **Wadenhoe** where several ancient-looking thatched cottages house a population of 100. From here the charming market town of Oundle is just 4 miles of easy pedalling away.

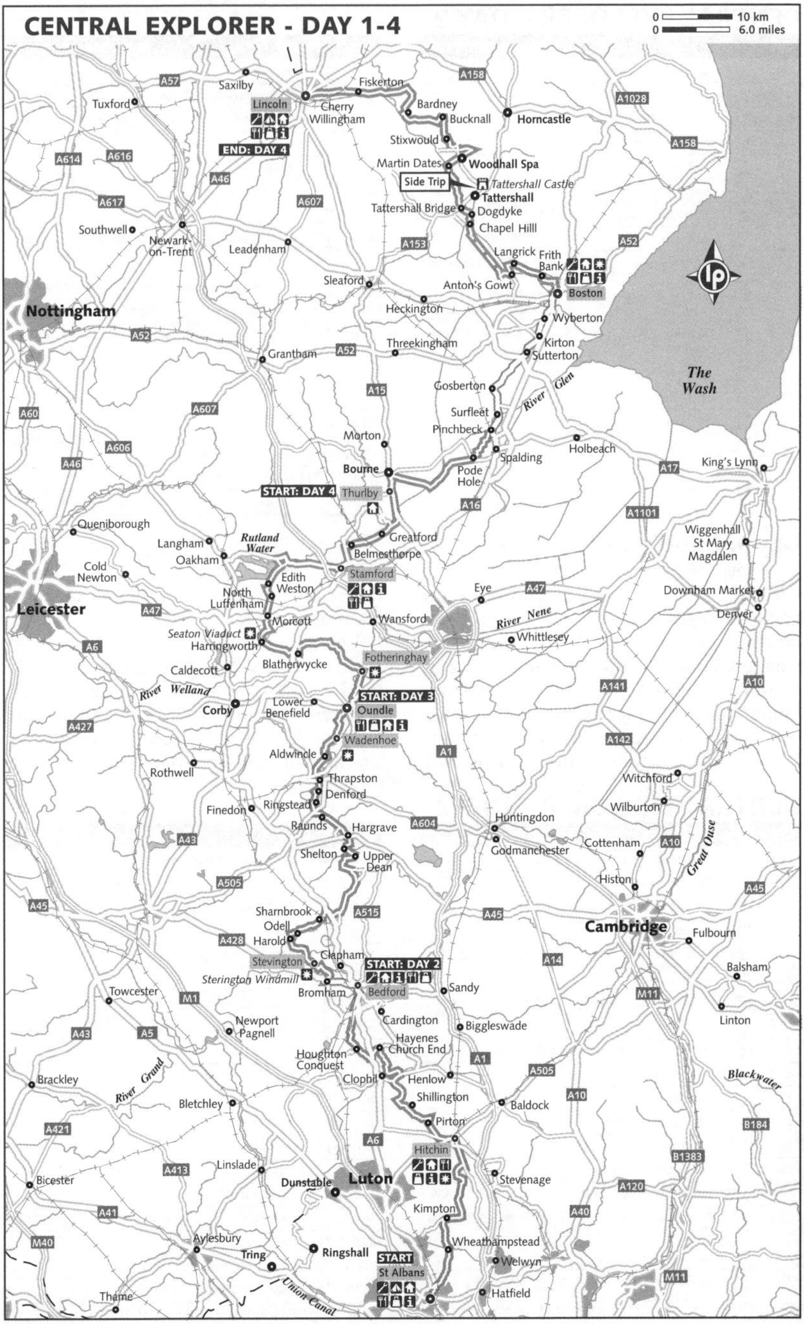

CENTRAL EXPLORER - DAY 1-4

0 —— 10 km
0 —— 6.0 miles

Tuxford
Saxilby
Fiskerton
A57
Lincoln
END: DAY 4
Cherry Willingham
Bardney
Bucknall
Horncastle
Stixwould
A1028
A158
A614
A616
A617
A46
A607
Martin Dales
Woodhall Spa
Side Trip
Tattershall Castle
Tattershall
Southwell
Newark-on-Trent
Leadenham
Tattershall Bridge
Chapel Hilll
Dogdyke
A153
A52
Frith Bank
Langrick
Sleaford
Anton's Gowt
Boston

Nottingham
A52
Heckington
Wyberton
Kirton
Sutterton
A60
Grantham
A52
Threekingham
A15
Gosberton
Surfleet
Pinchbeck
Spalding
Holbeach
A17
King's Lynn

The Wash

Morton
Bourne
START: DAY 4
Thurlby
Pode Hole
A16
Wiggenhall St Mary Magdalen
A606
A46
Queniborough
Langham
Rutland Water
Oakham
Greatford
Belmesthorpe
Stamford
Eye
A47
River Nene
Wansford
Whittlesey
Downham Market
Denver
Cold Newton
North Luffenham
Edith Weston
Morcott
Leicester
A6
A47
Seaton Viaduct
Harringworth
Blatherwycke
Fotheringhay
START: DAY 3
Oundle
A1
A141
A10
Caldecott
Lower Benefield
Wadenhoe
Witchford
Wilburton
Corby
Aldwincle
Thrapston
Denford
Huntingdon
A142
Rothwell
Finedon
Ringstead
Hargrave
A604
Godmanchester
Cottenham
A10
A45
Raunds
Shelton
Upper Dean
Histon
A43
A505
Sharnbrook
Odell
Harrold
A515
A45
Cambridge
Fulbourn
A45
Stevington
Sterington Windmill
Clapham
Bromham
START: DAY 2
Bedford
Sandy
A14
M11
Balsham
Towcester
M1
Cardington
Biggleswade
A1
Linton
A43
A5
Newport Pagnell
Hayenes Church End
Houghton Conquest
Clophill
Henlow
A505
A10
Blackwater
B184
Brackley
Bletchley
Shillington
Pirton
Baldock
A6
A421
Linslade
Hitchin
Stevenage
A120
Bicester
A413
A6
Kimpton
Wheathampstead
A40
M11
M40
A41
Dunstable
Luton
Welwyn
Aylesbury
Tring
Ringshall
START
St Albans
Hatfield
Thame
Union Canal

CENTRAL ENGLAND

CENTRAL EXPLORER – DAY 2

CUE		GPS COORDINATES	
start	Bedford tourist office	52°8'9"N	0°28'1"W
0 miles	go W on Horne Lane		
0.0	(100yd) A428		
0.3	A428 'to Northampton'		
2.3	'to Bromham'		
3.1	'to Stevington', Bromham	52° 8'41"N	0°31'39"W
5.8	'to Carlton', Stevington	52°10'7"N	0°33'16"W
7.5	'to Carlton'		
9.4	Harrold	52°12'4"N	0°36'37"W
10.0	'to Odell'		
11.0	★ Odell	52°12'33"N	0°35'20"W
13.0	'to Milton Ernest', Sharnbrook	52°13'33"N	0°32'39"W
13.5	'to Rushden'		
14.0	A6 'to Bedford'		
14.2	'to Riseley'		
16.6	'to Swineshead'		
17.0	'to Dean'		
17.7	'to Dean'		

CUE CONTINUED		GPS COORDINATES	
18.2	'to Dean'		
19.5	'to Shelton', Upper Dean	52°17'45"N	0°28'2"W
20.8	'to Lower Dean', Shelton	52°18'30"N	0°29'4"W
21.3	pass 'to Little Dean' road		
21.9	B645		
22.5	'to Hargrave'		
24.3	B663		
25.2	'to Thrapston', Raunds	52°20'17"N	0°32'49"W
25.8	'to Thrapston'		
26.7	'to Denford', Ringstead	52°21'54"N	0°33'2"W
27.8	Denford	52°22'40"N	0°32'37"W
29.2	unsigned road, Thrapston	52°23'45"N	0°32'2"W
29.5	'to Islip'		
30.3	A6116 'to Lowick'		
30.5	'to Aldwincle'		
32.8	'to Wadenhoe', Aldwincle	52°25'32"N	0°31'24"W
{33.9 ●●	Wadenhoe 1 mile ↺}		
37.6	unsigned roads (dogleg)		
38.0	Oundle tourist office	52°28'50"N	0°28'17"W

Day 3: Oundle to Thurlby

2½–4 hours, 40.6 miles

Although today is a relatively short ride, the route manages to take in three counties – Northamptonshire, Rutland (England's smallest county) and Lincolnshire. Cute country lanes lead you from sandstone Oundle through a landscape rich in royal, industrial and social history via Rutland Water to another sandstone town, Stamford. The only places heavy traffic raises its ugly head is as you cross the A47 before Morcott and on the broad A606 into Stamford.

Your first stop of the day after just 3 miles should be the village of **Fotheringhay**. The local castle, sadly long since demolished, was famous for two royal connections. Richard III was born here in 1452, and it was here in 1587 that Mary Queen of Scots

CENTRAL EXPLORER – DAY 3

CUE		GPS COORDINATES	
start	Oundle tourist office	52°28'50"N	0°28'17"W
0 miles	go NE on North St		
0.9	(1st exit) A605 'to Peterboro'		
1.2	'to Tansor'		
3.1	★ Fotheringhay	52°31'36"N	0°26'23"W
9.1	Wood Lane		
11.6	'to Laxton', Blatherwycke	52°33'1"N	0°34'4"W
12.5	'to Laxton'		
15.4	'to Seaton', Harringworth	52°33'57.27"N	0°38'54"W
{15.6 ★	Seaton Viaduct}		
15.8	B672 'to Morcott'		
16.9	▲ 0.5 miles hard climb		
18.0	A47/'to S Luffenham' (dogleg)		
18.1	'to Morcott village'		
18.4	'to Edith Weston', Morcott	52°35'47"N	0°38'14"W
20.4	T-junction, North Luffenham	52°37'17"N	0°37'16"W
20.8	'to Edith Weston'		
21.6	'to Rutland Water', Edith Weston	52°38'15"N	0°37'53"W

CUE CONTINUED		GPS COORDINATES	
{22.1 ★	Rutland Water picnic area (LHS)}		
22.2	go NE on Rutland Water bikepath		
23.6	cross the dam		
24.4	exit on car park road		
24.7	A606 'to Stamford'		
30.3	B1081 Scotgate		
30.6	Red Lion Square		
30.8	Stamford	52°39'8"N	0°28'50"W
	St Mary's St		
	(430yd) St George's St		
30.9	St Paul's St		
31.1	A6121 'to Bourne'		
32.6	'to Belmesthorpe'		
33.1	Belmesthorpe	52°40'45"N	0°27'34"W
34.0	'to Greatford' (dogleg)		
36.4	Greatford	52°41'37"N	0°23'33"W
37.9	'to Bourne'		
38.9	A15 'to Bourne'		
40.3	High St, Thurlby		
40.6	Thurlby YHA	52°44'17"N	0°22'17"W

lost her head after outstaying her welcome as guest-prisoner of Queen Elizabeth I. The old oak staircase she descended on the morning of her execution now graces the Talbot Hotel in Oundle. The castle may have gone but people are still drawn here by the site's strong historical associations.

Within the hour you should reach the spot where the route passes beneath the amazingly long **Seaton Viaduct,** stretching out over hay meadows beside the River Welland. Each of the 82 arches arch measures a whopping 12m (40ft) and the structure completely dominates the valley it spans. Today it's mostly used by freight trains, though in summer you may see the odd steam train puffing its way across.

Beyond the route's lone hill (16.9 miles) on the far side of the valley comes the day's top landscape feature, the great reservoir of **Rutland Water** (22.1 miles). Depending on when you left Oundle, this is a superb spot to down bikes and grab a picnic table to admire the views. Suitably refuelled, continue around the popular perimeter bikepath, which, although rough, should still be negotiable on narrow tyres.

One of the East Midlands' most attractive towns is Stamford, a good final destination for the day with plentiful accommodation and facilities. Stopping here, however, will

make the next day's ride more challenging at 78.5 miles. The village of Thurlby 10 miles further on only has a YHA, but your legs will thank you for it on Day 4.

Day 4: Thurlby to Lincoln
4½–7½ hours, 68.7 miles

A potentially long day, this ride involves crossing the **Lincolnshire fens,** flat as a board and very easy going. For those inclined towards inclines, this level landscape may seem dull, but for the cyclist who mulls over the problems of the world while eating up road, this day will be a philosophical experience.

A vast area of marshland, the Fens were reclaimed in the 17th century using an ambitious system of drains and rivers. Constituting much of eastern England, the fertile black soil here, found in just a handful of places around the world, produces a large share of the nation's harvest. If Kent is the garden of England, Lincolnshire is its industrial-scale vegetable patch, picked and pruned by an army of Poles and Czechs.

After around two hours you should reach **Boston**, the only large town you'll pass through today. Here the route joins NCN 1, which it follows for two more days as far as York. (Hessle to York is NCN 65, the White

CENTRAL EXPLORER – DAY 4

CUE			GPS COORDINATES	
start		Thurlby YHA	52°44'17"N	0°22'17"W
0 miles		go E on High St		
0.3	↰	A15 'to Bourne'		
1.9	↱	'to Spalding', Bourne	52°46'5"N	0°22'38"W
2.3	↱	South Fen Rd		
5.4	↰	'to Spalding'		
9.7	↰	A151 'to Bourne'		
9.8	↱	'to Pinchbeck'		
10.7		'to Pinchbeck'		
12.7	↱	Rotten Row, Pinchbeck	52°48'51"N	0°10'2"W
12.8	↰	Church St		
16.9	↑	B1397 'to Kirton', Gosberton	52°52'9"N	0°9'42"W
22.9		Kirton	52°55'42"N	0° 3'29"W
24.9		Wyberton	52°57'5"N	0°2'37"W
26.0	↰⊙	A16 'to town centre'		
26.4	↱⊙	A16 'to town centre/Grimsby'		
27.0	↰	High St 'to town centre' (NCN)		
27.3	★	Boston	52°58'39"N	0°1'25"W
	↰	Market Place		
27.4	↙	NCN 'to Wide Bargate'		
27.6	↰	Tawney St		

CUE CONTINUED			GPS COORDINATES	
27.8	↱	Norfolk St		
28.0	↰	B1183 Horncastle Rd		
29.1	↰	at NCN sign		
30.6	↰	'to Langrick', Frith Bank	53° 0'21"N	0°3'11"W
33.5	↰	B1184, Langrick	53°1'20"N	0° 6'22"W
34.2	↰	B1192 'to Boston'		
35.0	↱	'to Chapel Hill', Aston's Gowt		
41.5		Chapel Hill		
41.9	↱	'to Tattershall'		
47.4	↱	B1191, Martin Dales	53° 8'36"N	0°14'22"W
47.9	↰	'to Stixwould'		
51.3	↰	'to Bardney', Stixwould	53°10'37"N	0°14'37"W
53.1	↰	B1190		
53.8	↰	'to Bardney', Bucknall	53°12'14"N	0°14'59"W
58.2	↱	B1202 'to Stainfield', Bardney	53°12'38"N	0°19'27"W
59.5	↰	follow NCN		
67.1	↑⊙	Greetwell Rd/Eastgate		
68.4	↱	East Bight		
68.6	↰	Bailgate		
68.7		Lincoln tourist office	53°14'3"N	0°32'21"W

Rose Route.) Excellent NCN signposting makes navigation a doddle. Call a lunch halt in Boston (27.3 miles) where there are ample restaurants, pubs and 'greasy spoon' cafes. A major wool port in the Middle Ages, it was from here that the founding fathers of America made their first attempt to escape religious persecution. The 88m-high (288ft) tower of the St Botolph's Church, often dubbed 'the Boston Stump', can be seen for miles around. With a full belly, Boston won't hold you for long and you'll soon leave the town behind to press on through the Fens.

Some 90 minutes out of Boston you may have time to take a short there-and-back detour to **Tattershall Castle**, (☎ 01526 342543), an impressive 15th-century red-brick structure in the care of the National Trust. Otherwise NCN 1 will lead you unerringly through small fenland villages,

across dykes, over bridges, and along arrow-straight roads to Lincoln, whose cathedral towers beckon you in from around 20 miles as they have other travellers and pilgrims for the last 900 years.

Day 5: Lincoln to Hessle
4–6 hours, 55.61 miles

Road traffic evaporates on the 500ft-ridge of the rural Lincolnshire Wolds. The only sounds are those of sheep, birdsong and the occasional buzz of light aircraft from Humberside Airport. The views are long and fine, both westwards into the Lincolnshire Fens and eastwards to the sea ports and resorts. Two pieces of off-road bridleway are negotiable on narrow tyres if you take care. The first, north of Lincoln (2.2 miles), is almost 1 mile with some potentially tyre-shredding flints. The second (39.9 miles) is longer, over 2 miles and OK in the dry.

CENTRAL EXPLORER – DAY 5

CUE			GPS COORDINATES	
start		Lincoln tourist office	53°14'3"N	0°32'21"W
0 miles		go N on Bailgate		
0.3	↰	Westgate		
0.4	↱	Burton Rd		
1.6	↑⊙	B1398		
2.2	↱	rough bridleway		
2.9	↰	A15		
3.1	↱	unsigned road eastward		
4.7	↰	A46		
5.0	↱	'to Nettleham'		
5.6	↰	unsigned road, Nettleham	53°15'53"N	0°29'26"W
7.5	↰↱	'to Stainton' (dogleg), Scothern	53°17'3"N	0°26'59"W
8.4	↰	'to Stainton'		
9.7	↰	'to Wickenby', Stainton by Langworth	53°17'11"N	0°24'31"W
11.9		Snelland	53°18'37"N	0°23'5"W
13.1	↰	'to Friesthorpe', Wickenby	53°19'22"N	0°22'4"W
14.1	↱	'to Linwood'		
15.9	↰	'to Linwood'		
17.0	↰	B1202 'to Market Rasen', Linwood	53°21'42"N	0°20'5"W
19.0		Market Rasen	53°23'15"N	0°20'15"W
19.6	↰	'to Walesby'		
21.6	↰↱	'to Thoresway' (dogleg), Walesby	53°24'56"N	0°17'44"W
	↰	(55yd) 'to Thoresway'		
{21.9	★	Ramblers Church (RHS)}		
22.9	↰	'to Thoresway'		
23.8		B1225 'to Thoresway'		
24.0	↱	'to Thoresway'		
24.4	↰	'to Thoresway'		

CUE CONTINUED			GPS COORDINATES	
25.9		Thoresway	53°27'13"N	0°14'32"W
30.5	↰	'to Swallow', Beelsby	53°29'57"N	0°10'56"W
32.7	↱	unsigned road, Swallow	53°30'45"N	0°13'43"W
37.6	↰	unsigned road, Great Limber	53°33'44"N	0°17'29"W
39.9	↱	unsigned bridleway		
40.9	↑	bridleways		
42.1	↑	at house (tarmac)		
42.2	↰	at house		
43.1	↱	unsigned road, Barnetby	53°34'33"N	0°24'30"W
44.1		Melton Ross	53°34'54"N	0°23'7"W
48.1	↰↱	unsigned roads (dogleg), Burnham	53°38'21"N	0°23'54"W
50.8	↰	'to Barton'		
51.8	↰	A1077		
51.9	↱	George/King St, Barton-upon-Humber	53°41'1"N	0°26'22"W
	↰	(50yd) Catherine St (Soutergate)		
52.0	↱	Queens Ave		
52.2	↰	Butts Rd		
52.4	↱	Waterside Rd		
52.7	↱	Far Ings Rd		
53.0	↰	far bikepath under bridge		
	↑	(20yd) cross Humber bridge		
54.8	↰	North Bank 'to Hessle'		
54.9	↑	NCN 1 'to Hull'		
55.0	↑	track under bridge		
55.0	↱	Woodfield Lane		
55.4	↰	Southfield		
55.6	↰	Southgate		
{	●●↑	Hull 12 miles ↻}		
55.61		Hessle	53°43'23"N	0°26'7"W

North of Lincoln the NCN 1 crosses the traffic-plagued A15 and A46 where you should watch out for hurtling trucks. Otherwise there are just more quiet back roads to look forward to where the only sound is the buzz of your tyre tread on the tarmac.

The only town of any size you'll encounter today is **Market Rasen**, well-known in betting shops around the land for its racecourse. Just beyond the hour mark you reach the first real hill on the entire ride so far, the climb out of Walesby (21.6 miles) up the Wolds, which passes the squat **Ramblers Church**, adopted by the national walking group in 1914 as their place of worship. Having ascended to a dizzying altitude for this part of the world, the route undulates through drowsy hamlets to the River Humber.

Dropping down off the ridge, the imposing **Humber Bridge** piers come into view. Though planned throughout the 20th century, this crucial bit of infrastructure was only completed in 1981, and at the time its 1-mile central span was the longest in the world (it's since sunk to fifth though it's still the longest you can cross on foot). Over 120,000 vehicles roar across it every day and pay for the privilege, but cyclists cross gratis via the separated pedestrian track, giving you space to enjoy the view.

At Hessle NCN 1 turns east to finish at Hull, 6 miles on – follow the signs. (This route turns west on the NCN 65.) Overnighting in Hessle avoids retracing your pedal strokes the next day, but carrying on into Hull gives a vastly greater number of eating and sleeping options.

Day 6: Hessle to York
3–5 hours, 49 miles

After six days of heading north, today the route swings west towards the wilds of Yorkshire, but before things get hilly there's more pleasant fenland to cross in the East Riding. The signposting pointing the way along NCN 65 makes navigation simple but takes cyclists off-road at several points. All of these sections are manageable on touring

CENTRAL EXPLORER – DAY 6

CUE		GPS COORDINATES	
start	Southgate, Hessle	53°43'23"N	0°26'7"W
0 miles	go N on NCN 65		
0.3	Swanland Rd		
1.2	Jenny Brough Lane		
2.2	B1231		
3.1	Kemp Rd		
3.2	West End Main St, Swanland	53°44'17"N	0°29'31"W
4.4	unsigned road (at quarry)		
5.3	unsigned road, Melton	53°43'31.36"N	0°31'46"W
6.2	Welton	53°43'59"N	0°32'56"W
7.2	Kidd Lane		
7.5	unsigned road, Elloughton	53°44'31"N	0°33'45"W
7.7	Elloughton Main St		
8.6	cross A63 bridge		
10.6	'to Broomfleet'		
12.8	rough track, Broomfleet	53°44'4"N	0°39'51"W
16.5	Blacktoft	53°42'27"N	0°43'17"W
18.5	'to Laxton'		
21.6	'to Kilpin'		
22.2	Kilpin	53°43'58"N	0°49'49"W
23.4	'to Howden'		
24.1	A614		
	(100yd) unsigned road, Howden		
28.2	Barmby on the Marsh		
28.4	on tidal barrage		

CUE CONTINUED		GPS COORDINATES	
28.6	on rough track		
29.6	unsigned road (leave river)		
29.9	Hemingbrough		
30.2	unsigned road, Hemingbrough	53°46'2"N	0°58'44"W
30.6	A63		
31.0	'to Cliffe'		
32.0	on rough track		
33.9	A19, Selby	53°47'2"N	1° 4'7"W
34.0	Pond St (2nd left)		
34.1	Bungalow Rd		
	(100yd) join bikepath to rail trail		
35.0	follow 'to York' bikepath		
36.5	unsigned road (past 'road closed')		
37.0	bikepath		
37.9	unsigned road, Riccall	53°50'0"N	1° 3'33"W
38.8	rail trail 'to York'		
44.7	'to York', Bishopthorpe	53°55'15"N	1° 6'0"W
45.3	'to York Centre'		
46.9	cross to footpath on far side		
46.9	(50yd) bikepath 'to city centre'		
47.6	Terry Ave/Skeldergate		
48.3	North St/Wellington Row		
48.8	under Lendal Bridge (up stairs)		
48.9	cross Lendal Bridge/Museum St		
49.0	St Leonards Place/Exhibition Square		
49.0	York tourist office		

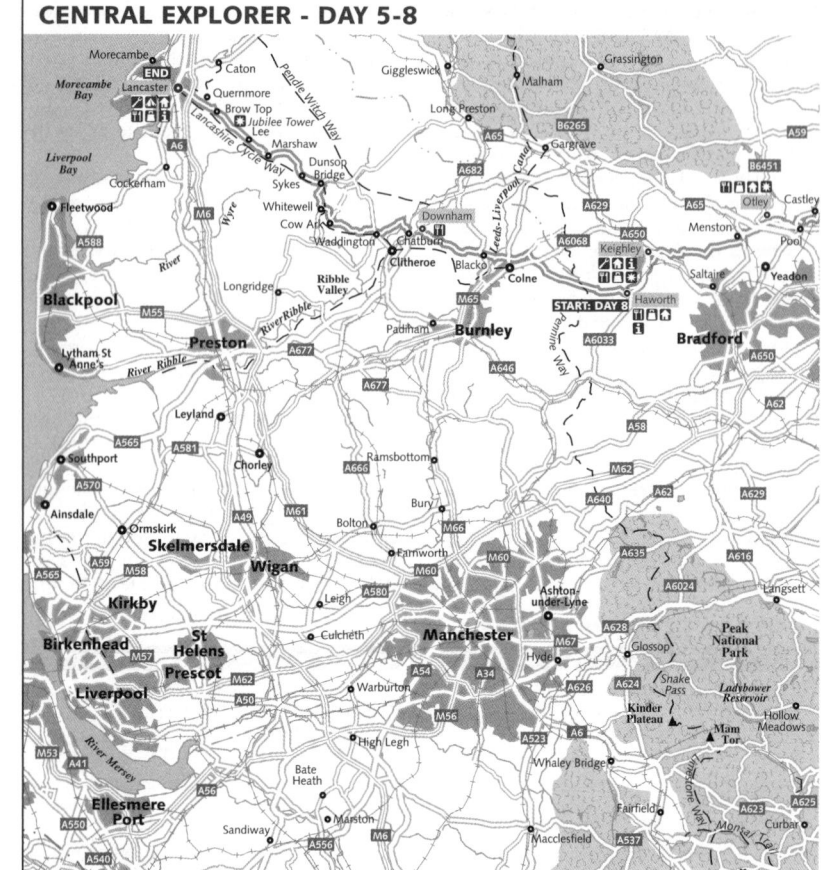

CENTRAL EXPLORER - DAY 5-8

bikes, though after rain taking an alternative road route may be advisable.

The route follows the River Humber then the River Ouse as far as **Selby** (33.9 miles), a handy island of civilisation for a lunch break. It's also the location of **Selby Abbey**, a magnificent Norman monastery church, more akin to one of the great northern cathedrals. The Benedictine monastery was the first to be founded in the north after the Norman Conquest and though dissolved by Henry VIII in 1539, the building survived as the town's parish church. It's a truly stunning building and well worth taking an hour or two off the saddle to explore.

Passing into North Yorkshire beyond Selby, the route follows the line of a dis-

used railway (34.1 miles), then off-road bikepaths into the heart of York.

Day 7: York to Haworth
3–5 hours, 47.6 miles

This route hits the hills of Yorkshire hard and finishes at the high village of Haworth. Away from the NCN signposting, make sure you keep your wits about you to navigate some tricky sections around Castley and Menston. Beyond Wetherby the landscape changes dramatically and the first sighting of the Pennines, the 'backbone of England', is from Kearby Cliff along Wharfedale (21.9 miles).

After Otley (32.5 miles) the route turns drastically upwards on the direct route over bleak **Rombalds Moor** to Keighley (pronounced 'keith-ley'). Striking views of Yorkshire valleys and hilltops and the steep descent make the climb worthwhile, so grit your teeth for some fast downhilling on the tops of the bars.

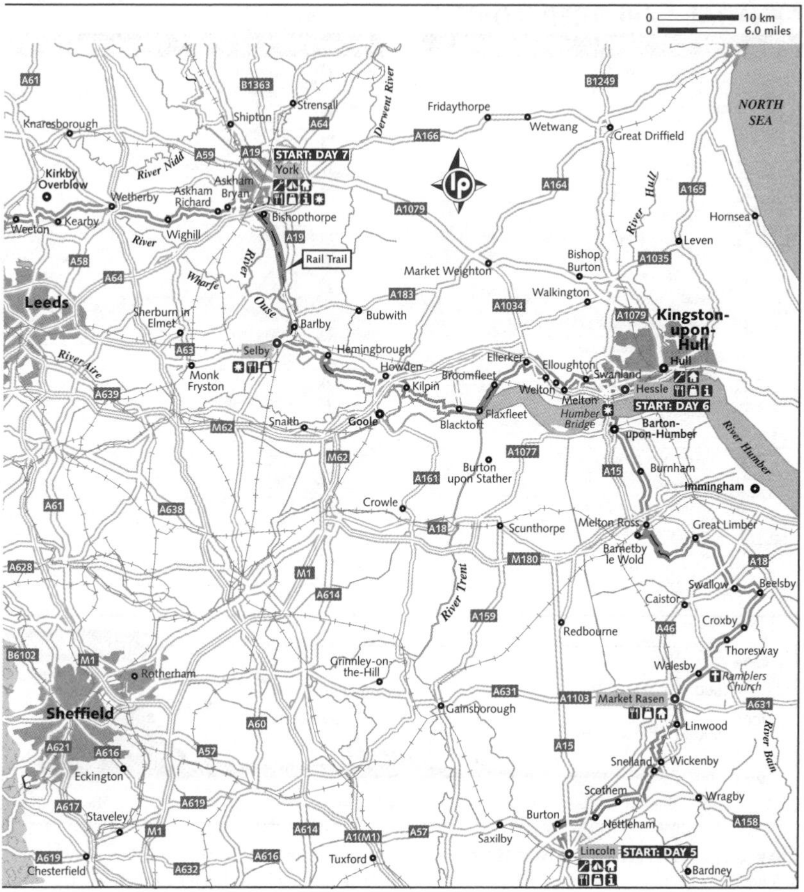

At the heart of the rural triangle between Leeds, Bradford and Harrogate, **Otley** is the obvious lunch halt on today's route. Thomas Chippendale, the celebrated furniture maker, was born and learnt his skill here. The town has a strong printing heritage, which can be seen at the **Otley Museum** (☎ 01943 461052). From there it's less than an hour's pedalling to Keighley where a highly recommended seasonal alternative to climbing the

narrow and busy A629 to Haworth is to let a steam train take the strain, in the shape of a 20-minute ride on the quaint **Keighley & Worth Valley Railway** (☎ 01535 645214; www.kwvr.co.uk; single ticket £4.50, bikes free). Travelling through the heart of Brontë country, trains run every 45 minutes at weekends throughout the year and every day from mid-June to the end of August. The railway serves both the local community and tourists alike.

Once at Haworth train station, cross the footbridge and continue 350 yards up Butt Lane. At the top, turn left into Rowdon Rd. After 175 yards, turn right at cobbled Main Rd – the tourist office is at the top after 530 yards.

CENTRAL EXPLORER – DAY 7

CUE			GPS COORDINATES
start		York tourist office	53°57'42"N 1°5'7"W
0 miles		retrace inward route on bikepath	
3.1	⤷	bikepath 'to Acomb'	
3.4	↑	pavement bikepath	
3.7	⤷	A1036 'to City Centre'	
4.1	↰ ⊙	(2nd exit) Moor Lane	
4.4	↰ ⊙	unsigned road	
6.25	↰	'to Askham Richard', Askham Bryan	53°55'44"N 1°9'38"W
6.6	⤷	'to Askham Richard'	
7.6		Askham Richard	53°55'28.78"N 1°11'2"W
12.2	⤷	'to Wetherby', Wighill	53°54'58.83"N 1°16'35"W
16.9	↰	Victoria St 'to town centre'	
	↰	(100yd) High St	
17.0	⤷	A661 'to Harrogate', Wetherby	53°55'40"N 1°23'8"W
17.5	↰	'to Sicklinghall'	
	▲	1.5 miles moderate climb	
21.9	↰	'to Harewood'	
	⚠	0.5 miles steep descent	
22.5	↑	'to Harewood', Kearby	53°54'59"N 1°29'32"W
23.3	↰	'to Harewood'	
23.8	↰	A61 'to Leeds'	

CUE CONTINUED			GPS COORDINATES
24.0	⤷	'to Weeton'	
25.8		Weeton	53°55'2.53"N 1°33'55"W
27.0	↰	'to Castley'	
29.4	↰	A658 'to Pool'	
29.6	⤷	A659 'to Otley', Pool	53°54'5"N 1°37'37"W
(32.5	★	Otley)	
33.1	↑ ⊙	'to Menston'	
34.4	↰ ⊙	A65 'to Menston'	
	▲	3 miles steep climb	
35.0	⤷	'to Keighley'	
35.4		Menston	53°53'10.94"N 1°43'47"W
36.4	↰	'to Keighley'	
36.6	⤷	'to Keighley'	
40.0	⚠	1.5 miles steep descent	
41.6	⤷	'to Keighley'	
42.9	↑ ⊙	'to town centre'	
43.4	★	Keighley	53°51'56"N 1°54'35"W
44.0	↰	A629	
46.3	⤷ ⊙	B6142 'to Haworth'	
47.1	↑	Bridgehouse Lane (cross river)	
47.3	↰	Main St (cobbled)	
47.6		Haworth tourist office	53°49'53"N 1°57'21"W

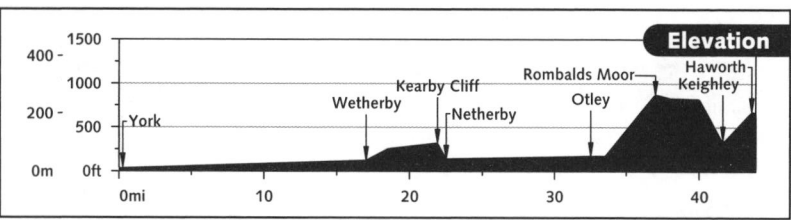

Day 8: Haworth to Lancaster
3–5 hours, 47 miles

This grand tour of England reaches a veritable climax today as we finish the Pennine crossing and descend to Morcambe Bay. This is not a ride to be tackled in bad weather, although there are towns and villages in the valleys along the way where you can shelter.

WARNING

Heavy lorries frequent the road between Healaugh and Wetherby. Prepare for a battering over Rombalds Moor during bad weather or a headwind as cyclists are fully exposed. Stock up on supplies, money and bike parts at Keighley, as Haworth is only small.

Windy conditions on the hilltops are a real danger and should not be taken lightly. Otherwise just enjoy the stunning views and wild landscapes this day offers, when you've caught your breath, that is.

This is by far the toughest day of the tour and starts with the traverse of **Haworth Moor** into Lancashire, just a taste of things to come, however. The ride along the desolate Two Laws Rd is breathtaking and the route is joined at Water Sheddles Reservoir by the Brontë Way long distance hiking path. The second major climb (9.8 miles) and the steepest of the whole trip is above Blacko beside Pendle Hill heading into the **Forest of Bowland.** The third ascent (30.7 miles), a long but not so high pass called the Trough of Bowland, is rewarded with a long run towards Lancaster, and the fourth climb (35.3

CENTRAL EXPLORER – DAY 8

CUE		GPS COORDINATES		CUE CONTINUED		GPS COORDINATES	
start		Haworth tourist office	53°49'53"N 1°57'21"W	21.1	↱	B6478 'to Newton', Waddington	53°53'27"N 2°24'53"W
0 miles		go NW on West Lane		21.6	↰	Cross Lane 'single track road'	
0.0	▲	2.5 miles moderate climb		23.8	↰	'to Whitewell'	
7.2	↑	Emmott Lane, Laneshaw Bridge	53°51'47"N 2°7'17"W	24.6	↱	unsigned road, at Micklehurst farm	
8.2	↱	uphill past the houses		25.7	↰	'to Lancaster', Cow Ark	53°54'12"N 2°30'1"W
8.3	↰	Castle Rd (downhill)		26.9	↱	'to Trough of Bowland'	
8.4	↘	at houses (not Ford Rd)		31.1	↰	'to Trough of Bowland', Dunsop Bridge	53°56'44"N 2°31'10"W
9.2	↑	Regent Ave (cross A56)		32.7	▲	1 mile hard climb	
9.3	↑◎	Red Lane		37.2		Lee	53°59'29"N 2°39'39"W
10.8	↱	'to Barnoldswick'			▲	0.5 miles hard climb	
11.1	↰	'to Blacko' (at Cross Gaits Inn)		42.0	⚠▲	1.5 miles steep descent	
11.4	↱	A682 'to Gisburn', Blacko	53°52'15"N 2°13'1"W	43.2	▲	0.8 miles steep climb	
11.7	↰	Wheathead Lane 'to Downham'		44.5	↱	'to city centre'	
11.8	▲	1.5 miles hard climb		45.7	↰	East Rd/Nelson St 'to centre'	
16.7	★	Downham	53°53'40"N 2°19'45"W	46.1	↰	Dalton Square/Thurman St	
	↰	unsigned road		46.3	↱	King St 'to tourist office'	
17.7		Chatburn	53°53'35"N 2°21'6"W	47.0	↰	Meeting House Lane	
	↰↱	unsigned rd/'to Grindleton' (dogleg)			↱	(20yd) Castle Hill	
18.8	↰	'to Waddington'		47.0		Lancaster tourist office	54° 2'56"N 2°48'14"W

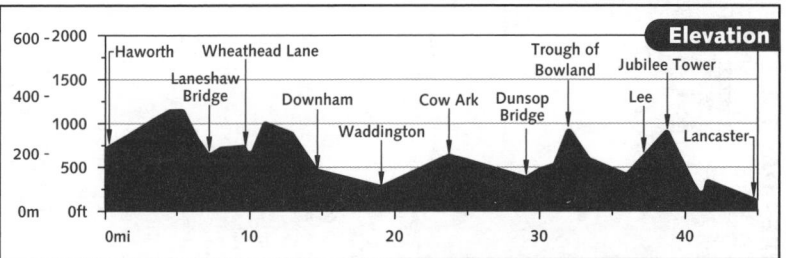

miles) is up to **Jubilee Tower**, erected in 1887 to mark Queen Victoria's 50th year on the throne and affording wide-screen views across much of Lancashire and Morecambe Bay. The short-but-steep fifth ascent (42.3 miles) is the 'sting in the tail'.

A good place to take on much needed lunch-time calories is the **Assheton Arms** (☎ 01200 441227) in Downham after 14.7 miles. This stone-built village on the far side of Pendle Hill has a conservation order, which bans 21st-century house adornments such as statellite dishes and plastic windows.

If you've completed the entire route from St Albans, pats on the back and air punches all round. You now have a valid excuse to head to one of Lancaster's or Morecambe's pubs for a well-deserved pint.

THE MARCHES, CHESHIRE & LANCASHIRE

Duration 5 days
Distance 258.9 miles
Difficulty moderate
Start Chepstow (p166)
Finish Lancaster (p172)

Summary A diverse five-day pedal which takes you from the tranquillity of the Welsh border to the drama of the Long Mynd and the urban sprawl of Merseyside to end on the sand flats of the Lancashire coast.

Travelling the length of the Welsh–English border, this varied and stimulating route begins in the beautiful Marches, climbs the Long Mynd, traverses the Cheshire Plain, burrows its way through Liverpool's urban

CENTRAL ENGLAND

THE MARCHES, CHESHIRE & LANCASHIRE - DAY 1-2

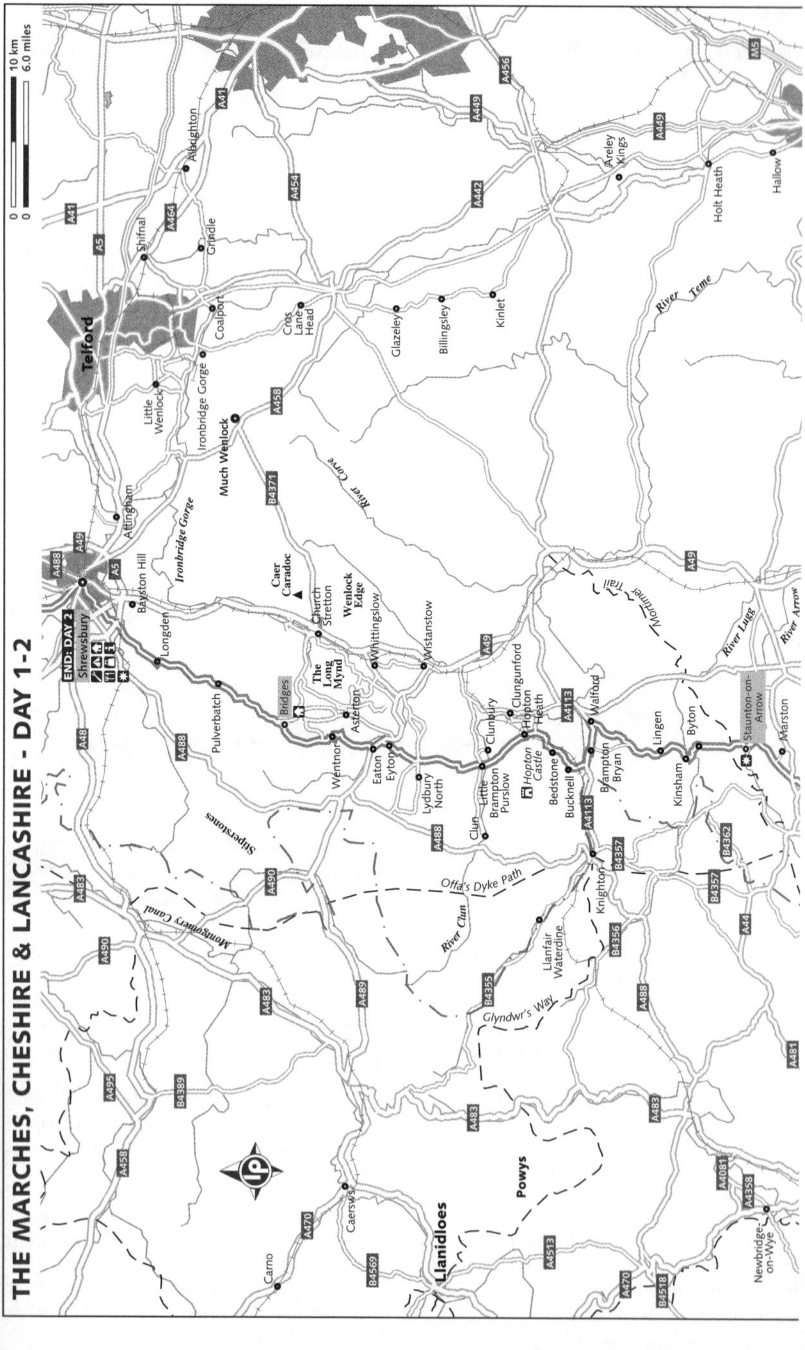

0 10 km
0 6.0 miles

A41

Albrighton

Shifnal

Cosford

A5

A464

A41

A454

A449

A442

Areley
Kings

Holt Heath

A449

Hallow

River Teme

Telford

Little
Wenlock

Ironbridge Gorge

Coalport

Cros
Lane
Head

Glazeley

Billingsley

Kinlet

A458

Much Wenlock

B4371

River Corve

A48

A49

A5

Atcham

Ironbridge Gorge

Caer
Caradoc

Church
Stretton

Wenlock
Edge

Whittingslow

Wistanstow

A49

Northall Trail

River Lugg

River Arrow

A49

END: DAY 2
Shrewsbury

Bayston Hill

Longden

The
Long
Mynd

Acton
Scott

Clungunford

Hopton
Heath

A4113

Walford

Lingen

Byton

Staunton-on-
Arrow

Marston

A48

Pulverbatch

A488

Bridges

Wentnor

Eaton

Clunbury

Hopton
Castle

Bedstone

Bucknell

Brampton
Bryan

Kinsham

Eyton

Lydbury
North

Little
Brampton

Purslow

Clun

B4385

B4357

A4113

A4362

Stiperstones

A483

A490

A488

River Clun

Offa's Dyke Path

Knighton

B4355

A44

B4356

A4357

Montgomery Canal

A489

A483

Llanfair
Waterdine

A4488

A481

A495

B4389

A483

B4355

Glyndwr's Way

A458

Carno

Caersws

A470

B4569

Llanidloes

A4513

Powys

A470

B4518

A4081

A4358

Newbridge-
on-Wye

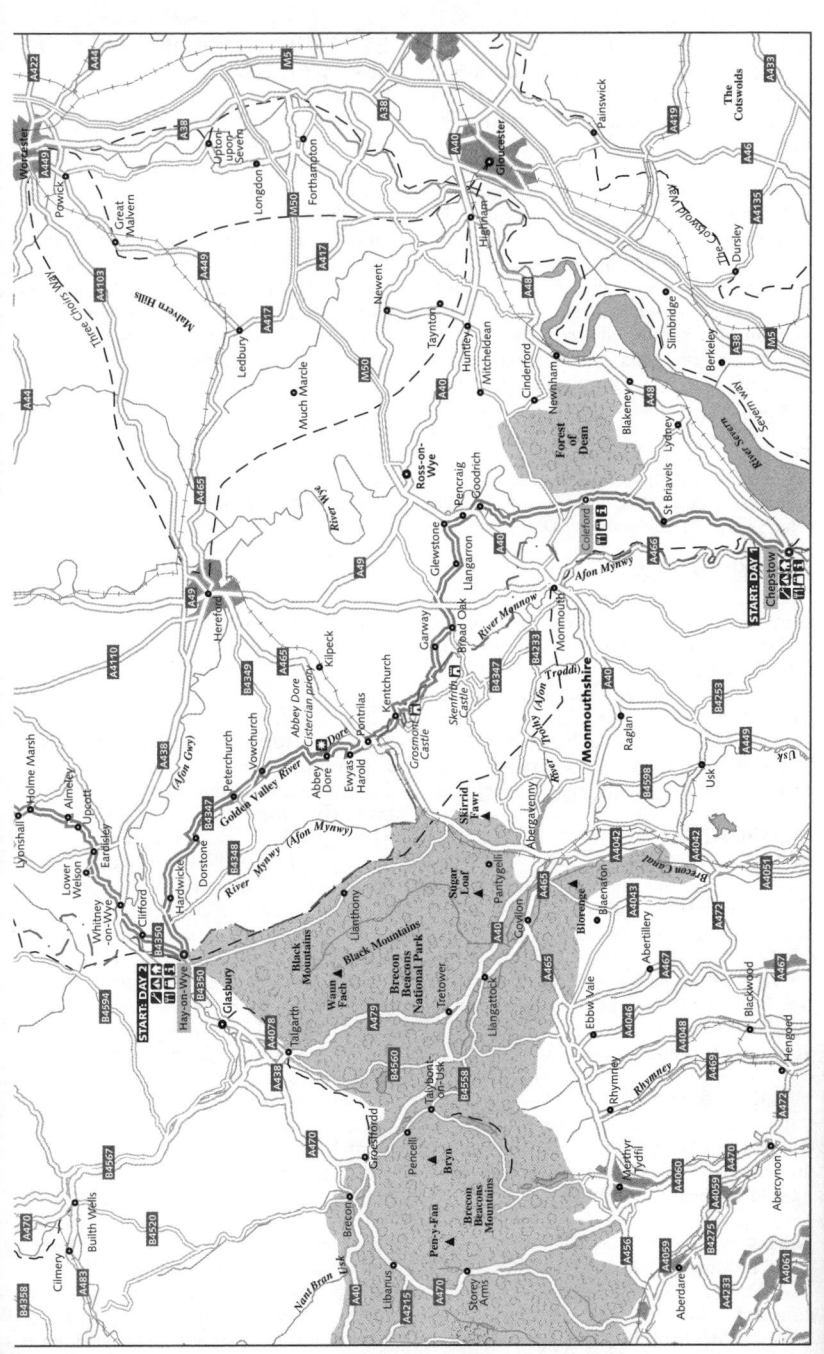

sprawl and ends on the Lancashire coast. Once fiercely fought over, the border region called the Marches (from the Old English *mearc*, meaning frontier) is today one of the most peaceful parts of the country, though the memory of more turbulent days lives on in castle ruins, which pepper the region. Other highlights include loading your bike onto the famous ferry across over the Mersey (everyone hums the song while crossing the river) to the Liverpool waterfront, fascinatingly historic Chester and bookish Hay-on-Wye renowned across the land for its literary bent. This tour truly has something for everybody, from inspiringly austere landscapes and quaint market towns, to the home of the Beatles and old fashioned British 'fun by the sea'.

This ride also links with the Through the Midlands ride (p141), later in this chapter, which starts at Shrewsbury (Day 2).

ENVIRONMENT

The England–Wales border follows a north-south course up the outlying areas of the Welsh mountain ranges. After Shrewsbury (Day 3) the altitude drops to sea level, with mosses and meres (lakes) around Ellesmere formed during the Ice Age. The Wirral Peninsula (Day 4) is a half-rural, half-industrial promontory separated from Liverpool by the mighty River Mersey.

PLANNING
When to Cycle

The summer months are warmest, but carry good water- and wind-proofs as the Marches are prone to heavy rainfall and Merseyside and Lancashire are exposed to strong south-westerlies gusting off the Irish Sea. The landscape is almost entirely rural, so look forward to some riding among spring blooms and autumn hues.

What to Bring

All the featured towns have bike shops, but carry spares and snacks for the remote stretches between Chepstow, Hay-on-Wye and Shrewsbury.

Maps

OS Travelmap – Road 1:250,000 *Wales and West Midlands* (sheet 6) and *Northern England* (sheet 4) are the best maps available for this ride.

GETTING TO/FROM THE RIDE
Chepstow (start)
TRAIN

To join up with the Avon to Thames ride (p66) in Bristol (£14.40; 90 minutes, hourly) take an **Arriva** (www.arrivatrain swales.co.uk) train to Severn Tunnel Junction then change onto a Taunton-bound **First Great Western** (www.firstgreatwest ern.co.uk) service to Bristol Temple Meads. London Paddington (£53; two-three hours, hourly) can be reached via Newport (same train companies) and travel to Cardiff (£8.10, 45 minutes, hourly) to join up with the Lôn Las Cymru ride (p184).

BICYCLE

Chepstow is a halt on the End-to-End ride (see the Land's End to John O'Groats chapter p306). It also lies on NCN 4, the Celtic Trail, which runs westwards along the south coast of Wales to Fishguard and eastwards to London.

Lancaster (finish)

See the Central Explorer ride (p172) for details on getting to/from Lancaster.

THE RIDE
Day 1: Chepstow to Hay-on-Wye
3½–6 hours, 54.7 miles

The first stretch of this five-day border raid takes you from Wales into England and back again to finish at Hay-on-Wye. This full day is about exploring the beautiful undulating farmland of the frontier that hints at wilder country to the west.

The first stretch is along the sometimes busy B4228 to the small town of Coleford (12.6 miles). The traffic combined with the steep climb can make the first few miles tricky. You'll be standing on the pedals once again as you pound out of Coleford to Symonds Yat, a dramatic viewing point overlooking the River Wye and a good place to pause for refreshments. You'll need them. Beyond Symonds Yat take care on the A40 before Pencraig (19.5 miles) where it may be worth using the footpath.

From Pencraig to Kentchurch the route heads towards, then tightly hugs the border but without actually crossing to the other side. Navigation is fiddly on this stretch and you'll have to stay alert so as not to miss a turning. An easy and short side trip

THE MARCHES, CHESHIRE & LANCASHIRE – DAY 1

CUE		GPS COORDINATES	
start	Chepstow tourist office	51°38'37"N	2°40'24"W
0 miles	go N on Bridge St		
0.0	(20yd) Castleford Hill (cross R Wye)		
0.8	↰ B4228 'to Coleford'		
	▲ 5 miles gradual climb		
12.6	Coleford	51°47'36"N	2°37'2"W
12.7	↱ 'to Symonds Yat'		
13.9	↰ B4432 'to Symonds Yat'		
{15.6	★ Symonds Yat}		
15.6	▲ 1 mile steep descent		
16.6	↱ 'to Goodrich'		
17.8	↱ 'to Goodrich'		
18.4	↰ 'to Goodrich'		
19.5	↱ A40 'to Ross'		
19.9	↰ 'to Glewstone', Pencraig	51°53'3"N	2°38'2"W

CUE CONTINUED		GPS COORDINATES	
20.6	↰ 'to Llangarron', Glewstone	51°53'45"N	2°38'34"W
22.6	↱ 'to St Weonards', Llangarron	51°53'13"N	2°41'4"W
23.8	↱▲ 'to St Weonards' (don't miss turn)		
24.5	↰ B4521		
26.4	↱ 'to Garway'		
32.6	B4347		
34.2	↰ 'to Hay-on-Wye'		
34.4	↰↱ A465/B4347 'to Hay' (dogleg)		
35.2	Ewyas Harold	51°57'7"N	2°53'27"W
36.8	★ Abbey Dore	51°58'15.94"N	2°53'49.31"W
43.1	↰ B4348 'to Hay-on-Wye'		
44.8	Dorstone		
52.2	↰ B4348 'to Hay-on-Wye'		
54.7	Hay-on-Wye tourist office	52° 4'23"N	3°7'37"W

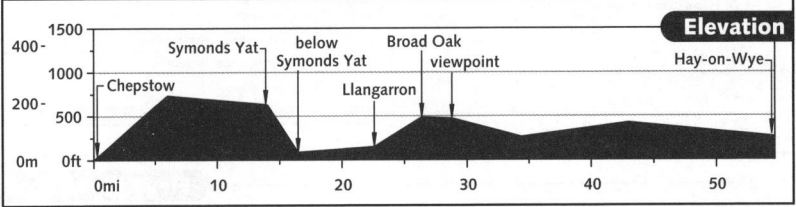

Elevation chart: Chepstow, Symonds Yat, below Symonds Yat, Llangarron, Broad Oak viewpoint, Hay-on-Wye

from Broad Oak is to the ruins of **Skenfrith Castle** just across the England–Wales line. It was built in the 11th century to guard over one of the main routes between the two countries during hostilities following the Norman Conquest. Back on the main route, get ready for some panoramic views of the surrounding hills just after Broad Oak. Shortly before Kentchurch the route passes **Grosmont Castle** ruins, which along with Skenfrith and White Castle form the three points of the triangular Three Castles Trail. After around two to three hours you should roll into **Abbey Dore** where the 12th-century **Cistercian priory** is the star attraction. It's also a good place to detach foot from pedal for a bite to eat.

The rest of the day is spent on the slight downhill gradient of the wide **Golden Valley** with some easy cruising to Hay-on-Wye.

Day 2: Hay-on-Wye to Shrewsbury
4–6½ hours, 61.65 miles

From the quaint toll bridge outside Hay-on-Wye to the swoop down off the Long Mynd, this exciting route proceeds through a delightfully jumbled landscape of green hills where peace prevails. With no towns of any size on the route and very few sights to distract you, today is all about an exhilarating ride through beautiful hill country. It may be a good idea to stuff a packed lunch into your panniers as eating options along the way are somewhat limited and you'll need a calorie boost at just the right time to get you to the end.

One of the prettiest villages en route to Shrewsbury is **Staunton-on-Arrow** (17.8 miles) with some folksy half-timbered cottages and a Victorian church. Veer off the route at the small village of Hoptonheath (33.4 miles) for a brief side trip to the ruined hulk of **Hopton Castle**, built in the 12th century and the scene of a bloody massacre during the English Civil War. There's a little adventurous section beyond Byton (20.5 miles) where the trees create a canopy over the broken road before a short, steep descent. But it's the **Long Mynd** south of Shrewsbury that will leave a lasting impression of the day as the heathered

CENTRAL ENGLAND

THE MARCHES, CHESHIRE & LANCASHIRE – DAY 2

CUE		GPS COORDINATES	
start	Hay-on-Wye tourist office	52° 4'23"N	3°7'37"W
0 miles	go NW on Oxford Rd		
0.1	B4350		
4.0	A438 'to Hereford'		
5.4	'to Brilley'		
6.1	'to Eardisley'		
8.5	A4111/'to Almeley' (dogleg), Eardisley	52° 8'11"N	3°0'20"W
10.4	'to Almeley'		
10.7	'to Lyonshall', Almeley	52°9'28"N	2°58'35"W
12.9	A480		
13.6	'Trail' on bend, Lyonshall	52°11'38"N	2°58'15"W
17.2	after River Arrow (not 'to Shobdon')		
17.8	Staunton-on-Arrow	52°14'11"N	2°55'27"W
17.9	'to Shobdon' (not 'to Stansbatch')		
20.5	Byton	52°16'17"N	2°55'29"W
	thru farm (not 'Private Rd')		
21.3	unsigned road (opp The Forge)		
27.4	A4113 (no sign)		
28.6	Brampton Bryan	52°20'46"N	2°55'33"W
29.5	B4367 'to Bucknell'		
33.4	'to Clun', Hopton Heath	52°23'29"N	2°54'38"W

CUE CONTINUED		GPS COORDINATES	
36.1	'to Kempton' (cross B4368)		
37.5	B4385		
39.7	'to Eyton' (on left bend)		
40.0	'to Plowden'		
41.1	Eyton	52°30'0"N	2°55'21"W
	unsigned road (not 'to Plowden')		
42.0	A489		
42.5	'to Wentnor'		
43.0	1 mile moderate climb		
45.0	'to Bridges', Wentnor	52°31'43"N	2°54'35"W
45.9	(no sign)		
48.3	Bridges	52°33'45"N	2°53'47"W
	2 miles moderate climb		
52.9	Pulverbatch	52°36'57"N	2°51'5"W
56.0	Longden	52°39'7"N	2°49'36"W
61.1	Coleham Head		
61.2	over English Bridge		
61.3	Wyle Cop (cobbled climb)		
61.4	High St (cobbled road)		
61.6	The Square		
61.65	Shrewsbury tourist office	52°42'27"N	2°45'15"W

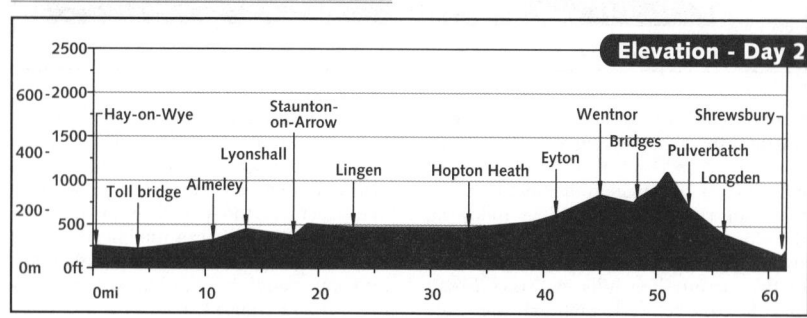

Elevation - Day 2

Hay-on-Wye · Toll bridge · Almeley · Lyonshall · Lingen · Staunton-on-Arrow · Hopton Heath · Eyton · Wentnor · Bridges · Pulverbatch · Longden · Shrewsbury

hills rise up around you. This rolling barrel of upland is crossed via a long valley climb and a hacking but exhilarating descent off the northern slopes. Halfway along in a steep valley lies the little village of Bridges where, one minute off the route, the **Bridges Long Mynd YHA** (☎ 01588 650656; r from £13) in a converted schoolhouse offers an alternative place to stay to the centre of Shrewsbury. The hostel offers secure bicycle storage and has a limited number of pitches on site. For a mountain bike route close by, see The Long Mynd boxed text (p161) later in this chapter. Your efforts throughout the day are rewarded with a long freewheel down into Shrewsbury.

Day 3: Shrewsbury to Chester
3–4½ hours, 43.7 miles

After two relatively tough days, today is far easier on the legs and quite a good deal shorter. From Shrewsbury the route drops nearer to sea level and uses quiet, country roads to bypass populated areas. It is a gentler landscape that leads over the Shropshire plain through a finger of Wales into Cheshire to the superbly preserved town of **Chester**. As with yesterday's ride, there are few sights to leave the saddle to see, meaning you can go at a slower pace and still make it to Chester in time for high tea.

The best place on the route for a lunch stop and the only town on today's ride is the

THE MARCHES, CHESHIRE & LANCASHIRE – DAY 3

CUE		GPS COORDINATES	
start	Shrewsbury tourist office	52°42'27"N	2°45'15"W
0 miles	go E on The Square		
0.0	(50yd) High St		
0.2	Bellstone/Barker St		
0.4	Smithfield Rd 'to Ellesmere'		
0.7	Chester St 'to Baschurch'		
1.0	B5067 'to Baschurch'		
8.0	'to Ruyton-XI-Towns'		
8.8	Baschurch	52°47'36"N	2°51'14"W
10.6	Weston Lullingfields	52°49'7"N	2°51'16"W
13.4	Bagley	52°50'25"N	2°53'9"W
16.1	'to Ellesmere', Hordley	52°52'16"N	2°55'19"W
17.7	Tetchill	52°53'17"N	2°54'28"W
19.5	main street (dogleg), Ellesmere	52°54'26"N	2°53'37"W
19.6	A528 'to Wrexham'		
{	mere (lake) 1 mile ↺}		

CUE CONTINUED		GPS COORDINATES	
20.7	'to Penley'		
23.6	A539/'to Halghton' (dogleg), Penley	52°57'7"N	2°51'58"W
25.2	'to Halghton'		
25.4	unsigned road (not 'to Halghton')		
25.9	A525		
26.1	'to Mulsford'		
27.3	unsigned road (at T-junction)		
27.5	'to Threapwood'		
28.1	'to Threapwood'		
28.7	Threapwood	53°0'5"N	2°50'6"W
29.0	B5069 'to Bangor'		
29.3	'to Farndon'		
29.6	'to Farndon'		
36.0	B5130 'to Chester'		
42.7	Boughton		
43.3	Grosvenor Park Rd		
43.7	Chester tourist office	53°11'30"N	2°53'33"W

attractive Shropshire market town of **Ellesmere** (19.6 miles). A short side trip off the route will take you to a *mere* (lake) in what is known as Shropshire's lake district. Five other glacial *meres* and several 'mosses' lie to the east (there are no hills), all linked by the Llangollen canal. At **Ellesmere's tourist office** (☎ 01691 622981, The Mereside) a display explains their prehistoric formation, interesting but not essential information if you just want to take it easy.

The sights and smells of cattle farming never retreat far. The straight approach to Chester along the B5130 has high-speed traffic but at least you can relax about navigation until you hit the city's southern outskirts.

Day 4: Chester to Southport
3–5½ hours, 52 miles

Today is all about Liverpool – reaching it, crossing it and making good your escape. The ride's perhaps unlikely attraction lies in arriving on the Mersey ferry and following bike routes and rail trails all the way from the city centre to the outskirts and away. With a rural start and finish, it is a unique way to say you've seen this slowly rejuvenating but still slightly crest-fallen city without overnighting there. If you plan on stopping in Liverpool itself, make sure you are armed with a chunky chain and axe-proof lock with which to secure you two-wheeled buddy from the 'scallies'.

Tear yourself away from beautiful Chester to make your way along the Wirral into Birkenhead. You'll be travelling along quite a major A road (A540) but the nearby M53 motorway siphons off most of the traffic. En route be sure to call a brunch break at the **Eureka Cyclists Cafe** (☎ 0151 339 5629; www .eurekacyclistscafe.co.uk; Two Mills, Parkgate Rd, Woodbank) located at the intersection of the A540 and A550. This friendly place has been serving tea and snacks to passing cyclists since 1929, and you're guaranteed a warm welcome. They also stock cycling maps and guides to help you navigate your way through Merseyside.

Having arrived at the Mersey, catch the famous ferry across from the **Woodside terminal** to **Pier Head terminal** (£1.45, bikes free; 10-20 minutes; hourly) to get an uninterrupted view of the waterfront. This includes the **Cunard Building** and the **Royal Liver Building** (pronounced as in 'alive') crowned by the famous 5.5m (18ft) **copper liver birds**, Liverpool's instantly recognisable symbol.

Immediately south of the terminal lies the redeveloped **Albert Dock,** now a colonnaded walkway of cafes, shops and museums, which also houses the famous **Liverpool Tate Gallery** and the **Beatles Story**. The **tourist office** (☎ 0151 707 0729; Anchor Courtyard), in the far corner of Albert Dock, has information on the sights and nightlife in the city

CENTRAL ENGLAND

CENTRAL ENGLAND

THE MARCHES, CHESHIRE & LANCASHIRE - DAY 3-5

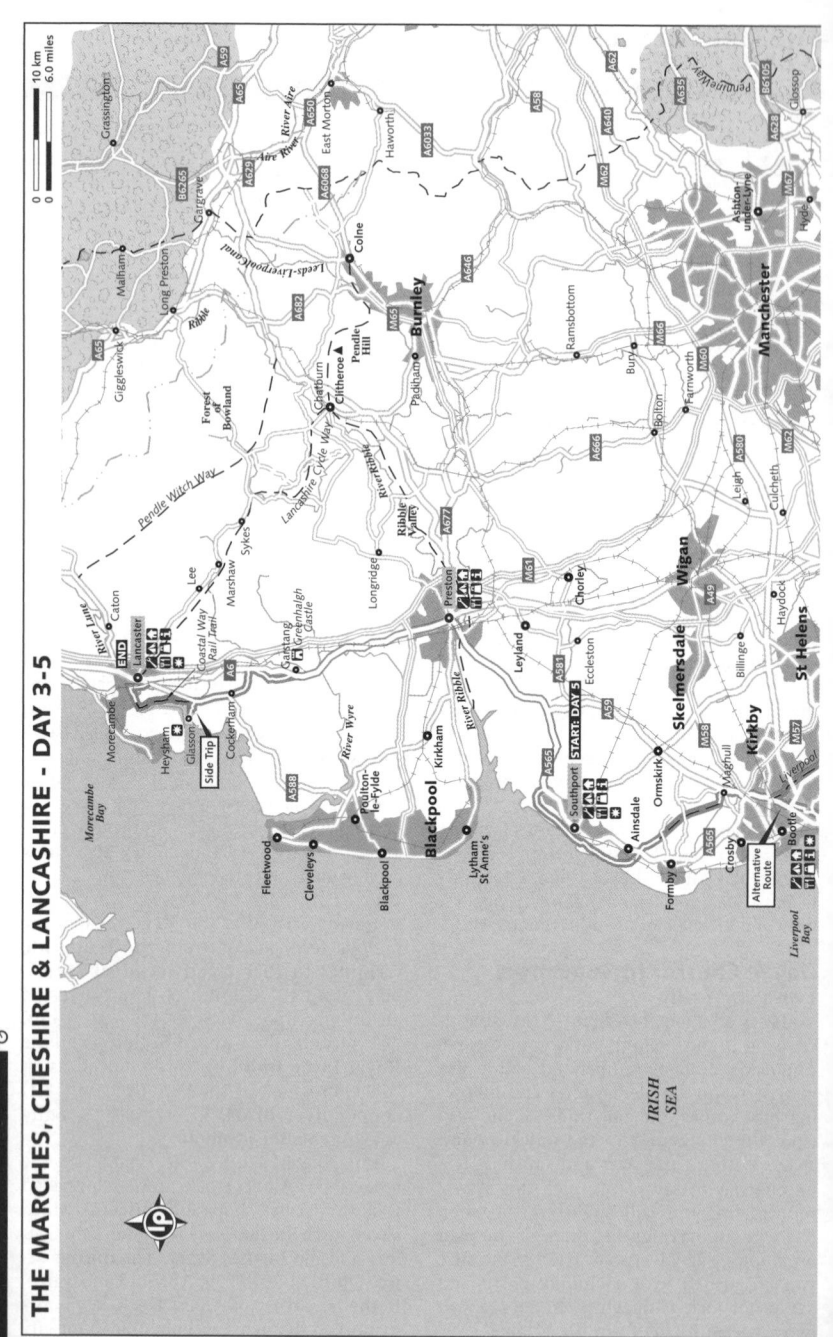

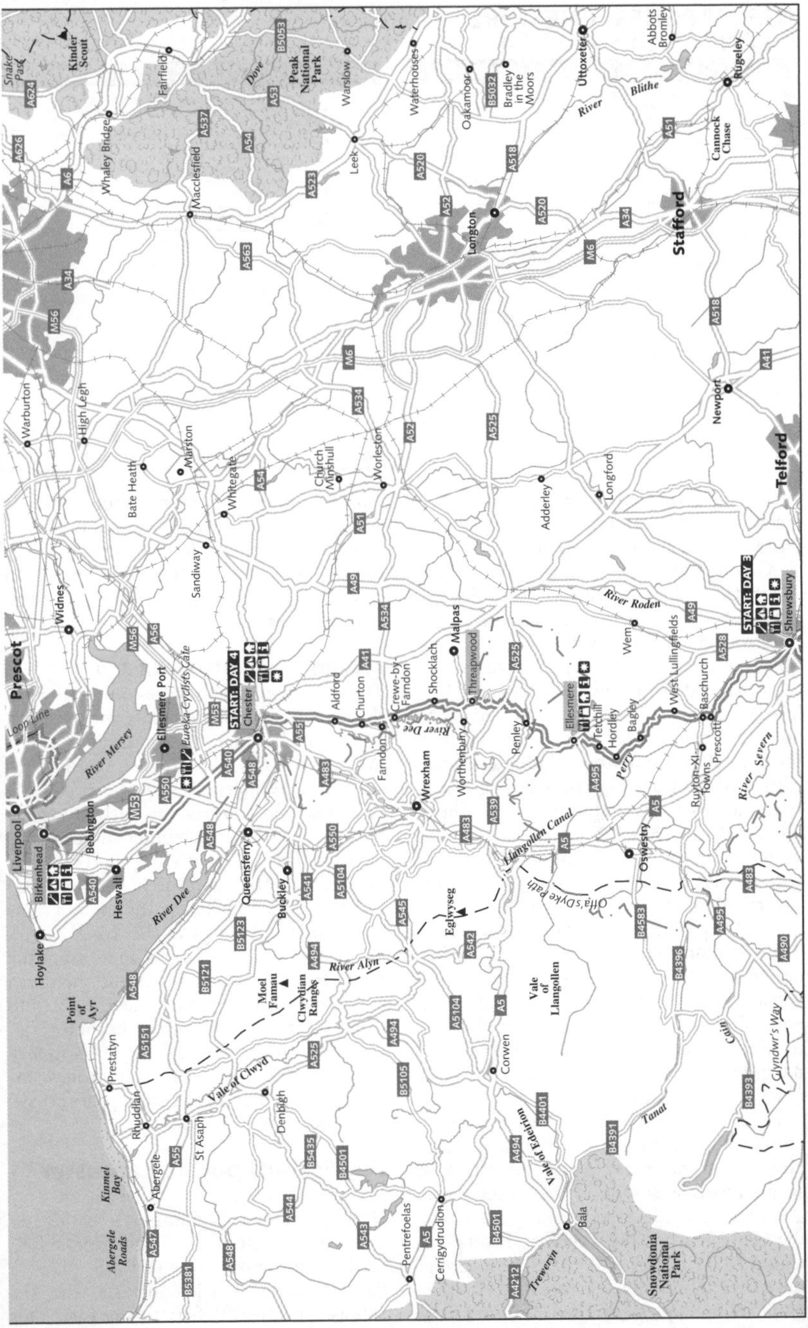

START: DAY 4
Chester
Eureka Cyclists Café
START: DAY 3
Shrewsbury
Prescot
Liverpool
Birkenhead
Bebington
Hoylake
Heswall
Widnes
Warburton
High Legh
Bate Heath
Marston
Whitegate
Sandiway
Church Minshull
Worleston
Ellesmere Port
River Mersey
Loop Line
River Dee
Queensferry
Buckley
Aldford
Churton
Farndon
Crewe-by-Farndon
Shocklach
Malpas
Threapwood
Worthenbury
Wrexham
Penley
Ellesmere
Tetchill
Hordley
Bagley
Perry
West Lullingfields
Wem
River Roden
Baschurch
Prescott
Ruyton-XI-Towns
River Severn
Oswestry
Llangollen Canal
Offa's Dyke Path
Eglwyseg
Vale of Llangollen
River Alyn
Moel Famau
Clwydian Ranges
Point of Ayr
Prestatyn
Rhuddlan
St Asaph
Vale of Clwyd
Denbigh
Abergele
Kinmel Bay
Abergele Roads
Corwen
Vale of Edeirion
Bala
Tryweryn
Snowdonia National Park
Pentrefoelas
Cerrigydrudion
Tanat
Cain
Glyndwr's Way
Adderley
Longford
Newport
Telford
Stafford
Longton
Cannock Chase
Rugeley
Abbots Bromley
River Blithe
Uttoxeter
Bradley in the Moors
Oakamoor
Waterhouses
Warslow
Leek
Macclesfield
Whaley Bridge
Fairfield
Peak National Park
Dove
Kinder Scout
Snake Pass
M56
M53
M6
A34
A6
A626
A624
A537
A54
A53
B5053
A523
A520
A518
B5032
A52
A51
A34
A518
A41
A525
A534
A51
A49
A563
A56
A55
A540
A548
A550
A483
A5
A495
A528
A539
A541
A5104
A545
A542
A494
B5123
B5121
A5151
A525
B5105
B4501
B5435
A544
A543
A547
B5381
A4212
B4401
B4391
B4393
B4396
B4583
A490

THE MARCHES, CHESHIRE & LANCASHIRE – DAY 4

CUE		GPS COORDINATES	
start	Chester tourist office	53°11'30"N	2°53'33"W
0 miles	go W on Little St John St		
0.4	↱⊙ 'to Birkenhead'		
1.1	↰⊙ follow signs 'to Hoylake (A540)'		
9.5	↱▲ Damhead Lane (not B5151)		
10.0	↑ Lydiate Lane (cross B5133)		
10.2	↰ B5151		
16.2	↱ 'to town centre'		
16.3	↱ Singleton Ave		
{16.7	↰🚉 Borough Rd (follow signs 'to town centre')		
17.8	↑⊙ (1st exit) 'to Woodside MFs'		
	{follow signs 'to Woodside MFs'}		
18.6	↰ ferry terminal		
	{catch ferry to Pier Head, Liverpool}		
18.6	↱ James St		

CUE CONTINUED		GPS COORDINATES	
	{follow Trans Pennine Trail/NCN 56 signs}		
{	●●↑ Albert Dock 1 mile ↺)		
25.7	↰ join Liverpool Line Loop		
	{follow Liverpool Line Loop/NCN 62 signs}		
34.3	↱ A59/Ormskird Rd		
35.4	↰ Leeds & Liverpool canal		
36.6	↱ Aldrin's Lane/Chapel Lane		
38.2	↰↱ Sefton Lane/'to Southport' (dogleg)		
	{follow Cheshire Line Path signs}		
43.8	↰ N Moss Lane (leave Cheshire Line)		
44.7	↱ unsigned road		
46.1	↱ A565		
46.2	↰ follow 'Southport tourist route' signs		
51.2	↱ follow 'to town centre' signs		
51.7	↰ Lord St		
52.0	Southport tourist office	53°38'51"N	3° 0'20"W

and the hip **Liverpool Cycle Centre** (☎ 0151 708 8819; 9 Berry St), 1 mile southeast of Pier Head, has a cafe called **the Hub**.

A riverfront cycle route continues from Albert Dock alongside the docks southward as far as Festival Park (6.6 miles return). This riverfront ride links up with the main ride a mile later in Sefton Park. The first section of the urban ride from the ferry terminal follows 7.1 miles of bikepaths signposted NCN 56 Trans Pennine Trail in Liverpool. Passing the huge 20th-century neo-Gothic Anglican **cathedral** (20.1 miles), it runs through back roads, across parks and even along a short piece of **Penny Lane** (22.6 miles), immortalised by the Beatles, to connect at Childwall with the second part of the urban route, the **Liverpool Loop Line** rail trail (25.7 miles).

The Loop Line, part of the coast-to-coast Trans Pennine Trail (NCN 62), was abandoned in 1964 and fell derelict before conversion work began in 1988. Via cuttings, embankments and bridges the trail leads northwards around the city outskirts for 8.6 miles as far as the A59 Warbreck Moor (34.3 miles) at Aintree.

Here the route passes **Aintree Racecourse**, the venue for the world famous Grand National every April (on which it seems nearly everyone in the country has a flutter). A mile after joining the road, the route reaches the **Leeds & Liverpool Canal** (35.3 miles) and turns west along the towpath for a mile. Across fields to Maghull it finally picks up the Cheshire Lines

Path (38 miles), a rural rail trail that leads across drained farmland towards the coast. The route continues to track the course of the old railway along the sand-dune lined coastal road to Southport, using well-maintained bikepaths.

ALTERNATIVE ROUTE: VIA A59

The Liverpool Loop Line rail trail runs through urban embankments and a tunnel, and is safest ridden during daylight hours. Women soloists in particular should consider the A59 alternative route, a preferable option should you have no wish to experience Liverpool's dreary inner suburbs.

Using this alternative from Liverpool city centre out to Aintree is much shorter (5.5 miles) than the bikepaths and rail trails (15.7 miles). However, the road carries heavy traffic. To follow the route from the ferry terminal, take James St and turn left into Derby St (18.8 miles), right into Cook St (18.9 miles) – which becomes Victoria St – to the roundabout (19.5 miles). Take the A59 'to Ormskirk' and follow it for 5 miles. Rejoin the main route at A59 Warbreck Moor (34.4 miles).

Day 5: Southport to Lancaster
3–5 hours, 46.9 miles

Having partaken of Southport's seaside fun and sandy beach, it's out into Lancashire's verdant lowlands and the Fylde plain, a flat landscape, which contrasts with the 500m-high (1640ft) fells to the east. This

THE MARCHES, CHESHIRE & LANCASHIRE – DAY 5

CUE		GPS COORDINATES
start		Southport tourist office	53°38'51"N	3° 0'20"W
0 miles		go N on Lord St
0.2		Bold St
0.4		Promenade
0.6	◎	Promenade
1.0		Fairway
1.3	◎	follow 'to Preston' signs
12.6	◎	(2nd exit) 'to Longton'
13.0		Longton	53°43'12"N	2°47'29"W
14.0		Hutton	53°43'57"N	2°46'14"W
17.4		A59 'to Preston'
17.8		'to Blackpool'
49.8		(32yd) 'to Riversway/Docklands'
18.3	◎	'to Marina'
{	●●↑	dock & marina 1.5 miles (↺) }
18.9	◎	Pedders Way
19.7		A5085
20.2		Tulketh Brow (not T Rd)
20.4		B6241 'to Garstang'
21.4		B6241 'to Garstang'
22.6	◎	B5411 'to Woodplumpton'

CUE CONTINUED		GPS COORDINATES
24.6	↑	B5269
24.8	⚠	Hollowforth Lane (no sign)
25.5		T-junction (no sign)
26.1		unsigned road
28.0		unsigned road
28.7		A6 'to Lancaster', Bilsborrow	53°51'13"N	2°44'41"W
30.5		B6430 'to Garstang'
32.7	◎	B6430 'to Lancaster, Garstang	53°54'2"N	2°46'27"W
37.9		A588 'to Glasson Dock', Cockerham	53°57'47"N	2°49'1"W
40.2		B5290 'to Glasson Dock'
41.9		join Coastal Way rail trail
{	●●↑	Glasson Dock 1 mile (↺) }
45.1	↑	New Quay Rd
46.3		follow 'to City Centre' signs
		(22yd) track thru lawns
46.4		bikepath
46.6		unsigned road (uphill)
46.8	↑	beside castle
46.9		Lancaster tourist office	54°2'56"N	2°48'14"W

is a densely populated corner of the British Isles and while the route does its best to shun big roads and built-up areas, some are unavoidable.

From Southport, the A565 coastal road has views over the Ribble Estuary to Lytham St Anne's. It leads eventually to the A59, which has a cycle path most of the way to Preston. To avoid the noise and fumes of traffic as it tears by, you could take a longer route via country lanes, but navigation is fiddly and you'll have to rejoin the A59 at Tartleton any way as the unbridged River Douglas blocks your way. Having arrived on the outer limits of **Preston**, a short detour (18.3 miles) takes you to the riverside dock and marina, now a shopper's paradise. It's a timely place for a half-time break, either at the chip stall beside the marina, or a pub. A more rural option comes 10 miles on at **Owd Nell's Tavern** (☎ 01995 640010) on the canalside before the A6 turn at Bilsborrow (28.7 miles).

Between Preston and Lancaster is Garstang, a semi-attractive market town overlooked by the ruins of **Greenhalgh Castle** standing between the town and the M6 motorway. It was besieged during the English Civil War but there's not much to admire save for its rurally picturesque location.

A short interlude on the thundering A6 is compensated by a quick side trip to **Glasson**, a little harbour town on the mouth of the tidal River Lune, from where the tranquil Lancashire Coastal Way rail trail leads right into Lancaster's St George's Quay.

THROUGH THE MIDLANDS

Duration 3 days
Distance 152.1 miles
Difficulty moderate
Start Shrewsbury (p176)
Finish Oundle (p175)
Summary Castle-dwelling phantoms and the echoes of Britain's industrial past accompany you on your cross-country journey via the stately homes, scenic reservoirs and thick forest of England's midriff.

This trans-midland jaunt explores the lesser-known historic and scenic side of England's heartland, bypassed more often than not by most Brits en route to more mainstream beauty spots. Generally considered post-industrial and dull, this swathe of Blighty was once blighted by the furnaces of industry, but following its decline since the Industrial Revolution's heyday, most areas

CENTRAL ENGLAND

THROUGH THE MIDLANDS

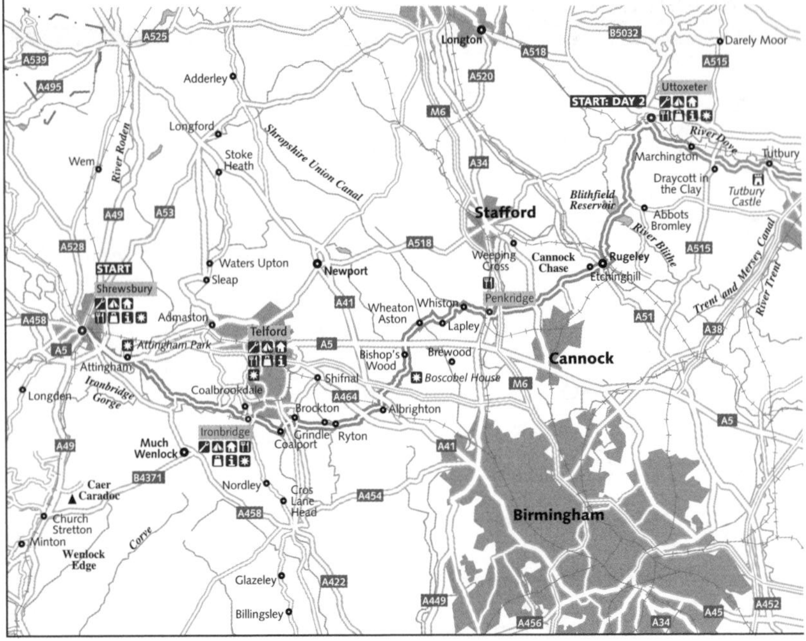

are recovering, rejuvenating and replanting. The region's historical focus on industrial activity and innovation has evolved in more recent times into a vibrant and well-funded arts scene. The prosperous market-town pockets never lost their rural charm and the countryside remains as soothing as ever. As the route proceeds from Shropshire through Staffordshire, Leicestershire and Rutland to Northamptonshire, it traces valleys guarded by castles, dips into atmospheric old towns and explores areas of unexpected wilderness, as well as weaving a path that comes within striking distance of numerous cities but in the end stays well clear.

Pedalling this itinerary, there are numerous drags rather than significant hills, although the roads are never flat for long. Be prepared for the contrast between the quiet lanes and the occasional thundering A-road which you should negotiate with care. Note that this ride can also be linked with the Peak District ride (p146) later in this chapter (which starts at Uttoxeter), and the Central Explorer ride (p131) at Oundle.

PLANNING
When to Cycle

This is a lowland, largely sheltered ride that can be done at almost any time of year, although the summer months are obviously best.

What to Bring

The little towns and villages en route have all necessary supplies and bike shops are plentiful. Campsites can be found at each overnight stop as well as in between stops, so packing the camping gear makes sense.

Maps

The OS Travel map 1:250,000 *Wales and West Midlands* (sheet 6) and *East Midlands & East Anglia* (sheet 5) cover all the counties through which the ride passes.

GETTING TO/FROM THE RIDE
Shrewsbury (start)
TRAIN

Shrewsbury has good connections with Manchester (£17.20, one hour 20 minutes, hourly) and bikes are carried free of charge and without reservations. From London Marylebone there are five direct services (£40, 3½ hours) otherwise change at Crewe (£42.40, 2½ hours, twice hourly). The first leg is with Virgin Trains who require reservations for bikes in transit. The second part of the journey is with more laid-back Arriva Trains Wales whose services carry cycles, no questions asked.

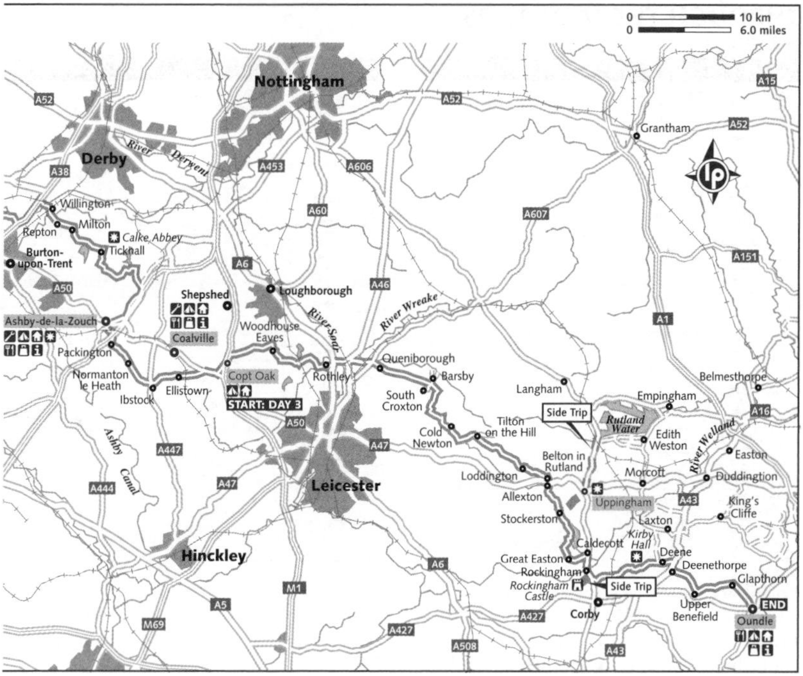

BICYCLE
Shrewsbury is on the Marches, Cheshire & Lancashire ride earlier in this chapter (p131).

Oundle (finish)
TRAIN
The nearest train station to Oundle is Peterborough, 11 miles away on the A605. The station straddles the east coast mainline and there are very fast and frequent connections to London Kings Cross (£23.20; one hour, every 10-20 minutes), Newcastle-upon-Tyne (£79.10; 2½ hours, twice hourly) and Edinburgh (£96; 3 hours 45 minutes, hourly).

BICYCLE
Oundle links up with Day 3 of the Central Explorer ride (p120) earlier in this chapter.

THE RIDE
Day 1: Shrewsbury to Uttoxeter
4–6½ hours, 59.5 miles

This is generally a gentle day of carefree riding through pleasant countryside with a bit of a wild section at Cannock Chase. There are a number of places you could squeeze the brake lever for some exploration along the way, and with almost 60 miles to cover, an early start may be in order.

Rolling on out of Shrewsbury the route passes close to **Attingham Park** (☎ 01743 708123), a regal 18th-century National Trust property fronted by four building-high Doric columns. From there the elevated road to **Ironbridge** has fine views of the meandering River Severn and the Welsh hills. The picturesque town is considered the birthplace of the Industrial Revolution and takes its name from the world's first iron bridge,

THROUGH THE MIDLANDS – DAY 1

CUE			GPS COORDINATES	
start		Shrewsbury tourist office	52°42'24"N	2°45'16"W
0 miles		go E to High St		
0.0	⌐►	(100m) High St		
0.1	↙	Wyle Cop		
	↰	(55yd) cross English Bridge		
0.3	⌐►	'to all routes'		
1.3	⌐►◎	(3rd exit) A5064 'to Emstrey'		
5.4	⌐►	B4380 'to Ironbridge'		
12.3	⌐►↰	A4169/'to Ironbridge' (dogleg)		
14.3	★	Ironbridge	52°37'39"N	2°29'7"W
14.8	↰	'to Blists Hill' (before bridge)		
15.6	⌐►	'to Coalport'		
16.4	↰	unsigned road		
	▲	0.7 miles steep climb		
17.6	⌐►	B4176 'to Sutton Maddock'		
18.4	↰	'to Ryton'		
23.3	↰	'to Albrighton'		
23.5	⌐►	A464 'to Wolverhampton'		
23.6	⌐►	'to Albrighton'		
24.7	↰	'to Cosford', Albrighton	52°38'6"N	2°16'42"W

CUE CONTINUED			GPS COORDINATES	
25.8	↰	A41 'to Whitchurch'		
26.0	⌐►	Sydnal Lane		
26.4	↰	'to Brewood'		
{29.1	★	Boscobel House}		
	↰	(22yd) unsigned road		
33.4	⌐►	'to Lapley'		
33.7	↰	'to Lapley'		
36.1	⌐►	Whiston 'to Penkridge'		
38.2	⌐►	A449, Penkridge	52°43'32"N	2° 6'57"W
39.0	↰	B5012 'to Cannock'		
40.0	⌐►◎	'to Cannock'		
40.6	⌐►	'to Rugeley'		
42.6	↑	'to Rugeley' (cross A34)		
	▲	1 mile moderate climb		
{44.5	●●⌐►	Cannock Chase visitor centre 4 miles ↺)		
48.2	⌐►↰	'to Uttoxeter' (dogleg)		
53.6	↰	B5013 'to Uttoxeter'		
58.7	⌐►	A518 'to Uttoxeter'		
59.2	↰◎	B5027 'to Stone'		
59.5		Uttoxeter tourist office	52°53'53"N	1°51'57"W

bolted together over the Severn in 1779. The End-to-End ride (see the Land's End to John O'Groats chapter p305) crosses the route here and there's lots to see and do (see Towns & Facilities, Ironbridge p342 for tourist office details).

Bucolic country lanes wend their way to the town of Albrighton and on to **Boscobel House** (29.1 miles; ☎ 01902 850244), this time a romantic 17th-century hunting lodge under the protective wing of English Heritage. It was here in 1651 that Charles II successfully hid from his parliamentary enemies by scarpering up the nearby 'Royal Oak' (a tree, not a pub) before spending an uncomfortable night in the attic priest hole (the house had been used to hide Catholics for the previous two decades).

Stomachs will be rumbling by **Penkridge** (38.2 miles), a good place as any to fill the hole as the town has at least five pubs serving grub. A good intake of carbs is essential as next comes the climb into the forests of **Cannock Chase**, a place well deserving of its status as an 'area of outstanding natural beauty'. The forests here are crisscrossed with tracks ideal for mountain biking. You'll emerge from the greenwood at the medium size town of Rugeley, beyond which the quiet B5013 leads right across the middle of **Blithfield Reservoir** with some

wide-screen watery views opening up on both sides. You can put the map away now as the simple run in to Uttoxeter sticks to the B5013 all the way.

Day 2: Uttoxeter to Copt Oak
2½–4½ hours, 41.1 miles

A short day, where historic buildings and beauty spots crop up time and again in an area where redundant open-cast coalmines have been recycled into the National Forest. Despite the region's dense population the route easily skirts around the big cities and keeps things firmly on the back roads.

The first few miles out from Uttoxeter follow the meanders of the prettily named River Dove. After around half an hour you should roll into Tutbury (9.9 miles) where the ruined turrets of **Tutbury Castle** overlook the river. Run by the Duchy of Lancaster, it's a regular ghoulish venue for ghost hunts and is known as one of the most haunted castles in England.

The route now squeezes its way between the large towns of Burton-on-Trent to the south and Derby to the north to arrive at Ticknall. Along a track from the village stands **Calke Abbey** (22.1 miles; ☎ 01332 863822), which is not an abbey at all, but a flamboyant Baroque mansion known as 'the house time forgot'. Collections and fur-

THROUGH THE MIDLANDS – DAY 2

CUE		GPS COORDINATES
start	Uttoxeter tourist office	52°53'53"N 1°51'57"W
0 miles	go SW on Carter St	
0.3	'to Stoke'	
0.8	B5017 'to Marchington'	
	(22yd) Wood Lane 'to racecourse'	
4.1	Church Lane, Marchington	52°52'26"N 1°47'57"W
6.0	A515/'to Tutbury'	
9.9	Tutbury	52°51'24"N 1°41'10"W
13.9	A38 'to Derby'	
15.5	'to Willington'	
15.8	B5008 'to Willington'	
16.7	B5008 'to Repton', Willington	
17.9	'to Milton', Repton	52°50'23"N 1°33'1"W
22.0	A514 'to Ticknall'	
22.1	Ticknall	52°48'41"N 1°28'52"W
	B5006 'to Ashby'	
23.0	'to Staunton Harold'	
24.4	'to Calke'	

CUE CONTINUED		GPS COORDINATES
25.3	Calke	52°47'50"N 1°27'16"W
26.2	B587 'All major routes'	
27.7	B587 'to Ashby'	
29.8	A511 'to Ashby'	
30.7	'to castle', Ashby de la Zouch	52°44'47"N 1°28'24"W
	castle	
31.2	'to Packington'	
31.8	'to Packington'	
32.5	'to Normanton', Packington	52°43'45"N 1°27'58"W
36.7	'to Ellistown'	
38.3	'to Bardon' (dogleg), Ellistown	52°41'57"N 1°22'3"W
39.5	'to M1/Leicester'	
39.9	B585 'to Coalville'	
40.3	A511 'to M1'	
41.0	B591 'to Shepshed/Copt Oak'	
41.1	Copt Oak	

nishings were kept under dust-sheets for centuries, by an eccentric family, before the National Trust took over in the late 1980s.

Either side of Ticknall extend the reservoirs of Foremark (where there's a cafe) and Staunton Harold (where there's a picnic site en route at 25.7 miles).

Ashby-de-la-Zouch (30.7 miles; pronounced 'zoosh') is the only bona fide town you'll encounter all day. It received its very un-British name from a Breton nobleman who inherited the estate in the 12th century. Top tourist dog here is the English Heritage-run **castle** (☎ 01530 413343), which boasts a distinct and climbable 15th-century tower as well as a network of secret passageways. It was partly dismantled after yielding to siege by the parliamentary forces during the Civil War, hence its ruined state. From here much of the route traverses the **National Forest**, an ambitious land-regeneration project due to mature later this century. Woodland and country parks have been planted for people and wildlife over a rectangular area of 20 miles by 10 miles, stretching from Burton-on-Trent to Charnwood Forest.

The day finishes at Copt Oak (see Central England Towns & Facilities p168) on the edge of Charnwood Forest, a piece of high forest land with rocky outcrops that was barely inhabited until the 19th century. Pedal the 4 miles into Coalville for a wider choice of places to kip and munch.

Day 3: Copt Oak to Oundle
3½–5½ hours, 52.52 miles

This picturesque ride begins with a climb through Charnwood Forest, passes the well-to-do outlying villages of Leicester and explores fine countryside as far as Tilton. There are numerous short (0.5 miles) climbs and descents en route, and a couple of heavy traffic sections. At Rockingham village (36.4 miles) hill and traffic combine, unfortunately at odds with the historic backdrop. Walk your bike if you don't want to struggle uphill with the HGVs.

Having picked your way out of the forest eastbound out of Copt Oak, you're liable to run into traffic as you arc across the top of Leicester. Past Queniborough things quieten down and you enter a sparsely populated area of hills and sheep farms. Somewhere between the villages of Loddington and Belton-in-Rutland your wheels will cross the dividing line twixt Leicestershire and Rutland, England's dinkiest county.

SIDE TRIP: UPPINGHAM & RUTLAND WATER

With time to spare, from Stockerston it's worth diverting 2.9 miles from the route to visit the beautifully atmospheric Rutland sandstone town of **Uppingham**. Well-heeled townsfolk from Leicester and Peterborough flock at weekends to its main street lined with sturdy stone buildings to

THROUGH THE MIDLANDS – DAY 3

CUE		GPS COORDINATES
start	Copt Oak	
0 miles	go N on previous day's route	
0.0	⌐► (44yd) B591 'to Woodhouse Eaves'	
0.5	⌐► 'to Woodhouse Eaves'	
0.8	▲ 1.4 miles moderate climb	
3.5	⌐► 'to Swithland'	
4.6	⌐► 'to Swithland'	
7.7	◄⌐ 'to Cossington'	
8.2	⌐► 'to Cossington', Rothley	52°42'33"N 1°8'12"W
10.3	↑ A607 'to Queniborough'	
16.7	⌐► 'to Baggrave Hall'	
18.3	◄⌐ 'to Cold Newton'	
19.2	⌐► 'to Cold Newton'	
20.6	▲ 0.5 miles hard climb	
22.0	◄⌐ B6047 'to Tilton'	
22.4	⌐► 'to Loddington', Tilton on the Hill	52°38'38"N 0°54'12"W
22.8	◄⌐ 'to Loddington'	
26.5	◄⌐ 'to Launde'	
26.7	⌐► 'to Belton'	
28.8	◄⌐ A47 'to Uppingham'	
29.2	⌐► 'to Allexton'	
29.3	◄⌐ 'to Stockerston'	

CUE CONTINUED		GPS COORDINATES
{ ●●⌐►	Uppingham & Rutland Water 12.8 miles (↻)}	
31.1	◄⌐ 'to Stockerston'	
31.3	⌐► B664 'to Stoke Dry'	
31.9	◄⌐ 'to Great Easton'	
34.3	◄⌐ 'to Great Easton'	
36.4	⌐► A6003 'to Corby'	
37.1	Rockingham	52°31'5"N 0°43'30"W
	▲ 0.5 miles steep climb	
38.0	◄⌐⊙ A6116 'to Corby'	
{ ●●⌐►	Rockingham Castle 0.6 miles (↻)}	
38.1	◄⌐⊙ 'to Stamford'	
39.0	◄⌐ 'to Deene, Kirby Hall'	
40.9	◄⌐ 'to Kirby Hall'	
{41.6 ●●	◄⌐ Kirby Hall 0.5 miles (↻)}	
42.8	⌐► 'to Deene'	
43.7	⌐► A43 'to Corby'	
43.9	◄⌐ 'to Benefield'	
44.3	◄⌐ 'to Benefield', Deenethorpe	52°30'59"N 0°35'27"W
46.7	◄⌐ 'to Oundle'	
{49.5	⌐► 'to Oundle'}	
51.5	⌐► West St (at cross)	
51.52	Oundle tourist office	52°28'50"N 0°28'16"W

peruse well-endowed antique shops and to ponder purchases in numerous little coffee shops. The local Uppingham Independent School is one of the poshest in the Midlands but the exquisite historical interiors are off limits to the prying public (the grounds can be explored).

With quite a bit more time you might kick yourself for missing **Rutland Water**, 3.5 miles beyond Uppingham along the A6003. This man-made reservoir is circled by a rideable path, near many picnic spots.

Another much shorter side trip is to **Rockingham Castle** (38 miles; ☎ 01536 770240) for some living history and cream teas – go right at the roundabout at the top of the hill above Rockingham and the entrance is 100 yards further on the right. The handsome and imposing fortification has guarded the Welland Valley above the village of Rockingham for 900 years. In Tudor times Henry VIII granted it to the ancestor of the family that still lives there today. A 19th-century family friend was none other than Charles Dickens who is thought have based Chesney Wold in the novel *Bleak House* on this stately pile.

A few miles further on is **Kirby Hall** (41.6 miles; ☎ 01536 203230), a stunning Elizabethan stone mansion in the safekeeping of English Heritage. From here just under 10 miles separate you and the end of your Midlands meanderings at Oundle.

PEAK DISTRICT

Duration 2 days
Distance 83.4 miles
Difficulty moderate–demanding
Start Uttoxeter (p180)
Finish Langsett (p172)
Summary Take a ride on England's wild side with this traverse of the country's favourite national park, its steep gradients rewarding cyclists with widescreen views of an inspiringly remote hillscape.

Wending an undulating path south-north across Britain's most popular national park, this is a full-blooded introduction to some of England's wildest and most beautiful upland areas. Although not for the unfit or faint-hearted, the untamed scenery, stone-built villages and easy sections of rail trail complement and relieve the sometimes gruelling ascents. This is a real adventure on two wheels and if this doesn't get your heart thumping, have someone check there's a pulse at all.

Many (even the vast majority of Brits) assume that the Peak District is so called thanks to its peaks – it isn't. Historians think the area takes its name from an Anglo-Saxon tribe, the Peacsaetna, who once lived here. However, one thing is for sure – thanks to its proximity to northern England's population hotspots (Manchester, South and West Yorkshire) it's the busiest national park in Europe and, incredibly, the second busiest in the world after Mt Fuji. But don't let this put you off, as even the bank holiday multitudes easily disperse into this 555-sq-mile of crinkled terrain.

HISTORY

As well as being a playground for cycle tourists and mountain bikers, the Peak District is the nursery of many a pro British racer. Roadies are often spotted on climbs they know like 'the back of their hand'.

The **Tour of the Peak** is an annual pro-am road race, and several steep climbs in the area are venues in the autumn hill climb season. Rounds of the national mountain bike series have been held beside Redmires Reservoir near Sheffield.

ENVIRONMENT

The Peak National Park is an area of high land riven by deep dales with the conurbations of Manchester and Sheffield running hard against its flanks. It divides into distinct geological halves: the southern limestone White Peak dominated by grazing and quarrying, and the harsher northern gritstone Dark Peak, a glowering high moorland.

PLANNING
When to Cycle

Providing you wear good weatherproof gear, the skies and frosts of the autumn and winter months can be thrilling. In spring and summer things are mellower but a spot of rain in the valley can mean a storm on the top. Always be prepared for bad weather and seek shelter in a dale village if in doubt.

Weekends are busy with visitors from the cities, but during the summer weeks the peaks are quieter than the coastal resorts.

What to Bring

In good weather carry waterproofs, water and snacks (pubs and village shops get a little 'thin on the ground'). In winter the peaks can get snowed in, so in bad weather carry emergency clothing and rations.

Maps

Recommended maps for general route planning include the OS Travelmap – Road 1:250,000 *Northern England* (sheet 4), *East Midlands & East Anglia* (sheet 5) and *Wales and West Midlands* (sheet 6). For more detailed overviews of the peak district be sure to get your hands on OS Explorer – Active 1:25,000 *Dark Peak Area* (sheet 1) and *White Peak Area* (sheet 24).

Cycle Hire

Derwent Cycle Hire (☎ 01433 651261; Fairholmes Car Park, Derwent, Bamford) **Parsley Hay** (☎ 01298 84493; Parsley Hay, Buxton) **Ashbourne Cycle Hire** (☎ 01335 343156; Mapleton Lane, Ashbourne) will be more than happy to lend you one of their bikes on which to hurtle round the Peak District. All three charge around £12 to £17 an adult per day for mountain or touring bike and you'll need to show photo ID.

Information Sources

The **Peak District & Derbyshire Tourist Board** (☎ 01298 25106; www.visitpeakdistrict.com) collects and disseminates information on the wider region, while the **Peak District National Park Authority** (www.peakdistrict.org) sits upon a veritable mine of meticulously compiled visitor information.

GETTING TO/FROM THE RIDE
Uttoxeter (start)

TRAIN

Trains run regularly to Uttoxeter from Derby (£8.30; 22 minutes, hourly) and from Crewe (£6.80; 50 minutes, hourly), which both enjoy frequent connections to London and Scotland. **East Midlands Trains** (www.eastmidlandstrains.co.uk) on this route (Derby to Crewe) carry bikes free of charge.

BICYCLE

Uttoxeter is the start of Day 2 on the Through the Midlands ride (p141), earlier in this chapter

CENTRAL ENGLAND

PEAK DISTRICT

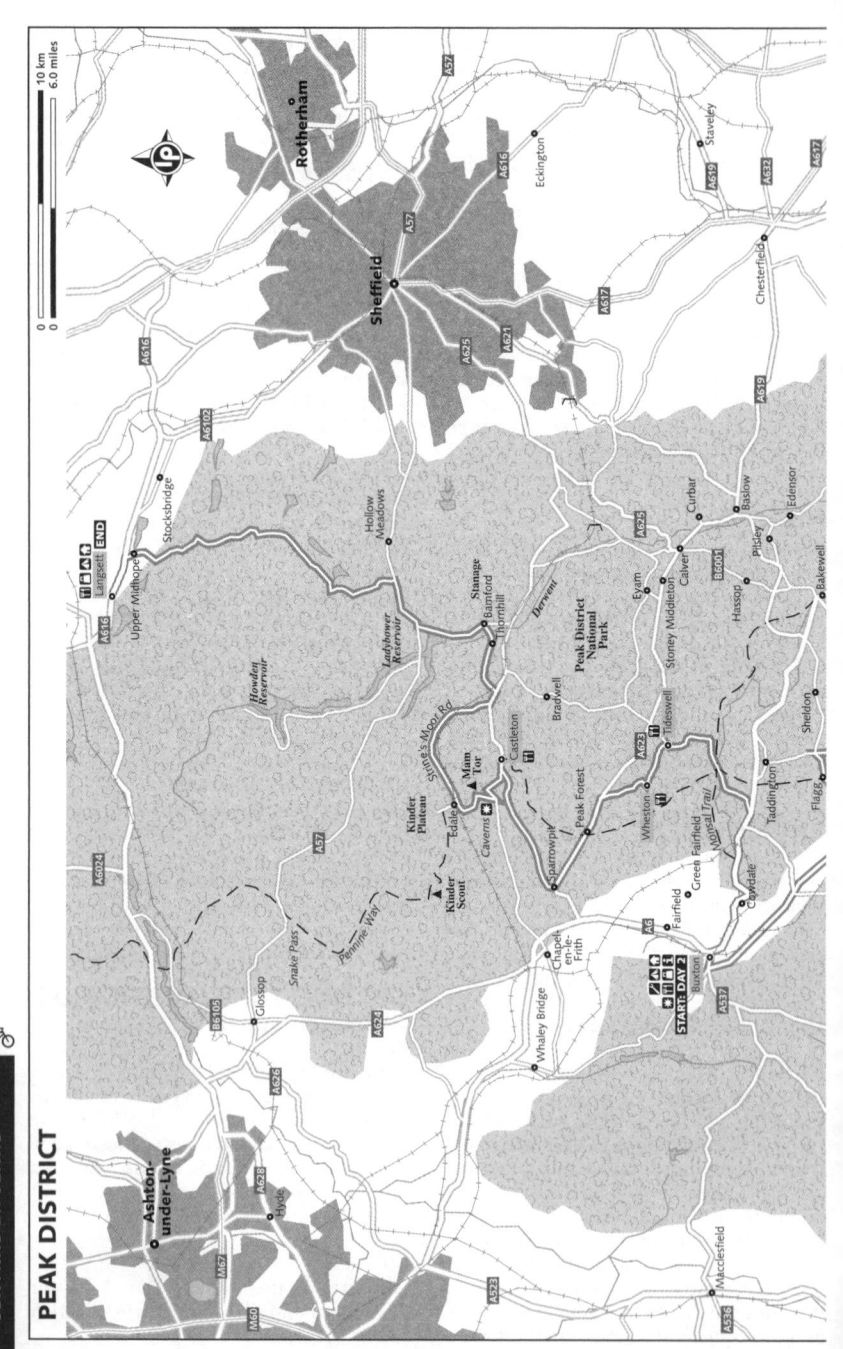

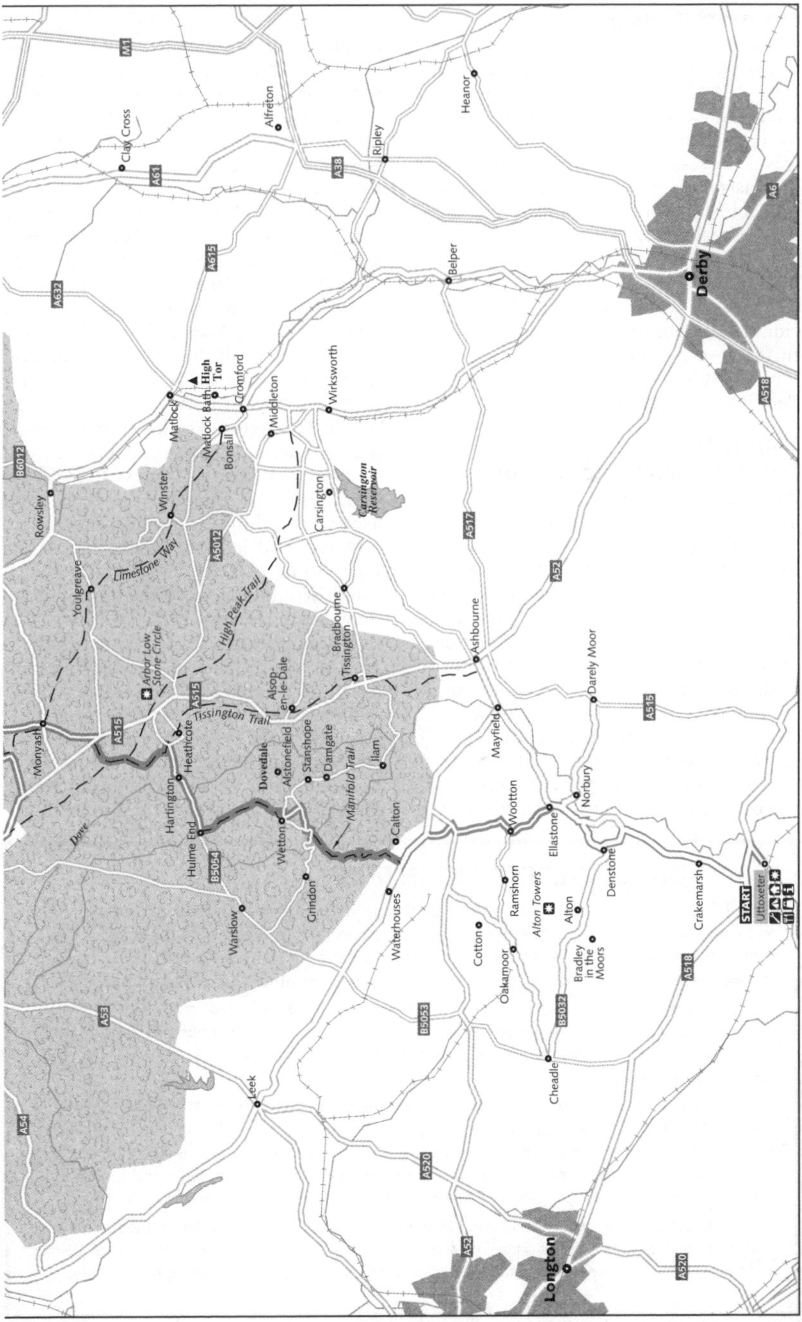
M1
Clay Cross
A61
Alfreton
A38
Ripley
Heanor
A632
A615
Belper
Derby
A6
A518
High Tor
Matlock
Matlock Bath
Cromford
Middleton
Wirksworth
Bonsall
B6012
Rowsley
Winster
A5012
Carsington
Carsington Reservoir
Youlgreave
Limestone Way
High Peak Trail
Arbor Low Stone Circle
A517
A52
Bradbourne
Tissington
Alsop-en-le-Dale
Ashbourne
Darely Moor
Monyash
A515
Heathcote
Tissington Trail
Hartington
Dovedale
Alstonefield
Stanshope
Damgate
Manifold Trail
Ilam
Mayfield
Norbury
Dove
Hulme End
B5054
Wetton
Calton
Wootton
Ellastone
Grindon
Waterhouses
Ramshorn
Alton Towers
Alton
Denstone
Crakemarsh
START
Uttoxeter
Warslow
Cotton
Oakamoor
Bradley in the Moors
B5032
A518
A53
B5053
Cheadle
Leek
A54
A520
A52
Longton

Langsett (finish)

TRAIN

Trains run from Penistone to Sheffield (£4.10, 45 minutes, hourly) and Huddersfield (£4.20, 34 minutes, hourly) for connections all over the country. Bikes travel free on **Northern Trains** (www .northernrail.org) with two to three spaces available on each service and a 'first come first served' policy.

BICYCLE

To link up with the Central Explorer ride (p120), continue from Langsett for a further (very strenuous and quite unenjoyable) 40 miles northwards through the Pennines to Keighley

THE RIDE
Day 1: Uttoxeter to Buxton

2½–4 hours, 39.82 miles

The first day may be short on miles but it's certainly big on stunning scenery, fascinating rail trails, hilly terrain and general adventure. This route reveals the sheer beauty of the southern Peak District and whets the appetite for Day 2. The roads undulate increasingly and the hills require a sturdy push on the pedals. Take care on the short sections of A-roads, particularly at the A523 at the right turn into the Manifold Trail (if you choose to ride on the road).

Warm up on the roads north of Uttoxeter for the trip's first challenge, the short but steep ascent of Weaver Hills. You may have come to this corner of the UK for the untamed solitude of the Peak District, but no one can pass this way without being aware of the irresistible pull of **Alton Towers**, the country's largest theme park – 4 miles west of Ellastone (8.3 miles). Ignoring the temptation to take rides of a different sort, turn off the A523 at Waterhouses to join the scenic 8 miles of the **Manifold Trail**, a rail trail that runs through the steep-sided Manifold Valley and one of the first disused lines to be converted in the 1930s. The fast-flowing Manifold River keeps the track company all the way to Hulme End (22.9 miles). Get ready for a climb past pretty Hartington to the final open stretch of the **Tissington Trail**, another disused railway line, which runs to Ashbourne. In its heyday, it carried express trains from Manchester to London. However, you leave this behind at Parsley Hay where a lonely road leads a mile to the **Arbor Low Stone Circle**, a Neolithic henge comprised of a circle of weathered white limestone blocks and one of Derbyshire's most significant prehistoric sites. If the weather is playing ball, this can be a scenic diversion for a picnic lunch among the stones.

This is true White Peak country, a landscape of green fields, dry-stone walls and ever-changing skies. Make the most of it while enduring more pedal pushing after Monyash before the descent into Buxton.

MAM TOR: 'SHIVERING MOUNTAIN'

Mam Tor (514m/1695ft), some say, is like a battlefield where man has clashed with nature and come off second best. Below the mountain's eastern face, to the right of the route, is the collapsed road, the twisted and broken remnants of what once was the A625, its craggy steps striking evidence of landslips, which have earned the peak its other name, 'Shivering Mountain'.

The road was originally built in 1817 as an alternative to the 20% gradient of Winnats Pass, which climbs out of the Hope Valley nearby. But the weathering of the mountain is a continual process, and after countless repairs the boys from the black stuff gave up in 1979 and the road was left to its fate.

The landslides are caused by the unstable combination of Edale Shales at the base of the cliff and Millstone Grits above which can be seen protruding from the face. In the wet, the shales revert to their original muddy form and unseat the sandstones and gritstones. This mix was also responsible for the great crash that exposed Mam Tor's face way back in geological time. The debris can be seen in the uneven land that spreads out over half a mile from the cliff base.

The ramparts of the breezy but impregnable 5th-century BC Iron Age Hillfort on the summit have also been damaged by slippage. The site commands one of the best views of the Peak District, and humanity's job there is to maintain the path against hiking boots as much as rolling rocks.

PEAK DISTRICT –DAY 1

CUE		GPS COORDINATES	CUE		GPS COORDINATES
start	Uttoxeter tourist office	52°53'53"N 1°51'57"W	13.7	lane before main road (A523)	
0 miles	go NE on Carter St		14.7	A523 (stay on pavement)	
0.1	Market Place		14.8	Manifold Way	
0.2	Bridge St/Church St/Dove Bank		21.4	after tunnel on small road	
0.3	Town Meadows Way		22.9	B5054, Hulme End	53° 7'51"N 1°50'51"W
1.0	B5030 'to Rocester'		24.7	unsigned road, Hartington	53° 8'26"N 1°48'35"W
2.0	'to Crakemarsh'			1 mile moderate climb	
3.5	unsigned road, Combridge		26.5	Tissington Trail	
4.3	unsigned road (at letterbox)			(100m) go N on bikepath	
5.1	'to Denstone'		28.5	rejoin unsigned road (dogleg)	
6.2	unsigned road, Denstone	52°57'53"N 1°51'28"W	28.6	A515/'to Monyash' (dogleg)	
6.3	'to Ashbourne'		31.6	'to Flagg'	
6.4	'to Ellastone'		33.2	'to Chelmorton'	
6.7	'to Prestwood'		35.0	A5270 'to Buxton'	
8.0	'to Wootton'		36.0	A515 'to Buxton'	
8.7	unsigned road			(200yd) B5053/'to Harpur Hill'	
9.1	'to Weaver Hills', Wootton	53° 0'10"N 1°50'31"W	37.2	'Heathfield Nook'	
9.9	'to Weaver Hills' (easy to miss)		37.7	A515 'to Buxton'	
10.4	1 mile steep climb		39.7	Market Place/Hall Bank	
12.1	A52 (no sign)		39.8	The Crescent	
12.8	unsigned road		39.82	Buxton tourist office	53°15'33"N 1°54'50"W

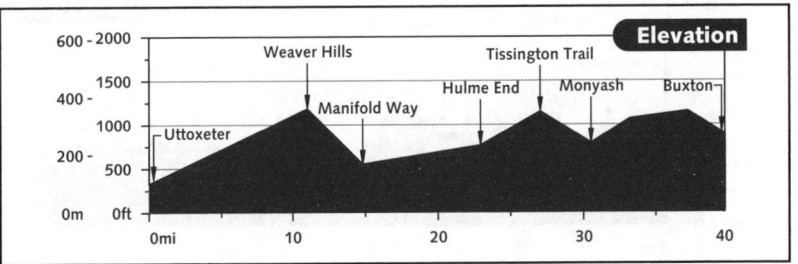

Elevation chart. Labelled points: Uttoxeter, Weaver Hills, Manifold Way, Hulme End, Tissington Trail, Monyash, Buxton. Vertical axis in metres (0m–600) and feet (0ft–2000); horizontal axis 0mi–40.

Day 2: Buxton to Langsett
3–4½ hours, 43.6 miles

Beyond any doubt, this is an adventurous day's cycling, with lots of strenuous climbing rewarded by exhilarating descents and jawdroppingly gorgeous views. The major climbs come out of Buxton, Miller's Dale, up to Mam Tor and along the glorious **Strine's Moor Rd**. 'Strines' is hallowed in local cycling lore – it has three steep sections and saves the biggest for last. Major descents include the 183m (600ft) drop from Mam Tor into Edale and hell-for-leather altitude losses on Strines. With all that climbing, you can afford to take the day steady as the distance is not great and there are cafes and pubs aplenty – these come in the first half of the day at Tideswell, Edale and Hope.

The first 7.6 miles of the day are about getting back into the **Peak District National Park** and the climbs out of Buxton and up to Wormhill.

SIDE TRIP: LITTON MILL

At 7.6 miles take a right turn into Miller's Dale to visit Litton Mill, a water powered cloth factory set up by Needham and Frith in 1782. Locating a mill in a remote valley where there was no workforce or raw materials was possibly not the best business plan the bank manager had ever seen, and they gradually went bankrupt in a bid to stay afloat they employed child paupers from the surrounding parishes, and one of these was Robert Blincoe whose life as a child labourer was published in 1832 as *The Memoirs of Robert Blincoe*. It's thought Dickens may

PEAK DISTRICT –DAY 2

CUE			GPS COORDINATES	
start		Buxton tourist office	53°15'33"N	1°54'50"W
0 miles		go E on The Crescent		
0.1	⌐↑⌐	Spring Gardens (dogleg)		
0.6	↑◉	A6/Bakewell Rd		
0.6	↰◉	A6 'to Stockport'		
1.1	⌐↑	Waterswallows Rd 'to Wormhill'		
1.6	▲	3 miles hard climb		
2.2	⌐↑	'to Wormhill'		
7.6		Miller's Dale	53°15'21"N	1°47'38"W
{	●●↰	Litton Mill 3 miles (↺) }		
8.0	▲	1 mile moderate climb		
9.9	↰↑	'to Wheston', Tideswell	53°16'36"N	1°46'28"W
10.1	↰↑	'to Wheston'		
11.6	⌐↑	'to Peak Forest', Wheston	53°17'3"N	1°48'8"W
12.9	↰↑	A623 'to Stockport'		
13.9	⌐↑	'to Perryfoot', Peak Forest	53°18'36"N	1°49'51"W
15.6	⌐↑	unsigned road		
	▲	1 mile moderate climb		
17.7	↰↑	'to Chapel-en-le-Frith'		

CUE CONTINUED			GPS COORDINATES	
{	★	caverns}		
{17.9	●●⌐↑	destroyed road 1 mile (↺)}		
18.4	⌐↑	'to Edale'		
	▲	2 miles steep climb		
18.7	⚠▲	1.5 miles steep descent		
25.8	↰↑	unsigned road, Hope	53°20'53"N	1°44'33"W
25.9	↰↑	'to Aston'		
	▲	1 mile steep climb		
27.9	↰↑	'to Ladybower', Thornhill	53°20'55"N	1°42'18"W
29.4	↰↑	A6013 'to Glossop'		
30.3	⌐↑	A57 'to Sheffield'		
	▲	1.5 miles moderate climb		
32.0	↰↑	'to Strines Moor'		
34.5	▲	1 mile steep climb		
37.5	▲	1 mile steep climb		
39.0	▲	1 mile hard climb		
40.6	↰↑⚠	unsigned road (easy to miss)		
42.6	↰↑	'to Langsett'		
43.5	↰↑	A616		
43.6		Langsett	53°30'1"N	1°40'52"W

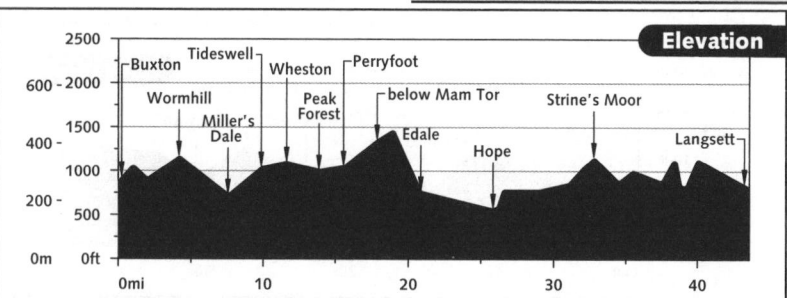

have based Oliver Twist on the real-life Blincoe. Litton Mill has now been converted into posh apartments and holiday accommodation, but it's still worth a look.

From Miller's Dale it's a hard uphill slog for almost 10 miles to just below **Mam Tor** (see the boxed text Mam Tor: 'Shivering Mountain' p150). Here you can dismount to take a tour of one of the spectacular if sometimes claustrophobic caverns – the **Blue John** (☎ 01433 620638), the **Treak Cliff** (☎ 01433 620571) or the **Speedwell** (☎ 01433 620638). This is also the best place on today's route to call a lunch halt.

Just after Mam Tor you can turn off to see the wrecked A625 (see the boxed text' p150). From here it's a brake-block smouldering freewheel drop to the village of Hope, which will hopefully rest your

legs for Strines. The day ends with a descent into Langsett, and you should take care with traffic coming in to the finish as the route uses the busy main road between Manchester and Sheffield.

A COTSWOLDS TRIANGLE

Duration 4 days
Distance 195 miles
Difficulty moderate
Start Jordans (p171)
Finish Oxford (p175)

Summary Stratford's Shakespeare, Oxford's Blenheim and Cirencester's Romans form the three historical corners of this chiefly gentle jaunt through England's most affluent hill country.

Ducks dabbling in the village ford and aged cottages glowing in the afternoon sun, rich cream teas in every town and monster 4WDs on the school run – the Cotswolds is England at its most persistently quaint and subtly well-to-do. This ancient hill country with its toffee-coloured limestone villages and sheep dotting the verdant landscape is chocolate-box Britannia, an understated vision of England many city-dwellers never see. Few can blame celebrities from Liz Hurley to Rolling Stone Brian Jones seeking out this corner of rural bliss far from the London paparazzi's cameras.

Starting in Buckinghamshire, this route crosses the ridges of the Chilterns and drops to the university town of Oxford. Thereafter it becomes a triangle, exploring the countryside and towns en route to Cirencester and Stratford-upon-Avon and returning through Oxfordshire. In an alternately gentle and wild landscape lie some of the south's quaintest villages, the majority proudly cared for and preserved by conservation orders.

'Where there's muck there's brass goes' the English saying, and the Cotswolds farm-to-field roads are lined with the stuff (muck that is) so take care after rain.

ENVIRONMENT

The Cotswold Hills form a wedge of upland that slopes up from the east in Oxfordshire to peak at 300m (1000ft) in the west at an escarpment above Cheltenham in Gloucestershire. As the land rises countless minor river valleys cut deep shafts into the Jurassic limestone and sandstone from which the honey-coloured villages are built. The area became prosperous in the Middle Ages when wool from Cotswolds sheep was a prized commodity throughout Europe. Many of the most charming cottages were originally for weavers, who diverted streams for processing fleeces, to run past their doorways. Production in the area continues to this day, though it's only just commercially viable due to rock bottom wool prices.

The Chiltern Hills of Day 1 are a chalk ridge cloaked in magnificent beech woods, with a rich history stretching back to Roman times. They can also be enjoyed by walkers on a long-distance walking route called the Ridgeway Path.

PLANNING
When to Cycle

The adage 'Stow-on-the-Wold, where the wind blows cold' says it all really – in winter the high Cotswolds are exposed. However, riding any other time of year here is enjoyable, and spring and summer are best when the countryside and villages burst forth in blossom.

Maps

Predeparture, arm yourself with the OS Travelmap – Road 1:250,000 *South East England* (sheet 8), which shows the region in ample detail.

Information Sources

The **Cotswolds District Council** (☎ 01451 831082; tourism@cotswold.gov.uk; Trinity Rd, Cirencester) produce an annual guide to the area called *The Cotswold Visitor Guide*.

GETTING TO/FROM THE RIDE
Jordans (start)
TRAIN

Seer Green station is 1 mile away on the London Marylebone-Bicester line (£7.30; 30 minutes, half-hourly). Go east (right) from the station for 0.75 miles and then left at the junction into Jordans. To reach High Wycombe, trains from London Marylebone are fast and frequent (£9.50; 30-50 minutes, half-hourly). Both lines are operated by **Chiltern Trains** (www.chilternrailways .co.uk) and bikes are carried free of charge in the passenger carriages during off-peak periods.

BICYCLE

By starting from Jordans you get to explore the pleasant wooded Chiltern Hills and the winding River Thames before embarking on the Cotswolds. However it is possible to start the ride at High Wycombe (8 miles from Jordans), which has a greater number of transport connections and places to stay. To pick up the route (3.5 miles away) take the A404 from High Wycombe south towards Marlow. At the A40 motorway roundabout take the A4010 Aylesbury Rd that exits the High Wycombe side of the motorway and follow that past the John Lewis store. Go left at the next mini-roundabout and continue, crossing over the motorway to the B482. Pick up the route there (next cue 16.9 miles).

CENTRAL ENGLAND

A COTSWOLDS TRIANGLE

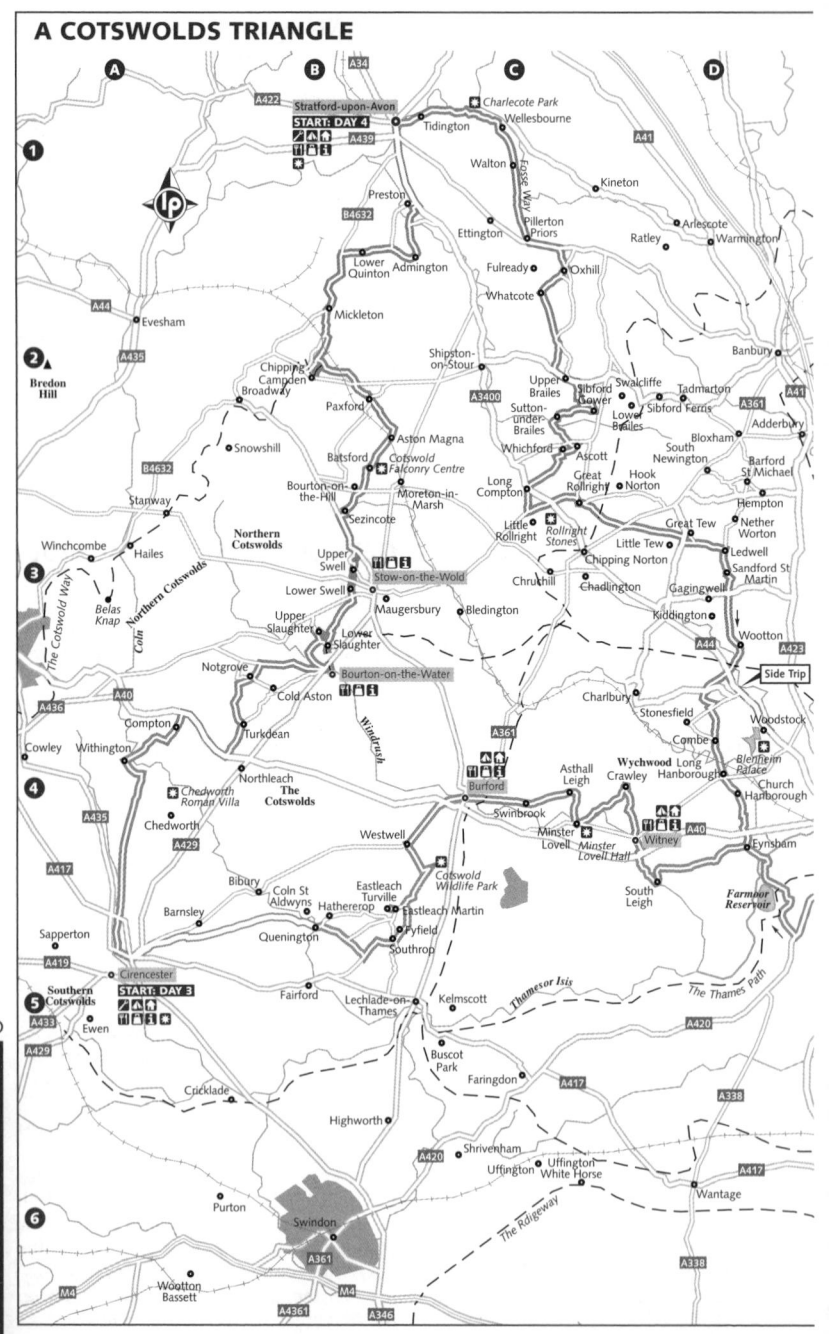

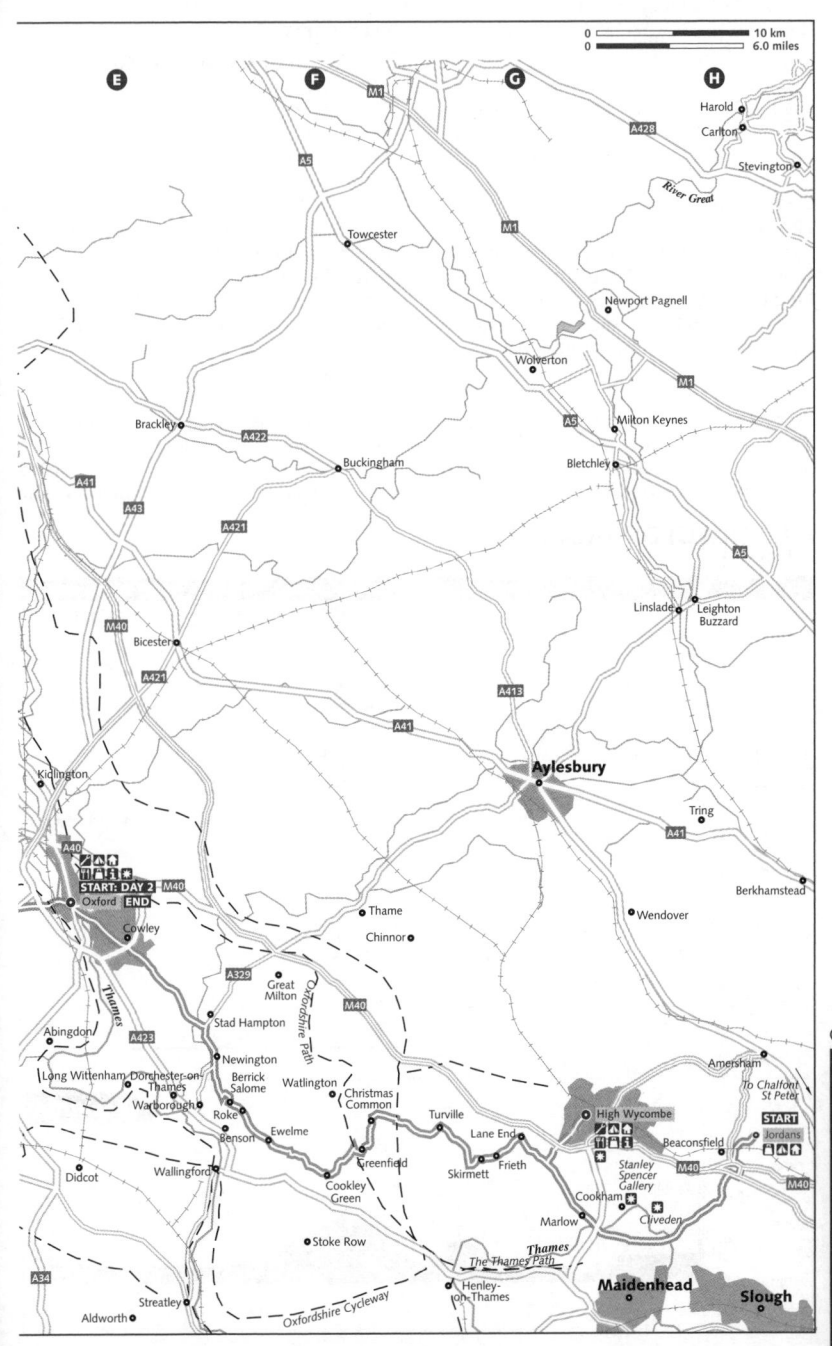

To ride the 25 miles from central London follow the A4020 (Marble Arch, Notting Hill, Shepherds Bush, Ealing, Southall, Hayes, Hillingdon, Uxbridge) to Denham, then join the A40, continue to Gerrards Cross, and turn right 2.5 miles beyond to Jordans.

Oxford (finish)
TRAIN
Oxford lies on the London Paddington-Worcester line (£22.50, one hour, hourly). **First Great Western** (www.firstgreatwestern.co.uk) allow bikes to be carried free in passenger carriages during off-peak periods.

BICYCLE
To cycle back to London, just do the first day of this ride only from finish to start then reverse the cycling route from London to Jordans as described above.

THE RIDE
Day 1: Jordans to Oxford
3–5 hours, 45.3 miles
This day strikes out through a handsome wooded landscape over the hills into Oxfordshire and the county town of Oxford. Be prepared for steep ups and downs, and even the odd hairpin bend as you traverse the Chiltern Ridge, climbing and descending to cross the twisting Thames at pretty Cookham (8.5 miles) and at Marlow with its flamboyant bridge. The final effort ascends from Turville to an altitude of 240m (800ft) at Christmas Common. Following a cruise downhill, you reach Oxfordshire.

Start the day by leaving the hushed prosperity of Jordans, perhaps saying hi to local Ozzy Osbourne as he heads to the village shopk. No sooner is the raging M40 behind you than you arrive at the day's first stop, the

A COTSWOLDS TRIANGLE – DAY 1

CUE			GPS COORDINATES	
start		Jordans YHA	51°36'34"N	0°35'35"W
0 miles		go W on unsigned road		
0.1	↰	Welders Lane		
1.1	↱	A40 'to High Wycombe'		
1.8	↰⊙	A355 'to Slough'		
2.6	↱	'to Burnham'		
3.8	↑	'to Littleworth Common'		
4.8	↱	'to Wooburn'		
5.1	↰	Heathfield Rd		
6.2	↱	'to Hedsor'		
{	★	Cliveden House}		
7.3	↰	'to Cookham'		
7.7	↰	A4094 'to Marlow'		
8.5	★	Cookham	51°33'44"N	0°42'21"W
	↱	'to Cookham Dean'		
12.0	↱	'to Marlow'		
12.2		Marlow		
12.4	↱	'to Bourne End'		
12.5	↰	B482 'to Lane End'		
16.9	↰	'to Frieth', Lane End	51°37'8"N	0°50'3"W

CUE CONTINUED			GPS COORDINATES	
19.6	↱	unsigned road, Skirmett	51°36'8"N	0°52'50"W
20.4	↰	'to Turville'		
21.0		Turville	51°36'49"N	0°53'34"W
22.4	▲	3.7 miles moderate climb		
24.7	↰	'to N'bed', Christmas Common	51°38'1"N	0°58'7"W
26.5	↱↰	B480/B481 (dogleg)		
27.2	↱	'to Ewelme', Cookley Green		
30.1	↱	'to Ewelme'		
30.8	↱	'to Benson', Ewelme	51°37'8"N	1° 4'15"W
32.2	↱	'to Berrick Salome'		
35.2	↱	A329 'to Stadhampton'		
37.0	↰	B480 'to Oxford'		
44.2	↑	High St 'to city centre'		
44.9	↑	Queen St		
45.1	↱	New Inn Hall St		
45.2	↰	George St		
45.3	↱	alley to bus station		
45.3		Oxford tourist office	51°45'14"N	1°15'26"W

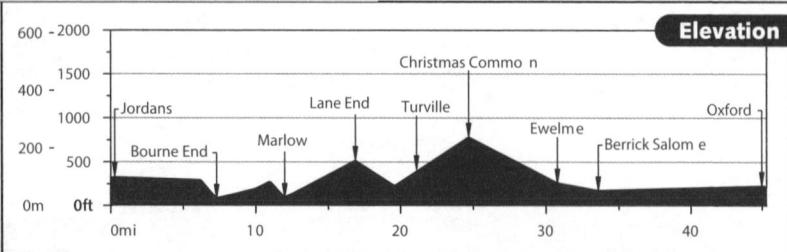

Elevation

Christmas Commo n

Lane End   Turville
Jordans

Ewelme
Marlow

Oxford
Bourne End
Berrick Salom e

600 - 2000

1500

400 -
1000

200 -
500

0m   0ft

0mi   10   20   30   40

stately National Trust property of **Cliveden** (☎ 01494 755562). Set on a scarp (steep hillside face) above the River Thames this country pile once belonged to the wealthy political Anglo-American Astor family. The building itself is now a hotel but the grounds and gardens are open for the public to admire. Just down the road in Cookham, drop into the **Stanley Spencer Gallery** (☎ 01628 471885; High St, Cookham) where works by this local 20th-century English painter, renowned for his images of the world wars, are exhibited.

With the medium-size town of Marlow a memory, you enter the Chilterns where things get hilly in the shape of two quite sharp ascents before the delightfully named Christmas Common (a local joke goes that here it's Christmas every day). Stop here for a pub lunch at the **Fox & Hounds** (☎ 01491 612599) where the sandwich menu is ideal for famished velocipedists. From here it's easy riding along the relatively traffic-free B480 into Oxford.

Day 2: Oxford to Cirencester
3–4½ hours, 43.4 miles

Today has all the right elements for a quintessential day out in the Cotswolds, though

most of the ups and downs in the road are over quite quickly. Be prepared for overtaking Land Rovers on minor roads, and don't underestimate the speed of oncoming traffic when crossing the A40 at Burford and approaching the finish at Cirencester.

The hills will suddenly envelope you beyond Witney in the valley of the River Windrush. The roads become narrow and views of the exposed downs, dry-stone walls and farmland contrast with the cosy buildings nestling in the dips. Just 2 miles northwest of Witney stands **Minster Lovell Hall**, an impressive 15th-century manor house, which now stands in ruins

After around two hours you should reach the handsome High St of **Burford**, more or less the halfway point of today's ride and a natural midday halt. After a quick lunch in any of the cafes and pubs here, visit the town's tourist office (☎ 01993 823558 The Brewery, Sheep St), peruse the antique shops and take a bit of a breather before hitting the road again.

Beyond Burford, the **Cotswold Wildlife Park** (☎ 01993 823006) just over a mile southeast of Westwell is well worth a stop if you have time. Hundreds of animal species from all corners of the globe occupy

A COTSWOLDS TRIANGLE – DAY 2

CUE		GPS COORDINATES		CUE CONTINUED		GPS COORDINATES	
start	Oxford tourist office	51°45'14"N	1°15'26"W	18.3	↰ 'to Swinbrook'		
0 miles	go W on Gloucester Green			20.1	↰ unsigned T-junction		
0.0	↰ (22yd) Worcester St/Hythe Bridge St			20.3	↱ 'to Burford'		
0.2	↑ A420 Botley Rd			22.6	★ Burford	51°48'27"N	1°38'12"W
3.1	↱ B4017 'to Eynsham'				↰↱ A361 to 'tourist office' (dogleg)		
3.6	↱ 'to Eynsham'			22.7	↰ Tanners Lane		
5.7	↰ 'to Eynsham'			23.1	↱ A40 (use footpath)		
7.2	cross toll bridge (free)			23.2	↰ 'to Westwell'		
7.4	↰⊙ 'to Stanton Harcourt'			24.9	↱ 'to Aldsworth', Westwell	51°47'18"N	1°40'31"W
7.9	↰⊙ 'to Stanton Harcourt'			27.0	↰ 'to Fyfield, Southrop'		
9.3	↰ 'to Witney'			28.5	↱ unsigned crossroad		
10.6	South Leigh	51°46'33"N	1°26'1"W	29.1	↰ 'to Southrop', Eastleach Martin		
11.1	↰ 'to Witney'			{ ●●↑ Eastleach Turville 0.5 miles ↺}			
12.2	↰ 'to Witney'			30.4	↱ 'to Southrop'		
13.5	↰⊙ B4022 'to Crawley', Witney			30.7	↑ 'to Fairford', Southrop	51°43'47"N	1°42'43"W
	↱⊙ (50yd) B4022 'to Charlbury'			32.3	↱ 'to Macaroni Woods'		
13.8	↑⊙ 'to Crawley'			40.5	↰ B4425 'to Cirencester'		
15.1	Crawley	51°48'21"N	1°30'24"W	42.9	↑ follow 'to town centre' signs		
15.6	↰ 'to Burford'			43.2	↱ South Way 'to tourist info'		
16.8	★ Minster Lovell	51°47'49"N	1°32'44"W	43.3	↰ Dyer St (QA House)		
17.1	↱ unsigned road (T-junction)			43.4	Cirencester tourist office	51°43'0"N	1°58'1"W
17.3	↰ 'to Asthall Leigh'						

160 acres around Bradwell Grove manor house. Rhinos replace Cotswolds sheep here to crop the lawns and there's even a penguin enclosure.

Continue another 4.2 miles through peaceful farmland to the village duo of **Eastleach Martin** and **Eastleach Turville**. Here only a clapper bridge across the River Leach separates their respective parish churches. Finish the day on Akeman St, a 2000-year-old stretch of Roman road, which runs almost dead straight into the Roman town of Cirencester.

Day 3: Cirencester to Stratford-upon-Avon
3½–5½ hours, 51.4 miles

Riding north along the fat end of the Cotswolds wedge means numerous steep climbs and descents across valleys that

A COTSWOLDS TRIANGLE – DAY 3

CUE			GPS COORDINATES
start		Cirencester tourist office	51°43'0"N 1°58'1"W
0 miles		go W on Market Place	
0.0	⌐→	(100yd) Dollar St (by church)	
0.4	▲	7.5 miles gradual climb	
9.2		Withington	51°50'19"N 1°57'23"W
9.3	⌐→	'to Compton Abdale'	
11.6		Compton Abdale	51°50'51"N 1°54'48"W
12.9	↰	'to Hazleton'	
13.2	⌐→	A40 'to Oxford'	
14.5	↰	'Unsuitable for goods vehicles'	
15.7	↰	'to Notgrove'	
	▲	1 mile moderate climb	
17.8	⌐→	'to Notgrove'	
18.3	⌐→	'to Cold Aston'	
18.5	↰	'to Bourton'	
18.8	⌐→	'to Ford' (after crossing A436)	
20.3	↑	ford the River Windrush	
20.4	⌐→	unsigned road (not B4068)	
	▲	0.5 miles moderate climb	
21.7	⌐→	'to Bourton'	
22.0	↰	'to Upper Slaughter'	
22.5	⌐→	'to Lower Slaughter'	
{	●●↰	Upper Slaughter 0.6 miles (↻) }	
23.3	↰	unsigned road, Lower Slaughter	51°54'6"N 1°45'48"W
{	●●⌐→	Bourton-on-the-Water 2 miles (↻) }	
25.3	⌐→ ↰	'to Upper Swell' (dogleg), Lower Swell	51°55'41"N 1°44'55"W
{	●●↑	Stow-on-the-Wold 2 miles (↻) }	

CUE CONTINUED			GPS COORDINATES
	⌐→	(30yd) 'to Upper Swell'	
26.3	↰	B4077 'to Ford'	
	⌐→	(30yd) 'to Donington Brewery'	
27.0	⌐→	'to Broadway'	
	↰	(30yd) 'to Broadway'	
27.3	↰	A424 'to Eavesham'	
28.0	⌐→	'to Sezincote'	
28.2	↰	'to Sezincote'	
30.2	↰	A44 'to Evesham'	
30.4	⌐→	'to Paxford'	
30.6	⌐→	'to Aston Magna'	
32.3	↰	'to Aston Magna', Batsford	52° 0'10"N 1°43'45"W
33.5	⌐→	'to Warwick', Aston Magna	52° 1'9"N 1°42'48"W
33.8	↰	'to Paxford'	
35.6	⌐→	unsigned road, Paxford	52°2'18"N 1°43'56"W
35.8	↰	'to Chipping Campden'	
36.6	↰	B4035 'to Chipping Campden'	
38.1	↰	unsigned one way road	
38.3	⌐→	B4081, Chipping Campden	52°3'7"N 1°46'42"W
39.2	⌐→	'to Mickleton'	
41.1	⌐→	B4632, Mickleton	52°5'21"N 1°46'4"W
41.7	⌐→	'to Ilmington'	
43.2	↰	'to Quinton'	
44.6	⌐→	'to Admington'	
45.3	↰	'to Preston'	
47.3	⌐→	'to Stratford'	
48.0	↰	A3400 'to Stratford'	
51.1	↰	'to town centre'	
51.4		Stratford tourist office	52°11'33"N 1°42'9"W

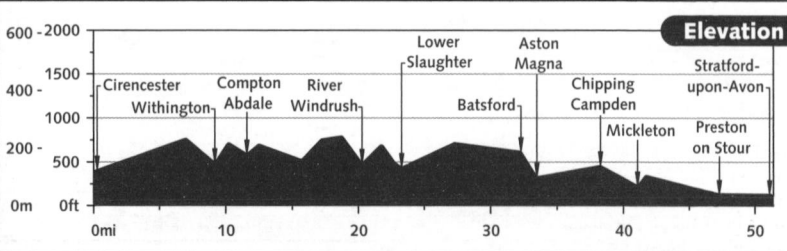

Elevation

Cirencester — Withington — Compton Abdale — River Windrush — Lower Slaughter — Aston Magna — Batsford — Chipping Campden — Mickleton — Stratford-upon-Avon — Preston on Stour

A COTSWOLDS TRIANGLE – DAY 4

CUE		GPS COORDINATES
start	Stratford tourist office	52°11'33"N 1°42'9"W
0 miles	go E 'to Tiddington'	
0.1	B4086 'to Tiddington'	
1.2	'to Wellesbourne', Tiddington	52°12'0"N 1°40'39"W
4.7	A429 'to Stow'	
5.0	'to Walton'	
5.3	'to Walton'	
5.4	'to Walton'	
6.8	unsigned road, Walton	52°10'35"N 1°35'2"W
9.1	'to Pillerton'	
9.3	'to Pillerton Priors'	
10.5	unsigned road, Pillerton Priors	52°7'37"N 1°34'24"W
10.6	A422 'to Stratford'	
10.9	'to Stow'	
	(20yd) unsigned road	
11.9	'to Whatcote', Fulready	52°7'8"N 1°35'41"W
13.4	'to Brailes', Whatcote	52°5'56"N 1°33'50"W
17.0	B4035 'to Banbury', Upper Brailes	52°3'32"N 1°33'29"W
17.1	'to Sutton, Stourton'	
18.5	'to Stourton' Sutton-under-Brailes	52°2'2"N 1°33'46"W
19.1	'to Whichford', Stourton	52°1'43"N 1°34'7"W
	(30yd) 'to Whichford'	
19.5	'to Long Compton'	
	0.5 miles steep climb	
20.9	'to Long Compton'	
21.8	dangerous bend on junction	
22.2	'to Woodstock', Long Compton	51°59'34"N 1°34'56"W
23.0	'to Little Rollright'	
23.2	1 mile climb	
23.8	'to Little Rollright'	
24.1	'to Rollright Stones'	
{24.4	Rollright Stones}	

CUE CONTINUED		GPS COORDINATES
24.9	A3400/'to Great Rollright' (dogleg)	
25.7	'to Great Rollright'	
26.1	'to Hook N'ton', Great Rollright	
27.2	'to Chipping Norton'	
27.8	'to Chipping Norton'	
28.0	'to Heythrop'	
28.7	A361 'to Banbury'	
28.9	'to the Tews'	
31.4	'to Ledwell'	
31.6	'to Ledwell'	
33.4	'to Sandford'	
34.4	Sandford St Martin	51°56'10"N 1°23'26"W
34.7	'to Glympton'	
39.0	'to Bletchingdon'	
39.2	'to King's Head Inn', Wootton	51°52'32"N 1°21'52"W
39.3	unsigned road	
40.2	'to Charlbury' (dogleg)	
{	Blenheim Palace 2 miles	
40.7	'to Stonesfield'	
41.8	'to Combe'	
44.1	'to Long Hanborough'	
44.7	Long Hanborough	51°49'27"N 1°23'39"W
44.8	A4095 'to Bicester'	
44.9	'to Church Hanborough'	
46.0	Church Hanborough	
46.4	'to Eynsham'	
48.1	cross A40/B449 'to Standlake' (dogleg)	
48.7	Eynsham	51°46'50"N 1°22'28"W
49.1	B4044 'to toll bridge/Botley'	
53.0	B4044 'to Oxford'	
53.4	A420 'to city centre'	
54.8	dismount & cross Worcester St	
	thru passage to Gloucester Green	
54.9	Oxford tourist office	51°45'14"N 1°15'26"W

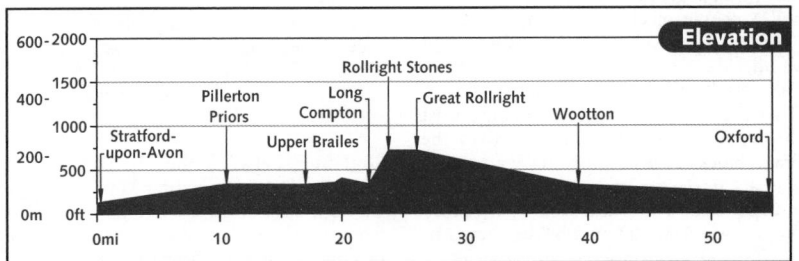

Elevation

Rollright Stones
Pillerton Priors
Long Compton
Great Rollright
Wootton
Stratford-upon-Avon
Upper Brailes
Oxford

600 - 2000
400 - 1500
1000
200 - 500
0m 0ft

0mi   10   20   30   40   50

shelter sleepy villages, several of which can be visited on short side trips. Watch out for high-speed traffic on the A40 (13.2 miles) and a very rough surface on the road down to the River Windrush (20.3 miles).

It's mostly uphill as far as Withington as you push north out of Chichester, so break the climb at **Chedworth Roman Villa** (☎ 01242 890256), a must-see for anyone with a soft spot for things Romano-British.

Located a mile east of the route on the River Coln, it's one of the largest Roman-era villas in the country with unbelievably well preserved mosaic floors and over a mile of walls. The on-site museum exhibits finds made during excavations at the site throughout the 20th century.

The interestingly-titled village of Upper Slaughter is pretty despite its name, and Lower Slaughter has a perfectly preserved line of stone cottages with a babbling brook running past their doorways. Other popular Cotswolds towns such as quaint **Bourton-on-the-Water** and sizable **Stow-on-the-Wold** are also worth short detours off the route and both are great for a lunch stop on your pilgrimage to the Bard. Around half and hour's pedalling north of Stow-on-the-Wold you may want to call a brief halt at Batsford, home to the **Cotswold Falconry Centre** (32.3 miles; ☎ 01386 701043) where you can take a peek at their veritable flock of vultures, owls and hawks.

From Batsford it's a steady run around the base of prominent Meon Hill (41.7 miles) to Stratford-upon-Avon. As you cross the River Avon into Stratford, glimpse the water frontage of the **Royal Shakespeare Theatre** on the left, where performances of the Bard's plays take place most days of the week. In the summer tourist stampede make sure you've booked your ticket in advance.

Day 4: Stratford-upon-Avon to Oxford

3½–6 hours, 54.9 miles

The return leg to Oxford passes for the most part through gentler farmland, but there are still a couple of climbs to watch out for. This is a potentially long ride, especially if you decide to make a day of it at Blenheim Palace, so be ready for an early reveille.

No sooner have you left behind the tourist throngs of Stratford-upon-Avon than the brake blocks will be pinching your wheel rims at **Charlecote Park** (☎ 01789 470277), a magnificent Tudor mansion by the River Avon. Owned for 700 years by the Lucy family, it's said they once caught Shakespeare poaching on their land. Tours are guided.

Just after Walton your tyres will leave their mark on the **Fosse Way** (9.1 miles) a laser-straight Roman road, which once linked Exeter with Lincoln. Further on, a climb (23.2 miles) takes you up to the Bronze Age

Rollright Stones. A circle of stones called 'the King's Men' (said to dance at midnight) stands on one side of the road, a monolith named 'the King's Stone' on the other.

SIDE TRIP: BLENHEIM PALACE

Spare an afternoon, if time permits, to visit one of England's greatest stately homes, **Blenheim Palace** (☎ 08700 602080; www .blenheimpalace.com) a triumphant Baroque fantasy designed by Sir John Vanbrugh and Nicholas Hawksmoor between 1705 and 1722. The land and funds to build the house were granted to John Churchill, Duke of Marlborough, by a grateful Queen Anne after his decisive victory at the Battle of Blenheim. Now a Unesco World Heritage Site, Blenheim (pronounced *blen*-num) is home to the 11th duke and duchess. Highlights include the east gate, the Great Court and landscaping by the English master Capability Brown. Allow several hours to admire and wander. Ample cafes and restaurants are on hand.

If it's swelteringly hot, why not take a cooling dip in **Farmoor Reservoir**, which the route skirts just beyond Eynsham (48.7 miles). Things also start to hot up on the roads as you approach Oxford and it's impossible to avoid the traffic.

CHILTERN RIDGE

Duration 3–4½ hours
Distance 45.2 miles
Difficulty moderate
Start Luton (p173)
Finish High Wycombe (p171)

Summary Pedal up steep gradients, cross thick forests and wizz through well-to-do villages on a ride which hugs a procession of hills just a few miles out of London.

Stretching between the Home Counties towns of Luton and High Wycombe, the Chiltern Hills form a ridge that rises out from the plains around the northwest edge of London. Straightforward to reach from the capital for a day trip or even a long afternoon ride, this short route can be tacked onto the Cotswolds Triangle (p152) ride earlier in this chapter. The ride is especially memorable in the autumn when the beech forests cloak the slopes in a coppery blaze.

ENVIRONMENT

The slopes are a mixture of open chalk downland and ancient beech woodlands that have been worked for hundreds of years.

PLANNING

When to Cycle

Spring fills the woods with bluebells and summer graces the fields with golden crops, but if there is one time to ride the Chilterns, it's autumn, when the turning leaves paint the hillsides glorious copper hues and the smell of wood smoke is in the air. On the weekends the HGV count on the main roads drops almost to nil, but near the picnic spots day-trippers come out in force.

What to Bring

Although a mountain bike is best for tackling the four sections of off-road bridleway, they can also be negotiated in the dry on skinny-tyres.

Maps

The OS Landranger maps 1:50,000 *Aylesbury & Leighton Buzzard* (sheet 165) and *Reading & Windsor* (sheet 175) show a large bridleway network for mountain biking, and the more detailed OS Explorer maps 1:25,000 *Chiltern Hills East* (sheet 172) and *Chiltern Hills North* (sheet 181) are also recommended.

Bike Hire

As there's nowhere to rent mountain bikes in Luton itself, see the London chapter (p37) for details of cycle hire companies in the capital.

Information Sources

The **Chilterns Conservation Board** (☎ 01844 355500; www.chilternsaonb.org; The Lodge, Station Rd, Chinnor) oversees the Chilterns 'area of outstanding natural beauty' and publish leaflets and maps to the area.

GETTING TO/FROM THE RIDE

Luton (start)

TRAIN

Luton is home to London's fourth airport and is easily reached by train from London St Pancras (£14; 35 minutes, every 15 minutes). Bikes go free, but can't be carried during the weekday evening commuter exodus from 4pm to 7pm.

High Wycombe (finish)

See the A Cotswolds Triangle ride (p152) for details on getting to/from High Wycombe.

THE RIDE

This ride has long views out over Bedfordshire and Buckinghamshire, taking in off-road sections, low-gear climbs and a few interesting off-route distractions along the way. There are four sections of off-road

---

MOUNTAIN BIKING: THE LONG MYND

The bare hills of south Shropshire are ideal for mountain biking and weekends year round see hundreds hitting the trails of the Long Mynd, a ridge that rises to almost 510m (1700ft). To tackle the myriad tracks, which crisscross the area, you'll need to be forearmed with the OS Explorer map 1:25,000 *The Long Mynd and Wenlock Edge* (sheet 217). Treat any ride as a day in the mountains, making a note of the weather forecast before you set off and carrying warm and waterproof clothing and extra rations. Keep to the bridleways to preserve the area's delicate eco-system. Mountain bikes can be hired from **Terry's Cycles** (☎ 01694 723302; 6 Castle Hill, All Stretton).

With a good map and compass you can fashion your own adventure, but this sample 12.4-mile circular ride shows off the Long Mynd massif at its best. Starting out from **Church Stretton tourist office** (☎ 01694 723133; Church St) make your way out of town along the B4370 to Little Stretton. There turn right onto a track, which takes you to Minton then head northwest onto the Minton Batch, a narrow uphill track which hugs the side of a hill. Towards the top where the land flattens turn right onto the ancient Portway Rd, pass Pole Bank and follow this round to Cross Dyke. From here continue on the road to Plush Hill where you should turn right onto a track that takes you into All Stretton. The B4370 will lead you safely back into Church Stretton.

CHILTERN RIDGE

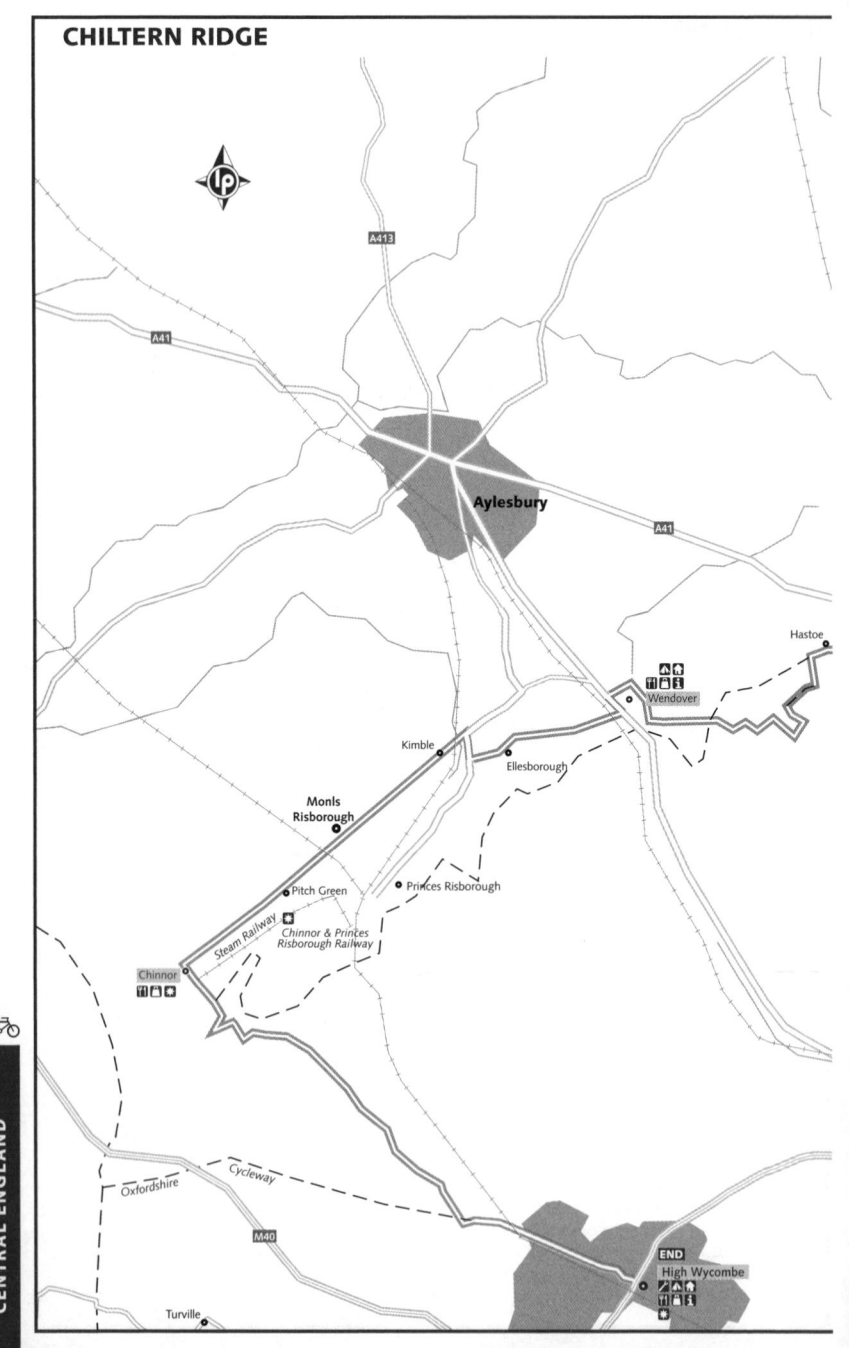

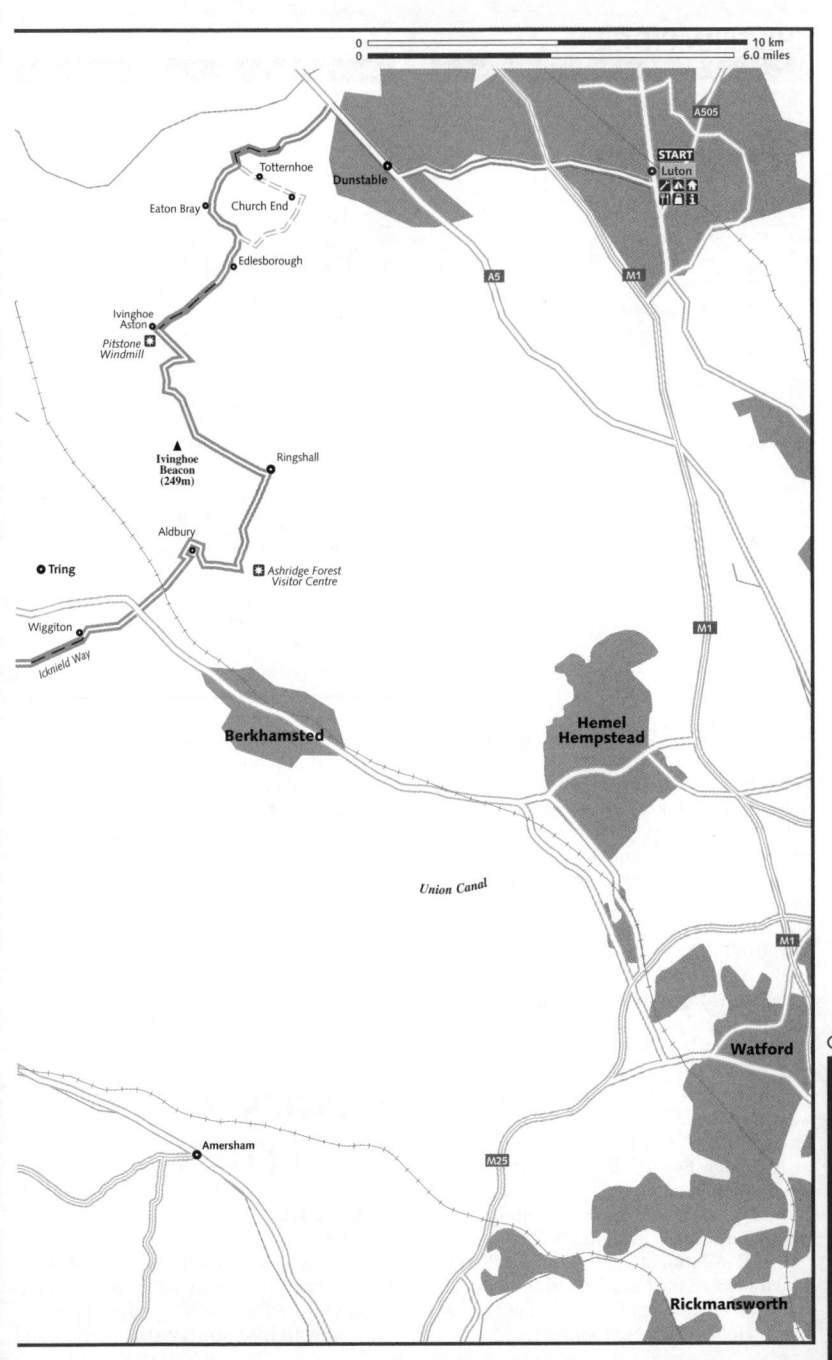

CHILTERN RIDGE

CUE		GPS COORDINATES
start	Luton main train station	51°52'55"N 0°24'49"W
0 miles	go W on Station Rd	
0.0	(200yd) Guildford St	
	(350yd) Bridge St	
0.2	'all routes'	
0.6	A505 follow 'to Dunstable' signs	
4.7	A5 'to Milton Keynes'	
6.0	'to Sewell'	
6.8	rough bridleway	
7.6	bridleway (at T-junction)	
7.7	main bridleway (turns sealed)	
7.9	'to Dunstable'	
8.9	Eaton Bray	
9.4	'to Edlesborough'	
10.2	bridleway (at T-junction)	
11.4	return to road, Ivinghoe Aston	51°51'11"N 0°37'1"W
12.0	B489 'to Ivinghoe Beacon'	
12.3	'to Ivinghoe Beacon'	
	1 mile moderate climb	
14.8	'to Berkhamsted', Ringshall	51°49'5"N 0°34'22"W
(15.8	Ashridge Forest visitor centre)	
16.5	'to Aldbury'	
17.7	Aldbury	51°48'9"N 0°36'7"W
	unsigned road (not 'to Tring')	

CUE CONTINUED		GPS COORDINATES
18.8	cross the Grand Union Canal	
	0.5 miles moderate climb	
19.9	'to Champneys', Wigginton	51°46'59"N 0°38'19"W
	(50yd) 'Dead End', Wick Rd	
20.1	'Wick Farm' bridleway	
20.9	'to Hastoe' (chain across track)	
21.0	'Icknield Way', Hastoe	
22.0	'Private Road' tarmac bridleway	
22.8	rejoin road	
23.3	Gilberts Hill	
23.5	'to Wendover'	
23.9	'to Hale'	
26.1	'to Village Centre'	
26.6	A4011 'to Aylesbury'	
	(50yd) 'to P Risboro', Wendover	51°45'46"N 0°44'28"W
29.6	A4010 'to Chinnor (B4009)'	
30.1	B4009 'to Chinnor'	
35.9	'to Lewknor'	
36.2	Chinnor	51°42'3"N 0°54'31"W
(36.6	steam railway)	
37.1	1m moderate climb	
37.5	'to Bledlow Ridge'	
40.2	Bledlow Ridge	51°40'19"N 0°50'52"W
42.6	A40 'to High Wycombe'	
45.2	High Wycombe train station (RHS)	51°37'46"N 0°44'44"W

bridleway, the first being the roughest. They all can become quite boggy after persistent rain when they are unsuitable for anything but mountain bikes.

Having accomplished your 6-mile getaway from Luton and Dunstable on fast roads, things improve immediately you leave the rumbling A5 to Sewell (6 miles). One of the first sights you pass is **Pitstone Windmill**, one of Britain's oldest, built in 1627. After some steady flat riding, the pedal to the top of **Ivinghoe Beacon**, popular with kite flyers and gliders who use the updraft as a launching place, is worth the exertion for the panoramic vistas.

Having drunk in the views and in hot weather possibly the contents of your water bottle, it's just a few downhill miles to **Ashridge Forest** and the visitor centre (15.8 miles) where you'll find information about walks through the surrounding beech wood and more refreshments. The wood is part of the National Trust **Ashridge Estate**, which formed the backdrop to some scenes from *Harry Potter and the Goblet of Fire* and *Sleepy Hollow* starring Johnny Depp.

Navigation can get tricky in the middle section of the route so keep your map reading senses sharp. After around three hours you should make **Chinnor** (36.2 miles), home to the headquarters of the Chilterns Conservation Board (see Chiltern Ridge/ Information p161) and one end of the **Chinnor & Princes Risborough Railway** (☎ 01844 354117) along which weekend steam trains snort and whistle year round. After Chinnor get ready for some low-gear action on today's most hard-hitting climb up Chinnor's Hill, rewarded with a relaxing glide into High Wycombe.

TOWNS & FACILITIES

BEDFORD
☎ 01234 / pop 79,190

Multicultural and mildly historic Bedford enjoys a riverside setting on the banks of the Great Ouse. Although the centre of town is overrun with high street chain shops, wander a little further to find a host of interesting sites connected to the town's most famous export John Bunyan (1628–88), the 17th-century nonconformist preacher and author of *The Pilgrim's Progress.*

Information

Located in a grand annex of the town hall, the ultra-friendly **tourist office** (☎ 01234 221712; www.visitbedford.co.uk; Town Hall, St Paul's Sq) can help find accommodation in and around Bedford and stocks a free guide to places with a Bunyan connection. In an adjacent room there's also a free audio tour on Bedford's history.

Supplies & Equipment

For outdoor kit, the nationwide chains **Blacks** (☎ 01234 742029; 13 Harpur St) and **Millets** (☎ 01234 357375; 3 West Arc, Church St) do the trick. The experienced mechanics at **Bedford Cycles** (☎ 01234 351525; 54-56 Midland Rd) will have your two-wheeled pal back on the road in no time, and they also sell a range of accessories, clothing and, of course, new bikes. One of the most central supermarkets is cheap and cheerful **Wilkinson's** (29-41 High St), or if you are lucky enough to arrive in town on a Wednesday or Saturday don't miss the even cheaper fresh produce **market,** which wraps itself around the Church of St Paul.

Sleeping & Eating

Gennaro's (☎ 0845 521 2216; Ram Yd; pizzas £8.25-11, pasta £9-12). Bedford has quite a large Italian community, and this lively, tightly-packed place tucked down an alleyway off High St keeps them in pasta, pizza and wine in characterful surroundings. The downstairs dining rooms have more atmosphere than the rather bland upstairs overflow space, or you can dine al fresco in the yard outside. The £4.95 lunch menu is as good a deal as you'll find anywhere in town.

    Tokyo (☎ 01234 266100; 21 Greyfriars; dinner-buffet adult/child £12.90/6.50) is a bright, cheery Japanese restaurant, which has a sushi conveyor the runs the length of the room as well as serving a wide range of à la carte dishes. The evening buffet is excellent value and includes sushi, tempura, dumplings and noodle dishes.

    Litten Tree (☎ 01234 330901; 53–55 High St; mains £5-8.50) is a humungous modern pub-eatery where filling bellies with grub and ale is the only thing on punters' minds. Starting with morning coffee and pastries, they move on to all-day full English and 'build your own' breakfasts, fish and chips, chilli con carne, tikka masala – you get the idea.

    Swan Hotel (☎ 01234 346565; www .bedfordswanhotel.co.uk; The Embankment; s/d/tr £130/135/155) it's not often a town's plushest establishment welcomes cyclists with open arms, but the Swan next to the bridge over the Ouse is different. Storage space for up to ten bikes means your wheels are safe, leaving you to savour this gorgeously elegant hotel's restaurant, bar, lush guestrooms and amazing Roman-style spa pool. Ask for a room with views of the River Ouse upon which swans bob and rowers heave.

    Elms Guesthouse (☎ 01234 353844; www.bedfordbedandbreakfast.com; 24 De Parys Ave; s £29-35, d/tw £45-55, tr £60-70) this is the best of a handful of B&Bs on De Parys St with generously cut, high-ceilinged rooms, original Victorian fireplaces and a large yellow-painted breakfast room. Cyclists are made very welcome.

    Hertford House (☎ 01234 350007; 57 De Parys Ave; s from £30 d/tr £80/£50) is next on the list if the Elms is full. This alternative B&B just up the road has decidedly pokey, unimaginatively decorated but functional rooms where the beds fill a good 70% of the floor space. Most rooms are en suite, there's semi-secure cycle storage outside, but when we visited the staff on duty hardly spoke any English.

BUXTON

☎ 01298 / pop 24,112

The former spa town of Buxton in Derbyshire has a peaceful central knot of handsome Georgian buildings that contrasts with heavy quarrying on the outskirts and the thundering A6 that runs near the centre.

Information

Buxton's **tourist centre** (☎ 01298 25106; www.highpeak.gov.uk; Pavilion Gdns, St John's Rd) at the beautiful Pavilion Gardens can help with accommodation.

Supplies & Equipment

For cycle parts aim your handlebars towards **Mark Anthony's Cycles** (☎ 01298 72114; 115 Spring Gdns) at the far end of the pedestrianised shopping street (Spring Gdns) and over the roundabout. Branches of national outdoor shops **Millets** (☎ 01298 25660; 53-55 Spring Gdns) and **Yeomans Outdoors** (☎ 01298 74330; 41 Spring Gdns) are also located handily in the pedestrianised zone.

Sleeping & Eating

Lime Tree Park (☎ 01298 22988; www.lime treeparkbuxton.co.uk; Dukes Dr; sites £14) about a mile south of the centre along the A515 this incredibly well-equipped campsite has all the right boxes tourist office ked. Ultra-modern shower blocks, friendly wardens and proximity to a local supermarket mean it got a big 'thumbs up' from all the campers we spoke to.

Roseleigh Hotel (☎ 01298 24904; www .roseleighhotel.co.uk; 19 Broad Wlk; s/d incl breakfast from £33/70) this gorgeous family-run B&B in a spacious old terraced house has lovingly decorated rooms, many with fine views out onto the ducks paddling in the picturesque Pavilion Gardens lake. The owners are a welcoming couple, both seasoned travellers, with plenty of interesting tales to tell. There's a large guest lounge full of travel guides and maps for browsing and a large Paddington bear if you get lonely.

Old Hall Hotel (☎ 01298 22841; www.old hallhotelbuxton.co.uk; the Square; s/d incl breakfast £65/100) has a tale to go with every creak of the floorboards at this genial, history-soaked establishment, supposedly the oldest hotel in England. Mary, Queen of Scots, was held here from 1576 to 1578, and the wood-panelled corridors and rooms are as well appointed and elegant as they must have been in her day.

Columbine Restaurant (☎ 01298-78752; Hall Bank; mains £11-13) perched on the slope leading down to the Crescent, this excellent understated restaurant is top choice among Buxtonites in the know. It delivers large portions of excellent local produce including some good vegetarian choices.

Art Cafe (☎ 01298 23114; sandwiches and snacks £3-6.75; 9.30am-5pm Apr-Sep, to 3pm Oct-Mar) housed on the second floor of the Pavilion, with beautiful views over the gardens, this little spot is a great place to enjoy a coffee and some homemade cakes whilst perusing the works by local artists that are splashed across the walls.

Old Sun Inn (☎ 01298 23452; 33 High St), the pick of the town's watering holes, and it retains an Edwardian-era ambience. Low ceilings, antique light fittings, flagstone floors and a different crowd in every cranny of this warren-like ale-house make it 'the' place to head for a pint – not to mention the surprisingly sophisticated pub grub.

CHEPSTOW

☎ 01291 / pop 14,195

Lying on the Welsh side of the steep-sided River Wye, Chepstow is a small and pretty town with an impressive 1000-year-old castle. It originally prospered on waterborne trade from the nearby Severn estuary, and later as a typical market town though it's best known today for its racecourse. The name comes from the Old English 'chepe' and 'stowe' meaning marketplace.

Information

The friendly **tourist office** (☎ 01291 623772) is located in the castle car park. Ask about local walking and cycling trails.

Supplies & Equipment

Chepstow's lone cycle shop is **559 Cycles** (☎ 01291 626126; 4 Manor Way) just off Bank St. It's closed both Wednesdays and Sundays.

Sleeping & Eating

George Hotel (☎ 01291 625363; Moor St; s/d £50/60) beside the city gate, the 17th-century George has well-decorated if slightly chintzy rooms with high ceilings. The restaurant is popular with residents and non-residents alike.

Castle View Hotel (☎ 01291 620349; www.hotelchepstow.co.uk; Bridge St; s/d £55/77) this old coach house opposite the castle is looking smarter and fresher for its refurbishment and the upgrading of the in-house restaurant is a welcome touch. The Cottage Suite is now the best room in the house with dark furnishings and views across to the castle.

The Boat Inn (☎ 01291 628192; The Back; mains £8-18) regarded by locals as the best pub in Chepstow has good vibes, warm yellow walls, a great riverside location with tables outside and a flavoursome menu featuring several choices for vegetarians.

Petrus (☎ 01291 626868; 18 The Back; mains around £16) this smart new eatery boasts a riverside location and a strong Mediterranean influence. The 48-cover, black-and-white-motif dining room looks elegant with a black onyx carved figure as its central feature. The all-day tapas bar offers lighter snacks.

Coffee No 1 (☎ 01291 637403; www .coffee1.co.uk; 1-2 Beaufort Sq) is good for a coffee or a pre-departure breakfast. This branch of a local chain brings an espresso-fuelled shot of top-notch coffee culture to south Wales. It's a light, airy place where mothers with babies and pensioners (and cyclists) are all made welcome by the smiley staff.

CHESTER
☎ 01244 / pop 80,130

This northwest tourist hotspot is famous for its complete red-sandstone walls, which encircle a handsome town centre based on an ancient cross pattern. Radiating out from this are the half-timbered, double-level rows, often called Britain's first shopping malls and dating from medieval times. Prosperous and picturesque, the town nurtures clichés about the quaintness of Olde Englande while slipping plenty of consumerism into the equation. The first tourist guide to the city was produced in 1781!

Information
Chester's tourist office (☎ 01244-351609; www.visitchester.com; Vicar's Ln) can tell you anything you want to know about the city and operates a special weekday accommodation hotline (☎ 0845 073 1324).

Supplies & Equipment
Chester has many outdoor shops. These include **Blacks** (☎ 01244 318398; 23 Northgate) and **Field & Trek** (☎ 0870 838148; 46 Bridge St). **Dave Miller's** bike shop (☎ 01244 326506; 14 Frodsham St) can be found just off Foregate and is best for repairs.

Sleeping & Eating
Chester Southerly Campsite (☎ 01244 671308; Balderton Ln, Marlton-cum-Lache)

is located around 3 miles south along the A483, and has basic but clean facilities and friendly owners. Oddly only adults are allowed here.

Chester Backpackers (☎ 01244 400185; www.chesterbackpackers.co.uk; 67 Boughton; dm from £13.50) comfortable dorm rooms with nice pine beds in a typically Tudor white-and-black building. It's just a short walk from the city walls and there's also a pleasant garden.

Chester YHA (☎ 0870 770 5762; 40 Hough Green; dm £19.95) is located in an elegant Victorian home about a mile from the city centre. This hostel has a variety of dorms that sleep from two to ten people – there's also a cafeteria, a kitchen, cycle storage and a shop on the premises.

Katie's Tea Rooms (☎ 01244 400322; 38 Watergate St) is a stone-walled tearoom located inside a historic building and is the place to go for a light lunch. Tea and scones cost £3.80. After 5pm it turns into **MD's Restaurant**, a Continental eatery with a pretty tasty menu. The restaurant is open for dinner from Tuesday to Saturday, and a two-course meal will set you back around £13.

Falcon (☎ 01244 314555; Lower Bridge St; mains from £5.50) is an old-fashioned boozer with a lovely atmosphere. The surprisingly adventurous menu offers up dishes such as Jamaican peppered beef or spicy Italian sausage casserole – great for both a pint and a bite.

Old Harker's Arms (☎ 01244 344525; www.harkersarms-chester.co.uk; 1 Russell St; mains £9-14) is another old-style boozer with a gourmet kitchen. This is the perfect place to tuck into Cumberland sausages or a Creole rice salad with sweet potatoes and then rinsing your palate with a pint of Waddies, as Wadworth Ale is know round here. It also does bar snacks and sandwiches.

CIRENCESTER
☎ 01285 / pop 15,861

It's hard to imagine today, but thanks to the wool trade Cirencester was for a time one of the most important towns in northwest Europe. The old Market Place is overlooked by a fine abbey church and several buildings and hotels dating back to those days of yore. To the Romans it was Corinium, a town they founded at the crossroads of Akeman St, Fosse Way and Ermin Way.

Information
The **tourist office** (☎ 01285 654180; Park St) is located in the museum and has a leaflet detailing a guided walk around the town and its historic buildings.

Supplies & Equipment
Millets (☎ 01285 651250; 3 Cricklade St) near the tourist office are Cirencester's sole purveyor of adventure kit. **Ride 24/7** (☎ 01285-642247; 6 The Woolmarket), is the most central bike shop, but ironically doesn't quite live up to its name as it's closed Sundays (they're probably out riding).

Sleeping & Eating
Hoburne Cotswold Holiday Park (☎ 01285 860216; www.hoburne.com; Broadway Ln, South Cerney; sites £13.50-32) is a full-on holiday park with a heated outdoor pool, an amusement arcade and a whole assortment of other facilities to keep happy campers just that. However the top summer rate for pitching a tent is extortionate.

Old Brewhouse (☎ 01285 656099; www .theoldbrewhouse.com; 7 London Rd; s £50-55, d £65-70) set in a charming 17th-century town house, this lovely B&B has bright, pretty rooms with cast-iron beds and subtle, country-style florals or patchwork quilts. The beautiful garden room even has its own patio.

No 12 (☎ 01285 640232; www.no12 cirencester.co.uk; 12 Park St; d £85) is a Georgian townhouse right in the centre of town with gloriously unfussy rooms kitted out with a tasteful mix of antiques and modern furnishings. Think feather pillows, merino blankets, extra long beds, slick modern bathrooms and a host of little extras to make you smile.

Jesse's Bistro (☎ 01285 641497; Black-jack St; mains £12.50-21.50) is hidden away in a cobbled stableyard with its own fish-monger and cheese shop. Jesse's is a great little place with flagstone floors, wrought-iron chairs and mosaic tables. The modern menu features a selection of great dishes, but the real treat is the fresh fish and meat cooked in the wood-burning oven.

Piazza Fontana (☎ 01285 643133; 30a Castle St; mains £9-17) an authentic family-run Italian joint is hidden away in a courtyard. This place serves up a great selection

of traditional pastas, meat and fish dishes just done to perfection. It's well worth seeking out for its informal atmosphere but top notch service.

COPT OAK & COALVILLE
☎ 01530 / Coalville pop 30,000

Copt Oak is a quiet hamlet on the edge of Charnwood Forest, with a dire pub and no accommodation to speak of. If you're not camping, head to the nearby former mining town of Coalville (4 miles in total – take the Whitwick Rd from the crossroads and turn left after 2 miles) where you'll find lodgings and limited eating options.

Information
Coalville **tourist office** (☎ 01530 813608; Snibston Discovery Pk, Ashby Rd) stocks heaps of information on what to see and do in the surrounding area as well as accommodation lists.

Supplies & Equipment
Coalville Cycles (☎ 01530 832179; 28 Belvoir Rd) is in the heart of town. If you're self catering, there's a **Morrisons** supermarket (Whitwick Rd) just off the A511 by-pass to the north of the town centre.

Sleeping & Eating
Meadow Farm Marina (☎ 01509 816035; Houston Cl, Barrow upon Soar; sites £10) is the nearest campsite to Copt Oak and enjoys a tranquil riverside location 6 miles away in Barrow upon Soar. Facilities are clean and well-maintained but after a day in the saddle it may be easier just to head into Coalville to find digs.

Saint Joseph's Cottage (☎ 01509-503943; www.stjosephscottage.co.uk; Abbey Rd, Oaks in Charnwood; B&B £25-30) located 3 miles northeast of Coalville, is an old country house with two twin rooms and a single, all with shared facilities. The owners could not be more welcoming and the hearty breakfast is prepared with locally sourced produce, which will set you up nicely for a day's ride.

Hermitage Park (☎ 01530 814814; www .hermitageparkhotel.co.uk; Whitwick Rd; d £67.50-80.50) is a boxy hotel, generally regarded as the best in town with clean if bland rooms. Temporary home to an army of sales-reps during the week, rates tumble by a whole 8% at weekend. Cycles can be left overnight in the luggage room.

Bhujon Tandoori (☎ 01530 510449; 40 High St; mains £6-8). In best Leicestershire tradition, this tandoori restaurant serves up poppadums, curries and rice dishes for consumption indoors or to takeaway.

The Wise Plaice (23-25 Hotel St) is a sit-down fish and chip shop that also serves kebabs and burgers.

HAWORTH
☎ 01535 / pop 6100

Once home to the Brontë sisters, this erstwhile weaving village perches on the side of a steep valley. Thanks to its literary connection, Haworth is usually second port of call after Stratford-upon-Avon on the literary tourist trail meaning summer crowds toting copies of *Wuthering Heights* and *Jane Eyre*.

Information
The **tourist office** (☎ 01535 642329; www .haworth-village.org.uk; 2-4 West Ln) has an excellent supply of information on the village, the surrounding area and, of course, the Brontë's.

Supplies & Equipment
If you're in serious need of repairs, bike spares or other cycle-related gear, the nearest bike shop is **Aire Valley Cycles** (☎ 01535 610839; www.airevalleycycles .com; 4 Campbell St) in nearby Keighley which lies on the route.

Sleeping & Eating
Upwood Holiday Park (☎ 01535 644242; www.upwoodpark.co.uk; sites £10) take mainly caravans and camper vans, but has some space for small tents. Located a mile southeast of the village.

Haworth YHA (☎ 0870 770 5858; www .yha.org.uk; Longlands Dr; dm £14) is a big old house with a games room, lounge, laundry and most importantly, cycle store. It's on the northeastern edge of town, off Lees Lane.

Haworth House (☎ 01535 643374; 6 Church St; s/d from £25/50) tucked along the alley beside the church, this place has mostly spacious rooms with a New Age vibe, though the smaller, cheaper rooms are pretty cramped. Breakfast (£3-4 extra) is served in your bedroom.

Weaver's Restaurant with Rooms (☎ 01535 643822; www.weaversmallhotel .co.uk; 15 West Ln; s/d £60/100, mains £12-18) is a stylish and atmospheric restaurant serving local specialities such as black pudding, sausage and mash. Upstairs are three comfy bedrooms, two with views towards the moors.

HAY-ON-WYE
☎ 01497 / pop 1400

Nestled just inside Wales on the northern slopes of the Black Mountains, Hay-on-Wye is an eccentric little place known as the 'town of books' thanks to its 39 bookshops and Britain's leading annual literary festival which takes place here.

Information
The hit-and-miss **tourist office** (☎ 01497 820144; Oxford Rd) is on the main drag through town. Staff can help with accommodation bookings.

Supplies & Equipment
Bike supplies and a repair service are available at **Paddles & Pedals** (☎ 01497 820604; 15 Castle St) in the town centre. The shop also hires out bikes as well as kayaks for trips on the River Wye. In the same street you'll also find the excellent **PSM Outdoors** (☎ 01497 820022; 7 Castle St), which stocks a huge selection of outdoor gear, maps and cycling equipment.

Sleeping & Eating
Booking well ahead during the annual **Hay Festival** (late May) is essential as the town teems with visitors at this time.

Radnor's End (☎ 01497 820780; Radnor's End; camping £5 per person per night) is a small campsite found down on the river, just two minutes' ride northwest of the centre on the Clyro Rd.

The Start (☎ 01497 821391; www.the start.net; s/d £35/70) peacefully set on the fringes of town, is a beautiful 18th-century house, just a five-minute walk from the centre across Hay Bridge. The rooms are comfortable and the setting, away from the centre in a quiet, riverside enclave, adds to the tranquil atmosphere.

The Bear (☎ 01497 821302; www.the bearhay.co.uk; Bear St; d from £70, s/d without bathroom £31/56) is homely and rustic with exposed stone walls and original beams, plus a liberal sprinkling of books – this former coaching inn remains a popular choice. It only has four rooms, of which two are en suite, and excels at breakfast with organic, fair trade and vegetarian-friendly options to kick start the day.

The Granary (☎ 01497 -820790; Broad St) is popular and welcoming, with a bustling country-kitchen cafe with a staple choice for breakfasts, snack lunches and coffees. It's great for vegetarians and families, with menus for both, while the huge upstairs gallery offers extra seating. Free wi-fi internet is a welcome new addition.

Oscars Bistro (☎ 01497 821193; High Town) for lunches and snacks, plus a good range of vegetarian options, Oscars is a popular option for a quick bite in the heart of town.

Blue Boar (☎ 01497 820884; Castle St) the pick of the pubs in town, this cosy and traditional inn is the ideal place to while away an afternoon with a decent pint of Timothy Taylor's ale, a home-cooked lunch of Glamorgan sausage, served with plum chutney and new potatoes, and a good book. Food is served all day with hearty fare and mains around £11.

HESSLE & HULL
☎ 01482 / Hull pop 250,000
'It's never dull in Hull' read the T-shirts in the tourist office. They lied. Kingston-upon-Hull, to use its posh full name, is a major port with a population of 250,000, many employed in the docks handling freight and passengers on the ferries to the Dutch ports of Rotterdam and Zeebrugge. The town is way off the tourist trail, but has an old town and marina with a certain charm, and features quirky trails by which to plot two local mainstays – fish and ale. Hessle dates from Anglo-Saxon times, and is an ordinary little town with a very limited choice of accommodation and eating options. Pedal on to Hull where there's much more variety.

Information
Despite the dearth of visitors to the town, Hull does have a **tourist office** (☎ 01482 223559; www.hullcc.gov.uk; 1 Paragon St), which books accommodation free of charge.

Supplies & Equipment
The large **Winfields Megastore** (☎ 01482 587088; 273 Hessle Rd) is an outdoor gear geeks heaven around 5 miles along the Hessle Rd near Pickering Park. The most central bike shop is **Freetown Sports** (☎ 01482 589066; 70-76 Prospect St).

Sleeping & Eating
Dorchester Hotel (☎ 01482 343276; 273-277 Beverly Rd; dm/s/d/tw £17.50/40/50/50) sounds grand, but this is a no-frills crash pad 1 mile north of the train station. Bikes can be stored and rooms are bookable through Hostelworld (www.hostelworld.com).

Clyde House Hotel (☎ 01482 214981; www.clydehousehotel.co.uk; 13 John St; s/d £30/50) overlooks leafy Kingston Square, and is close to the New Theatre. This is one of the best B&B options in the city centre – the rooms are nothing fancy, but are tidy and comfortable, and the owners are friendly and helpful.

Kingston Theatre Hotel (☎ 01482 225828; www.kingstontheatrehotel.com; 1-2 Kingston Sq; s/d/tw from £45/65/80) is a slightly more formal hotel sharing the same central location. This place offers charming if not quite memorable rooms – upgrade to a suite if you're looking for a little leg room.

McCoy's (☎ 01482 327757; Colonial Chambers, Princes Dock St; mains £3-5) is a home-grown alternative to Starbucks and serves excellent coffee, and a breakfast menu that ranges from porridge, to a vegetarian fry-up, to scrambled egg with smoked salmon. Freshly baked cakes and pastries are served throughout the day, with salads and sarnies at lunch.

Hitchcock's Vegetarian Restaurant (☎ 01482 320233; 1 Bishop Lane, High St; per person £15). The word 'quirky' could have been invented to describe this place – an atmospheric maze of small rooms, an all-you-can-eat vegetarian buffet whose theme – Thai, Indian, Spanish, whatever – is chosen by the first person to book that evening, BYOB, and no credit cards. But hey – the food is excellent and the welcome is warm. Bookings necessary.

Cook's Endeavour (☎ 01482 213844; 5 Scale Ln; two–/three-course dinner £25/30) is set in a quaint 15th-century building – the oldest surviving house in Hull. This wittily named place specialises in local produce, including Yorkshire beef and Whitby crab, prepared in traditional English style.

HIGH WYCOMBE
☎ 01494 / pop 118,229

Hemmed in by steep wooded hillsides, Buckinghamshire's largest town has a semi-attractive setting. The town was once renowned for furniture production and has a museum showcasing chairs made here over the centuries. Otherwise it's a pretty unspectacular place but with sufficient eating and sleeping options to make it a viable end-of-ride overnight stop.

Information

The town's **tourist office** (☎ 01494 421892; Paul's Row) is bang in the heart of town and has a wealth of info on High Wycombe and the Chiltern Hills to the north.

Supplies & Equipment

Bring all wonky wheels and dud derailleurs to **Cycle Care** (☎ 01494 447908; 225 Desborough Rd) just off the West Wycombe Rd (A4010). The High Street double act of **Blacks** (☎ 01494 510185; 38-42 Frogmoor) and **Millets** (☎ 01494-522100; 4-5 Church St) flog all you could ever need for a day in the great British outdoors.

Sleeping & Eating

Highclere Farm Country Park (☎ 01494 875665; www.highclerefarmpark.co.uk; New Barn Ln, Seer Green, Beaconsfield; sites £16) is the nearest campsite to High Wycombe, 7 miles east along the main A40 road.

Abbey Lodge (☎ 01494 471013; www.abbeylodgehotel.co.uk; Priory Rd; s/d/tw £75/89/89) has 31 rooms at this town centre hotel, which are basic and a touch on the cramped side but perfectly survivable for a night. To keep you entertained there's free wi-fi, at least 50 channels on TV and a satisfying full English breakfast to look forward to in the morning.

The Bell (☎ 01494 525588; www.thebellonline.co.uk; 41 Frogmoor; rooms £55-85) is a cosy grade II listed guesthouse and pub with stylishly fitted out rooms, some with exposed beams, a somewhat out of place menu of Thai staples and real ale on tap. Breakfast is a rather cheeky £5 extra and

we were assured space (probably chained to the beer barrels) could be found somewhere for bikes.

Cliffton Lodge Hotel (☎ 01494 440095; 210 West Wycombe Rd; mains £10-15) has a good standard hotel restaurant serving an inimitably heavy British menu, changed little in 30 years, featuring culinary delights such as gammon with pineapple, lamb curry and breaded scampi.

ASK (☎ 01494 528244; 17 High St; pasta £6-9, pizzas £6-8.50) is a large chain with restaurants across the country, and has superb Italian food, well-designed interiors, usually great service and satisfied diners – it hardly ever feels like a chain. The pasta is freshly cooked for each dish, pizzas are generously topped and there's always an interesting list of specials.

JORDANS
☎ 01494 / pop 500

This sprawling village of tree-shaded lanes, posh houses and high fences is an exclusively hushed community, a mere 5 miles from the end of the London Underground. Jordans played a role in English Quaker history and meetings for worship were first held regularly at Jordans Farm (now the defunct Old Jordans Guesthouse) from 1659, attended by luminaries such as William Penn (founder of Pennsylvania), George Fox (founder of Quakerism) and James Naylor (one of the first Quaker preachers). The only place to stay is the YHA and to grab a pre-ride bite to eat you'll need to travel into Chalfont St Peter just over a mile to the east.

Information

The nearest **tourist office** is in High Wycombe 7 miles away to the west along the A40.

Supplies & Equipment

There's a **Budgens** Supermarket (Bishops House, Market Pl) in Chalfont St Peter. Nearby **Chalfont Home Stores** (☎ 01753 886367; Burnham House, Market Pl) stock a few bike bits but nothing that will rescue you from serious mechanical failure.

Sleeping & Eating

The simple **Jordans YHA** (☎ 0845 371 9523; Welders La; dm £13.95) is up the hill behind the former Quaker guesthouse. Tents can be pitched in the grounds in July and August. Chalfont St Peter has several decent places to eat including **Spice** (☎ 01753 885889; 10 Market Pl; mains £7.50-14), a clean-cut Bangladeshi restaurant serving curry-and-rice dishes, and the **Flames Restaurant & Takeaway** (☎ 01494 891169; 21 High St; meals from £4) dispensing filling kebabs, chips and burgers.

LANCASTER
☎ 01524 / pop 45,960

Lancashire's county seat is handsome Lancaster, lined with Georgian buildings that lend the place an air of austere gentility. Folks have done business here since Roman times, but none more successfully than during the 18th century when Lancaster was a key port in the slave trade. Despite city status, Lancaster has a compact small-town atmosphere and is only a few pedal turns away from the stunning vistas of the Lake District and Morecambe Bay.

Information

Lancaster's excellent **tourist office** (☎ 01524 841656; www.citycoastcountry side.co.uk; 29 Castle Hill) is brimming with brochures and booklets including some on local cycle routes. Staff can help with accommodation.

Supplies & Equipment

Yeomans Outdoors (☎ 01524 388929; 16 New St) and a large outdoor gear discount store called **Mountain Warehouse** (☎ 01524 63801; 43-45 Market St) are the best shops to take on essential camping equipment, waterproofs and alike. **Bicycle Magic** (☎ 01524 844389; 103 Penny St) can work wonders with warped wheels and bust brakes.

Sleeping & Eating

New Parkside Farm (☎ 01524 770723; Caton Rd, Denny Beck) in the Lune Valley at Caton is the nearest campsite to Lancaster. It's accessible by rail trail from Lancaster, or turn north off the Central Explorer ride (p120), 3 miles before Lancaster at Quernmore.

Wagon & Horses (☎ 01524 846094; 27 St George's Quay; s/d £35/48) is a pleasant pub near the Maritime Museum with five

comfortable rooms upstairs – only one is en suite, but all have river views.

Sun Hotel & Bar (☎ 01524 66006; www .thesunhotelandbar.co.uk; 63 Church St; s/d from £45/65) is an excellent hotel in a 300-year-old building with a rustic old world look that stops at the bedroom door – a recent renovation has resulted in eight pretty snazzy sleeping quarters. The pub downstairs is one of the best in town and a top spot for a bit of grub – there are three different menus to choose from, with meals from £8 to £15.

Whale Tail Cafe (☎ 01524 845133; www.whaletailcafe.co.uk; 78a Penny St; mains £6), is a gorgeous first-floor vegie restaurant with an elegant dining room and a more informal plant-filled yard for lunch on a sunny day. The spicy bean burger is particularly good.

Old John of Gaunt (☎ 01524 32358; 53 Market St; mains £5-6) is your one stop for traditional pub grub, decent ale and live music.

LANGSETT & PENISTONE
☎ 01226 / Penistone pop 8500

Langsett is a hamlet on the A616 above Langsett Reservoir. It has a shop that doubles as a cafe, a hostel and a good pub with lodging. The little town of Penistone (4.5 miles away) has many more facilities.

Supplies & Equipment

Stock up on camp food and muesli bars at the **Co-op** (26 Market St) in Penistone. There's no bike shop in Pensitone, so if you're unlucky enough to arrive with mechanical problems you'll have to head to Barnsley, 6.5 miles east along the A628 Barnsley Rd. There the **Barnsley Bicycle Centre** (☎ 01226 287770; 16 Doncaster Rd) will see you right.

Sleeping & Eating

Woodland View Caravan site (☎ 01226 761906; 322 Barnsley Rd, Hoylandswaine; sites £5) located around 2 miles northeast of Penistone just off the Barnsley Rd, this small, low-key site has OK facilities and some relaxing walks in the surrounding woodland.

Langsett YHA (☎ 01226 761548) is a basic hostel that lies up a quiet track beside the village cafe. Open in July and August only, there is cycle storage available.

Cubley Hall (☎ 01226 766086, Mortimer Rd; s £60-70, d £75-82) around 1½ miles from Langsett, south of Penistone over the steep little road from Midhopestones, lies this superb country house hotel that has a pub, a restaurant and ornately done out oak panelled rooms.

The Waggon and Horses Inn (☎ 01226 763147; Langsett; s/tw £42/68, mains £7-10) in Langsett has en suite rooms, top-notch home-cooked bar food, real ale and views over the reservoir.

LINCOLN
☎ 01522 / pop 85,595

The under visited hilltop city of Lincoln has a history going back 2000 years with both the Romans and Normans having set up shop on this strategic site. It is dominated by Britain's third largest cathedral, which looms over the medieval city centre as it tumbles away down steep cobbled streets to the river below.

Information
The main **tourist office** (☎ 01522 873213; www.visitlincolnshire.com; 9 Castle Hill) is at the top of the hill between the cathedral and the castle. There's another branch at the Cornhill (☎ 01522 873256) on High St.

Supplies & Equipment
Get tooled up and ready for the weather at **Yeomans Outdoors** (☎ 01522 545630; 352 High St). For bike repairs and spares look no further than **Cycle Sport** (☎ 01522 870100; 383-384 High St).

Sleeping & Eating
Hartsholme Country Park (☎ 01522 873578; Skellingthorpe Rd; sites £7-15) is a decent camping ground with OK facilities. The main draw here is that it's next to a sprawling nature reserve, filled with lovely lakes, woods and meadows. It's 3 miles southwest of the train station.

Admiral Guest House (☎ 01522 544467; 16-18 Nelson St; s/d £30/50) suffers from a mismatched, chintzy interior, but is good value, well located, and run by friendly, knowledgeable hosts.

The Old Bakery (☎ 01522 576057; www.theold-bakery.co.uk; 26-28 Burton Rd; rooms from £53) is a wonderful guesthouse, set above an excellent restaurant,

with four sweet, characterful rooms. The welcome is warm but unobtrusive and the delicious breakfasts feature goodies such as homemade muffins.

Castlegate Restaurant (☎ 01522 541000; Union Rd; mains £9.95-19.95), this former coach house has a prime position right outside Lincoln Castle gate. There's elegant, fine dining on offer as well as a bar and lighter snacks throughout the day.

The Old Bakery (☎ 01522 576057; www .theold-bakery.co.uk; 26-28 Burton Rd; mains £14.50-20.50) is an old bakery conversion in the shadow of Lincoln Castle's walls, and is one of the town's most popular restaurants. The dining room, which opens up into an airy, slate-floored conservatory, serves award-winning, local produce, impeccably presented, including very addictive bread.

Brown's Pie Shop (☎ 01522 527330; 33 Steep Hill; pies £6.50-10.75) not strictly a pie shop – this restaurant dishes up large servings of speciality pies, steaks and other hearty fare. Eat in the bustling, bright, white dining room, or in a lovely brick-vaulted basement area for candle-lit evenings. The local wild-rabbit and beef and stout pies are particularly tasty.

LONDON
See the London chapter (p37) for information on accommodation and other services, and getting to/from the city.

LUTON
☎ 01582 / pop 184,370

Luton is a sizable working town officially 32 miles north of London though these days it's almost like a far-flung suburb of the capital. The town regularly comes high up in the list of '50 worst towns in the UK to inhabit' and, not too surprisingly, attracts few tourists. Once known for its hat industry, its name is now synonymous with London's third airport (and a shocking '80s pop song) and the number of passengers needing to reach the town means it enjoys good transport links to the capital.

Information
Luton's **visitor information centre** (☎ 01582 401579; www.luton.gov.uk; St. Georges Sq) is housed in the town's main library and is open year round.

Supplies & Equipment

A branch of the nationwide outdoor chain store **Millets** (☎ 01582 724514; Arnedale Centre) is buried in the bowels of the town's main shopping mall. Top dog among Luton cycle shops is **Cycle King** (☎ 01582 723333; 56-66 Dunstable Rd) just off the ring road.

Sleeping & Eating

Belzayne (☎ 01582 736591; 70 Lalleford Rd; B&B from £19), the hosts at the Belzayne are used to cyclists, having put up the Irish national cycling squad three times. Comfortable rooms are great value and the breakfast is a hearty English feast.

easyHotel (www.easyhotel.com; Guildford St; rooms from £25) the future is orange at easyHotel, a spin-off from the successful low-cost airline, easyJet. Usually full of budget airline passengers with 4am flights to the Mediterranean and Eastern Europe, this is not a bad place to stay at all though cycle storage could be more than the staff can handle. In typical easyJet fashion, the earlier you book, the less you pay. Rooms are small and must be booked online.

The Royal Hotel (☎ 01582 400909; www.theroyalhotelluton.com; 1 Mill St; s/d/tr £59/69/79) occupying an impressive Georgian corner building near the train station, the grandly named Royal offers honestly priced business standard rooms in the heart of town. The hotel restaurant serves decent grub and bikes can be stored in the luggage room.

Man Ho (☎ 01582 723366; 72 Dunstable Rd; set menus £6-18) is the best place in Luton to feast on huge portions of inexpensive Chinese fare or get a takeaway menu for a little over a tenner.

MANCHESTER

☎ 0161 / pop 394,270

Probably best known around the world for its football team, this urban sprawl responsible for giving the world Oasis, the Bee Gees and Coronation Street is also a testimony to northern England's industrial decline and revival. Derelict factories rub shoulders with opulent Victorian buildings, rusting railway tracks and motorway flyovers with flashy bars and nightclubs. Things may have improved in recent decades with warehouses given new life as overpriced des-res apartment blocks, and the city centre redeveloped, but travel out of the centre in most directions and you'll hit urban deprivation before long.

You're highly unlikely to fall in love with Manchester at first sight, but after a while the vibrancy of England's self-styled northern capital might just break down your resistance.

Information

Manchester's **tourist office** (☎ 0871 222 8223; www.visitmanchester.com; Town Hall Extension, St Peter's Sq) sells tickets for all sorts of guided walks, which operate almost daily year-round, as well as helping out with accommodation and other general info queries.

Supplies & Equipment

Manchester's long-established central bike shop is **Harry Hall Cycles** (☎ 0161 236 5699; www.harryhallcycles.co.uk; 69 The Arches, Whitworth St West) where clued-up staff provide excellent service seven days a week. The city has an entire shopping centre's worth of outdoor shops waiting to kit you out. These include **Cotswold Outdoor** (6a Oxford Rd), **Nomad Travel Store** (66-68 Bridge St) and the **North Face Store** (Wellington Mill, Duke St).

Sleeping & Eating

Manchester YHA (☎ 0161 839 9960; www .yha.org.uk; Potato Wharf; dm incl breakfast from £13.50) is a purpose-built canalside hostel in the Castlefield area, and is one of the best in the country. It's a top-class option with four- and six-bed dorms, all en suite, as well as a host of good facilities.

Manchester Backpackers' Hostel (☎ 0161 865 9296; 64 Cromwell Rd; dm £15) is a very pleasant private hostel in Stretford, 2 miles south of the city centre, with cooking facilities, a TV lounge and some doubles. It's a cinch to get to from the city centre via Metrolink (Stretford stop).

The Ox (☎ 0161 839 7740; www.theox .co.uk; 71 Liverpool Rd; d/tr from £55/75), not quite your traditional B&B (breakfast is extra), but an excellent choice nonetheless: nine ox-blood-red rooms with tidy amenities above a fine gastro-pub in the heart of Castlefield. It's the best deal in town for the location.

Eighth Day (☎ 0161 273 4878; 111 Oxford Rd; mains around £5) new and most definitely improved after a major cleanup, this environment-friendly hang-out is a favourite with students and sells everything to make you feel good about your place in the world, from fair trade teas to homeopathic remedies. The vegetarian- and vegan-friendly menu is substantial.

Al Bilal (☎ 0161 257 0006; 87-81 Wilmslow Rd; mains £7-14) it's a given that you cannot leave Manchester without tucking into a curry along Wilmslow Rd, aka the Curry Mile – as famous as Bradford or Birmingham is for its Indian cuisine. There are so many great ones to pick from – and some pretty awful ones too – but Al Bilal will treat you and your tummy just right with their excellent dishes.

Lass O'Gowrie (☎ 0161 273 6932; 36 Charles St; mains around £6), a Victorian classic off Princess St that brews its own beer in the basement. It's a favourite with students, old-timers and a clique of BBC employees who work just across the street in the Beeb's Manchester HQ.

Getting There & Away

Virgin Trains (☎ 0845 722 2333; www.virgintrains.co.uk) operate express services up and down the west coast mainline between Glasgow (£60; 3½ hours, 4 daily) and London Euston (£115, 3 hours, twice hourly). Cycles go free but you must make a reservation prior to travelling.

OUNDLE

☎ 01832 / pop 5345

One of the best examples of a honey-coloured sandstone Northamptonshire market town, Oundle (pronounced *own*-del to rhyme with 'town') rises above the watery meadows of the River Nene. Quaint to the hilt, its layout and period buildings have been preserved in architectural formaldehyde for the past 200 years, and the town makes a very pleasant stop on the journey north with ample board and lodgings.

Information

The town's excellent **tourist office** (☎ 01832 274333; 14 West St) has accommodation and restaurant lists and hands out leaflets mapping out relaxing walks by the River Nene.

Supplies & Equipment

Very basic bike supplies are available at **Owen & Hartley** (☎ 01832 272591; North St). For self catering supplies there's a **Tesco Express** (6 Market Pl) on the main square.

Sleeping & Eating

The nearest campsite to Oundle is **Ferry Meadows** (☎ 01733 244526; Ham La, Peterborough; sites £15) around 9 miles away on the southwest outskirts of Peterborough. This Caravan Club site has a very small tent area and there have been reports of staff being reluctant to take campers at all.

Ashworth House (☎ 01832 275312; www.ashworthhouse.co.uk; 75 West St; s/d/tw £40/30/35) is an award-winning B&B with immaculate en suite rooms and a Fairtrade breakfast.

The **Talbot Hotel** (☎ 01832 273621; New St; s/d £80/100, mains £7-11) is the town's classiest act with 35 beautiful period rooms sporting bags of character and a smart restaurant. Its staircase came from the demolished Fotheringhay Castle (p124), and is the flight of steps Mary Queen of Scots is supposed to have descended in 1587 on her day of execution. There should be no problem storing a few bikes.

If you're looking for a cheap night out after some hard pedalling try **China Town** (☎ 01832 272347; 6-8 New St; mains £5.50-8), a Cantonese restaurant that has a cosy maroon, cream and exposed stonework exterior.

A little further along is Oundle's best pub, **The Ship** (☎ 01832 273918; 18 West St; sandwiches £4.50, mains £6-10), or continue on into the main square to find the inviting **Coffee Tavern** (34 Market Pl; sandwiches £4, breakfast £5, mains £5-7.25), which packs in two floors of small cafe tables, exposed beams and walls lined with old prints. It's usually busy with munching locals, always a good sign.

OXFORD

☎ 01865 / pop 143,016

Oxford's handsome old centre belies the fact that this famous university town is also an industrial city with a sizable population. It sits at the confluence of the Rivers Thames and Cherwell, both good for punting, and boasts the smallest cathedral in the country.

The university was established in the 12th century when the Anglo-Normans were refused permission to study at the Sorbonne in Paris, then the centre of European scholar-ship. The first three colleges Balliol (pronounced 'bay-liol'), Merton and University were founded during the 13th century – others have been established at a rate of about three a century since then and today 36 colleges cater for around 14,500 undergraduates. The exquisite architecture and the town's riverside setting attract hordes of tourists in the high season, as well as the world's zippiest brains year round.

Information

Oxford's busy **tourist office** (☎ 01865 252200; www.visitoxford.org; 15-16 Broad St) stocks a *Welcome to Oxford* (£1) brochure and can book accommodation for a £4 fee plus a 10% deposit.

Supplies & Equipment

Replace conked out clobber and kit at **Go Outdoors** (☎ 01865 246551; 426 Abingdon Rd) located around a mile south of the city centre. **Bikezone** (☎ 01865 728788; 6 Lincoln Hse, Market St) is just one of many bike shops in the city that carry out repairs.

Sleeping & Eating

Oxford Camping & Caravanning Club (☎ 01865 244088; www.campingandcaravanningclub.co.uk; 426 Abingdon Rd; sites £9.25), this well-run campsite is conveniently close to the city centre but consequently lacks character and can be noisy. It's a popular spot however, especially on weekends, so book well in advance.

Central Backpackers (☎ 01865 242288; www.centralbackpackers.co.uk; 13 Park End St; dm £16-19) is a good budget option right in the centre of town, this small hostel has basic but bright and simple rooms sleeping 4 to 12 people. There's a small but decent lounge with satellite TV, a rooftop terrace, free internet and cycle storage.

Oxford YHA (☎ 01865 727275; 2a Botley Rd; dm/d £21.95/55.95) is bright, well-kept, clean and tidy, and one of Oxford's best budget option with simple but comfortable dorm accommodation, private rooms and loads of facilities including a restaurant, library, garden, laundry and a choice of lounges. All rooms are en suite

and are bright and cheery and there's even room for two-wheelers.

Edamame (☎ 01865 246916; 15 Holywell St; sushi £2.50-3.50, mains £6-7), you'll find this tiny Japanese place by looking for the queue out the door as you head down Holywell St, and it's well worth the wait. The food here is simply divine with the best rice and noodle dishes in town and sushi (Thursday night only) to die for.

Jamie's Italian (☎ 01865 838383; 24-26 George St; mains £8-18) is celebrity chef Jamie Oliver's new 'neighbourhood' restaurant – an all rustic Italian with wooden crates of freshly made pasta tempting you from the windows and a menu of authentic but affordable Italian dishes. Packed since opening, the crowds come as much for the name as the heaped plates of bruschetta and the steaming bowls of pasta.

Jam Factory (☎ 01865 244613; www .thejamfactoryoxford.com; 27 Park End St; mains £8-12) is an arts centre, bar and restaurant rolled into one. The Jam Factory is a laid-back, boho kind of place with changing exhibitions and hearty breakfasts, an excellent value £10 two-course lunch and an understated menu of modern British dishes.

SHREWSBURY
☎ 01743 / pop 67,126

The county town of Shropshire sited on a strategic bluff in a 340-degree loop in the River Severn is famous for its half-timbered Tudor buildings and mesh of medieval winding streets. The lack of a major attraction, an armaments factory or port saved Shrewsbury from WWII bombs and, largely, from death by tourism. Shrewsbury's most famous son is Charles Darwin who was born here in 1809 and educated at the renowned local public school.

Information

The town's **tourist office** (☎ 01743 281200; www.visitshrewsbury.com; Rowley's Hse, Barker St) was relocated at the end of 2008 while the Music Hall where it normally lives is renovated. It is scheduled to move back in late 2010.

Supplies & Equipment

There are two first-rate bike shops in town: **Dave Mellor Cycles** (☎ 01743 366662; www.thecycleshop.co.uk; 9a New St), owned by the manager of the national mountain bike squad, and **Stan Jones Cycles** (☎ 01743 343775; www.stanjonescycles.co.uk; 17a Hills Lane). Outdoor supplies are taken care of by the trusty high street duo **Blacks** (☎ 01743 368272; 27 Shoplatch) and **Millets** (☎ 01743 353686; 6-7 Mardol Head).

Sleeping & Eating

Severn House Campsite (☎ 01743 850229; Montford Bridge; sites £9) is the nearest campsite to Shrewsbury, situated around 4 miles northwest along the B4380.

164 (☎ 01743 367750; www.164bedand breakfast.co.uk; 164 Abbey Foregate; s/d £35/54, with bathroom £45/58) despite the age of the building you won't find any chintz or faux Tudor interiors here. This B&B celebrates its lovely 16th-century timber frame with bright colours, contemporary fabrics and a quirky mix of artwork. As an extra treat, breakfast is served in bed.

Tudor House (☎ 01743 351735; www .tudorhouseshrewsbury.com; 2 Fish St; s/ d from £69/79) if you're feeling nostalgic, this creaky medieval house has old-world charm by the bucket load. The building is festooned with floral window boxes and its handful of traditional oak-beamed rooms are turned out in high-shine fabrics, some with spindly metal-framed headboards entwined with flowers. Not all rooms have an en suite.

Good Life Wholefood Restaurant (☎ 01743 350455; Barracks Passage; mains £3.50-7) healthy, freshly prepared vegetarian food is the name of the game, in this cute little refuge off Wyle Cop. Favourites include quiches, nut loaf and slightly less health conscious cakes and desserts.

Three Fishes (☎ 01743 344793; 4 Fish St) is a quintessential creaky Tudor alehouse, with a jolly owner, mellow regulars and hops hanging from the 15th-century beamed ceiling. No music here, just plenty of good value real ales on tap and solid bar food.

Armoury (☎ 01743 340525; www .armoury-shrewsbury.co.uk; Victoria Ave; mains £9-17), there's a great warmth and conviviality to this converted riverside warehouse. Towering bookshelves, old pictures and curios help straddle the divide between posh restaurant and informal pub, large, curved windows invite in sheds of light, while a plethora of blackboard menus invite you to sample wines, guest ales and hearty British dishes.

SOUTHPORT
☎ 01704 / pop 99,456

Southport is a pleasant holiday town with little of the tackiness that besets many English resorts. A broad Victorian boulevard lined with well-kept gardens runs parallel to a beachfront where seaside entertainments distract the masses. Miles of sand dunes and woodland along the coast support rare flora and fauna as well as British sun-seekers.

Information

The **tourist office** (☎ 01704 533333; www .visitsouthport.com; 112 Lord St) can be found outside the town hall, is open year round and operates a free accommodation booking service.

Supplies & Equipment

NE Mosscrop (☎ 01704 228805; 78 Bispham Rd) is the nearest bike shop to the town centre but is a fair way out near Meol's Cop train station. For outdoor paraphernalia try **Caravan & Camping** (☎ 01704 531405; 78-80 Eastbank Rd).

Sleeping & Eating

Riverside Holiday Park (☎ 01704 228886; www.riversideleisurecentre.co.uk; Southport New Rd, Banks; sites £16-18) is a large caravan park near the village of Banks, 3 miles north of town. Facilities are of a high standard but things can get busy (and noisy) in summer.

Royal Clifton Hotel (☎ 01704 533771; www.royalclifton.co.uk; Promenade; s/d from £55/95), the most obvious choice of digs in Southport, the impressive white turreted building of the town's top hotel houses semi-luxurious rooms, a very good deal for the price. Special offers are common, though as a cyclist staying one night your unlikely to benefit.

The **Vincent Hotel** (☎ 01704 883800; www.thevincenthotel.com; 98 Lord St; d from £99) is a new, sleek and quite unexpected design hotel, a breath of fresh air after floral-patterned B&Bs and musty rooms above pubs. Minimalist decor, bathrooms of tile, glass and chrome and polite efficient service make this one of the best

CENTRAL ENGLAND

places to rest your head on the northwest coast. Downstairs the smart **V-deli** opens from breakfast until late night cocktails.

Forge Brasserie (☎ 01704 500522; Queen Anne St; mains £10-20) is tucked away in a side street just off Eastbank St. Flamboyant staff serve an à la carte and a daily specials chosen from the fresh fish counter. This includes exotica from around the world such as blackspotted grouper. A lunchtime fish and chips in shandy batter may be exotic enough, even for some from other parts of the UK.

Owens (☎ 01704 501522; www.owensthe restaurant.co.uk; 9b Hougton St; pizzas £8-10, mains £9-16), this plush Italian job has tables lined long, plates piled high and diners kept happy. The decor is clean cut and stylish without a chequered tablecloth or Chianti bottle in sight. The lunchtime soup and sandwich menu (£4.95) is a great deal.

Darcy's (☎ 01704 543290; 52 Eastbank St) is a great little old-style traditional tea and dining rooms with dark wooden floors and Victorian decor, serving a large choice of tea and light snacks. One of the more interesting places in town for a pre-departure nibble.

ST ALBANS
☎ 01727 / pop 114,710

St Albans is a well-to-do little town dating back 2000 years to Roman times when the settlement of Verulamium lay at the bottom of the hill upon which the magnificent cathedral and abbey church now stand. This contains the shrine of St Alban a Roman soldier beheaded in AD 209 for his beliefs and England's first Christian martyr.

Information
The **tourist office** (☎ 01727 864511; www .stalbans.gov.uk; Market Pl) is in the grand town hall in the marketplace. It stocks the St Albans City Trail, a free guide to the town's historic buildings.

Supplies & Equipment
Cycledelik (☎ 0845 371 2870; www.cycle delik.com) is the UK's first company offering roadside assistance and home servicing for bikes! They operate mostly within the M25 doughnut, but as they're based in St Albans, it's worth giving them a call if you bike conks out here. Hopefully more branches

will be opening soon across the country. For more classic workshop-based repairs try **Addiktion Cycles** (☎ 01727 858841; 97 Victoria St) . You're spoilt for choice when it comes to outdoor stores. **Cotswold Outdoor** (☎ 01727 847888; 91 Victoria St) and **Millets** (☎ 01727-856328; 19-21 French Row) are probably the safest options.

Sleeping & Eating
Black Lion Inn (☎ 01727 851786; www .theblacklioninn.com; 198 Fishpool St; s/d from £55/65) is just a few turns of a bike wheel from the city centre. This traditional inn puts up guests in rooms with many period features and feeds them on British and international grub in the very snazzy **Savanna Restaurant**.

Park House (☎ 01727 811910; www .parkhouseonline.co.uk; 30 The Park; s/d £35/55) has bright rooms with crisp white linens, white wicker chairs and subtle floral patterns, which give this small B&B a fresh and airy feel. It's set in a quiet residential area within walking distance of town and is a good deal for the price.

Mantra (☎ 01727 811115; 6 The Collonade; mains £9-12) features excellent modern Japanese food on the menu at this slick joint where sushi, sashimi and maki compete with wonderful curries, noodles and grills. You'll probably have to make a return visit to fit it all in.

Lussmanns Eatery (☎ 01727 851941; Waxhouse Gate; mains £7-16) is a bright, modern restaurant just off the high street and is enduringly popular with locals despite ample competition around town. It serves a menu of mainly Mediterranean dishes in a bright, modern space with oak, leather and metal decor.

Ye Olde Fighting Cocks (☎ 01727 869152; 16 Abbey Mill Ln) is reputedly the oldest pub in England, and this unusual octagonal-shaped inn has oodles of charm. Oliver Cromwell spent a night here, stabling his horses in what's now the bar – underground tunnels lead to the cathedral. Drink in this historic atmosphere while you nurse your pint.

STRATFORD-UPON-AVON
☎ 01789 / pop 22,187

Stratford is a thriving town and a major halt on the tourist trail courtesy of several

Tudor houses associated with Shakespeare's life and theatres devoted to his work. The willow tree-lined river with paddling swans is attractive, though with the sheer number of visitors, you're lucky to get much feeling of intimate discovery here.

Information

The **tourist office** (☎ 0870 160 7930; www .shakespeare-country.co.uk; Bridgefoot) is helpful, open all year but overrun in summer with Shakespeare devotees. A new-fangled 24-hour interactive kiosk allows you to book accommodation out of hours. There's a £3 charge plus 10% deposit to book accommodation through the office.

Supplies & Equipment

Field & Trek (☎ 0870 838 7340; Town Sq) supply Stratfordians and visitors with tents, sleeping bags and other camping essentials. If your bike has turned into a 'comedy of errors', let **The Cycle Studio** (☎ 01789 205057; Guild St) in the very heart of the town put things right.

Sleeping & Eating

Vacancies can be hard to find, especially during summer. If there's no room at any of the following try the tourist office.

Stratford Touring Park (☎ 01789 201063; www.stratfordtouringpark.com; Luddington Rd; two-person sites £11) is a campsite just off Evesham Rd.

Stratford-upon-Avon YHA (☎ 0870 160 7930; Hemmingford Hse, Alveston; dm incl breakfast members/nonmembers £19.95/22.95) is a four-star YHA, situated in a large, 200-year-old mansion 1.5 miles east of the town centre along Tiddington Rd and has room for storing cycles.

Ambleside Guest House (☎ 01789 297239; www.ambleseguesthouse.co.uk; 41 Grove Rd; s/d from £30/50) is a lovely non-frilly B&B, with spotless, homely rooms, amiable hosts who know everything that's going on around town, and great big organic breakfasts.

Vintner Wine Bar (☎ 01789 297259; 5 Sheep St; mains £6.95-12.95) is a quirky space full of beams, exposed brick, and tucked away spaces with low ceilings to bang your head on. There's a relaxed atmosphere and a tasty menu of burgers, grills and pastas with some good vegetarian options.

Dirty Duck (☎ 01789 297312; Waterside), officially called the **Black Swan**, is an enchanting riverside alehouse that should be on your list of must-visit pubs in Stratford. It's a favourite post performance thespian watering hole, and has a roll call of former regulars (Olivier, Attenborough etc) that reads like an actors' *Who's Who*. The adjoining restaurant (11am-10pm) is good value.

Cox's Yard (☎ 01789 404600; Bridgefoot) large riverside complex with a pub, cafe and music venue. It's a lovely place to enjoy a coffee, drink or a full-blown meal while watching the swans glide past.

THURLBY & STAMFORD

☎ 01780 / Stamford pop 19,500

Thurlby is a tiny village and unless you're staying at the local YHA, you're better of shopping in the beautiful town of Stamford, 10 miles back. A maze of streets lined with medieval and handsome Georgian properties in uniform honeycomb sandstone, Stamford never fails to impress and you may find you're in no hurry to continue as you explore its architectural delights and frozen-in-time emporia.

Information

The **tourist office** (☎ 01780 755611; 27 St Mary's St) is in the Stamford Arts Centre, and helps with accommodation. They can also arrange guided town walks and chauffeured punt trips.

Supplies & Equipment

Outdoor and work wear shop **George Alan** (☎ 01780 763327; 1 Red Lion Sq) stocks basic kit. **Richardsons** (☎ 01780 480455; 7 North St) is a local chain of traditional small-town bike store where repairs are carried out by a man in brown overalls and pencil behind his ear. If you're self catering, **Tesco Metro** (46-51 High St) is a handy place to shop for supplies.

Sleeping & Eating

Thurlby YHA (☎ 01778 425588; 16 High St; dm £9.95) is located where the day's ride finishes at this relative outpost 10 miles on from Stamford. When it's full you can camp in the grounds.

Gwynne House (☎ 01780 762210; www .gwynnehouse.co.uk; 13 King's Rd; rooms

£55-90), the rooms at this guesthouse may have touches of 1990s flower-patterned chintz and the building housing them may not be overly inspiring, but the owners make guests feel welcome, there's free wi-fi and all rooms are en suite.

Rock Lodge (☎ 01780 481758; www .rock-lodge.co.uk; 1 Empingham Rd; s/d £70/90) is an imposing Edwardian townhouse that sits haughtily above clipped green lawns, and the welcome is all smiles. The country casual rooms are well looked after and breakfasts (complete with homemade jams) are excellent.

Cloisters (☎ 01780 755162; 9 St Mary's St; pizzas £5.25-9, pasta £7-8) is an Italian restaurant on busy St Mary's St, with minimalist modern leather-and-wood interior that focuses all the attention on the delicious food served here. Simple pizzas and pastas can be washed down with a vintage from the expertly compiled wine list.

The Tobie Norris (☎ 01780 753800; www.tobienorris.com; St Paul's St; pizzas £7-10, mains £7-12) – sometimes you stumble upon a British pub that knocks the stuffing out of you – this is one of them. From the wood-panelled lounge to the large beer garden, and from the red leather boxbenches upstairs to the huge exposed beams in the roof, this place oozes character by the beer barrel and has even won awards for it interiors. As the local CAMRA (Campaign for Real Ale) pub of the year in 2008 it takes its beer seriously. The only surprise here is the Italian menu, which doesn't quite segway into the historic surroundings.

Raj of India (☎ 01780 753556; 2 All Saints St; mains £7-12.50) has a striking gold and black front, behind which it has been serving the good folk of Stamford expertly prepared India dishes for the past 25 years. Poppadoms, pickles and a range of Indian and Bangladeshi dishes.

UTTOXETER

☎ 01889 / pop 12,000

This small market town in East Staffordshire has a name that has been spelt 78 different ways throughout its history, with many still unsure of the number of t's or where exactly they go. It's home to a nationally known racecourse and to the manufacturer of the famous yellow earth-diggers, JCB, a name everyone can spell.

Information

Visit Uttoxeter's **Heritage Centre** (☎ 01889 567176; www.enjoystaffordshire.com; 34-36 Carter St) for tourist information and accommodation listings.

Supplies & Equipment

Uttoxeter Cycle Centre (☎ 01889 567608; 62 Carter St) is just along from the Heritage Centre. There's a **Tesco** supermarket (Brookside Rd) opposite the train station if you're sourcing your own provisions.

Sleeping & Eating

Around 10 miles north of Uttoxeter is Alton Towers, one of the UK's top theme parks, which attracts fun-seekers in their millions. Most visitors opt to stay in nearby villages meaning ample supply but heavy occupancy, especially in the school summer holidays. There are a limited number of places to stay in Uttoxeter itself.

Uttoxeter Racecourse Caravan Site (☎ 01889 564172; Wood La; sites £5.20 plus £4.25 per adult) is located in the centre of the racecourse oval half a mile east of town, call ahead as they close for race days once or twice a month (though you might still be let in).

Oldroyd Guest House (☎ 01889 562763; www.oldroyd-guesthouse.com; 18-22 Bridge St; s/d £30/50) is a welcoming family-run B&B near the train station with light, airy but slightly cramped rooms. Comfortable and well-situated, we were assured room could found for bikes overnight.

The White Hart (☎ 01889 562437; Carter St; rooms £50/70; mains £6-10) is a fully refurbished 16th-century coaching inn boasting decent rooms though breakfast is an extra £3.95. The extensive menu of filling British pub grub and some more sophisticated dishes is just what you want to see after a hard day in the saddle.

Indulgence Coffee Lounge (☎ 01889 568064; 1 Lions Buildings, Market Pl) is a relaxed coffee shop serving light lunches and lip smacking desserts under exposed beams.

YORK

For information on facilities in York, see the Towns & Facilities section (p258) in the Northern England chapter.

Wales

- Ride the relatively traffic-free **Taff Trail** to the fairytale **Castell Coch** (p184)
- Cycle around lakes, through river valleys and over rolling hills in picturesque **Brecon Beacons National Park** (p188).
- Check out more than 120 bikes and memorabilia at the **National Cycle Exhibition** (p189) in Llandrindod
- Get off the bike and tramp through the mist aiming for the desolate summit of **Snowdon** (p182), Wales' highest peak
- Explore locations used in hit TV series *Dr Who* and *Torchwood* against the stunning backdrop of the revitalised **Cardiff Bay** (p206)

TERRAIN

Rolling hills and gentle uplands yielding to rugged ranges around Snowdonia National Park to the northwest and the Brecon Beacons and Black Mountains in the south.

Telephone Code: ☎ 029	www.visitwales.com

There's never been a better time to hop on your bike and start exploring Wales on two wheels. Cyclists will love the 1000 miles of cycle paths on the National Cycle Network (NCN) and arguably the best mountain biking in the UK. As well as its natural attractions, Wales boasts national parks, World Heritage sites, medieval castles, and dozens of beaches that provide endless opportunities for off-road entertainment. The valleys of southern Wales are home to many historic places including, Caerphilly's colossal 13th-century castle.

Ride through picturesque woodland, switch gears navigating switchbacks and climbs, then weave down adrenaline-pumping descents on some of the steepest and most challenging terrain in the Brecon Beacons National Park. Following any of the dedicated biking trails throughout Wales will have you rolling through spectacular countryside scenery, up mountainous slopes, and across valleys strewn with summer wildflowers. The Cardiff to Brecon and Brecon Beacons Gap on the Lôn Las Cymru ride are great places to start.

With a backdrop of pine-covered hillsides, cascading waterfalls spilling into crystal clear lakes, and awe-inspiring mountain vistas, it's no wonder Betws-y-Coed is often called the outdoor adventure capital of Wales (see Views from the Valley ride). Whether you prefer pedalling leisurely along ancient pathways or humping it across rugged trails, Wales has something for everyone to experience.

ENVIRONMENT

At 170 miles in length and 60 miles in width, Wales is surrounded by the sea on three sides and England to the east. There are two main mountain systems: the Black Mountains and Brecon Beacons in the south, and the more rugged glaciated mountains of Snowdonia in the northwest, deeply cut by narrow river valleys. These areas are joined by the hills and uplands of the Cambrian Mountains, which run north–south through much of central Wales. At 1085m (3650ft), Snowdon is the highest peak in England and Wales. With the exception of the island of Anglesey, there's no avoiding the hills on almost any tour through Wales.

PLANNING

If you are cycling on the high hills or open moors at any time of year it's essential to be prepared with rain gear and warm clothing, even in summer. Good maps, a compass, some water, food or energy bars are also vital. Pick up a copy of *Cycling Wales*, a free, comprehensive booklet describing cycling opportunities, tour operators and bike-friendly accommodation throughout the country.

Place Names

With its seemingly unpronounceable chains of consecutive consonants, Welsh is closely related to Cornish and Breton, and more distantly related to Irish Gaelic,

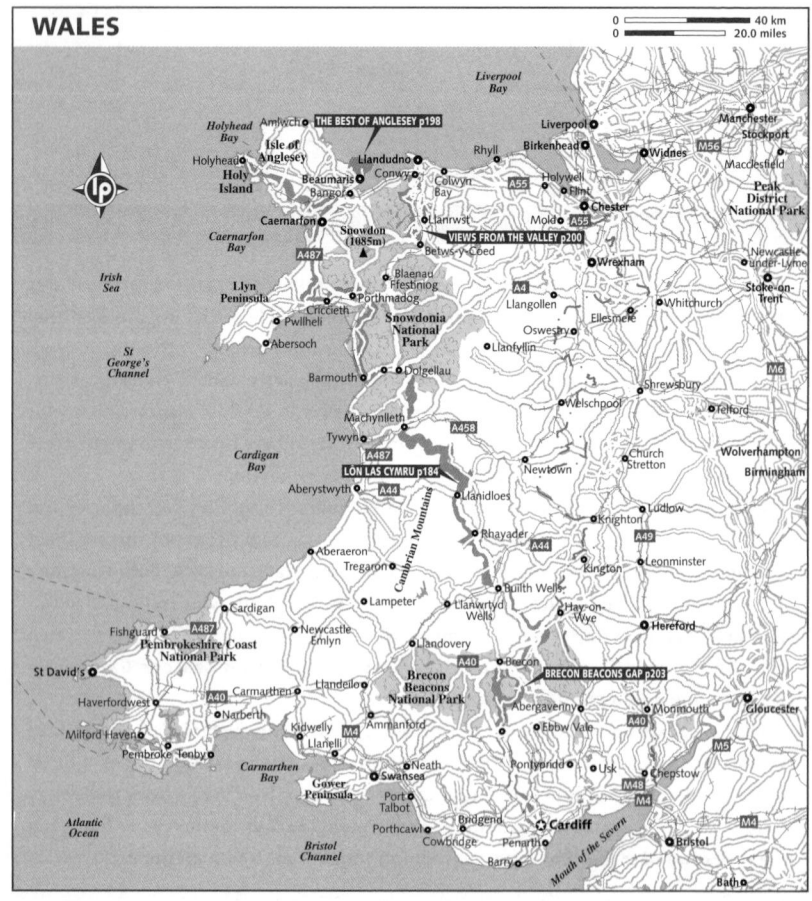

WELSH (CYMRAEG)

All vowels except y can be short or long. A circumflex accent (eg ê) lengthens the vowel sound:

- a   long, as in 'far', *tad* (father)
- a   short, as in 'ham', *mam* (mother)
- e   long, as in 'whey', *hen* (old)
- e   short, as in 'ten', *pen* (head)
- i   long, as in 'marine', *mis* (month)
- i   short, as in 'pin', *prin* (scarce)
- o   long, as in 'more', *môr* (sea)
- o   short, as in 'fond', *ffon* (walking stick)

- w   long, as the 'oo' in 'moon', *swn* (sound)
- w   short, as the 'u' in 'put', *gwn* (gun)
- y   has three possible pronunciations: as the 'i' in 'marine', *dyn* (man); as the 'i' in 'pin', *cyn* (before); as the 'u' in 'run', *dynion* (men)
- oe   as the 'oy' in 'annoyed', *coed* (wood)
- u   as the 'i' in 'pimp', *pump* (five)

Welsh consonants are similar to their English counterparts, but there are a few exceptions:

- c   always hard, as in 'cat', *cwm* (valley or corrie)
- ch   as in Scottish loch, *fach* (small)
- dd   as 'th' in 'them', *mynydd* (mountain)
- f   as in 'of' (not as in 'if'), *fach* (small)
- ff   as in 'off', *ffenestr* (window)

- g   as in 'go', *gwyn* (white)
- th   as in 'three', *byth* (ever)
- ll   there is no exact equivalent sound in English; it's somewhere between the English 'l' and Scottish 'ch' (as in loch) – a little like the 'tl' in 'antler', *llyn* (lake)

WORDS & PHRASES

If you're feeling brave, here are a few expressions you might try out in the Welsh-speaking parts of the country (word stress is usually on the second-last syllable in Welsh pronunciation):

- Good morning   *Bore da*
- Good afternoon   *Prynhawn da*
- Good night   *Nos da*
- Hello   *Sut mae or S'mae*
- Please   *Os gwelch in dda*
- Thanks   *Diolch*
- I don't understand   *Dw i ddim in deall*
- Cheers!   *Iechyd da!*
- (very) good   *da (iawn)*

- How much   *faint?*
- Bike shop   *beic siop*
- Women   *Merched*
- Men   *Dynion*
- Entrance   *Mynedfa*
- Open   *Ar Agor*
- Closed   *Ar Gau*
- Exit   *Allanfa*

Check the Glossary (p397) for common words cyclists may encounter. If you'd like a more comprehensive guide to Welsh, get a copy of Lonely Planet's *British Phrasebook*.

Manx Gaelic and Scottish Gaelic. The language as it is spoken today, although later influenced by French and English, seems to have been more or less fully developed by the 6th century, making it one of Europe's oldest languages.

Information Sources

The following websites have cycling info:
- www.cycling.visitwales.com
- www.sustrans.co.uk

GETTING THERE & AWAY

Cardiff, the Welsh capital, is 155 miles from London and the region's gateway. Unless you are driving (or biking from southwest England, Bristol is just 50 miles to the southeast), your bus, train or plane will more than likely debunk you here.

Flights from London and mainland Europe arrive at **Cardiff International Airport** (☎ 01446 711111; www.info .cwlfly.com), 12 miles southwest of the city centre. **Cardiff Central Train Station** (☎ 0845 6061 660; www.national rail.co.uk; off Penarth Rd) is on the main InterCity London to Swansea route. Trains connect Cardiff with Pembroke Dock via Tenby – Milford Haven via Haverfordwest – and Fishguard Harbour (for Rosslare in Ireland). Cardiff Valley Lines has regional services (from Cardiff Central or Queen St) to Merthyr Tydfil, Aberdare, Pontypridd, Treherbert, Rhymney and Coryton.

GATEWAY

See Cardiff (p206).

LÔN LAS CYMRU

Duration 7 days
Distance 261.7 miles
Difficulty moderate–demanding
Start Cardiff
Finish Holyhead

Summery From the bustling southern capital of Cardiff to the fertile flats of Anglesey and Holyhead up north, this epic ride traverses the length of Wales and is 'the' way to experience the country.

One of the jewels of the NCN, the classic Lôn Las Cymru (Welsh National Route) provides a wonderful means of experiencing much of Wales' finest scenery up close. Traveling the length of the country, this is the most diverse, and interesting, cycling route in Wales. The described route starts in Cardiff – an alternative route beginning in Chepstow (not described) meets the main route just outside Glasbury.

PLANNING

This cycling route is well signed with plenty of transport and accommodation options along the way. Predictably, this tour is fairly hilly throughout, especially in mid Wales. With that in mind, the days are intentionally short. Try and get out over the summer months, which offer the longest and warmest days and the best chance of fine weather.

Maps

Sustrans produces two excellent maps at 1:100,000 detailing the route, *Lôn Las Cymru – south*, from Cardiff or Chepstow to Builth Wells, and *Lôn Las Cymru –*

north, from Builth Wells to Holyhead. They are available from tourist offices along the route or from **Sustrans direct** (www .sustrans.org.uk). For the first day, the Taff Trail is covered by a set of six pamphlets detailing the route, with maps and lots of information about sights encountered along the way.

GETTING TO/FROM THE RIDE
Cardiff (start)

See Wales Getting There & Away (p206) for information about getting to/from Cardiff.

Holyhead (finish)
FERRY

There are regular ferry services between Holyhead and Dublin. **Stena** (☎ 0870 570 7070) and **Irish Ferries** (☎ 0870 513 4324) both have several daily crossings.

TRAIN

There are frequent train services from Holyhead to Cardiff (£55, five hours), London (£80, 4½ hours) and several Welsh destinations.

THE RIDE
Day 1: Cardiff to Brecon
5–7 hours, 51 miles

Utilising a combination of traffic-free trails, rail and canal paths, as well as quiet country roads, the **Taff Trail** links the heart of Cardiff with the principal gateway of the wonderfully scenic Brecon Beacons National Park. If only cycling out of all capital cities could be so easy! Once into leafy **Bute Park**, the path joins the **River Taff** and travels upstream, staying more or less beside the river until you're clear of Cardiff's urban fringe. The only hazards on the shady path are numerous dog-walking pedestrians also out enjoying the tranquil surroundings.

From the unremarkable village of Tongwynlais, the route climbs sharply up to spectacular **Castell Coch**, a fairytale fortress perched high on the wooded slopes behind the town. Predominantly a 19th-century creation by William Burges the ostentatious interiors display a 'spare no expense' approach. It's a wealthy man's medieval fantasy. From the castle car park, a steep path leads to the top of the wooded hillside before descending to join a rail trail that extends most of the remaining distance

LÔN LAS CYMRU – DAY 1

CUE		GPS COORDINATES	
start	Cardiff Castle entrance	51°28′48″N	3°10′43″W
0 miles	go west on Castle St		
0.2	into Bute Park		
	(50yd) follow path to river		
0.8	join path closest to River Taff		
3.5	'Taff Trail'		
4.0	'Taff Trail'		
5.5	path under road bridge		
5.9	under road bridge		
6.1	Merthyr Rd		
6.2	'to Castell Coch', Tongwynlais	51°32′8″N	3°14′58″W
6.5	'to Castell Coch'		
{6.8	Castell Coch}		
	(50yd) steep trail from car park		
⚠	0.9 miles dirt road		
6.9	'Taff Trail' (at top of hill)		
7.7	join rail trail (at bottom of hill)		
8.9	rail trail		
9.4	'Taff Trail'		
9.5	thru gate onto rail trail		
13.1	Cemetery Rd		
13.2	A4054, Pontypridd	51°36′4″N	3°20′59″W
17.0	B4275 'to Abercynon'		
17.1	unsigned road		
17.3	join path beside fire station		
⚠	3.3 miles dirt road		
18.7	stay on rail trail		
20.5	'Taff Trail'		
20.6	over bridge and thru underpass		
	(50yd) at top of steps		
22.1	'Taff Trail' (on descent)		
27.5	cross A4102, Merthyr Tydfil	51°44′51.19″N	3°22′41.30″W

CUE CONTINUED		GPS COORDINATES	
27.6	along road		
27.7	join riverside path, 'Taff Trail'		
28.0	join road, 'Taff Trail'		
28.1	'to Brecon'		
{	Cyfarthfa Castle}		
29.0	Old Drill Hall Rd		
29.1	lane beside churchyard		
31.9	join road, 'Taff Trail'		
32.9	along dam wall		
33.1	at end of dam wall		
33.4	'to Talybont-on-Usk'		
33.6	thru gate		
⚠	2.4 miles bumpy dirt road		
36.0	join road by edge of reservoir		
37.9	by camping area		
⚠	0.7 miles dirt road		
38.6	unsigned road		
▲	600yd moderate climb		
39.2	gated dirt road		
⚠	3.8 miles dirt road		
44.2	along dam wall		
44.5	join narrow road		
45.8	narrow lane 'Taff Trail'		
46.6	'to Brecon'		
47.7	'to Plas Pencelli', Pencelli	51°54′56″N	3°19′7″W
49.2	by churchyard, Llanfrynach	51°55′20″N	3°20′46″W
49.9	'to Brecon'		
50.3	join canal towpath at lock		
50.5	Rich Way		
50.6	The Watton		
50.7	Glamorgan St		
	(50yd) Wheat St/B4520		
50.9	by Kwik Save supermarket		
51.0	Brecon TIC (end of car park)	51°56′54″N	3°23′34″W

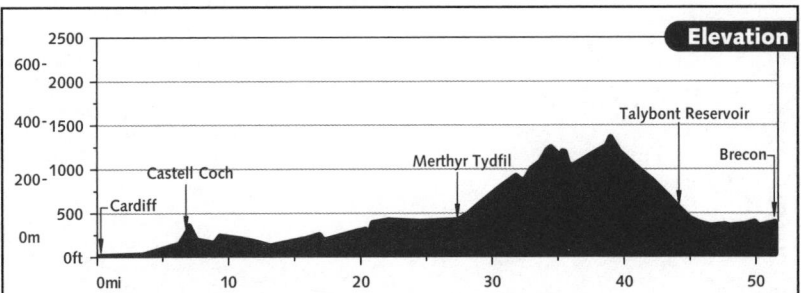

into Pontypridd. Unless you're in need of a drink or other supplies, however, it's easiest to stay on the A4054 instead of following the signed route through the town centre.

Near Abercynon turn off the A4054 (left) by a **fire station** and follow the Taff Trail as it parallels the river once more. The traffic-free path meanders through a very

WALES

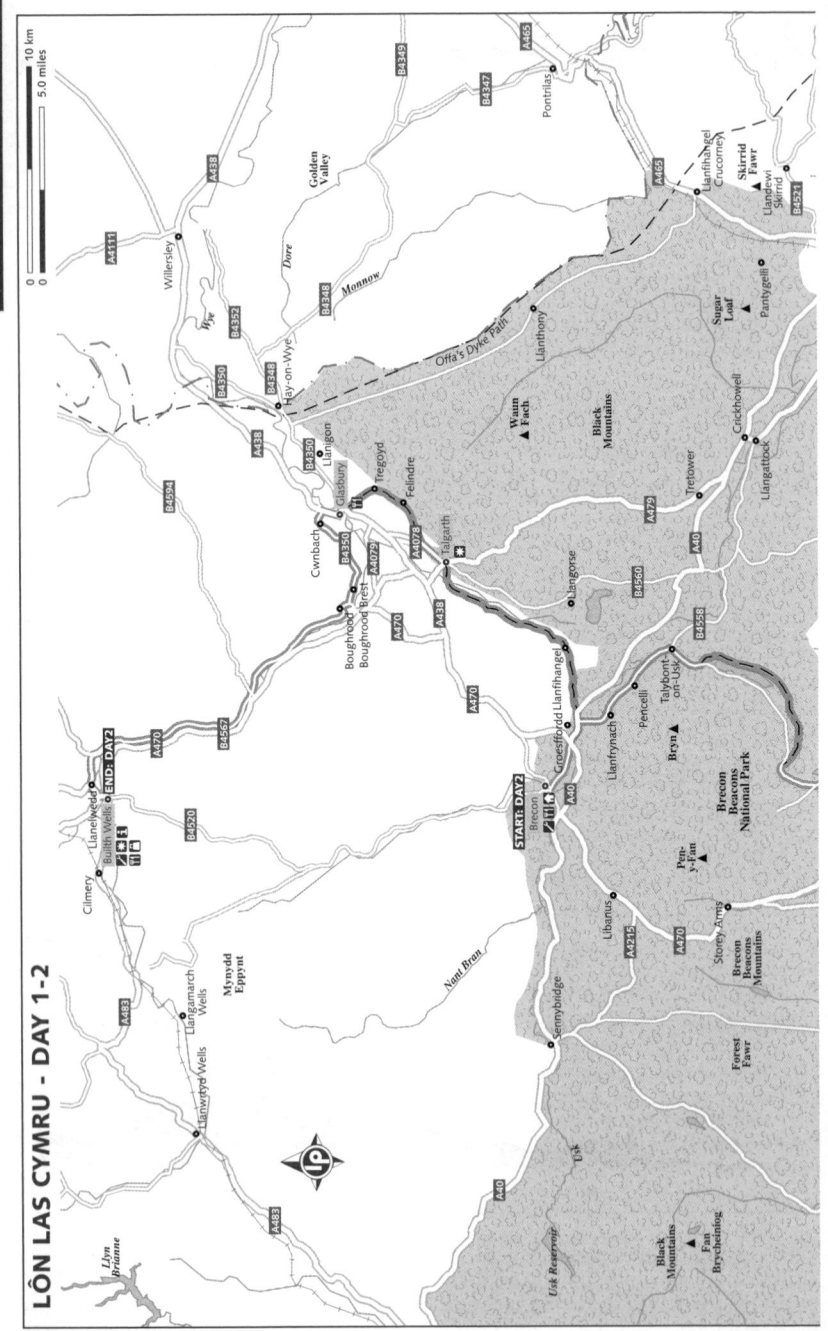

LÔN LAS CYMRU - DAY 1-2

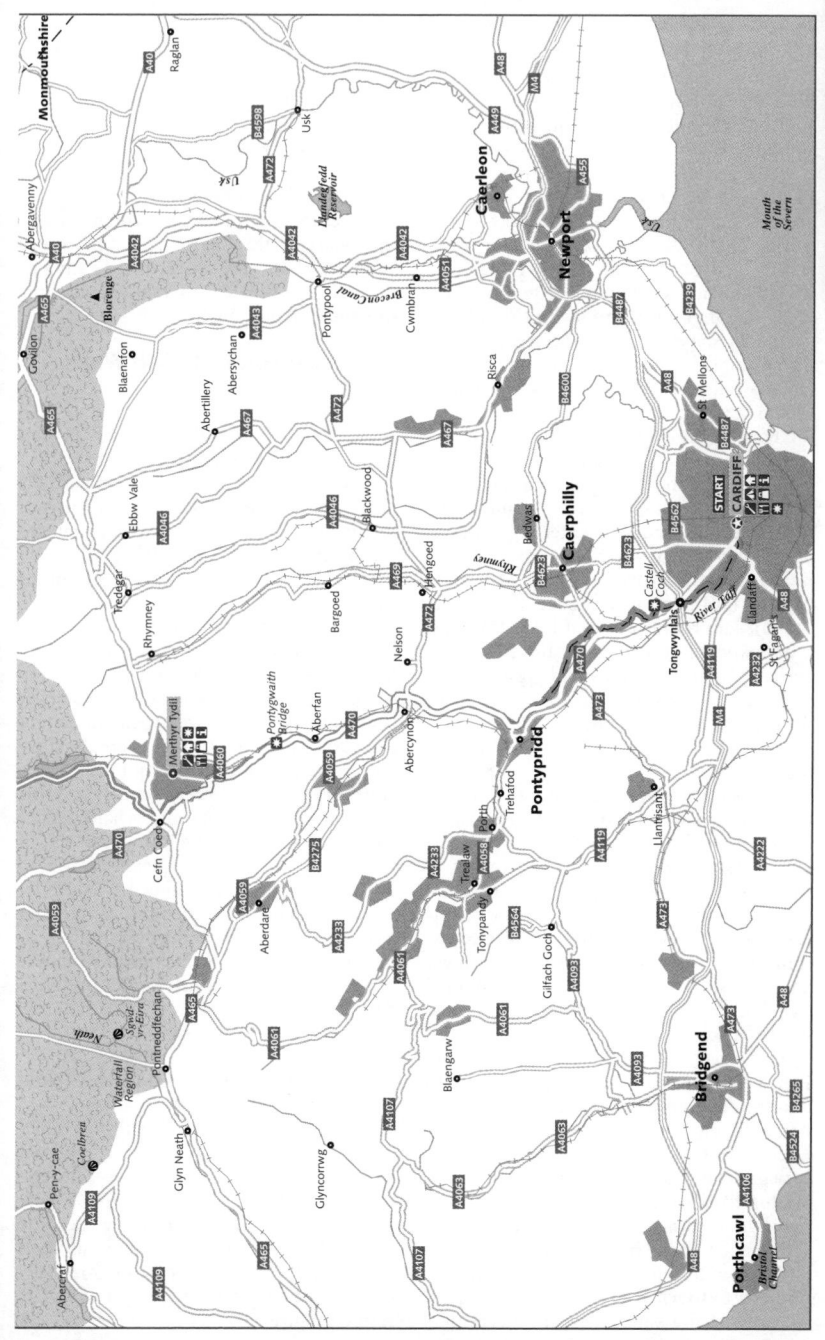

scenic wooded section before crossing the humpbacked **Pontygwaith Bridge**. Here, a flight of steps heads away from the Taff River and into more open scenery, passing a string of former coal-mining settlements along the valley below.

At 27.5 miles you arrive in **Merthyr Tydfil**. During the 19th century, the town was home to one of the largest ironworks in the world. That's all long gone, but Merthyr, at the head of the Taff Valley, remains a sizeable town it's a good place for an overnight stay if you want to tackle the ride in two easier stages. Unlike Brecon it also has the advantage of a rail link back to Cardiff. On the outskirts of town, pass **Cyfarthfa Castle**, a grand residence built in 1825 for the boss of the Merthyr Tydfil ironworks, which is now museum and art gallery.

Once out of the Taff Valley, the nature of the landscape changes: leave the industrial settlements behind and enter the wilder, more spectacular environs of **Brecon Beacons National Park**. Behind **St John's Church** (at the northwest edge of Merthyr Tydfil), join a rail trail that leads through a dramatic gorge carved by the River Taf Fechan. The river is crossed by way of the magnificent **Pontsarn Viaduct**, a relic of the Merthyr to Brecon railway, whose seven stately arches soar up to 28m (92ft) above the valley floor.

Not long after the path rejoins the road is the **Pontsticill Reservoir** (Llyn Taf Fechan) – cycle across the dam wall to join a road signed **Talybont-on-Usk**. At the top of a short climb, the Taff Trail once again heads off-road, joining a bumpy, stony track that traverses the hillside. This section affords some great views of the reservoir below, and across the water to the Brecon Mountain Railway, chugging along on the opposite bank.

The track rejoins the road beside the **Pentwyn Reservoir** and begins to climb once more, eventually rising to the highest point on the trail 39 miles into the day. The descent that follows is awesome, the very gradual gradient maximising the payoff for hard-won height. Inspiring views make good company from the head of the valley and along the Talybont Reservoir. Sit back and enjoy the scenery – there's no need to touch your pedals for the next 5.2 miles. On a sunny day, the steep hills

covered in pines cascading down to meet the blue water's edge are reminiscent of the Norwegian fjords.

The descent ends as the route splits from the trail (walkers only), crosses the dam wall, joining a series of quiet lanes that travel through the small villages of Aber, Pencelli and Llanfrynach. At the Brynich Lock, leave the road and pass colourful narrow boats on the final miles into **Brecon**, a quaint Welsh market town. The smooth towpath runs beside the serene Monmouthsire and Brecon Canal.

Day 2: Brecon to Builth Wells
3–4 hours, 32.4 miles

The route out of town follows the Taff Trail along the Monmouthshire and Brecon Canal, before turning off (left) at the lock and heading up into the lush, green hills near Groesffordd. Busy little **Talgarth** is the first substantial settlement encountered during the day, a friendly village home to the imposing 14th-century **St Gwendoline's Church**.

After a short stint on the moderately busy A4078, turn back onto a quiet country lane that leads through Felindre and on to Tregoyd. Continue past the outdoor activity centre and turn left at the crossroads, about 875 yards further on (this is where the alternative route from Chepstow joins the ride). **Glasbury**, with a couple of good pubs, is the next village of any size and a handy place to break for lunch. The rest of the ride is relatively easy and very pleasant, passing fertile pastures and shadowing the River Wye (Afon Gwy) for much of the way. After a short final stretch on the busy A481, pass by the **Royal Welsh Showground**, home of the giant Royal Welsh Show, and cross a bridge over the River Wye to end the day in the centre **Builth Wells**.

Day 3: Builth Wells to Llanidloes
3½–4 hours, 32.4 miles

Although there aren't any really big climbs, progress throughout the day is rarely easy as the route never stays on level ground for long. After leaving town on a path along the banks of the River Wye head up into lush green hills. The numerous short climbs are rewarded with some fine views of Builth Wells surrounded by a collage of fertile pastures.

LÔN LAS CYMRU – DAY 2

CUE			GPS COORDINATES	
start		Brecon TIC	51°56'54"N	3°23'34"W
0 miles		go south thru Bethel Square		
	↰	(100yd) Lion St		
0.1	↑	The Watton		
0.2	↱	Rich Way 'to canal & theatre'		
0.3	↰ ⊙	unsigned road (past theatre)		
	↑	(40yd) join canal path		
2.4	↰	B4558 'to Groesffordd'		
2.7	↱	'to Llanfihangel'		
5.1	↘	'NCR8', Llanfihangel	51°56'49"N	3°17'21"W
9.6	↱	High St 'to town centre'		
9.9	★	Talgarth	51°59'45"N	3°13'56"W
	↑	(60yd) Hay Rd		
10.2	↱	A4078 'to Hay-on-Wye'		
11.0	↱	'NCR8'		
12.7		Felindre	52° 1'20"N	3°11'21"W
13.8		Tregoyd	52° 1'21"N	3° 9'50"W
14.3	↰	'NCR8' (after activity centre)		

CUE CONTINUED			GPS COORDINATES	
14.6	↱	'NCR8' (second turn-off)		
15.1	↘	'NCR8'		
15.9	↱	'NCR8'		
16.1	↱	A438 'to Glasbury'		
	↰	(100yd) A438 (over bridge)		
16.2	↰	B4350, Glasbury	52° 2'43"N	3°12'4"W
19.6	↰	B4350 'to Boughrood'		
20.0	↱	Station Rd, Boughrood	52° 2'42"N	3°16'20"W
20.6	↘	'NCR8'		
21.9	↘	'NCR8'		
24.6	↰	B4567 'to Builth Wells'		
30.4	↰	A481 'to Builth Wells'		
31.3	↰	A481		
31.7	↰ ⊙	'to tourist information'		
32.0	↙	High St (cross bridge)		
32.2	↱	'to tourist information'		
32.3	↱	The Strand		
32.4		Builth Wells TIC	52° 8'59"N	3°24'8"W

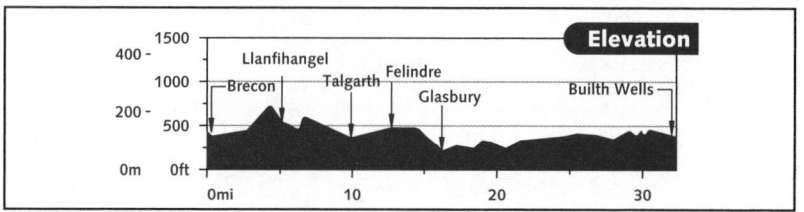

Elevation chart showing Brecon, Llanfihangel, Talgarth, Felindre, Glasbury, Builth Wells along the route from 0mi to 30mi, with elevation scale in m (0m, 500, 1000, 1500) and ft (0ft, 200, 400).

The River Wye is never far from the day's route. Cross it shortly before entering **Newbridge-on-Wye** (7.1 miles), then follow it up the spectacular Wye valley for much of the day. There's a 1.9-mile off-road section along a grassy track that starts 10.2 miles from Builth Wells. Although it's relatively smooth, the surface can get soft and muddy in the wet. As the track steadily gains height, there are some great views through occasional breaks in the dense pine forest.

Beyond **Rhayader** – one of the larger towns of the day, with a good selection of lunch spots – the quiet road continues to shadow the River Wye. The scenery is particularly stunning here as the valley narrows and high hills tower overhead. The route bids farewell to the River Wye at Llangurig. After a short steep climb, followed by an enjoyably long descent, catch your first glimpse of another fine waterway (Britain's longest river in fact), the Severn (Afron Hafren – where afron means 'river').

SIDE TRIP: NATIONAL CYCLE EXHIBITION
1 hour, 8.4 miles

It would be a shame to cycle through this part of the country and not check out the **National Cycle Exhibition** (☎ 01597 825531; Temple St) in Llandrindod Wells. Occupying the historic Automobile Palace, now known as the Tom Norton building, there are more than 120 bikes on display, ranging from penny farthings to the very latest high-tech offerings recreations of Victorian and Edwardian cycle shops – and tributes to British cycling greats Tom Simpson (1965 professional road race world champion) and Barry Hoban, winner of eight Tour de France stages.

From **Newbridge-on-Wye**, follow the B4358 and continue east as it joins the A4081. The road forks about two miles further on. Take the right fork, continuing south on the A4081/Spa Rd into Llandrindod Wells. The museum is centrally located, facing the crossroads where the A4081 joins the A483/Temple St.

WALES

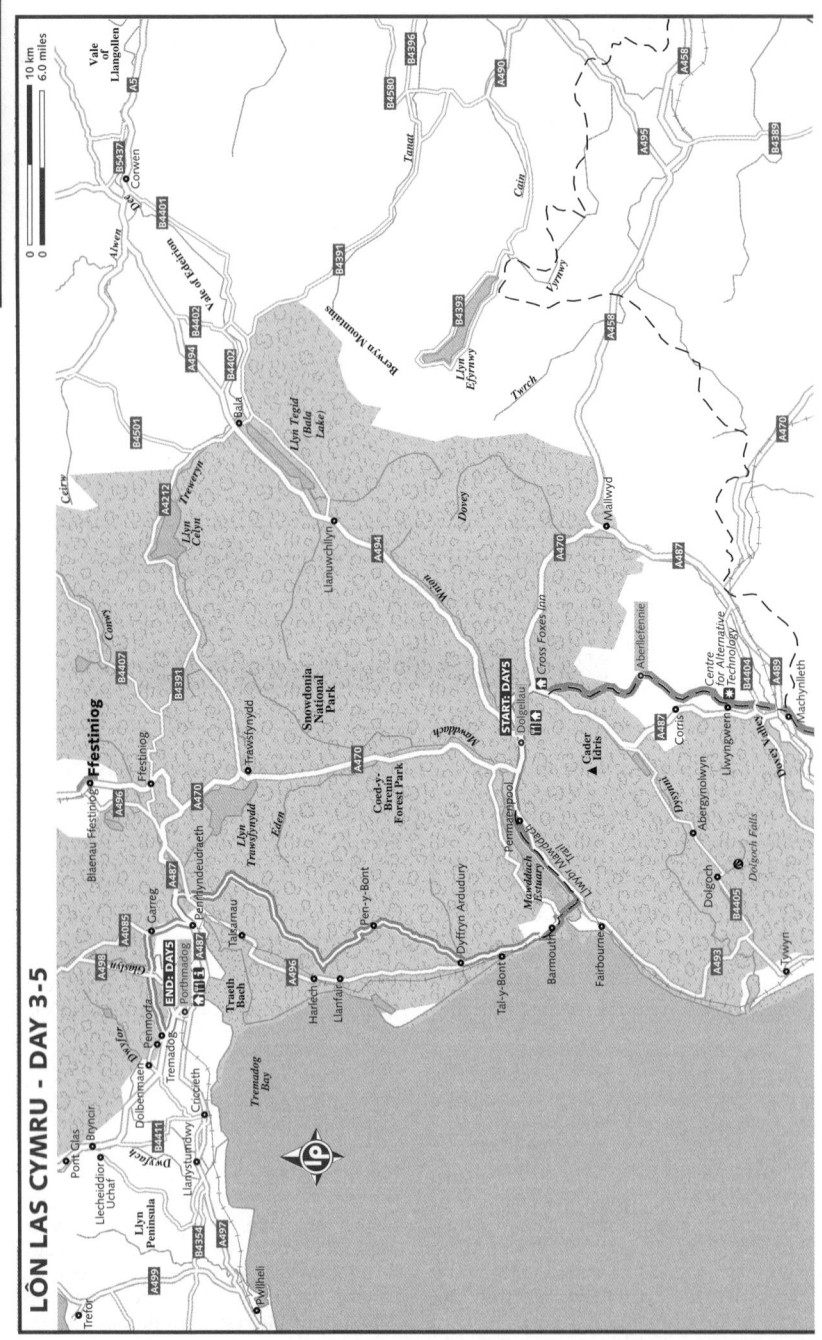

LÔN LAS CYMRU - DAY 3-5

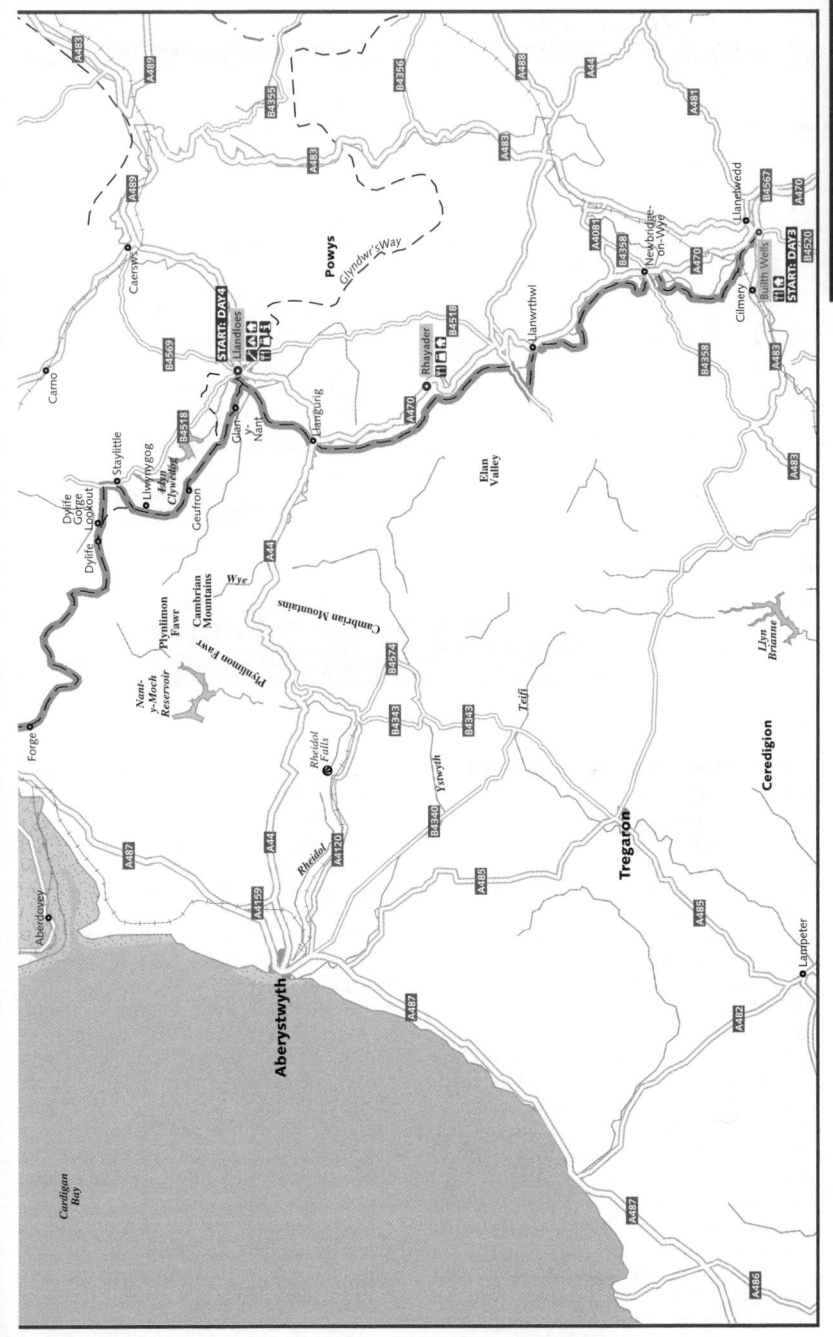

WALES

LÔN LAS CYMRU – DAY 3

CUE		GPS COORDINATES
start	Builth Wells TIC	52°8'59"N 3°24'8"W
0 miles	go W on river path behind TIC	
0.6	walk over footbridge	
	(40yd) Golf Links Rd	
4.2	'to Newbridge-on-Wye'	
5.0	'to Newbridge-on-Wye'	
6.6	A470	
7.1	Newbridge-on-Wye	52°12'48"N 3°26'28"W
{	National Cycle Exhibition 8.4 miles }	
7.4	B4358 'to Beulah'	
7.7	'to Llysdinam' (over bridge)	
7.8	1.2 miles moderate climb	
9.3	'NCR8'	
10.2	join grassy track	
	1.9 miles grassy track	
	1.5 miles moderate climb	

CUE CONTINUED		GPS COORDINATES
13.6	'to Elan village', Llanwrthwl	52°16'30"N 3°33'54"W
	600m moderate climb	
13.7	'to Elan village'	
14.0	'to Elan village'	
16.2	'to Rhayader'	
16.4	B4518	
	1000yd moderate climb	
17.4	'NCR8', Rhayader	
17.9	'NCR8'	
20.0	1200yd moderate climb	
27.6	A44, Llangurig	52°24'22"N 3°36'20"W
27.7	Cae Capel (by Blue Bell Inn)	
	600yd hard climb	
32.3	Shortbridge St (over bridge)	
32.4	Longbridge St (at old market hall)	
32.4	(18yd) Llanidloes TIC	52°26'57"N 3°32'23"W

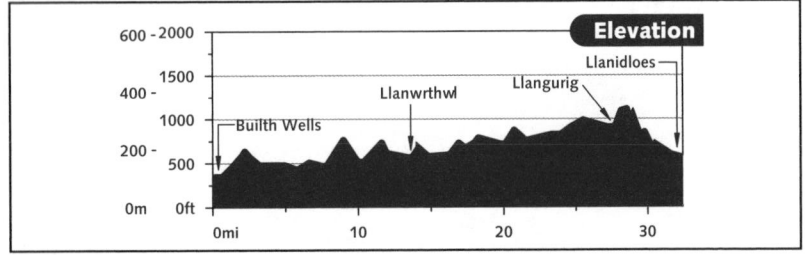

Day 4: Llanidloes to Dolgellau
4–4½ hours, 38.8 miles

This is a testing day at times, with two major climbs. You start gaining height shortly after leaving Llanidloes, travelling up a lush valley with the River Severn away to your left. The route winds its way through the Hafren pine forest with large stands of plantation timber flanking the road. A **picnic area** with toilet facilities (7 miles from Llanidloes) provides a good spot to take an early breather.

Once out of the woods, turn off the B4518 and join a narrow mountain road, coming to a roadside rest area and lookout over the dramatic **Dylife Gorge** (13.2 miles). The first of the day's substantial climbs commences shortly after: a testing 1.4-mile ascent on a lonely road up to the highest point (509m/1669ft) of the whole tour.

A fantastic 4.3-mile descent follows with some great views from numerous vantage points along the way. The downhill trend continues for the rest of the journey into **Machynlleth**. A sizeable town, and once the ancient capital of Wales, it's a cosmopolitan place and a nice stopover for a drink or snack. The influence of the area's refreshing alternative lifestylers is evident on High St.

After a short stint on the A487, turn off onto a quiet, rolling road. It passes the **Centre for Alternative Technology** (CAT; ☎ 01654 702400; www.cat.org.uk), an outstanding 40-acre site established in 1974, dedicated to promoting sustainable technology and energy conservation. There are plenty of things to see and do – you could easily occupy half a day. If you feel like lingering longer, there's a really nice riverside camping ground across the road at Llwyngwern Farm.

The 'Scandinavian' landscape of steep, pine-covered hills changes briefly but dramatically just after **Aberllefenni** as you cycle through a slate quarry with giant piles of the grey stone stacked beside the road.

LÔN LAS CYMRU – DAY 4

CUE		GPS COORDINATES	
start	Llanidloes TIC	52°26′57″N	3°32′23″W
0 miles	go SW on Longbridge St		
	(40yd) Shortbridge St		
0.1	Pennygreen Rd (over bridge)		
3.0	'to Staylittle'		
11.2	Llwynygog	52°34′55″N	3°31′28″W
11.7	B4518 'to Llanbrynmair'		
12.6	'to Machynlleth'		
{13.2 ★	Dylife Gorge Lookout}		
14.0 ▲	1.4 miles hard climb		
22.6	'to Machynlleth', Forge	52°34′35″N	3°48′52″W
23.6	A489		
23.8 ★	Machynlleth	52°35′26″N	3°51′12″W
	'to Dolgellau'		

CUE CONTINUED		GPS COORDINATES	
24.6	A487 over bridge		
25.1	'to Llanwrin'		
25.2	'to Centre for Alt Tech'		
{26.7 ★	Centre for Alternative Technology (RHS)}		
	'NCR8'		
27.9	Ceinws	52°38′15″N	3°50′26″W
29.5	Bridge St, Corris	52°39′9″N	3°50′33″W
31.2	thru slate quarry, Aberllefenni	52°40′24″N	3°49′11″W
31.3 ▲	2.5 miles hard climb		
32.9 ⚠	1.9 miles gravel track		
34.8	A487		
36.0	'to Tabor'		
38.5	Arran Rd		
38.8	Dolgellau TIC		

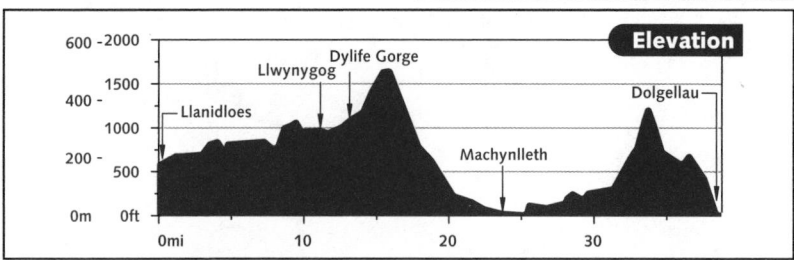

Elevation

It also marks the beginning of the day's second major climb. The road becomes a rough track, a mixture of slate shards and grass. It's steep, rough and slippery, so unless you have fat tyres and an abundance of energy, you'll probably have to push your bike most of the way up. Thankfully, getting down the other side is considerably easier, the predominantly grassy path a little bumpy in places but definitely rideable. The final two miles in to sleepy **Dolgellau**, where you spend the night, are a nice end-of-day downhill reward.

Day 5: Dolgellau to Porthmadog
3–3½ hours, 35.3 miles

After several days of cycling through the Welsh interior it's time to hit the coast! A short distance out of Dolgellau, the route joins the **Llwybr Mawddach Trail**, a relatively smooth rail trail along the scenic shores of the **Mawddach Estuary** – take your time, this is some of the best cycling on the trip.

A toll bridge (60p) leads to the coast at **Barmouth**, a traditional seaside resort

enjoying a dramatic setting between the mountains and the sea. The various amusement arcades, snack bars and guesthouses along the promenade look a bit grim, but there are plenty of places to grab refreshments. At the end of the promenade, climb briefly and join the A496 for a traffic heavy stint of peddling. You escape the congestion of the motorway at **Dyffryn Ardudury**, and climb on quiet lanes into sheep-grazing country, where the green hills are crisscrossed by a myriad of dry-stone walls. A multitude of gates can make progress frustrating at times. A nice descent through a lush patch of woods leads to a nice respite, but get ready: it leads to the start of the major ascent of the day, a gradual 4.3-mile climb. The upside is, the haul up has great views over Tremadog Bay as you approach the summit.

Back on level ground, another toll bridge (free this time) crosses the River Dwyryd into Penrhyndeudraeth. Here, join the A4085 to start the easy, but indirect final leg into the busy seaside town of **Porthmadog**.

WALES

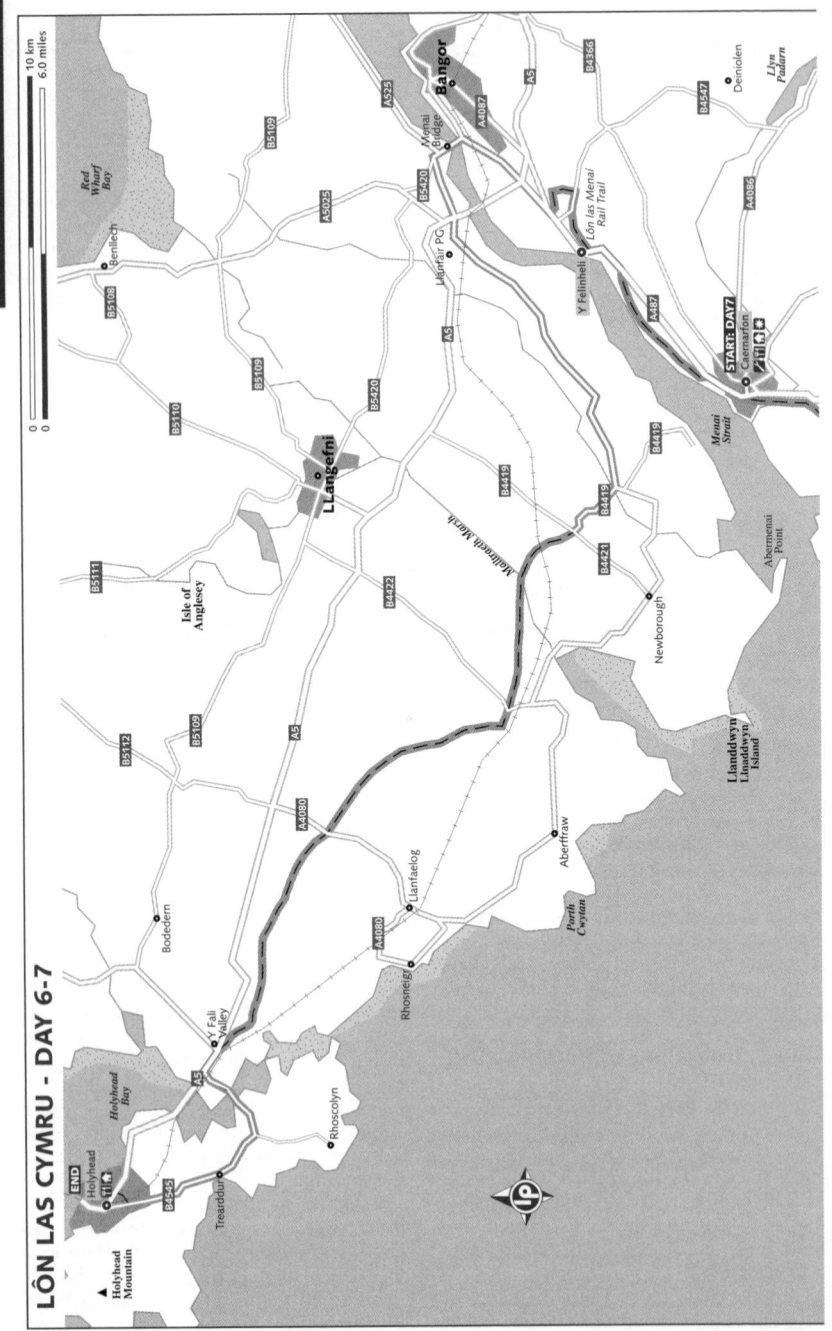

LÔN LAS CYMRU - DAY 6-7

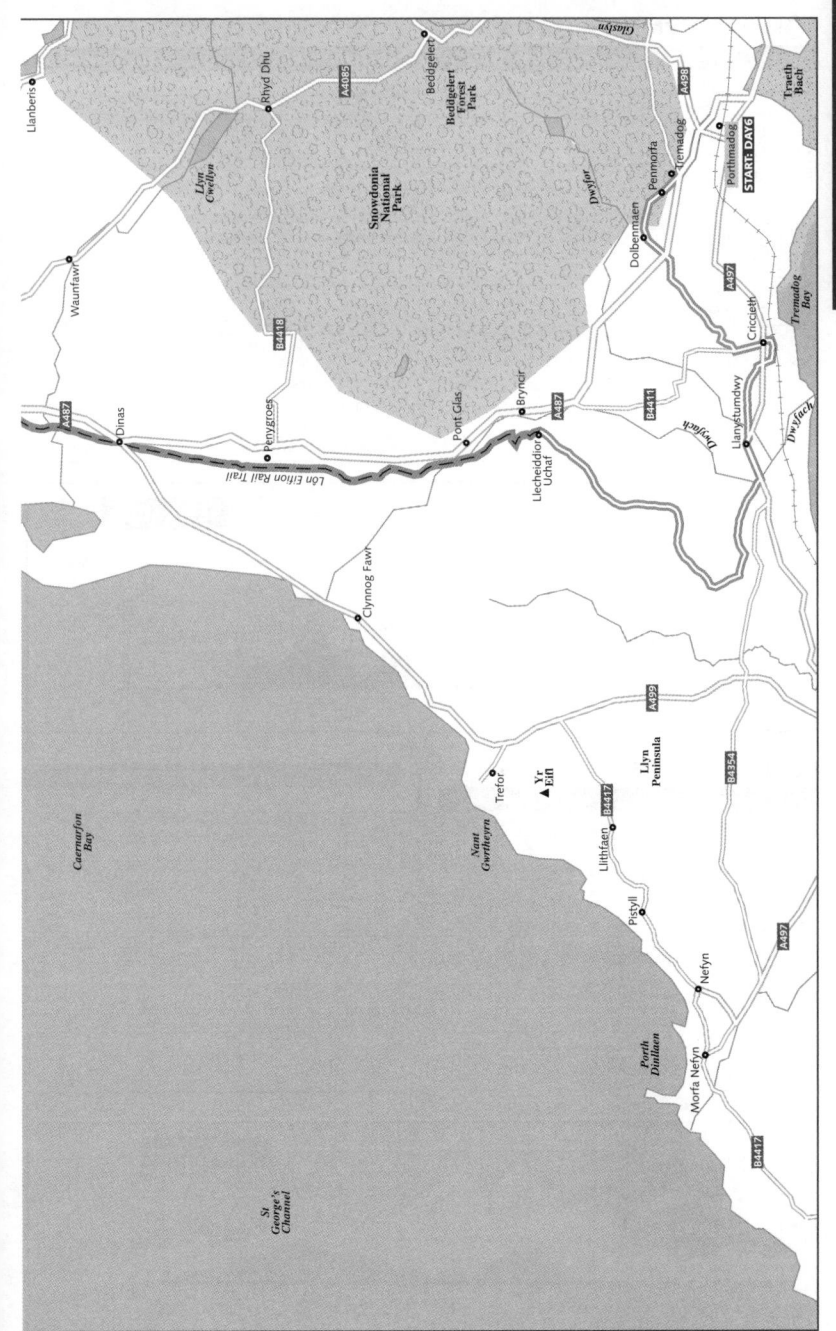

WALES

LÔN LAS CYMRU – DAY 5

CUE			GPS COORDINATES	
start		Dolgellau TIC	52°44'32"N	3°53'7"W
0 miles		go west on Cader Rd		
1.0	⬏	'to Barmouth'		
1.1	⬑	Llwybr Mawddach Trail		
8.1	⤢	alongside railway line		
8.7	↑	over toll bridge		
9.3	⬑	along waterfront, Barmouth	52°43'26"N	4°3'43"W
10.9	⤢	cross railway line		
	⬎	(40yd) 'NCR8' (up hill)		
11.0	⬑	A496		
14.0		Tal-y-Bont	52°46'27.18"N	4° 5'33.73"W
14.9	⬏	Ffordd Capel (opp Station St), Dyffryn	52°47'16"N	4°5'48"W
	▲	1100yd hard climb		
16.1	⤢	narrow lane 'NCR8'		
16.3	⬏	'NCR8'/Ffordd Briws		

CUE CONTINUED			GPS COORDINATES	
16.7	⬑	'to Llanbedr'		
17.2	⬏	'NCR8'		
18.6	⬏	'to Cwym Bychan' (over bridge)		
18.7	▲	4.3 miles moderate climb		
19.6	⬑	'to Harlech'		
21.4	⬏	'to Talsarnau'		
24.5	⬏	'NCR8'		
25.4	▲	1400yd moderate climb		
27.1	↑	cross A496		
28.2	⬏	A4085 'to village centre'		
28.3		Penrhyndeudraeth	52°55'47"N	4°3'58"W
30.2	⬑	B4410 'to Tremadog', Garreg	52°57'18"N	4° 4'0"W
31.9	⬑	A498 'to Porthmadog'		
34.0	⬑	'to Porthmadog', Tremadog	52°56'21"N	4° 8'29"W
35.3		Porthmadog TIC	52°55'30"N	4° 7'43"W

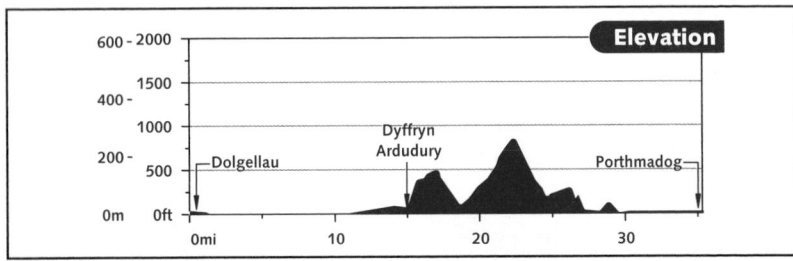

LÔN LAS CYMRU – DAY 6

CUE			GPS COORDINATES	
start		Porthmadog TIC	52°55'30"N	4° 7'43"W
0 miles		go north-west on High St		
1.3	⬑	A487 'to Caernarfon', Tremadog	52°56'21"N	4°8'34"W
2.2		Penmorfa	52°56'35"N	4° 9'44"W
2.4	⬏	'to Hen Lon'		
	▲	1400yd moderate climb		
3.2	⬏	'NCR8'		
5.0	⬎	'NCR8'		
5.1	↑	cross A487		
7.3	⬑	B4411		
8.5		Criccieth	52°55'2"N	4°13'52"W

CUE CONTINUED			GPS COORDINATES	
8.7	⬏	Castle St		
{	★	Criccieth Castle}		
9.8	⬏	'NCR8'		
11.1	⬏	'NCR8' (bridge), Llanystumdwy	52°55'16"N	4°16'7"W
11.5	⬏	'to Talhenbont Hall'		
11.5	⬑	(40yd) 'to Talhenbont Hall'		
12.6	⬏	'to Bryncir'		
15.9	⬑	'NCR8'		
16.7	⬏	'Llecheiddior U' (thru farm yard)		
17.2	⬎	join Lôn Eifion rail trail		
29.6	⬎	follow street around castle		
29.8		Caernarfon TIC	53° 8'25"N	4°16'37"W

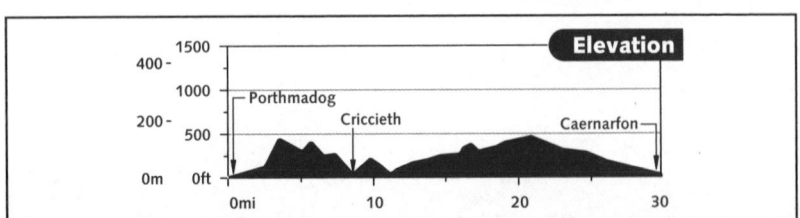

Day 6: Porthmadog to Caernafon
2½–3 hours, 29.8 miles

After a short backtrack to **Tremadog**, the route takes to quiet roads through the hills around Penmorfa, before meeting the coast at **Criccieth**, a relaxed seaside resort with a decidedly more genteel feel than Porthmadog. At Bryncir, join the **Lôn Eifion rail trail**, following the bed of a line closed in 1964. The surface is good, a combination of compacted gravel interspersed with bitumen sections. After a high point (at 20.8 miles), the remainder of the day is wonderfully easy, a gradual downhill all the way to the end of the ride. Near **Caernarfon**, the path emerges from the trees and the awesome sight of **Caernarfon Castle** just a few hundred yards ahead.

Day 7: Caernarfon to Holyhead
3½–4 hours, 42 miles

The exit from Caernarfon is traffic-free as you join the **Lôn Las Menai rail trail** down by Victoria Dock. It follows the route of the old Bangor to Caernarfon line, closed since 1972. The easy, pleasant route travels along the shores of the **Menai Strait** (Afon Menai) and onto the road at the waterfront in **Y Felinheli**.

Travelling on a series of quiet lanes, climb gently into the green hills behind Bangor. Watch for route markers here, as navigation is tricky in places. Soon after crossing the A4087 is the **Menai Suspension Bridge**, designed by Thomas Telford. An engineering marvel when it opened in 1826, the bridge, at 579ft long and 30m

LÔN LAS CYMRU – DAY 7

CUE		GPS COORDINATES
start	Caernarfon TIC	53° 8'25"N 4°16'37"W
0 miles	go east on Castle Ditch	
	(50yd) Greengate St	
0.2	along Victoria Dock	
0.5	join Lôn Las Menai rail trail	
2.8	'to Y Felinheli'	
4.5	Bangor St, Y Felinheli	53°11'13"N 4°12'18"W
4.7	'NCR8' (by war memorial)	
4.8	join Lôn Las Arfon rail trail	
5.6	'to Bangor'	
5.7	Ffordd Fodolydd/'NCR8'	
	1.9 miles moderate climb	
6.8	'NCR8'	
7.1	Ffordd Yr Hafod/'NCR8'	
8.1	Penrhos Rd	
8.5	'NCR8' (opp car dealer)	
8.7	A487 'to Menai Bridge'	
9.7	Holyhead Rd (over bridge)	
10.1	A4080, Menai Bridge	
10.4	A4080 'to Caergybi'	
11.9	A4080, Llanfair PG	53°13'16"N 4°12'30"W
{13.3}	Plas Newydd (LHS)	
14.0	'to Llanddaniel Fab'	
15.3	'NCR8', Llanddaniel Fab	53°12'35"N 4°15'18"W

CUE CONTINUED		GPS COORDINATES
17.6	by post box	
18.9	B4419	
	(20yd) at village store, Llangaffo	53°11'24"N 4°19'43"W
21.2	'NCR8' (parallel with canal)	
22.1	'NCR8'	
23.7	B4422, Bethel	53°12'25"N 4°24'5"W
	(50yd) 'NCR8'	
24.2	'to Soar'	
25.2	Soar	53°13'15"N 4°25'14"W
26.7	Dothan	53°14'26"N 4°25'58"W
28.3	'NCR8'	
29.1	'NCR8'	
32.1	Minffordd Rd	
32.6	Llanfihangel-yn-Nhowyn	53°16'8"N 4°31'0"W
34.0	'NCR8'	
34.8	Lôn Ty Main	
35.6	'NCR8'	
36.1	B4545 (by rail crossing)	
37.0	Four Mile Bridge	
39.1	at Lon Towyn Capel, Trearddur	53°16'58"N 4°36'44"W
40.9	Cyttir Rd	
41.4	(50yd) Llanfawr Rd	
42.0	Holyhead rail/ferry terminal	53°18'34"N 4°37'44"W

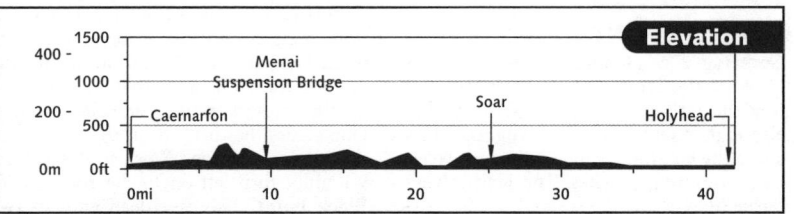

(100ft) high, is still a most impressive sight. Once across the rushing tidal waters of the strait, you arrive in the imaginatively-named town of Menai Bridge, first port of call on the island of Anglesey – at 276 sq miles, the largest island in England and Wales.

Cycling along the moderately busy A4080, the view back across the Menai Strait, spanned by its two bridges and with the craggy peaks of Snowdonia in the background, is really a sight to behold. Just up the road is (take a deep breath) is **Llanfairpwllgwyngyllgogerychwyrndrobwllllandysiliogogogoch** (Llanfair PG for short), the village with the longest name in Britain. You can deviate off the route into the centre of town for the obligatory photo next to the sign at the train station – there's not much else worth seeing. Anglesey is the flattest region in Wales, and the remainder of the route is relatively easy passing a succession of small villages on quiet country lanes.

THE BEST OF ANGLESEY

Duration 1½–2½ hours
Distance 16.9 miles
Difficulty easy
Start/Finish Beaumaris
Summary A fantastic short and easy spin around Anglesey with 360-degree views of the Menai Strait, ocean and the island's lush velvet fields.

Following one of four signposted routes on the island, this is a fantastic short ride making the most of Anglesey's limited elevation to provide near 360-degree views of the Menai Strait, ocean and the island's fertile green fields. The historic buildings of holy Penmon Priory and magnificent Beaumaris Castle ensure there's plenty to see off the bike.

ENVIRONMENT

Covering 276 sq miles, Anglesey (Ynys Môn) is the largest island in Wales and England. It's the flattest part of Wales, although there are some rugged cliffs along the coastline, which has some excellent swimming beaches. The land is very fertile here.

PLANNING

Be sure to pick up a copy of the *Rural Cycling on Anglesey* pamphlet, which describes this and three other signposted routes on the island. It's available from tourist offices.

GETTING TO/FROM THE RIDE
Beaumaris (start/finish)
TRAIN

The closest train station is six miles away at Llanfair PG, on the north Wales coastal railway line to Holyhead (the end of the Lôn Las Cymru ride described earlier). About seven trains run from Cardiff per day (4-5½ hours; the 9.45pm train takes 9 hours).

BICYCLE

Beaumaris is 4.3 miles from the Menai Bridge, passed on the final day of the Lôn Las Cymru ride (p184). If riding from Bangor, turn right at the roundabout just over the bridge and follow the moderately busy but very scenic A545 along the coast. Llanfair PG is only a short distance (west) from Menai Bridge on the A4080 – turn left before the bridge.

THE RIDE

This easy day ride takes about two hours and starts and ends in the popular holiday town of **Beaumaris**, known for its brilliant castle, gorgeous scenery and happening sailing and water sports centre. The well-signed route begins from the **Beaumaris Leisure Centre**, a few hundred yards from the tourist centre on Castle St. The quiet lane, which climbs gently away from town towards Llanfaes, affords a spectacular view of **Beaumaris Castle**, with green fields in the foreground and the peaks of Snowdonia behind. High hazel hedges on either side of the road act as an effective buffer from the wind, which often blows hard.

A summit is reached on the outskirts of Llanddona, although the road continues to undulate. Head towards a tall communications mast, from where a spectacular vista of Red Wharf Bay, Menai Strait and the peaks of the mainland unfold. The fine view continues as the route gradually descends. Don't miss the turn-off on the left (at 7.6 miles), near the top of a steep descent. At 9.1 miles turn left on to the road out to **Black Point**. This is a dead end, so you

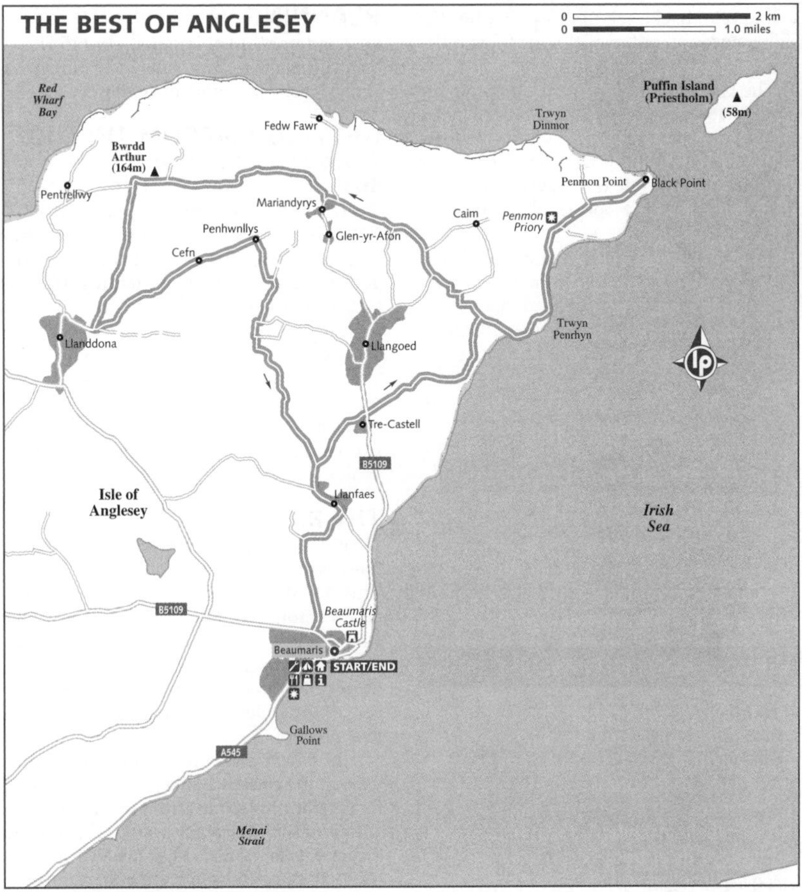

WALES

THE BEST OF ANGLESEY

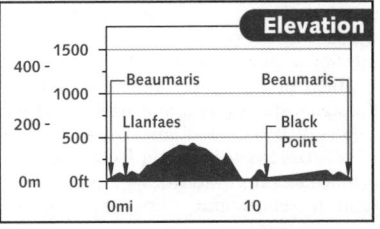

CUE			GPS COORDINATES	
start		Beaumaris Leisure Centre	53°15'51"N	4°5'30"W
0 miles		go south from leisure centre		
0.1	⌐	Rating Row		
0.2	⌐	Church St		
0.3	⌐	'Telor'		
1.3	⌐	Ffordd Eglwys		
1.5	⌐	'Telor', Llanfaes	53°16'44"N	4° 5'45"W
2.2	▲	2.8 miles gradual climb		
3.0	⌐	'Telor'		
5.0	⌐	'to Llangoed'		
7.6	⌐	'Telor' (at start of descent)		
9.1	⌐	join coast road		
{10.2	★	Penmon Priory & dovecote}		
	⚠	0.8 miles dirt road		
11.0		Black Point	53°18'37"N	4° 3'0"W

CUE CONTINUED			GPS COORDINATES	
		{retrace outward route}		
13.0	↑	towards Beaumaris		
15.2	⌐	towards Beaumaris		
		{retrace outward route}		
16.9		Beaumaris Leisure Centre	53°15'51"N	4°5'30"W

WALES

will have to backtrack to this point, but the sights encountered over the next few miles make it well worth the effort.

The road to Black Point soon meets the coast, before leading to a scattering of heritage buildings at the site of **Penmon Priory**. Along the way, enjoy fabulous views over the Menai Strait all the way to Llandudno's Great Orme, a spectacular limestone headland.

The former monastic outpost, which is still considered by many to be a very holy place, was initially established on nearby Puffin Island, but was moved to Penmon by the 6th-century head of the monastery, St Seiriol. Many of the original buildings were demolished by the Danes in the 10th century.

After backtracking to the Black Point turn-off, the lane turns inland and climbs briefly. Cross the B5109 and enter Llanfaes for the second time, retracing the first leg of the route back into Beaumaris. For a change of scenery, take the B5109 back into town. It's not as quiet, but is fairly scenic and follows the coast.

VIEWS FROM THE VALLEY

Duration 2 days
Distance 36.2 miles
Difficulty moderate–demanding
Start/Finish Conwy

Summary Short and sweet, but also challenging, this scenic two-day ride from Conwy to the popular inland resort of Betws-y-Coed and back provides a spectacular introduction to northwest Wales' mountainous interior.

Keeping to the scenic, wooded hills as much as the picturesque Conwy Valley itself, this short but far from easy two-day ride takes you to the popular inland resort of Betws-y-Coed. The ride from Conwy avoids main roads as far as possible and is a great way to experience the mountainous interior of northwest Wales.

Much of the route follows sections of the signposted (brown-and-white markers) Conwy Valley Cycle Route, which consists of two circuits originating from Llanrwst, one heading north to Conwy and the other south to Penmachno.

PLANNING

OS Landranger Map 1:50,000, No 115 *Snowdon*, covers the Conwy Valley and northwest Wales, including most of Anglesey.

GETTING TO/FROM THE RIDE
Conwy (start/finish)
BUS

There are two **National Express** (☎ 0870 580 8080) buses a day from London and frequent services between Llandudno, Bangor and Caernarfon. Only folding bikes in bags will be carried.

TRAIN

Conwy's small train station is now only used by regional trains. Llandudno Junction, about a mile away (just over the River Conwy), is the closest station on the north Wales coastal railway line to Holyhead.

THE RIDE
Day 1: Conwy to Betws-y-Coed
1¾–3 hours, 16.1 miles

This ride starts in picturesque little **Conwy**, at the mouth of the River Conwy. You would think a ride along a river valley would be pretty flat, but much of this leg, however, meanders through the hills to the east of the valley floor, making for a tough ride most of the way to Llanrwst.

The B5106 starts to climb shortly after leaving the **tourist office**, and it's not long before the first of a series of brown-and-white markers' sign the way to the **Conwy Valley Cycle Route**. Keep an eye out for these as the ride follows the signed route right through to Llanrwst.

The B5106 isn't particularly busy but it's nice all the same to turn off (at 2.5 miles) onto a quiet lane that climbs steadily, providing some good views of the broad River Conwy (Afon Conwy) away to the left.

A swift descent brings you alongside the waterway after 4.3 miles – cross to the other bank, entering the village of Tal-y-Cafn. This is where the killer hill of the day commences, an unrelenting 1.6-mile climb, so steep in places you may have to get off and push.

Beyond the small lake, **Llyn Syberi** – a popular local fishing hole and a nice place to rest – the road emerges from the trees, providing an appreciation of the height you've gained.

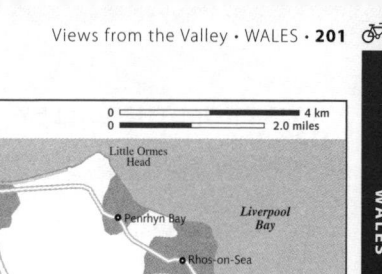

VIEWS FROM THE VALLEY

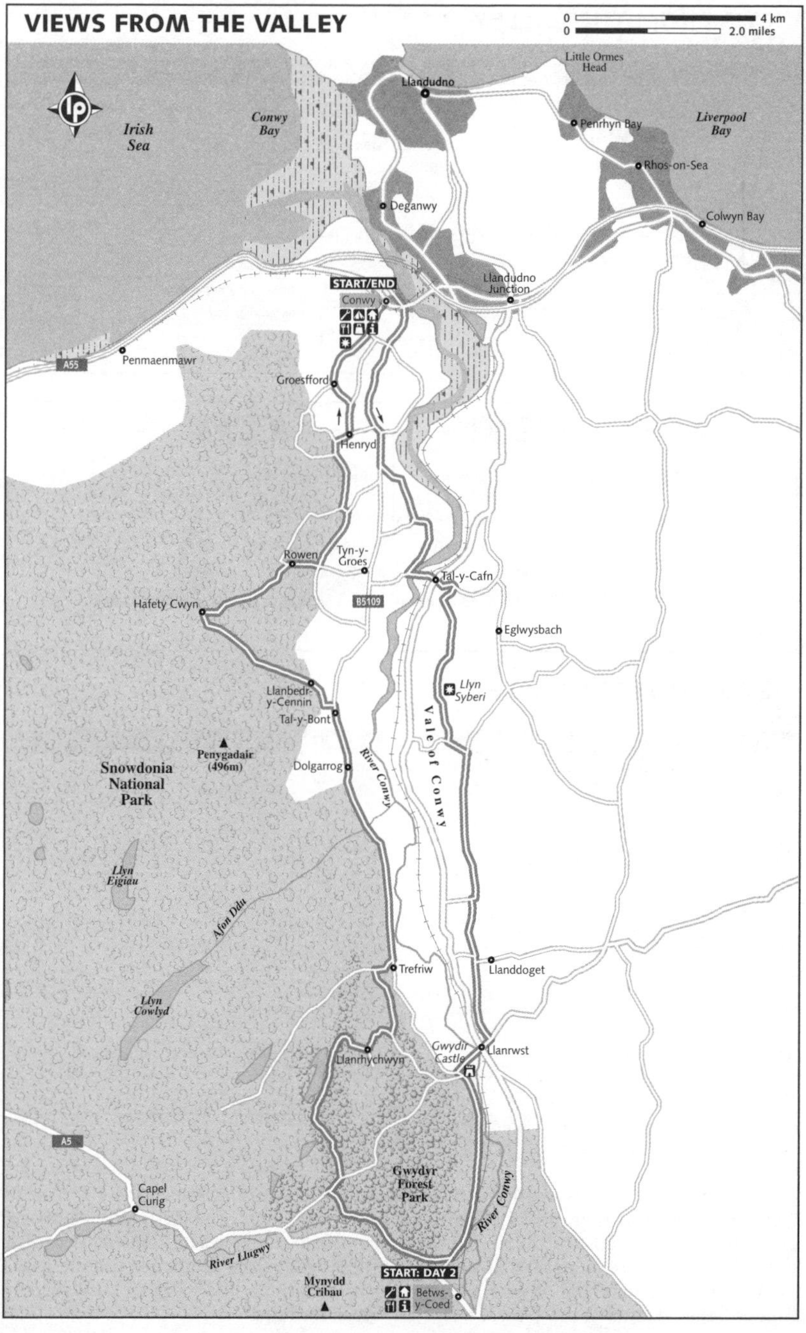

| 0 | | 4 km |
| 0 | | 2.0 miles |

Irish Sea

Conwy Bay

Little Ormes Head

Llandudno

Penrhyn Bay

Liverpool Bay

Rhos-on-Sea

Deganwy

Colwyn Bay

Llandudno Junction

START/END
Conwy

Penmaenmawr

A55

Groesfford

Henryd

Rowen

Tyn-y-Groes

Tal-y-Cafn

Hafoty Cwyn

B5109

Eglwysbach

Llyn Syberi

Vale of Conwy

Llanbedr-y-Cennin

Tal-y-Bont

Penygadair (496m)

Dolgarrog

River Conwy

Snowdonia National Park

Llyn Eigiau

Afon Ddu

Llyn Cowlyd

Trefriw

Llanddoget

Gwydir Castle

Llanrwst

Llanrhychwyn

Capel Curig

A5

River Llugwy

Mynydd Cribau

Gwydyr Forest Park

River Conwy

START: DAY 2
Betws-y-Coed

VIEWS FROM THE VALLEY
- DAY 1

CUE			GPS COORDINATES
start		Conwy TIC (by castle roundabout)	53°16'49"N 3°49'35"W
0 miles		go S on B5106 'to Trefriw'	
2.5	↰	at Groes Inn	
	▲	0.7 miles hard climb	
4.3	↰	over bridge	
4.5		Tal-y-Cafn	53°13'41"N 3°49'4"W
	▲	1.6 miles hard climb	
4.6	↘	'CVCR'	
4.8	↱	'to Ffordd Llyn Syberi'	
6.1	↙	'CVCR'	
6.2	↰	'CVCR'	
7.4	↰	'to Plas Iwrwg' (on descent)	

CUE CONTINUED			GPS COORDINATES
7.8	↱	'CVCR'	
9.6	↱	'to Llanrwst'	
12.0	↱	'to town centre'	
12.2	↘	Watling St	
12.3	↱	alongside river, Llanrwst	53° 8'15"N 3°47'53"W
12.4	↰	over bridge	
12.8	↰	B5106 'to Betws-y-Coed'	
(13.0	★	Gwydir Castle)	
15.9	↑	cross Pont-y-Pair bridge	
	↰	(40yd) High St/A5	
16.1	↰	'to TIC'	
16.1		(80yd) Betws-y-Coed TIC	53°5'35"N 3°48'4"W

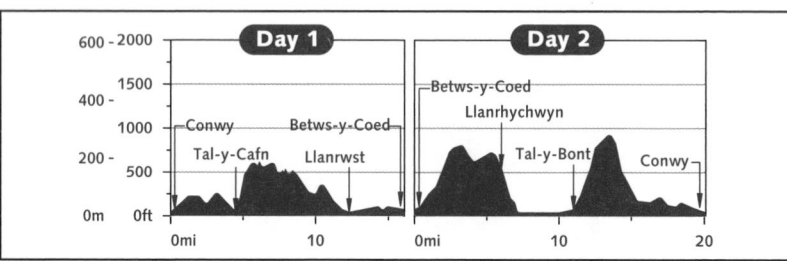

VIEWS FROM THE VALLEY
- DAY 2

CUE			GPS COORDINATES
start		Betws-y-Coed TIC	53°5'35"N 3°48'4"W
0 miles		go south-west towards A5	
	↱	(80yd) High St/A5	
0.2	↱	cross Pont-y-Pair bridge	
0.2	↰	(40yd) Capel Curig Rd (after bridge)	
0.3	▲	2.4 miles hard climb	
2.4	↱	unsigned road	
2.7	↰	'to Llanrhychwyn'	
(4.0	★	Llyn Geirionydd)	
5.6	↘	'to Llanrhychwyn'	
6.0	↰	'to Trefriw', Llanrhychwyn	53° 8'9.90"N 3°50'5.11"W
6.9	↱	at public phone & mail box	
7.1	↰	B5106, Trefriw	53°9'6"N 3°49'28"W
10.0		Dolgarrog	53°11'7"N 3°50'27"W
11.0	↰	'to Llanbedr-y-Cennin', Tal-y-Bont	53°12'8"N 3°50'51"W

CUE CONTINUED			GPS COORDINATES
11.1	▲	2.4 miles very hard climb	
11.5		Llanbedr-y-Cennin	53°12'29.23"N 3°51'25.47"W
13.5	↱	through gate	
15.4		Rowen	53°13'47"N 3°51'52"W
16.3	↰	'to Henryd'	
16.4	↱	'CVCR'	
17.2	↱	'to Henryd'	
17.5	↰	'CVCR', Henryd	53°15'18"N 3°50'42"W
18.1	↰	'CVCR'	
18.4	↱	Hendre Rd, Groesffordd	53°15'57"N 3°50'50"W
19.3	↘	St Agnes Rd	
19.6	↰	Sychnant Pass Rd	
	↱	(20yd) Mount Pleasant/Town Ditch Rd	
19.9	↙	Castle St	
20.1		Conwy TIC	53°16'49"N 3°49'35"W

There are some fine views of the valley below and the bald high peaks of Snowdonia to the west. Most of the remaining miles to Llanrwst are mercifully downhill.

The main commercial centre of the Conwy Valley, **Llanrwst** is a pleasant, size-able place without the touristy feel of its near neighbours. The shady park – just over the small humpbacked Pont Mawr bridge, attributed to the renowned architect and local lad, Inigo Jones – is an ideal place to break for lunch.

The final few relatively flat miles into **Betws-y-Coed** along the B5106 pass quickly and it almost comes as a surprise to round a bend and see the sign welcoming you to town. Betws (as it's known and pronounced) has been Wales' most popular inland resort since Victorian days, and it still pulls in the crowds over summer. Walkers flock to the town to enjoy its picturesque woodland setting and tramp along the numerous trails snaking through the **Gwydyr Forest**. The centre of town swells with sightseers enjoying cream teas and checking out the latest kit in the numerous outdoor equipment shops lining the main thoroughfare.

Day 2: Betws-y-Coed to Conwy
2–3 hours, 20.1 miles

After a night in Betws, you return to Conwy via a different mountain route. Like the Day 1 leg, this stage (although relatively short) can be tough at times, with a couple of steep, long climbs to tackle. Leave Betws-y-Coed via the Pont-y-Pair bridge. The quiet road shadows the River Llugwy as it climbs, steeply at times, up into the pines of the tranquil Gwydyr Forest. The route levels and arrives at picturesque **Llyn Geirionydd**, an incredibly pretty lake surrounded by forest, popular with local waterskiers.

Hard-won height is shed rapidly on an exhilarating descent down from the hills, dropping back to the valley floor at the village of Trefriw. The next few miles of flat cycling along the B5106 give you a chance to catch your breath for the tough ascent ahead.

Leaving the B5106 behind at Tal-y-Bont, it's time to head for the hills yet again. If you're not feeling very energetic, turn right opposite the pub in Llanbedr-y-Cennin (11.5 miles) and follow a less strenuous route (signed 'Conwy Valley Route') to Rowen.

Slogging up the hill, however, your extra efforts are soon rewarded with some memorable views back over the valley with the coast, Conwy and the bald higher peaks of Snowdonia's Carneddau Range all in view.

The tough 2.4-mile climb propels you to a lofty 290m (951ft), summiting as you strike off along a gated road through pastures of grazing sheep. You can relax on the steep descent into peaceful **Rowen** – just keep an eye out for oncoming traffic on the narrow lane. The remaining miles back into Conwy are very pleasant and relatively easy, travelling along quiet back roads through the tiny settlements of Henryd and Groesffordd. Leave behind the countryside not far from Conwy's city walls. A quick trip through busy streets leads back to the tourist centre, the magnificent castle and the end of the tour.

MOUNTAIN BIKE RIDES

Wales has some good mountain biking, especially around Brecon Beacons National Park. **Brecon**, the principal town in the park, where the ride described here starts and ends, is an attractive, market village. It's popular with weekend walkers and mountain bikers.

Brecon Beacons Gap

This 21.4-mile ride (about three hours) is one of the all time classics of the Beacons suitable for mountain bike novices and experienced riders alike. It climbs high into the heart of the Brecon Beacons National Park following the **Gap route**, a former (possibly Roman) main road, between the desolate

---

THE WALLS OF CONWY

Conwy is a town justly proud of its walls, and it has rather a lot of them. The walls of Conwy Castle stand alone and proud unshielded and unsullied by modern architectural neighbours as is often the case with Europe's surviving castles.

The medieval fortified walls of Conwy Town are also considered the finest in Britain, and not just by the locals. The majestic walls that have guarded the town for centuries are almost completely intact and now enjoy World Heritage protection to ensure they'll stand for as long as time and gravity allow.

BRECON BEACONS GAP

CUE			GPS COORDINATES
start		Brecon TIC	51°56'54"N 3°23'25"W
0 miles		go south thru Bethel Square	
	↰	(100yd) Lion St	
0.1	↑	The Watton	
0.2	↱	Rich Way 'to canal & theatre'	
0.3	↰ ◎	unsigned rd (past theatre)	
	↑	(40yd) join canal towpath	
2.4	↱	join road at Brynich Lock	
2.8	↱	'to Llanfrynach'	
3.5	↱	lane by churchyard, Llanfrynach	51°55'17"N 3°20'44"W
5.0	↱	B4558, Pencelli	51°54'56"N 3°19'7"W
6.1	↱	'Taff Trail'	
6.9	↙	'Taff Trail'	
8.1	↰	along dam wall	
8.4	↱	'Taff Trail'	
	⚠	3.8 miles dirt road	

CUE CONTINUED			GPS COORDINATES
▲		5.2 miles moderate climb	
12.2	↰	sealed road	
12.8	↱	road (after cattle grid)	
⚠		4.9 miles dirt road & track	
	↙	(100yd) 'Taff Trail'	
13.0	↙	grassy track (thru gate)	
13.8	↙	stony track (at road)	
14.3	↙ ▲	cross stream (steep dip)	
{15.8	★	The Gap & Pen-y-Fan trailhead}	
17.5	↑	thru gate	
18.0	↘	unsigned road	
18.4	↰	100yd after crossing bridge	
20.6	↱	B4601/Orchard St	
21.1	↰	Wheat St/B4520	
21.3	↱	Mount St (by supermarket)	
21.4		Brecon TIC (end of car park)	51°56'52"N 3°23'17"W

peaks, starting and finishing in the attractive town of Brecon. The terrain is rideable in all seasons but take precautions in bad weather conditions. The Gap takes you up to 600m (1968ft) above sea level and is very open and windswept. Technically, the going is mostly uncomplicated, with a tricky gulch halfway up The Gap Rd and some formidable rock steps on beginning the descent from The Gap itself. Also worthy of note is the descent from the top of the **Brinore Tramway** to the valley bottom just up stream of the **Talybont Reservoir**. The track varies from smooth grass to start with, to gravel, rocks and ruts. Finally, at the bottom, you have to ford the river where floods have washed away the bridge. In periods of high water levels, opt for a short cut along the **Taff Trail** (p184) to the top end of the forest.

TOWNS & FACILITIES

BETWS-Y-COED
☎ 01690 / pop 1000

Alpine-like Betws-y-Coed (Betws), the self-styled eastern gateway to Snowdonia National Park, blossomed as Wales' most popular inland resort during Victorian days and has remained a popular spot ever since. Betws, meaning 'sanctuary in the wood', takes its name from the 14th-century St Michael's Church at the heart of town. New

in 2008, the Penmachno Mountain Bike Trail is a 12-mile forest biking trail.

Supplies & Equipment
Beics Betws (☎ 01690 710766; www.bike wales.co.uk; Tan Lan; half-/full-day £15/18) provides hire bikes and route information.

Sleeping & Eating
The **Vagabond Bunkhouse** (☎ 01690 710850; www.thevagabond.co.uk; Craiglan Rd; dm/breakfast £14/4; reception 7.30-10am & 4.30-5.30pm) is a new, independent hostel located next to a gurgling waterfall at the heart of town. Simple dorm rooms but decent facilities, including a bar, drying room and bike storage, make it a welcome newcomer.

Plas Derwen (☎ 01690 710388; Holyhead Rd), all-day food in pleasant surroundings mark out Plas Derwen as a rising star. The food is homemade with local produce and weekly specials, and can be enjoyed in the modern and airy cafe or on the al fresco terrace. Upstairs five simple but tasteful rooms, three en suite, are available for B&B (r from £50).

BRECON (ABERHONDDU)
☎ 01874 / pop 8500

The stone market town of Brecon is the principal transport centre for the national park. Boasting winding streets and a languid river crossing, it is as handsome as it is traditionally Welsh.

Supplies & Equipment
BiPed Cycles (☎ 01874 622296; www
.bipedcycles.co.uk; 10 Ship St) hires mountain bikes and has lots of cycling advice.

Sleeping & Eating
The best all around place for food and sleep
is the **Bridge Cafe** (☎ 01874 622024; www
.bridgecafe.co.uk; 7 Bridge St; mains around
£5; rooms around £50; breakfast & lunch
only) serves beautifully prepared organic
and fair trade food using local ingredients.
The three adjoining B&B bedrooms are
spacious with feather pillows, Egyptian cotton sheets and rustic colour schemes. Room
one is the best, a large en suite with a sofa
bed and DVD player.

BEAUMARIS
☎ 01248 / pop 2000
The best base for visiting the island, Beaumaris boasts an attractive waterfront location and a romantic castle lording it over a
pretty collection of Georgian buildings, all
set against the magical Snowdonia backdrop. It has lots of infrastructure and is
home to some excellent little boutiques,
delis, cafes and galleries. The town abounds
with history and is today growing in popularity with a new generation as a centre for
water sports, sailing and walking.

Sleeping & Eating
Cleifiog (☎ 01248 811507; www.cleifiog
bandb.co.uk; Townsend; s/d from £75/45)
is a homely and smarter-than-average B&B,
set in an historic building to the eastern end
of Castle St – this place is a little gem. The
three rooms (one en suite) abound with
original features and period fittings, while
breakfast mixes healthy options with a traditional cooked meal. The owner displays
her artworks around the house.

  Courts (☎ 01248 810565; Regent Hse,
Church St; mains £12-15; 11am-3pm &
6-9pm, Wed-Mon) Renamed from The
Courtyard, the menu retains its European
brasserie motif and reliance on local produce in sleek, refined surroundings. Dinner dishes boast fish and meat specials.
There are special menus for both vegetarians and children.

  Sarah's Delicatessen & The Coffee Shop
(☎ 01248 811534; 11 Church St; breakfast
& lunch only; Mon-Sat) is an excellent deli

and champions local produce, such as cheese
and ales, with a well-stocked selection of
treats. They recently opened a small cafe
round the corner has daily specials (try the
Anglesey dressed crab), good coffee and
heavenly desserts.

BUILTH WELLS
☎ 01982 / pop 2350
Once a significant spa town, today Builth
Wells is an honest agricultural centre and is
unlikely to detain you too long. It's pleasant
enough however, especially down near the
river. It springs to life in mid-July when
the cream of Wales' agricultural community converges on the showgrounds for the
Royal Welsh Show.

Sleeping & Eating
The Greyhound Hotel (☎ 01982 553255;
www.thegreyhoundhotel.co.uk; 3 Garth
Rd; s/d £55/80), a friendly local pub with
comfortable, non-fussy rooms and decent
bar meals at lunch and dinner, this is a reliable option. Catch the local male choir who
rehearse here on Monday nights.

  The Lion Hotel (☎ 01982 553311; www
.lionhotelbuilthwells.com; 2 Broad St; d/tw
£98/120) is the smartest option in town.
This recently refurbished hotel has contemporary rooms with nice, homely and
a wood-panelled dining room for upscale
lunches and dinners. Some rooms have
disabled access.

  Calon Wen (☎ 07792 812739; 3 Groe St;
mains £10; noon–9.30pm, Mon-Sat) This
smart little bistro's menu has shifted to take
on a more Mediterranean motif, plus lots of
fish and steak mains. By day you can take
coffee on the leather couches and watch the
world go by.

CAERNARFON
☎ 01286 / pop 9600
Dominated by a magnificent castle that vies
with Conwy's as the most impressive in
Wales, Caernarfon is an attractive, historic
market town well worth exploring. The
tourist office has details of cycling trails
around Caernarfon.

Supplies & Equipment
Beics Menai (☎ 01286 676804; www.beics
menai.co.uk; Slate Quay; bikes per day per
adult/child £19/11) hires bikes.

WALES

Sleeping & Eating

Black Boy Inn (☎ 01286 673604; www
.welsh-historic-inns.co.uk; Northgate St; s/
d £50/70; mains £10; lunch & dinner only)
Despite the rather offensive sounding name,
this is actually a great place to either sleep
or eat. Dating from 1522, the creaky but
atmospheric rooms at this traditional inn
have original wooden beams and panelling.
Less creaky is the reliable selection of bar
meals and evening mains with an emphasis
on fresh fish specials and real ales.

Totters (☎ 01286 672963; www.totters
.co.uk; 2 High St; dm incl breakfast £15,
rooms £45) is a great independent hostel
and by far the best budget option in town,
and has modern, clean and welcoming
dorms. The 14th-century arched basement
hosts a long table for communal dining with
atmosphere, while the attic family room has
en-suite facilities and more mod cons.

CARDIFF

☎ 029 / pop 317,500

The capital of Wales since only 1955, the
city has embraced its relatively new role
with vigour, emerging as one of Britain's
leading urban centres in the 21st century.
Cardiff's strengths are a redefined cityscape,
a creative buzz, a cultural renaissance and a
vibrant nocturnal life that seems well above
standard for a city of its size. The striking
74,500-seat Millennium Stadium (which
hosted the Rugby World Cup final, the 2001
FA Cup final and will host football matches
from the 2012 Olympic Games), and the
massive Cardiff Bay redevelopment, are the
most tangible signs of Cardiff's transforma-
tion. The city as a whole has since risen
Phoenix-like from the waters as a testament
to the city's capacity for reinvention.

Supplies & Equipment

For cycling spares and repairs, visit
Reg Braddick Cycles (☎ 2049 0137; 59-61
Broadway).

Sleeping & Eating

NosDa@Cardiff Backpackers (☎ 2034
5577; www.nosda.co.uk; 98 Neville St,
Riverside; dm with breakfast from £18) is
a stalwart of the Cardiff budget scene. This
independent hostel was the original cheap
place to stay with well-maintained facilities
and a central location.

NosDa@the Riverbank (☎ 2034 8866;
www.nosda.co.uk; 53-59 Despenser St; s/
d from £35/55) is a slightly smarter sister
property to NosDa@Cardiff Backpackers
(above), it offers a upscale hostel experience
with more privacy, home-cooked meals at
the **Tafarn cantina and** a cool live music
venue, the **Underground Sound Lounge**.

The **Parc Hotel** (☎ 0870 333 9157; www
.thistle.com; Park Pl; d from £80) is a really
smart, contemporary hotel located right at
the heart of the main shopping area with
tasteful rooms, good facilities and helpful
staff. Ask about cheaper weekend rates
when the business travellers vacate the
premises.

The **Plan** (☎ 2039 8464; 28-29 Morgan
Arcade; lunch only) is a small but satisfying
place is a haven for healthy options: specialist teas and fair trade coffees, vegetarian and vegan options, and lots of organic,
local produce. Sip a coffee and browse the
Guardian newspaper over a hearty vegetarian breakfast (£4).

Zerodegrees (☎ 2022 9494; www.zero
degrees.co.uk; 27 Westgate St; lunch & dinner only) is the latest opening in town – a
huge microbrewery-cum-restaurant combining all-day food with six, lip-smacking,
artisan-crafted beers. Try the Black Lager
with hints of caramel and coffee. Pizza and
salads complement the beers, as does the
house speciality, the kilo pots of mussels
(£13). The setting is bright, buzzy and striking with huge vessels of fermenting beer
bubbling away in the window. Catch the
happy hour (4-7pm, Mon-Fri) for a £2
pint.

Zushi (☎ 2066 9911; www.zushicardiff
.com; The Aspect, 140 Queen St; plates
£1.70-3.50; lunch & dinner on Mon-Sat,
lunch only Sun) is a happening conveyor-
belt sushi bar with a big menu of colour-
coded plates. It attracts a mixed crowd from
office groups to minor local celebrities, attracted by the fresh, good-value food. Bento
boxes to go from £6.

CONWY

☎ 01492 / pop 4000

Conwy is all about the castle. The approach
to the castle gate is highly theatrical, with
three bridges spanning the river. But while
the castle, one of Wales' finest and a Unesco
World Heritage Site, remains one of the

essential visits in north Wales, the town of Conwy itself feels like a major letdown. Still, despite the eerie quiet that descend upon the place after the shops shut, it will do for shut-eye. You're leaving in the morning anyway.

Sleeping & Eating

Try the **Bryn Guest House** (☎ 01492 592449; www.bryn.org.uk; Sychnant Pass Rd; s/d £45/65), located under the highest point of the town walls. The period Victorian home with traditional fittings has four comfy rooms with great views. The owner will cater for all dietary needs, including preparing a vegan-friendly breakfast.

Grab dinner at the **Bistro Conwy** (☎ 01492 596326; Chapel St; mains around £15; dinner only) is a local favourite with a big menu that blends modern and traditional Welsh dishes – boasting ambiance and quality service.

DOLGELLAU

☎ 01341 / pop 2680

The fairly sleepy pace of things in Dolgellau today belies an eventful history. It was here in the 15th century that Owain Glyndwr assembled his rebel Welsh parliament and since then the town has played host to persecuted Quakers, fortune-seeking gold miners and well-to-do 19th-century English tourists out to see the wonders of nearby Cadair Idris (892m/2928ft), the second-highest peak in Snowdonia National Park. The centre of town is a series of small squares surrounded by austere grey buildings built of local dolerite and slate.

Sleeping & Eating

Dylanwad Da (☎ 01341 422870; 2 Smithfield St; 10am-3pm & 7-9pm daily Easter–Oct, Thu-Sat Nov-Mar) is an informal wine and tapas bar by day, and contemporary restaurant by night. This well-run locals' favourite has been serving up high-quality food for over 20 years. Daily specials include local produce and vegetarian options (mains around £14).

Ffynnon (☎ 01341 421774; www.ffynnon townhouse.com; Love Ln; s/d £80-95/120-150) is a boutique guesthouse and about as family friendly as you will find. But, with a keen eye for contemporary interior design and a super-friendly welcome, it feels both homely and stylish at the same time. Three contemporary rooms, the boldest with an Oriental theme, are now joined by a fourth room with a free-standing bath. The drawing room is a sun-soaked space to relax over coffee and weekend papers.

HOLYHEAD

☎ 01407 / pop 12,000

Holyhead has had a rough time and remains primarily a hub for ferry passengers rather than a place to visit, but the first signs of regeneration are evident with the 2006 opening of the Celtic Gateway bridge, linking the train station to the main street. The inscription reads: 'Pass this way with a pure heart' – it's certainly a more attractive entrance to the town.

Sleeping & Eating

Yr Hendre (☎ 01407 762929; www.yr-hen dre.net; Porth-y-Felin Rd; s/d £45/50) is the best of the town's B&Bs. It is professionally run and homely with some modern touches. The hearty breakfast will set you up for the day's ride.

LLANIDLOES

☎ 01686 / pop 2300

One of the prettiest towns in mid Wales, Llanidloes was formerly a centre for the local flannel and lead-mining industries, but now manages to pick up its fair share of tourists. The town's four principal streets meet at the half-timbered market hall, built around 1600.

Information

The town itself is set gracefully on the River Severn, and has a **tourist office** (☎ 01686 412605) and all the services a visitor might need. Llanidloes also has a good range of accommodation and several good pubs – if you have time, it's an ideal spot for a rest day.

Sleeping & Eating

The pick of the B&Bs is **Dyffryn Glyn Guest House** (☎ 01686 412129; www.dyf frynglyn.co.uk; rooms from £25), a modernised farmhouse 2 miles out of town with gorgeous views, friendly owners and a head start on the next day's walk.

Another good choice is **Lloyds Hotel** (☎ 01686 412284; www.lloydshotel.co.uk; rooms from £38), on the southeast edge of town, where helpful staff dispense key information about local sights and characters.

Many of Llanidloes' pubs offer meals – try the walker-friendly **Angel** (☎ 01686 412381; High St; mains from £6; lunch & dinner). On the main street there's a good takeaway serving fish and chips, and a **Spar** supermarket open late.

PORTHMADOG

☎ 01766 / pop 4500

Most non-cyclists visit Porthmadog, a busy seaside town, for two reasons: to catch the Ffestiniog Railway to Blaenau Ffestiniog and to visit the nearby village of Portmeirion. The town makes a good base for both. Porthmadog is proud to maintain a tradition of local independent businesses. It is home to the **Purple Moose Brewery** (☎ 01766 515571; www.purplemoose.co.uk; Madoc St), one of Wales' best-known microbreweries, which produces four lip-smacking ales.

Sleeping & Eating

Yr Hen Fecws (☎ 01766 514625; www .henfecws.com; 16 Lombard St; s/d from £49/67; mains £16; dinner only) stylishly restored, this stone-cottage restaurant, with rooms, remains the most characterful place to stay in town. The seven rooms feature exposed-slate walls and fireplaces, while the elegant restaurant serves excellent bistro dishes with fresh fish specials.

Snowdon Lodge (☎ 01766 515354; www.snowdonlodge.co.uk; Church St, Tremadog; dm/d incl breakfast £16.50/40) is a friendly independent hostel located in the historic house where TE Lawrence (Lawrence of Arabia) was born on August 16, 1888. The rooms are mainly simple dorms but some private rooms are available and a continental breakfast is included in the price. Good communal facilities. Located 1 mile north of Porthmadog on the A498D.

Northern England

HIGHLIGHTS

- Join a fleet of like-minded cyclists heading from **sea to sea** (C2C) on Britain's most popular cycle route (p226)
- Leave a single tyre track across the wide golden beaches of **Northumberland** as you ride along the coast from castle to castle (p211)
- Lean your bike against 2000-year-old **Hadrian's Wall** as you explore Roman forts and temples (p210)
- Experience the timeless beauty of the Yorkshire Dales along the **Yorkshire Dales Cycleway** (p234)
- Rest on a soft bed of heather after scaling the steep gradients of the **North York Moors** (p241)

TERRAIN

Predominantly hilly, with larger peaks in the Northern Pennines, Yorkshire Dales and Lake District. Gentle hills and low-lying plains along the east coast, except for the high uplands of the North York Moors.

Telephone Code: ☎ 0191	www.visitenc.com

Rugged open spaces, big Nordic skies and chilly nights out 'on the razzle', bizarre dialects, far-flung abbeys and golden beaches by a Viking sea – this is England's glorious north, an independently minded region with a fascinating past and rousing vistas. With more square miles of national park than any other part of the UK, whole counties of wind-swept and forgotten landscapes and history by the horned helmet–load, there's no more satisfying way to enjoy the north than from the saddle of a two-wheeler.

The northeast is comprised of North Yorkshire, Durham and Northumberland, while over the Pennines, Cumbria fills outs England's northwest corner. From North Yorkshire's celebrated Yorkshire Dales and North York Moors, to the splendid isolation of the Northumberland National Park and the legendary beauty of the Lake District – in this part of the world it's not hard to escape the clutches of urban life. Throw in Yorkshire's stately homes and abbeys, Northumberland's coast and castles and World Heritage-listed Hadrian's Wall, and it's plain to see why the north is a cycling destination you don't want to miss.

Although the north possesses a mere handful of towns of any size, the region's population centres are surprisingly vibrant places, with hedonistic Newcastle, quaint Durham and history-soaked York all fascinating places to linger. Things are not as happening on the western side of the Pennines but the poetry-inspiring hills and lakes more than make up for any urban shortcomings.

HISTORY

In the centuries leading up to the Roman invasion, the area from the River Humber to the Firth of Forth was ruled by a confederation of Celtic tribes known as Brigantes. The Romans were the first to attempt to delineate a border with Hadrian's Wall in AD 122, but the struggle between north and south didn't end until the Act of Unity in the early 18th century.

In the 9th century the Danes made York their capital and ruled the Danelaw – all of England north and east of a line between Chester and London. Later, William the Conqueror found the north to be rebellious and difficult and responded with brutal thoroughness. After 500 knights were mas-sacred at Durham, William burnt the city and York, and devastated the surrounding countryside. It took the north generations to recover.

Following their successful invasion of Britain in 1066, the Normans left a legacy of spectacular fortresses and the marvellous Durham Cathedral. Regarded by many as the greatest Norman building in England, it's architecture and setting contributed to the cathedral's listing as one of Britain's first World Heritage sites. The region prospered on the medieval wool trade, which sponsored the great cathedral at York and enormous monastic communities, the remains of which can be seen at Rievaulx and Fountains' Abbeys.

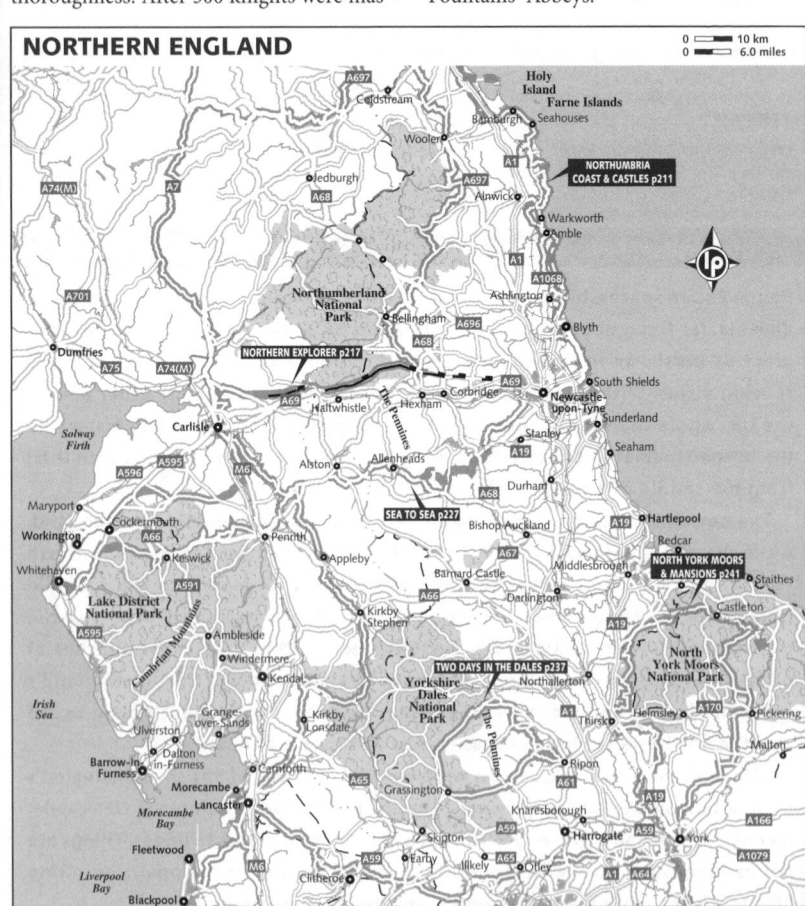

NORTHERN ENGLAND

ENVIRONMENT

The dominant geographic feature is the Pennine Hills that form a north-south spine dividing the region, with Cumbria and Lancashire to the west and Yorkshire, Durham and Northumberland to the east. Even away from the Pennines much of the region is hilly with plenty of challenging climbs in and around the Lake District, the Yorkshire Dales and Moors, and Northumberland's Cheviot Hills. The Scottish border traces a diagonal line southwest from Berwick-upon-Tweed to Carlisle.

PLANNING
When to Cycle

It's cold up north, and even in summer a chilly breeze brings the temperature down a notch or two. Travelling by pedal power is most pleasant in these parts from late spring until early autumn but at both ends of this time scale you'll experience ground frosts, especially at higher altitudes.

Maps

As ever, the superb Ordnance Survey maps are the best to source before putting foot to pedal. Northern England is covered by the OS Travel Map – Road 1:250,000 *Southern Scotland and Northumberland* (sheet 3) and *Northern England* (sheet 4).

Cycling Events

Bike Week (www.bikeweek.org.uk) is the best time to catch a cycling event in the north, with rides and rallies taking place in Newcastle, Middlesbrough and many smaller towns. For details of the **CTC York Cycle Show** see Cycling Events in the Central England chapter (p120).

Information Sources

The **Yorkshire Tourist Board** (www.yorkshire.com), the **Northeast England Tourist Board** (www.visitnortheastengland.com) and **Cumbria Tourism** (www.golakes.co.uk) are the official providers of tourist information from the Humber (Yorkshire), to the border with Scotland. They offer a comprehensive and eclectic coverage of regional and visitor information.

GATEWAYS

See Carlisle (p250) and Newcastle-upon-Tyne (p253).

NORTHUMBRIAN COAST & CASTLES

Duration 2 days
Distance 107 miles
Difficulty easy–moderate
Start Newcastle-upon-Tyne
Finish Berwick-upon-Tweed

Summary Off-road and on-road, through sand dunes and past dramatic castle ruins, these two days explore a desolately romantic coastline of empty golden beaches, islands of colourful puffin colonies and wind-whipped lighthouses.

Wide golden sands where the Vikings once dragged their longboats ashore, ancient castles looming out over the North Sea, islands of orange-billed puffins and wind-battered fishing villages – Northumberland's coastline is a magically forgotten place and ideal for an enjoyable two days on the pedals. Northumberland is one of the wildest, least spoilt of England's counties – and thanks to its strategic position adjoining the Scottish border – is home to more castles and battlefield sites than just about anywhere in the country. This relatively easy ride heads north from Newcastle, following country lanes and coastal paths on the journey up to the city of Berwick-upon-Tweed. Mighty fortresses at Warkworth, Alnwick, Dunstanburgh and Bamburgh and many natural features of the coastline provide ample reason to leave the saddle to explore. On the rare summer day when the weather's hot, a dip in the North Sea will cool you down, literally in an instant.

PLANNING
When to Cycle

Although locals flock to the coast over summer, Northumberland's charms remain largely undiscovered by the rest of the country, making this a ride that can be enjoyed when roads in tourist hot spots such as the Lake District are choked with visitors. The longer daylight hours and warmer days between June and September offer the best touring conditions. The winter months can be bleak, with many attractions closed from November to March.

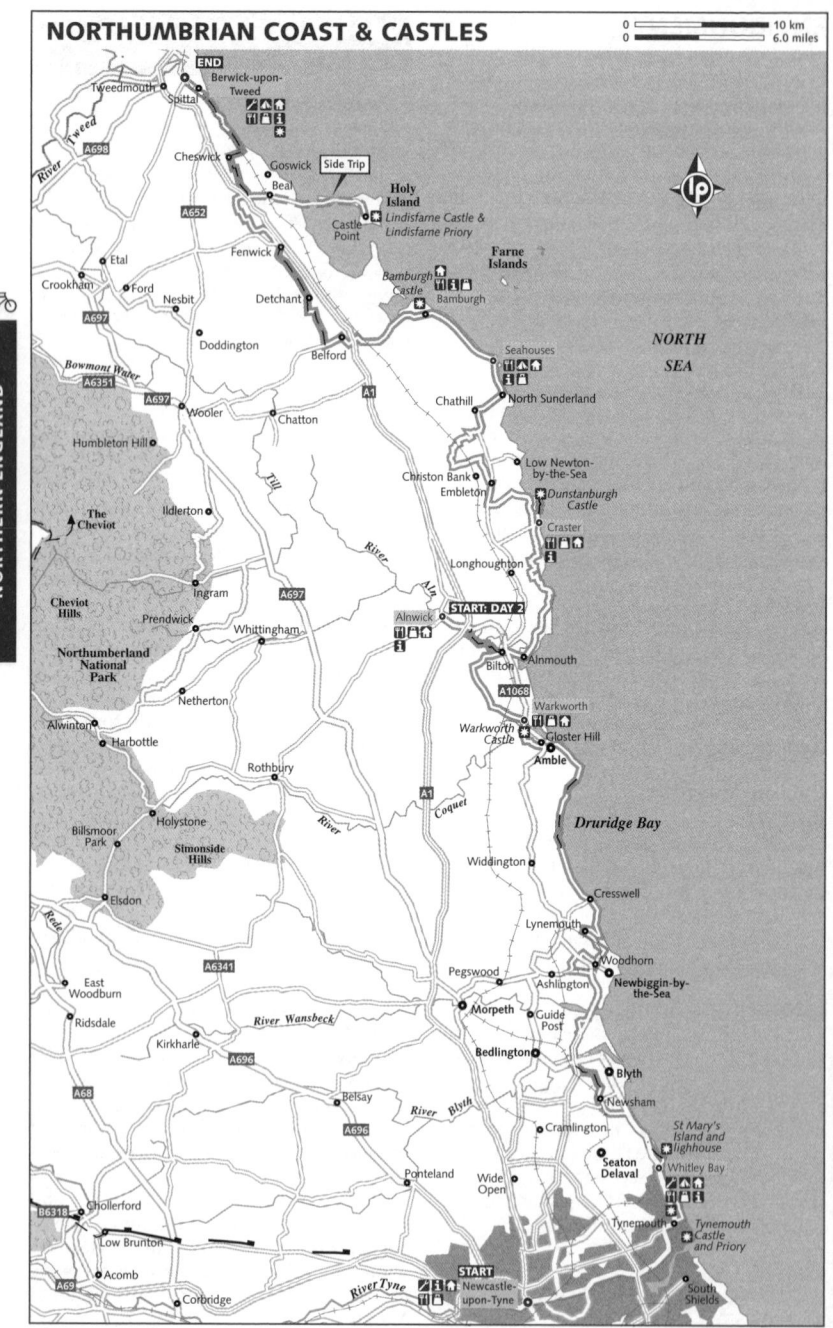

NORTHUMBRIAN COAST & CASTLES

0 — 10 km
0 — 6.0 miles

NORTHERN ENGLAND

THE BORDER REIVERS

Those who fret about modern-day levels of crime should thank their lucky stars they didn't live in the borderlands during the 400 years when the rapacious Reivers were around. The Reivers were brigands whose backgrounds differed but who had in common a complete disregard for the governments of England and Scotland. For the Reivers, sheep rustling and burning the homes of their enemies was a way of life and, as a result, northern Cumbria and Northumberland, the southern Scottish Borders and Dumfries and Galloway are littered with minor castles and tower-houses, as people struggled to protect themselves. It wasn't until James VI of Scotland succeeded Elizabeth I of England, and united the two countries, that order was finally reasserted.

The Reivers are credited with giving the English language such nice words as 'blackmail' and 'bereaved'. And if your surname is Armstrong, Carruthers, Dixon, Elliot, Henderson, Johnstone, Maxwell, Nixon, Scott, Taylor, Wilson or Young, there's a good chance you're descended from a Reiver.

What to Bring

Several sections of the ride lead along bumpy bridleways (used by walkers, horse riders and cyclists) and sandy coastal tracks. Although these are for the most part rideable on a touring bike, if you have the option tackle the ride on a mountain bike.

Maps

The OS Travel Map – Tour 1:100,000 *Northumbria* (sheet 14) covers the entire region in superb detail and is likely to prove invaluable for keeping you on the straight and narrow when negotiating tricky navigation on some sections of the ride. The NCN *Coast & Castles South* cycle route map, published by Sustrans, traces the NCN 1 from Newcastle to Edinburgh. The AA *Tyne & Wear Street by Street* atlas may also be useful for picking your way to the coast.

Information Sources

Visit **Northumberland** (www.visitnorthumberland.com) is the official source of information on England's most northerly county.

GETTING TO/FROM THE RIDE
Newcastle-upon-Tyne (start)

See Towns & Facilities (p253).

Berwick-upon-Tweed (finish)
TRAIN

Berwick is on the main east coast London-Edinburgh line operated by **National Express East Coast** (☎ 08457 225333; www.nationalexpresseastcoast.com). There are frequent services north to Edinburgh and

south to Newcastle, York and beyond. All services require (free) cycle reservations to be made at least 24 hours before you travel. Services from Berwick include:

Destination	One-way	Duration
Edinburgh	£16.00	50 minutes
London Kings Cross	£100.50	4 hours
Newcastle	£19.30	50 minutes
York	£49.10	1 hour 50 minutes
Peterborough	£89.00	3 hours

BICYCLE

The route to Wooler, Bellingham, Carlisle, Cockermouth and Whitehaven from Berwick is described in the Northern Explorer ride (p217).

THE RIDE
Day 1: Newcastle-upon-Tyne to Alnwick

4½–6 hours, 55 miles

Although today's ride isn't too physically taxing, the first part involves some tricky navigation through the suburbs of Newcastle. This entails negotiating a confusing web of traffic-free paths and moderately busy roads, and it would be easier to leave this relatively uninteresting section out, load your bike onto the Metro and simply start at the coast. However, it seems the bosses of Tyne and Wear's suburban rail system consider bikes a health and safety risk, so you'll have to ride. As an alternative to the described route, you can also cycle along the southern bank of the Tyne,

NORTHUMBRIAN COAST & CASTLES – DAY 1

CUE		GPS COORDINATES
start	Quayside, Newcastle (under Tyne Bridge)	54°58'6"N 1°36'22"W
0 miles	go E (downstream) along Quayside	
1.3	↘ St Lawrence Rd	
1.9	↘ onto riverside path	
3.1	↘ onto bikepath	
3.3	↰ unsigned road (by factory)	
3.8	↑ Wincomblee Rd (pass Malaya Dve)	
4.0	↱ White St	
4.9	↱ ⊙ Neptune Rd/A186	
7.2	↱ ⊙ Bewicke St	
7.6	↱ ⊙ Eastern Terrace	
8.0	↑ Howdon Rd/A187	
8.5	↱ ⊙ Coble Dene (to ferry terminal)	
8.9	↰ on path across park	
9.7	↱ ⊙ Howdon Rd/A187	
10.5	↑⊙ Charlotte St	
10.8	↱ Brewhouse Bank	
10.9	↰ join waterfront path	
11.8	↑ join coast road/Pier Rd	
(	★ Tynemouth Castle and Priory}	
{14.5	★ Whitley Bay}	
16.1	↱ 'to St Mary's Island'	
16.7	↰ join track at end of promenade	
17.3	↑ track emerges at car park	
17.5	↱ ⊙ A193 'to Blyth'	
20.4	↰ ⊙ A1061 'to Newcastle'	
21.5	↱ ⊙ Newcastle Rd 'to Newsham'	
22.3	↰ Wharton St	
22.3	↱ (50yd) join track at end of street	
23.9	↙ A193 (by supermarket)	
23.9	↰ (40yd) 'to Bedlington Station'	
24.1	↑ join bikepath beside A189	
24.7	↘ path crosses under A189	
24.8	↙ on path 'to Bedlington Station'	
25.2	↱ join road 'to East Sleekburn'	

CUE CONTINUED		GPS COORDINATES
25.5	↑ Moorland Ave (cross A189)	
26.1	↘ 'to West Sleekburn'	
26.2	↰ 'to West Sleekburn'	
27.0	↱ 'to Ashington' (by school)	
27.4	↱ loop onto path by A189	
30.1	↙ 'to Woodhorn' (cross road)	
30.2	↱ onto bikepath 'to Druridge Bay'	
32.3	↱ ⊙ Albion Terrace, Lynemouth	55°12'49"N 1°32'32"W
35.0	Cresswell	55°14'7"N 1°32'24"W
36.9	↑ coast road 'to Druridge Bay'	
37.6	⚠ thru gate, 200yd dirt track	
37.8	↱ track joins road	
39.3	↱ car park & road behind dunes	
40.7	⚠ 0.5 miles dirt track	
41.8	↱ Links Rd	
43.6	↱ ⊙ Church St	
43.8	↱ 'to Warkworth', Amble	55°20'6"N 1°34'54"W
44.0	↰ Gloster Hill	55°20'01"N 1°35'34"W
44.6	↱ 'to Warkworth'	
45.4	↱ 'to Warkworth'	
45.9	★ Warkworth	55°20'45"N 1°36'40"W
46.2	↰ 'to Alnmouth' (cross bridge)	
47.0	↱ 'to Alnmouth'	
47.5	↰ 'to Alnmouth'	
48.2	↱ 'to Alnwick'	
49.0	↘ 'to Alnwick'	
49.2	↱ unsigned road	
50.1	↱ 'to Alnmouth'	
51.1	↰ on descent	
51.9	↑ ignore 'no through road' sign	
52.1	↰ thru double wooden gates	
	⚠ 1.5 miles dirt rail trail	
53.3	↙ onto broader farm track	
53.6	↰ A1068	
55.0	Alnwick tourist office	55°24'47"N 1°42'25"W

following the Keelmans Way and C2C (Sea to Sea) markers to Jarrow, where you cross back to the north bank using the Tyne Pedestrian Tunnel.

From the **Quayside**, beneath the arching **Tyne Bridge**, follow the riverside path east past some new apartment and restaurant developments, with a brief stint on the road before picking up the path again. The next few miles head through a rather bleak landscape of factories and industrial sites with occasional stretches on moderately busy roads. If you get lost, just keep the compass pointing east and you'll hit sand and water soon enough.

Beyond the ferry terminal the route travels through North Shields, returning to the waterfront at **Fish Quay**. A pedestrian promenade leads the final mile to the official C2C end-point marker, just across from **Tynemouth Castle & Priory** (☎ 0191 257 1090). This English Heritage site, perched on a dramatic headland overlooking the mouth of the River Tyne, contains the remnants of castle walls and a gatehouse, within which stand the impressive remains of a Benedictine priory founded in 1090. If you're lucky, from here you may see one of the humungous container ships which dock in the Tyne for repairs, or the huge ferry bound for Norway.

From Tynemouth, the road follows the coast through to the grand old seaside resort of **Whitley Bay**. Pop music buffs will get a kick out of seeing the dome of the old Spanish City amusement park, the inspiration for the famous Dire Straits song 'Tunnel of Love'. The whole complex was receiving a much-needed make-over at the time of research. North of the shops and amusements a wonderfully wide stretch of sandy beach extends (at low tide) towards picture-perfect **St Mary's Island** dominated by a gleaming white **lighthouse** (☎ 0191 200 8650). Between tides you can pedal across the causeway to clamber up the 137 steps to the lantern room for spectacular vistas up and down the coast.

The route follows the coast before turning inland to somewhat dishevelled Newsham, where a bumpy bridleway leads along the back of a row of houses to link up with the A189.

A good cycle path signed with blue NCN route markers runs alongside the motorway, the route leading past various foul-smelling industrial installations to Lynemouth. Things finally start to look up again when the route hits the coast, running just behind the dunes of curving **Druridge Bay**. Quiet roads and scenic coastal tracks hug the sand line right through to the pleasant fishing town of Amble.

Just beyond Amble comes perhaps the (man-made) highlight of today's ride in the shape of imposing **Warkworth Castle** (☎ 01665 711423), a formidable 14th-century fortress with a large keep (the innermost and strongest structure or central tower of a medieval castle), full of narrow passageways and dark rooms to explore. The attractive village itself, situated on a meander of the River Coquet, is also well worth a wander.

On the run into Alnwick a perhaps unnecessary bit of fiddly navigation along country lanes can be avoided by sticking to the not-exceptionally-busy A1068, which crosses the A1 on the edge of the town.

Day 2: Alnwick to Berwick-upon-Tweed

5–6 hours, 52 miles

A long day this may be, but with flat coastal terrain most of the way you shouldn't arrive at your overnight stop in Berwick-upon-Tweed too dead beat. Set the alarm for an early start so you have plenty of time to soak up the many sights along the way.

From Alnwick retrace back to Bilton, and beyond Boulmer join a coastal path to Craster, following (as for much of the day) the reassuring blue signs marking NCN 1. Although things get quite bumpy at times, the scenic traffic-free path running just behind the dunes is suitable for all but the most heavily laden of cyclists. An alternative road route via Longhoughton is also signed.

After 12.5 miles the route turns left towards Embleton, although before that it's well worth making the half-mile side trip into Craster to visit **Dunstanburgh Castle** (☎ 01665 576231), a 14th-century fortress with a spectacular coastal backdrop. From Craster, it's a 1-mile walk north along a coastal path to the castle.

The route runs inland on a mix of traffic-free paths and quiet road to Seahouses (25.4 miles), a busy coastal resort and departure point for trips out to see the puffins and grey seal colonies of the **Farne Islands** – a wonderful experience with time and weather permitting. More golden strands and grassy dunes guide you onwards to the seaside hamlet of Bamburgh. Sitting on top of a basalt crag rising from the sea, **Bamburgh Castle** (28.6 miles; ☎ 01668 214515) is an awesome sight, its massive hulk dominating the coast for miles. Largely a late 19th-century creation of the Armstrong family, its interior isn't quite as impressive as some of the other castles of Northumbria.

Beyond Belford (34.8 miles), navigation can be awkward with the route following a number of grassy bridleways and paths. At times you are literally riding through fields, making for a bumpy ride, especially if you don't have the benefit of fat tyres. Heavily laden cyclists may prefer to stick to the on-road route between Belford and Detchant (37.9 miles).

After crossing the A1 near Beal, follow a stony railway service road alongside the main Edinburgh line, before crossing (take care!) and following a road down to the Cheswick golf course. A grassy bridleway begins just before the rail line and runs parallel with it for around 1.9 miles, emerging at a rough road by the coast. A short distance on, another very scenic bridleway heads along a narrow strip of grass hugging

NORTHUMBRIAN COAST & CASTLES – DAY 2

CUE		GPS COORDINATES
start	Alnwick tourist office	55°24'47"N 1°42'25"W
0 miles	go E on Bondgate Within	
	{retrace previous day's route}	
3.9	↰ 'to Bilton'	
4.1	Bilton	55°23'34"N 1°38'11"W
4.3	↑⊙ 'to Alnmouth'	
5.0	↰⊙ B1339 'to Craster'	
6.0	↱ 'to Boulmer'	
8.2	↱ Boulmer	55°25'19"N 1°34'52"W
	⚠ 2.3 miles dirt track	
10.5	↑ path meets coast road	
12.2	↱ 'to Craster'	
12.5	↰ 'to Embleton'	
	●●↱ Dunstanburgh Castle walk 1 mile ↻	
12.8	↱ 'to Embleton'	
13.0	↱ 'to Embleton'	
13.4	↑ thru gate onto concrete path	
14.5	↰ 'to Embleton'	
15.3	↱ 'to Seahouses'	
15.4	Embleton	55°29'43"N 1°38'7"W
15.6	↘ Station Rd (cross B1339)	
16.6	↰ B1340 'to Seahouses'	
16.9	↱ 'to Seahouses'	
18.2	↘ 'to Seahouses'	
18.8	↗ 'to Seahouses'	
20.7	Chathill	55°32'10"N 1°42'22"W
21.3	↰ 'to Seahouses'	
22.1	↗ 'to Seahouses'	
23.3	↘ 'to Seahouses'	
23.6	↗ 'to Seahouses'	
25.2	↑⊙ 'to Bamburgh'	

CUE CONTINUED		GPS COORDINATES
25.4	↑⊙ 'Bamburgh coastal route', Seahouses	
28.6	↑★ B1342, Bamburgh	55°36'24"N 1°43'1"W
34.1	↑ 'to Belford', cross A1	
34.8	↰ B6349 'to Wooler', Belford	55°35'42"N 1°49'2"W
35.1	↱ 'public bridleway'	
35.8	↑ thru gate onto grassy pathway	
	⚠ 2 miles dirt/grass path	
36.2	↑ thru gate, stay on path	
36.4	↘ onto forest track	
36.9	↱ bridleway 'to Detchant'	
37.4	↗ thru gate (follow fence line)	
37.8	↱ bridleway joins road	
37.9	↰ 'to Fenwick', Detchant	55°37'19"N 1°51'53"W
40.7	↰ B6353, Fenwick	55°39'14"N 1°53'47"W
40.9	↗ unsigned road	
42.2	↑ cross A1, 'to Beal'	
43.0	↰ onto road alongside railway line	
	⚠ 1.4 miles dirt road	
	●●↑ Holy Island 9.5 miles ↻	
44.2	↱ cross rail line at crossing	
44.4	↰ to golf course	
45.8	↱ 1.9 miles grassy bridleway	
47.7	↘ onto rough road by coast	
48.7	↗ 1.4 miles grassy bridleway	
50.8	↑ Dock Rd (by Albion Inn)	
51.5	↗ Main St	
51.6	↗ over bridge (first of three)	
51.8	↑ West St (walk; one-way)	
51.9	↰ Marygate High St	
52.0	Berwick-upon-Tweed tourist office	55°46'12"N 2°0'14"W

the tops of coastal cliffs and joining the black top again at Spittal (50.1 miles).

The three bridges across the River Tweed make for an impressive first view of Berwick. Cross over the first (built in 1634) and after pushing your bike up one-way West St, emerge at Marygate, the town's main shopping street.

SIDE TRIP: HOLY ISLAND
1 hour, 9.5 miles (RT)

Lying on the other side of a 3-mile causeway across fascinating muddy flats, tiny Holy Island is a beacon for tourists, even in low season. St Aidan founded a monastery in this cut-off location in AD 635, and it soon became a major centre of Christianity and learning. The exquisitely illustrated Lindisfarne Gospels, which originated here, can be seen in the British Library in London. The two principal sights are the ruins of **Lindisfarne Priory** (☎ 01289 389200), consisting of the remains of the priory's church and the 13th-century St Mary the Virgin Church, and **Lindisfarne Castle** (☎ 01289 389244), built in 1550 on a rocky hillock at the southern end of the island and restored by Sir Edward Luytens in 1903.

The island is completely cut off from the mainland when the causeway is submerged at high tide. Check the causeway notice board for tide times or call **Berwick tourist office** (☎ 01289 330733). If you don't want to detour off the main route, visit Holy Island later by catching twice-daily bus 477 back from Berwick. It's possible to spend a whole day on the island visiting the sights, wandering the grassy hills, taking photographs of Bamburgh Castle and lunching in one of the quaint tearooms.

NORTHERN EXPLORER

Duration 5 days
Distance 201.5 miles
Difficulty moderate
Start Berwick-upon-Tweed
Finish Whitehaven

Summary A blockbuster coast-to-coast route that dips into Scotland, traces Hadrian's Wall, calls at Roman forts and clambers into the Lake District before swooping down to the Cumbrian shore.

Travelling a winding route from the North Sea to the Irish Sea, this route is less popular and not as taxing as the classic C2C, but takes in a wealth of history and the rugged and lonely landscapes of northern England's far-flung uplands. From the splendid solitude of the Northumberland National Park, to the numerous Roman sites along Hadrian's Wall, the fine city of Carlisle, and the celebrated beauty of the northern Lake District – this ride presents a different face for every day. Tackle it in combination with the C2C (p227) and Northumbrian Coast & Castle (p211) rides for a giant circular tour of the best England's far north has to offer.

PLANNING
When to Cycle
Much of the ride, especially through Northumberland, is well off the beaten track so with the possible exception of Cockermouth, you shouldn't have too many problems finding accommodation even during peak periods. If possible, try to ride the leg from Bellingham to Carlisle midweek as the B6318 can carry a lot of tourist traffic on weekends. Summer, with its warmish weather and light nights, is the pick of the seasons as many attractions close from November to March.

What to Bring
As neither Wooler nor Bellingham have cycle repair shops, make sure you stuff your panniers with plenty of bike spares and that your set of wheels for the five days is in general good health. You'll be riding over 136 miles coast-to-coast, with no opportunity to buy spares or fix faults (unless you do it yourself), so ride prepared. In spring and

autumn, plan for nippy nights and morning frosts in the hills.

Maps
Navigation is fairly straightforward throughout this ride, especially from Carlisle where the ride follows the well-signed Reivers' cycle route. It may be worth getting hold of two route maps – available from Sustrans and local tourist offices – the NCN *Hadrian's Cycleway* and the *Reivers Cycle Route,* which are useful if you intend a more thorough exploration of the area. Otherwise OS Travel Map – Road 1:250,000 *Southern Scotland & Northumberland* (sheet 3) and *Northern England* (sheet 4) show the area in sufficient technicolor detail.

Information Sources
Visit Northumberland (www.visitnorthumberland.com) and the **Cumbrian Tourist Board** (www.golakes.co.uk) are the official sources of tourist information for the counties through which this route passes. Much of this ride follows the **Reivers Route cycle path** (www.reivers-guide.co.uk) whose online guide is extremely helpful. The route takes you from the North Sea to Kielder Water: Europe's largest man-made lake.

GETTING TO/FROM THE RIDE
Berwick-upon-Tweed (start)
TRAIN
See p213 for details on getting to and from Berwick.

Whitehaven (finish)
TRAIN
Whitehaven is a stop on the Cumbrian Coast line, which runs from Carlisle (£8.50; one hour, hourly) to Barrow-in-Furness, and inland east to Lancaster (£16; 2½ hours, three daily). Both Lancaster and Carlisle are on the main Glasgow-London Euston west coast mainline operated by Virgin Trains (☎ 08457 222333; www.virgintrains.co.uk) who require you to hold a (free) reservation to take your bike on their services.

BICYCLE
The route from Whitehaven to Newcastle, via Keswick, Penrith and Allenheads is described in the C2C ride (p227).

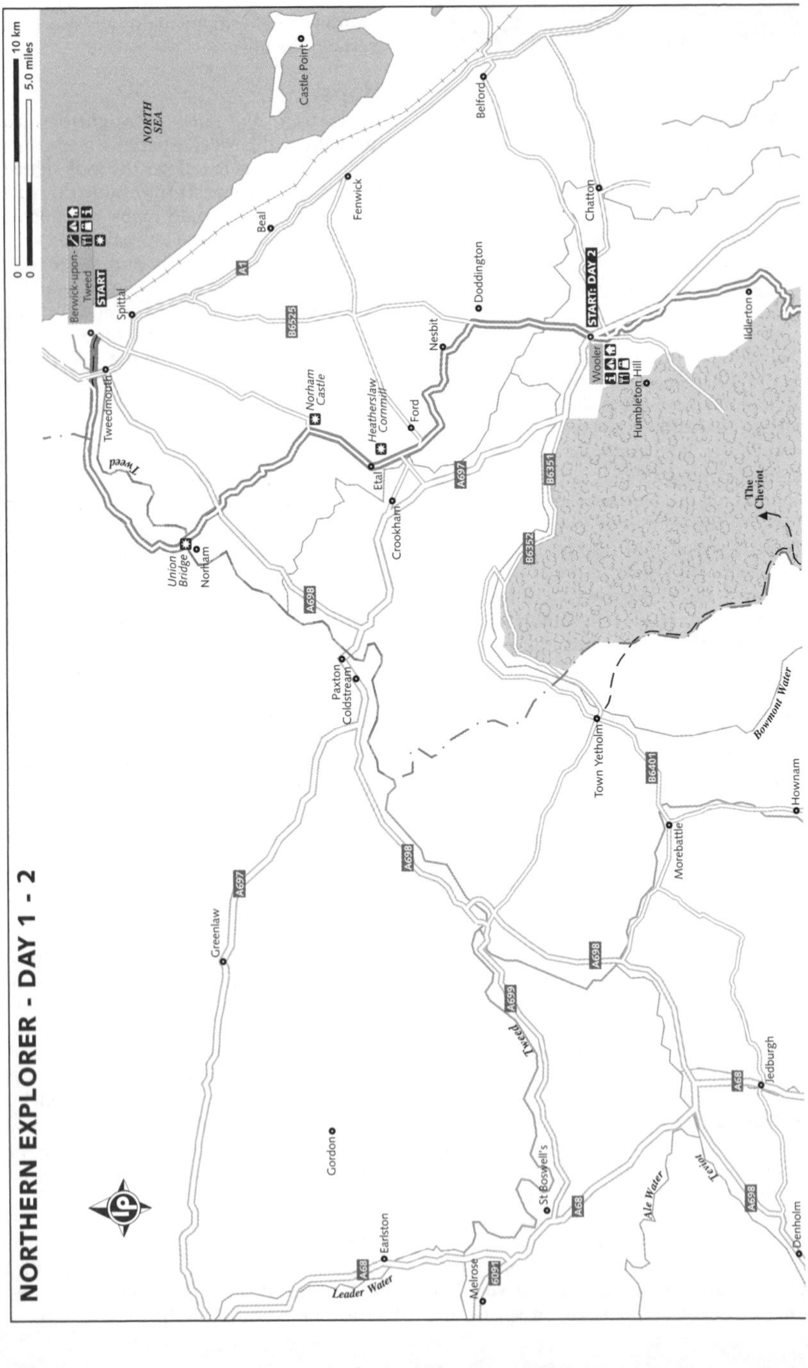

NORTHERN EXPLORER - DAY 1 - 2

NORTH SEA

Castle Point

Belford

Beal

Fenwick

Chatton

Berwick-upon-Tweed
START

Spittal

A1

B6525

Doddington

Iddlerton

Tweedmouth

Norham Castle

Heatherslaw Cornmill

Nesbit

START: DAY 2

Wooler

Humbleton Hill

Ford

B6351

Tweed

Union Bridge

Norham

Etal

A697

Crookham

B6352

The Cheviot

A698

Paxton
Coldstream

Town Yetholm

Bowmont Water

Greenlaw

A697

B6401

Hownam

Morebattle

A698

A698

A698

A699

Tweed

Jedburgh

A68

Gordon

St Boswell's

Ale Water

A698

Teviot

Denholm

Earlston

A68

A58

Melrose

B6j

Leader Water

10 km
5.0 miles

0
0

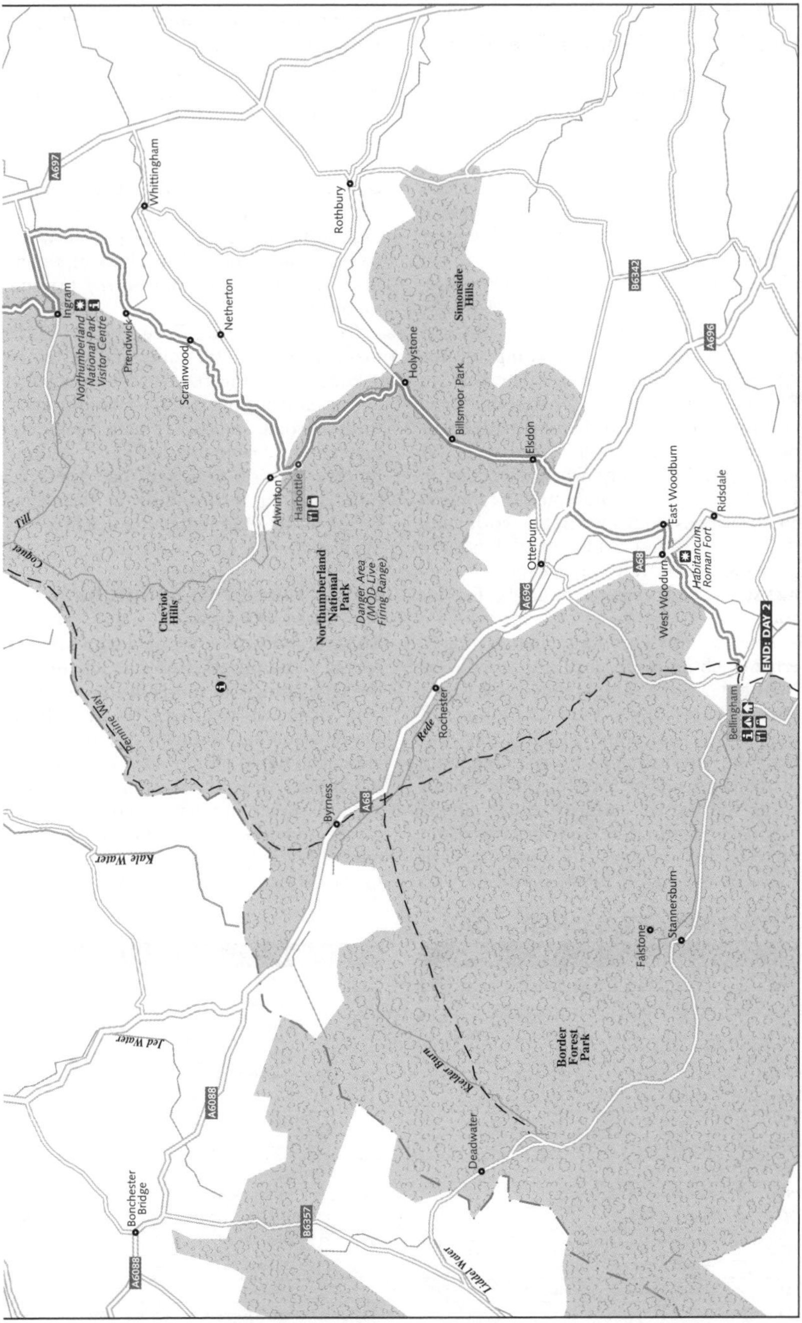

A697

Whittingham

Rothbury

Ingram

Northumberland National Park Visitor Centre

Prendwick

Netherton

Scrainwood

Simonside Hills

Holystone

Billsmoor Park

Alwinton

Harbottle

Elsdon

East Woodburn

Ridsdale

Otterburn

A68

Habitancum Roman Fort

West Woodburn

A696

Till

Coquet

Cheviot Hills

Northumberland National Park

Danger Area (MOD Live Firing Range)

Pennine Way

Rede

Rochester

Bellingham

END: DAY 2

Byrness

A68

Kale Water

Stannersburn

Falstone

Border Forest Park

Kielder Burn

Jed Water

A6088

Bonchester Bridge

B6357

A6088

Deadwater

Liddel Water

B6342

A696

THE RIDE
Day 1: Berwick-upon-Tweed to Wooler
2½–3½ hours, 29.9 miles

This is a short and relatively easy day of cycling, heading briefly over the border into Scotland and finishing at the foot of the rolling green Cheviot Hills. There are few real climbs, only one short off-road stretch and a few places where the road surface deteriorates significantly.

You'll get a feel for just how close Berwick is to Scotland when you cross the border after just 3.8 miles on the way to Paxton, shortly after turning off the A1. However, you're soon safely back in Blighty after the route crosses the small and somewhat forlorn **Union Bridge** suspended over at the River Tweed at the 7.1 mile point. Incredibly, when it opened in 1820 its tiny span represented the longest chain suspension bridge in the world, and it's still the oldest bridge of its kind still carrying traffic (although cars can only just squeeze between the bollards at either end).

After a brief visit to England's northern neighbour your next stop should be **Norham Castle** (11.4 miles; ☎ 01661 881297), now under the watchful eye of English Heritage. Built in 1160 this dramatic set of ruins stands as a vivid reminder of the centuries of bloody conflict towns along the border endured. Much of the original structure has been destroyed but there is still enough standing to make it a good stopping-off point, especially with the self-guided audio tour. Another English Heritage castle can be found in the village of **Etal** (18.4 miles) where the visitor centre prides itself on an award-winning display on the Battle of Flodden (fought at nearby Branxton Moor), although not much of the fortress still remains. As you leave the village you'll pass the **Heatherslaw Cornmill** (☎ 01890 820488), a fully functional water mill on the banks of the River Till, where you can take a tour of the clunking timber machinery before retiring to the tearoom for a cuppa.

Heading towards Ford, turn off the main road after 20.1 miles and cycle past a farm where the road becomes rougher and eventually turns into a bumpy track through some woods. It's quite sandy and may be unrideable in a few short sections. Emerge back on to sealed road after 22.3 miles, heading for Doddington, the rolling B6525 leading the remaining distance into Wooler.

Day 2: Wooler to Bellingham
4½–5½ hours, 47.6 miles

Today is almost 50 miles of blissful solitude, rolling along on quiet back roads through the undulating Cheviot Hills, the sound of your chain whirr through the gears being the only sound. No towns of any real size are encountered all day so pack a pannier lunch for a spot of roadside dining. The short climb out of town is a good warm-up for the numerous short uphill bits throughout the day. While there are no huge ascents to tackle en route, they're not called the

NORTHERN EXPLORER – DAY 1

CUE		GPS COORDINATES	
start	Berwick tourist office	55°46'12"N	2°0'14"W
0 miles	go NW on Marygate		
0.4	↘ B6461 'to Kelso'		
1.1	↰ A1 'to Paxton'		
2.1	↱ B6461 'to Paxton'		
3.8	Scottish border		
6.1	↰ 'to Horncliffe'		
7.1	English border		
7.7	↱ 'to Norham'		
9.0	↱ 'to Norham'		
[11.4	★ Norham Castle]		
12.0	↰ B6470 (no sign), Norham	55°43'10"N	2°9'41"W
12.6	↱ unsigned road		
14.3	↙ 'to Etal', Grindon	55°41'48"N	2°8'11"W
14.8	↘ 'to Etal'		

CUE CONTINUED		GPS COORDINATES	
14.9	↙ 'to Etal'		
17.2	↙ 'to Wooler'		
18.4	★ Etal	55°38'53"N	2°6'58"W
19.8	↑ 'to Ford'		
20.1	↱ rough unsigned road		
20.5	↘ enter woodland (by farm)		
	⚠ 1.8 miles dirt track		
22.3	↱ track comes out at road		
22.5	↰ 'to Doddington'		
24.1	↙ 'to Doddington'		
26.4	↱ 'to Wooler', Doddington	55°35'11"N	2°0'11"W
29.1	↰ South Rd		
29.8	↱ Church St 'to town centre'		
29.9	↰ Padgepool Pl		
29.9	Wooler tourist office	55°32'47"N	2°1'6"W

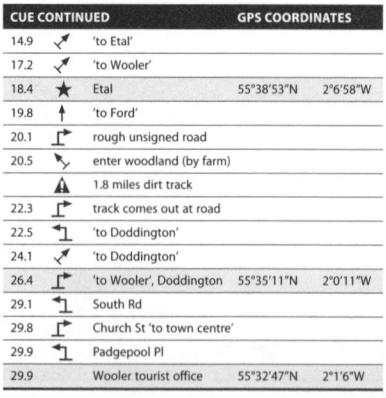

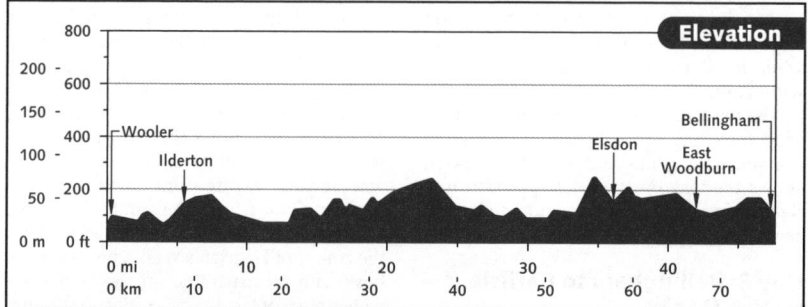

NORTHERN EXPLORER – DAY 2

CUE			GPS COORDINATES	
start		Wooler tourist office	55°32'47"N	2°1'6"W
0 miles		go SE on High St		
0.0	↗	(40yd) Cheviot St		
2.2	⚠	ford		
2.6	↗	unsigned road		
2.9	↰	unsigned T-junction		
3.7	↱	A697 'to Morpeth'		
4.4	↱	'to Ilderton'		
5.5	↑	past village buildings, Ilderton	55°29'29"N	1°58'29"W
6.3	↑	thru gate on to path		
	⚠	700yd grassy path		
6.7	↗	back on to road		
8.9	↗	unsigned road		
9.2	↰★	Ingram NP Centre (RHS)		
11.2	↱	cross stream via footbridge		
11.7	↰	unsigned road		
11.8	↱	'to Glanton', Branton	55°29'29"N	1°58'29"W
13.0	▲	700yd moderate climb		
13.4	↱	'to Great Ryle'		
13.7	↗	'to Great Ryle'		
15.3	↱	'to Prendwick'		
17.3	↘	'to Alnham', Prendwick	55°24'15"N	1°59'51"W
18.3	▲	0.7 miles moderate climb		

CUE CONTINUED			GPS COORDINATES	
19.3	↗	'to Alwinton'		
20.0	↗	'to Eilaw'		
20.5	↑	thru gate		
21.5	↰	by quarry, Biddlestone	55°22'6"N	2°3'49"W
21.6	↱	unsigned road		
22.8	↱	'to Alwinton'		
24.9	↰	just before river		
26.2		Harbottle	55°20'9"N	2°6'11"W
27.7	↱	'to Holystone' (before Sharperton)		
28.3	↘	'to Elsdon', Holystone	55°19'6"N	2°4'23"W
30.9	↱	B6341 'to Elsdon'		
33.4	▲	1.2 miles hard climb		
36.1	↗	'to Newcastle', Elsdon	55°14'2"N	2°6'0"W
36.1	↰	(50yd) 'to Newcastle'		
36.4	↗	'to Newcastle'		
	▲	0.7 miles moderate climb		
37.6	↱	A696 'to Jedburgh'		
38.4	↰	'to East Woodburn'		
42.0	↗	'to W Woodburn', East Woodburn	55°10'31"N	2°8'48"W
42.9	↱	A68 'to Jedburgh'		
43.0	↰	'to Bellingham', West Woodburn	55°10'31"N	2°10'11"W
47.0	↱	Bellingham tourist office	55°8'36"N	2°15'19"W

Cheviot Hills for nothing, and the day as a whole can be quite testing.

A short distance beyond Ilderton the sealed road, barred by a gate, comes to an end, and there's a short section of rough bridleway with a ford to negotiate (use the footbridge), before rejoining the bitumen for the journey into Ingram. Here you'll find a national park centre (☎ 01665 578248) with lots of information and displays on the **Northumberland National Park**, which extends almost wholly devoid of humans for 405 sq miles to the west. It's slightly off the route but well worth

the short detour. The main route continues through the rolling green hills of heather in myriad shades on virtually traffic-free roads, with only the sound of the occasional bleating sheep (and the odd earth-shakingly loud jet fighter) to fill your ears. Even at the height of summer the feeling of solitude is remarkable.

A couple of the bigger climbs of the day are encountered near Elsdon (36.1 miles), with the biggest a fairly tough 1.2-mile ascent starting 2.7 miles short of the village. After a brief stint of traffic dodging on the A696 you'll arrive at West Woodburn where the faint remains of **Habitancum Roman Fort** lie next to A68, itself the erstwhile Roman Dere Street linking Scotland with York.

The final miles are fairly gentle, the gated road travelling through paddocks of grazing sheep. A gentle but welcome descent shows the way on the final approach into Bellingham, a good way to end a tiring but rewarding day.

Day 3: Bellingham to Carlisle
6–7 hours, 58.6 miles

This long day heads along the most interesting sections of Hadrian's Wall with heaps of history to see along the way, so rise early to make the most of this ride through

the outer limits of the Roman Empire. The countryside south of Bellingham is scenic and very lush, with the road passing green fields and numerous pockets of woods as it follows the course of the River North Tyne. The road rolls along throughout the day with a few moderate climbs to puff and wheeze your way up from time to time.

Near Chollerford the route joins the B6318, the fast road that most closely follows the course of Hadrian's Wall. Things can get busy with tourist traffic on this none-too-wide stretch of tarmac, especially on summer weekends, and cyclists should take care. The upside is that it offers a direct route to all the best sights on the wall, the first of which is reached almost immediately.

NORTHERN EXPLORER – DAY 3

CUE			GPS COORDINATES	
start		Bellingham tourist office	55°8'36"N	2°15'19"W
0 miles		go E on Woodburn Rd		
0.5	↰	High St		
6.1	↰	'to Barrasford', Wark	55°5'15"N	2°13'16"W
6.4	↱	over bridge, 'to Barrasford'		
10.7		Barrasford	55°3'17"N	2°7'57"W
12.2	↱	'to Chollerford'		
13.6	↱	A6097 'to Chollerford'		
14.0	↰⊙	B6318 'to Hadrian's Wall'		
{14.3	★	Chesters Roman Fort}		
	▲	1 mile moderate climb		
15.2	▲	0.6 miles moderate climb		
{22.7	★	Housesteads Fort & Museum}		
25.5		Once Brewed	54°59'47"N	2°23'13"W
{	●●↰	Vindolanda site 3 miles ↻}		
31.7	↱	B6318 'to Gilsland', Greenhead	54°58'55"N	2°31'57"W
33.7	↱	B6318 'to Walton', Gilsland	54°59'28"N	2°34'29"W
34.0	↰	B6318 'to Roadhead'		
35.1	↰	'to Lanercost'		

CUE CONTINUED			GPS COORDINATES	
{40.0	★	Birdoswald Fort}		
38.4		Banks East Turret		
40.1	↙	'to Walton'		
{	★	Lanercost Priory}		
41.4	↰	'to Walton'		
42.9	↱	'to Kirkcambeck', Walton	54°58'20"N	2°44'56"W
43.0	↘	'to Solmain'		
48.1		Heathersgill	54°59'47"N	2°49'1.59"W
50.8		Smithfield	54°58'46"N	2°52'28"W
53.1	↱	'to Carlisle'		
55.5	↱	'to Houghton'		
55.6	↰	'to Houghton' (cross M6)		
55.5		Houghton	54°55'34"N	2°55'28"W
56.9	↱	B6264 'to Carlisle'		
58.8	↱	Warwick Rd 'to City Centre'		
58.9	↱	Lowther St		
59.0	↰	Bank St		
59.0	↱	(50yd) English St		
59.1		Carlisle tourist office	54°53'41"N	2°56'11"W

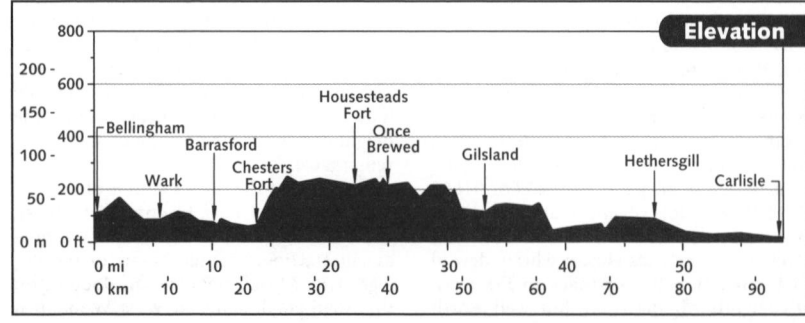

Elevation

Chesters Roman Fort & Museum (13.8 miles; ☎ 01434 681379) houses the remnants of a Roman cavalry fort where you can wander and explore the foundations of the barracks and bathhouse. The latter comes complete with a luxurious underfloor heating system, which must have been stoked up daily to warm the cockles of soldiers from sunnier climes. The museum, with its extensive collection of Roman artefacts and inscribed stones, is a good place to start. Like most of the wall sites you'll need to use a bit of imagination as few buildings have remained intact.

The next major Roman site is **Housesteads Roman Fort & Museum** (22.2 miles; ☎ 01434 344363). The ruins here aren't quite as extensive or well preserved as Chesters, but its setting perched high on a ridge is spectacularly dramatic. From here it's not far to pedal to the interestingly named **Once Brewed** (25 miles), a settlement with a national park visitor centre (☎ 01434 344396) and a youth hostel. The **Vindolanda** site (☎ 01434 344277), a 3-mile return side trip signposted from the visitor centre, offers a fascinating glimpse into the daily life of a Roman garrison town. The **Roman Army Museum** is displays personal belongings of people who lived at Vindolanda 2000 years ago and puts some flesh on the bones of Britain's stony Roman heritage. The museum is just one part of this large, extensively excavated site, which includes impressive parts of the fort and town and reconstructed turrets and a temple. Parts of the site are still undergoing excavation and there are ambitious and well-funded plans to turn it into an even bigger and more interactive tourist attraction than it already is.

Beyond Greenhead (31.2 miles) much of the traffic is thankfully siphoned away by the A69, with the route continuing to follow the much quieter B6318 through to Gilsland. Two miles on you pass an impressive, largely intact section of the wall containing the well-preserved **Birdoswald Fort** (35 miles; ☎ 01697 747602) overlooking the beautiful Irthing Gorge, before arriving at Lanercost (39.6 miles) where the veritable feast of ancient sites continues. If you've not developed 'temple fatigue' by this stage, make a brief visit to **Lanercost Priory** (☎ 01697 73030), from which Edward I briefly ruled the kingdom

in the early 14th century. From Lanercost the route to Carlisle follows quiet roads through Walton, Hethersgill and Smithfield, a bridge over the M6 leading into Houghton on the outskirts of Carlisle itself. Traffic increases on the approach to the city centre so it's a good idea to use the dual-use paths where possible.

Day 4: Carlisle to Cockermouth
4–5 hours, 46.7 miles

While yesterday was all about stopping to ogle at 2000-year-old walls and forts, today's eyeball pleasure can be found in the rounded peaks of the Lake District National Park's northern extremities. Navigation initially looks challenging, but as you'll be following the blue signposted **Reivers Route** all the way, you can happily stash the map in the panniers for this day's pedalling. The route out of car-plagued Carlisle leads along the banks of the River Eden on a traffic-free, bumpy pathway. A flight of steps leads away from the river on to an industrial estate, but the urban clutter is soon left behind as the road flanked by hedgerows heads out into the picturesque Cumbrian countryside.

A number of small villages punctuate the route but the tearooms and pubs of **Hesket Newmarket** (27.6 miles) provide the best spot to break for lunch and sample some hearty Cumbrian fare. Fans of CAMRA (Campaign For Real Ale) may know the **Hesket Newmarket Brewery** (☎ 01697 478288), which produces some fine bitters and porters (a dark, sour bitter). Sadly the brewery tours only take place on weekday evenings. Beyond the village you enter the Lake District National Park and the terrain becomes hillier, with a number of small climbs to negotiate. The landscape is one of green pastures, dry stone walls and nonchalant woolly sheep staring at odd two-wheeled humans from the fields.

As the route climbs up towards the Caldbeck Fells the countryside takes on a less manicured, exposed appearance, with sheep grazing on the common land beside the road. Some classic lakeland views over **Bassenthwaite Lake** can be enjoyed as you pass through Fellend Farm, a freewheeling drop heading down to the A591. Those not fond of gradients will be pleased to learn that the trend is most definitely downhill from here

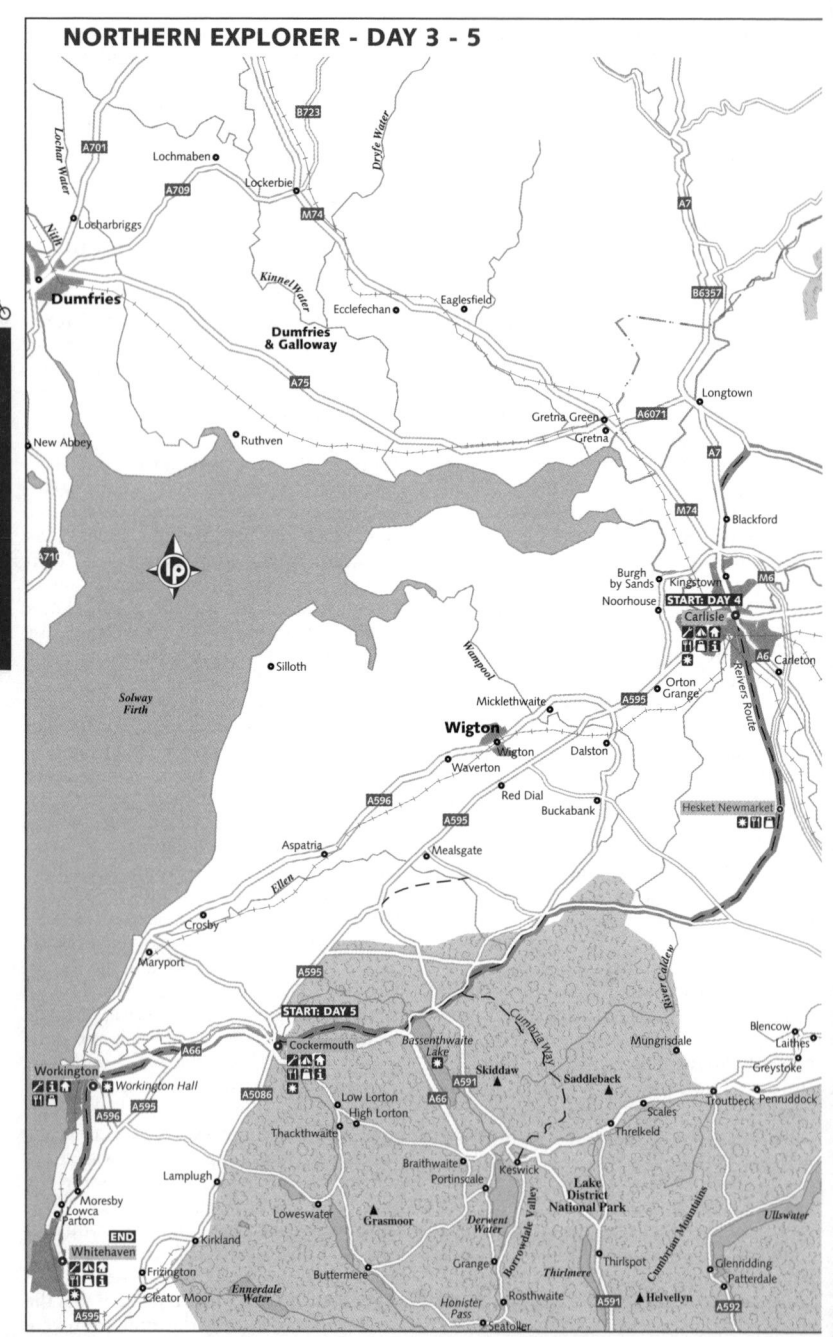

NORTHERN EXPLORER - DAY 3 - 5

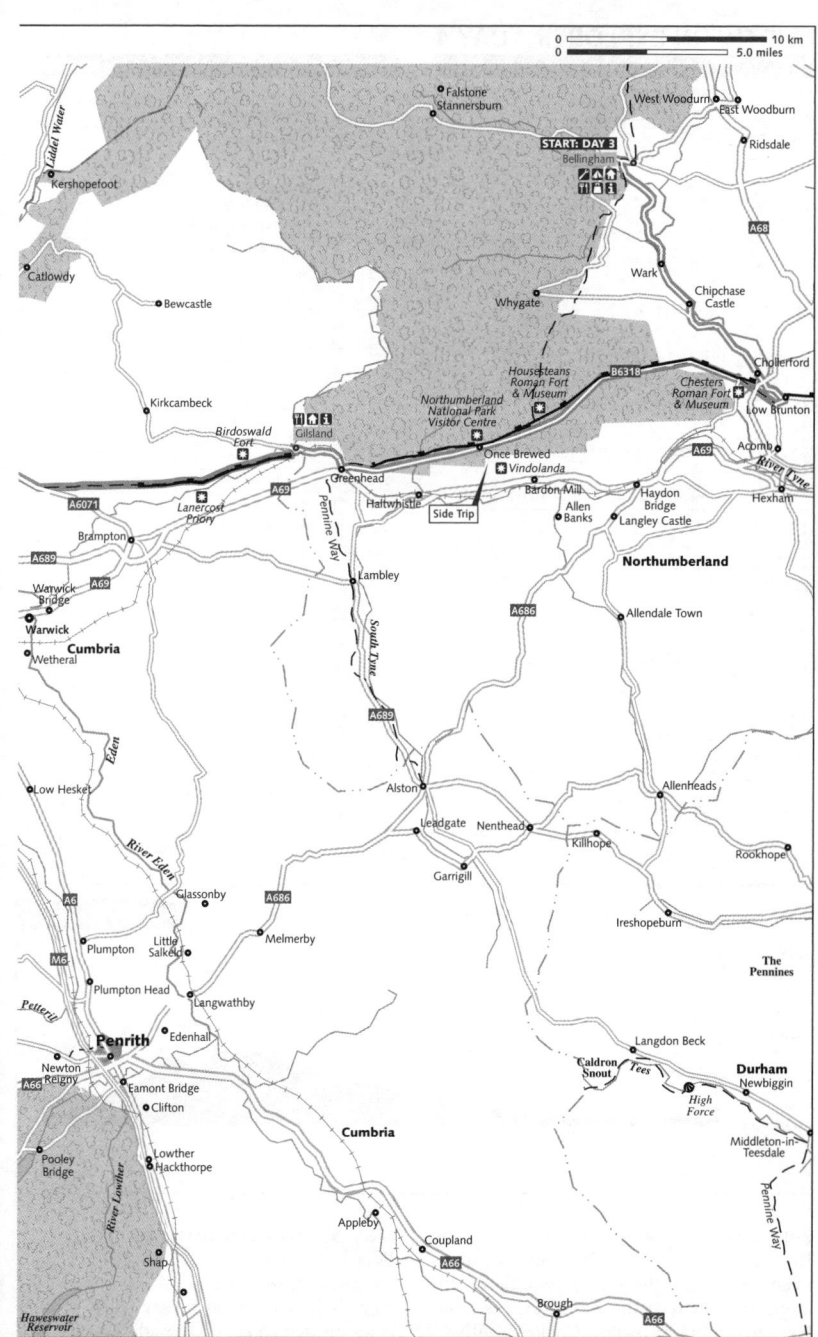

NORTHERN EXPLORER – DAY 4

CUE			GPS COORDINATES	
start		Carlisle tourist office	54°53'41"N	2°56'11"W
0 miles		walk N on Scotch St		
0.2	↰	West Tower St		
0.3	↱	under A595		
	↑	join bikepath in Bitts Park		
0.4	↰	alongside River Eden		
	⚠	1.7 miles dirt bikepath		
0.7	↱	20yd after bridge		
1.8	↙	stay next to river		
2.0	↑⚠	up flight of steps		
2.0	↙	(30yd) at top of steps		
2.1	↘	on to road		
2.4	↱	Thomas Lane		
2.4	↰	(20yd) Marconi Rd		
2.5	↱	Burgh Rd		
4.5	↙	'to Beaumont', Kirkandrews		
5.2	↱	unsigned road		
5.3	↘	'to Burgh', Beaumont	54°55'27"N	3°1'5"W
6.8	↘	unsigned road		
8.7	↘	Burgh by Sands	54°55'16"N	3°3'31"W
10.2	↘	B5307 'to Carlisle'		
10.5		Moorhouse	54°54'5"N	3°2'32"W
10.7	↱	'to Great Orton'		
12.1	↘	'to Great Orton'		
12.5		Great Orton	54°52'43"N	3°2'52"W
12.8	↘	'to Dalston'		
14.8	↰	A595 'to Carlisle'		
14.8	↰	(30yd) 'to Dalston'		
15.4	↰	'to Dalston'		
16.2	↱	'to Dalston'		
16.8	↰	unsigned road		
17.5	↱	B5299, Dalston	54°50'28"N	2°59'3"W
18.5	↙	B5299 'to Welton'		

CUE CONTINUED			GPS COORDINATES	
18.8	↘	at top of short climb		
19.3	↘	'to Rose Castle'		
20.2	↘	'to Raughtonhead'		
20.8	↙	at top of short climb		
21.1	↱	'to Sowerby Row', Raughton Head	54°47'20"N	2°58'13"W
23.3	↱	'to Hesket Newmarket'		
23.6	↙	'to Hesket Newmarket'		
24.7	↰	B5305 'to Penrith'		
25.0	↱	'to Hesket Newmarket'		
26.3	▲	800yd moderate climb		
27.6	↙	The Street, Hesket Newmarket	54°44'17"N	3°1'34"W
27.7	↘	unsigned road		
29.0	▲	800yd steep climb		
29.5	↱	'to Fell Side'		
32.9	↰	B5299 'to Aspatria'		
33.2	↘	'to Keswick'		
34.0	↰	'to Orthwaite'		
36.0	↱	'to Cockermouth'		
36.2	↘	'to Cockermouth'		
37.4	↱	'to Uldale'		
37.6	↘	'to Ireby'		
37.7	↰	by house with large wall		
39.6	↱	'to Bothel'		
39.7	↑	cross A591		
41.9	↰	'to Cockermouth'		
43.0	↰	cross bridge over River Derwent		
43.2	↱	'to Cockermouth'(broken sign, not Keswick)		
46.4	↱	Castlegate Dr		
46.6	↰	St Helens St (bottom of hill)		
46.6	↱	(30yd) Market St		
46.7		Cockermouth tourist office	54°39'47"N	3°21'41"W

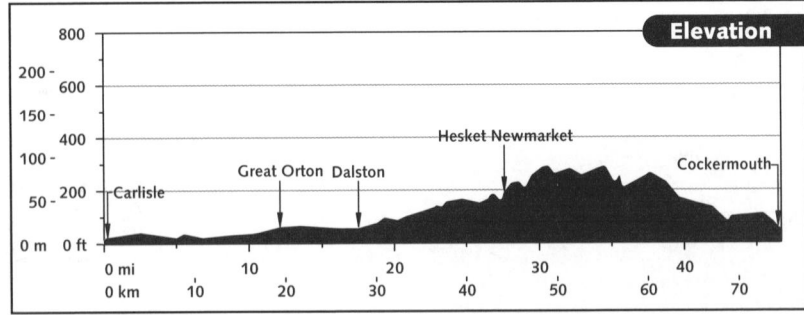

Elevation chart showing the route from Carlisle through Great Orton, Dalston, Hesket Newmarket to Cockermouth. Vertical axis in metres (0 m, 50, 100, 150, 200, 800) and feet (0 ft, 200, 400, 600, 800). Horizontal axis in miles (0 to 40+) and km (0 to 70).

until the end of the ride. After crossing the River Derwent there's a short steep climb to negotiate before the final downhill stretch along Isel Rd into the beautiful tree-lined Georgian market town of Cockermouth.

Day 5: Cockermouth to Whitehaven

1½–2½ hours, 18.7 miles

Almost half of today's very short section is along dedicated cycle paths, meaning a

NORTHERN EXPLORER – DAY 5

CUE			GPS COORDINATES
start		Cockermouth tourist office	54°39′47″N 3°21′41″W
0 miles		go on N on Market St	
0.1	↰	St Helens St	
0.1	↰	(30yd) Main St	
0.2	↱	Bridge St	
0.4	↑	on lane beside soccer pitch	
0.5	↰	lane at back of soccer pitch	
2.4	↘	join C2C bikepath	
3.2		Great Broughton	54°40′11″N 3°26′14″W
3.4	↘	'to Camerton'	
4.6		MOD facility	
6.1	↱	unsigned road, Camerton	54°39′48″N 3°29′41″W
6.4	↰	join C2C path at top of climb	
6.5	↑	on either fork	
7.6		Seaton	54°39′44″N 3°31′29″W
9.2	↑	rejoin C2C bikepath	
9.6	↑	over bridge	
10.0		Workington	54°38′37″N 3°33′8″W
10.2	↑	rejoin C2C bikepath	

CUE CONTINUED			GPS COORDINATES
10.9	↗	on bikepath	
11.3	↰⊙	leisure centre car park	
11.4	↱	join NCN 10 bikepath	
12.2	↘	under bridge	
12.8	↗	on bikepath	
12.9	↱	join road (no sign)	
13.0	↰	'to Lowca'	
	▲	0.8 miles gradual climb	
13.8	↰	NCN 10 (top of hill)	
14.7	↗	NCN 10	
15.5	↘	NCN 10 (end of path)	
15.7	↰	NCN 10	
15.8	↱	Foundry Rd 'to Parton'	
16.6	↱	join coastal path below cliffs	
17.9	↱	Bransty Rd	
18.0	↘	George St	
18.1	↱	Church St	
18.1	↰	(50yd) Duke St	
18.3	↱	Scotch St	
18.4	↱	Roper St	
18.7		Whitehaven tourist office	54°32′51″N 3°35′29″W

relatively stress-free ride away from traffic. The route beats a hasty retreat out of Cockermouth and has you pedalling scenic country lanes within a few miles. Beyond Great Broughton the pastoral scenery is briefly interrupted as the quiet lane flanks a barbed wire fence protecting a Ministry of Defence (MOD) store.

Leaving the small village of Camerton, a short steep climb leads onto a traffic-free rail path (6.4 miles), passing under a number of old stone bridges on the way into sizeable Seaton (7.6 miles). However it's not long before the picturesque rural scenery yields to a more industrial landscape, punctuated by power pylons, smokestacks and large wind turbines.

With the coast in sight the route crosses the River Derwent into the relatively nondescript former steel-producing town of Workington, and continues on pathways through the outskirts where you'll find **Workington Hall**, a castle to which Mary Queen of Scots fled after the Battle of Langside. Heading back out into the countryside, the final few miles follow part of the NCN10 along a scenic path below coastal cliffs, before entering Whitehaven – site of one of England's first modern banks opening in 1786 – and following a well-signed route through a system of one-way streets to the tourist office.

SEA TO SEA (C2C)

Duration 4 days
Distance 130.6 miles
Difficulty moderate–demanding
Start Whitehaven
Finish Newcastle-upon-Tyne
Summary From the Irish to the North Sea, go with the wind and a merry two-wheeled throng as you climb the fells of the Lake District and tickle the backbone of England before the swoop to the coast.

Stretching from the Irish Sea to the chilly North Sea across the lumpy northern reaches of England, this long distance route with a neat text-speak title is Britain's most popular bike ride. One of the jewels in the National Cycle Network (NCN) crown, this challenging coast-to-coast journey showcases the great work being done by Sustrans and the enormous potential of dedicated cycling trails. Over a third of this ride follows traffic-free paths, allowing for a safe and thoroughly enjoyable cycling experience. If you're planning to do just one ride in the northern half of Britain, this should be it.

There's something about the sense of achievement gained from travelling from one side of the country to the other that

NORTHERN ENGLAND

C2C:GR8!

Created in 1994, the C2C is Britain's most-ridden cycling route and one of its best organised. It's estimated that between 12,000 and 15,000 cyclists a year complete the official 140-mile Sustrans route from Whitehaven to either Jarrow or Sunderland, only 4% of which leads along main roads.

In cycling circles it's commonly believed that the C2C is best ridden from west to east, as this is the way the wind usually blows and there are shorter ups and longer downs. There may be something in this as most of those who have set record times for the C2C have begun in White-haven, with some reaching the North Sea in an amazing 10 or 12 hours. The route described here doesn't set out to break any records, but sets a pace that gives you ample time to admire the landscape, as well as a series of quite unexpected modern sculptural works commissioned for the route by Sustrans and local authorities through which the C2C passes. These include bridges with an artistic flourish, scrap-iron cows and steel men (near Sunderland's Stadium of Light).

Other than two wet wheels (rear dipped in the Irish Sea, front in the North Sea), a memento of your achievement and proof that you completed the ride is the official 'I did the C2C' T-shirt, which Sustrans sends out on production of a card stamped six times along the way. On meeting another cyclist wearing a Sustrans T-shirt you could always ask: 'C2C:U2?'

captures the imagination, and this ride travelling west to east from Whitehaven to Newcastle is no exception. It's a wonder-fully varied and at times challenging tour taking in the classic beauty of the Lake Dis-trict, solitude and space of the North Pen-nines and urban vitality of Newcastle. The official signed C2C route also provides for Workington and Sunderland as alternative start/finish points.

PLANNING
When to Cycle
Although much of this ride is on traffic-free paths and generally off the beaten track, Kes-wick and the whole Lake District can get ex-tremely busy over the peak summer period. The C2C route itself is also proving very pop-ular with lots of groups tackling sections of it over the weekend. Try to ride midweek and preferably outside the summer holidays.

What to Bring
As sections of this ride are very popular, especially over summer weekends, try to book accommodation ahead, especially in Allenheads, as there are few alternatives if you arrive late and everywhere is full. Al-though there are several off-road sections, cyclists on touring bikes shouldn't encounter problems.

Cycle Hire
Whitehaven's **Haven Cycles** (☎ 01946 63263; Preston St, Whitehaven) are situated handily near the beginning of the C2C and offer bike hire as well as a repair service and accessories. At the other end of the route **Tyne Bridge Bike Hire** (☎ 0191 277 2441; The Guildhall, Quayside, New-castle-upon-Tyne) hire bikes (£15 per day) as well as racks, panniers, pumps and lights.

Maps
There's a small library of route guides and maps available to Britain's most popular cycling route. The bible for C2Cers is the NCN *Sea to Sea Cycle Route Map* produced by Sustrans, an essential companion for this ride providing easy-to-read full-colour maps of the main and alternative routes, as well as other valuable information. It's available direct from Sustrans, local bike shops and many tourist offices.

Information Sources
Before setting off, check out the invaluable online *C2C Guide* (www.c2c-guide.co.uk), which has heaps of information on accom-modation, routes, preparation and many other aspects of doing the C2C.

GETTING TO/FROM THE RIDE
Whitehaven (start)
See p257 for information on getting to and from Whitehaven.

Newcastle-upon-Tyne (finish)
See Towns & Facilities (p253).

THE RIDE
Day 1: Whitehaven to Keswick
3–4 hours, 32.1 miles

The route described here sets off from Whitehaven tourist office, but the official start of the C2C is down on the quayside by what looks like a six-metre-tall steel C2C stencil. Many cyclists have their photographs taken by this striking chunk of public art to prove they began at the beginning. A C2C tradition dictates you should dip your back tyre in the Irish Sea before setting off. Though mile-poor don't underestimate this first day's ride, as you'll climb from sea level to almost 300m (985ft) in the space of 12 miles. You'll also want to stop and admire the striking views every two minutes.

A few pedal strokes and you'll have fled the clutches of the industrial Cumbrian coast and be on your way towards some of England's most attractive landscapes. The route out of Whitehaven follows the signed C2C trail along a series of pathways, a great traffic-free start to the ride though the multitude of paths can complicate navigation at times. Climb gradually but steadily as the bikepath, part of the West Cumbrian Cycle Network, follows the bed of an old mineral railway, with a number of interesting sculptural trail-markers punctuating the route.

The real lakeland deal meets the eye beyond Kirkland (10.9 miles) where the gradual ascent continues as you follow quiet country lanes past Keltonfell Top. Views of the bald rounded tops of the Lake District's

SEA TO SEA – DAY 1

CUE			GPS COORDINATES	
start		Whitehaven tourist office	54°32′51″N	3°35′29″W
0 miles		go S on Preston St (behind tourist office)		
0.3	↑⊙	Preston St		
0.3	↰	(40yd) 'C2C' bikepath		
0.9	↱	along street		
1.1	↱	onto bikepath		
1.5	↙	'to C2C'		
1.6	↘	stay on bikepath		
1.9	↑	Croasdale Ave		
1.9	↰	(50yd) Wasdale Close		
2.0	↑	stay on main bikepath		
2.3	↘	'Whitehaven to Ennerdale'		
4.2	↘	'to Frizington'		
7.8	↑	'to Rowrah'		
9.1	⚠	1 mile dirt road		
9.2	↱	onto gravel bikepath		
10.1	↰	unsigned lane		
10.4	↱	by school		
	▲	1.4 miles moderate climb		
10.9		Kirkland	54°32′56″N	3°26′9″W
11.8	↰	'C2C'		
13.1	↱	bottom of hill		

CUE CONTINUED			GPS COORDINATES	
13.5	↱	'to Loweswater'		
14.0	↱	'to Loweswater', Lamplugh	54°34′29″N	3°24′38″W
15.7	↙	start of descent		
	⚠	1.1 miles steep descent		
16.4		Waterend	54°36′2″N	3°19′11″W
18.2	↰	'to Thackwaite'		
21.5	↱	'to Buttermere'		
21.6	↱	'to Buttermere', Low Lorton	54°37′8″N	3°18′54″W
21.6	↰	(50yd) 'to Keswick'		
22.2	↱	'to Boon Beck Scales', H. Lorton	54°37′15″N	3°17′52″W
	▲	1.1 miles hard climb		
23.8	↱	B5292, 'to Keswick'		
{25.3	★	Whinlatter Forest Visitor Centre}		
27.6	↱	'to Newlands', Braithwaite	54°36′8″N	3°11′28″W
28.1	↘	'to Swinside'		
28.5	↰	'to Ullock'		
29.3	↘	'to Keswick'		
29.9	↘	towards A66, Portinscale		
30.2	↱	A66		
30.4	↙	B5289		
32.1		Keswick tourist office	54°36′6″N	3°8′20″W

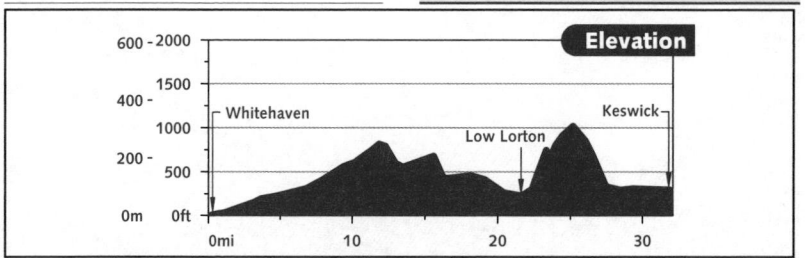

Elevation

(Elevation profile showing route from Whitehaven through Low Lorton to Keswick, with y-axis marked 0m/0ft, 200–500, 400–1000, 1500, 600–2000, and x-axis marked 0mi, 10, 20, 30)

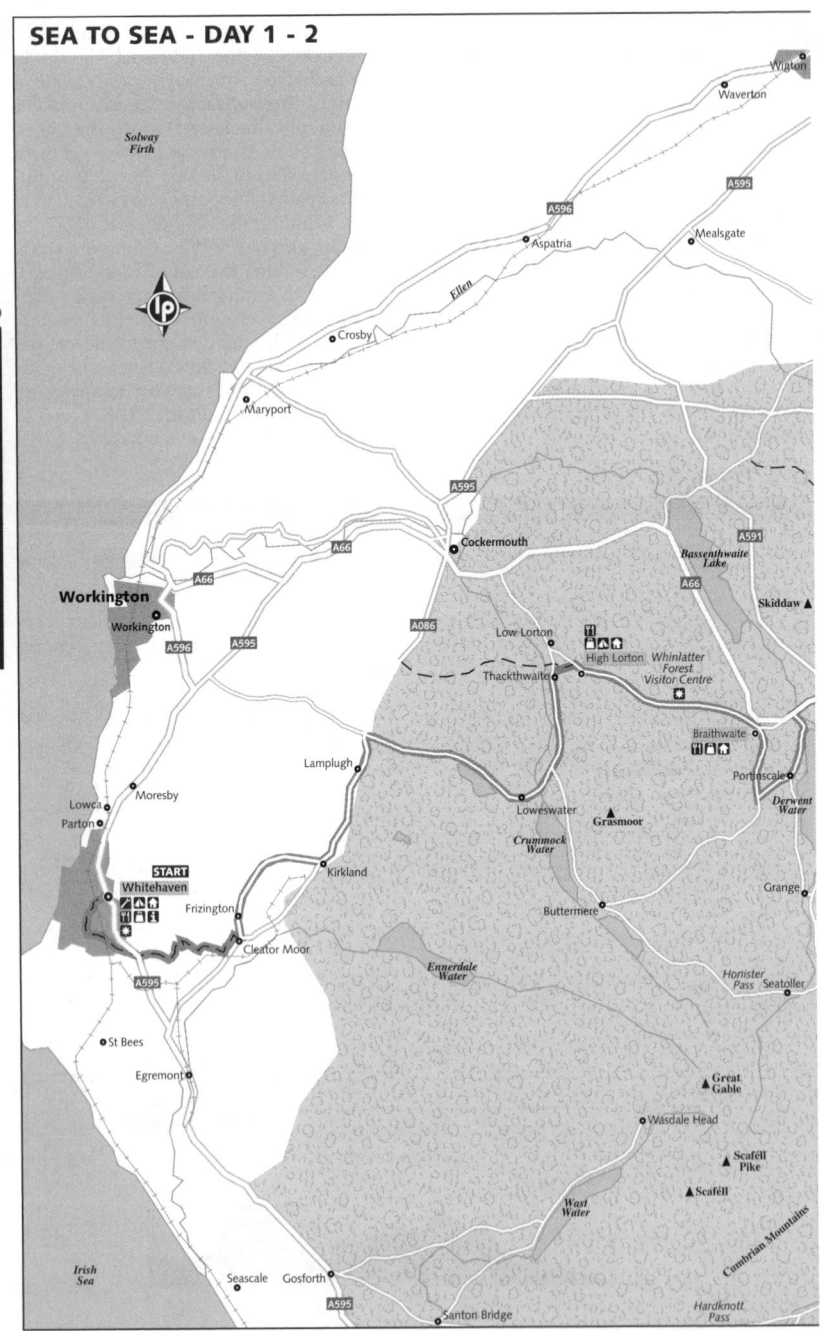

SEA TO SEA - DAY 1 - 2

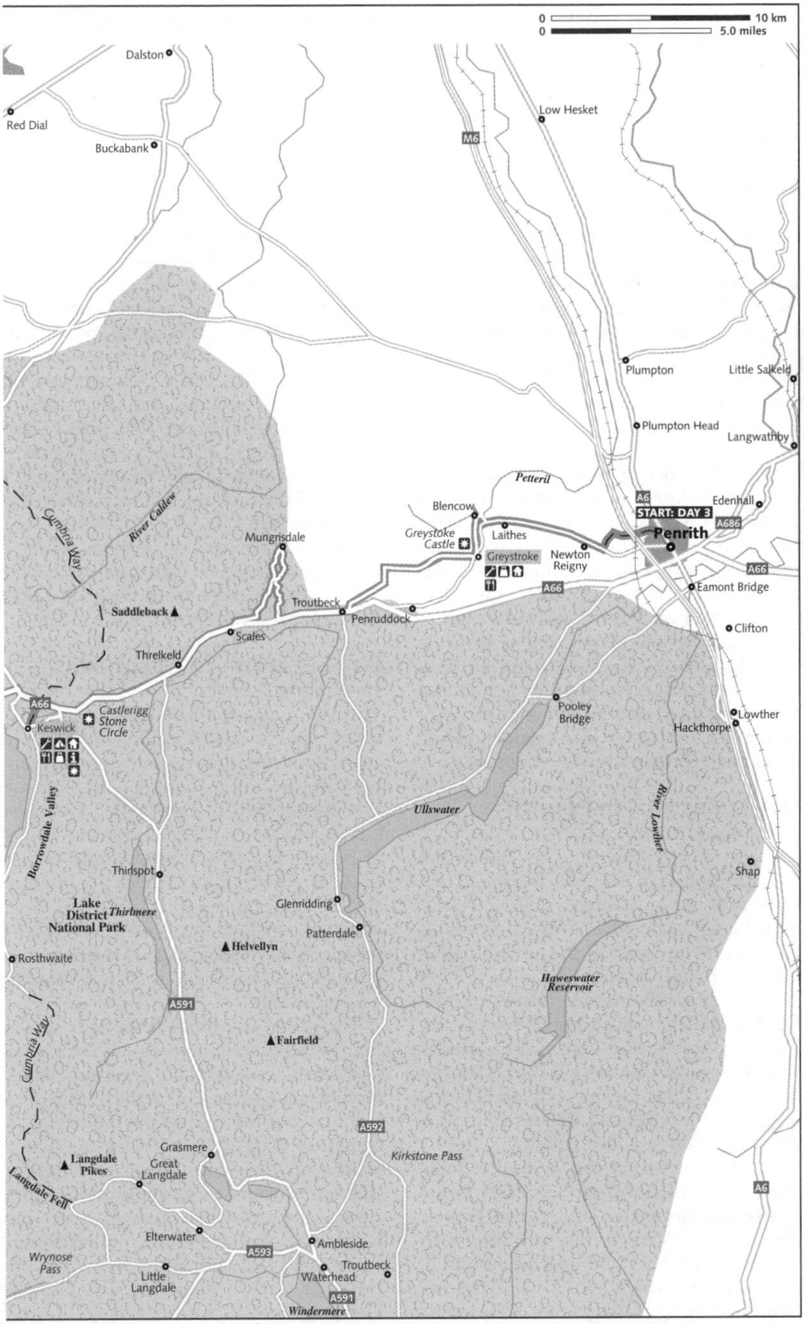

NORTHERN ENGLAND

0 ————— 10 km
0 ————— 5.0 miles

Dalston

Red Dial

Buckabank

Low Hesket

M6

Plumpton   Little Salkeld

Plumpton Head

Langwathby

Petteril

Cumbria Way

River Caldew

Blencow   Edenhall

Greystoke Castle   Laithes

Greystoke   A6

A686

START: DAY 3

Penrith

Mungrisdale   Newton Reigny

A66

A66

Saddleback ▲

Troutbeck   Eamont Bridge

Penruddock

Scales   Clifton

Threlkeld

A66

Castlerigg Stone Circle

Keswick

Pooley Bridge

Lowther

Hackthorpe

Borrowdale Valley

River Lowther

Ullswater

Shap

Thirlspot

Glenridding

Lake District National Park

Thirlmere

Patterdale

▲ **Helvellyn**

Rosthwaite

Haweswater Reservoir

A591

Cumbria Way

▲ **Fairfield**

A592

Kirkstone Pass

A6

Grasmere

▲ **Langdale Pikes**   Great Langdale

Langdale Fell

Elterwater   Ambleside

A593

Wrynose Pass   Troutbeck

Little Langdale   Waterhead

A591

Windermere

many peaks, flashes of water between them, open up in front of you, before the route drops down to tiny **Loweswater**. The quiet road bordered by forest on one side and glassy surface of the water on the other gets very up close and personal with the lake, providing an opportunity to plop in and practice your breaststroke.

Just after Low Lorton (21.6 miles) a testing steep climb over the Whinlatter Pass reaches the high point of the day near the **Whinlatter Forest Visitor Centre** (25.3 miles; ☎ 017687 78469), which has an audio-visual presentation on the surrounding forest. Colour-coded walking trails head off from here into the coniferous forest, planted over the last 60 years. From the top of Whinlatter Pass a bracing, brake-annihilating descent ends at the village of Braithwaite (27.6 miles).

Beyond Ullock, a peacefully shady lane through the forest leads the final mile into Portinscale, nestled on the banks of **Derwent Water**. It's worth stopping here to admire one of Britain's most breathtakingly beautiful bodies of water, cupped by the misty peaks of the Lake District, it's surface punctuated with several islands (one of which is inhabited). The access road leading into Keswick town centre is reached after a short and noisy spell on a pathway alongside the A66, itself a C2C route from Workington to Middlesbrough (Britain's very own Route 66).

Day 2: Keswick to Penrith
2½–3 hours, 23.9 miles

Today's snappy ride roughly traces the smooth asphalt of the A66 from Keswick to Penrith but only actually joins it briefly after Mungrisdale. Most of the first half of the route is up, most of the second half is down – an ideal day of pedalling.

Leaving Keswick, the route follows a traffic-free rail trail along the tranquil River Greta. There are some steep steps to negotiate as well as a few gates, but despite these obstacles it makes for great cycling with many of the original rail bridges and shelters still intact along the shady, wooded pathway.

Shortly after emerging at the A66 the route passes the turn-off (3.6 miles) to the **Castlerigg Stone Circle**, a sacred Bronze Age meeting place, before continuing to Threlkeld (4.2 miles). Beyond the village the quiet country lane climbs briefly, passing farms and sheep grazing on the hillsides. At

Scales you can take the convoluted but scenic route via Mungrisdale or stick to the A66 if the weather is not playing ball. Minor roads and another short stretch alongside the A66 eventually lead to the village of **Greystoke** (16.9 miles), whose Gothic church greets you from afar. **Greystoke Castle**, closed to the public and hidden behind high walls, gave its name to Edgar Rice Burroughs's fictional Earl of Greystoke whose son was raised by apes to become the chest-beating, tree-swinging Tarzan. Oddly the village makes little of its literary and silver screen connections. Just after the turn to Blencow, call a halt in Greystoke, call a halt at the **Greystoke Cycle Cafe** (☎ 17684 83984; www.greystokec yclecafe.co.uk) where a hot drink and a stamp for your Sustrans' C2C card will be waiting for you. Their welcoming Cyclists' Barn with towels, oil, bike pumps, maps and even free juice for frame bottles is almost too good to be true.

The final stretch into Penrith, along a public bridleway, emerges at busy Scotland Rd, a short distance from the pink sandstone of the town centre.

Day 3: Penrith to Allenheads
4½–5½ hours, 33.5 miles

This is a tough day involving some of the biggest climbs in this guide, and heading away from the lakes up into the ruggedly beautiful northern Pennines. Setting the tone for the day, it starts with a climb on quiet roads through Edenhall to the village of Langwathby (4.9 miles). A little farther on just out of Little Salkeld, a couple of ancient **stone circles** (Long Meg and Little Meg) are signed off the route. There's nothing spectacular to see but they're interesting spots to take a break and prepare for the big hills up ahead.

The going gets tough, especially in the wet, as the route joins a rough track after 11.8 miles. Things don't get much easier when it emerges back on to the bitumen 1.4 miles later at the start of the mother of all climbs up **Hartside**. The ascent to almost 600m (1969ft) is gradual but prolonged – stop to rest your legs a couple of times and admire the views that just get better the higher you go. Once at the top, relax with a cup of tea and take in the view from the **Hartside Cafe**, reputedly the highest in England (15.9m/52ft).

SEA TO SEA – DAY 2

CUE		GPS COORDINATES	
start	Keswick tourist office	54°36'6"N	3°8'20"W
0 miles	go NE on Station Rd		
0.1	cross A5271, Station Rd		
0.3	bikepath by swimming pool		
0.3	(40yd) join rail trail behind pool		
⚠	3.2 miles dirt section		
3.5	A66 (path parallel)		
{3.6 ●●	Castlerigg Stone Circle 4.6 miles ↻}		
3.6	(50yd) 'to Threlkeld'		
4.2	Threlkeld	54°37'7"N	3°3'16"W
4.3	before A66		
▲	700yd moderate climb		
5.0	A66 (path parallel)		
5.9	unsigned road, Scales	54°37'44"N	3°1'53"W
8.9	'C2C', Mungrisdale		
11.0	A66 'to Penrith' (bikepath)		

CUE CONTINUED		GPS COORDINATES	
12.4	A66 (bikepath parallel)		
13.4	'to Hutton Roof'		
14.1	'to Greystoke'		
16.9 ★	'C2C', Greystoke	54°40'10"N	2°52'10"W
18.6	Blencow	54°41'13"N	2°50'57"W
19.1	'to Laithes'		
19.6	Laithes	54°41'20"N	2°49'57"W
20.8	Newton Reigny	54°40'43"N	2°48'35"W
22.0	'Public Bridleway Penrith'		
⚠	1.1 miles dirt road		
22.1	straight thru college		
22.6	pass under M6		
22.6	(40yd) unsigned bridleway		
23.1	under railway		
23.4	Scotland Rd		
23.8	Corney Square		
23.9	Penrith tourist office	54°39'55"N	2°45'14"W

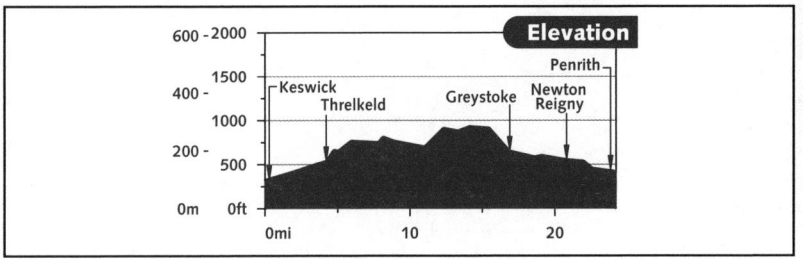

NORTHERN ENGLAND

For every up there's a down, but this one, most of the way from Hartside into Garrigill (23.2 miles), doesn't last long enough and only leads to another ascent. From Garrigill the official C2C route leads along a very crumbly, steep track through a quarry. A better option, especially if it's wet or you're on a touring bike, is the alternative sealed route described here, which leads you up Dowgang Hush. It's still no picnic, however, and is very steep in places.

A rapid descent brings you to Nenthead, one of the highest villages in England and once the most significant lead mining centre in the north Pennines. The **Nenthead Mines Heritage Centre** (☎ 01434 382037) in the village provides an insight into what was once a vital industry for the region. After Nenthead comes another climb, the ascent reaching the summit of Black Hill (609m/1998ft) at 28 miles, the highest point on the C2C. Obviously (and mercifully) it's downhill almost all the way

from here, with just an excuse of a climb to conquer before the final tumble (down 'romantically named' Slag Hill) into drowsy Allenheads.

Day 4: Allenheads to Newcastle-upon-Tyne

4–5 hours, 41.1 miles

Day 3's hill-conquering exertions are justly rewarded on this final leg with some wonderfully long downhill sections. Check your brakes are in order, as you're gonna need 'em. Most of today is off-road on dedicated cycle trails, allowing you to escape the four-wheelers and enjoy the barren northern vistas undisturbed.

The day starts, however, with a strenuous post-breakfast 1.1-mile climb out of Allenheads so make sure you've had your porridge. This is followed by a magnificent, long, gradual descent past long-abandoned lead workings down into the village of **Rookhope** (6.1 miles). Here you are

SEA TO SEA - DAY 3 - 4

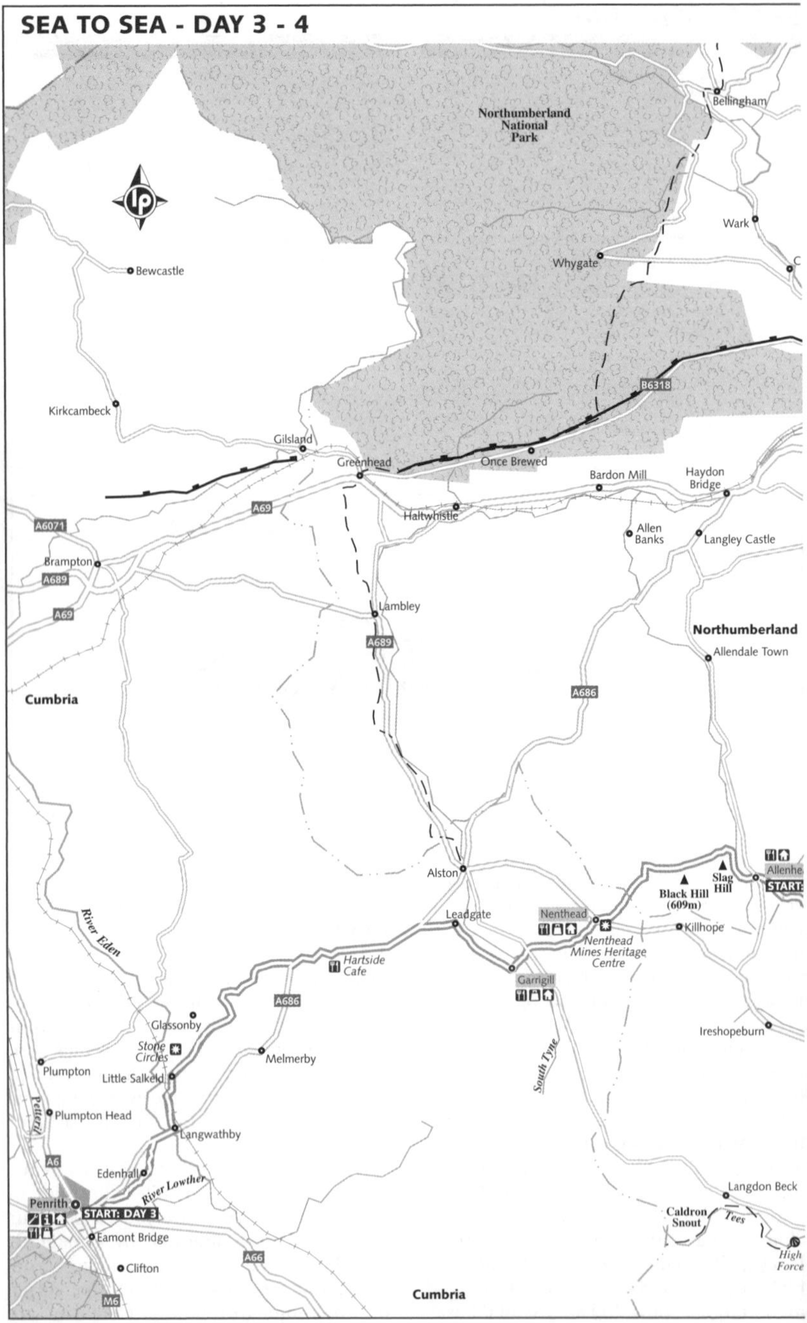

Northumberland National Park

Bellingham

Wark

Whygate

Bewcastle

Kirkcambeck

Gilsland

Greenhead

Once Brewed

B6318

Bardon Mill

Haydon Bridge

A6071

A69

Haltwhistle

Allen Banks

Langley Castle

Brampton

A689

A69

Lambley

A689

Northumberland

Allendale Town

A686

Cumbria

Alston

Leadgate

Nenthead

Black Hill (609m)

Slag Hill

Allenhe

START

Hartside Cafe

A686

Nenthead Mines Heritage Centre

Killhope

River Eden

Glassonby

Stone Circles

Melmerby

Garrigill

South Tyne

Ireshopeburn

Plumpton

Little Salkeld

Plumpton Head

Langwathby

River Lowther

Edenhall

Penrith

START: DAY 3

Eamont Bridge

Langdon Beck

Caldron Snout

Tees

High Force

Clifton

A66

Cumbria

M6

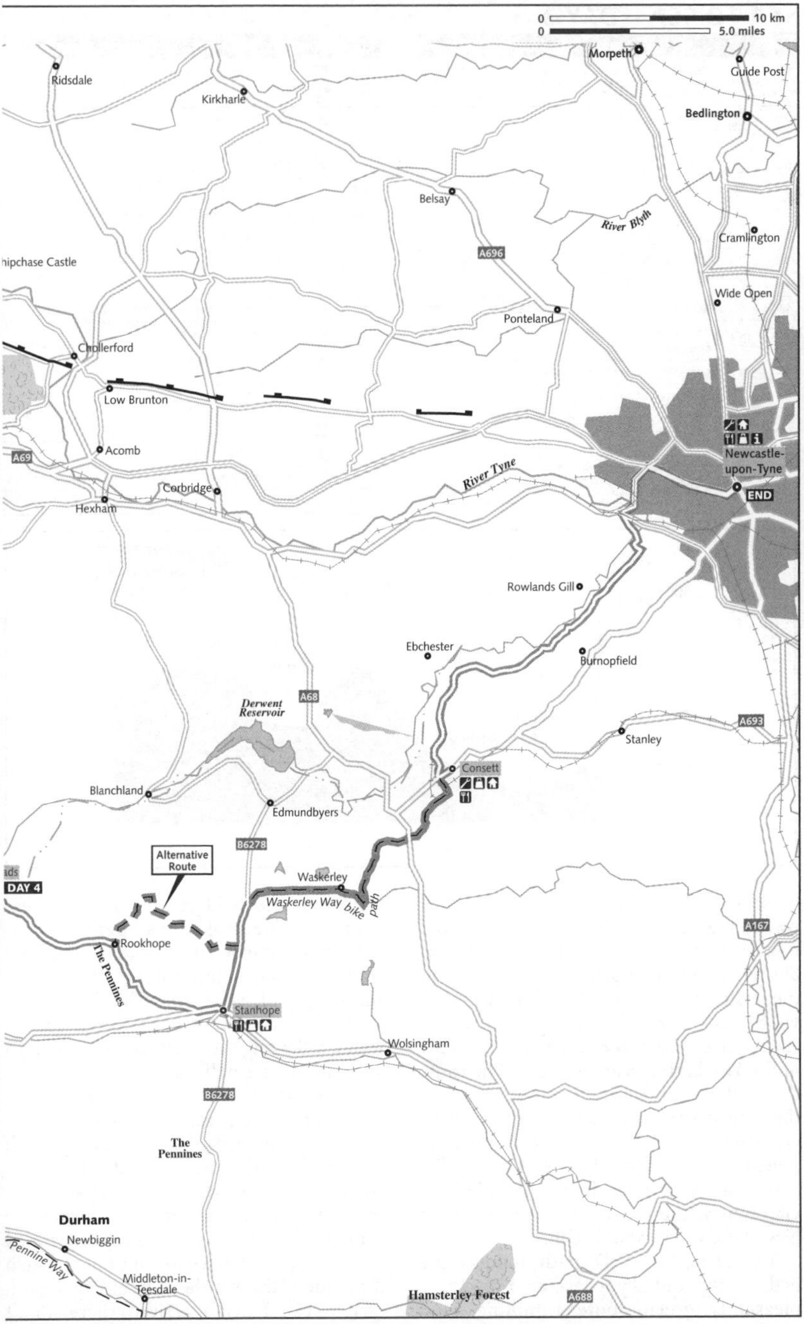

0 [_____] 10 km
0 [_____] 5.0 miles

Ridsdale

Kirkharle

Morpeth

Guide Post

Bedlington

Belsay

River Blyth

Cramlington

A696

hipchase Castle

Wide Open

Chollerford

Ponteland

Low Brunton

River Tyne

Newcastle-
upon-Tyne

A69

Acomb

END

Corbridge

Hexham

Rowlands Gill

Ebchester

Burnopfield

*Derwent
Reservoir*

A68

Stanley

A693

Blanchland

Consett

Edmundbyers

Alternative
Route

ds

DAY 4

Waskerley

Waskerley Way bike path

A167

The Pennines

Rookhope

B6278

Stanhope

Wolsingham

A688

B6278

**The
Pennines**

Durham

Newbiggin

Pennine Way

Middleton-in-
Teesdale

Hamsterley Forest

NORTHERN ENGLAND

SEA TO SEA – DAY 3

CUE			GPS COORDINATES	
start		Penrith tourist office	54°39′55″N	2°45′14″W
0 miles		go SE on Marketgate		
0.0	↱	(40yd) Burrowgate		
0.2	↑	Fell Lane		
0.6	↳	Beacon Edge		
2.2	↱	A686, 'to Alston'		
2.6	↗	'to Edenhall'		
3.1	↘	by West Lodge		
3.8	↘	'C2C', Edenhall	54°41′5″N	2°40′32″W
4.4	↳	A686		
4.9	↘	at Langwathby	54°41′42.49″N	2°40′2″W
6.6	↗	'to Glassonby', Little Salkeld	54°43′7″N	2°40′29″W
7.1	●● ↱	Long Meg Stone Circle 0.7 miles ↺		
8.1	↗	'C2C' (start of descent)		
8.7	↱	'C2C' turn-off (on descent)		
11.0	↳	'to Alston'		
11.8	↑	'Public Byway – Selah Bridge'		
⚠		1.4 miles dirt road		

CUE CONTINUED			GPS COORDINATES	
13.2	↳	rough track joins road		
14.4	↱	A686		
▲		1.5 miles hard climb		
15.9		Hartside Cafe		
19.1	↙	'C2C'		
20.1	↳	'to Garrigill', Leadgate	54°47′14″N	2°27′22″W
23.2	↱	'to Alston', Garrigill	54°46′5″N	2°23′54″W
23.6	↳	'to Nenthead'		
▲		1.9 miles hard climb		
26.5	↳	bottom descent		
26.7	↳	'to Stanhope', Nenthead	54°47′16″N	2°20′30″W
★		Mines Heritage Centre		
▲		1.3 miles hard climb		
27.3	↱	'to Allenheads'		
28.0		highest point on C2C		
28.9	↳	'C2C'		
▲		1.1 miles hard climb		
32.3	↳	'to Allenheads'		
33.5		Allenheads village shop	54°48′10″N	2°13′10″W

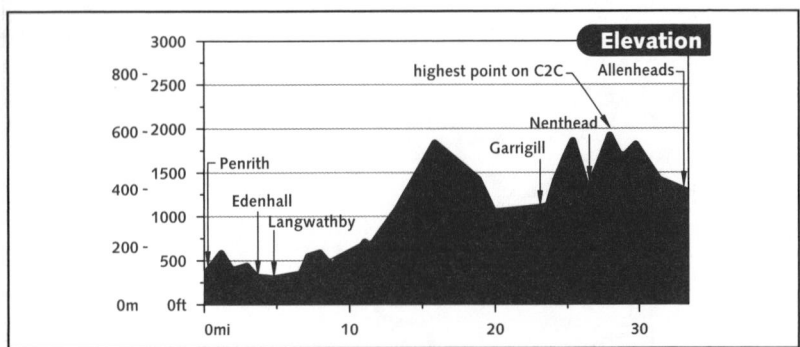

presented with a choice of routes – one way follows a steep, rough trail up an old railway incline, but without a fat and knobbly-tyred mountain bike it's best to stick to the less jarring, touring-bike friendly route via Stanhope, which itself involves a few stiff climbs. The two reunite near the start of the **Waskerley Way** bikepath. The route then follows this traffic-free trail, taking in the rugged, expansive scenery of the northern Pennines all the way (predominantly downhill) to Consett. Here the C2C splits with one branch heading to Sunderland via Stanley, the other (described here) to Newcastle via Rowlands Gill.

The Derwent Walk path follows the bed of the old Tyne Valley railway, a pleasantly green route rumbling over numerous old bridges and Victorian-era viaducts. The traffic-free path is broken momentarily at Rowlands Gill but soon resumes, continuing all the way to the fringes of Newcastle. The final stages of the ride can be difficult to navigate at times, following the Keelmans Way along a succession of small pathways with occasional short stretches on suburban roads. Once across the River Tyne, however, you are practically in the heart of the city with only a short distance to pedal from the trendy Quayside area up to Grey's Monument, the central shopping area and the tourist office. But to say you've truly cycled from C2C, you'll have to continue through Tyneside all the way the coast at Tynemouth (see p213). Having arrived there, don't

SEA TO SEA – DAY 4

CUE		GPS COORDINATES	
start	Allenheads village shop	54°48'10"N	2°13'10"W
0 miles	go E up hill past shop		
0.0 ▲	1.1 miles hard climb		
6.1 ▲	Rookhope	54°46'50"N	2° 5'50"W
6.4 ↘	C2C alternative route		
▲	1.6 miles steep climb		
10.0 ⬑	A689, 'to Stanhope'		
10.7 ⬑	B6278 'to Edmondbyers', Stanhope	54°44'49"N	2°0'23"W
▲	2 miles hard climb		
12.6 ↗	dirt road by abandoned buildings		
⚠	10.9 miles dirt road		
13.4 ↑	Waskerley Way (main C2C route)		
21.5 ↑	cross A68, continue on path		
22.6 ↘	on path		
23.3 ↘	keep sculpture on right		
23.5 ⬑ ⊚	A692		
23.7 ↑⊚	Genesis Way		
24.0 ⬑	'C2C 14'		
24.2 ⌐	'C2C 14'		
24.4 ↑	Derwent Walk (bikepath on left)		
24.7 ⌐	bikepath joins street		
24.7 ⬑	(30yd) rejoin Derwent Walk path		
29.9 ↑	Derwent Walk path		
32.1 ↑	Burnopfield Rd		

CUE CONTINUED		GPS COORDINATES	
32.3 ↑	A694 (path on right), Rowlands G.	54°55'18"N	1°44'20"W
32.5 ↗	rejoin Derwent Walk path		
35.4 ↑	path emerges by rugby ground		
35.5 ⬑	Hexham Rd		
35.5 ↗	(50yd) 'C2C'		
35.6 ↗	join pathway 'the Hurrocks'		
35.8 ⬑	cross bridge over stream		
35.8 ⬑	(30yd) over bridge		
36.1 ↗	under road bridge		
36.2 ↗	pathway, signed '14'		
36.3 ↘	path alongside waterway		
36.8 ⌐	cross ped. bridge (by rail lines)		
37.2	Metro Centre		
37.7 ⬑	Cross Lane (path joins road)		
37.8 ⌐	Handy Dr/A1114		
38.0 ↑	Colliery Way		
38.2 ↘	onto path		
39.2 ⬑	onto path 'Keelmans Way'		
40.4 ⬑	cross Swing Bridge over R. Tyne		
40.4 ⌐	(50yd) over bridge		
40.5 ↘	Quayside		
40.6 ↗	Dean St/Grey St		
41.0 ⌐	New Bridge St W, Grey's Monument		
41.1	Newcastle tourist office	54°58'22"N	1°36'48"W

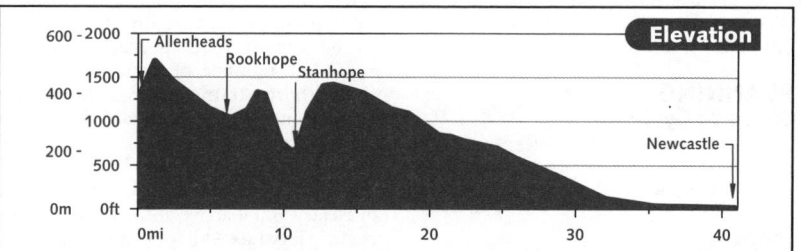

Elevation chart showing route from Allenheads, Rookhope, Stanhope to Newcastle.

forget to dip your front tyre in the North Sea as a symbolic end to one of Europe's great cycle journeys.

TWO DAYS IN THE DALES

Duration 2 days
Distance 66.8 miles
Difficulty moderate–demanding
Start/Finish Ripon
Summary A two-wheeled loop through James Herriot's landscape of sheep, dry stone walls and lonely ridge-top tracks with dramatic vistas across the Dales National Park.

A cyclist is rarely the fastest moving object in today's world, but in the Dales, where villages have changed little since their entry in the Doomsday Book and life is still dictated by the harshness of the weather and the lifecycle of the sheep, things move as slowly as the changing of the seasons. This circular ride is a great introduction to this landscape of picturesque sheep-dotted valleys and charming market towns which make up the Yorkshire Dales National Park. The route rarely runs on level, ground with several challenging climbs leading out of one dale and into the next. With that in mind, each day has been kept deliberately short.

Much of the ride follows the Yorkshire Dales Cycle Way, a 128-mile circular route that continues south to Skipton and east to Ingleton. It's easy to construct some excellent longer rides by combining sections of both routes.

ENVIRONMENT

Austere stone villages – streams and rivers cutting through the hills – wide, empty moors – and endless lines of stone walls dividing the landscape into a checkerboard of green pastures populated by wandering sheep – this is the region made famous by James Herriot and the TV series *All Creatures Great and Small.* The Dales can be broken into northern and southern halves: in the north the two main dales (valleys), Swaledale and Wensleydale, run parallel and east–west. In the south, north–south Ribblesdale is the route taken by the Leeds–Settle–Carlisle railway line, which provides access to a series of attractive towns. Wharfedale runs parallel to the east.

The high tops of the hills are exposed moorland, and the sheltered dales between them range from narrow and sinuous Swaledale through to broad and open Wensleydale and Wharfedale and rugged Littondale and Ribblesdale.

PLANNING
When to Cycle

Like the Lake District, the Dales are a major tourist magnet, so it's best if possible to avoid weekends and the peak summer period.

Maps

The best maps to carry with you are undoubtedly the OS Explorer maps 1:25,000 *Yorkshire Dales: N & Cen areas* (sheet OL30) and *Nidderdale* (sheet 298).

Information Sources

The **Yorkshire Dales National Park Authority** (☎ 01756 751600; www.yorkshiredales.org.uk) looks after all aspects of visiting the Dales, from accommodation to volunteering for conservation projects.

GETTING TO/FROM THE RIDE
Ripon (start/finish)
TRAIN

The closest train station is at Thirsk, a stop on the main London-Edinburgh line, 11.5

miles away east along the A61. There are frequent trains to Thirsk from York (£8.10; 20 minutes, twice hourly), a busy railway hub that can be reached from just about anywhere in the country.

BICYCLE

Ripon is an easy 28½-mile ride from York. Follow the route out of the city detailed in Day 1 of the North York Moors & Mansions ride (p241) and continue on back roads through Linton-on-Ouse, Lower Dunsforth, Boroughbridge and Skelton. From Thirsk avoid the A61 by cycling the back roads through Sowerby, Dalton, Topcliffe, Rainton and Sharrow, an easy ride of 16.1 miles (see also the Day 1 map for the North York Moors & Mansions ride p241).

THE RIDE
Day 1: Ripon to Kettlewell
3½–4½ hours, 35.5 miles

The first day of this two-day circuit is meagre on miles but big on terrain, and by the end of it you'll know you've been on a substantial bike ride! The strenuous rolling route propels you high into the heart of the dales with the undulating hills of Nidderdale beginning soon after Ripon.

The narrow road to Masham carries a modest number of cars, but beyond Grewelthorpe traffic thins as the narrow country lane travels a postcard dales landscape of rolling green fields, boxed by dry stone walls and cropped by hardy unshorn sheep. Shortly after a fairly tough climb out of Healey you'll arrive at the gates of 12th-century **Jervaulx Abbey** (17 miles; ☎ 01677 460391). A profusion of wildflowers (over 200 species) bloom in between the stones of the privately owned Cistercian ruins of a monastery plundered during Henry VIII's 'dissolution' of the 16th century. It's a pleasant place to take a break and there's a small tearoom at the visitor centre serving delicious homemade cakes.

A grand Gothic church surrounded by a large graveyard marks your arrival in **East Witton** (18.7 miles), a pretty village with a huge green dotted with mature trees. There's also an inn and small store, the last for quite a distance. The hills loom larger as the day progresses – the quiet lane climbing steadily and leaving the lush green pastures behind for a wilder landscape of open graz-

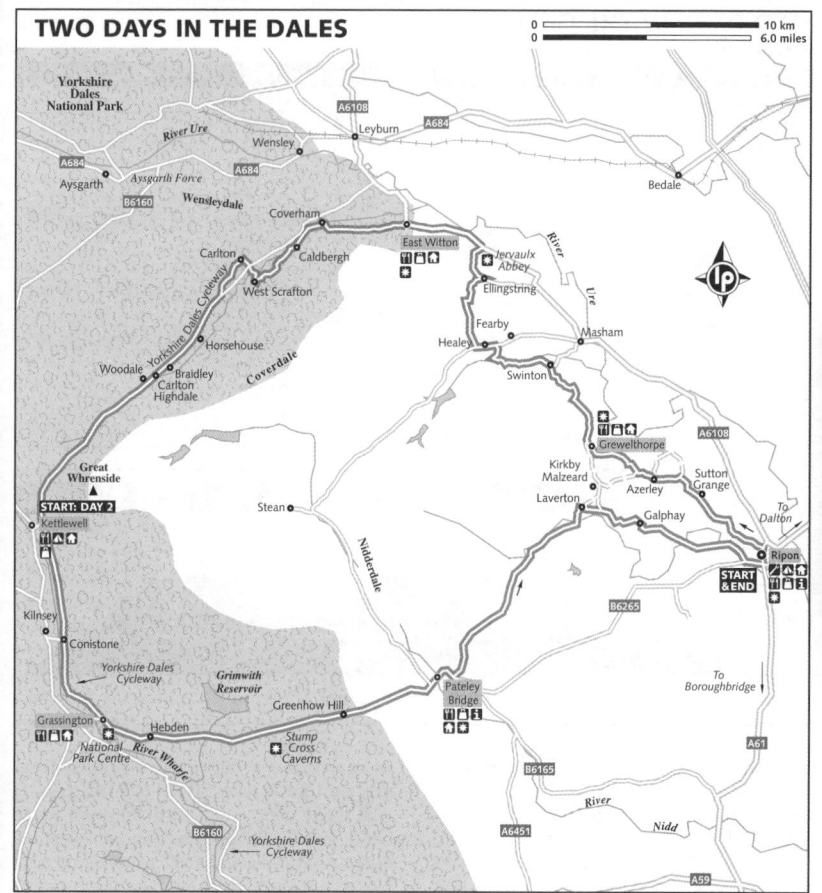

TWO DAYS IN THE DALES

ing land roamed by wandering livestock. In fact the greatest hazard on this section of the route comes not from the odd car or tractor but from the sheep, hedgehogs and pheasants who seem to consider the road a good place sit, and the odd farm dog yapping at your spokes.

From just past West Scrafton the route hooks up with the **Yorkshire Dales Cycleway** along the ridge above Coverdale. This is perhaps one of the best bits of cycling you might ever do, with the road dipping and diving, passing through seemingly medieval Caucasus-style stonebuilt farmsteads and hamlets along the way. Sheer magic. The day's biggest ascent starts a short distance out of Horsehouse

at the beginning of this wonderful stretch and the single-track road bounces all the way to Kettlewell. Care is needed to keep your speed under control on the final twisting descent, which at times boasts a frighteningly steep, brake-block-burning gradient of one in four.

Day 2: Kettlewell to Ripon
3–3½ hours, 31.3 miles

Today is just as dramatic as Day 1, with more punishing ascents and views to astonish. Are your brakes and lowest gear in working order? Then off we go.

From Kettlewell a quiet, gently rolling lane runs parallel with the River Wharfe through Conistone to Grassington, a size-

TWO DAYS IN THE DALES – DAY 1

CUE		GPS COORDINATES
start	Ripon tourist office	54°8'4"N 1°31'15"W
0 miles	go W on Kirkgate (walk)	
0.1	Fishergate/North Rd	
0.3	College Rd	
0.7	Kirkby Rd	
5.0	'to Grewelthorpe'	
6.7	Grewelthorpe	54°10'52"N 1°38'55"W
7.0	'to Masham'	
8.5	'to Swinton'	
9.6	unsigned road	
9.8	'to Fearby', Swinton	54°12'46"N 1°40'21"W
11.2	unsigned road	
11.8	'to Healey'	
12.3	'to Healey'	
12.6	Healey	54°13'14"N 1°43'28"W

CUE CONTINUED		GPS COORDINATES
12.9	'to Ellingstring'	
	0.7 miles hard climb	
14.9	'to Jervaulx'	
16.8	A6108, 'to Middleham'	
{17.0	Jervaulx Abbey (RHS)}	
18.7	leave A6108, East Witton	54°16'10"N 1°46'45"W
21.4	'to Caldbergh'	
	2.2 miles moderate climb	
24.2	West Scrafton	54°14'54"N 1°53'23"W
25.1	'to Kettlewell'	
27.3	Horsehouse	54°13'39"N 1°55'43"W
30.1	2.7 miles hard climb	
32.8	2.5 miles steep winding descent	
35.3	village road	
35.5	Kettlewell village store	54°8'48"N 2°2'52"W

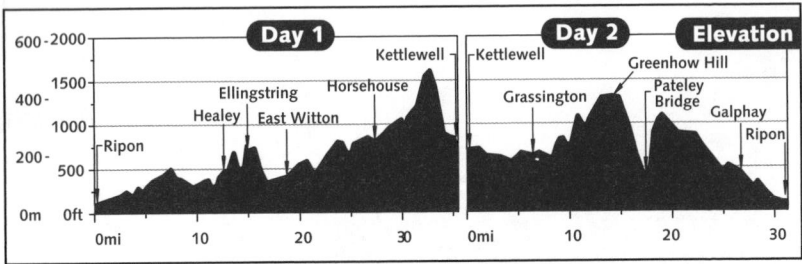

able village and home to the **National Park Centre** (☎ 01756 751600). Here you can pick up piles of information relating specifically to the Yorkshire Dales National Park. The route splits from the Yorkshire Dales Cycleway at Hebden (8.2 miles) from where the B6265 begins to climb, with a number of stiff ascents over the next five miles. The **Stump Cross Caverns** (12.2 miles, ☎ 01756 727780) is an interesting place to take a well-earned breather. The limestone caves, in which animal remains as old as 90,000 years have been found, are open for self-guided and guided tours. If you're no budding speleologist, grab a drink in the cafe instead.

The road continues to climb beyond the caves, with the steady gain in altitude gradually reflected in the transition to a landscape of open moors. A high point is reached at the aptly named settlement of Greenhow Hill (14.1 miles), beyond which numerous roadside vantage points provide excellent views out over spectacular **Nidderdale**. Hard-won height is quickly shed on the

enjoyable, but at times frighteningly steep, descent into Pateley Bridge (17.4 miles).

A lively dales town straddling the River Nidd, **Pateley Bridge** has a sound selection of shops and places to eat fronting its narrow and steep high street. The climb out of Pateley Bridge will test even the strongest of riders, and although you'll more than likely have to get off and push in places, the brutal gradient does provide a direct and a relatively short route out of the valley.

At the top your hard work is rewarded with more stunning views of Nidderdale and the rooftops of Pateley Bridge below. The lonely road travels along the open heather-topped moor beside dry stone walls and fields of woolly sheep before descending into greener countryside near Laverton (24.9 miles).

The final miles, with the exception of a small climb just beyond Galphay, are fairly effortless, bringing you out on to the moderately busy B6265 near the outskirts of Ripon. Follow the well-signed route back into the centre of town.

TWO DAYS IN THE DALES
– DAY 2

CUE			GPS COORDINATES
start		Kettlewell village store	54° 8'48"N 2°2'52"W
0 miles		go S past Kings Head pub	
0.1	↰	'to Conistone' (at maypole)	
3.3		Conistone	54°6'10"N 2° 1'48"W
6.4	★	Grassington	54° 4'17"N 1°59'53"W
8.2		Hebden	54°3'52"N 1°57'42"W
	▲	0.6 miles hard climb	
9.9	▲	0.7 miles hard climb	
11.5	▲	1.6 miles hard climb	
{12.4	★	Stump Cross Caverns}	
14.1		Greenhow Hill	54°4'25"N 1°49'43"W
14.9	⚠	2.1 miles steep descent	
17.4		Pateley Bridge	54°5'12"N 1°45'27"W

CUE CONTINUED			GPS COORDINATES
	▲	1.2 miles steep climb	
17.6	↘	Old Church Lane	
20.6	↰	'to Laverton'	
24.3	↰	'to Laverton'	
24.9	↱	'to Galphay', Laverton	54°9'18"N 1°39'7"W
25.4	↱	'to Galphay'	
26.0	↘	'to Galphay'	
26.7		Galphay	54°8'58"N 1°36'53"W
29.9	↰	B6265 'to Ripon'	
30.8	↑⊙	Park St	
31.1	↑	Westgate (push; one-way)	
31.2	↑	Market Place South	
31.2	↘	(50yd) Kirkgate	
31.3		Ripon tourist office	54°8'4"N 1°31'15"W

NORTH YORK MOORS & MANSIONS

Duration 4 days
Distance 139.7 miles
Difficulty moderate–demanding
Start/Finish York
Summary Gradient-junkies will love this orbital ride of the heather-clad moors dotted with country piles and ruined abbeys.

Tracing a ring around the North York Moors National Park, the contrasts between the northern and southern sections of this ride are dramatic, with each day presenting a fresh series of landscapes. As you pedal northwards the lush, gently rolling green fields of the Hambleton and Howardian Hills, dotted with numerous stately homes, are replaced by isolated stone cottages and remote villages weathered by the harsh environment of the stark but beautiful North York Moors. The route returns via Pickering and the palatial splendour of stately Castle Howard. The ancient Aelred, Abbot of Rievaulx Abbey described the area thus: 'Everywhere peace, everywhere serenity, and a marvellous freedom from the tumult of the world.'

This is a testing ride at times with numerous long and steep climbs up, into and across the moors. With that in mind, many of the days described below are intentionally short. Much of the route from York to Swainby follows the Sustrans White Rose, Hull to Middlesbrough, cycle route (No 65, 66). Watch for the blue and white markers.

PLANNING
When to Cycle
The North York Moors are at their best from July to early September when the heather blooms in an explosion of purple. Be mindful that the Yorkshire weather can change at a moments notice. Even in the summer hill fog and storms can blow into the moors.

Maps
There is a wide range of cartography available covering the North York Moors and the surrounding area. For some, the OS Travel Map – Road 1:250,000 *Northern England* (sheet 4) will suffice, but you could also choose more detailed maps such as the OS Explorer maps 1:25,000 *North York Moors Western Area* (sheet OL26) and *North York Moors Eastern Area* (sheet OL27). Possibly more convenient for the cyclist is OS Travel Map – Tour 1:100,000 *North York Moors* (sheet 2), which shows the entire region on one sheet.

GETTING TO/FROM THE RIDE
York (start/finish)
TRAIN
National Express East Coast (☎ 08457 225 333; www.nationalexpresseastcoast.com) operate fast trains up and down the country along the east coast mainline to London Kings Cross (£78.20; 2¼ hours, twice hourly), Edinburgh (£72.10; 2½ hours, twice hourly), Berwick-upon-Tweed (£49.10; one hour 50 minutes, twice hourly) and Newcastle-upon-Tyne (£31.80; one hour, twice hourly).

NORTHERN ENGLAND

THE RIDE
Day 1: York to Thirsk
3½–4½ hours, 39.3 miles

This first day is relatively easy going, but like every section of this ride there's plenty to see and do off the bike. Although only just over 39 miles long, allow plenty of time if you want to leave the saddle to explore.

The exit from York is very cycle friendly, travelling the first few miles on a path alongside the River Ouse. After nine miles, you pass symmetrically Georgian **Beningbrough Hall** (☎ 01904 472027), one of many splendid period homes in the area that's open to the public and under the protective wing of the National Trust. Keep an eye out for the turnoff before Linton-on-Ouse, which, unlike the many low-flying planes from the nearby RAF base, is easy to miss. A short stretch on a bumpy public bridleway and quiet country lanes leads to **Easingwold** (20.3 miles), a buzzing little Georgian market town with plenty of places around the central grassed square to grab some lunch. Alternatively take a short excursion to the village of Crayke two miles to the east, to the excellent **Durham Ox** (☎ 01347 821506), declared Pub of the Year for 2008. The food's some of the best you'll taste in a British tavern.

Out of Easingwold the route hits higher ground, nothing too serious but plenty of draining little ups and downs. One of the off-pedal high spots of the day is **Newburgh Priory** (26 miles; ☎ 01347 868435), a fine

NORTH YORK MOORS & MANSIONS – DAY 1

CUE			GPS COORDINATES	
start		York train station	53°57'28"N	1°5'32"W
0 miles		go N on Station Rd/A1036		
0.2	↘	join riverside bikepath/footpath		
0.4	⌐	cross river via rail bridge		
3.3	↰	into laneway		
4.2	↰	'to Beningbrough'		
6.6	↘	'to Beningbrough'		
7.2	↰	'to Newton-on-Ouse'		
7.9	↰	'to Beningbrough'		
9.0	★↙	at Beningbrough Hall		
10.5	↰	Newton-on-Ouse	54°2'1"N	1°13'15"W
10.6	↗	'to Linton-on-Ouse'		
11.1	⌐	Linton Woods Lane (before village)		
13.5	↑	'Public Bridleway' (by farm)		
	▲	0.5 miles dirt road		
14.4	↗	'to Easingwold', Youlton	54°3'54"N	1°15'5"W
15.9		Alne	54°4'58"N	1°14'30"W
19.6	⌐	Station Rd, 'to Easingwold'		
19.9	⌐◎	Long St		
20.2	↰	Chapel Lane		
20.3		Easingwold	54°7'9"N	1°11'35"W
20.8	↗	Mill Lane 'to Crayke'		

CUE CONTINUED			GPS COORDINATES	
21.0	↰	Oulston Rd 'to Coxwold'		
23.3	↰	'to Coxwold'		
	▲	1.6 miles moderate climb		
24.5		Oulston	54° 9'44"N	1° 9'49"W
{26.0	★	Newburgh Priory}		
26.6	⌐	'to Byland', Coxwold	54°11'14"N	1°10'53"W
28.2	↰	'to Kilburn'		
	★	Byland Abbey		
29.6		Oldstead	54°12'44"N	1°11'17"W
30.5	↑	'low level route', route splits		
30.6	↰	'to High Kilburn'		
31.7	⌐	'to Thirsk'		
32.0	↰	'to Bagby', Kilburn	54°12'36"N	1°12'53"W
	★	Mouseman Centre		
34.2	↑	'to Thirsk'		
35.2	↘	'to Bagby'		
36.9	⌐	Moor Lane 'to Thirsk'		
38.4		Sowerby	54°13'50"N	1°20'44"W
38.7	↗	join bikepath		
39.0	↑	Castlegate		
39.2	↰	Kirkgate (off market place)		
39.3		Thirsk tourist office	54°13'58"N	1°20'36"W

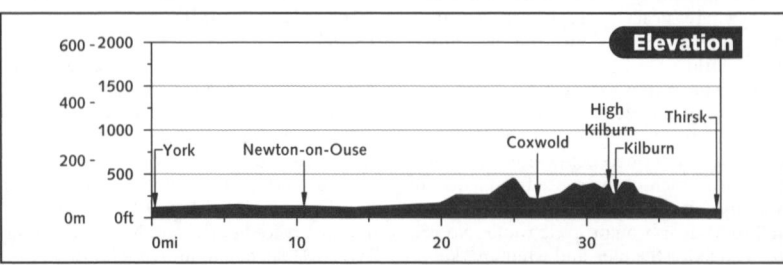

Elevation

York — Newton-on-Ouse — Coxwold — High Kilburn — Kilburn — Thirsk

HEATHER & GROUSE

As you cycle the North York Moors you can't help but notice the beautiful carpet of heather, which covers the landscape. This area possesses the largest expanse of heather moorland in England, made up of three species called ling (the most widespread, pinkish-purple flower), bell heather (deep purple) and cross-leaved heather (or bog heather, which prefers wet ground, unlike the first two, and tends to flower earlier). In wet and boggy areas you'll also find cotton grass, sphagnum moss and even carnivorous sundew plants.

Although they appear wild, the moors have traditionally been managed to provide an ideal habitat for the red grouse, a famous game bird who lives in blissful peace and ignorance for most of the year until the 'Glorious Twelfth', the beginning of the shooting season, which lasts until 10 December. Don't be too concerned if you see the moors ablaze – managing moorland involves periodically burning the heather. While grouse nest in mature growth, they feed on the tender shoots of new plants, which sprout after fires.

stately home, built on the site of an Augustinian priory. The house, reputed to hold the entombed body of Oliver Cromwell, stands amid much manicured greenery of the impressive gardens. A little further down the road, not far from the picture perfect village of Coxwold, stand the skeletal remnants of **Byland Abbey** (☎ 01347 868614), once one of Yorkshire's greatest and erstwhile home to 200 Cistercian monks.

Following the White Rose low-level route pass through Kilburn (32 miles) and get a close-up view of Britain's largest **White Horse**, first etched out on the hillside by the local schoolmaster in 1857. Interestingly it was covered over during World War II to prevent the Luftwaffe from using it as a landmark for navigation. Kilburn is also where Robert Thompson produced his famous fine oak furniture complete with the trademark mouse carved into each handcrafted piece. The furniture factory is still going strong and you can learn all about the man and his furniture at the **Mouseman visitor centre** (☎ 01347 869102), housed in Thompson's original workshop.

Leave the White Rose route (33 miles), continuing through Bagby and over the busy A19 to enter Thirsk via Sowerby on quiet but unremarkable back roads.

Day 2: Thirsk to Castleton

3½–4½ hours, 37.7 miles

Despite a short initial stretch on busy Stockton Rd, it's not long before you're away from the traffic, cycling along quiet hedge-lined lanes and edging up into the green Hambleton Hills. Beyond Kepwick the route enters the Silton Forest pine plantation and climbs sharply on a rough gravel single-track forestry road, emerging to reveal a dramatically different landscape. This section could be tricky for heavily laden cyclists so take it easy.

Welcome to the North York Moors National Park, a lonely open expanse of heather-carpeted hills that's wild and bleak, but undeniably beautiful. Your first taste of the moors is a brief one though, with the route quickly descending back into greener surrounds at Cod Beck Reservoir on the way into Swainby.

During the short stretch on the busy A172 look out for the curiously pointed peak directly in front of you. This is **Roseberry Topping**, Cleveland's most famous hill, whose shape is the result of a mine collapse in the early 20th century. Its odd shark's fin shape can be seen up to 60 miles away and most Teesiders make at least one pilgrimage to the top per lifetime. The ride is largely level to Great Broughton (24.6 miles) but becomes increasingly lumpy beyond it. Just out of Battersby **Captain Cook's Monument** atop Easby Moor is visible for miles around. Captain James Cook, arguably the Northeast's greatest achiever and most famous son, was born in Marton – now a suburb of Middlesbrough, educated in nearby Great Ayton and gained his sea legs at Whitby on the North Yorkshire coast.

A couple of tough gradients around Kildale (30.4 miles) and out of Commondale lead back up into characteristic moors scenery with a final ascent from Castleton train station, a stop on the scenic Middlesbrough-Whitby (Esk Valley) line, heading into the village proper.

NORTH YORK MOORS & MANSIONS

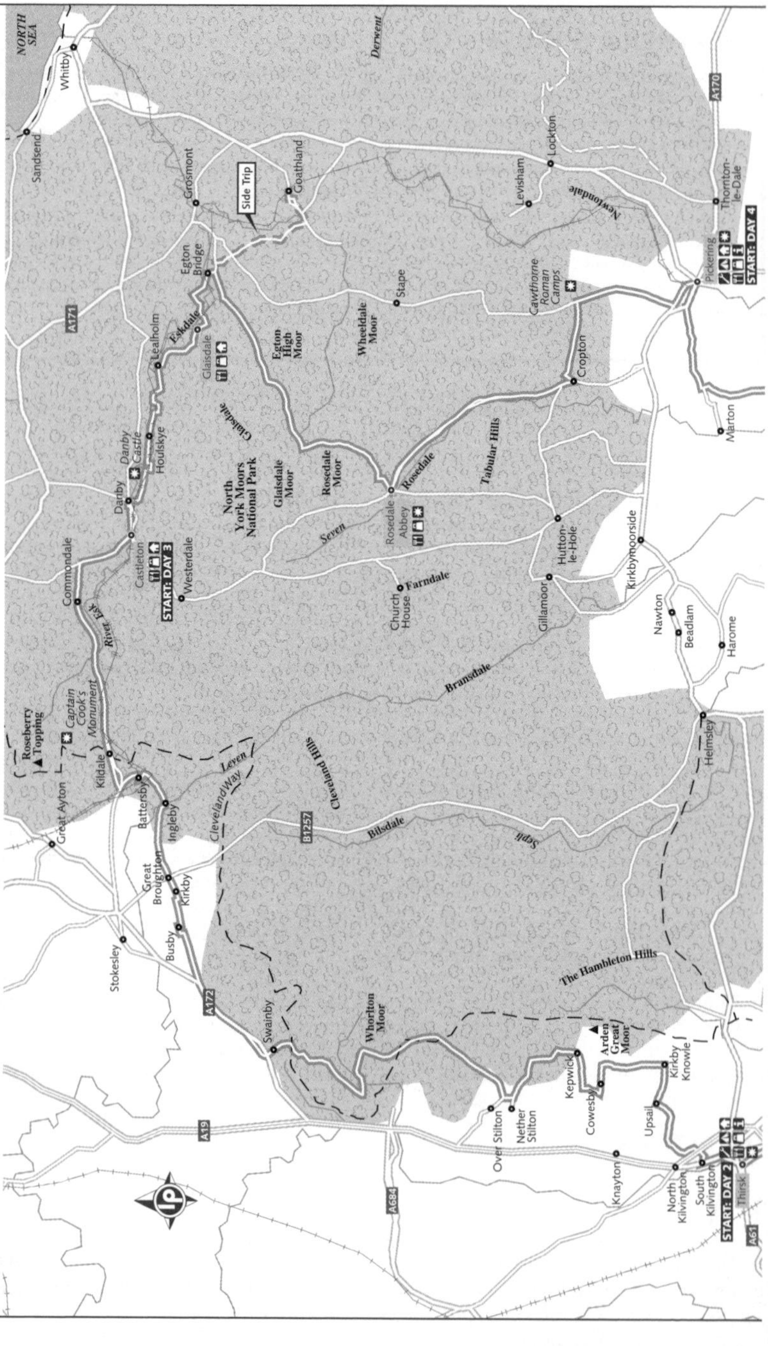

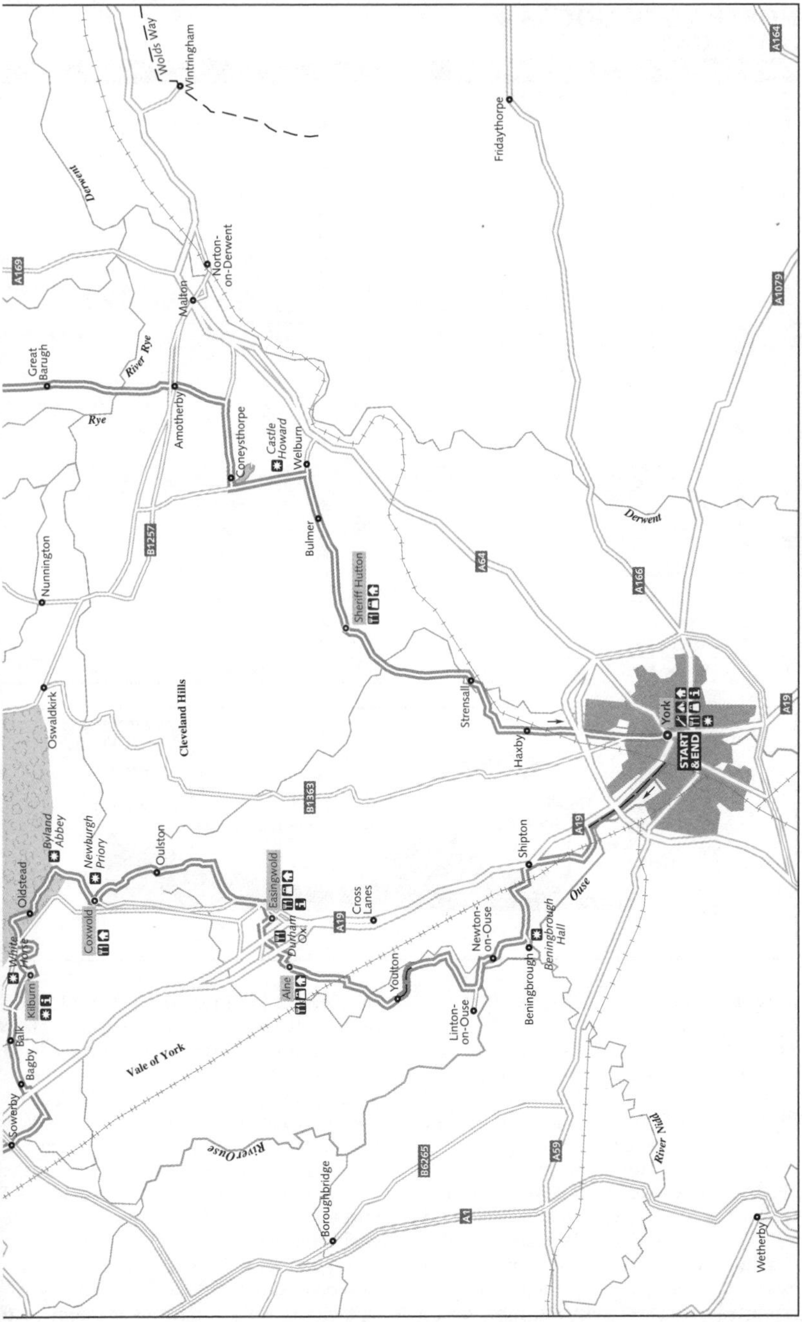

Wolds Way

Wintringham

Fridaythorpe

A164

A169

Derwent

Norton-
on-Derwent

Malton

A1079

Great
Barugh

River Rye

Amotherby

Rye

Coneysthorpe

Castle
Howard

Welburn

Derwent

Nunnington

B1257

Bulmer

Sheriff Hutton

A64

A166

Cleveland Hills

Strensall

York

A19

Oswaldkirk

Haxby

START
& END

Byland
Abbey

Newburgh
Priory

Oulston

B1363

Shipton

A19

Ouse

White

Oldstead

Coxwold

Essingwold

Cross
Lanes

Newton-
on-Ouse

Beningbrough
Hall

Kilburn

A19

Durham
Ox

Beningbrough

Balk

Aine

Youlton

Bagby

Linton-
on-Ouse

Sowerby

Vale of York

River Ouse

A59

River Nidd

Boroughbridge

B6265

A1

Wetherby

NORTH YORK MOORS & MANSIONS – DAY 2

CUE			GPS COORDINATES	
start		Thirsk tourist office	54°13'58"N	1°20'36"W
0 miles		go SE on Kirkgate		
0	↰	(60yd) Market Place		
0.1	↰	Millgate		
0.3	↘	Stammergate		
0.4	↰◎	Stockton Rd/A19 North		
1.4	↰	'to Upsall'		
3.1	▲	1.2 miles moderate climb		
4.3		Upsall	54°16'44"N	1°18'24"W
5.3		Kirby Knowle	54°16'42"N	1°16'58"W
7.2	↰	'to Kepwick', Cowesby	54°18'7"N	1°17'8"W
8.1	↰	'to Kepwick'		
9.0	↘	'to Silton', Kepwick	54°18'43"N	1°16'42"W
10.4	↰	'to Over Silton'		
10.5	↗	'NCN 65'		
11.3		Silton Forest		
	⚠	1.7 miles dirt road		
11.7	▲	0.7 miles steep climb		
12.0	↑	unsigned track		
12.7	↰	gravel path exits forest		
13.0	↑	'to Swainby'		
14.0	↗	unsigned road		
	⚠	1.6 miles dirt road		
14.7	↰	'NCN 65'		
15.4		Cod Beck Reservoir		

CUE CONTINUED			GPS COORDINATES	
15.6	↰	join road		
16.7	⚠	0.5 miles steep descent		
18.5		Swainby	54°15'47"N	1°29'0"W
18.7	↗	cross over stream		
18.8	↑	Gold Hill Loop Rd		
19.9	↰	A172		
21.5	↰	'to Kirkby'		
21.6	↘	'to Kirkby'		
22.7		Busby	54°27'2"N	1°13'4"W
23.9		Kirkby	54°26'46"N	1°10'13"W
24.6		Great Broughton	54°26'57.57"N	1°9'27"W
26.6	↑	'to Kildale'		
27.0	↰	'to Kildale', Ingleby	54°26'58"N	1°6'18"W
28.5		Battersby	54°27'35"N	1°4'56"W
{28.8		view of Captain Cook monument}		
29.1	↗	'to Kildale'		
30.4		Kildale	54°28'34"N	1°3'48"W
32.5	▲	700yd steep climb		
34.3		Commondale		
	▲	0.5 miles steep climb		
35.6	↰	'to Castleton'		
36.3	⚠	0.9 miles steep descent		
37.2	▲	700yd steep climb		
37.6	↰	High St		
37.7		Castleton post office	54°27'48"N	0°56'26"W

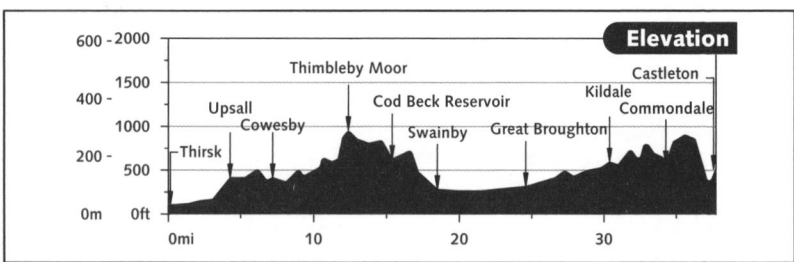

Day 3: Castleton to Pickering
3½–4 hours, 31.3 miles

This is a short but strenuous day through some of the most evocative scenery in the North York Moors. Gradients are frighteningly steep and some of the most precipitous in Britain, so get ready for pain.

Just out of Danby and situated at the head of Eskdale, 14th-century **Danby Castle** (☎ 01287 669219) – where Henry VIII courted his sixth wife Catherine Parr – is visible high on the hillside above. Some extremely steep ascents around Glaisdale are rewarded with show-stopping views over a chequerboard of green fields. Out of Egton Bridge (10.5 miles) the gradient is so steep that the road would possibly be considered a wall in the flatter parts of the southeast. Keeping the pedals moving is particularly punishing here, and you'll more than likely have to get off and push. Having conquered the hill lap up some of the finest vistas the moors have to offer, with vast expanses of purple heather and even glimpses of the steely North Sea beyond.

A breakneck descent heads down into **Rosedale Abbey** (19.2 miles), a pretty village blessed with numerous tearooms and

NORTH YORK MOORS & MANSIONS – DAY 3

CUE		GPS COORDINATES
start	Castleton post office	54°27'48"N 0°56'26"W
0 miles	go E on the High St	
1.5	Danby	54°28'6"N 0°54'33"W
2.1	Moors Centre tourist information centre	
3.5	↘ 'to Lealholm'	
3.8	Houlsyke	54°27'41"N 0°51'55"W
5.8	⌐→ 'to Glaisdale', Lealholm	54°27'32"N 0°49'31"W
6.1	←⌐ 'to Glaisdale'	
6.3	▲ 0.6 miles hard climb	
7.8	↑ 'to Egton', Glaisdale	54°26'19"N 0°48'23"W
8.6	▲ 700yd very steep climb	
9.3	⌐→ 'to Egton Bridge'	
10.5	⌐→ 'to Goathland', Egton Bridge	54°26'10"N 0°45'41"W

CUE CONTINUED		GPS COORDINATES
10.7	⌐→ 'to Rosedale'	
{	●●↘ Goathland 8.7 miles ↻ }	
11.2	▲ 1.4 miles very steep climb	
17.5	▲ 800yd hard climb	
18.1	⚠ 1.2 miles steep descent	
19.2	←⌐ 'to Pickering', Rosedale Abbey	54°21'14"N 0°53'12"W
24.1	▲ 800yd hard climb	
24.5	↘ 'to Sutherland', Cropton	54°17'27"N 0°50'21"W
{26.6	★ Cawthorne Camps (LHS)}	
27.0	⌐→ 'to Pickering'	
30.5	←⌐ Middleton Rd	
30.8	↗ Potter Hill	
30.9	←⌐ Southgate	
31.3	Pickering tourist office	54°14'44"N 0°46'47"W

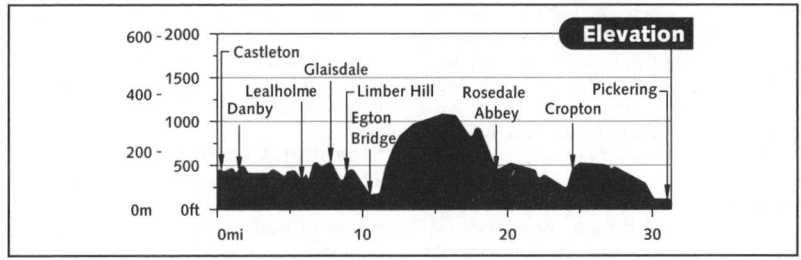

Elevation

bakeries servicing the needs of car-bound day trippers. Very little of the 12th-century nunnery from which the village takes its name remains, with just a few remnants visible behind the church. The route avoids the infamous Rosedale Chimney, a hill boasting one of the steepest gradients in Britain, by taking the scenic route along moor-hemmed **Rosedale** to Pickering. The final few miles of the ride beyond Cropton are predominantly downhill. En route you'll wizz past the **Cawthorne Roman Camps** (26.6 miles), a rare Roman site in these parts where excavations have revealed a well-preserved settlement. From there let the wheels roll as you plunge from the hillsides down to the Vale of Pickering and into the town itself.

SIDE TRIP: GOATHLAND
1½ hours, 8.7 miles (RTN)
If you were a fan of the TV series *Heartbeat*, you will no doubt not want to pass up the chance to see with your very own eyes the village of Goathland, which played a star-

ring role as Adensfield, and where much of the series was filmed. It lies around 4.3 miles from Egton Bridge (signed at 10.7 miles), although getting there involves a punishing climb. Goathland is also a stop on the North Yorkshire Moors Railway, so if you don't fancy backtracking, load your bike on the train and put your feet up for the scenic steam-hauled journey into Pickering.

Day 4: Pickering to York
2½–3 hours, 31.4 miles
Mile-wise this is a short and easy day allowing plenty of time to explore the splendour of stately Castle Howard, for many the man-made highlight of this ride. There's some relief for legs, brakes and *derailleur* as the terrain flattens out into the Vale of York.

The briefest of stints on the semi-busy A170 out of Pickering delivers you to quiet tracks through a pleasant and relatively flat rural scene. Navigation can be a nuisance on these weaving and intersecting country lanes but just keep the compass pointing south if

NORTHERN ENGLAND

NORTH YORK MOORS & MANSIONS – DAY 4

CUE			GPS COORDINATES
start		Pickering tourist office	54°14'44"N　0°46'47"W
0 miles		go W on Eastgate/A170	
0.0	↑⊙	(20yd) 'to Thirsk'	
1.0	↰	'to Marton'	
3.0	↘	'to Riseborough'	
4.3	↘	'to Great Barugh'	
6.8		Great Barugh	54°12'27"N　0°51'19"W
10.5		Amotherby	54°9'4"N　0°51'13"W
10.6	▲	1 mile moderate climb	
11.8	↱	'to Castle Howard'	
13.6		Coneysthorpe	54° 7'55"N　0°54'42"W
14.0	↰	'to York'	
{14.9	★	Castle Howard}	

CUE CONTINUED			GPS COORDINATES
16.0	↱	'to Sheriff Hutton'	
17.0		Bulmer	54°5'57"N　0°56'3.20"W
17.7	▲	800yd moderate climb	
20.2	↗	'to York', Sheriff Hutton	54° 5'20"N　1°0'25"W
20.4	↰	'to Strensall'	
24.5	↱	unsigned road, Strensall	54° 2'24"N　1°2'7"W
25.6	↱	'to York'	
27.3	↑⊙	cross A1237(T), 'to Huntington'	
30.5	↱⊙	Monkgate	
30.8	↱	Lord Mayor's Walk	
31.1	↰	Gillygate	
31.3	↑	St Leonards	
31.4		York tourist office	53°57'44"N　1°5'6"W

NORTHERN ENGLAND

you get lost, and sooner or later you'll hit the B1257. Hopefully this will be at Amotherby (10½mi) where you begin a steady but fairly gentle climb, providing some attractive views back over the Yorkshire countryside.

At 14.9 miles, not far from Coneysthorpe, a large obelisk in the middle of the road marks the entrance to **Castle Howard** (14.9 miles; ☎ 01653 648444). Generally regarded as one of the north's finest country houses, it's definitely worth parting foot from pedal to explore the majestic interiors and sprawling, manicured grounds. The house was the setting for the TV series *Brideshead Revisited*, and pulls in tourists by the coachload. Visit during the week when finding some space to appreciate the aristocratic grandeur is surprisingly easy. There's a bicycle parking area close to the entrance.

Beyond Castle Howard the route continues on quiet lanes to Sheriff Hutton, which has a substantially older castle of its own. Inevitably traffic begins to increase on the approach to York, but thankfully a bike-path begins in Huntington and continues for most of the way into the city centre.

TOWNS & FACILITIES

ALLENHEADS
☎ 01434 / pop 200
A former lead-mining town and reputedly England's highest village, Allenheads today is a small, sleepy place nestled in a valley high up in the lonely northern Pennines.

Despite its drowsy existence, some local businesses are well keyed up for the arriving armies of muddy and famished cyclists tackling the C2C route.

As Allenheads is a big stop on the C2C, with very limited sleeping and eating options, booking ahead is essential.

Sleeping & Eating
Thorn Green Bunkhouse (☎ 01434 685200; dm £18) is just the sort of place you want waiting for you at the end of a hard day in the saddle. The price includes a dorm bed, bedding and breakfast, there's room to store away cycles and it's one of the best places along the route to meet up with other C2C-ers to swap stories and advice.

Allenheads Inn (☎ 01434 685200; B&B £30-39) – the small bars are so chock full of bric-a-brac, smutty postcards and memorabilia at this rather eccentric place that retrieving your drink from the other side of the bar becomes a real test of skill. Rooms are of a decent standard and, handling over 2000 cyclists a year, this old inn at the epicentre of the village is well geared up for those in transit from sea-to-sea.

The Hemmel (☎ 01434 685568; meals £5.50-8.50; closed Mon) is an all-day cafe serving breakfasts, snacks and drinks, and is popular with cyclists passing through or starting out from Allenheads. It's behind the Heritage Centre.

ALNWICK
☎ 01665 / pop 7770
Northumberland's historical county town is a pretty cobbled affair huddling

beneath a colossal medieval castle. The town boasts the county's most popular tourist attraction, the Alnwick Gardens, as well as the legendary and unmissable Barter Books second-hand bookshop, which has taken over the old railway station in its entirety.

Information
Open year round, Alnwick's **tourist office** (☎ 01665 511333; 2 The Shambles) is housed in a handsome building by the market place. Sometimes called the 'British Library of second-hand books', **Barter Books** (☎ 01665 604888; Alnwick Station) stocks titles on local history and a limited range of old maps.

Supplies & Equipment
Self-caterers should head for **Morrisons** (Fenkle St) the most centrally located supermarket. Get geared up at **North North East** (☎ 01665 510753; 8-10 Fenkle St), the best source of outdoor kit in Alnwick. There's no cycle shop in town.

Sleeping & Eating
White Swan (☎ 01665 602109; Bondgate Within; s/d £95/130) is Alnwick's top address – this 300-year-old coaching inn right in the heart of town. Rooms and facilities are of a high standard but this hotel stands out for the elaborately decorated dining room, which has stained-glass windows pinched from the *Olympic*, sister ship to the *Titanic*.

Lindisfarne Guesthouse (☎ 01665 603430; 6 Bondgate Without; B&B £35) is just one of several similar guesthouses along Bondgate Without offering bed and breakfast.

Market Tavern (☎ 01665 602759; 7 Fenkle St) is an atmospheric pub where the huge beef stottie (bread cake) will more than replace the calories you've burnt up on the ride so far.

Ye Old Cross (☎ 01665 602735; Narrowgate; mains around £7) is possibly the best drinking spot in town and is imaginatively known as 'Bottles' after the dusty glass receptacles in the window.

BELLINGHAM
☎ 01434 / pop 1230
Bellingham is a fairly nondescript village but a popular overnight halt for walkers and cyclists thanks to its position on the Pennine Way and cross-country cycling routes. It's the closest settlement of any size to Kielder Water and is surrounded by some striking landscapes, especially to the south.

Information
The village's unexpectedly good **tourist office** (☎ 01434 220616; Station Yd, Woodburn Rd) is open year round and stocks a discomfiture of information on the surrounding area.

Sleeping & Eating
Brown Rigg Caravan & Camping Park (☎ 01434 220175; sites £10) offers soft grassy tent pitches on the outskirts of town towards Hexham.

YHA Bellingham Bunkhouse (☎ 01434 220258; Demesne Farm; dm £15) is housed in a converted stone-built barn – this self-catering YHA hostel may look like a frugal affair from the outside, but inside you'll discover comfy bunks, under floor heating and a fully equipped kitchen. Bikes stay for free and you can pitch your tent nearby if the bunkhouse is full.

Cheviot Hotel (☎ 01434 220696; www .thecheviothotel.co.uk; Bellingham; B&B £32) is Bellingham's top place to stay. It has flowery en suite rooms, a decent restaurant and a handy location at the heart of the village. The owners can arrange all sorts of activities in the Cheviots and can store bikes for no extra charge.

Riverdale Hall Hotel (☎ 01434 220254; www.riverdalehallhotel.co.uk; Bellingham; s/d £69/116) is a cosy country house hotel set in spacious grounds a short distance to the west of the village by the North Tyne River. Even if you're not staying here, book a table at the superb award-winning restaurant, one of the best places to eat between Newcastle and Edinburgh.

BERWICK-UPON-TWEED
☎ 01289 / pop 12,870
England's northernmost town occupies a dramatic location overlooking the estuary of the River Tweed. Berwick's perfectly preserved ring of 16th-century defensive walls hint at its turbulent history, caught between the warring English and the marauding Scots who passed the town back and forth 13 blood-soaked times between

the 12th and 15th centuries. Not surprisingly Berwick shows both an English and Scottish side and even the local football team play in the Scottish league.

Information

The **tourist office** (☎ 01289 330733; www.berwick-upon-tweed.gov.uk; 106 Marygate) can book accommodation.

Supplies & Equipment

Friendly **Wilson Cycles** (☎ 01289 331476; 17a Bridge St) not only sell and repair bikes but also double up as an unofficial cycling information centre with detailed info on rides in the area. Surprisingly the only outdoor stockists in Berwick is the austerely named **Government Surplus Store** (☎ 01289 306808; 38 West St), which sounds as though it should sell egg powder and air raid shelters, but in fact stocks a range of basic camping and survival gear as well as policemen's helmets, Union Jack flags and other items you probably won't find at your local supermarket.

Sleeping & Eating

Seaview Caravan Park (☎ 01289 305198; Billendean Rd, Spittal; sites £8.50) is a well equipped caravan park with a small camping area overlooking the sea, just five minutes' ride south of central Berwick.

Berwick Backpackers (☎ 01289 331481; www.berwickbackpackers.co.uk; 56-58 Bridge St; dm/s/d from £12.95/15.95/38) is an excellent hostel – basically a series of rooms in the outhouses of a Georgian home around a central courtyard – has one large comfortable dorm, a single and two doubles, all en suite. Highly recommended.

No 1 Sallyport (☎ 01289 308827; www.1sallyport-bedandbreakfast.com; 1 Sallyport, off Bridge St; rooms £110-170) is one of the best B&Bs in England. Sallyport has only six suites – each carefully appointed to fit the theme.

King's Arms Hotel (☎ 01289 307454; www.kingsarms-hotel.com; Hide Hill; s/d from £69/99) – Berwick's most prestigious digs enjoy a central location and the hotel restaurants serve up large portions of local and international fare for a few pounds.

Reivers Tryst (☎ 01289 332455; 119 Marygate; lunch £4-7, dinner £8-12) offers a hearty breakfast through to homemade pies

for lunch, and the likes of lemon sole in the evening. This place specialises in classic British cuisine – nothing fancy, but very good.

CARLISLE

☎ 01228 / pop 70,400

A handy base for exploring the north of the Lake District and Hadrian's Wall, far-flung Carlisle is a sleepy but oddly engaging place, certainly worth half a day's exploration. Straddling the west coast mainline it's one of the easiest places in Cumbria to reach from all points south and from Scotland.

Information

Carlisle's **tourist office** (☎ 01228 625600; www.historic-carlisle.org.uk; Greenmarket; 9.30am-5pm Mon-Sat, 10.30am-4pm Sun) offers a free accommodation booking service if you come in person.

Supplies & Equipment

For all things bike, Botchergate is the place to head where well stocked **Palace Cycles** (☎ 01228 523142; 120-124 Botchergate), **Hollymill Cycles** (☎ 01228 513909; 140 Botchergate) and **Whiteheads Cycle Centre** (☎ 01228 526890; 128 Botchergate) all engage in healthy competition for the cyclist's pound. For camping and other outdoor gear there's a handy branch of **Millets** (☎ 01228 529206; 59 English St) or try **Field and Trek** (☎ 0870 333 9458; 66 English St) in the same street.

Sleeping & Eating

Dalston Hall Caravan Park (☎ 01228 710165; www.dalstonhall.co.uk; Dalston; sites £8). Spend a night under rustling nylon at this basic campsite, south of Carlisle on the route to Cockermouth. The facilities are of the no-frills ilk and the ground can get very spongy after a day or three of rain.

Carlisle YHA (☎ 01228 597352; Old Brewery Residences, Bridge Ln; Jul-Sep; s £21) provides a cheap roof for you and your two-wheeled buddy – this excellent hostel has single rooms in self contained flats in the former Theakston's Brewery building.

Cornerways (☎ 01228 521733; www.cornerwaysguesthouse.co.uk; 107 Warwick Rd; s £30-35, d £55-65) is a cheery corner guesthouse offering reliable B&B rooms (not all are en suite). Period touches (including a tiled Victorian hallway) elevate it above Carlisle's bog-standard B&Bs.

Number 31 (☎ 01228 597080; www .number31.co.uk; 31 Howard Pl; s/d from £65/95) oozes opulence. Choose from three colour-coded rooms: blue is classically old-fashioned with polished wooden bed and upmarket wallpaper; yellow is cosily coun-trified, with flower-print quilt and half-tester bed; red has a touch of Zen thanks to its Japanese-print bedspread and dragon headboard.

Prior's Kitchen Restaurant (☎ 01228 543251; lunches £4-6; 9.45am-3pm/4pm Mon-Sat) is hidden in the old monks' mess hall – this cosy little cafe is always a favour-ite stop for jacket spuds, club sandwiches and homemade quiches – and it does a mean cream tea, too.

Alexandros (☎ 01228 592227; 68 War-wick Rd; mezze £3-6, mains £10-16) – go Greek with authentic mezze, grilled kebabs and calamari at this ever-popular restau-rant on Warwick Rd – just remember that smashing your plates is reserved for special occasions.

Le Gall (☎ 01228 818388; 7 Devonshire St; mains £5-12) – despite the Gallic name, this town-centre bistro brims with world flavours. Italian panini and pasta, Mexican wraps and Cumbrian standards fill the spe-cials board.

Teza Indian Canteen (☎ 01228 525111; 4a English Gate Plaza; mains £7.95-13.95) – this 21st-century Indian stands out from Carlisle's other curry houses like a Bol-lywood superstar in a crowd of extras. It shimmers with chrome, plate glass and modern art, and champions a new breed of Indian cuisine – try the slow-cooked lamb in pickled ginger.

Getting There & Away

Carlisle sits on the London Euston-Glasgow west coast mainline as well as serving as the terminus for several regional railways. **Virgin Trains** (☎ 08457 222 333; www .virgintrains.co.uk) operate hourly services from Carlisle to London Euston (£123.50, 3¼-4¼ hours) and Glasgow (£43.20, 1¼-1½ hours) line. Cycles go free but you must have a reservation. **Northern Rail** (☎ 0845 000 0125; www.northernrail.org) run trains along the Cumbrian Coast Line to Lancas-ter (£23, 3-4 hours) and the Tyne Valley

Line to Newcastle-upon-Tyne (£12.10, 1½ hours), which traces Hadrian's Wall. Cycles can be taken onto Northern Rail trains for free and without a reservation but storage space is very restricted.

CASTLETON
☎ 01287 / pop 500

A small moors village of stone cottages, Castleton boasts a surprising number of services for its size. There's not a lot do here besides resting your weary legs and checking over the bike, though the parish church with furniture by Robert 'Mouse-man' Thompson is worth a look. The village straddles one of the most scenic rail routes in the UK, the **Esk Valley Railway** between Middlesbrough and Whitby.

Information

The closest tourist office is at the **Moors Centre** (☎ 01439 772737; www.visitthe moors.co.uk) just out of Danby. It's the national park's HQ and has interesting ex-hibits on the natural history of the moors as well as a cafe, an accommodation booking service and a huge range of local guide-books, maps and leaflets.

Supplies & Equipment

Self-catering sustenance can be sourced at the **Co-op** food store (High St).

Sleeping & Eating

Greystones (☎ 01287 660744, 30 High St; B&B £23) is a three-star stone-built family-run guesthouse offering cosy digs with safe bike parking. Full English or continental breakie and a warm welcome from the own-ers is guaranteed.

Duke of Wellington Inn (☎ 01287 660351; www.danby-dukeofwellington.co .uk; s/d from £45/70; mains £7-8) is situated in nearby Danby – this handsomely refur-bished coaching inn, which was used as a recruitment centre during the Napoleonic Wars, was built in 1732 and has nine well-appointed en suite bedrooms. Downstairs there's a traditional pub with warming real fire, cooling Yorkshire bitters.

Castleton Tea Rooms (2 Station Rd) is a popular cafe among walkers, cyclists and locals. Enjoy a cuppa with a sandwich or freshly baked cake or go for the full-on all-day-breakfast (£4.95).

COCKERMOUTH
☎ 01900 / pop 7800

Best known as the birthplace of the writer William Wordsworth, Cockermouth is an attractive Georgian market town well positioned for exploring some of the prettiest areas of the northwest, especially Crummock Water and Buttermere.

Information
Cockermouth's **tourist office** (☎ 01900 822634; Town Hall, Market St) is open year round and books local accommodation free of charge.

Supplies & Equipment
Cockermouth's sole outdoor shop is **Angling & Outdoor** (☎ 01900 823071; www .anglingandoutdoor.co.uk; 37 Market Pl) though a large part of the store is occupied with fishing paraphernalia. **Derwent Cycles** (☎ 01900 822113; 4 Market Pl) take care of worndown brake blocks and dodgy *derailleurs*, or you could try the cheekily named **4play Cycles** (☎ 01900 823377; 25-31 Market Pl).

Sleeping & Eating
Violet Bank Holiday Home Park (☎ 01900 822169; Simonscales Ln; sites £11) hosts mostly caravans and pine lodges but has a small area for tents – it's located around half a mile south of Cockermouth centre.

Cockermouth YHA (☎ 0845 371 9313; Double Mills; dm £13.95) occupies a restored 17th-century watermill 10 minutes' walk from the town centre – it boasts a cycle storeroom.

Trout Hotel (☎ 01900 823591; www .trouthotel.co.uk; Crown St; s/d £60/90) – from the beautifully furnished rooms to the top-notch **Derwent Restaurant**, this stylish hotel ticks all the right boxes. Cycles can be stashed in the luggage room while you indulge in some well-earned off-saddle R&R. The hotel also takes its green credentials seriously with a comprehensive environmental policy.

Taste of India (☎ 01900 822880; 72 Main St; mains £7-10) is hidden away in a secluded courtyard behind a red gate on Main St – enjoy all kinds of curries inside the stone-built restaurant or around the trickling fountain on rare warm evenings. There's a 10% discount on takeaways.

Tarantella Restaurant (☎ 01900 822109; 22 Main St; pizzas £10, pasta £9) is an unexpectedly slick Italian joint with smart leather chairs, trendy tableware and beige walls. The food is well prepared, the service polite and, unless you've overdone it with the *vino rosso*, the bill relatively painless.

KESWICK
☎ 017687 / pop 5000

With its picturesque setting sandwiched between the rounded peak of Skiddaw and beautiful Derwent Water, attractive Keswick is a busy hub for outdoor activities of all kinds. On summer weekends the town heaves with walkers, cyclists and tourists, so if you're not camping, book ahead.

Information
The tourist office (☎ 017687 72645; Moot Hall, Market Pl; 9.30am-5.30pm Apr-Oct, 9.30am-4.30pm Nov-Mar) is based in the early 19th-century Moot Hall and provides a free local booking service for personal callers.

Supplies & Equipment
Keswick Mountain Bikes (☎ 017687 80586; repairs 74407; www.keswickbikes.co.uk) is based at three locations around Keswick. The workshop and hire centre (Southey Hill) does what it says, but it's worth calling ahead in summer to make sure they can fit your conked out bike into their busy schedule. The other two premises (Henderson's Yd & 18 Otley Rd) are cycle shops specialising in high-spec mountain bikes and accessories. The only other bike shop in town is **Whinlatter Bikes** (☎ 017687 74412; www .whinlatterbikes.com; 7 Tithebarn St) where repairs may be slightly cheaper. Keswick has more outdoor shops than you can shake a hiking pole at, and the town centre has quite possibly the highest concentration of them in the UK. **Millets** (85-87 Main St), **Blacks** (53-57 Main St) and **Cotswold** (16 Main St) as well as local company **Rathbones** (36 Main St & 13 Market St) are standard outdoor stockists but there are many more independent shops and discount stores around.

Sleeping & Eating
Castlerigg Farm Campsite (☎ 017687 72479; www.castleriggfarm.com; Castlerigg Farm just off A591; sites £7) – waking up to the panoramic views of the mist-wreathed

mountains from this basic but popular campsite is an experience not to be missed.

Keswick YHA Hostel (☎ 0870 770 5894; keswick@yha.org.uk; Station Rd; dm £22.95) is fresh from a refit – this former woollen mill is now one of Lakeland's top YHAs. Some of the dorms, doubles and triples have balconies over the river and Fitz Park, and the hostel has all the facilities a discerning backpacker could wish for.

Cumbria House (☎ 017687 73171; www.cumbriahouse.co.uk; 1 Derwent Water Pl; rooms £52-64) has a charming Georgian surroundings and an admirable eco-policy. fair trade coffee, local produce and a 5% discount for car-free guests make this a smart option. Secure bike storage is also available.

Lakeland Pedlar Wholefood Cafe (☎ 017687 74492; www.lakelandpedlar .co.uk; Hendersons Yd; mains £3-10) caters for both cyclists and vegetarians at this homely cafe, noted for doorstep sandwiches, homemade soups, vegie chillies and ultra-crumbly cakes. It's situated below a branch of the Keswick Mountain Bike empire.

Dog & Gun (☎ 017687 73463; 2 Lake Rd; mains around £8) is where russet-faced farmers rub shoulders with cyclists and hikers at Keswick's top pub – a wonderful place dotted with hunting prints, faded carpets and well-worn wood. The grub's honest and uncomplicated – mainly goulash, stews, steaks and pies.

KETTLEWELL
☎ 01756 / pop 285

A stop on both the Dales Way Footpath and the Yorkshire Dales Cycleway, picture perfect Kettlewell is understandably popular with walkers and cyclists. Book accommodation well in advance in the summer months. As locals will tell you at any opportunity, Kettlewell recently played a starring role in the film *Calendar Girls* starring Helen Mirren.

Supplies & Equipment
Take on supplies at the multitasking **village store** (☎ 01756 760221), which provides B&B in one double room (£24 per person) and internet access (£1 per half hour). **Over & Under** (☎ 01756 760871; www.overand under.co.uk; Low Hall) is an outdoor shop, which also sells a limited selection of bike spares and accessories.

Sleeping & Eating
Fold Farm Campsite (☎ 01756 760886; sites £8) is just two fields and a basic shower block, but has great Dales views and is very near to the village.

Kettlewell YHA (☎ 0845 371 9025; bed £11.95) is an excellent hostel based in an 18th-century stone house in the middle of the village, with modern facilities, bike storage and meals.

King's Head Inn (☎ 01756 760242; The Green; B&B £40) is a traditional pub with delicious food made from locally sourced produce, hand pulled ales, and rooms where you can sleep it all off.

Littlebeck B&B (☎ 01756 760378; www .little-beck.co.uk; The Green; B&B £34) is a gem of a place, with three beautifully kept rooms, a welcoming lounge and friendly hosts.

Blue Bell Inn (☎ 01756 760230; rooms £55) is a 17th-century coaching inn with possibly the best food in the village, a cosy bar with roaring fire and four basic but comfortable rooms above.

NEWCASTLE-UPON-TYNE
☎ 0191 / pop 189,900

The largest city in North East England and the region's unofficial capital, Newcastle has long since cast off its dreary rain-soaked image to become a vibrant metropolis. This has been helped along by a huge student population, generous government handouts for much needed regeneration and the arrival in the city of some cutting edge art galleries and entertainment venues. Despite gentrification, Newcastle has retained its inimitable Geordie spirit and, as anyone who's been on the famous Bigg Market of a Saturday eve will confirm, some of the most unfettered nightlife in the UK.

Information
The town's **tourist office** (☎ 0191 277 8000; www.newcastlegatehead.com; Central Arc, Market St) provides a booking service as well as other assorted tourist sundries with a Geordie welcome. There's another branch down on the Quayside.

Supplies & Equipment
Tiso Outdoor (☎ 0191 222 0020; 100-104 Grainger St) on one of the city centre's busiest shopping streets stocks a vast range of

outdoor gear and plan to add cycle accessories and spares in 2009. **Millets** (☎ 0191 232 1100; 121-125 Grainger St) and the **Army & Navy Surplus Store** (☎ 0191 261 6474; 50-52 Pilgrim St) supply less high-tech gear. The most central place for basic bike bits is **Halfords** (☎ 0191 269 9470; Unit 3a Newgate Centre, Newgate St) or you could try **Denton Cycles** (☎ 0191 272 3386; 259 Scotswood Rd) near Central Station.

Sleeping & Eating

Sandhaven Caravan Park (☎ 0191 454 5594; Sea Rd, South Shields) is the only site anywhere near Newcastle where you can pitch a tent. The location just a few yards short of South Shields sandy beach is superb and you can join the Northumbrian Coast & Castles ride by taking the Shields ferry (£1.10) across the Tyne or passing under the river via the pedestrian tunnel.

Newcastle YHA (☎ 0191 281 2570; 107 Jesmond Rd; dm from £11.25) in a Victorian townhouse, only a 15-minute walk north of the city centre. It has ample overnight storage space for velocipedes but a limited number of beds, so booking ahead is advisable.

Albatross Backpackers In! (☎ 0191 233 1330; www.albatrossnewcastle.com; 51 Grainger St; dm £16.50-22.50) has 177 beds, a long list of well-maintained facilities and a city centre location - it's no surprise the Albatross was voted 'England's best hostel' in 2007 by fans of Hostelworld. The hostel has storage space for 30 bikes inside and around 80 outside.

Adelphi Hotel (☎ 0191 281 3109; www .adelphihotelnewcastle.co.uk; 63 Fern Ave; s/d £40/60) though not much from the outside, inside the Adelphi has seven basic but well maintained rooms with en suite facilities and a hearty breakfast to set you up for the day's ride.

Big Mussel (☎ 0191 232 1057; www .bigmussel.co.uk; 15 The Side; mains £6-12) offers mussels and other shellfish - all served with chips - a very popular choice at this informal diner. There are pasta and vegetarian options as well, and students get 15% off everything. There's another branch (☎ 0191 261 8927) on Leazes Park Rd.

Paradiso Caffe Bar (☎ 0191 221 1240; 1 Market Ln; mains £7.50-14) is hidden away in a small alley off Pilgrim St - this is one of the city's best loved spots. Great food, a £10 all-you-can-eat buffet and a fabulous alfresco balcony keeps this place full almost all of the time.

Comfort Food Co (☎ 0191 261 1525; 24 Pudding Chare) is bang in the centre of the city. This small but popular eatery cooks up mouth-watering modern British fare made using only locally sourced meat and vegetables of the highest quality. The staff are clued-up about the dishes they're serving, quite a rarity in the UK.

Getting There & Away

National Express East Coast (☎ 08457 225 333; www.nationalexpresseastcoast.com) are better known for operating the UK's intercity coach network, but currently hold the franchise to run trains on the east coast mainline between London and Edinburgh. Big express trains hurtle between Newcastle and London Kings Cross (£98; three hours, every 30 minutes), Berwick (£19.30; 45 minutes, hourly), Edinburgh (£43.20; 1½ hours, every 30 minutes) and York (£21.90; one hour, several per hour). Cycles are carried free of charge but you should ideally make a reservation at least 24 hours before you travel.

PENRITH

☎ 01768 / pop 14,756

Once the capital of Cumbria and built of pinky-red sandstone, the bustling market town of Penrith is still the principal northern gateway to the Lake District and the North Pennines.

Information

The **tourist office** (☎ 01768 867466; pen. tic@eden.gov.uk; Middlegate) houses a small town museum displaying archaeological finds.

Supplies & Equipment

Poorly pushbikes in need of some love should be wheeled to **Arragons** (☎ 01768 890344; Brunswick Rd) who promise to have you back on the road within 48 hours or lend you a suitable bike if they don't. For all things outdoor look no further than **Penrith Outdoor Pursuits** (☎ 01768 891383; www.penrithoutdoorpursuits.com; 37 Middlegate).

Sleeping & Eating

Brandelhow (☎ 01768 864470; www.bran delhowguesthouse.co.uk; 1 Portland Pl; s £32.50, d/tw £65) offers plain, uncomplicated rooms, all in pine and neutral beige, with lots of little luxuries (mini-fridges, biccies, bath-robes). Tuck into a sit-down tea with a slice of Grandma's Courting Cake or Lanie's Expedition Flapjack.

Brooklands (☎ 01768 863395; www .brooklandsguesthouse.com; 2 Portland Pl; s £30-35, d £65-75) is next door to Brandelhow – another top-notch Victorian guesthouse. Some rooms feature pine fourposters and rich purples, while others go for soothing magnolias and flower prints. For the full swank-factor you'll want the fluffy-pillowed suite, with brass bedstead and wall-mounted TV.

Bank House (☎ 01768 868714; www .bankhousepenrith.co.uk; Graham St; s £38, d £68-76) is an unpretentious Cumbrian guesthouse that does all the basics right (including a kingly breakfast of coiled Cumberland sausage and fresh-baked granary loaf). The rosy-pink twin room might be too lacy for some, but the other doubles are more neutral, with DVD players and wooden bedframes.

No 15 (☎ 01768-867453; 15 Victoria Rd; lunches £6-10) – look no further for lunch in Penrith than this zingy little cafe-cumgallery. There are fifteen specials to choose from behind the counter, plus a bevy of artisan teas, cakes and sarnies, and you can check out local art and photography in the gallery annexe.

Yanwath Gate Inn (☎ 01768 862886; Yanwath; mains £15.95-18.95) is 2 miles south of town – this award-winning inn has scooped a clutch of culinary prizes for its grub-to-grub. Wood panels and A-frame beams conjure a convincingly rural atmosphere, and the menu ranges the fells in search of local smoked venison, salt lamb and crispy pork belly, chased down with a delicious selection of Cumbrian cheeses.

PICKERING

☎ 01751 / pop 6600

This bustling Yorkshire market town attracts large numbers of summer tourists who come for the Norman castle and to ride the North York Moors Railway, a rare survivor from Britain's age of steam.

Information

The **tourist office** (☎ 01751 473791; www .ryedale.gov.uk) is just off the main street (A170) and stocks all the usual details including information on the North York Moors Railway.

Supplies & Equipment

Pickering Cycle Centre (☎ 01751 472581) round the corner from the tourist office repair two-wheelers and sell a range of accessories and spares. Nearby **Ryedale Rambler** (☎ 01751 475183; www.ryedalerambler .com; 17 Market Pl) is the best outdoor stockist in town.

Sleeping & Eating

The **Black Bull Caravan Park** (☎ 01751 472528; www.blackbullpark.co.uk; sites £15) is situated 1 mile south of Pickering on the Malton Rd (A169). There's a strip of B&Bs on tree-lined Eastgate (the A170 to Scarborough), and a few more on Westgate (heading towards Helmsley). Decent options include the flower-clad

Rose Folly (☎ 01751 475067; www .rosefolly.freeserve.co.uk; 112 Eastgate; s/d £30/55), with lovely rooms and a beautiful breakfast conservatory, and **Eleven Westgate** (☎ 01751 475111; www.elevenwest gate.co.uk; 11 Westgate; d £60-68), a pretty house with patio and garden.

The **White Swan Hotel** (☎ 01751 472288; www.white-swan.co.uk; Market Pl; s/d from £110/145; mains £9-15) successfully combines a smart pub, a superb restaurant serving local dishes with a continental twist, and a luxurious boutique hotel all in one. The nine modern rooms in the converted coach house boast LCD flatscreen TVs and other stylish paraphernalia that add to the luxury found throughout.

RIPON

☎ 01765 / pop 16,000

This typical Yorkshire market town is a great base from which to tackle both the North York Moors and the Yorkshire Dales, and is worthy of half a day's exploration in its own right.

Information

Ripon's **tourist office** (☎ 0845 389 0178; www.visitripon.org; Minster Rd) opposite the cathedral is efficient, welcoming and hands out unusually detailed information on the town and surroundings, as well as booking accommodation.

Supplies & Equipment

Strangely named **Moonglu** (☎ 01765 601106; 57 Blossomgate) deal mostly in high-spec mountain bikes but can repair any kind of cycle given a bit of notice. **Yeoman's Outdoors** (☎ 01765 609136; 7 Queen St) is a well-stocked outdoor shop open every day of the week. Stock up on edibles at the central **Sainsbury's** (5 Market Pl East).

Sleeping & Eating

Riverside Meadows Caravan Park (☎ 01765 602964; Ure Bank Top; sites £14) is located around five minutes' ride out of the town centre – there is ample room for tents and bikes, superbly maintained facilities and entertainment at weekends in the on-site pub. There is a minimum two-night stay at weekends.

Unicorn Hotel (☎ 01765 602202; www.unicorn-hotel.co.uk; Market Pl East; s/d £45/80) is a two-star 30-room hotel with some very plush rooms, a posh restaurant and a superb central location.

Riverside Hotel (☎ 01765 603864; 20-21 Iddesleigh Tce, Boroughbridge Rd; s/d from £28/60) has the fragrance and ambience of a northern granny's house – time at this cosy guesthouse is like staying with distant Yorkshire relatives with dubious taste in interior furnishings and an appetite for fry-ups. Cycle storage may be possible but call ahead to make sure.

Black Bull (☎ 01765 602755; 6 Old Market Pl; mains £6-7) is a typical Yorkshire market town tavern serving traditional northern belly fillers such as bangers and mash, pork chops with apple sauce, and fish and chips. They also do generously filled sandwiches for £3.50.

One-eyed Rat (☎ 01765 607704; 51 Allhallowgate) is listed in the *Good Beer Guide* and stocks an impressive range of real ales and continental lagers – this is a good place to come for a pint after a gruelling day in the saddle.

Golden Lion (☎ 01765 602598; 69 Allhallowgate) is a gastro pub serving a contemporary fusion of northern English and international fare while retaining a

Yorkshire tavern ambience complete with wrought iron tables, wall lamps and gruff barman polishing glasses behind the bar.

THIRSK
☎ 01845 / pop 9100

Like Ripon on yonder side of the A1 motorway, Thirsk is a fine-looking Yorkshire market town that grew rich on cross-country trade. Today it's best known as the erstwhile home of the late James (Alf) Wight, author of the ever popular James Herriot stories, which brought a taste of rural Yorkshire to homes across the UK and beyond

Information

Thirsk's **tourist office** (☎ 01845 522755; 49 Market Pl) is on the main square.

Supplies & Equipment

Somerfields supermarket (32 Market Pl) is as good a place as any in town for self-caterers to stock up on foodstuffs.

Sleeping & Eating

Thirsk Racecourse Caravan Park (☎ 01845 525266; Thirsk Racecourse) is the nearest campsite to the centre of Thirsk, and is right by the racecourse on the road leading to the railway station.

Three Tuns Hotel (☎ 01845 523124; www.the-three-tuns-thirsk.co.uk; Market Pl; rooms from £50) is a coaching inn best known as having hosted the Wordsworths on their honeymoon in 1802 (you can still stay in the room they occupied). Accommodation is comfortable if unspectacular and there's a decent restaurant downstairs.

Fourways Guesthouse (☎ 01845 522601; www.fourwaysguesthouse.co.uk; Town End; s/d from £30/55) is a large family-run B&B close to the town centre.

White Horse Cafe (☎ 01845 522786; Market Pl) next to the clock in the middle of Market Place is a popular choice for sit-down fish and chips, pies, mushy peas and the like.

WHITEHAVEN
☎ 01946 / pop 25,500

More of a gritty working town than some of its tourist-dependent neighbours to the east, Whitehaven isn't worth a lengthy stay but does possess a small collection of restored heritage buildings, a small harbour and ample opportunities for stocking up on supplies and equipment.

Information

Whitehaven's first-rate **tourist office** (☎ 01946 598914; Market Hall, Market Pl) has tons of detailed information on the town, is open year round and is very cycle savvy. Staff sell a number of cycling maps including the official Sustrans' *Sea to Sea* route map. Sadly, puncture repair kits have disappeared from their otherwise well-stocked shelves.

Getting There & Away

Whitehaven is a stop on the Cumbrian Coast Line between Carlisle (£8.50; one hour, hourly) and Lancaster (£20.50, 2½ hours, hourly) where two Central England routes (Central Explorer p120 and The Marches Cheshire & Lancashire p131) end.

Supplies & Equipment

Haven Cycles (☎ 01946 63263; Preston St) is conveniently close to the C2C cycle route heading south. Branches of **Yeomans Outdoors** (☎ 01946 599737; 72 King St) and **Millets** (☎ 01946 694655; 19-20 King St) stock the standard selection of tents, sleeping bags and outdoor clothing. Take on provisions at the large **Tesco** (Bransty Row) just a short walk or ride north of the town centre.

Sleeping & Eating

Seacote Park Campsite (☎ 01946 822777; www.seacote.com; The Beach, St Bees; sites £14) is located on the coast at St Bees around 3½ miles away – this is the nearest campsite to Whitehaven.

    The Georgian House (☎ 01946 696611; 9-11 Church St; s/d £79/89) boasts immaculate rooms and gleaming bathrooms at this perfectly renovated Georgian townhouse in a quiet central street – the perfect end to a hard day in the saddle or a last gasp of comfort before a C2C slog.

    Waverley Hotel (☎ 01946 694337; www.thewaverleyhotel.co.uk; Tangier St; s/d from £32/52) – rooms may be basic and cramped at this central hotel, but the price is about right and there's secure storage for two-wheelers.

    Zest Harbourside (☎ 01946 66981; West Strand; mains £4-8) enjoy a snack-and-share menu of international favourites and Cumbrian mainstays as well as full-blown pasta dishes, vegie options and local meat dishes under trendy bare light bulbs at this lively quayside eatery.

    Ali Taj (☎ 01946 693085; 34 Tangier St; mains £5-8) – boast to your friends back home that you've eaten at West Cumbria's first Indian restaurant.

    Arrighis (Market Pl) is a Whitehaven institution – locals have been queuing up here for over a century to get their fix of fish 'n' chips.

WOOLER

☎ 01668 / pop 1857

A small town built from local stone and situated at the edge of the Northumberland National Park, Wooler has the Cheviot Hills as a scenic backdrop. The town itself is a pleasant enough overnight halt with a good range of accommodation options for its size.

Information

Wooler's spanking new **tourist office** (☎ 01668 282123; The Cheviot Centre, 12 Padgepool Pl) is at the top of the High St as you enter the town centre.

Supplies & Equipment

The best place for self-caterers to stock up is the **Co-op** (High St). Wooler, somewhat surprisingly as the self-styled 'gateway to the Cheviots', has neither an outdoor shop nor a cycle repair place.

Sleeping & Eating

Highburn House Holiday Park (☎ 01668 281344; www.highburn-house.co.uk; Burnhouse Rd; sites £12) is situated on the approach road into the town (on the cycling route), this attractive campsite is ringed with tranquil Northumbrian upland vistas.

    Cheviot YHA (☎ 01668 281365; 30 Cheviot St; dm £14) is the most northerly YHA hostel in England is a basic but comfortable affair, cycle friendly and close to the town centre.

    Black Bull (☎ 01668 281309; 2 High St; d/tw £40/50) is a large pub, good for a quick beer, basic meals (£6.50) including several sound vegie options, and has clean and comfortable rooms upstairs. There are slightly higher room rates at weekends.

Trotters Family Bakers (5 Market Pl) is a typical northern family bakery selling a range of cheap cakes, rolls, and savouries, and very popular with the locals – always a good sign.

Market Place Cafe (☎ 01668 282282; 22 Market Pl; snacks £4.50) is good for lunches and light meals including the usefully calorific all-day breakfast (£4.25).

YORK
☎ 01904 / pop 181,100

Sightseeing in York should not be overlooked in a hurry to get on to the Pennines. This cathedral and university city is the historic capital of the north, with evidence of power and prosperity from different periods in the buildings, streets and town walls. It suffers from a high number of tourists – book your accommodation ahead – but a rather un-English air of liveliness and contentment suffuses the place. To its further credit, York likes bikes and about 10% of people cycle to work along miles of dedicated pathways.

Information
York Visitor Centre (☎ 01904 550099; www.visityork.org; De Grey Rooms, Exhibition Sq) enjoys a central location and there's another branch at the train station.

Supplies & Equipment
York has an embarrassment of outdoor shops to choose from including **Yeomans Outdoors** (☎ 01904 640822; 22 Colliergate) and **Blacks** (☎ 01904 654979; 23 Colliergate). If your bike runs into bother in York turn to **Tony Boswell Cycles** (☎ 01904 410405; 133 Tang Hall Ln) or **Life Cycle** (☎ 01904 798848; 128 Borrough Bridge Rd) for assistance.

Sleeping & Eating
Rowntree Park (☎ 01904 658997; Terry Ave; sites £8.30) is situated on the banks of the River Ouse a mile south of the city centre and gets the thumbs up from most who stay here.

York Backpackers (☎ 01904 627720; www.yorkbackpackers.co.uk; 88-90 Micklegate; dm/d from £14/35) is housed in a Grade I Georgian building that was once home to the High Sheriff of Yorkshire. This large and well-equipped hostel was closed for refurbishment at the time of research, but should be open for 2009.

York YHA Hostel (☎ 0870 770 6102; www.yha.org.uk; 42 Water End, Clifton; dm £18.50) was originally the Rowntree (Quaker confectioners) mansion – this handsome Victorian house makes a spacious YHA hostel, with most of the rooms being four-bed dorms. It's about a mile northwest of the city centre.

Blake Head Vegetarian Cafe (☎ 01904 623767; 104 Micklegate; mains £4-6) is a bright and airy space at the back of a bookshop, filled with modern oak furniture and funky art, the Blakehead offers a tempting menu of daily lunch specials such as crispy bean burger with corn relish or hummus and roast red pepper open sandwich – great ginger and lemon cake too.

Melton's Too (☎ 01904 629222; 25 Walmgate; mains £9-13) is a comfortable, chilled out, booth-lined cafe-bar and bistro – this place serves everything from cake and cappuccino to tapas-style snacks, to a three-course dinner of Whitby crab, braised beef with Yorkshire pudding – and local strawberries with clotted cream.

Living Room (☎ 01904 461000; www.thelivingroom.co.uk; 1 Bridge St; mains £9-15) snapped up a hot location when it opened back in 2004, and has been making the most of its balcony tables overlooking the river ever since. The menu focuses on quality versions of classic dishes from around the world from fish and chips and steak and ale pie to Thai fish cakes and Peking duck. Sunday brunch served noon to 6pm.

Scotland

- **Skye**'s the limit as you take a two-wheeled adventure around the coast of Scotland's most celebrated island (p265)
- Pedal along solitary glens, around deep lochs and over mountains in the **Scottish Highlands** (p282)
- Kick down the stand at the eerie Machrie Moor standing stones on the mysterious **Isle of Arran** (p265)
- Enjoy a two-wheeled spin to the whine of the bagpipes around **Edinburgh**'s grand old city centre (p264)
- Seek out clandestine passageways and lost rooms in **Traquair House**, Scotland's oldest inhabited dwelling (p292)

CYCLING EVENTS

- **Bike Week** (www.bikeweek.org.uk).
- **Edinburgh Bike Film Festival** (www.bicyclefilmfestival.info) is held during Bike Week.
- **CTC Grampian Rally** (www.ctcgrampian.org.uk).

TERRAIN

Gentle through the central lowlands around Edinburgh and Glasgow – undulating with some steep sections on the islands and in the Highlands.

Telephone Codes: ☎ 0131 / 0141	www.visitscotland.com

Nowhere else in the UK can you escape a petrol-fuelled civilisation better than in Scotland – a paradise of back country cycling, wild camping and island-hopping fun. From the lonely purple moors alongside dark lochs, the convoluted coast and a rash of islands to the highest peaks of the Grampians and Cairngorms, the countryside is littered ancient forts and monuments to beautiful old abbeys and castles with plenty of opportunity to leave the saddle and explore.

A land with one of the most distinctive brands in the world, Scotland is proud of its traditional and wholly unique culture of single malts, *ceilidhs* and instantly recognisable symbols. The two big cities, Glasgow and Edinburgh, are as diverse as anywhere in the UK, awash with Indian curry houses, Polish grocery stores and top-notch culture – a pleasant surprise to many visitors.

The main obstacle to carefree cycling in Scotland is the weather – at best unpredictable, at worst as rough and wild as the landscape. Pack woollens and the mercury will rise like a swarm of midges, lightweight lycra and the June snow will catch you short. But be sure of one thing in Britain's most northerly reaches – if it's not raining now, it soon will be.

HISTORY

Although inhabited for around 6000 years previously, the Celtic Picts, whose loose tribal organisation survived until the 18th century in the clan structure of the Highlands, were the first people to really leave their mark on Scotland. They famously never bowed to Rome, resulting in the building of Hadrian's Wall from where the legions could keep an eye on this unruly bunch. Another Celtic tribe, the Gaels (or Scots), arrived from Northern Ireland (Scotia) in the 6th century. By the time the Normans arrived, most of Scotland was loosely united under the Canmore dynasty.

Despite almost continuous border warfare, it wasn't until a dispute over the Can-

more succession that England's Edward I attempted the conquest of Scotland. Beginning with the siege of Berwick in 1296, fighting finally ended in 1328 with the Treaty of Northampton, which recognised Robert the Bruce as king of an independent Scotland. Robert, more Norman than Scottish in his ancestry, cemented an alliance with France that would complicate the political map for almost 400 years.

In 1542 Scotland's James V died, leaving his two-week-old daughter Mary to be proclaimed queen. Henry VIII of England decided she would make a suitable daughter-in-law, and his armies ravaged the Borders and sacked Edinburgh in a failed attempt to force agreement from the Scots (they called

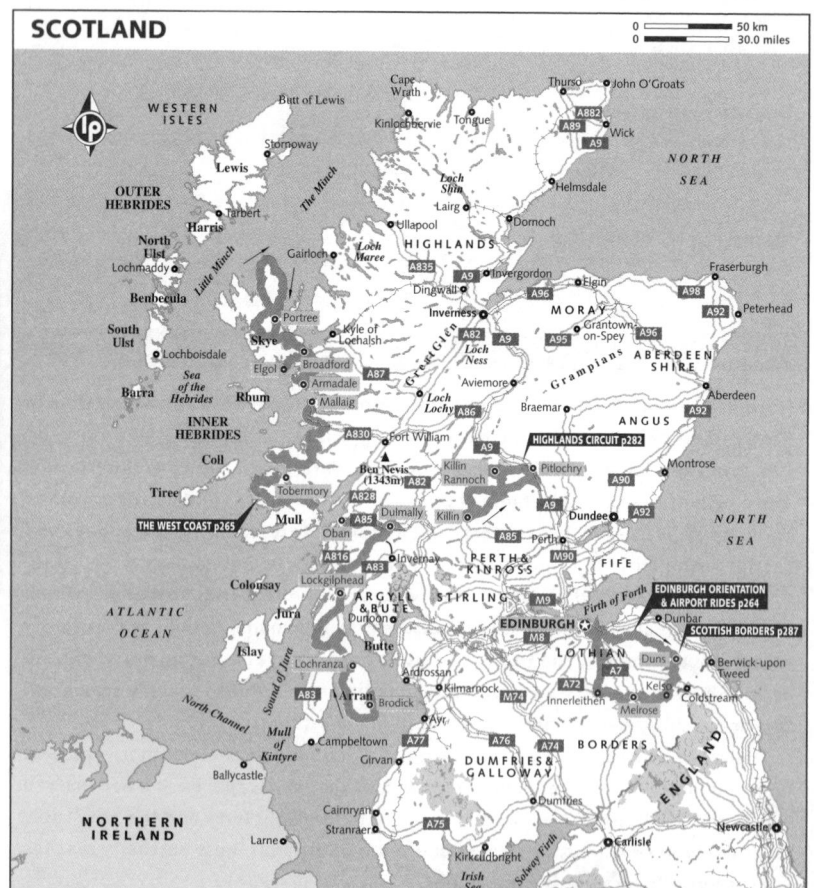

MARK BEAUMONT: GLOBAL CYCLIST

As circumnavigators of the globe go, Mark Beaumont, born and raised in Fife, is up there with the best. On 15 February 2008 Mark rode his bike to the Arc de Triomphe in Paris – nothing special you might think, but this was the conclusion of a trip that had taken him 18,000 miles around the globe in 194 days and 17 hours. Not only was this a new world record for circumnavigating the earth by bike, he utterly obliterated the old record by a massive 82 days! His journey was, as you might expect, not without incident. In Louisiana he was downed by a motorist (whose son helped him fix his bike) and later that day he was robbed in a motel full of drug dealers. But Mark came through this and more to complete his amazing trial of endurance.

Mark's feat is an inspiration for anyone setting off on a bike ride of any length, and after days in the saddle, a few sore bits and couple of punctures, your admiration for the man will grow even more. For more on Mark's amazing achievement visit www.pedallingaround.com.

it the Rough Wooing). At 15, Mary married the French dauphin and duly became Queen of France as well as Scotland, until forced to abdicate in favour of her son, James VI. She was imprisoned but escaped and fled to England's Queen Elizabeth (her cousin), who locked her in the Tower of London. Nineteen years later, at the age of 44, Mary was beheaded for allegedly plotting Elizabeth's death, but when the childless Elizabeth died in 1603 Mary's son united the two crowns for the first time as James I of England and James VI of Scotland.

In 1707 after complex bargaining (and buying a few critical votes), England persuaded the Scottish Parliament to agree to the union of the two countries under a single parliament. The Scots received trading privileges and retained their independent church and legal system. The decision was unpopular from the start, and the exiled Stuarts promised to repeal it. Jacobites (Stuart supporters) led two major rebellions in 1715 and in 1745, when Bonnie Prince Charlie failed to extend his support beyond the Catholic Highland clans. The Jacobite cause was finally buried at the Battle of Culloden (1746), after which the English set out to destroy the clans, prohibiting Highland dress, weapons and military service.

In the mid-19th century overpopulation, the collapse of the kelp industry, the 1840s potato famine and the increased grazing of sheep by the lairds (landowning aristocrats) led to Highlanders being forced off their land in what became infamously known as the Highland Clearances. After WWI Scotland's ship, steel, coal, cotton and jute industries began to fail, and, though there was

a recovery during WWII, since the 1960s they have been in terminal decline.

In the 1970s and '80s, North Sea oil – Scottish oil, as many will tell you – gave the economy a boost. Despite the bonanza, Thatcherism failed to impress the Scots and from 1979 to 1997, Scotland was ruled by a Conservative government for which the majority of Scots didn't vote. Following the victory of the Labour Party in May 1997, a referendum on the creation of a Scottish Parliament was overwhelmingly supported by voters. For the first time since 1707, the Scottish Parliament opened in Edinburgh on 1 July 1999. Since then the Scottish National Party (SNP), under their leader Alex Salmond, has been a thorn in the side of the Labour government both in Edinburgh and at Westminster, taking control of the Scottish Parliament in the 2007 Scottish elections.

ENVIRONMENT

About half the size of England, Scotland is often described in terms of three regions: The Southern Uplands are the fertile coastal plains and range from the English border to Edinburgh and Glasgow. Within the triangle from Glasgow to Edinburgh and Dundee are the Central Lowlands, containing the industrial belt and most of the population. The northern two-thirds of the country comprise the Highlands and Islands.

Among the Highland mountain ranges of sandstone, granite and metamorphic rock are almost 300 peaks over 900m (3000ft), known as 'Munros' after the man who listed them. At 1343m (4406ft) Ben Nevis, in the western Grampians, is Britain's highest mountain. The Great Glen is a fault line running northeast from Fort William to Inverness containing a chain of freshwater lochs, including Loch Ness. Of Scotland's 790 islands, only 130 are inhabited. The inner and outer Hebrides are off the west coast – to the north are the Orkney and Shetland groups.

Despite its wild, uncultivated appearance, the Scottish countryside has been dramatically altered by humans. Much of Scotland was once covered by Caledonian forest (a mix of Scots pine, oak, birch, willow, alder and rowan), but only 1% now remains. Today almost three-quarters of the country is uncultivated bog, rock and heather, with peat covering almost two million acres. Fast-growing conifer plantations have been encouraged in recent decades, despite serious ecological drawbacks. The ubiquitous heather brings a purple haze to the moors during August. Other summer flowers include bluebells (Scotland's national flower), thistles (also a common emblem), yellow flag, wild thyme, yarrow and gorse.

Changes to the environment and hunting have taken their toll on native Scottish animals, many of which are now rare or extinct. Some of the more common species include the red deer (which has an over-population problem), hairy Highland cattle, red squirrels, foxes, hares and minks. Grouse graze the heather on the moors, which gamekeepers burn to encourage new shoots and thereby attract birds (see the Heather & Grouse box in the Northern England chapter p243). Less common is the black, turkey-like capercaillie, largest

of the grouse family, which prefers heavily wooded areas.

Scotland, with 80% of Britain's coastline, is also home to millions of seabirds, including the comical puffin. Whales and seals are frequently seen in Scottish waters, while Scottish salmon, along with trout, are found in many rivers and lochs.

CLIMATE

With a cool temperate climate, Scotland has changeable and localised weather with the west considerably wetter than the east. Rainfall in the Highlands can be up to 3000mm (prompting the wry observation: 'If you can see the mountains, it's about to rain, if you can't, it already is'). May and June are generally the driest months, but be prepared for rain any time. Its proximity to the Gulf Stream means that the west coast is milder than the east (the average summer high being around 19°C). Considering its northerly latitude, the whole country's climate is milder than it should be.

PLANNING
When to Cycle

Summer may be the best time to tour on two wheels due to the temperature, but it also brings with it the bane of any outdoor enthusiast in Scotland – midges.

What to Bring

Mosquito (midge/mozzie) repellent is an absolute necessity in many parts of Scotland in summer and early autumn, and if you think Scotland's mozzies (see boxed text Alba's mozzies p269) won't get to you after that road trip through Africa, rest assured, after

---

WARNING

Be conscious of the following when cycling in Scotland:

o Take particular care if you're cycling or walking off-road during the grouse hunting season, which opens on 12 August. Avoid areas where shooting is in progress (look out for signs or check with local tourist offices).

o Deer stalking also takes place from August to October. Again, call the local tourist office for detailed information.

o Scottish weather can change quickly and dramatically. It's essential to carry adequate protective clothing and food, particularly in the Highlands.

o Outside the main tourist season (Easter to October), services and accommodation may close. Especially in remote areas, it's advisable to phone ahead.

RIDING TO/FROM EDINBURGH AIRPORT

With an ever-increasing number of international flights landing at Edinburgh Airport, the chances of you arriving, bike bag in hand (or perhaps better on a trolley) is far greater than it was a decade ago. The busy airport lies around 8 miles west of the city centre and the direct route from the airport is main roads all the way. The ride is quick and easy, if not especially scenic, and takes up to an hour to complete. See also the Edinburgh Orientation ride map (p266) for greater detail on central Edinburgh.

AIRPORT TO CITY

Although the route runs entirely along busy main roads, there are shared bicycle paths or Greenway (bike/bus) lanes for much of the way. The route is almost a straight road running west-east and requires little explanation. Between the airport and the Maybury Rd intersection (3 miles) cyclists are required to use the sometimes-bumpy shared footpath along the roaring A8. Initially the path is only on the south side of the road, but continues on the north side after crossing a footbridge (2 miles). From Maybury Rd, Greenway lanes continue to the city.

Take particular care at roundabouts, especially at the huge and busy Gogar roundabout (2.6 miles) and in shopping areas where the Greenway fizzles out to make way for parking.

CITY TO AIRPORT

When riding to the airport from the city, detour onto George St (via St David St) to avoid Princes St where there is no bike lane on the north side and traffic can be particularly heavy. Particular care is needed at the one-way section through Torpichen Place and Morrison St (1.2 miles). Use the middle lane, but beware of heavy traffic.

---

the first night in a lochside campsite you'll be sprinting to the nearest chemist's to stock up on DEET. Things get so bad that some travellers resort to face masks and even mosquito nets. If you wear your hair cropped, a hat is also a good idea. Some people who have never been bitten by a midge previously can develop a severe allergic reaction resulting in acute swelling. If this happens you should get to a doctor who will prescribe you antibiotics to take down the inflammation.

Maps

For a general overview of the country, the best map to get hold of is the OS Travel Map – Tour 1:500,000 *Scotland* (sheet 12). The OS Travel Map – Road 1:250,000 *Northern Scotland, Orkney & Shetland* (sheet 1), *Western Scotland & The Western Isles* (sheet 2) and *Southern Scotland & Northumberland* (sheet 3) divide the country neatly into three regions and provide a lot more detail.

Cycling Events

The now well-established **Bike Week** (www .bikeweek.org.uk) sees a multitude of events taking place across Scotland. Held during Bike Week, the **Edinburgh Bike Film Festi-**

val (www.bicyclefilmfestival.info) offers four days of assorted bike-themed documentaries and shorts from around the world. Out in 'the sticks', the **CTC Grampian Rally** (www.ctcgrampian.org.uk) involves several shortish runs with every night ending in a traditional *ceilidh* (dance).

Information Sources

The **Scottish Tourist Board's** (www.visit scotland.com) *Cycling in Scotland* booklet (free from tourist offices and the website) contains basic cycling information, useful organisations and some cyclist-friendly accommodation. Look for the 'Cyclists Welcome' symbol in regional accommodation guides – this guarantees secure bike storage, drying facilities for wet gear and even a hot drink on arrival! The section of the website dedicated to cycling (http:// cycling.visitscotland.com) is crammed with valuable information.

As ever, **Sustrans** (☎ 0131 539 8122; www.sustrans.co.uk) is the best source of information on the NCN north of the border. The **Edinburgh Bicycle Cooperative** (☎ 0131 331 5010; www.edinburghbicycle .com) is also a good starting point for country-wide information.

The **Cyclists' Touring Club for Scotland** (CTCS; www.ctcscotland.org.uk) is the umbrella organisation for the 200 or so Scottish District Associations. **Spokes** (☎ 0131 313 2114; www.spokes.org.uk) is a volunteer-run cycle advocacy group for Edinburgh and the Lothians. It runs rides on the first Sunday of the month and distributes regular new leaflets in bike shops and hostels. **Undiscovered Scotland** (www.undiscoveredscotland.co.uk) is an excellent website that points the way to some of the more off-the-beaten-track locations, many of which lie close to the routes described below.

GATEWAYS

See Edinburgh (p294) and Glasgow (p296).

EDINBURGH ORIENTATION
Duration 1½–2½hours
Distance 15.7 miles
Difficulty easy
Start/Finish Edinburgh (p294)
Summary An urban figure of eight through the Scots capital taking in museums, royal residences and the city's largest green space en route.

Edinburgh's characterful city centre is a compact, bike-friendly place with acres of green space and abundant cycle lanes. This easy introduction squeezes the historic Old Town, wide open spaces, city views and leafy bikepaths into less than 16 miles of riding. Cycling is a relatively popular way of getting around the city – especially among cash-strapped students – meaning you won't often be riding alone.

PLANNING
When to Cycle

Queen's Drive is closed to cars on Sunday, making it the best riding time. Avoid midweek morning and afternoon rush hour traffic.

Maps

There are countless maps of the Scottish capital on sale across the land, but one of the best, most compact and cheapest is the AA's *Pocket Map Edinburgh,* which will fit snugly into any handlebar map pocket and won't take up space in the panniers when you're finished with it. The *Edinburgh City Cycle Map* published by **Spokes** (www.spoke.org.uk) is now in its eighth edition and is an essential companion for anyone planning to put foot to pedal in the Scottish capital. It can be ordered online.

Information Sources

The **Edinburgh Tourist Board** (www.edinburgh.org) serves up classic tourist info on the city. For information with a cycling flavour, **Cycling Edinburgh** (www.cyclingedinburgh.wordpress.com) pools a huge amount of information, news, views and basically anything cycle-related happening in the Scottish capital and beyond on one website. As well as a bike shop, The **Edinburgh Bicycle Cooperative** (www.edinburghbicycle.com) also serves as an information centre with details on all aspects of cycling in Scotland, route ideas and cycling advice. Another source of offbeat info is the **Edinburgh paths** website (http://edinburghpaths.info), which brings together many obscure route maps, ideas and articles.

THE RIDE

Keeping mostly to quiet streets and bikepaths, this ride's main hazards or perhaps just annoyances are frame-rattling cobbled streets, the odd chicane and ill-positioned barriers. Oh, and one set of steps. Apart from Holyrood Park there's little climbing to be done. Though the ride is short, it's wise to start early to allow time for the attractions en route. Most come in the first half.

Starting at the Edinburgh tourist office, the **Royal Scottish Academy** (RSA), with artwork by academy members, and the **Scottish National Gallery** sit at the bottom of the Mound (0.25 miles). On the **Royal Mile** (High St) between **Edinburgh Castle** (300yd west off the route) and the Queen's official residence in Scotland, the **Palace of Holyrood House**, sights include **St Giles Cathedral** (0.6 miles), **John Knox House** (1 mile), dating from 1490, and attractive **Canongate Kirk** (1.1 miles). **Our Dynamic Earth**, an interactive, multimedia journey of discovery through Earth's history from the Big Bang to the present day, is a 160-yard-detour west along Holyrood Rd.

Holyrood Park is the city centre's main green expanse where there are great city views from Queen's Drive and walking tracks leading to the summit of **Arthur's Seat** (251m/823ft).

Back through the city's West End, the **Dean Gallery** (7.5 miles) features contemporary art and sculpture. It's on Belford Rd, near the impressive **Scottish National Gallery of Modern Art**, which has exciting exhibits of 20th-century works. Entry to the bikepath off Ravelston Dykes is near a bus stop, but not obvious. Use the gate.

Turn south off the bikepath onto Granton Rd, then right onto busy Ferry Rd, then left into Arboretum Rd. You'll pass the **Botanic Garden** and the cafes of Stockbridge before walking down the steps by the bonny Water of Leith. Up a steep wee *brae* (hill) from Dean Village is the West End and Princes St (use the green centre lane).

THE WEST COAST

Duration 10 days
Distance 424.7 miles
Difficulty moderate–demanding
Start Brodick (Isle of Arran)
Finish Armadale (Isle of Skye)
Summary This island-hopping cycle odyssey delivers you to the lonely roads and unpeopled landscapes of Britain's Celtic fringe, where Gaelic whirrs through the whisky-scented air and voiceless standing stones tell of ancient clans.

Using Arran, Mull and Skye like three giant stepping stones, this island-hopping adventure is one of the most exciting and visually dazzling cycle routes in the British Isles. This 10-day expedition will see you load your bike onto five ferries, seek out countless standing stones, roll along undulating, coast-hugging roads hemmed by drinkably pure lochs, and sample Scotland's finest product at the Talisker Distillery. Heritage centres and folk museums beckon from the side of the single-track roads, giving an insight into life here over the millennia, and cosy guesthouses are warm with the hospitality of today's islanders.

Following the 18th-century Highland Clearances, the area remains sparsely populated (except by sheep) and the roads, for the most part, are lightly trafficked. This ride needs some predeparture preparation as the midges are waiting for you, but the sun probably isn't.

ENVIRONMENT

Scotland's Western Highlands are the wettest part of Europe, but things don't get too cold, and particularly on the more southerly islands the mild, moist conditions give rise to lush vegetation. Much of the area is covered in peat bogs, which act as a sponge, absorbing run-off from the hills.

Widespread sheep grazing and conifer plantations have taken their ecological toll on the Highlands' indigenous forests. Remnants of ancient oak forests can be seen on the Ardnamurchan peninsula by

ROADS IN SCOTLAND: KNOW YOUR A, B, SINGLE-TRACK

One of the joys of the Scottish Highlands and islands is cycling on isolated single-track roads. They invariably lead through delightful scenery, but the main plus for the cyclist is the relative absence of cars. In a world obsessed with going faster, motorists generally avoid the long winding drive along a single-track B-road (where the only option is to slow down) in favour of the blink-and-miss-it sprint along a straight, boring, evenly-graded A-road. Evenly-graded, however, is what B-roads are not. While most A-road hills are long, steady climbs at worst, narrow B-roads and unclassified tracks typically rock and roll with steeper gradients.

Courtesy has special significance on a single-track road and it's essential to know your single-track protocol. Passing places located at regular intervals are the only spots wide enough for two road users to pass (even, in many cases, when one is a bicycle). The accepted practice is for the road user closest to the passing place to pull over to the left (never to the right), allowing the other to pass. You're also legally required to pull over to enable a closely following vehicle to pass. Take care, however, not to be driven off the road by somebody overtaking at a place not designated for passing.

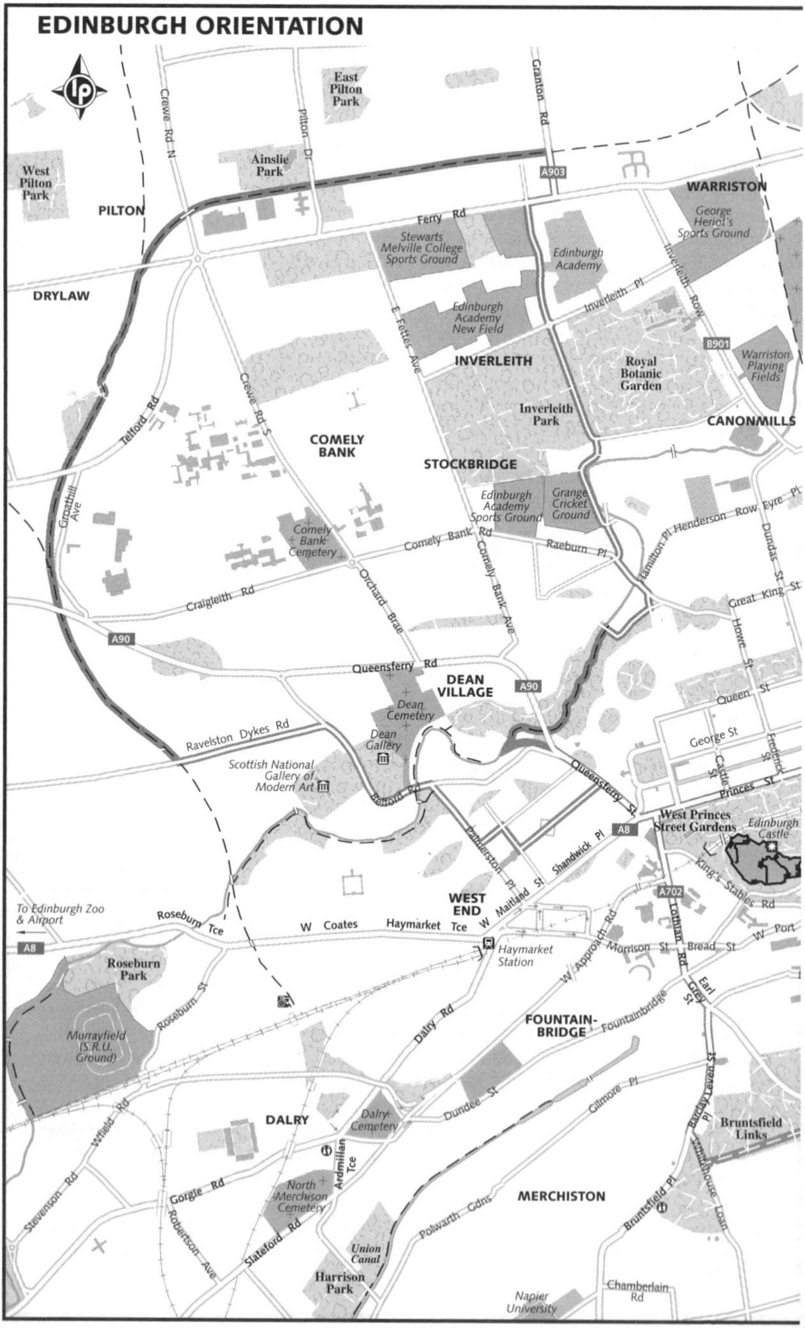

EDINBURGH ORIENTATION

SCOTLAND

East Pilton Park

West Pilton Park

Ainslie Park

PILTON

WARRISTON

George Heriot's Sports Ground

Ferry Rd

DRYLAW

Stewarts Melville College Sports Ground

Edinburgh Academy

Edinburgh Academy New Field

INVERLEITH

Royal Botanic Garden

Warriston Playing Fields

COMELY BANK

Inverleith Park

CANONMILLS

STOCKBRIDGE

Comely Bank Cemetery

Edinburgh Academy Sports Ground

Grange Cricket Ground

Great King St

Comely Bank Rd

Raeburn Pl

Craigleith Rd

Orchard Brae

Queensferry Rd

DEAN VILLAGE

A90

Ravelston Dykes Rd

Dean Cemetery

Dean Gallery

Scottish National Gallery of Modern Art

Queensferry Rd

George St

Princes St

Queen St

West Princes Street Gardens

Edinburgh Castle

To Edinburgh Zoo & Airport

A8

Roseburn Tce

W Coates

Haymarket Tce

WEST END

A8

King's Stables Rd

A702

Roseburn Park

Haymarket Station

Morrison St

Bread St

W Port

Murrayfield (S.R.U. Ground)

Dalry Rd

FOUNTAIN-BRIDGE

Fountainbridge

DALRY

Dalry Cemetery

Dundee St

Gilmore Pl

Bruntsfield Links

Gorgie Rd

North Merchiston Cemetery

Ardmillan Tce

MERCHISTON

Bruntsfield Pl

Stevenson Rd

Robertson Ave

Slateford Rd

Union Canal

Polwarth Gdns

Harrison Park

Napier University

Chamberlain Rd

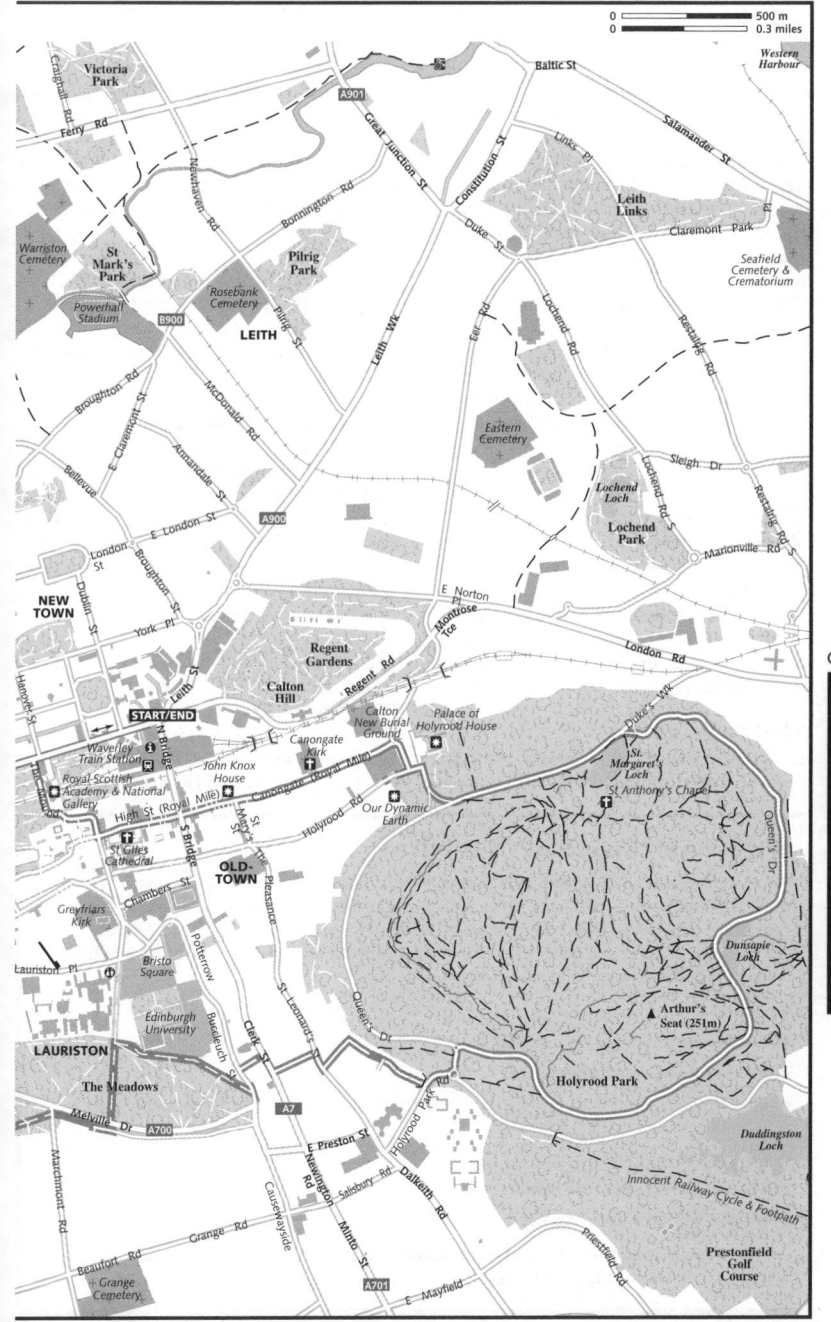

Loch Moidart and this area, only lightly grazed by sheep and deer, still supports animals such as pine martins, otters and wildcats. The Natural History Centre near Kilchoan has more information on local fauna.

One local insect that's difficult to miss during the summer period is the midge – a close relative of the mosquito. They're particularly prevalent in the early evening, in still, sheltered conditions, and are attracted to dark colours.

Not surprisingly, the west coast and islands are home to thousands of seabirds – seals and whales can also be seen. The famous Scottish wild salmon are threatened by disease and gene-pool dilution from commercial salmon farms, while shellfish and mackerel are in danger of being overfished.

PLANNING
When to Cycle
Plan to ride between May and September. The weather is most settled in summer (June-August), but this is the busiest tourist (and midge) season. Ferries and many other services decrease or close down completely between October and April.

What to Bring
An absolutely essential piece of kit in summer and early autumn is a good DEET-based insect repellent to see off Scotland's plague of midges. Forget this at your peril, especially if you're camping, though it can usually be sourced at any travel section of Boots and other large pharmacists. Waterproofs should also be packed alongside a three-season sleeping bag if spending night's outdoors, as even in summer the temperature can plummet under clear night skies.

Maps
The OS Travelmap – Road 1:250,000 *Western Scotland & the Western Isles* (sheet 2) and *Southern Scotland & Northumberland* (sheet 3) are essential pieces of cartography to take along.

Information Sources
The southern part of this ride comes under the **Southern Scotland Tourist Board** (☎ 0870 835 8558 www.visitsouthern scotland.com). North of Kintyre, the **Highlands of Scotland Tourist Board** (☎ 01997 421160; www.visithighlands.com) takes over. Both have a wealth of information in brochure and website form.

GETTING TO/FROM THE RIDE
Brodick (start)
TRAIN & FERRY
Before setting off it's always best to contact **Traveline Scotland** (☎ 0871 200 2233; www.travelinescotland.com) to make sure

WILD CAMPING IN SCOTLAND

Wild camping is relatively common in Scotland and a cheap way to go. You can camp free on public land (unless it's specifically protected) and in many instances on private land as well. Wild camping is generally accepted in most areas, provided it's away from houses and cultivated land, permission has been given by the landowner (where possible), it's unobtrusive and the area is left in the condition in which it was found.

If you are camping wild:

o Practise 'minimum impact' camping.

o Avoid camping immediately beside water courses.

o Be scrupulous about toilet hygiene: bury excrement; go at least 30 yards from water; and carry out tampons and sanitary pads.

o Carry out all rubbish.

o Use fuel stoves rather than lighting wood fires.

o Minimise disturbance to vegetation and wildlife.

For more information, contact the **Mountaineering Council of Scotland** (☎ 01738 493942) and ask for their *Wild Camping Code* leaflet.

ALBA'S MOZZIES

A close but vastly more irritating relative of the mosquito, the Scottish midge is pest number one for walkers, cyclists and campers in summer and early autumn. The 3mm-long female of the *culicoides impunctatus* species is normally vegetarian, but needs a drop of protein-rich blood to lay her eggs. These mini-vampires aren't fussy whether the donor is human or animal, and a shaggy Highland cow or bare-legged cyclist are donors of equal worth to the midge on heat.

The only way to defend yourself against these blood-thirsty squadrons is to spray your body and clothes with a DEET-based anti-mozzie spray. Some find the little blighters so annoying they veil themselves with face nets, and these can be especially useful to the cyclist who can't keep relinquishing the handlebars to shoo them away. You may see midge-zappers in campsite shower blocks and hotels often have plug-in devices to keep them out of rooms. The problem is so bad some years that a website (www.midgeforecast.co.uk) has been set up to give accurate predictions on midge numbers region by region.

the services listed below are actually running. **Scotrail** (☎ 0845 601 5929; www .firstgroup.com/scotrail) trains from Glasgow Central station (Argyle St) to Ardrossan harbour (£6.85; 45 minutes) connecting with the ferry to Brodick several times daily. Connecting services are also shown in the ferry timetable. Trains also run to Ardrossan from Edinburgh (£17.20; two hours, twice hourly). **Caledonian MacBrayne** (CalMac; ☎ 08000 665000, www.calmac .co.uk) is Scotland's main ferry operator. Its packaged 'Island Hopscotch' tickets are superb deal and much cheaper than buying individual tickets for the five ferry crossings. Buy 'Hopscotch 5' (Ardrossan-Brodick, Lochranza-Claonaig) for £7.25, and 'Hopscotch 7' (Oban-Craignure, Tobermory-Kilchoan, Mallaig-Armadale) for £9.30. Bikes travel free.

BICYCLE

It's possible to cycle from Glasgow to Ardrossan via the NCN (39 miles). The best map to use is the *Glasgow to Carlisle Cycle Route* (sheet 7B) published by Sustrans.

Armadale (finish)
TRAIN & FERRY

The 'Hopscotch 8' ticket includes return ferry from Armadale to Mallaig on the west coast. Ferries sail eight times daily (mid-May to mid-September only) with a vastly reduced service in winter. **Scotrail** runs daily services from Mallaig to Glasgow (£29.60; 5½ hours, three daily), which connect with the ferry. To get to Edinburgh change at Glasgow. Leave the train at remote

Crianlarich (£22; 3¼ hours from Mallaig) to start the Highlands Circuit ride.

THE RIDE
Day 1: Brodick to Lochranza
3½–5½ hours, 42.4 miles

Packing in a wild variety of landscapes into its modest area, Arran is sometimes described as 'Scotland in miniature'. Blessed with mild temperatures but a relatively high rainfall, the island goes from lush farmland in the south to rugged mountains in the north, via sea cliffs and wonderfully sandy beaches. As is often the case in the Scottish Islands, the east coast is more sheltered than the west and it's no coincidence that the main towns of Brodick, Lamlash and Whiting Bay were founded here, protected from the cutting winds. Where there are people, there's traffic, but away from the population centres you'll often have the asphalt to yourself. Skirting the rim of the island, there are just a few moderate climbs to negotiate, most notably in the east and south. Some of the coastal views are simply awe-inspiring and benches have been thoughtfully placed at scenic points along the road.

The ride south out of Brodick is one of the few parts of the route that doesn't follow the line of the shore. In fact the entire first 2 miles are through thick pine forest until you break out at the coastal hamlet of Margnaheglish. From Lamlash (3 miles) a summer-only **ferry** (☎ 01770 600998) runs to tiny **Holy Island** just off the coast. The island is owned by the Samye Ling Tibetan Centre and used as a retreat, but day visits are allowed.

SCOTLAND

THE WEST COAST - DAY 1 - 5

SCOTLAND

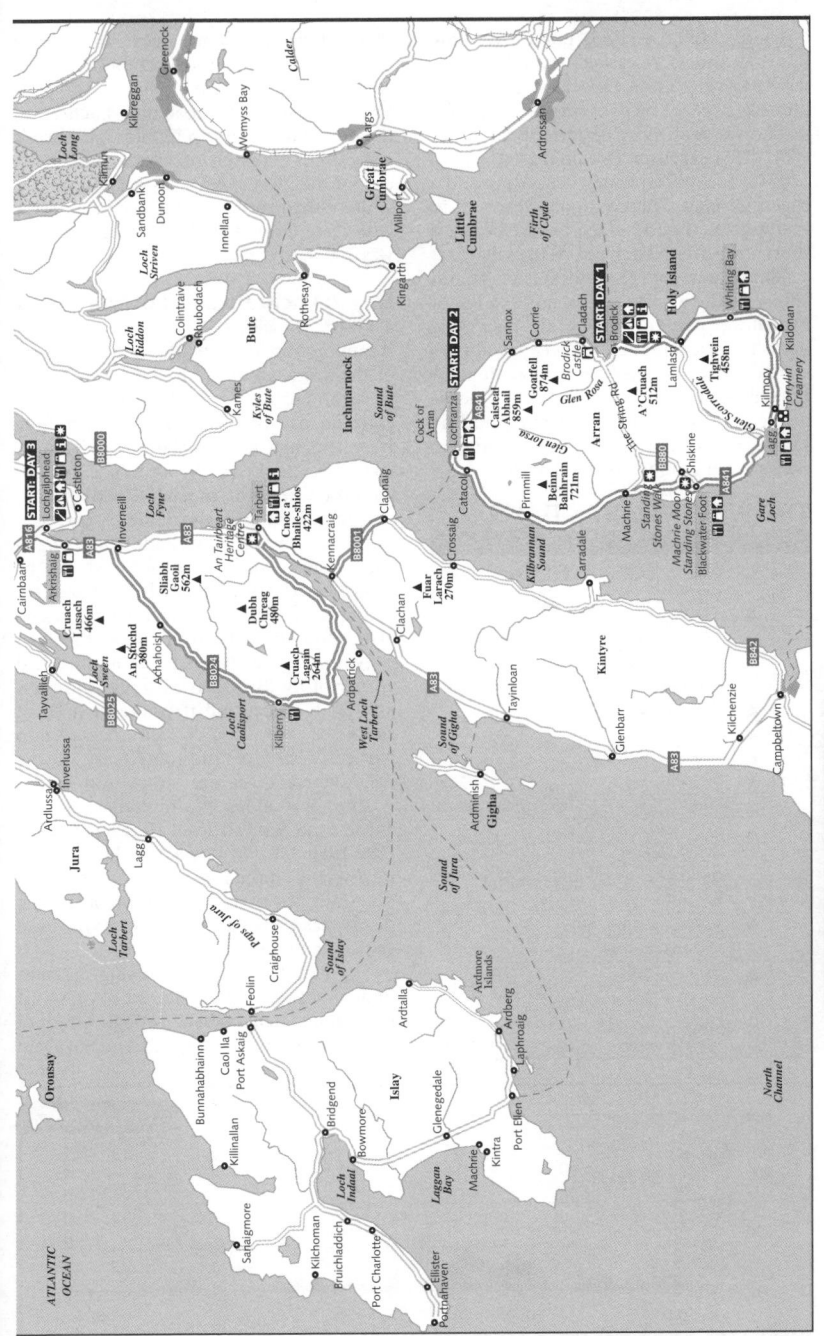

SCOTLAND

There's quite a climb out of Whiting Bay (6.9 miles) rewarded 10 miles along the A841 with a brake block-singeing drop into Lagg (16.9 miles). Arran is known for its cheeses, and shortly before the descent, visit the **Torrylinn Creamery** (☎ 01770 870240; 16.5 miles) which has a shop and a cheese display. There's a good tearoom in shady Lagg, a good place to rest before a short steep climb back out of the village.

Blackwaterfoot (23.8 miles) is the largest village on the west coast and more or less at the halfway point of today's ride, it's a good place to pause for lunch, especially as there's a small store, a bakery and a tearoom. A 1.5-mile walking track (at 27.7 miles) leads to the impressive **Machrie Moor standing stones,** the pick of Arran's many Neolithic sites erected around 6000 years ago.

THE WEST COAST – DAY 1

CUE			GPS COORDINATES	
start		Brodick tourist office	55°34′34″N	5°8′18″W
0 miles		go S on A841		
0.9	▲	0.8 miles moderate hill		
3.0	↗	'to Whiting Bay', Lamlash	55°31′57″N	5°7′44″W
4.2	▲	1.2 miles moderate climb		
6.9	▲	Whiting Bay	55°29′25″N	5°5′42″W
8.0	▲	2.4 miles moderate climb		
10.8	▲	440yd moderate climb		
13.1	▲	1.7 miles moderate climb		
16.5	★	Torrylin Creamery		
16.9		Lagg	55°26′42.07″N	5°13′59″W
18.5	▲	1 mile moderate climb		
23.8	↘	'to Blackwaterfoot'		
23.8		Blackwaterfoot	55°30′6″N	5°19′58″W
24.4	↗	'to Lochranza'		
27.7	★	Standing Stones walk (RHS)		
28.5		Machrie Bay tearooms		
32.9	▲	0.7 miles hard climb		
35.5		Pirn milesll		
39.9	★	Catacol	55°41′39″N	5°19′34″W
42.4		Lochranza post office	55°42′17″N	5°17′41″W

Apart from a short steep climb (32.9 miles), the terrain into Lochranza is relatively flat with striking views of the Kintyre Peninsula. Approaching Lochranza, the mountainous north unfolds and there's a stretch of attractive rocky coastline. Look out for the Twelve Apostles at **Catacol** – 12 whitewashed cottages built to house people who were cleared from the land to make way for sheep.

Day 2: Lochranza to Lochgilphead
4–6 hours, 44.7 miles

Assuming you haven't indulged in too much of the drink produced by Lochranza's Isle of Arran Distillery, you'll be up bright and early on day two to make the 30-minute ferry trip to Claonaig. Ferries to Kintyre leave from the pier at the western end of Lochranza. Check the timetable by the pier.

Apart from two short main-road sections, the route follows undulating single-track roads, which, though sealed, can be somewhat rough in parts. Be prepared for a couple of stiff climbs with superb views at the top and little traffic to bother you on your way. In this virtually uninhabited corner of the British Isles services are few and far between and if you're in need of snacks or cash you'd do well to divert into Tarbert, 1 mile off the route (east, on the A83) where there are shops and banks. A short way along the diversion towards Tarbert the **An Tairbeart Heritage Centre** (☎ 01880 820190) is also worth a stop for its displays on the area's history. There are occasional sheep shearing and woodturning displays as well as a restaurant serving local venison and oysters.

The B8024 is a cyclist's dream, narrow, undulating and almost devoid of cars as it runs along **Loch Tarbert** through woods of oak, birch, heather and spruce and out again

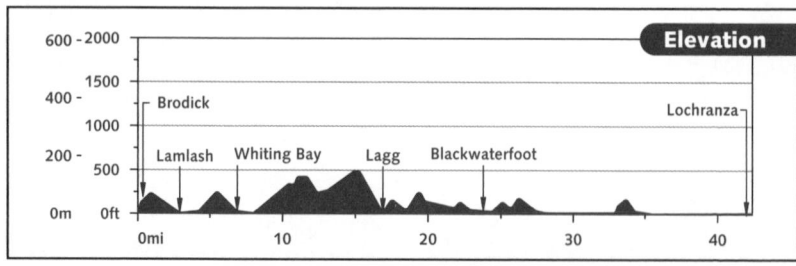

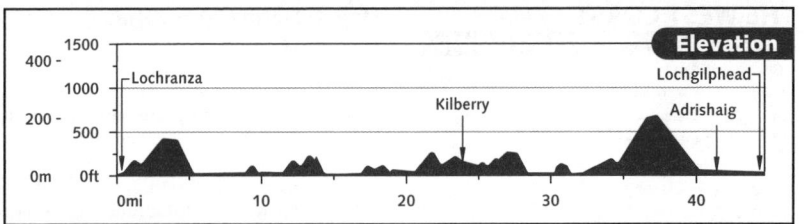

THE WEST COAST – DAY 2

CUE			GPS COORDINATES	
start		Lochranza ferry terminal	55°42′27″N	5°18′7″W
		{catch ferry to Claonaig}		
0 miles		go N on B8001		
0.1	↰	B8001 'to Tarbert'		
0.5	↱	B8001 'to Tarbert'		
1.7	▲	1.5 miles moderate climb		
5.3	↱	A83 'to Glasgow'		
10.0	↰	B8024 'to Kilberry'		
	●●↑	Heritage Centre 0.6 miles ↻		
	●●↑	Tarbert 2 miles ↻		
10.5	↰	B8024/'to Kilberry'		
12.8	▲	0.5 miles moderate climb		
20.6	▲	1.1 miles steep climb		
23.9		Kilberry	55°49′9″N	5°38′59″W
25.6	▲	1.4 miles moderate climb		
30.3	▲	760yd moderate climb		
34.6	↗	B8024		
	▲	2.7 miles moderate climb		
40.2	↰	A83 'to Glasgow'		
42.4	★	Ardrishaig		
44.3	◉↱	A83 'to Lochgilphead'		
44.7		Lochgilphead tourist office	56°2′10″N	5°25′55″W

into open, rocky country. A reasonably strenuous, undulating climb (20.6 miles) is rewarded with superb views out to sea and of Ardpatrick Point and Gigha Island to the south. After around two hours you should roll into the village of Kilberry (23.9 miles), little more than the whitewashed and red-roofed **Kilberry Inn** (☎ 01880 770223). This is a real gem whose warm welcome and renowned home-cooking make it hard to pass, especially at lunchtime.

There's little to distract you from the rousing Highland views as you follow the single track back to the coast and the A83. Fight the urge to turn back and do the whole thing again, and follow the main road into Ardrishaig. The **Crinan Canal** (42.4 miles) was cut late in the 18th century as a maritime shortcut between the Sound of Jura and Loch Fyne. There's a

lock where it intersects with the A83, but these days it's pleasure craft and fishing boats that hold up the traffic rather than the cargo vessels for which the canal was built. This amazing day of pedalling ends at Lochgilphead.

Day 3: Lochgilphead to Dalmally
3½–5 hours, 41 miles

There's easy riding, not too much traffic and lots to see in the first 10 miles through Kilmartin Glen. Traffic is lighter along the lovely, single-track B840 and there's only one serious climb before an easy run into Dalmally on busier main roads.

It's worth spending half a day covering the 10 miles (plus short side trips) along the A816. An information board (3.5 miles) describes the attractions around Kilmartin Glen, the first of which is **Dunadd**, the erstwhile focal point of the ancient kingdom of Dalriada. An access road (4.8 miles) leads to a 10-minute walk to the rocky outcrop atop which sit the remains of the fort. From the 6th to the 10th century Dunadd was home to the Scotti, a Celtic tribe who arrived from Ireland to occupy the west coast and later people the rest of Scotland. It was allegedly the location of the Stone of Destiny upon which Scottish kings and queens were crowned. The fort overlooks the 'great moss', **Moine Mhór Nature Reserve**, one of the few remaining raised peat bogs in Britain. A boardwalk through the moss extends just west of the route (side trip at 6.3 miles). Look out for the **Ballymeanoch standing stones** to the west on the way to Dunchraigaig (6.9 miles) where you'll discover a burial mound and rock carvings.

An alternative route (go left at 7.5 miles, then right 'to Slockavullin') passes more standing stones at **Lady Glassary Wood**, the **Temple Wood stone circle** and the **Nether Largie chambered cairn**.

SCOTLAND

THE WEST COAST – DAY 3

CUE		GPS COORDINATES
start	Lochgilphead tourist office	56°2'10"N 5°25'55"W
0 miles	go W on Lochnell St/A83	
0.4	A816 'to Oban'	
2.4	A816 'to Oban'	
3.5	Kilmartin Glen info board	
4.8	Dunadd Fort 900yd	
6.3	Moine Mhòr Reserve 2 miles	
(6.9	Dunchraigaig walk)	
7.5	Lady Glassary Wood 1.3 miles	
8.3	Kilmartin	56°7'58"N 5°29'8"W
9.6	Carnasserie Castle (LHS)	
9.8	B840 'to Ford'	
12.7	B840 'to Cladich', Ford	56°10'39"N 5°26'5"W
30.8	Portsonachan	56°20'25"N 5°9'16"W
32.0	0.75 miles hard climb	
34.2	'to Dalmally', Cladich	56°21'8"N 5°5'3"W
34.6	330yd steep climb	
34.7	A819 'to Oban'	
39.8	A85 'to Dalmally'	
40.9	'to Dalmally'	
41.0	Dalmally post office	56°24'8"N 4°57'50"W

It's 1.3 miles back to the main road and adds 1 mile to the route in total.

At the village of Kilmartin, the churchyard is notable for its 10th-century Celtic crosses and many medieval grave slabs. The award-winning **Kilmartin House Museum** (☎ 01546 510278) maps out one of Scotland's most important archaeological areas with audiovisual and fixed displays and is quite welcoming to cyclists. The **Glebe Cairn cafe** within the museum is open to everyone and serves morale-boosting espressos and snacks. On a hilltop north of Kilmartin rise the substantial remains of 16th-century **Carnassarie Castle** (9.6 miles) built by John Carswell, the first Protestant Bishop of the Isles.

Shortly after Carnassarie you leave the A816 and turn towards the Highlands. The low-grade road undulates gently by the side of beautiful Loch Awe (the longest in Scotland) for 19 miles, dipping through wee wooded glens and alongside bubbling burns, before climbing to meet the A819. As you approach the junction of the A819 and the A85 and the turn for Dalmally, look out for the dramatic lochside hulk of **Kilchurn Castle**. The ruins strike a quintessentially Scottish pose set against bald rounded mountains, its reverse image reflected in the mirror-smooth water.

Day 4: Dalmally to Oban
2–3 hours, 26.6 miles

This day's low mile count means you can turn down the pedal power and proceed at a slower pace to lap up the scenery. About half of today's short ride is on the busy (but otherwise pleasant and easy) A85. After that the main 'traffic' on the up-down single-track Glen Lonan Rd is four-legged. The steepest climb is a short one, followed by a winding descent into Oban. There are no services whatsoever after leaving the A85.

This is a very scenic day beginning in the mountains and then travelling along the northern shores of **Loch Awe**. Mountain views are best to the east, so it's worth stopping periodically to look back. Buried beneath Ben Cruachan (1126m/3693ft), 'the hollow mountain', is the **Cruachan hydroelectric power station** (8.4 miles). The **visitor centre** (☎ 01866 822618) runs tours underground to see what must be one of the country's most incredible feats of engineering and the attraction has won awards for its commitment to sustainable tourism and green approach. It could be worthwhile phoning ahead to make sure no maintenance work is taking place when you intend visiting. The spillway (10.9 miles) is a good spot to watch leaping salmon.

After the relative hurly-burly of the A85, the mood changes in Glen Lonan, which should perhaps be renamed 'Glen lonely'.

THE WEST COAST – DAY 4

CUE		GPS COORDINATES
start	Dalmally post office	56°24'8"N 4°57'50"W
0 miles	go E on main access road	
0.4	A83 'to Crianlarich'	
0.6	B8077 'to Stronmilchan'	
0.9	over bridge	
4.1	A85 'to Oban'	
4.7	Lochawe	
8.4	Cruachan Power Station	
14.5	Glen Lonan Rd (no sign)	
	1.9 miles moderate climb	
16.0	7 miles of cattle grids & sheep	
23.6	unsigned road	
24.0	'to Oban'	
	0.7 miles steep climb	
24.2	Rare Breeds Park	
24.7	1.2 miles steep/winding descent	
26.4	Soroba Rd/Combie St	
26.6	Argyll Square	
26.6	Oban tourist office	56°24'38"N 5°28'31"W

Its verdant rolling hills are Highland eye candy but the going can be slow with plenty of stubborn sheep to contend with, as well as the unhurried and eminently photogenic Highland cows. The last steep climb (24.2 miles) shouldn't pose too many problems before the swoop down into Oban.

Day 5: Oban to Tobermory

4–6 hours, 46.1 mlesi

There are no cycle repair workshops between Oban and Tobermory, so make sure everything is shipshape with the bike before loading it onto the ferry for the 40-minute crossing (six to eight daily) to Craignure. Weather permitting, today is scenically stunning, and with quiet, mostly single-track roads, cute villages and sandy beaches – you'll find the Isle of Mull cycling bliss.

Having disembarked in Craignure, you could take a short excursion on the dinky **Mull & West Highland Narrow Gauge Railway** (☎ 01383 728652) but as it heads in the opposite direction to the route, you'll need a return ticket and bikes are too bulky to fit in the carriages (leave them at the station). At the end of the 1.5-mile-long stretch of track lies the Scottish baronial-style **Torosay Castle** (☎ 01680 812421) set in exquisite gardens.

Heading out of Craignure the two-way A849 to Salen (10.5 miles) is easy riding with negligible amounts of traffic. Look right to admire the views across the Sound of Mull, left to gaze up at the peaks with unpronounceable Gaelic names that rise over 600m (1968ft). Just before Selen airstrip look out for the **Celtic cemetery** (9.1 miles). After Salen there are next to no services so stock up here if you didn't in Oban.

Traffic is almost nonexistent once you point your handlebars off the main road,

yet the views to the mountains across Loch na Keal and Loch Tuath are superb. Riding becomes more strenuous as the road heads northwest. The first climb (17.7 miles) is not too bad, but a swim at gorgeous and usually deserted **Calgary Beach** (32.6 miles) could be in order after working up a sweat on the second (27 miles). Calgary (33.2 miles) is barely a village, but somewhat surprisingly boasts an art gallery and a hotel.

Cutting inland, the **Old Byre Heritage Centre** (☎ 01688 400229) has exhibitions on Mull's human and natural history, a film and a welcoming tearoom. It's a 1.5-mile return side trip (37.5 miles) just before Dervaig – take the Torloisk turn-off, then the first left.

Two serious ascents rise between Dervaig and Tobermory. There's a welcome lookout (39 miles) shortly before the first summit and equally good views just be-

THE WEST COAST – DAY 5

CUE		GPS COORDINATES	
start	Oban ferry terminal	56°24'52"N	5°28'25"W
	{catch ferry to Mull}		
0 miles	go NW on A849		
0.0	Craignure	56°28'14"N	5°42'22"W
9.1	★ celtic cemetery		
11.2	↰ B8035 'to Gruline', Salen	56°31'1"N	5°56'51"W
13.7	⌐ B8073 'to Calgary'		
27.0	▲ 1.9 miles steep climb		
33.0	▲ 1.7 miles hard climb		
33.2	★ Calgary	56°34'48"N	6°16'37"W
37.5	●●⌐ Heritage Centre 1.5 miles ↻		
38.1	Dervaig	56°35'22"N	6°11'3"W
	▲ 1.4 miles hard climb		
41.0	▲ 1.2 miles steep climb		
45.1	↗ A848 'to Salen'		
45.4	↗ across river		
45.5	↰⊙ Main St		
	⚠ 650yd steep descent		
46.1	Tobermory tourist office	56°37'23"N	6°4'3"W

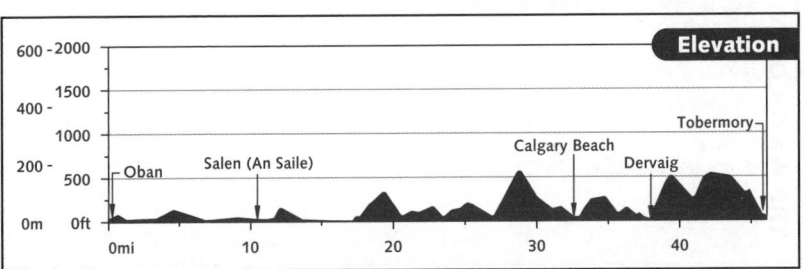

Elevation

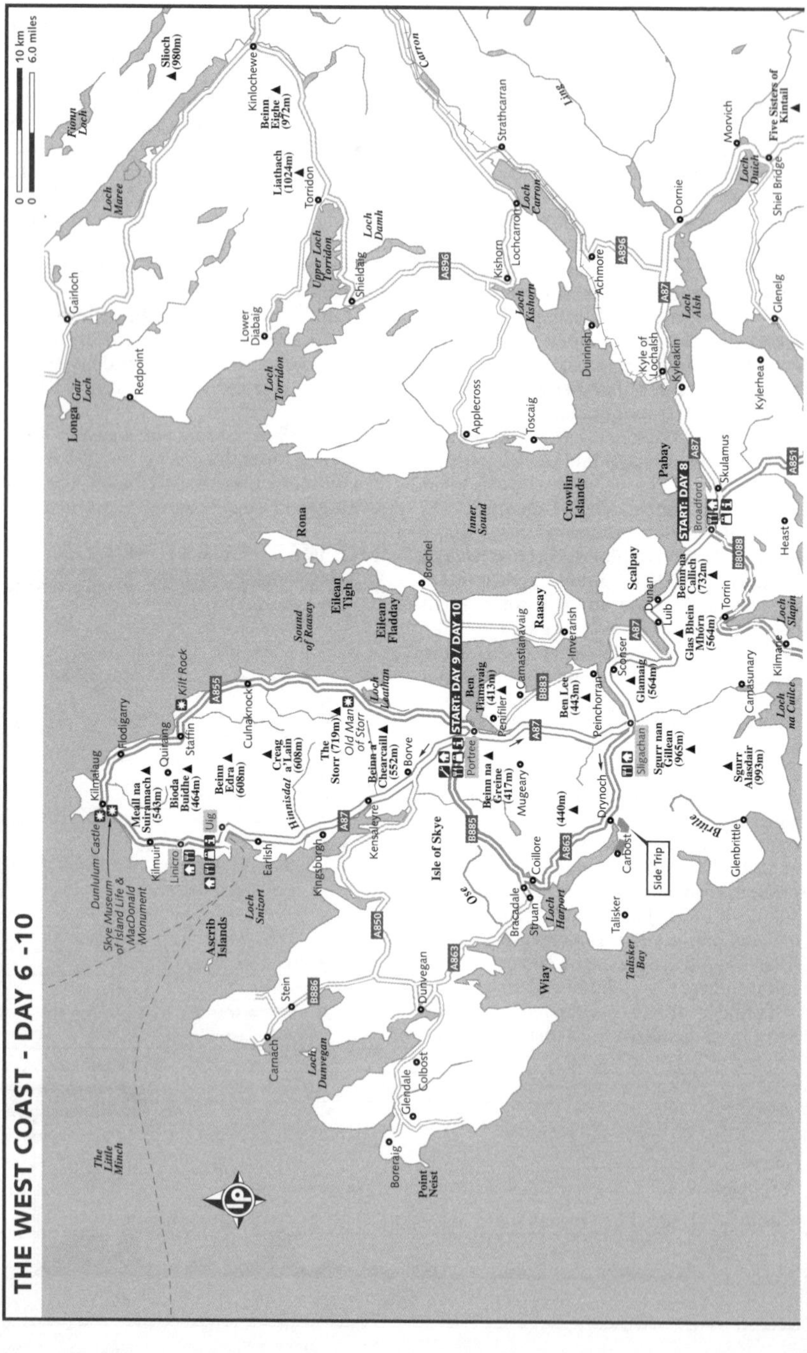

SCOTLAND

THE WEST COAST – DAY 6 -10

0 ___ **10 km**
0 ___ **6.0 miles**

Slioch (980m)

Fionn Loch

Loch Maree

Kinlochewe

Beinn Eighe (972m)

Liathach (1024m)

Torridon

Beinn Alligin (985m)

Carron

Strathcarron

Upper Loch Torridon

Shieldaig

Loch Damh

Loch Carron

Lochcarron

Achmore

Loch Kishorn

Kishorn

Morvich

Loch Duich

Five Sisters of Kintail

Gairloch

Lower Diabaig

Loch Torridon

A896

Dornie

A87

Shiel Bridge

Glenelg

Longa Gair Loch

Redpoint

Kishorn

Kyle of Lochalsh

A87

Loch Alsh

Kylerhea

Applecross

Toscaig

Duirinish

Kyleakin

A851

Kylakums

Rona

Brochel

Crowlin Islands

Inner Sound

Scalpay

Broadford

START: DAY 8

Pabay

Heast

Sound of Raasay

Eilean Tigh

Eilean Fladday

Raasay

Duirh

Beinn na Caillich (732m)

Glas Bhein Mhorn (564m)

Torrin

Loch Slapin

Kilt Rock

Flodigarry

A855

Culnaknock

Staffin

Quiraing

Loch Dubhan

Camastianavaig

START: DAY 9 / DAY 10

Raasay

Inverarish

Sconser

A87

B883

Glamaig (564m)

Ben Lee (443m)

Peinchorran

Luib

Kilmarie

Camasunary

Loch na Cuilce

Kilbride

Meall na Suiramach (543m)

Bioda Buidhe (464m)

Beinn Edra (608m)

Hisimdal (608m)

Creag a'Lain (608m)

The Storr (719m)

Old Man of Storr

Beinn a' Chearcaill (552m)

Borve

Portree

Ben Tianavaig (413m)

Peinifiler

A87

Sligachan

Sgurr nan Gillean (965m)

Sgurr Alasdair (993m)

Bràtail

Kilmuir

Uig

Linicro

Kingsburgh

Kensaleyre

Beinn na Greine (417m)

Mugeary

(440m)

Drynoch

Duntulm Castle

Skye Museum of Island Life & MacDonald Monument

Loch Snizort

Eabost

A850

Ose

Isle of Skye

Coillore

Sligachan

Side Trip

Glenbrittle

Ascrib Islands

Stein

B886

Carnach

Loch Dunvegan

Colbost

Glendale

Dunvegan

A863

Wiay

Struan

Bracadale

Sligachan

Loch Harport

Carbost

Talisker

Talisker Bay

The Little Minch

Borrg

Point Neist

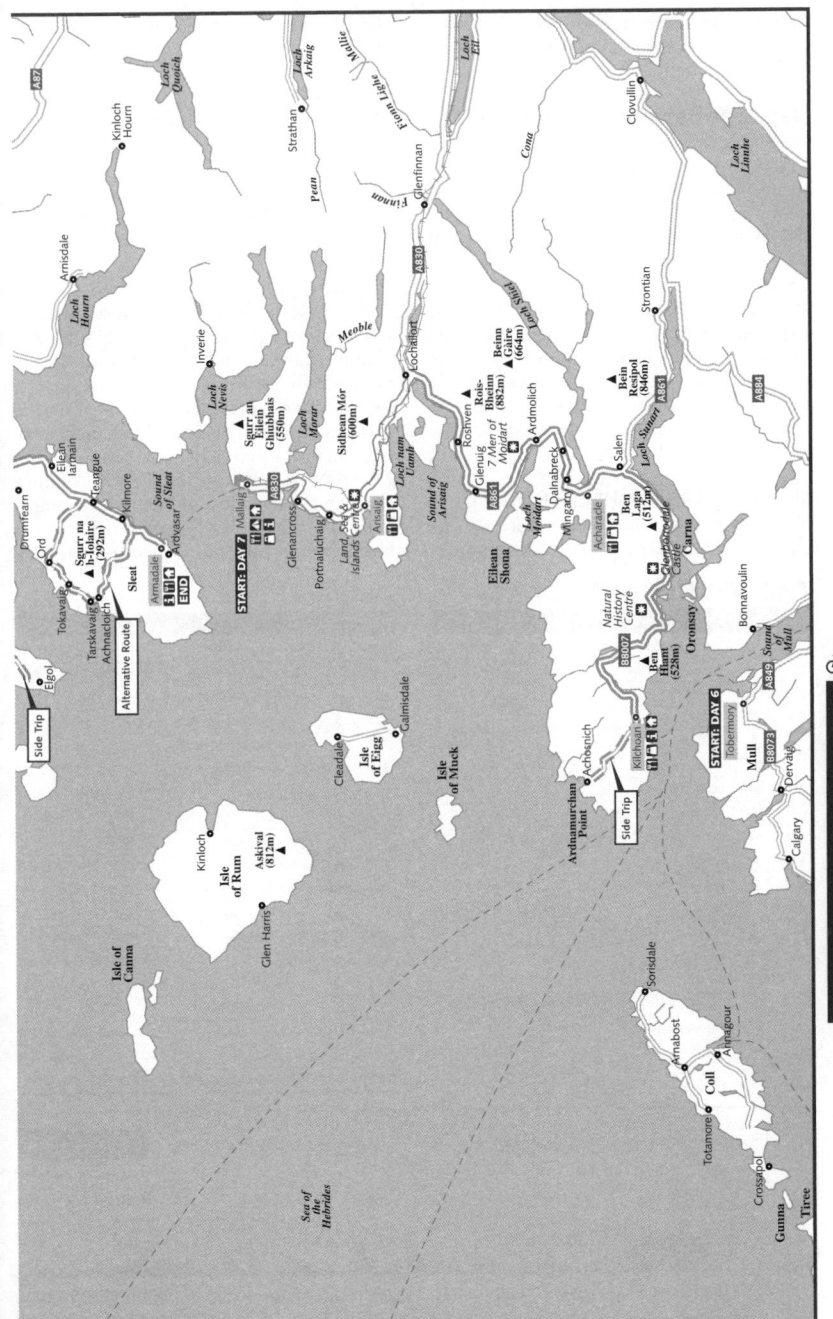

fore the top of the second. After that it's a downhill cycle slalom all the way to the sea and an overnight halt at Tobermory.

Day 6: Tobermory to Mallaig
5½–8 hours, 61.2 miles

Today, this island odyssey offers quiet roads to Lochailort through Scotland's absurdly scenic and sparsely populated 'empty quarter'. With over 60 miles to negotiate as well as numerous potential wayside halts, it's wise to catch an early ferry for the long and reasonably strenuous ride through Ardnamurchan (Calmac Ferries depart Tobermory from 7.20am, 10am Sunday). The day's serious climbing comes in the ride's first half and traffic increases somewhat when you turn onto the A830 to Mallaig, aka the road to the Isles.

SIDE TRIP: ARDNAMURCHAN POINT
No sooner have you come ashore at Kilchoan than a side trip beckons. **Ardnamur-**

chan Point is the British mainland's most westerly point, seven rolling miles west of the ferry on a coarse track. The strikingly lonely **lighthouse complex** (☎ 01972 510210) contains an interactive museum exhibition in the former head keeper's house and there's a cafe with seating indoors and out. It's well worth making the 14-mile round trip, but with over 60 miles to go to Mallaig, consider whether you're up to such an extended day in the saddle, especially if the sky looks ready to drop.

The road is forced inland just south of Kilchoan by **Ben Hiant** (528m/1732ft), Ardnamurchan's highest mountain, which sits dramatically on the shores of Loch Sunart. Settled by families for thousands of years, the surrounding fertile volcanic soils now support mainly sheep and cattle, following the eviction of families during the 18th-century Highland Clearances. Riding is surprisingly hard along the shore of Loch Sunart so you'll be glad of a breather at the **Natural History**

THE WEST COAST – DAY 6

CUE			GPS COORDINATES	
start		Tobermory ferry terminal	56°37'23"N	6°3'48"W
		{catch ferry to Kilchoan}		
0 miles		go NW on B8007		
0.9	⌐	B8007 'to Salen'		
	▲	3.2 miles moderate climb		
●●	↰	Ardnamurchan Pt 14 miles ↻		
4.2	↗	B8007 'to Salen'		
6.7	▲	750yd moderate climb		
11.0	★	Natural History Centre		
12.8	★	Glenborrodale Castle		
15.4	▲	650yd steep climb		
20.3		Salen	56°42'54"N	5°46'49"W
	▲	0.9 miles moderate climb		
20.5	↰	A861 'to Acharacle'		
	⚠	9.4 miles single-track road		
22.4		Acharacle	56°44'54"N	5°48'9"W
23.4	↗	A861 'to Lochailort'		
23.7	↘	A861		

CUE			GPS COORDINATES	
23.9	↗	A861 'to Lochailort'		
24.4		Mingarry	56°45'17"N	5°48'9"W
25.3	★	Illegal Moidart Museum		
26.5	▲	1.2 miles moderate climb		
29.9	★	7 Men of Moidart Memorial		
31.4	▲	1.5 miles steep climb		
33.3		Glenuig	56°49'44"N	5°49'10"W
42.1		Lochailort	56°52'41"N	5°40'0"W
42.3	↰	A830 'to Mallaig'		
42.8	▲	1.1 miles gradual climb		
46.0	★	Prince Charlie's cairn		
46.4	▲	1.1 miles gradual climb		
51.4	↘	A830 'to Mallaig'		
51.6	★	Arisaig	56°54'39"N	5°50'33"W
51.8	▲	0.75 miles steep climb		
57.2	▲	200yd steep climb		
57.6	⌐ ◎	A830 'to Mallaig'		
61.1	⌐ ◎	'to town centre'		
61.2		Mallaig tourist office	57°0'21"N	5°49'44"W

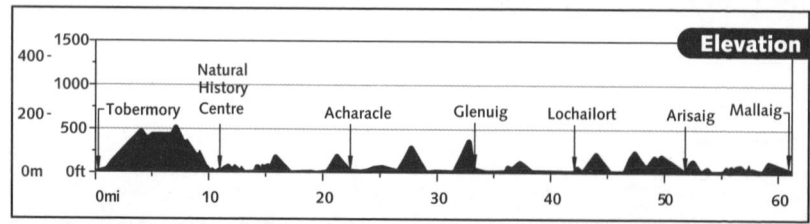

Centre (11 miles; ☎ 01972 500209) where you can grab a snack or lunch at the Antler Tearoom. A little further on, tall **Glenborrodale Castle** (12.8 miles) was once owned by Jesse Boot, pharmacist and founder of the Boots chemist chain, but is now a luxury hotel.

Acharacle (22.4 miles) offers some respite from the wilderness with a few shops and cafes. Your next brief stop should be on Loch Moidart at the memorial to the **Seven Men of Moidart** (29.9 miles) who joined Bonnie Prince Charlie in the ill-fated 1745 uprising. The local MacDonald clan were some of the Prince's strongest supporters.

Riding is easier along the sublime Loch Ailort and the road to the Isles, though there'll be more cars nosing past you from behind. Bonnie Prince Charlie's arrival and departure point in 1745–46 was at Loch nam Uamh and there's a cairn (46 miles) marking the start of a walk to the place he made his escape in 1746. Local natural and social history is the theme of Arisaig's **Land, Sea & Islands Centre** (☎ 01687 450263). Between here and Mallaig extend exquisite stretches of beach known as the 'Silver Sands of Morar', a fine place to camp.

Day 7: Mallaig to Broadford
1½–2½ hours, 27.5 miles

A 30-minute ferry hop from Mallaig to Armadale (see Day 10 p282 at the end of this ride for details about Armadale) and you've arrived on **Skye**, the most illustrious and evocative name in the Scottish Island phonebook. Armadale is at the end of the Sleat Peninsula, wooded and less rugged than other parts of the island and containing most of Skye's tallest and rarest trees. As you leave Armadale you'll notice that most of the road signs on Skye are printed in tongue-twisting Gaelic as well as English, as it's spoken by half the island's residents. There's even a Gaelic-language college a couple of miles from Armadale pier.

ALTERNATIVE ROUTE: VIA THE ORD ROAD

The easy, short run from Armadale to Broadford is interrupted with a more challenging and scenic section by detouring via the hilly (but virtually traffic-free) Ord Rd to the western side of the Sleat Peninsula (pronounced 'slate'). It offers magnificent views of the Sound of Sleat to the east and the Cuillins mountain range to the west but beware of the cattle grids.

Traffic is naturally busiest on the A851 at ferry times but it's quiet otherwise, leaving you to enjoy the quick trip up the coast then inland. The last 9 miles of the A851 is a new two-lane road, but parts of the pleasant old road (adjacent) are still accessible to bicycles (keep an eye out for access points). The final 1.5 miles to Broadford are via the relatively busy A87. If you haven't taken the alternative route via Ord, you'll be in Broadford in plenty of time for high tea.

Day 8: Broadford to Portree
3½–5½ hours, 42.1 miles

Skye's famous Cuillin Mountains may dominate the skyline, but the busy A87 remains relatively flat until Sligachan (18.6 miles). Escape the traffic at least briefly by taking the coastal Moll Rd (8.6 miles). The A863

THE WEST COAST – DAY 7

CUE		GPS COORDINATES	
start	Mallaig tourist office	57°0'21"N	5°49'44"W
0 miles	go N on Harbour View		
0.1	↱ 'to ferry'		
	{catch ferry to Armadale}		
0.3	go W on A851		
0.7	↘ A851, Armadale		
2.4	↰ 'to Achnacloich'		
	▲ 2.5 miles hard climb		
7.6	▲ 7.3 miles undulating terrain		
16.0	↰ A851		
26.0	↰ A87 'to Broadford', Skulamus		
27.5	Broadford tourist office	57°14'28"N	5°54'32"W

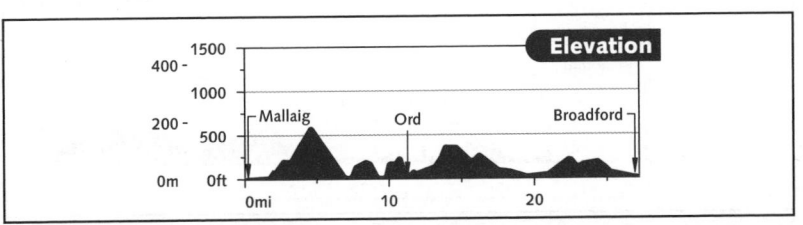

from Sligachan is considerably quieter than the A87, yet still A-road in character with relatively fast traffic and gentler gradients. In contrast, the B885 to Portree (31.8 miles) is single-track, lightly trafficked, winding and constantly undulating with some steeper grades in places.

SIDE TRIP: ELGOL (EALAGHOL)
2½–4 hours, 31 miles (RTN)

To flee the traffic on Skye means getting off the main roads, which generally involves returning via your outward route. In any case, the marvellous mountain scenery on the single-track Elgol Rd is worth seeing in both directions.

Take the Elgol Rd/B8083, 240 yards west of Broadford tourist office, and follow it through pleasant crofting countryside to Elgol. There are a couple of hills but nothing too taxing, except for the very steep first mile of the return journey from the Elgol wharf. Elgol has a shop, a tearoom and usually a waiting fish and chip van. If Elgol takes your fancy you can stay the night at **Coruisk House** (☎ 01471 866330; B&B £37.50) at the narrow end of town.

Closer to Broadford the skyline is dominated by the smooth slopes of the 'red hills'. The striking jagged black peaks that come into view around the village of Torrin and Loch Slapin are exquisite, but it's at the end of the road, right down at the Elgol wharf, that the spectacular Cuillin Range is best viewed.

Sligachan is a possible base from which to explore the Cuillins but apart from the bustling **Sligachan Hotel** (☎ 01478 650207), which caters mainly to climbers and walkers, there's not much else here, or anywhere for that matter until Portree. At Sligachan you could take the lazy option and head straight along the A87 into Por-

tree, but with plenty of time till sundown taking the long way round pays dividends of the scenic type.

SIDE TRIP: CARBOST & THE TALISKER DISTILLERY

Skye's only whisky producer is the **Talisker Distillery** (☎ 01478 640314) maker of an alluring, sweet, full-bodied single malt. The property has dramatic views of the Cuillins and is a short side trip away at Carbost (go left at 24.2 miles and follow the B8009) in a pretty crofting valley around Loch Harport. It involves some short hills and affords more excellent views of the Red and Black Cuillins. The fascinating tours include a free 70cl bottle of whisky and a taste of the 10-year-old single malt. After this, Skye may be hard to leave, in every sense of the word.

At Coillore take the lonely and sometimes rough B885, which passes along valleys and climbs through forests to end at Portree around 12 miles later.

THE WEST COAST – DAY 8

CUE			GPS COORDINATES	
start		Broadford tourist office	57°14'28"N	5°54'32"W
0 miles		go W on A87		
0.1	●● ↰	Elgol 31 miles ↺		
8.6	↱	'to Mol/Moll'		
14.5	⚠	quarry blasting		
15.0	↱	A87		
18.6		Sligachan	57°17'22"N	6°10'27"W
18.8	↰	A863 'to Dunvegan'		
19.9	▲	1.1 miles gradual climb		
24.2	●● ↰	Talisker Distillery 5.5 miles ↺		
	▲	1.9 miles gradual climb		
31.8	↱	B885 'to Portree'		
24.2	▲	2.1 miles hard hill		
37.6	▲	600yd moderate climb		
41.5	↱	A87 'to town centre'		
41.8	↘	'to town centre'		
42.1		Portree tourist office	57°24'43"N	6°11'36"W

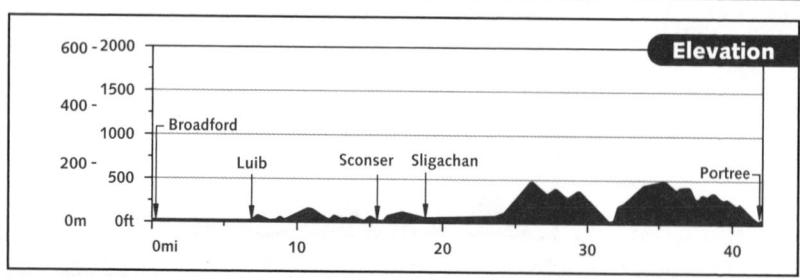

Day 9: Portree to Portree
4–6 hours, 49.7 miles

Skye's lonely Trotternish Peninsula offers some dramatic scenery north of Uig and particularly along the west coast. Traffic is reasonably light on this circular ride, especially after the Dunvegan turn-off (4.2 miles). Gradient junkies get their fix of climbs in the second half of the day.

Things just tick along nicely accompanied by views across the oddly-named Loch Snizort Beag until Uig (15.5 miles) the main settlement on the peninsula's west coast. Ferries to the Outer Hebrides leave from here and there are good views of these far-flung islands following the climb out of the village.

One place you should definitely squeeze the brakes is the unmissable **Skye Museum of Island Life** (22 miles; ☎ 01470 552206) at Kilmuir where the late 19th-century traditional crofting lifestyle has been dipped in formaldehyde. A group of shaggy thatch and stone cottages conceal peaty period interiors complete with household implements and somewhat unconvincing dummies in traditional Skye clobber. It's a fascinating place giving an insight into a way of life much more in tune with these harsh surroundings than that of today's islanders. A **monument** to Flora MacDonald (who helped Bonnie Prince Charles escape his defeat at the Battle of Culloden) strands in a nearby cemetery.

There are few services until Staffin (31.6 miles), but it's worth stopping for delicious homemade food at **Whitewave** (☎ 01470 542414) in Linicro (19.9 miles), a small cafe and outdoor centre that also does folk music, and offers B&B. With bellies full, more exploration awaits at 23.4 miles in the shape of **Dunlulum Castle** (three minutes' walk from the road), or at least its ruins, which command a strategic cliff top position looking out to sea and the Outer Hebrides.

It's a stark landscape around the peaty moors of the peninsula's northern end and at Flodigarry (28.4 miles), site of Flora MacDonald's home, brooding grey cliffs stand like a fort to the west, the weather-worn folds in the rock like the rouched skirts of austere Victorian aunts. After Staffin (32.2 miles) the ups become more serious, but the stunning scenery continues all the way back to Portree. Give the gears a breather to see spectacular **Kilt Rock** (a short aside at 34.3 miles) and look out for the dramatic obelisks of the **Old Man of Storr** (41.7 miles), which overlooks photogenic **Loch Leathan** (43.5 miles). The snaking **Island of Raasay** to the east comes into sharper focus as the end of the day at Portree looms.

THE WEST COAST – DAY 9

CUE			GPS COORDINATES	
start		Portree tourist office	57°24'43"N	6°11'36"W
0 miles		go W on Bridge Rd		
0.3	⌐►	Dunvegan Rd/A87 'to Uig'		
0.6	▲	2.8 miles gradual climb		
4.2	◄↗	A87 'to Uig'		
15.2	⌐►	A855 'to Staffin'		
15.5		Uig		
15.8	⌐►	A855 'to Staffin'		
15.9	▲	0.9 miles moderate climb		
22.0	★	museum & monument		
24.0	★	Duntulum Castle		
27.6		Flodigarry	57°39'45"N	6°15'30"W
31.0	↘	A855		
32.2		Staffin	57°37'35"N	6°12'22"W
32.5	▲	0.8 miles moderate climb		
33.7	●●⌐┐	Kilt Rock 200yd ↺		
37.7	▲	1.2 miles moderate climb		
40.7	▲	1.1 miles moderate climb		
49.6	┐	Bank St		
	⌐►	(100yd) Bridge Rd		
49.7		Portree tourist office	57°24'43"N	6°11'36"W

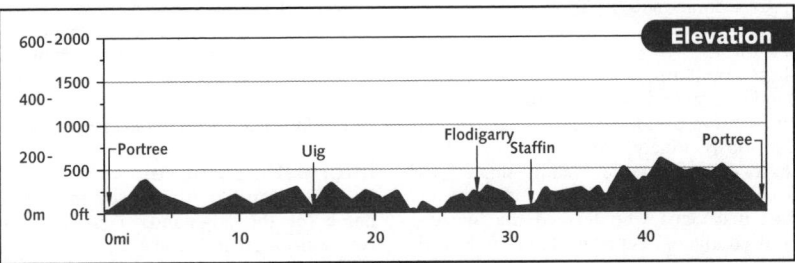

Elevation

Flodigarry
Staffin
Portree
Uig
Portree

THE WEST COAST – DAY 10

CUE		GPS COORDINATES	
start	Portree tourist office	57°24'43"N	6°11'36"W
0 miles	go W on Bridge Rd		
0.3	↘ A87 'to Kyleakin'		
3.0	▲ 4.3 miles gradual climb		
9.6	Sligachan	57°17'19"N	6°10'33"W
13.5	▲ 2.3 miles moderate climb		
26.4	Broadford		
	{retrace Day 7 route to Armadale}		
37.9	↑ A85		
43.4	Armadale Pier	57°3'52"N	5°53'42"W

Day 10: Portree to Armadale

3¼–5½ hours, 43.4 miles

Today is all about the return trip to Armadale via the A87. The route is straightforward, the riding easy (but with more traffic) and the navigator can have a day off. There's a long, gradual climb to 113m (371ft) after leaving Portree, but otherwise it's a pretty unmemorable road until the descent into Sligachan when moors and mountains begin to huddle around you.

Though the Moll Rd detour (at 13.5 miles) is a more enjoyable option, the most direct route between Sligachan and Broadford is to stick to the A87, but this involves a moderate ascent to 130m (426ft). Likewise, between Broadford and Armadale stay on the A85 instead of detouring through Ord.

HIGHLANDS CIRCUIT

Duration 3 days
Distance 126.8 miles
Difficulty moderate
Start/Finish Killin

Summary Let the lonely single-track high road guide you on this loop around the deep lochs, remote glens and ancient rounded mountains of Britain's most celebrated wilderness.

The mountains, lochs and glens of Scotland's Highlands combine to create Britain's most dramatically picturesque and gloriously lonely landscape, crossed by traffic-free and cycle friendly single-track roads. Once a stronghold of the famous tartaned clans who farmed the hillsides and conducted centuries-long feuds with their neighbours, the region's now peaceful, back-of-beyond atmosphere makes it ideal for adventurous and unhurried cyclists. This three-day circuit takes in three scenic lochs, the oldest tree in Europe, Scotland's longest and loneliest glen, plus a village so happening they named it Dull.

ENVIRONMENT

The National Trust for Scotland administers Ben Lawers' Nature Reserve, 6 miles north of Killin, which is also home to some rare alpine flora. A stand of ancient Caledonian Pine forest can be seen at the Black Wood of Rannoch just west of the Rannoch School (see Day 2 p285). Other things to watch out for include birds of prey, red deer, squirrels and pine martens in forested areas. Salmon and trout are found in the region's lochs and rivers, and one of the most quintessentially Scottish sights is of salmon flicking their way up the Pitlochry fish ladder.

PLANNING
When to Cycle

Ride between May and September, as the area is at its best during summer, especially later in the season when heather turns the moors a deep purple. Beware of grouse and deer hunting from mid-August to October if you're heading off-road, though it's extremely rare for a hunter to bag a cyclist by mistake.

What to Bring

Forget weatherproof gear or a good midge-repellent containing DEET or DMP at your peril, especially if you're camping. The earlier in spring or the later in autumn you arrive, the more pieces of warm attire you'll need.

Maps

The ride falls on the boundaries of the OS Travel Map – Road 1:250,000 *Northern Scotland* (sheet 1) and *Southern Scotland* (sheet 3). Perhaps better (and essential for mountain biking or walking) are OS Explorer 1:25,000 *Ben Lawers & Glen Lyon* (sheet 378), *Rannoch Moor & Ben Alder* (sheet 385) and *Pitlochry & Loch Tummel* (sheet 386).

Information Sources

Visit Highlands is the trendy marketing name for the Highlands Tourist Board (www.visithighlands.com) whose website is packed with ideas.

GETTING TO/FROM THE RIDE
Killin (start)
TRAIN
The **Scotrail** (☎ 0845 601 5929, www
.firstgroup.com/scotrail) West Highland
Line from Glasgow to Oban/Mallaig stops
at lonely Crianlarich station (£20.70; 1¾
hours, three daily). From Crianlarich to Killin it's an easy 14-mile ride. Go north from
the station and turn right (east) onto the
busy A85, signed 'to Perth'. Take the A827
(left) to Killin at 11.6 miles. The Breadalbane Centre and tourist office is on the left
after crossing the bridge into Killin.

BICYCLE
Killin to Perth is around 47 miles – go via
Lochearnhead (south of Lock Earn to St
Fillans) and Crieff, turning right ('to Mad-
derty') near the top of the hill. The minor
road rejoins the busy A84 just before Perth.
Perth is connected to Edinburgh by train
(£12.20; one hour 20 minutes, hourly). This
ride can be linked up from the end of the
West Coast ride by catching the train from
Mallaig to Crianlarich (£27.70; three hours
20 minutes, three daily).

THE RIDE
Day 1: Killin to Kinloch Rannoch
3–4½ hours, 33.4 miles
Today begins with the quiet, single-track
road along the southern shore of Loch Tay,
the second half, via the slightly busier B846,
heads over the shoulder of Schiehallion before a cracking descent through the heather
to Loch Rannoch.

The undulating, road that hugs the line
of Loch Tay dips and dives for 16.8 miles to
the town of Kenmore, passing little human
habitation and no cars en route. The surprisingly strenuous riding is tempered by
the magnificent Highland scenery, which

opens up around you. Look out for squirrels and other critters in the shady woods or
the other way to admire the gently curving
profile of the loch. **Ben Lawers**, Scotland's
ninth-highest peak rises above the loch
on the northern side, a dusting of snow
remaining on the very summit until late
spring.

If you've never heard of a 'crannog', all
will be explained at the intriguing **Scottish Crannog Centre** (16.4 miles; ☎ 01887
830583) where a reconstructed Iron Age
defensive homestead (a *crannog*) built on
lochs throughout Scotland, Ireland and
Scandinavia as long as 5000 years ago is
displayed

You should reach **Kenmore** (16.8 miles)
at the eastern end of the loch in around two
hours with stops. As the main settlement on
this part of the route, it's the best place to
refuel your legs with much needed calories
and carbs. The bar at the **Kenmore Hotel**
(☎ 01887 830205) is one option where you

HIGHLANDS CIRCUIT – DAY 1

CUE		GPS COORDINATES	
start	Killin tourist office	56°27'57"N	4°19'8"W
0 miles	go S over bridge		
0.1	↗↑↰ 'to South Loch Tay' (dogleg)		
7.6	▲ 0.75 miles steep climb		
12.3	▲ 400yd moderate climb		
15.1	Acharn	56°34'11"N	4° 1'38"W
{16.4	★ Crannog Centre}		
16.7	↘ 'to Killin'		
16.8	Kenmore	56°35'4"N	4° 0'2"W
17.3	↰ 'to Kinloch Rannoch'		
19.8	↰ B846 'to Kinloch Rannoch'		
20.4	▲ 4 miles moderate climb		
24.2	↰ Schiehallion Rd		
26.4	★ Maskelyn cairn		
32.6	↙ unsigned descent		
33.4	Kinloch Rannoch village square	56°42'2"N	4°11'14"W

SCOTLAND

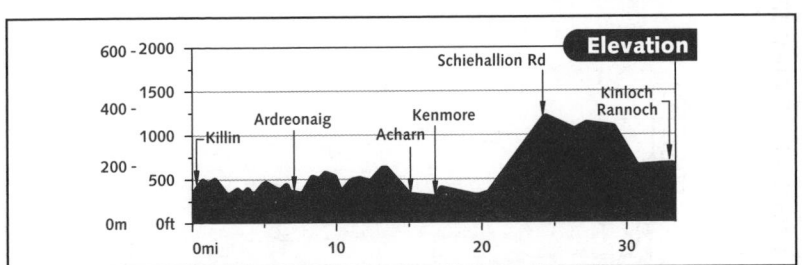

Elevation chart showing landmarks: Killin, Ardreonaig, Acharn, Kenmore, Schiehallion Rd, Kinloch Rannoch. Vertical axis in metres (0m–600) and feet (0ft–2000), horizontal axis in miles (0mi–30).

HIGHLANDS CIRCUIT

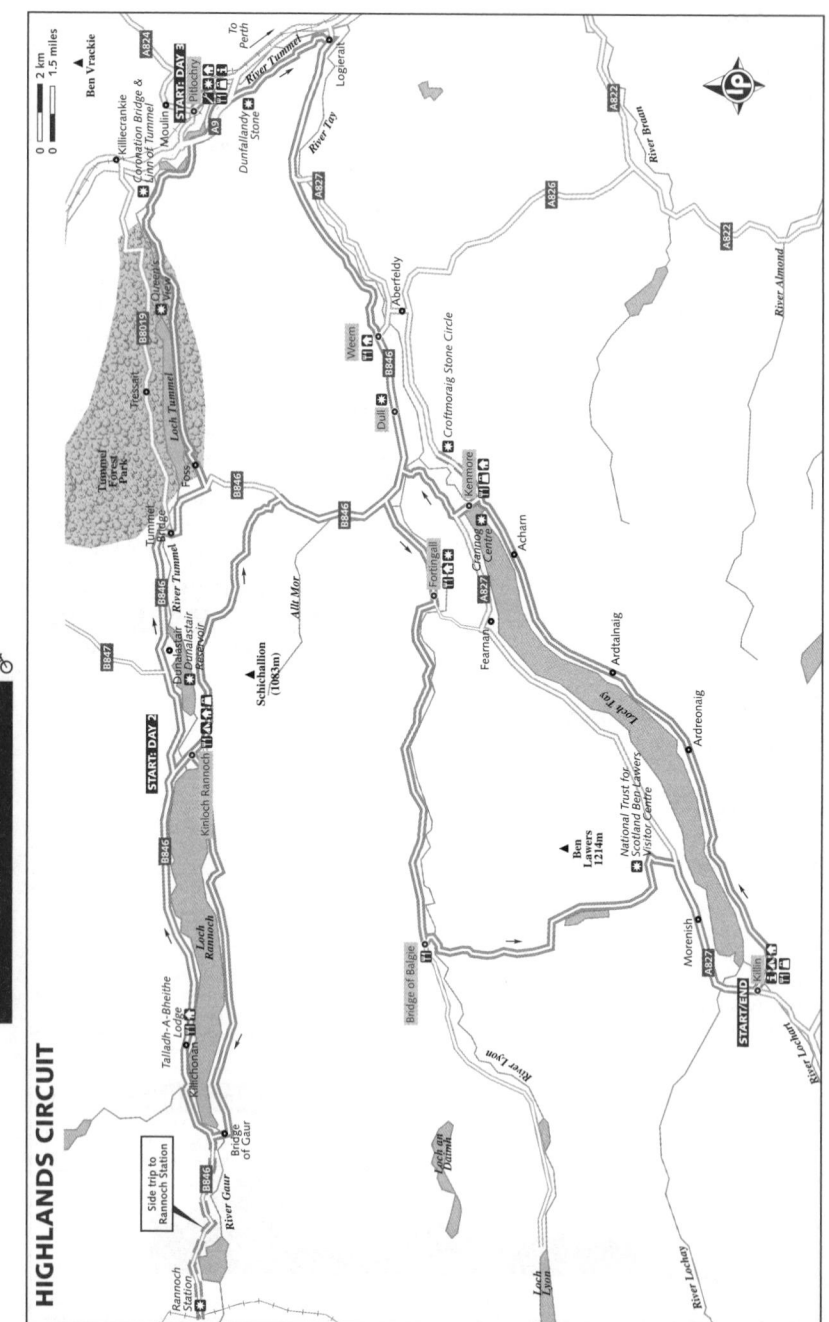

can enjoy sandwiches or a full-blown meal while you check out the Burns poem in the bar, allegedly written onto the wall by the man himself. If stone circles get you giddy, make a short side trip of the route to the **Croftmoraig Stone Circle**, 1.5 miles along the A827 from where it meets the single track road just outside Kenmore. It's one of the most complete examples in Scotland, only excavated in the 1960s.

With a satisfied belly there's not much to detain you in Kenmore save for the views down Loch Tay, so it's back into the saddle for, 4-mile climb up the shoulder of Schiehallion. Towards the end of the ascent to almost 400m (1312ft) things become more desolate. A cairn 2.2 miles along the Schiehallion Rd commemorates the Reverend Nevil Maskelyn, an astronomer who used Schiehallion's symmetry to calculate the earth's mass (but don't ask us how). Coming off Schiehallion, your efforts on the ascent are rewarded with a steep swoop down past Loch Tummel and into the tiny village of Kinloch Rannoch.

Day 2: Kinloch Rannoch to Pitlochry
3½–5½ hours, 45.4 miles

Kick off today with a gentle, untaxing 23-mile circuit of Loch Rannoch, followed by some climbing with several sheer ascents but none that last too long. You may run into a bit of traffic during the second half of the day, especially between Kinloch Rannoch and the village of Tummel Bridge (30.4 miles), but no services. You'll probably end up having lunch where you had breakfast, in Kinloch Rannoch around halfway through the ride.

Now virtually uninhabited save for a handful of modest dwellings on the north shore, the land cupping Loch Rannoch was once home to eight different clans – who, it would seem, were less than friendly. **Clan Trail** information boards (beginning at 0.6 miles) around the loch illustrate the lifestyle of these people for whom murdering their neighbours and engaging in all sorts of Highland mayhem seems to have been a lifestyle choice.

Thankfully peace reigns here now and you are left, unmolested by kilted axemen, to admire the beautiful views the loch's south side offers. The building of the once exclusive Rannoch School (5.2 miles), which closed in 2002, is one of only a small number on this side.

HIGHLANDS CIRCUIT – DAY 2

CUE		GPS COORDINATES	
start	Kinloch Rannoch village square	56°42′2″N	4°11′14″W
0 miles	go S over bridge		
0.1 ⌐►	'to south Loch Rannoch'		
5.2 ★	Rannoch School		
12.0 ⌐►	B846 'to Kinloch Rannoch'		
●●⌐↰	Rannoch Station 10 miles ↺		
16.2	Talladh-A-Bheithe Lodge		
23.2 ↰	B846, Kinloch Rannoch	56°42′0″N	4°11′26″W
25.9 ↑	'to Tummel Bridge'		
26.4 ▲	850yd steep climb		
31.1 ▲	1.2 miles moderate climb		
32.4 ↰	'to Foss'		
36.9 ▲	440yd gradual climb		
37.6 ▲	550yd steep climb		
39.6 ▲	550yd steep climb		
40.4 ⚠	800yd steep descent		
41.1 ★	Coronation Bridge walk		
41.5 ★	Lin of Tummel walk		
43.8 ↰	thru gate to bikepath		
44.0 ⌐►	thru gap in fence on bikepath		
44.3 ↘	join Foss Rd		
44.9 ↗	Bridge Rd		
45.1 ↰	'to Pitlochry'		
45.4	Pitlochry tourist office	56°42′5″N	3°43′47″W

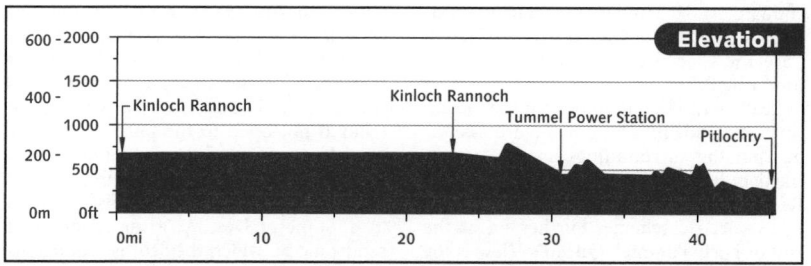

Elevation

Kinloch Rannoch · Kinloch Rannoch · Tummel Power Station · Pitlochry

HIGHLANDS CIRCUIT – DAY 3

CUE			GPS COORDINATES	
start	Pitlochry tourist office	56°42'5"N	3°43'47"W
0 miles	go E on Atholl Rd		
0.4	⌐	Bridge Rd 'to Forab'		
0.6	⌐↑	'to Logierait'		
1.1	★	Dunfallandy Stone		
4.9	⌐	A827 'to Aberfeldy', Longierait	56°39'15"N	3°42'58"W
7.8	⌐	'to Pitnacree'		
8.6		Strathtay	56°39'35"N	3°47'4"W
8.7	↑⌐	'to Weem' (dogleg)		
14.2	⤢	B846 'to Kinloch Rannoch'		
14.5		Weem	56°37'32"N	3°52'57"W
16.6	●●⌐	Dull 0.5 miles ↺		
19.0	⌐↑	'to Fortingall'		
21.8	★	Fortingall	56°35'52"N	4°3'32"W
22.4	⌐	'to Glen Lyon'		
26.7	▲	6.4 miles moderate climb		
33.8	⌐↑	'to Killin' (over bridge)		
	▲	4.5 miles moderate climb		
41.1	★	NTS visitor centre		
43.1	⤢	'to A827' (no sign)		
43.2	⌐	A827		
48.0		Killin tourist office	56°27'57"N	4°19'8"W

SIDE TRIP: RANNOCH STATION

This great side trip (at 12 miles) passes the glassy surface of small Loch Eigheach, where you'll discover Rannoch Station on the edge of wild Rannoch Moor (10 miles RTN). This is one of Britain's most remote train stations, which straddles the six-train-a-day West Highland Railway between Glasgow and Mallaig. At almost 1000m (3280ft) up and with nothing around it, the station feels like some far-flung outpost of the Trans-Siberian Railway serving nowhere in particular. Magic. Between March and October a tearoom and shop welcome curious visitors and the odd passenger.

The north bank of Loch Rannoch is more open and dotted with tiny sandy beaches where you can take a plunge if you're brave enough. At 16.2 miles, the gracious **Talladh-A-Bheithe Lodge** (☎ 01882 633203), once the Clan Menzies hunting lodge, is now a B&B.

Leaving Kinloch Rannoch for the second time, the pedalling becomes more strenuous but the surroundings are no less attractive. En route you'll pass **Dunalastair Reservoir**, part of the Tummel Garry hydro-electric scheme. Further on at the end of Loch Tummel, **Queen's View** is the

spot Queen Victoria viewed the loch during a tour of Scotland in 1866. The view from the lightly trafficked south bank is also pretty special.

One of the most spectacular sections of today's ride is the descent through the gorge to Pitlochry. Short five-minute walks to the **Coronation Bridge** (41.1 miles) spanning the River Tummel, and the **Linn of Tummel** (41.5 miles), a set of rocky rapids, provide opportunities to linger. Approaching Pitlochry, the route passes under the A9 and navigation becomes complicated. After 600 yards follow the bike signs left and through a gate onto a bikepath that leads to the town's access road.

Day 3: Pitlochry to Killin
4–6 hours, 48 miles

Initially undulating, today soon flattens out along the wide Tay Valley. Apart from a brief busy stretch after Logierait (4.9 miles) traffic is not intrusive. The highlight is the climb through beautiful Glen Lyon (22.4 miles), Scotland's longest and, some say, loneliest glen, and over the shoulder of Ben Lawers. The steady but mostly gentle (at least until the final 4.5 miles) ascent is lightly trafficked and gloriously scenic. (Note that wild camping is restricted through Glen Lyon).

Pedal just over a mile out of Pitlochry to view the ancient Pictish carvings of the **Dunfallandy Stone**. This 9th-century Christian symbol stone bears a cross surrounded by strange zoomorphic creatures and even elephants.

The names of some tiny Tay Valley villages will have you chuckling as you roll along. **Weem** (14.5 miles) is deliciously whimsical, Blairish might have once been topical, but **Dull** (16.6 miles) takes the shortbread, and road signs pointing the way to this tiny settlement provide an amusing photo opportunity. Appropriately, not a lot goes down in Dull, a place that's thought to have once been the de facto capital of Perthshire as the location of the area's first church. The small, unassuming kirk (church not open to the public) is visible from the main road, but better seen on a wee detour (0.5 miles return) through the village. Some claim that Dull also held the 'real' Stone of Destiny, a carved block of sandstone on which the Scottish monarchs

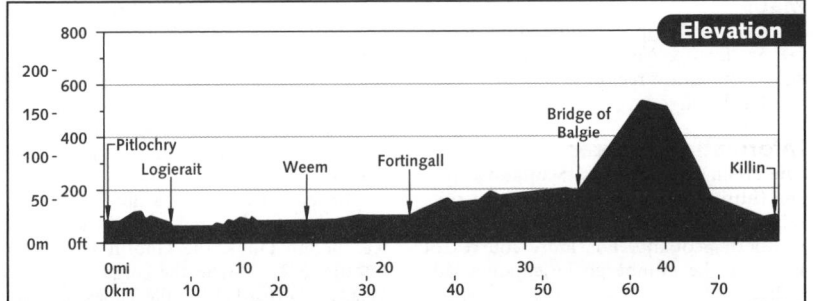

placed their feet during the coronation, and which was famously stolen on Christmas Eve 1950 from Westminster Abbey.

After around two hours you should arrive at the charcterful village of **Fortingall** (21.8 miles), famous for the **3000-year-old yew**, probably the oldest tree in Europe, which stands in the churchyard. Fortingall is virtually the last chance for a meal before plunging into the isolation of gorgeous **Glen Lyon**. This spectacular glen is one of Scotland's finest with peaks rising up above the road and river on both sides and burns tumbling down off the hillsides. Past Bridge of Balgie break the descent into Killin at the **National Trust** for Scotland **Ben Lawers Visitor Centre** (41.1 miles; ☎ 01567 820 397) where you can learn about the natural history of the surrounding Munros.

SCOTTISH BORDERS

Duration 3 days
Distance 125.6 miles
Difficulty moderate
Start/Finish Edinburgh (p294)

Summary From *burgh* to *burgh* this borderland hill circuit through once troubled Walter Scott country takes you to abbey ruins, stately homes and monuments to Scotland's good and great, before the return to Edinburgh's urban pleasures

The traffic-free B-roads and colourful market towns of the area – only an hour's pedalling from the capital – make the Borders between Edinburgh and England just the deal for a bit of carefree cycle touring. Somewhat unjustly, the region is often

passed over by travellers en route to the more obvious hotspots in the Highlands and islands further north. But here, in the big-space southern Lowlands with their bulging rounded hills, pine forests and stocky stone-built abbeys and *burghs* (a local word for town), the scenery is just as inspiring and history weighs down perhaps more heavily on the passing cyclist than in other more in-vogue bits of Alba.

ENVIRONMENT

Scotland and England are thought to have been part of separate continents until they collided around 400 million years ago (as they have many times since in a different way), bringing about the formation of the Southern Uplands. While 16% of the Borders are covered in forest, much is plantation timber with only a tiny proportion of the original ancient woodland remaining. Forest conservation laws were passed here as early as the 14th century. Other important local ecosystems include bogs rich in plant life and insects, and flower-filled grasslands. In the uplands heather-covered moors are burnt to encourage grouse, which feed on the new shoots.

Lifeblood of the region, the River Tweed and its tributaries form Britain's fourth-largest river system. Once the victim of industrial pollution, it is now one of Britain's least polluted major rivers supporting 16 fish species, otters, water voles (rodents) and various other fauna.

PLANNING
When to Cycle

The moors are prettiest in August, when the heather is flowering, but the ride is pleasant any time between April and September.

Maps

The OS Travel Map – Road 1:250,000 *Southern Scotland & Northumberland* (sheet 3) shows the entire region in glorious Technicolor detail.

Information Sources

The cycling pages of **VisitScotland's** website (http://cycling.visitscotland.com) contain a wealth of information on cycling in southern Scotland. For more sources of info, see the Edinburgh Orientation ride (p264).

THE RIDE
Day 1: Edinburgh to Duns
3–5 hours, 40.3 miles

The day starts with a test of your navigation skills through 5.5 miles of city streets and the attractive **Innocent Railway bikepath** (1.9 miles). The latter begins with a 550-yard tunnel curiously buried in a residential car park. From Musselburgh, the ride to Duns is via quiet country lanes mostly passing through undulating farming country, with some hefty climbs as far as East Saltoun.

Conveniently located around the halfway point of today's ride, and the last services before Duns, the **Goblin Ha Hotel** (☎ 01620 810244) in the gorgeously leafy village of **Gifford** (17.5 miles) does tasty bar meals and a fine real ale. The village has an attractive main street capped by the stocky whitewashed tower of the town's church.

Taking your leave of Gifford, there's a long climb, steep in parts, through the heather-coated moors of the **Lammermuir**

SCOTTISH BORDERS – DAY 1

CUE		GPS COORDINATES	
start		Edinburgh tourist office	55°57'10"N	3°11'25"W
0 miles		go W on Princess St		
0.3	⬏	The Mound		
0.3	▲	450yd moderate climb		
0.5	⬋	Bank St/George IV Bridge		
0.8	⬊⬒	Bristo Place		
0.8	⬏⬒	Lothian St		
0.9	⬋	Potterow/Chapel St		
1.3	⬏	Gifford Park/Rankeillor St		
1.5	⬑⬏	St Leonard's St/St L Lane		
1.6	⬐	signed path thru car park		
1.8	⬏	follow signs thru car park		
1.9	⚠	550yd tunnel		
		{follow Innocent Railway bikepath}		
4.3	⬏	Duddingston Park Sth		
4.4	⬐	Magdalene Dr		
4.9	⬐	Milton Rd		
5.8	⬐	Edinburgh Rd		
6.9	⬏⬐	High St (dogleg), Dalrymple Loan		
7.0	⬏	Inveresk Rd		

CUE CONTINUED		GPS COORDINATES	
7.1	⬐	A6124 'to Inveresk'		
7.9	▲	1.8 miles moderate climb		
8.7	⬋⬏	dogleg onto A6124		
10.1	⬏	A6093		
10.8	▲	1.6 miles moderate climb		
11.0	⬐	B6371		
11.4	⬏	'to Templehall'		
12.1		Templehall	55°52'38"N	2°54'57"W
12.6	⬋	unsigned road		
14.2	⬐	B6355 'to Gifford', East Saltoun	55°53'59.49"N	2°50'24.08"W
14.3	⬊	B6355 'to Gifford/Duns'		
18.0		Gifford	55°54'12"N	2°44'46"W
19.3	⬋	B6355 'to Duns'		
22.5	▲	760yd very steep climb		
23.8	⬊	B6355		
27.5	▲	330yd steep climb		
27.7	⚠	650yd steep descent		
38.8	⬋	A6112 'to Duns'		
40.0	⬏	Currie St		
40.1	⬐	South St (Market Square)		
40.3		Market Square, Duns	55°46'39"N	2°20'37"W

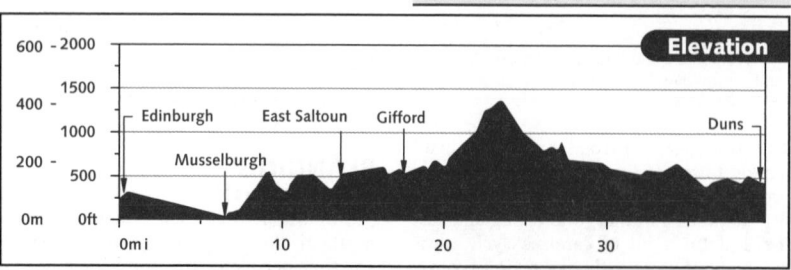

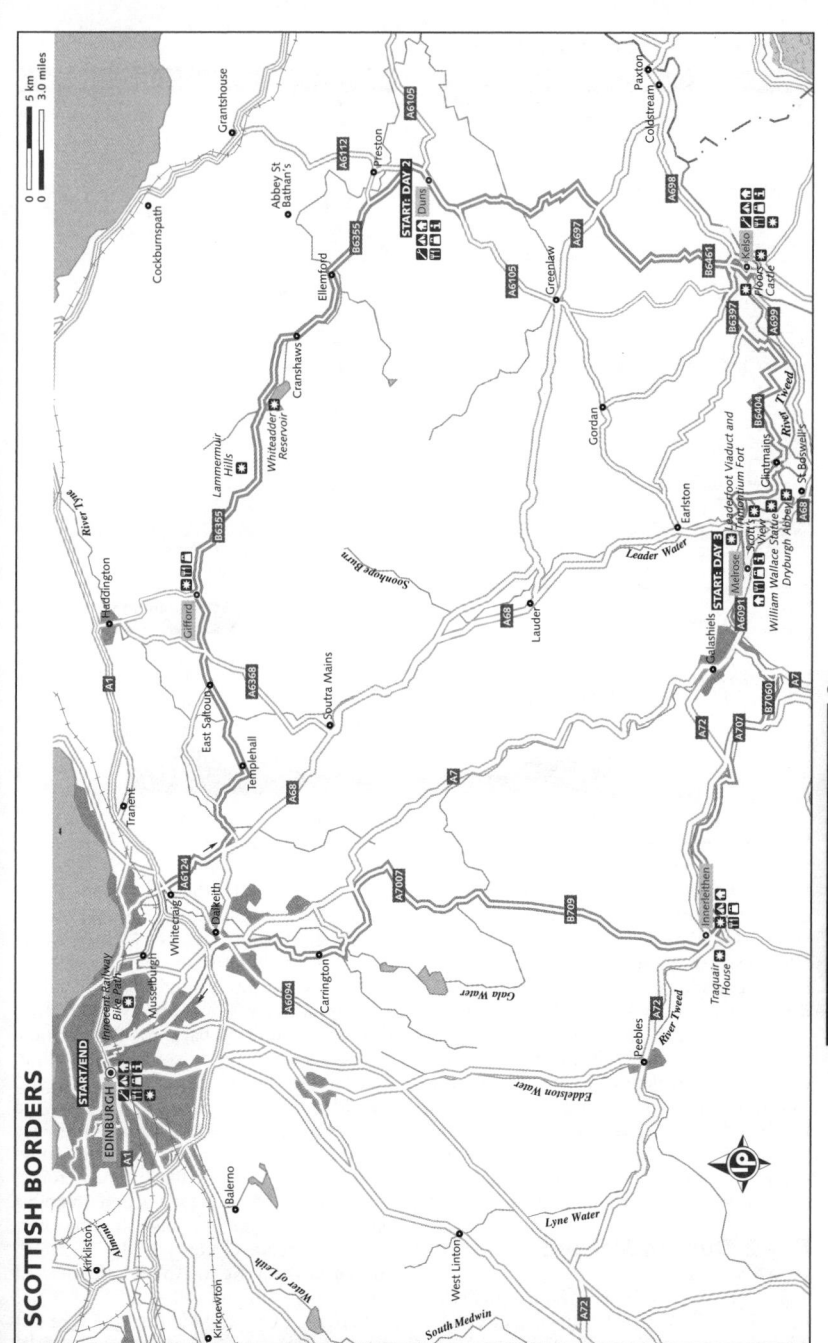

SCOTTISH BORDERS

SCOTLAND

SCOTTISH BORDERS – DAY 2

CUE		GPS COORDINATES	
start		Market Square, Duns	55°46'39"N 2°20'37"W
0 miles		go W on South St	
0.2	↘	A6105	
1.9	↰	'to Gavington'	
2.1	↱	'to Fogo'	
3.8	↱	'to Fogo'	
4.4	↱	unsigned lane	
5.3	↰	unsigned lane	
6.3	↱	unsigned lane	
6.9	↱	unsigned lane	
7.8	↱	'to Mersington'	
9.2	↱ ↰	A697/'to Hassington' (dogleg)	
10.2	↘	under power lines	
12.1	↘	unsigned lane	
12.7	↙	unsigned lane	
12.9	↰	unsigned lane	
14.2	↱	B6461 'to Kelso'	
16.7	◎ ↱	'to town centre'	
17.2	↱	Roxburgh St, Kelso	55°36'2"N 2°26'15"W

CUE CONTINUED		GPS COORDINATES	
17.5	★	Floors Castle	
17.7	↘	Edinburgh Rd/A6089	
18.9	↰	B6397 'Tweed bikepath'	
		(follow Tweed Cycleway signs to Melrose)	
28.0	↱ ▲	330yd steep climb	
	●●↑	Dryburgh Abbey 1.5 miles ↺	
26.9	↱	B6356	
	▲	440yd steep climb	
28.2	↱	B6356	
	▲	330yd steep climb	
28.6	★	Wallace's statue (LHS)	
29.3	▲	440yd moderate climb	
30.6	⚠	880yd descent to T-junction	
31.6	↱	unsigned road (past gate)	
	▲	650yd moderate climb	
32.0	★	Trimontium monument (LHS)	
32.2	⚠	thru gate	
32.3	↱	B6361, Newstead	
33.6		Melrose tourist office	55°35'58"N 2°43'9"W

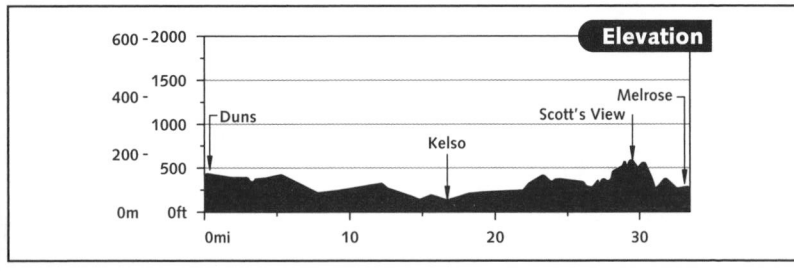

Hills. After around 8 miles the B6355 delivers you to the attractive **Whiteadder Reservoir**, a popular water sports venue. Shortly after the reservoir you cross the administrative boundary between East Lothian and Borders but the landscape doesn't change.

The hills between here and Duns can reach up to 400m (1312ft) in height and the landscape is streaked with stretches of pine forest. The road ducks and dives through heathered hills flecked with preoccupied sheep and guarded by the odd soaring wind turbine all the way to Duns, an attractive burgh and your overnight stop.

Day 2: Duns to Melrose

2½–4 hours, 33.6 miles

Things go downhill between Duns and Kelso, but only as far as the terrain is concerned. This pleasant ride along quiet country lanes is easy going, with the only busy stretch coming in the final three miles. There are several short climbs towards Melrose as the land becomes lumpier in character.

Beyond the interestingly named village of Fogo there's some knotty navigation through a mesh of back roads to handle so make sure you have your map head on. Within two hours of leaving Duns you should pitch up in **Kelso** (16.2 miles), a lively market town sitting at the confluence of the Rivers Tweed and Teviot. The **tourist office** (☎ 0870 608 0404; Town House, The Square) can advise you where to grab a bite to eat, and the only bike shop in town, **Simon Porteous Cycles** (☎ 01573 223692; Bridge St) near Kelso Abbey can sort out any niggles with your bike.

Between Kelso and Melrose a rash of fascinating sights await. First up, the gracefully turreted **Floors Castle** (☎ 01573 223333) just outside Kelso (17.5 miles) is Scotland's largest inhabited house, though there's no sense of habitation in the 10 rooms open to the public. It's home to the 10th Duke of Roxburghe whose ancestors built this magnificent country pile in 1721, nine dukes ago. Ten miles of pedalling brings you to the ruined 12th-century **Dryburgh Abbey** (☎ 01835 822381), the most beautiful of the Border abbeys, 0.75 miles off the route (at 28 miles). Most flock straight to the chapel where Sir Walter Scott is buried, but the rest of the site is fascinating for its surviving architecture, which conjures up images of 12th-century monastic life more successfully than its counterparts in nearby towns. Back on the main route, detour 200 yards to the **William Wallace statue** (28.4 miles) on the way to **Scott's View** (29.5 miles), Sir

Walter Scott's favourite spot overlooking the Tweed Valley and Eildon Hills.

The spectacular **Leaderfoot Viaduct** stands high over the River Tweed east of Melrose. Its slender piles and lofty arches were erected in 1865 for the Berwickshire railway, which closed in 1948. Nearby, the first-century **Trimontium** ('three mountains') **Fort** was one of the Romans' most important. The Trimontium monument (31.9 miles) marks the site of the now feint Roman ramparts.

Day 3: Melrose to Edinburgh
4–6½ hours, 51.7 miles
Beginning on bikepaths, the route joins the signed Tweed Cycleway, wiggles across the A7 and then via quiet roads traces the River Tweed and the A72 (but doesn't join it) through the Elibank and Traquair Forest.

SCOTTISH BORDERS – DAY 3

CUE		GPS COORDINATES	
start	Melrose tourist office	55°35'58"N	2°43'9"W
0 miles	go W on Buccleuch St		
0.2	Waverley Rd/B6374		
1.6	Tweedbank Dr		
1.7	'to Tweed Cycleway'		
	(60yd) bikepath		
2.6	Winston Rd		
4.0	0.9 miles gradual climb		
4.5	A7		
	(80yd) minor lane		
	(follow Tweed Cycleway signs)		
9.8	across bridge		
10.0	0.5 miles gradual climb		
17.7	Traquair Rd 'to Innerleithen'		
	Traquair House 1.7 miles ↺		
18.4	A72 'to Galashiels'		
18.5	Innerleithen post office	55°37'8"N	3°3'50"W
18.6	Leithen Rd/B709		
	7.4 miles gradual climb		
28.4	2 miles gradual climb		
33.2	'to Middleton'		

CUE CONTINUED		GPS COORDINATES	
35.0	unsigned lane		
36.7	unsigned lane		
37.8	B6372 'to Temple'		
38.4	'to Carrington'		
38.6	'to Carrington'		
39.7	'to Dalkeith', Carrington		
42.2	cross B704 'to Dalkeith'		
42.9	A7 'to Edinburgh'		
43.2	B6392 'to Eskbank'		
	use pedestrian ramp not roundabout		
44.1	B6392 'to Edinburgh'		
44.8	A772 'to city bypass'		
45.1	A772 'to city centre'		
45.8	Drum St/A772		
47.9	Claverhouse Dr		
48.3	Kirkbrae		
48.6	Liberton Brae/Mayfield Rd (dogleg)		
50.8	Forest Rd		
50.9	George IV Bridge 'to city'		
51.2	Bank St/The Mound		
51.4	Princes St		
51.7	Edinburgh, tourist office	55°57'10"N	3°11'25"W

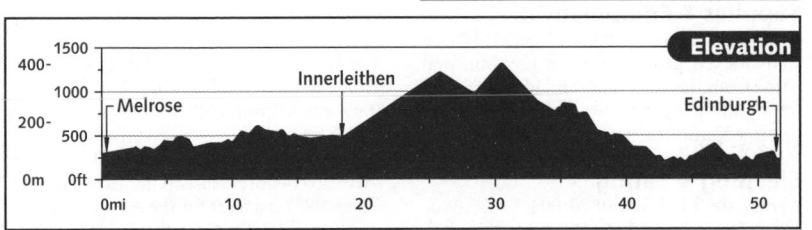

This is the scene until you reach Inner-leithen (18.4 miles).

Traquair House (☎ 01896 830323), a quarter mile from the Innerleithen turn-off (17.7 miles) claims to be the oldest in-habited house in Scotland. It makes a good picnic spot and there's a restaurant in the pleasant walled garden. The town's other at-traction is the National Trust for Scotland's **Robert Smail's Printing Works** (☎ 0844 493 2259), a fully functional Victorian let-terpress printing house, which provides a fascinating insight into this old-style print-ing process. There are no services between Innerleithen and the outskirts of Edin-burgh. In Innerleithen, the **Corner Hotel** (☎ 01896 831181, cnr High & Chapel Sts) has generous mains starting at £4.25, and there are fish and chip shops and a bakery nearby (High St).

From Innerleithen the long, gradual climb (starting at 18.6 miles) over the **Moorfoot Hills** is not particularly taxing, especially compared to some of the gradi-ents experienced earlier in the ride. There are widescreen views of Edinburgh and the Firth of Forth from the tops of the hills and the B709 and B7007 can feel blocked-in and pretty lonely. Coming down off the ridge, traffic becomes heavier the nearer to Edinburgh you get, but some roads boast well maintained cycle lanes.

TOWNS & FACILITIES

ARMADALE
☎ 01471 / pop 150

Armadale is a scattering of services around the ferry terminal. Ardvasar, 0.6 miles from the ferry terminal, is more of a real village.

Supplies & Equipment
Ardvarsar Stores (☎ 01471 844214) is a well-stocked grocery shop a few hundred yards from the ferry quay and ideally placed for building up supplies before venturing out to explore the island.

Sleeping & Eating
Armadale YHA (☎ 0870 004 1103; Ard-vasar, Sleat; dm £12.50-14) overlooking the Sound of Sleat, this is a well-maintained hostel with large single-sex dorms, cycle storage, a fully equipped kitchen and a din-ing area. It's very popular with cyclists and walkers so book early.

Ardvarsar Hotel (☎ 01471 844223; www.ardvasarhotel.com; Ardvasar, Sleat; B&B £42.50), the social hub of Ardvarsar rents out florally chintzy rooms for a rela-tively good rate and serves up inexpensive and filling bar meals during the day and a slap up, four-course dinner every evening in summer. It's an 875-yard ride from the ferry terminal.

Kinloch Lodge (☎ 01471-833214; www .kinloch-lodge.co.uk; d £150-275) is a stately foodie treat, dinner £42 belonging to cel-ebrated Scottish chef Claire MacDonald. Rooms have an elegant country-house feel with bird watercolours on the wall and plump beds. The drawing room has a selec-tion of whisky and cigars, so you can swig, puff and contemplate the view. It's 10 miles north of Armadale, 5 miles before the turn-off to the A87.

Pasta Shed (☎ 01471-844264; The Pier; mains £7-12) is beside the ferry pier in a cute little conservatory with a couple of outdoor tables. It serves well-prepared sea-food dishes, pizzas and sandwiches.

BROADFORD
☎ 01471 / pop 1050

Broadford is one of Skye's two main towns, the other being Portree. Really just a serv-ice town for the scattered communities of southern Skye, this straggling village is a good place to take on provisions.

Information
The **tourist office** (☎ 01471 822361) is opposite the Esso petrol station and seven-day supermarket.

Sleeping & Eating
Broadford SYHA (☎ 01471 822442; www .syha.org.uk; dm £14.50) has a great outlook over the bay and is set in a quiet spot away from the busy road in a modern building. Staff are helpful with local walks – long and short.

Tigh an Dochais (☎ 01471 820022; www.skyebedbreakfast.co.uk; 13 Harrapool; s/d £60/80) is a feast for the eyes, a chic new guesthouse looking like it's come straight to

Broadford from some Nordic architecture contest. All the rooms as well as the lounge boast glass walls – they're too big to call windows – which look right out over the shoreline and are so clean you'll bang your nose. It really is an extraordinary place, and comfort, not minimalism, inspires the interior decor. Book well ahead.

Skye Picture House (☎ 01471 822531; www.skyepicturehouse.co.uk; Ard Dorch; s/d £32/64) is about 7 miles north of Broadford right by the water, looking across at the island of Scalpay. The owners are avid photographers (and offer courses), so photography tomes and images decorate the wonderful guest lounge, which has memorable wraparound vistas – there's a telescope for bird- and otter-watching. The en-suite rooms have spacious bathrooms and offer unfussy comfort.

Creelers of Skye (☎ 01471 822281; mains £9-16, tapas £5-7) does quality seafood in an unpretentious atmosphere, and smaller tapas-style creations during the day. It's a friendly spot that doubles as an art gallery.

BRODICK
☎ 01770 / pop 621

Easily accessible by train and ferry from Glasgow, the port village of Brodick is where the vast majority of visitors to the Isle of Arran first land. Apart from shops and pubs, there's little real reason to linger in Brodick though some use it as a base from which to explore the island.

Information

There is an Isle of Arran **tourist office** (☎ 01770 303774; www.ayrshire-arran.com; Brodick Pier).

Supplies & Equipment

Brodick Cycle Hire (☎ 01770 302868; Glencloy Rd) and **Arran Power & Sail** (☎ 01770 302337; www.arranpowerand sail.com; Shore Rd) both loan out bikes with rates around £12-15 a day. For repair work, **Brodick Cycles** (☎ 01770 302460) is opposite the village hall.

Sleeping & Eating

Glen Rosa Farm (☎ 01770 302380; www .glenrosa.com; Glen Rosa; campsites per person £3.50) is set in n a lush glen 2.5 miles north of Brodick pier, this riverside site

offers basic camping in a lovely setting with cold water and toilets as the only facilities.

Fellview (☎ 01770 302153; fellview arran@yahoo.co.uk; 6 Strathwhillan Rd; rooms per person £25, bunkhouse per person £15) is a lovely warm house with friendly owners whom epitomise Scottish hospitality. As well as cosy B&B rooms there's a snug bunkhouse out the back with just two bunks, (you share the bathroom inside the house). Head north out of Brodick and take the left hand turn to Strathwhillan – Fellview is just up on the right.

Glencloy Farm Guesthouse (☎ 01770 302351; glencloyfarm@aol.com; Glencloy Rd; s/d £65/80) is perfect for families, with plenty of space for kids to run around in safety, plus animals to pet and videos for those cabin-fever rainy days,. Glencloy is a picturesque old farmhouse with free-range chickens in the garden (providing eggs for breakfast) and unfailingly hospitable and helpful owners.

Ormidale Hotel (☎ 01770 302293; Knowe Rd, Brodick) is a long-standing favourite among Arran hikers and climbers. The Ormidale is the best drinking place in Brodick, with Deuchars IPA and Arran Ales on tap, and a crumbling but atmospheric Victorian conservatory at the back where you can kick off your shoes and relax with a pint.

Creelers Seafood Restaurant (☎ 01770 302810; www.creelers.co.uk; Cladach, nr Brodick; mains lunch £9, dinner £15-18) is an award-winning restaurant, 1.5 miles north of Brodick, offering relaxed dining with the emphasis on seafood – sourcing all of its delicacies from Arran and the Western Isles. The **Smokehouse** next door sells seafood to go.

Brodick Bar & Brasserie (☎ 01770 302169; Alma Rd, Brodick; mains £8-15) is a bright, modern bar with a family-friendly brassiere. The Brodick offers an unpretentious menu of pizza, pasta, lamb, beef and fish dishes plus daily specials, with a separate kids' menu (high chairs available) and a decent wine list.

DALMALLY
☎ 01838 / pop 325

The small community of Dalmally is a spread out affair with the post office-cum-pharmacy coming closest to forming a focus for village life. There's also a store and the small 'suburb' of Glenview about 1 mile east. Otherwise, there isn't much here.

Supplies & Equipment
The Glenview store (☎ 01838 200348), 1 mile east along the A85 (follow the signs to Glenview), is the only source of food-stuffs and other supplies.

Sleeping & Eating
Inveraray YHA (☎ 01499 302454, Dal-mally Rd; dm £8), open March to October, is closest to Dalmally (turn right at Cladich, instead of left; from here it's 9 miles on the A819 to Inveraray).

The **Orchy Bank Guesthouse** (☎ 01838 200370, Stronmilchan Rd/B8077; B&B £25) is a tranquil farmhouse retreat by the river with eight traditionally furnished rooms with shared facilities.

Near the train station Dalmally's plush-est offering is the **Glenorchy Lodge Hotel** (☎ 01838 200312; d/tw £70-120; mains £8-18), which doubles up as the only place to eat in town. The restaurant does a great line in chunky scotch steaks.

DUNS
☎ 01361 / pop 2308
Duns is a small burgh on the edge of the Lammermuir Hills. Now a peaceful market town, it has been destroyed and rebuilt at least three times over the centuries. Market Square and surrounding streets is where the 'action' is six days a week, but when locals say Sunday is closing day, they mean it.

Information
As there's no tourist centre in Duns, try the **Jim Clark Room** (☎ 01361 883960; New-town St) or the notice board on the main square that features limited accommoda-tion listings and information on the Duns Town Trail.

Supplies & Equipment
The town's main supermarket is the **Co-op** (Market Sq) up the hill from Market Sq despite the address. It's one of the few busi-nesses in Duns to open on the Sabbath.

Sleeping & Eating
Black Bull (☎ 01361 883379; www.black bullhotelduns.com; 15 Black Bull St; s/d £55/80; mains £9) is located opposite the Co-op supermarket just a short walk from Market Sq – the Black Bull has light and airy rooms and a lively restaurant carpeted in purple and green tartan. The pub grub, evening dinners and blackboard specials, including local salmon dishes, are superbly prepared, but Wednesday is evidently cook's day off as there's no food.

The White Swan (☎ 01361 88338; www .whiteswan-hotel.co.uk; 31-32 Market Sq; s/d £40-70) is conveniently situated on Mar-ket Sq. Rooms at this pub-cum-hotel are a good deal if a touch on the small side. The staff are flexible about bikes overnighting in rooms.

Trotters Bakery (50 Market Sq) is a fam-ily-run baker's shop supplying this small Borders town with delicious oven-fresh bread, cakes and savoury snacks.

Border Baguettes (Market Sq; snacks £1.50-2.40) dispenses cheap no-nonsense filled baguettes, sandwiches, rolls and baked potatoes to lunching tourists and lo-cals, but once it's done, the doors are locked (around 3pm).

China Palace (☎ 01361 883100; 29-30 Market Sq; mains £7-8) is Duns' bit of ex-otica, a rather incongruous Chinese res-taurant where inexpensive Chinese dishes can be enjoyed in the gaudy interior or save 30% by taking away.

EDINBURGH
☎ 0131 / pop 430,000
Edinburgh is a city that just begs to be explored. From the vaults and wynds that riddle the Old Town to the pictur-esque urban villages of Stockbridge and Cramond, it's filled with quirky, come-hither nooks that tempt you to walk just that little bit further. And every corner turned reveals sudden views and unex-pected vistas – green sunlit hills, a glimpse of rust-red crags, a blue flash of distant sea. It's a place to put the guidebook away for a bit, and just wander.

There's more to Edinburgh than just sightseeing – there are top shops, world-class restaurants and a bacchanalia of bars to enjoy. All of the city's best sides come together in August at festival time, when it seems as if half the world descends on the Scottish capital for one enormous shindig. So get off your bike and party.

Information

Edinburgh & Scotland Information Centre
(☎ 0845 225 5121; Princes Mall, 3 Princes
St) offers an accommodation booking
service and internet access as well as housing a currency exchange desk, a gift and
bookshop. For excellent service and cycling
advice try the **Edinburgh Bicycle Cooperative** (☎ 228 3565; www.edinburghbicycle
.com; 8 Alvanley Tce, Whitehouse Loan).
Their website has route information and
maps for rides across the UK as well as
several useful links.

Supplies & Equipment

Tiso Outdoor (☎ 225 9486; 123-125 Rose
St) claims to be one of the biggest outdoor
stores in the UK. **Cycle Scotland** (☎ 556
1212; www.cyclescotland.co.uk; 29 Blackfriars St) has around a hundred bikes for
hire and depots throughout the Highlands.
A 24-speed touring bike plus helmet, repair kit and mechanical backup costs £120
per week, panniers and camping gear cost
extra and rates may be negotiable for longer
hire. The company also hires sturdy mountain bikes and organises group tours and
individually tailored cycling holidays
throughout Scotland.

Sleeping

Mortonhall Caravan & Camping Park
(☎ 664 1533; 38 Mortonhall Gate, Frogston
Rd; sites £15) is a first-rate campsite on the
southern edge of the city with spacious clean
facilities and lots of grassy pitches. Reception staff hand out maps of the city as well as
information on things to see and do.

Edinburgh Caravan Club Site (☎ 312
6874; www.caravanclub.co.uk; 35 Marine
Dr; sites £4.80-7.60, plus per person £4.60-
6) is 5 miles from the city – this caravan
park is nicely positioned overlooking the
Firth of Forth, and has excellent facilities. It's geared primarily to caravans, but
there are plenty of tent sites. It's essential
to book during summer, when no cars are
allowed in the tent area. Take bus 8A from
Broughton St.

Budget Backpackers (☎ 226 6351; www
.budgetbackpackers.com; 39 Cowgate, The
Grassmarket; dm £11-14, tw £44), this
unique spot piles on the extras, with bike
storage, pool tables, laundry, breakfast (£2
extra) and colourful chill-out lounge. You'll

pay a little more for four-bunk dorms, but
larger dorms are great value. The only
downside is that the prices increase by £2 a
night on weekends, but otherwise a brilliant
place to doss.

Edinburgh Central SYHA (☎ 524 2090;
www.syha.org.uk; 9 Haddington Pl, Leith
Wlk; dm £10-25.50, s/tw from £33/49) is
a modern purpose-built hostel, a half-mile
north of Waverley train station. It's a big
(300 beds), flashy, five-star establishment
with its own cafe-bistro as well as self-
catering kitchen, smart and comfortable
eight-bed dorms, private rooms, and mod
cons including key-card entry and plasma
screen TVs.

Greenhouse (☎ 622 7634; www.green
house-edinburgh.com; 14 Hartington
Gdns; s/d from £65/70), award-winning,
the Greenhouse is a wholly vegetarian and
vegan guesthouse, which uses organic and
genetically modified-free foods as much
as possible – the breakfast menu includes
home-made vegie sausages, scrambled tofu,
and pancakes with maple syrup – and even
the soap and shampoo are free of animal
products.

Eating

Monster Mash (☎ 225 7069; www.monster
mashcafe.co.uk; 4a Forest Rd; mains £5-7)
is where you will find classic British grub of
the 1950s – bangers and mash, shepherd's
pie, fish and chips – is the mainstay of
the menu at this nostalgia-fuelled cafe. But
there's a twist – the food is all top-quality
nosh freshly prepared from local produce,
including Crombie's gourmet sausages.
And there's even a wine list!

Engine Shed (☎ 662 0040; www.engine
shed.org.uk; 19 St Leonard's Lane; lunches
£3-6) is a vegetarian cafe in an ideal spot
for a cuppa and a bakery-fresh scone after
climbing Arthur's Seat. It's been set up to
help special-needs adults and as well as having their own bakery they also make their
own tofu, which is used plentifully through
curries.

Forest (☎ 220 4538; www.theforest.org
.uk; 2 Bristo Pl; mains £3-5) is a chilled-out
and comfortably scuffed-around-the-edges
antidote to squeaky-clean style bars –
this volunteer-run, not-for-profit art space
and cafe serves up humoungous helpings
of hearty vegetarian and vegan fodder,

ranging from burritos to falafel burgers and boasts free wi-fi.

David Bann (☎ 556 5888; www.david bann.com; 56-58 St Mary's St; mains £8-12) is on a one-man mission to convince the world that vegetarian food doesn't have to mean alfalfa and tofu. Bann has been thrilling locals with his sophisticated vegetarian cuisine for years. The Thai fritters are flavoured with ginger, lime, green chilli and sesame, while the tart of braised fennel, spinach and goat's-cheese curd is guaranteed to win converts.

L'Alba D'Oro (☎ 557 2580; www.lalba doro.com; 5-7 Henderson Row; fish supper £6-7) – pronouncing any place as Edinburgh's best chippie is always contentious, but with a busy knot of cars waiting for a parking space outside, this place gets the nod from many locals. But it's more than a chippie – you wouldn't expect a 300+ wine list at your average deep-fryer, nor could you get zesty prawn suppers or vegie haggis.

Getting There & Away

AIR

Edinburgh International Airport (☎ 0131 333 1000; www.edinburghairport.com) on the city's western fringes handles flights to and from over a hundred destinations worldwide including all the London airports, New York and most of continental Europe.

TRAIN

There are many **National Express East Coast** (☎ 722 5333; www.nationalexpress eastcoast.com) services to and from London (£101.40; five hours, up to twice hourly) and **Scotrail** (☎ 0845 601 5929; www .firstgroup.com/scotrail) trains to Glasgow (£10.80; 50 minutes, several hourly). Bikes are transported free of charge by both operators, but space may be limited on Scotrail and you must make a reservation with National Express East Coast.

BUS

Bikes other than the fold-to-nothing commuter type are not officially carried on buses in Scotland. However, depending on who you talk to, they may be taken (free) at the driver's discretion. Since buses are considerably cheaper than trains, it may be

worth checking, especially if you're on a tight budget (but don't rely on it). **Scottish Citylink** (☎ 0870 550 5050, www.citylink .co.uk) connects Edinburgh to even the remotest of towns across Scotland.

GLASGOW
☎ 0141 / pop 629,500

Scotland's biggest city has shrugged off its shroud of industrial soot and shimmied into a sparkling new designer gown. Ten years on from being named UK City of Architecture and Design 1999, Glasgow is flaunting its reputation as a capital of cool and has branded itself as 'Scotland with Style'. Like London, the city has re-discovered the river that made its fortune, and massive redevelopment is making the most of the Clyde waterfront in preparation for an expected flood of visitors – Glasgow will be hosting the Commonwealth Games in 2014, and is a soccer venue for the 2012 London Olympics. Though larger, hillier and less charming than Edinburgh, the city is quite cycle-friendly, with bike parking around inner areas and cycle routes within and surrounding the city.

Information

The **Tourist Office** (☎ 0141 204 4400; www.seeglasgow.com; 11 George Sq) can help with most Glasgow-related queries. There's another branch at the airport (☎ 0141 848 4440).

Supplies & Equipment

Dales Cycles (☎ 0141 332 2705; 150 Dobbies Loan) sell and hire all kinds of bicycles as well as stocking a vast array of bike spares and kit. **West End Cycles** (☎ 0141 357 1344; 16 Chancellor St) is a Partick-based bike shop where a service costs between £20 and £30. They also hire bikes for £15 a day or £85 a week. There's certainly no shortage of outdoor shops in Glasgow city centre with **Tiso** (☎ 0141 248 4877; 129 Buchanan St) and more hardcore **Adventure1** (☎ 0141 353 3788; 38 Dundas St) the most central.

Sleeping

Craigendmuir Caravan Park (☎ 0141 779 4159; www.craigendmuir.co.uk; Campsie View; two-person tent £14) is a well-equipped campsite just 6 miles northwest of the city centre on the A80, and only 547 yards from Stepps train station, with regular services to Glasgow Queen St station.

Euro Hostel (☎ 0141 222 2828; www .euro-hostels.co.uk; 318 Clyde St; dm £16-18, s/tw from £30/40) – we're tempted to add 'Eastern' at the start of this hostel's name, as it's a large institutional slab that wouldn't look out of place in Soviet-era Poland. Luckily it's close to Central Station, and as a former university hall of residence it almost always has a bed.

Glasgow YHA (☎ 0141 332 3004; www .syha.org.uk; 8 Park Tce; dm £15.50-20) is set in a charming town house perched on a hill overlooking Kelvingrove Park – this place is simply fabulous and one of Scotland's best official hostels. Dorms are mostly four to six beds and all have their own en suite – very posh. The common rooms are spacious, plush and good for lounging about.

Babbity Bowster (☎ 0141 552 5055; babbitybowster@gofornet.co.uk; 16-18 Blackfriars St; s/d £45/60) is smack bang in the heart of the trendy merchant city – the building's design is attributed to Robert Adam – this lively bar and restaurant offers accommodation in rooms with sleek furnishings and a minimalist design (no 3 is a good one). Staying here makes for an excellent Glaswegian experience.

Eating

Most of the city's best restaurants are clustered in the merchant city and the West End – many offer a two-/three-course lunch special and 'pretheatre' early-evening menus for as little as £8, a good way to sample the more expensive restaurants.

University Cafe (☎ 0141 339 5217; 87 Byres Rd; mains £3-6) first opened in 1918 and is still run by the same family (now fourth generation). This is a classic Glasgow cafe that has been serving fried breakfasts and ice cream floats to hungover students for almost a century.

Asia Style (☎ 0141 332 8828; 185-9 St George's Rd; mains £6-8) – don't be put off by the fluorescent lights and spartan decor – this little hole-in-the-wall serves the most authentic Chinese and Malaysian food in the city, seasoned with handfuls of fresh herbs and spices.

Wee Curry Shop (☎ 0141 353 0777; 7 Buccleuch St; two-course lunch £6, dinner mains £11) could there be a better illustration of Scotland's infatuation with Indian cuisine than a curry shop decked out in tartan? The Indian food is authentic though, so there's no fear of a faulty balti. The West End has another branch (☎ 0141 357 5280; 29 Ashton Ln), open for lunch and dinner (dinner mains £11), which offers similar rogan josh nosh.

Horse Shoe Bar (☎ 0141 221 3051; 17 Drury St ; three-course lunch £3.50) is a legendary city pub and popular meeting place dating from the late 19th century, which has hardly changed its appearance since then. It boasts the longest continuous bar in the UK, but its main attraction is what's served over it – real ale and the best-value lunches in town.

Getting There & Away

AIR

Glasgow has the luxury of two airports, **Glasgow International** (☎ 0141 887 1111; www.glasgowairport.com) 10 miles west of the city and **Prestwick** (☎ 0871 223 0700; www.gpia.co.uk) 30 miles southwest in Ayrshire. There are direct flights from Glasgow international to the Scottish islands as well as all the London airports, Vancouver and much of Europe. Prestwick deals mostly with no-frills Ryanair flights to Europe.

TRAIN

Virgin Trains operate tilting express Pendolino trains to London (£102; five hours, hourly) and Manchester (£60; three hours 40 minutes, four daily). You must make a (free) cycle reservation before boarding. Services to Edinburgh (£9.70, 50 minutes, several per hour) are operated by Scotrail whose liberal cycle policy means bikes are carried free of charge and without reservations.

BUS

Scottish Citylink (☎ 0870 550 5050, www .citylink.co.uk) run services from Glasgow to all major cities and many remote outposts across Scotland. Officially buses don't carry cycles but you may be able to persuade the driver to take you, especially if the luggage compartment is almost empty. Of course, don't buy a ticket in advance just in case you can't get on.

SCOTLAND

KILLIN
☎ 01567 / pop 700

Situated just west of Loch Tay, the village of Killin straddles the frothy Falls of Dochart, a series of rapids formed by the River Dochart. With more services and charm than Crianlarich, it's a better base from which to ride.

Information
The helpful, informative **tourist office** (☎ 0870 720 0627; Main St) is housed in the Breadalbane Folklore Centre.

Supplies & Equipment
The village store is the **Co-op** (Main St), the best place for stocking up on stuff for the pot. The superb **Killin Outdoor Centre** (☎ 01567 820652; www.killinoutdoor .co.uk; Main St) carries out repairs and hires bikes (£20 a day), as well as selling new and ex-hire bikes, outdoor kit and maps of the local area.

Sleeping & Eating
Cruachan Farm Caravan & Camping Park (☎ 01567 820302; www.cruachan farm.co.uk; North Loch Tay Side; sites £11) is set amid spectacular Scottish scenery around 3 miles along the Loch-hugging A827. This site has a large camping area, new shower blocks and a handy store at the nearby farmhouse. There's also a small coffee shop and restaurant for when the camping gas runs dry.

Braveheart Backpackers (☎ 07796 886899; dm £15, d £35-45) is tucked away alongside the Killin Hotel – these two adjoining cottages offer several types of room, all wood-clad with comfortable beds & bunks. There are particularly good en suite rooms for families, and the appealing kitchens and lounge area make it feel like a home rather than a hostel. They also rent out bikes and kayaks.

Falls of Dochart Inn (☎ 01856 820270; www.falls-of-dochart-inn.co.uk; bar meals £7-9 , dinner mains £11-15). Once you've conquered the hills hereabouts, reward yourself with a pint at this inviting historic inn. On a sunny evening it's a delight to sit outside watching the river cascade down its rocky course, but it's very cosy indoors too, with a classic old fireplace crackling away. There's bar food during the day, bolstered by some classier dishes such as venison or salmon roulade, available after 6pm. The rooms badly need a refit though.

KINLOCH RANNOCH
☎ 01882 / pop 256

A peaceful and remote backwater, the village of Kinloch Rannoch sits at the east end of stunningly beautiful Loch Rannoch. It's a tiny place with limited eating and sleeping options.

Sleeping & Eating
Kilvrecht Caravan & Campsite (☎ 01350 727284; Kinloch Rannoch; sites £3 per person) is an ultra-basic, no-frills camping ground, which enjoys a secluded spot 3 miles west of Kinloch Rannoch along the south shore road. Facilities are minimal here and there isn't even hot water, a fact which can make this a nippy experience, even at the height of a Scottish summer. It's popular with cyclists and walkers nonetheless.

Dunalastair Hotel (☎ 01882 632323; www.dunalastair.co.uk; Kinloch Rannoch; d from £110), a stunning hotel in the centre of the village, may be more luxurious than cycle tourists are used to, but go on, treat yourself. After freshening up in the luxurious gadget-packed room, stylishly done out in traditional Scottish patterns and colours, dine in the wood-panelled restaurant or 'tak a wee dram' in the whisky bar where you can warm the insides after a cold day on the road.

Bunrannoch Hotel (☎ 01882 632367; B&B £35) has a woodland setting on the outskirts of the village, this peaceful guest house has spacious airy rooms, some with wrought iron Victorian fireplaces and en suite bathrooms. Don't miss the dinner where dishes such as breast of duck in whisky, lemon and honey sauce, and bramble and almond tart are served in the high-ceilinged dining room. Bikes are stored outside.

LOCHGILPHEAD
☎ 01546 / pop 2600

You don't have to be much of a linguist to work out that Lochgilphead sits at the head of Loch Gilp, a sea loch attached to the much larger Loch Fyne. It also stands at the junction of the main roads to Loch Lomond and Oban, which form part of the route for Day 3 of the ride. While not a particularly humming place, it does have just enough facilities to make calling a halt to your pedalling easy enough.

Information

The small **tourist office** (☎ 01546 602344; Lochnell St) can be found on the waterfront.

Supplies & Equipment

The town's only cycle emporium is the excellent **Crinan Cycles** (☎ 01546 603511; www .crinancycles.co.uk; 1 Argyll St) is just back from the waterfront on the main drag. In addition to repair work they also hire out tourers for £12 a day or £45 a week. The **Co-op** supermarket (Oban St) is the best place to stock up if you're doing your own cooking.

Sleeping & Eating

Booking ahead in the summer months is probably advised, though the town has an ample supply of beds, meaning you should be able to turn up unannounced in spring and autumn and still find a place to lay your hat.

Lochgilphead Caravan Park (☎ 01546 602003; www.lochgilpheadcaravanpark .co.uk; Bank Park; sites £7-9 plus £2 per adult) is just a short walk from the shops and cafe. This well regimented caravan park has soft grassy tent areas and tiptop facilities including hot showers, a laundry and a bike shelter.

Kilmory Guesthouse (☎ 01546 603658, Paterson St; d/tw from £40/50) is a six-room B&B on the waterfront road with small, functional rooms (with TV), but only four rooms have en suite bathrooms. There are lower rates for single occupancy and the owners will rustle up a vegie (and even vegan) breakfast if you give them a bit of notice.

The Stag Hotel (☎ 01546 602496; www.staghotel.com; Argyll St; s/tw/d/tr £45/60/60/75) is a town centre inn with somewhat Spartan but moderately comfy rooms, including TV and en suite facilities. Rates are trimmed by £5-10 if you skip the breakfast and inexpensive meals are served downstairs in the bar. There's limited shelter for bikes.

The Argyll Hotel (☎ 01546 602221; www.argyll-hotel.com; 69 Lochnell St; s/d/ tw £37.50/60/60, mains £6.25-18.50) have en suite rooms and are generally well kitted out, the Argyll is as good a deal as you'll find in town. The snug restaurant serves a limited menu and provides an opportunity to sample Scotland's signature dish, Haggis, which comes with 'neeps and tatties', turnip and potatoes to you and me. You may be able to persuade staff to let you stash your bike in the beer cellar.

LOCHRANZA

☎ 01770 / pop 250

Lochranza is a beautiful little spot tucked alongside a narrow bay and surrounded by mountains. The ruined Lochranza Castle on its tiny peninsula is the central focus of the village.

Sleeping & Eating

Lochranza YHA (☎ 01770 830631; Lochranza; dm £13-15) is in the north of the island – this hostel has clean, spacious dorms, helpful owners and loads of information about Arran. Its worn furnishings are offset by the lovely views.

Lochranza Hotel (☎ /fax 01770 830223; Lochranza; d £50-76) is a long-established bastion of Arran hospitality, and has some rooms with outrageous pink floral decor, but they're a good size, sort of homely, and the rooms at the front (nos 1 and 10) have fantastic views.

Apple Lodge (☎ /fax 01770 830229; Lochranza; d £74-86) is the finest place to stay in Lochranza, with beautiful, individually furnished rooms, one with a four-poster bed, and a guest lounge that's perfect for curling up with a good book. And it makes all the difference when your hosts so obviously love their job.

Distillery Restaurant (☎ 01770 830264; Isle of Arran Distillery, Lochranza; mains £6-8) has a waterfall fountain that forms the centrepiece of the entrance hall at Arran's distillery, overlooked by a mezzanine floor with an attractive restaurant that serves a range of hearty, home-made dishes including burgers and lasagne.

Catacol Bay Hotel (☎ 01770 830231; Catacol; bar mains £7-10) is 2 miles from Lochranza – the bar here does great grub. The cheery service makes you feel like one of the islanders and in summer there are weekly *ceilidhs* with live music.

MALLAIG

☎ 01687 / pop 800

Primarily a fishing village rather than a tourist hotspot, most visitors en route to Skye and the small isles find themselves funnelled through Mallaig, which lies at the end of the railway line from the south. A heritage centre and Mallaig Marine World are minor distractions and most simply board the next boat bound for Armadale.

Information

Mallaig's small **tourist office** (☎ 01687 462064) can be found at the harbour.

Supplies & Equipment

As in many small Scottish towns, the best supermarket for self caterers is the **Co-op** (Station Rd). There's no bike shop.

Sleeping & Eating

Due to the sheer numbers of people passing through in summer, booking ahead is advised.

Silversands Portnaluchaig Campsite (☎ 01687 450269; Arisaig, Portnaluchaig; sites £8) – pitching a tent at this campsite on the famous Silver Sands of Morar is almost like wild camping with showers! Facilities are basic to say the least, you can pitch up almost anywhere and the sea breeze/wind/gale keeps the midges at bay. The views across to the island trio of Rum, Eigg and Muck are tremendous. The downside is that it's 7.1 miles from Mallaig but on the route.

Sheena's Backpackers Lodge (☎ 01687 462764; www.mallaigbackpackers.co.uk; Station Rd; dm £13.50) is a compact place with narrow dorms and with the kitchen upstairs.

Moorings Guest House (☎ 01687 462225; mooringsguesthouse@tiscali.co.uk; East Bay; s/d £27/54), a little farther along the main street has a cute front conservatory, faultless if uninteresting rooms, and good breakfasts with kipper and vegetarian possibilities – while admiring photos of rescued golden eagle chicks.

Cornerstone (☎ 01687 462306; mains £8-18) – sophistication is a stranger to the decor at the Cornerstone – lose the sauce sachets guys – but there are daily specials like squid straight off the boats, and it's got the best harbour views. They also run a chip shop out the back.

MELROSE

☎ 01896 / pop 1656

Melrose is the most charming and picturesque of the Border towns, lying at the foot of the heather-clad triple peaks of the Eildon Hills. It's a spick-and-span little place, with a tidy market square decked out with flower-filled hanging baskets, some attractive hotels and restaurants, and a famous rugby pitch that is host to the annual Melrose Sevens tournament. But its main attraction is Melrose Abbey whose ruins rise above the middle of the town, enticing walkers and cyclists to call an enjoyable halt.

Information

The **tourist office** (☎ 0870 608 0404; Abbey House), across from Melrose Abbey, has acres of print on tlocal and national topics.

Supplies & Equipment

Best for self-catering supplies is the **Alldays** convenience store (27 Market Sq).

Sleeping & Eating

Melrose SYHA Hostel (☎ 01896 822 521; www.syha.org.uk; Priorwood; dm £14-16) is just a stroll from the abbey (in fact you can glimpse it from the second floor). This Georgian mansion features tidy dorms complemented by a big garden and barbecue area. Not a party house, this hostel is mainly used by walkers looking to turn in early. From Market Square, follow the signposts to the A68.

Burts Hotel (☎ 01896 822285; www.burtshotel.co.uk; Market Sq; s/d from £60/116), set in an early-18th-century house it retains much of its period charm – with an enviable reputation – it has been run by the same couple for over 30 years. There's a welcoming bar that serves excellent meals, and roaring log fires in winter.

Townhouse (☎ 01896 822645; www.thetownhousemelrose.co.uk; Market Sq; s/d from £75/114) is Burts' more contemporary sister hotel across the square, the classy Townhouse has some of the most stylish rooms in town. There are two enormous 'superior' rooms with lavish furnishings – the one on the ground floor in particular has an excellent en suite, which includes a Jacuzzi.

Marmion's Brasserie (☎ 01896 822245; 5 Buccleuch St; mains dinner £13-15 , lunch £9–1), this atmospheric, wood-panelled niche serves snacks all day, but the lunch and dinner menus include gastronomic delights such as grilled venison, roast lamb and sea bass. At lunch the Cumberland sausage with mash and melted onions is a good choice.

Monte Cassino (☎ 01896 820082; Palma Pl; mains £8-17) is an Italian restaurant with an atmospheric setting in the old Victorian train station building. It dishes up reliably good pastas, pizzas and classic dishes such as chicken Milanese and *saltimbocca alla Romana*.

Russell's Restaurant (☎ 01896 822335; Market Sq; mains £5-7) is a stylish little tearoom/restaurant with a large range of snacks and more substantial offerings, including a hearty ploughman's lunch.

OBAN

☎ 01631 / pop 8120

Often dubbed 'the Gateway to the Isles', Oban is the most important ferry port on the west coast and one of the Highlands' largest communities. Built around the harbour, this pretty if slightly touristy town enjoys sweeping views to Kerrera and Mull. There's not a lot to see in Oban itself but it does offer some good restaurants and lively pubs for the island-hopping cyclist.

Information

Oban's tourist office (☎ 01631 563122; Argyll Sq) is busy and well-stocked, with internet access for visitors.

Supplies & Equipment

Bang in the centre of Oban you'll find **Outside Edge** (☎ 01631 566617; 6 MacGregor Ct), by far the town's best outdoor shop where staff know their breathable waterproofs from their Pac-a-Macs. **Evo Bikes** (☎ 01631 566996; www.evobikes.co.uk; 29 Lochside St) can put the bite back into your brakes as well as hiring out cycles for £14/50 per day/week.

Sleeping & Eating

Oban Caravan & Camping Park (☎ 01631 562425; www.obancaravanpark.com; Gallanachmore Farm; tent £12) is in a great position on a lovely green hillside above

the water, near the islet of Kerrera, 2.5 miles south of Oban towards Gallanach (turn right out of the ferry terminal) – this campsite is a top spot to stay. Two daily buses from Oban stop outside.

Oban Backpackers (☎ 01631 562107; www.scotlandstophostels.com; Breadalbane St; dm £13.50) – space isn't a worry at this sociable hostel – you could dock the Mull ferry in the enormous lounge, which features sofas sporting colourful fabric throws, a pool table, and a handpainted map of the coastline. The kitchen is also large, and the great dorms feature bottom bunks that you can actually sit on without banging your head. Powerful showers and a £1.90 breakfast make for painless mornings.

Kilchrenan House (☎ 01631 562663; www.kilchrenanhouse.co.uk; Corran Esp; s/d £40/80) boasts sea views on both sides, and this well-run property makes the most of them, with smart rooms, many of them brand new, with modern bathrooms. The vistas are magnificent, and really soothing. Room five is particularly memorable, with a four-poster bed and a great freestanding bathtub – another room features a loo-with-a-view. Porridge and kippers put in a welcome appearance at breakfast.

Cuan Mòr (☎ 01631 565078; 60 George St; mains £7-13) is right in the heart of town, the fresh, confident interior of this excellent bar-restaurant makes creative use of slate, driftwood, and wooden shellfish cases. The menu offers jazzed-up pub classics as well as vegie choices, crab cakes, and scallops to remind you of where you are. Fifteen wines by the glass and welcoming service keep punters smiling.

Seafood Temple (☎ 01631 566000; Gallanach Rd; dishes £6-15) – lobsters, langoustines, and locally-smoked salmon are just some of the seafood treats on offer at this recently-opened spot past the Manor House hotel at the southern end of town. The light wooden tables are tiered democratically, giving everyone a peek at the wonderful bay views.

Oban Inn (☎ 01631 562484; Stafford St) dates from 1790 – this pub overlooks the harbour by the North Pier. It's got a time-worn, historic feel with low wooden beams – there's a great mix of people here, with posh yachties comparing tidal charts with gruff local fisherfolk.

PITLOCHRY
☎ 01796 / pop 2564

Though often teeming with tourists, Pitlochry manages to retain the charm of a true Highland town. With two distillery tours and ample opportunities to purchase Scotland's favourite firewater, your memories of scenic Loch Faskally on which the town stands may be somewhat blurred.

Information

The efficient **tourist office** (☎ 01796 472215; 22 Atholl Rd) stocks ample information on the local area.

Supplies & Equipment

Escape Route (☎ 01796 473859; www .escape-route.biz; 3 Atholl Rd; bike hire half-/full-day £12/20) repair, rent out and sell new bikes as well as hiring cars. They also sell camping gear and outdoor accessories. There are several grocery stores in Pitlochry including the **Co-op** supermarket (W Moulin Rd).

Sleeping & Eating

Pitlochry Backpackers Hotel (☎ 01796 470044; www.scotlands-top-hostels.com; 134 Atholl Rd; dm/tw £15/50) – nailed in the centre of town, this facility-packed spot offers decent dorms as well as value en suite twins and doubles (beds not bunks). Cheap breakfast and a pool table are among the attractions, as is the convivial party atmosphere. The prices listed are for August – they drop a little in other months.

Tir Aluinn Guest House (☎ 01796 473811; www.tiraluinn.co.uk; 10 Higher Oakfield; s/d £30/60) is tucked away above the main street – this is a little gem of a place with bright rooms with easy-on-the-eye furniture, and an excellent personal welcome. There's a single, and a family room, and if they're full there are several others along this street.

Craigatin House (☎ 01796 472478; www.craigatinhouse.co.uk; 165 Atholl Rd; d standard/deluxe £70/80) is several times more tasteful than the average Pitlochry lodging, this noble house and garden is set back from the main road at the western end of town. Chic contemporary fabrics covering expansive beds offer a standard of comfort above and beyond the reasonable price – the rooms in the converted stable block are particularly inviting. Breakfast choices include whisky-laced porridge, smoked fish omelettes, and apple pancakes.

Moulin Hotel (☎ 01796 472196; www .moulinhotel.co.uk; Moulin; bar mains £6-11) is a mile away, but a world apart, this atmospheric hotel was trading centuries before the tartan tack came to Pitlochry. With its romantic low ceilings, ageing wood and booth seating, the inn is a wonderfully atmospheric spot for a house-brewed ale or a portion of Highland comfort food: try the filling haggis or venison stew. A more formal restaurant serves equally delicious fare, and the hotel has a variety of rooms (s/d £60/85) as well as a self-catering annexe. The best way to get here from Pitlochry is walking: it's a pretty uphill ride through green fields, and an easy roll down the slope afterwards.

Port-Na-Craig Inn (☎ 01796 472777; www.portnacraig.com; Port Na Craig; mains £8-17) is right on the river – this top little spot sits in what was once a separate hamlet. The delicious main meals are prepared with confidence and panache – scrumptious scallops or lamb steak bursting with flavour might appeal, but simpler sandwiches, kids' meals, and light lunches also tempt. Or you could just sit out by the river with a pint and watch the anglers whisking away

PORTREE (PORT RIGH)
☎ 01478 / pop 1920

Wee Portree is Skye's largest and liveliest town and generally regarded as the island's capital. The harbour is very pretty, the houses are brightly painted and there are superb views of the surrounding hills. Like other parts of Skye, there's a significant and increasing Gaelic-speaking population. The name (from the Gaelic for King's Harbour) commemorates the visit of James V who arrived here in 1540 to pacify the local clans.

Information

Tourist office (☎ 01478 612137; Bayfield Rd) is helpful, with accommodation booking, internet (£1 for 20 minutes) and foreign exchange.

Supplies & Equipment

Island Outdoors (☎ 01478 611073; The Green) is virtually the only outdoor shop on Skye. Nearby **Island Cycles** (☎ 01478 613121; The Green) can get your bicycle back on the road and hire out bikes. The **Co-op** supermarket (Dunvegan Rd), around half a mile northwest of the town centre, is open seven days a week.

Sleeping & Eating

Bayfield Backpackers (☎ 01478 612231; Bayfield; dm £14) is one of two hostels in town – this smart functional spot by the water has few frills but lots of sensible details like keycards, powerful showers, and lockable wire baskets under the comfortable bunks. The common room looks out over the bay – the kitchen is modern and clean, and the owner knows plenty about the island and can give good walking advice.

Braeside B&B (☎ 01478 612613; www .braesideportree.co.uk; Stormy Hill; d £54-60) – you'll know this bright spot by its flowerpots. Inside it's just as sweet, with ivy-patterned linen and a roomy residents' lounge that's good for meeting other guests. Breakfast is a treat with vegetarian options and plenty of choice – there's a reduction if you go continental. The good triple is ideal for small cycling groups.

Marmalade (☎ 01478 611711; www .marmaladehotels.com; Home Farm Rd; s/ d/family £100/120/125) – the tourist board will have a fit – doesn't this place know that accommodation in Scotland can only be named after trees or geographical features? Thankfully, that's not the only rule they break – the modern cafe chic, funky wire chandeliers in the bar, above-average breakfast, and laid-back staff are the perfect complements to the seven large light rooms, super-spacious bathrooms, grassy grounds, and long views. Prices drop sharply outside summer.

Cafe Arriba (☎ 01478 611830; Quay Brae; mains £5-10), colourful and fun, this upstairs cafe does inventive sandwiches served on a range of breads, bagels and croissants – stay-awhile views – and the best espresso in town. The all-day breakfast is a good-value calorie hit, and the range of daily specials and booze licence make it a good spot for casual dinner too.

Sea Breezes (☎ 01478 612016; Quay St; lunch £5-7, dinner £11-19) is down by the harbour, and run by a chef with a good local rep – he makes the effort to source island produce like organic Uist salmon or hand-dived scallops from Barra. Lunches are simpler, but all is tasty.

Bosville Hotel (☎ 01478 612846; 9 Bosville Tce) is very much the place to eat and drink in Portree – this offers three distinct but connected spaces, all of which deserve attention; the **Merchant Bar**, within the Bosville, is the most stylish drinking option in town.

The upmarket restaurant, **The Chandlery** (two-course dinner £32), serves up exquisite seafood concoctions, but the more affordable adjoining bistro (mains £7-13) isn't far behind, with a generous daily roast (£9), seafood specials (crunch into local langoustines if they're available) and a couple of dozen wines by the glass.

TOBERMORY

☎ 01688 / pop 750

Mull's low-rise capital is a picturesque fishing village and a major yachting centre with brightly painted houses gathered around a sheltered harbour. The village rises steeply from its colourful, much photographed harbour and is home to about two-thirds of the island's population. Things can get busy here mid-summer, so it pays to book ahead.

Information

Tobermory **tourist office** (☎ 01688 302182) will have moved to smart new harbourside premises by the time you read this.

Supplies & Equipment

The biggest food store in the village is the **Co-op** supermarket (33 Main St). **Browns Ironmonger** (☎ 01688 302020; 21 Main St) is a one-stop-shop for almost anything you could imagine. They even do bike repairs, hire mountain bikes and sell midge repellent and gas bottles for stoves.

Sleeping & Eating

Tobermory Campsite (☎ 01688 302624; www.tobermory-campsite.co.uk; Dervaig Rd; sites £6 per person) is located 1.7 miles east of the village. This friendly, low-tech camping ground enjoys a gently scenic position and soft turfy tent pitches.

Tobermory SYHA (☎ 01688 302481; www.syha.org.uk; Main St; dm £14) is one of the cute, colourful, waterfront buildings that win Tobermory a spot in every 'Highlands and islands' calendar. This simple and friendly hostel with creaky bunks and downstairs showers – a minor quibble – the big kitchen, laundry, drying room and lounge with view make up for it. It's a quiet, walker-oriented place but a midnight curfew is harsh when the good folk at the Mishnish Hotel don't shut for another hour after that.

Fàilte Guest House (☎ 01688 302495; www.failteguesthouse.com; 27 Main St; s/d from £32/64). Happiness in Tobermory is a cosy B&B on the pretty, colourful waterfront, and this welcoming choice fits the bill. The rooms are en suite and warmly decorated, with Asian-print bedcovers and lovely gleaming white bathrooms. The best face out to the water, and have huge windows to take advantage of the privileged view.

Highland Cottage (☎ 01688 302030; www.highlandcottage.co.uk; Breadalbane St; d £150-185) – intimate and personable, this small luxurious hotel sits on the hill above the harbour and offers friendly elegance, a warm welcome, and great food. It feels very cosy, with comfortable antique furniture in country-house style and rooms with a homelike feel. Dinner is a gourmet four-course affair (£42.50) that has a deservedly high reputation – non-guests are welcome but book ahead.

Mishnish Hotel (☎ 01688 302009; Main St; bar meals £5-9) – you might not find a better island pub than the legendary Mishnish, a nook-and-cranny setup behind a black facade. There's always good chat at the bar and an interesting mix of locals and tourists. Large pub meals offer plenty of value – posher fare is served upstairs.

Cafe Fish (☎ 01688 301253; The Pier, Tobermory; dinner mains £8-14) is located upstairs at the far end of the harbour – this fabulous newcomer offers simply prepared, delicious seafood. At lunchtime you can chow down on lobster wraps or crab sandwiches, the dinner options include a delicious fish pie and aromatic bowls of steamed mussels. Some of the food comes from the friendly owners' own boat.

Land's End to John O'Groats

- Snapping a photo in front of the famous **Land's End sign** (p310) to chronicle the start of your end-to-end journey
- Taking in the **lovely sea views** following the easy coastal roads between Land's End and Newquay (p307)
- Experience the freak tidal wave – creating surfer heaven – at the **Severn estuary** (p313)
- Toss a caber or have a Highland fling at the **Braemer Gathering** in September (p331)
- Collect stamps as you ride, to claim the official end-to-end certificate (p307)

Telephone Codes: ☎ 01736 / 01955   **www.endtoenders.co.uk**

Let us tell you, the longest cycling route in the UK is one heck of a ride. The adventures awaiting you upon embarking on a Land's End to John O'Groats adventure is nothing short of epic when it comes to British biking. The stuff, in fact, that travel writers dedicate entire books to. To hump the complete 1051.5-mile trail from Land's End in Britain's extreme southwest corner, to John O'Groats in the extreme northeast, is one legendary journey. An ambition harboured by many, that will surely gain you minor celebrity status among the UK's hard-core cycling crowd.

The route detailed here, one of many possible, balances quiet roads and scenery with accommodation choice and ease of navigation. Though it keeps mostly to quiet roads, there are some busier sections, especially around larger towns. The ride is broken into 20 days, averaging 52.6 miles per day, but could be varied according to fitness and time restraints. Alternative routes include the CTC's (Cyclists' Touring Club) three 1000 miles (or so) routes: a main road route – a scenic, YHA-based route, divided into 14 or 15 days – and a scenic B&B-based route. Some of the trip could also be done via Sustrans' NCN (National Cycle Network).

Cyclists traditionally do the ride from Land's End to John O'Groats. Not only are the winds more likely to be favourable, there's no riding into the midday sun. Heading south to north is apparently psychologically uphill – at least if you believe north is higher than south. It's probably not the best factor on which to base a directional decision. However, check the long-range forecast and do consider travelling north to south if, as sometimes happens, the wind is likely to be predominantly from the north.

LAND'S END TO JOHN O'GROATS

Duration 20 days
Distance 1051.5 miles
Difficulty demanding
Start Land's End
End John O'Groats

Summary Get ready for the ride of a lifetime, covering more than 1000 miles of soulful British countryside, this is the UK's epic cycle journey traversing the kingdom from Land's End to John O'Groats.

HISTORY

The first person to travel from one end of the British mainland to the other was Eliuh Burritt, an American, who walked from John O'Groats to Land's End in 'several weeks'. Robert Carlisle, who pushed a wheelbarrow to John O'Groats, was the first Briton on record to have made the journey. It was first cycled around 1880.

But the end-to-end craze didn't really gain momentum until the 20th century, with the advent of the motor car. Both bikes and cars were popular vehicles for the trip. With waves of end-to-enders coinciding with the release of new models, it appears that Land's End to John O'Groats became something of a test route.

Entries in the John O'Groats House Hotel's visitor book chronicle the development of motor cars and bicycles. Some of them, virtual essays (in beautiful copperplate), detail journeys made in little-known models brought out from the US or Germany.

The 20-odd visitor books are now held by the End-to-End Club, which is developing 'Miles of Memories' – an end-to-end hall of fame. Unfortunately, records stored at Land's End were destroyed by fire in 1985.

CLIMATE

Generally speaking, the temperature becomes cooler heading north. The coldest section is likely to be through the Grampian Mountains in Scotland, especially on the high passes.

Rainfall is greatest in the west and in hilly areas, for example, around the Pennines. However, in Britain, it can rain anywhere, anytime. The prevailing wind is from the southwest, though it's possible to get periods of northeasterlies.

PLANNING
When to Cycle

Although people have ridden end-to-end in the dead of winter, the ideal time is between April and mid-September. June is perhaps the best month: the roads – and accommodation – are less crowded than in July and August, the days are long, and the

END-TO-END RECORDS

Around 4000 people each year complete the journey from one end of Britain to the other, an estimated 75% of whom do it by bike. Most cyclists do the trip in two or three weeks.

Andy Wilkinson was much less patient – in 1990, he cycled 874 miles from Land's End to John O'Groats in 1 day, 21 hours, 2 minutes and 18 seconds, beating the previous record by 53 seconds. Pauline Strong holds the women's cycling record of 2 days, 6 hours, 49 minutes and 45 seconds. An early cycling record to be recognised was by GP Mills who, in 1891, rode the distance in 4 days, 11 hours and 17 minutes.

With so many people making the journey these days, you have to do something extra special to be noticed. People have spiced up the journey – and the record books – in all manner of ways: Steve Gilkes has done it several times on a motorised toilet (one wonders whether he was linked with the motorised bar stool) – another used a supermarket trolley. It's been done in a battery-powered Sinclair C5 in 80 hours and on roller skates in 9½ days. Penny farthings are relatively common, as are tricycles and tandems. In 1990, it was run in 26 days and 7 hours by Arvind Pandya – no great record in itself, apart from the fact that he was running backwards!

Raising money for charity is very common among end-to-enders – it's estimated that around 80% of those undertaking the trip (most of them locals) raise money – whether it's the primary purpose of the trip, or just an added extra.

LAND'S END TO JOHN O'GROATS

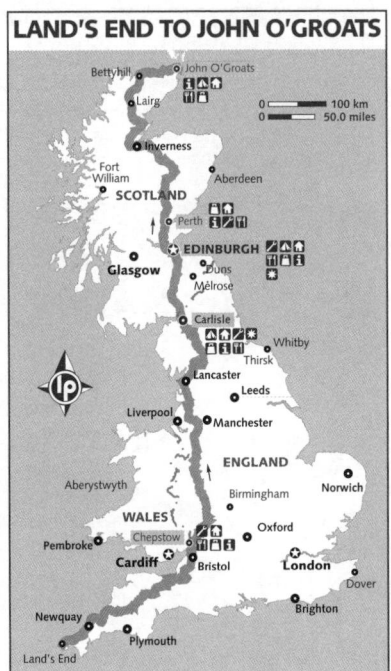

weather is more likely to be on your side than in spring or autumn. By mid-September, there can be snow on the Grampian's high passes.

What to Bring

Make sure your bike is in good working order – have it serviced before you go. Check that there's plenty of wear left in the tyres, rims and chain. Take some chain lubricant and a rag to keep it clean and oiled throughout the ride, plus emergency repair tools (see p23).

Remember to bring and fill out your transit or record sheet, to qualify for an official certificate.

Maps

The best supplementary maps are the Ordnance Survey (OS) 1:250,000 Travelmaster series. The ride is covered by sheets two, four, five, seven and eight – available from tourist information centres, and map and book shops. The OS Landranger series maps (1:50,000) are useful for providing detail in some areas.

Information Sources

For info on cycling from Land's End to John O'Groats online check out the following websites:

- www.sustrans.org.uk
- www.landsend-landmark.co.uk

GETTING TO/FROM THE RIDE
Land's End (start)

Unless you can convince a friend to drive you to Land's End, the best option is to catch the train to Penzance, about 9 miles from Land's End, and ride west from there. We suggest riding the fastest route from Penzance – via the often busy A30 – since Day 1 of the Land's End to John O'Groats ride returns to Penzance via more scenic (and quieter) B-roads.

TRAIN

The train journey from London to Penzance (around £70; five hours) is on **Great Western** services. Up to six bicycles are carried on each train – bikes booked at least two hours before departure cost £1. They're £3 if you book under two hours before departure.

John O'Groats (finish)

See p343 for information on getting to and from John O'Groats.

THE RIDE
Day 1: Land's End to Newquay
6–7 hours, 51.1 miles

While the surrounding scenery features granite cliffs running to the booming Atlantic surf and dramatic views, **Land's End** is in fact a much-visited, slightly generic tourist trap. Certainly, the town has a wild, isolated appeal but you'll have to

---

MEMORALISING THE TRIP

Both the CTC and End to End Club provide certificates on evidence of completion. Use the official record or transit sheet (or equivalent) to collect hostel stamps or date stamps from places of accommodation. CTC's certificate is free providing you buy a T-shirt or cloth badge – End to End Club charges a small fee, which includes a year's membership of the club.

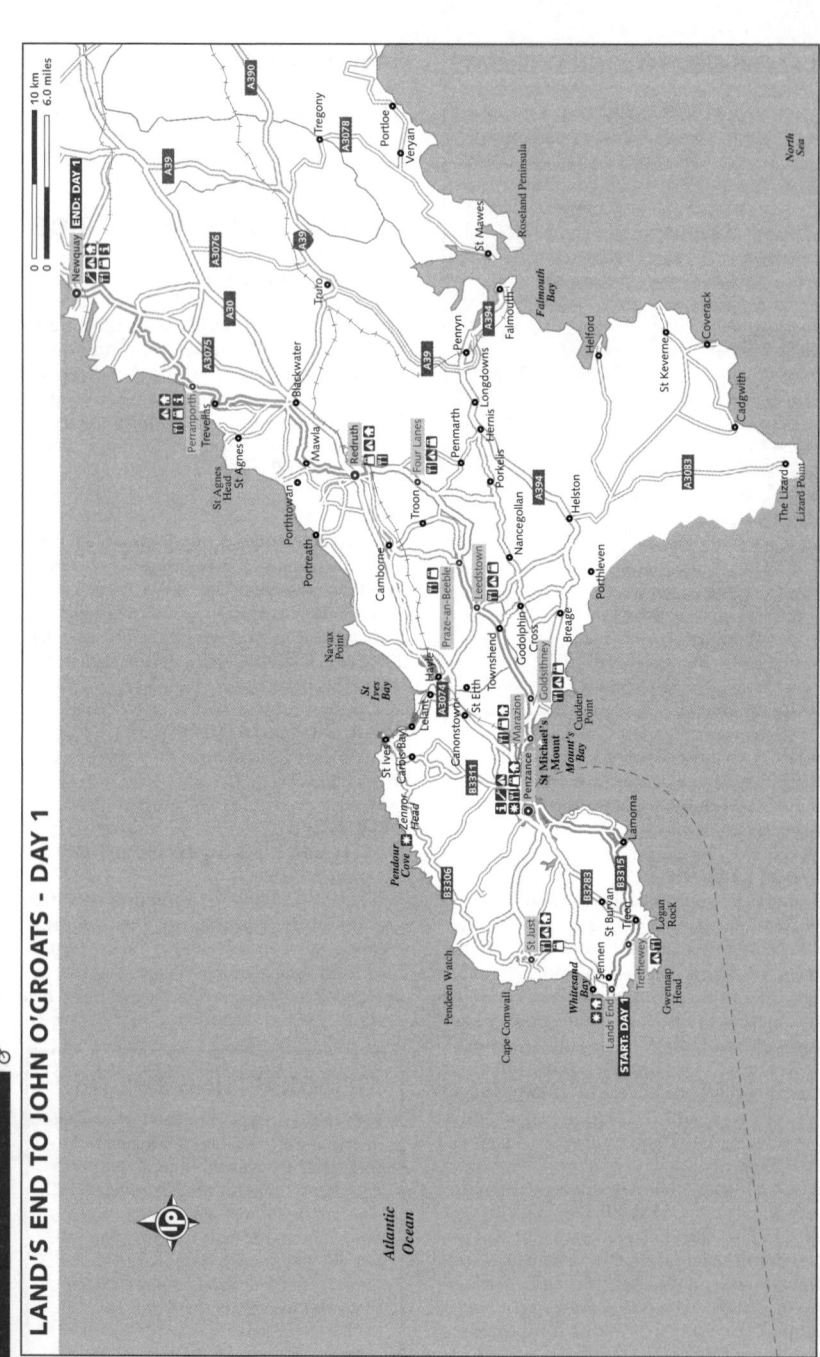

LAND'S END TO JOHN O'GROATS - DAY 1

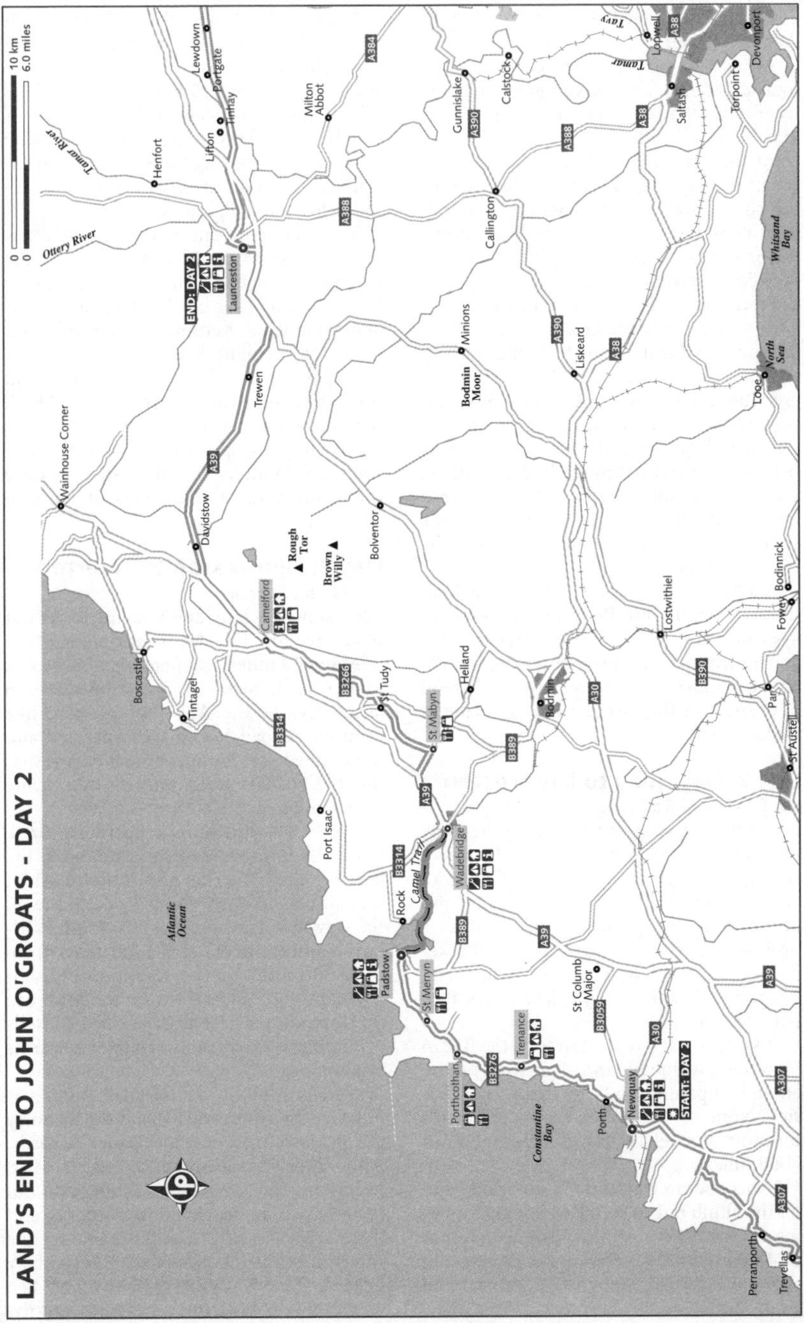

LAND'S END TO JOHN O'GROATS - DAY 2

10 km
6.0 miles

Lewdown

Portgate

Lifton

Tinhay

Milton Abbot

A384

Tavy

Lopwell

A38

Devonport

Torpoint

Salfash

Whitsand Bay

Gunnislake

A390

A38

Calstock

A388

Hemford

Ottery River

Tamar River

A388

A390

Callington

Minions

Liskeard

A38

Looe

North Sea

END: DAY 2

Launceston

A39

Trewen

Bodmin Moor

Wainhouse Corner

Davidstow

Rough Tor ▲

▲ Brown Willy

Bolventor

Lostwithiel

Fowey

Bodinnick

A30

Boscastle

Camelford

B3266

Tintagel

B3314

St Tudy

Helland

St Mabyn

Bodmin

B390

Par

St Austell

Port Isaac

B389

A39

Rock

Camel Trail

B3314

Wadebridge

Padstow

B389

St Merryn

St Columb Major

B3059

A39

Atlantic Ocean

Porthcothan

B3276

Treyarnon

A30

Constantine Bay

Porth

Newquay

START: DAY 2

A307

Perranporth

A3075

Trevellas

A302

⛢ **LAND'S END TO JOHN O'GROATS**

get out to the rugged cliffs overlooking the Atlantic Ocean to experience it.

All end-to-end (E2E) riders start their journey at the famous **signpost** (a photo by the resident concession holder will set you back £5), which is a short distance from the Land's End Hotel. This is a nice warm-up day, mostly on B-roads, featuring some lovely ocean views and interesting towns and villages. While there are no major climbs, there's a fair bit of the up-and-down terrain.

From Land's End to Penzance you'll see Cornwall countryside and the ocean off to the south and east. Along the Penzance waterfront and extending to Marazion there are wonderful views of **Mount's Bay**. Just past Marazion (15.6 miles) the route slices inland and, for about 15 miles, follows quiet B-roads. Be careful through Redruth – there can be quite a bit of traffic in the town centre, near the train station, and again on the short stretch on the A30 and A3075 in the 38- to 40-mile range.

A return to the coast, after the exhilarating downhill into Perranporth, precedes a steady climb and another niggling up-and-down before you rejoin the A3075 about 3 miles from **Newquay**. Be careful of traffic over this last section, especially in midsummer.

Day 2: Newquay to Launceston
5½–6½ hours, 49.8 miles

Leave Britain's surfing capital in the early morning. You've got another full day of riding through magnificent Cornwall countryside ahead of you – both on- and off-road. A busy morning for traffic is broken by a stint on the Camel Trail bikepath – the afternoon features wonderful hedge-lined lanes on the last miles into Launceston.

It's a hilly start to the day, with the B3276 between Newquay and Padstow taking enough dips and rolls to make you seasick. None of the climbs are long, but it's certainly a relief to join the **Camel Trail** (14.8 miles).

Expect some traffic in Wadebridge and on the climb out of it (take great care turning off the A39 on to the unsigned road at 22.4 miles), but look forward to quiet going through lovely **St Mabyn** (23.7 miles) and along the B3266.

Keep your wits about you during the 3-mile section on the A39 near equally quaint **Camelford**, but once you've taken the 'to Altarnun' turn, it's 15 miles of cycling bliss all the way to Launceston. The road climbs briefly, then flattens (for what seems an eternity), first passing the wide-open northern flank of Bodmin Moor before re-entering fields and hedgerows.

There's a 'blink-and-you'll-miss-it' interlude on the A395 (44.3 miles) before the left turn to arguably the day's highlight – the wonderful lane on the steep-sided hills above the River Kensey. Launceston, your home for the night, is well worth a wander. After parking your bike, stop and check out the **Launceston Castle** (☎ 01566 772365). Majestic even in ruin, it crowns the town centre, offering splendid views of the surrounding countryside. The castle was once the stronghold of the powerful Earls of Cornwall.

Day 3: Launceston to Tiverton
5½–7 hours, 52.3 miles

After some ducking and weaving to get out of Launceston, this day is very pleasant.

About 12 miles are spent on what passes as the 'back road' to Okehampton – an alternative to the A30 that is more like a minor A-road it's so well surfaced and maintained. Traffic moves fast as a result, but the road is wide and it's not really threatening.

Views of Dartmoor's northern flank gradually improve and for a moment, the longish climb to the A30 junction (16.4 miles) feels like it's going to continue all the way to 621m-high (2038ft) **High Willhays mountain**. After a brief blast from the A30 traffic, there's respite in pleasant Okehampton, where a stop at the **Museum of Dartmoor Life** (☎ 01837 52295) tells of the bleak expanse of Dartmoor and its inhabitants.

A longish climb out of Okehampton is followed by some truly delightful country riding, both on lanes and quiet B-roads. After a brief back-road deviation (40.8 miles), the final 10 miles into Tiverton can be busy. It's an up-and-down section, and there are some slow uphill corners on the way into Withleigh, where care is especially needed. The day ends with a long, fast downhill into **Tiverton** – have fun and fly.

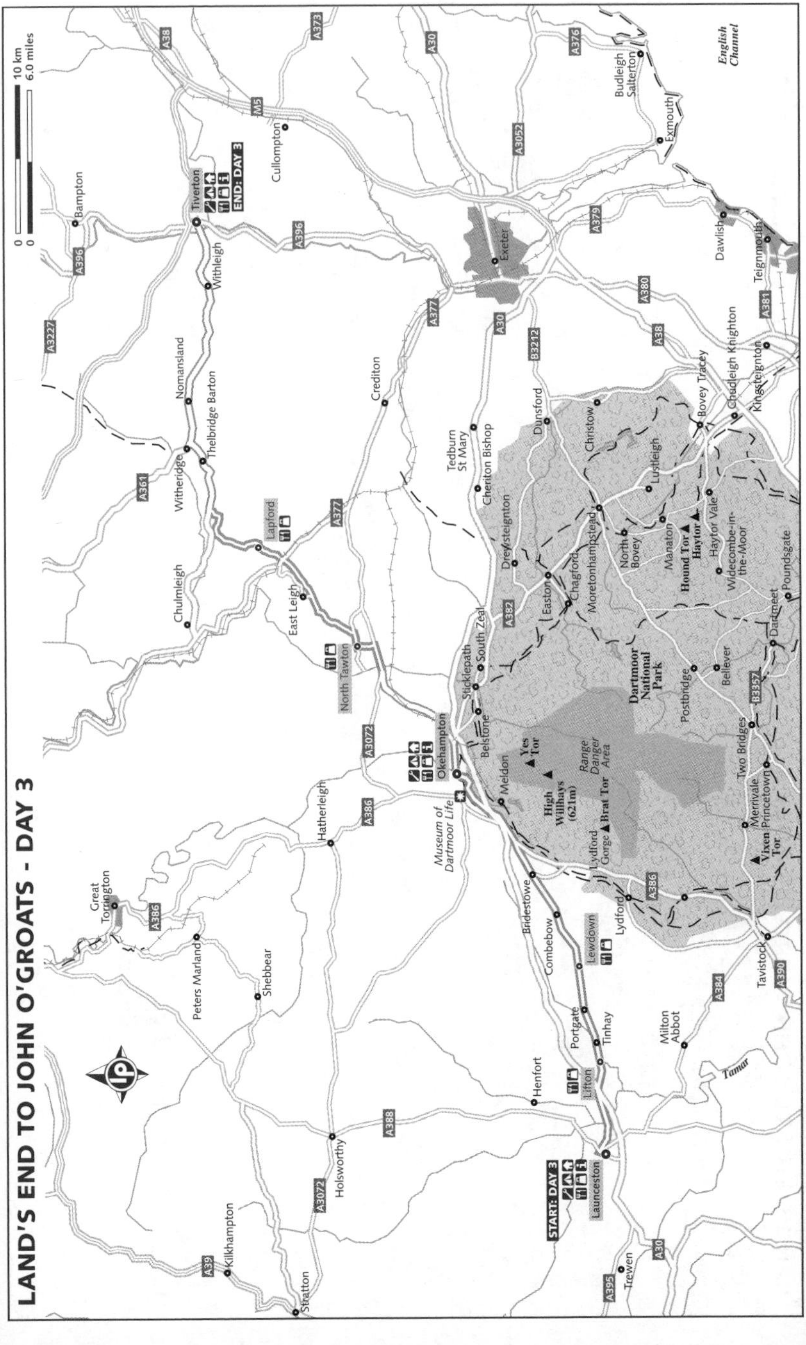

LAND'S END TO JOHN O'GROATS – DAY 3

0   10 km
0   6.0 miles

English Channel

A38
A373
A30
A376
M5
Cullompton
Budleigh Salterton
Exmouth
A396
Bampton
Tiverton
END: DAY 3
Withleigh
A396
A3052
A379
Dawlish
Teignmouth
A380
A381
A3227
Nomansland
Thelbridge Barton
Witheridge
Crediton
A377
Exeter
Tedburn St Mary
Cheriton Bishop
Dunsford
Christow
B3212
Chudleigh Knighton
Kingsteignton
A38
Bovey Tracey
A361
Chulmleigh
East Leigh
Lapford
A377
Drewsteignton
Chagford
Easton
Moretonhampstead
North Bovey
Lustleigh
Manaton
Hound Tor ▲
Haytor ▲
Haytor Vale
Widecombe-in-the-Moor
Poundsgate
North Tawton
A3072
Sticklepath
South Zeal
Belstone
Dartmoor National Park
Bellever
Dartmeet
B3357
Hatherleigh
A386
Okehampton
Meldon
Yes Tor ▲
Range Danger Area
Postbridge
Two Bridges
Museum of Dartmoor Life
High Willhays (621m) ▲
Lydford Gorge ▲
▲ **Brat Tor**
Merrivale
Princetown
▲ **Vixen Tor**
Great Torrington
A386
Peters Marland
Shebbear
Bridestowe
Combebow
Lydford
A386
Tavistock
A390
A384
Milton Abbot
Tamar
Henfort
Portgate
Tinhay
Lewdown
Lifton
A388
Holsworthy
A3072
Kilkhampton
A39
Stratton
START: DAY 3
Launceston
Trewen
A30
A395

LAND'S END TO JOHN O'GROATS

LAND'S END TO JOHN O'GROATS - DAY 4

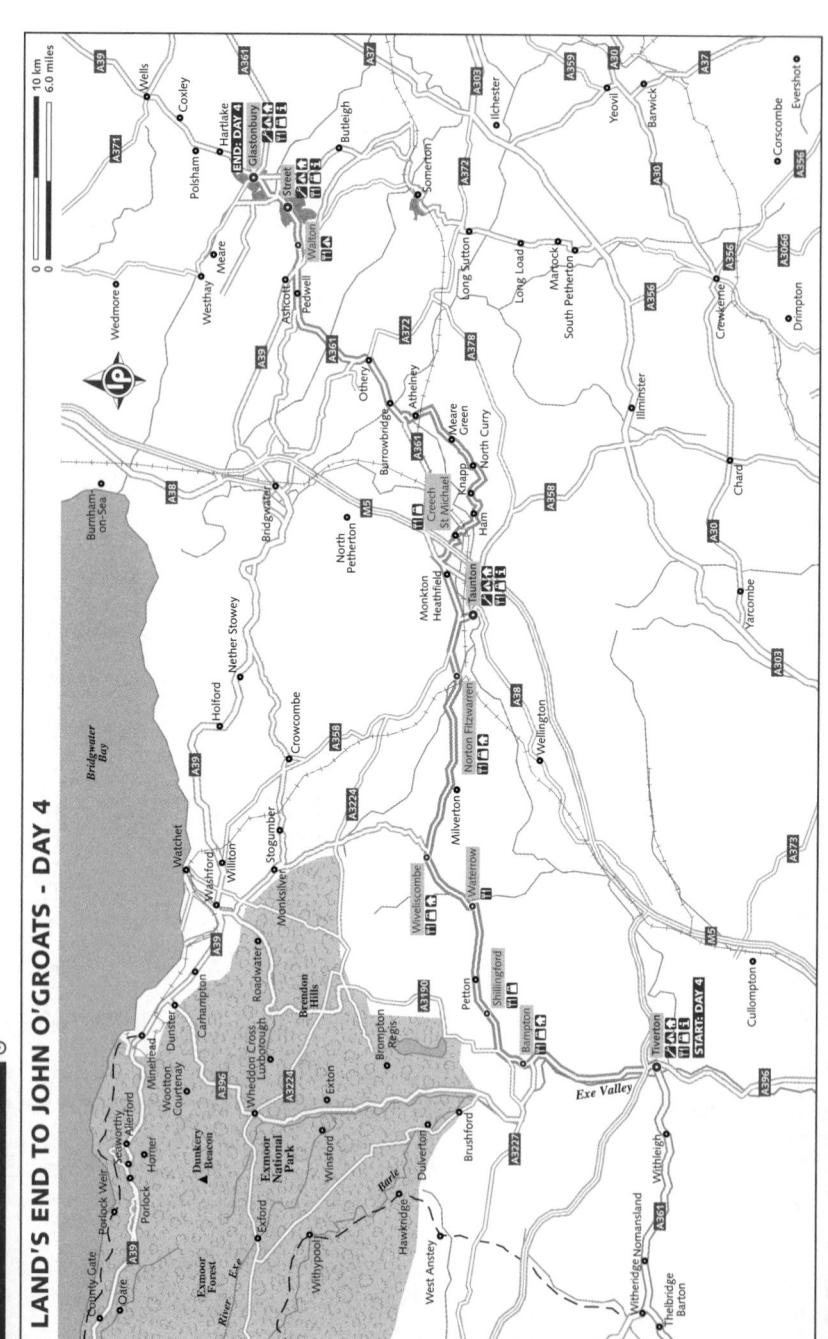

THRILL AT THE SEVERN BORE

For something like 24 days a year, a spectacular wall of water sweeps up the Severn estuary carrying surfers, canoeists and branches alike. One of the best tidal waves, or bores, in the world – it is formed because the funnel shape of the broad estuary can't dissipate the sudden volume of water quickly enough. With a good spring tide, low inland water and a wind coming off the sea, the wave can rise as high as 2m (6.5ft) as it rushes in noisily at 10mph. For the surfers, it's the longest rollers they've ever caught, swooshing them as far as the tidal weirs at Gloucester. For spectators, it's an excuse for a picnic and a chance to get your feet wet if you get too close.

There's a good view of the full bore at Minsterworth, Stonebench or Overbridge. Get there early to secure a spot if it's a weekend or bank holiday. The nascent bore can also be spotted en route on Day 6 at Newnham (17.4 miles).

The bore is best during the lunar cycles of January, February, March, April, July, August, September and October. The **Gloucester tourist office** (☎ 01452 421188) has times, or visit the **Environment Agency website** (www.environment-agency.gov.uk.envinfo/index.htm).

Day 4: Tiverton to Glastonbury
5½–7 hours, 52.9 miles

Generally, this is a busier day for traffic, with some noticeably noisy and less enjoyable sections to negotiate. While these A-road sojourns can be a little taxing, they typically allow a more direct route.

The day starts quietly enough with an undulating few miles, on lanes that are sometimes a bit rough, beside the tranquil River Exe. A short spell on the A396 (6 miles) near Bampton passes quickly, and afterwards there's a wonderful 6 to 7 miles on the B3227 heading for Wiveliscombe – its flat, wide and surrounded by wonderful scenery.

The day's major climbs come between the 15- and 22-mile mark. The first, leading up to **Wiveliscombe**, is steeper – the second is a gradual rise over 3.1 miles. Expect traffic, sometimes heavy, from outside Norton Fitzwarren (25.5 miles) all the way to the **Creech St Michael** turn-off (31.2 miles). Quiet, flat lanes afterwards will ease any road-stress, but take care navigating in this section. The ride's last 12 miles are spent on A-roads (the A361 & A39) and conditions vary depending on the time of day. Generally the A361 traffic isn't too bad – the A39 into new-agey **Glastonbury** can be busy during the morning and evening peak times and you should take extra care.

Day 5: Glastonbury to Chepstow
6–7½ hours, 57.4 miles

Extended flat sections make this long-ish day a fairly easy ride. The flats commence on the route out of Glastonbury. The B3151 is level and also very straight for extended sections – as a consequence traffic moves fast, but vision is good and the situation isn't worrying. The stiff pinch uphill into Wedmore comes as a bit of a shock, but it's easy going again from there to Cheddar.

The 4.7-mile climb up through striking **Cheddar Gorge** (13.8 miles) sounds daunting, but it's a gradual rise and you're conscious of the strain in only a few places. Once atop the **Mendip Hills** the views are splendid. Take care descending (20.3 miles) and save some breath for the last climb – the nasty, rearing ascent of **Dundry Hill** (25.9 miles).

It's slow going through **Bristol** on the cycle paths but worth it to miss the city traffic.

Once on NCN 4 (39.3 miles) it's flat riding practically all the way to **Chepstow** – the biggest climbs are on bridge cycle paths – where you'll stop for night five.

Day 6: Chepstow to Worcester
4–6½ hours, 58.6 miles

This long day tracks the course of the River Severn as it downsizes from a broad tidal estuary at the Welsh border to a gentle water meadow flowing through Gloucestershire. The first 20 miles are on the fast and narrow A48 – riding here will take nerve as the road is plagued by heavy trucks and overtaking cars. Riverside viewpoints on the way often feature a drinking hole or two. Good pubs en route can be found in

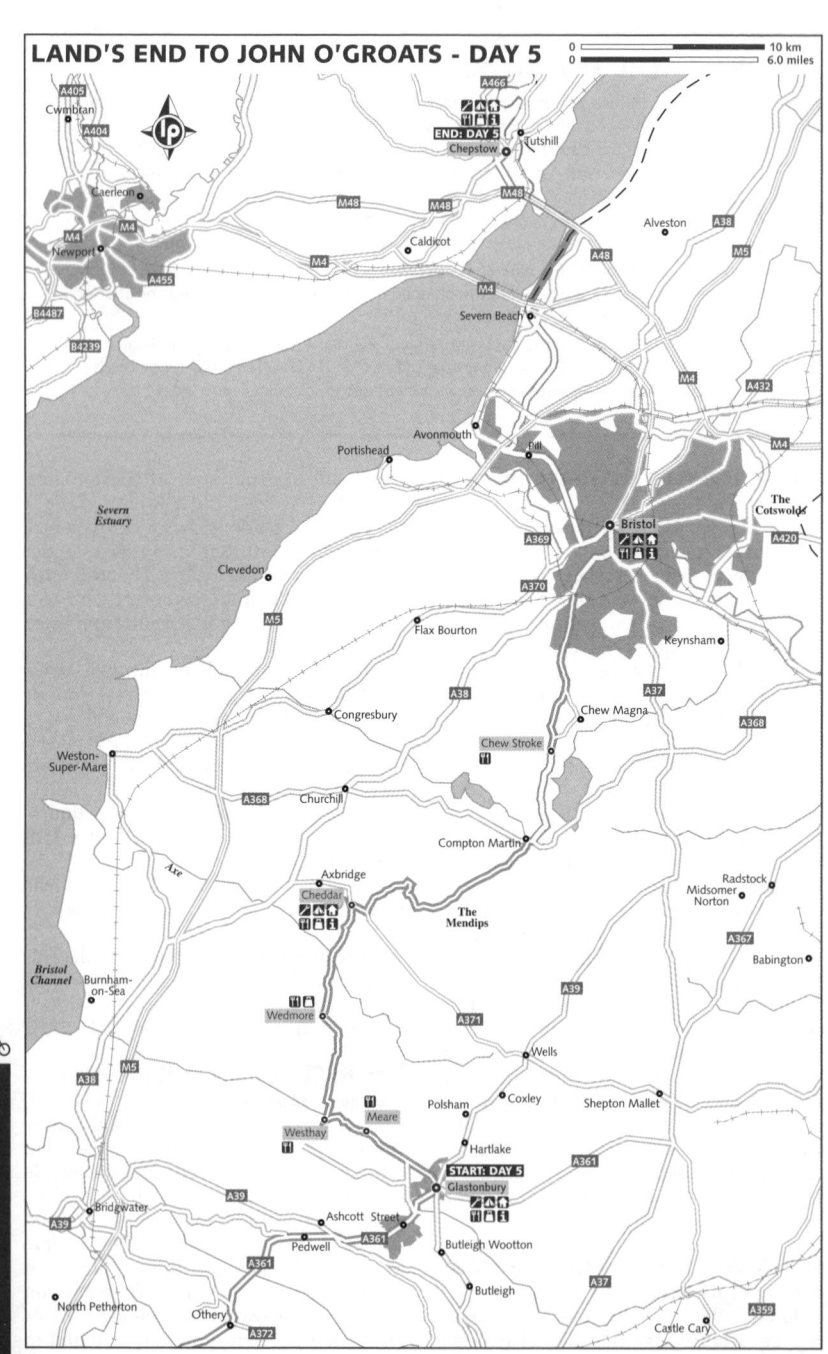

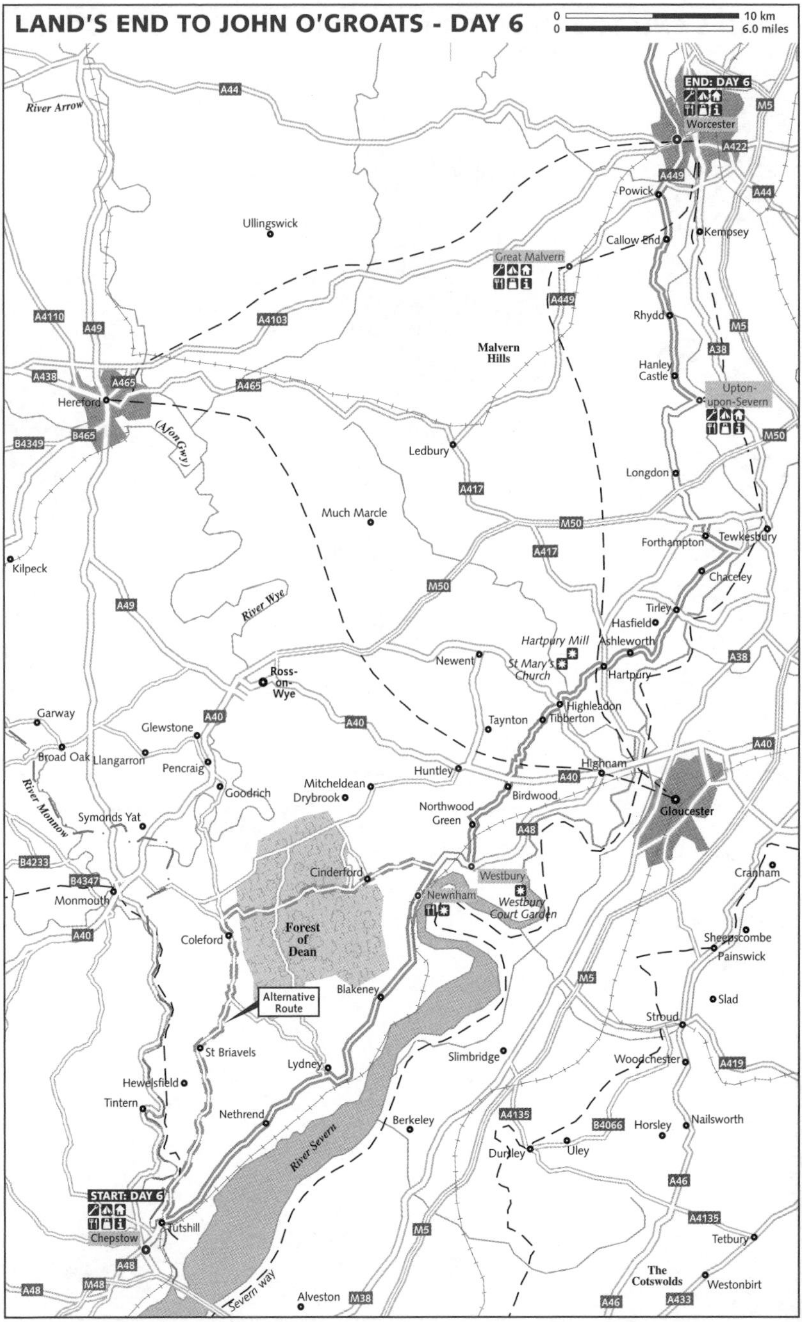

LAND'S END TO JOHN O'GROATS - DAY 6

0   10 km
0   6.0 miles

River Arrow

A44

END: DAY 6
Worcester
M5
A422

Powick
A449
A44

Ullingswick

Great Malvern

Callow End
Kempsey

A449

Rhydd
M5

A4110
A49
A4103

Malvern
Hills

Hanley
Castle
A38

A438
A465
A465
Hereford
Upton-
upon-Severn
M50

B465
(Afon Gwy)

Longdon
M50

Ledbury

A417

Forthampton
Tewkesbury

Kilpeck

Much Marcle
M50
A417

Chaceley

A49
River Wye

Tirley
Hasfield
Ashleworth
A38

Hartpury Mill
Newent
St Mary's
Church
Hartpury

Garway
A40
Ross-
on-
Wye
A40
Taynton
Highleadon
Tibberton
A40

Glewstone
Broad Oak
Llangarron
Pencraig
Goodrich
Huntley
Highnam
A40

Symonds Yat
Mitcheldean
Drybrook
Northwood
Green
Birdwood
Gloucester

B4233
B4347
Cinderford
A48

Monmouth
Westbury
Cranham

A40
Newnham
Westbury
Court Garden
Sheepscombe
Painswick

Forest
of
Dean
Alternative
Route
Blakeney
M5
Slad

Coleford
Stroud

St Briavels
Lydney
Slimbridge
Woodchester
A419

Hewelsfield
Tintern
Nethrend
Berkeley
A4135
B4066
Horsley
Nailsworth

Dursley
Uley
A46

START: DAY 6
Chepstow
Tutshill
River Severn
M5
A4135
Tetbury

A48
A48
Severn way
Alveston
M38
A46
The
Cotswolds
A433
Westonbirt

LAND'S END TO JOHN O'GROATS

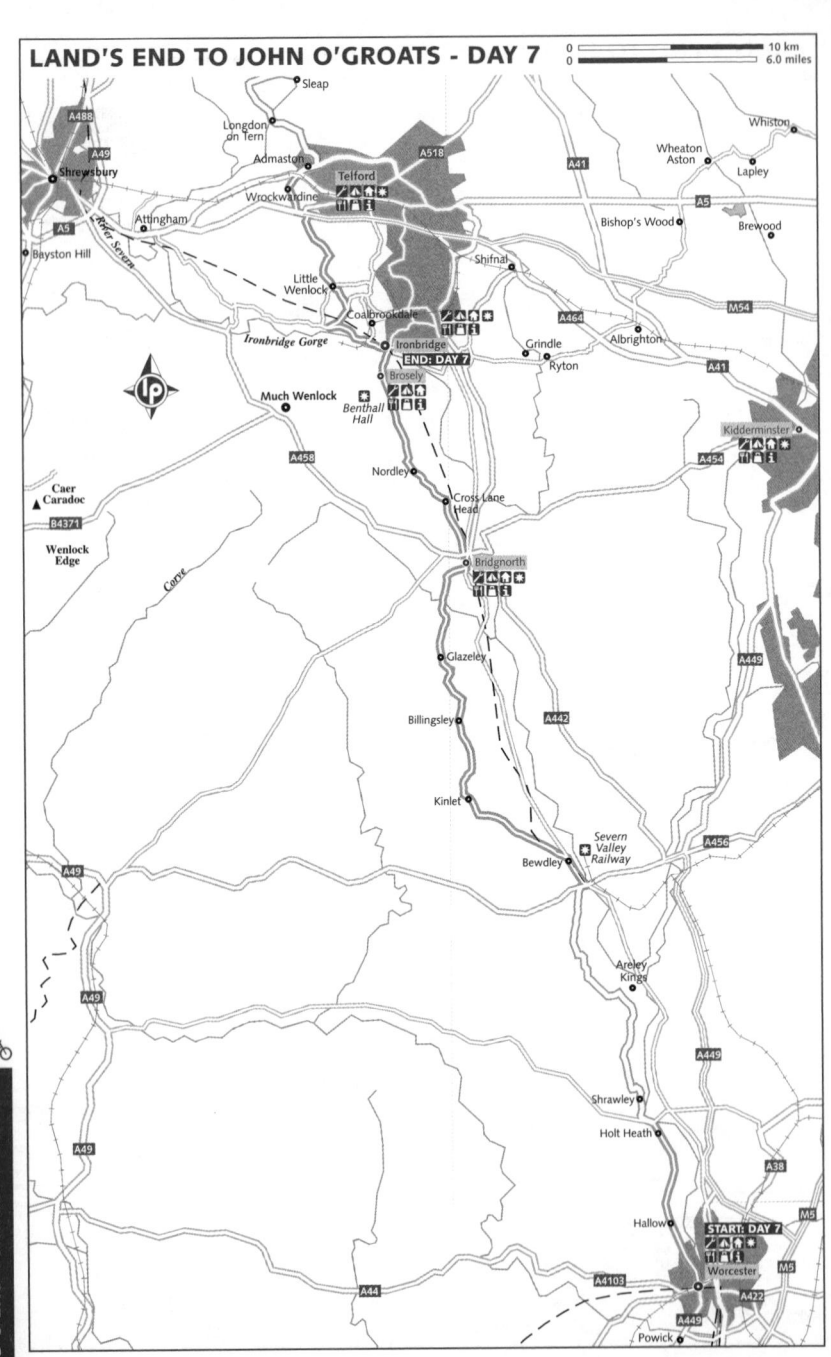

LAND'S END TO JOHN O'GROATS - DAY 7

Newnham (17.4 miles), **Ashleworth quay**, a side trip to the right just eastward of Ashleworth at 34.4 miles, and **Upton upon Severn** (47.5 miles).

Westbury Court Garden (20.1 miles; ☎ 01452 760461) is the only restored 17th-century Dutch water garden in the country and merits parting bum from saddle when the sun is shining. At Westbury-on-Severn the route changes character when the demanding A48 is swapped for the quite back roads of Gloucestershire. About 10 miles further on, grade–II-listed **Hartpury Mill** (not open to the public) and **St Mary's Church** enjoy an idyllically English setting. The rest of the day is an uninterrupted easy run, mostly along the semi-quiet B4211.

ALTERNATIVE ROUTE: VIA COLEFORD

A recommended less hazardous and mildly more scenic alternative route, if you have time, is to follow day one of the Marches, Cheshire & Lancashire ride (see p134 in the Central England chapter) to Coleford. After that take the very hilly B4226 to Cinderford passing through the **Forest of Dean** on the way. After Cinderford join the A4151, which meets the A48 not far from the Westbury-on-Severn turn-off.

Day 7: Worcester to Ironbridge
2½–4 hours, 40.5 miles

Today may be short but the climbs make up for it as you follow the River Severn on its way into Shropshire. The route traverses a landscape of valleys and forest as far as the spectacular Ironbridge Gorge. However, today's not all about rustic riding as the towns of Bewdley and Bridgnorth block the way, adding some urban diversion and providing an opportune lunch/coffee halt. Beware of heavy traffic on the A-roads leaving Worcester and the right turn at 7.7 miles. Thereafter, things quieten considerably.

The riding is persistently hilly, gaining height numerous times between streams that feed the Severn and towns that bridge it. A satisfying 16-mile stretch between the red sandstone towns of Bewdley and Bridgnorth starts with a steady climb through the **Wyre Forest** and continues with a rollercoaster road and good views before a long descent into Ironbridge. Some may be tempted to cheat by boarding the **Severn Valley Railway** (☎ 01299 403816), which steams its scenic way between

the two towns, hugging the twists and turns of the River Severn all the way. **Bewdley** is the most obvious place to take lunch.

If you still have the strength towards the end of the day's riding, **Benthall Hall** (☎ 01952 882159) near Broseley on the approaches to Ironbridge is a grand 16th-century manor in the care of the National Trust. Inside you can admire exquisite interiors with acres of oak panelling and an impressive carved oak staircase.

Day 8: Ironbridge to Northwich
4–6½ hours, 60.4 miles

Mile-rich, today is memorable for a major lung-busting ascent early on, a Cold War relic and some idyllic country lanes. You'll be mostly riding on quiet back roads though there are short bits on the A442 and the busy A41 to deal with.

With a 5-mile climb up the side of **The Wrekin** gaining 180m (590ft) directly out of Ironbridge, you say farewell to the Severn Valley for good. Between Waters Upton (15.2 miles) and Audlem (35.2 miles) are 20 miles of pretty rural lanes along the Rivers Tern and Weaver – cars are a rarity.

Just before Nantwich detour follow the rather amusing 'Secret Bunker' signs (to the left) to the fascinating **Hack Green Secret Nuclear Bunker** (40 miles; ☎ 01270 629219), declassified in the late 1990s and one of the most interesting sights along the entire E2E route. It was set up in 1976 as a hide-out for 135 civil servants and military personnel who would sit out a nuclear attack here. Experience a four-minute warning, watch genuine pre-strike TV broadcasts and see the decontamination room, before emerging again to find rural Cheshire still very much intact.

The route skirts the centre of **Nantwich**, which, if you haven't eaten already, has a good choice of places to fill the hole. Nearing the end of the day you pass through the semi-large but wholly uninteresting town of Winsford (52.9 miles) before the final push to your overnight stop at Northwich.

Day 9: Northwich to Lancaster
5–8½ hours, 78.8 miles

There are few distractions during this super long day dodging and negotiating the northwest's urban sprawls. With plenty of traffic for company get your head down

LAND'S END TO JOHN O'GROATS

LAND'S END TO JOHN O'GROATS - DAY 8

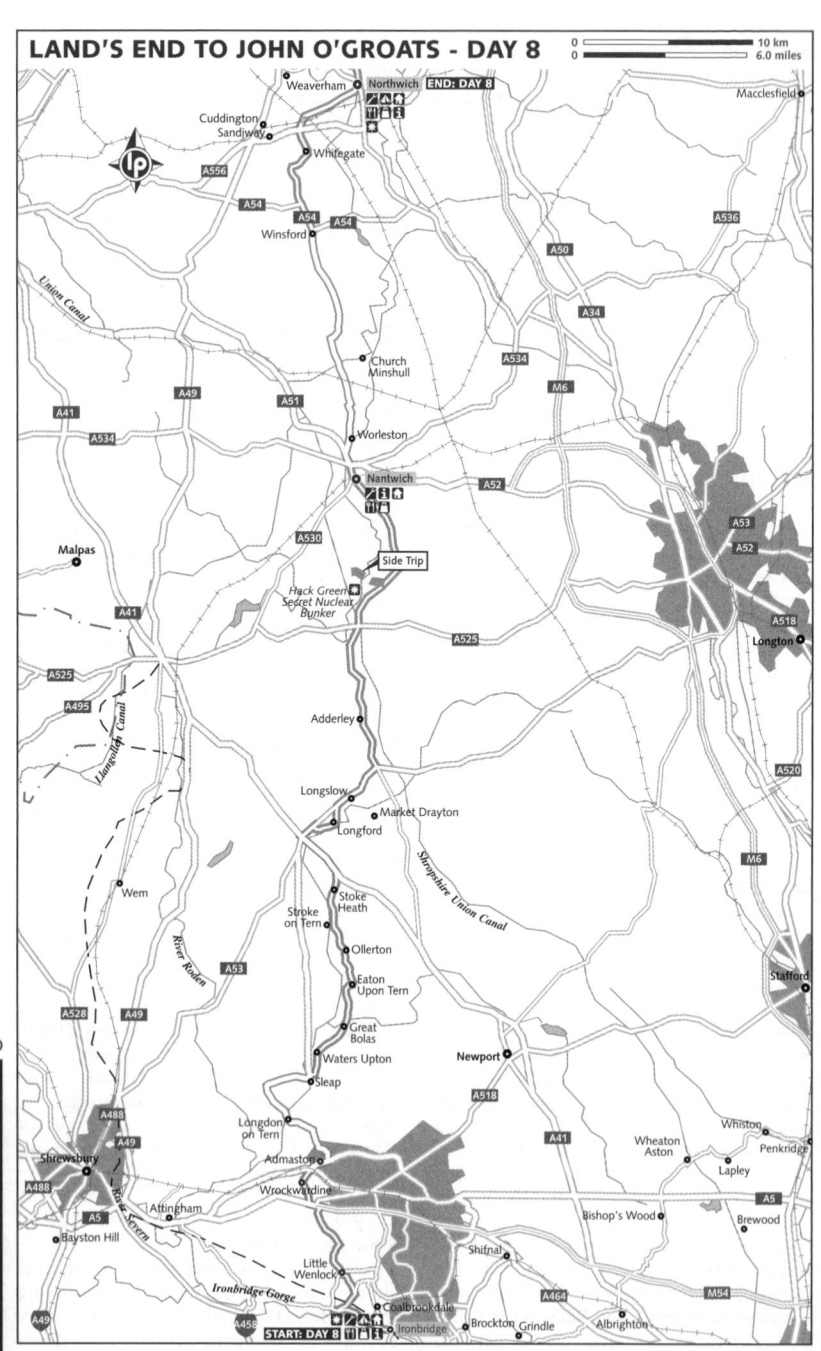

0 ——————— 10 km
0 ——————— 6.0 miles

END: DAY 8

Macclesfield

Weaverham
Northwich
Cuddington
Sandiway
Whitegate

A556

A54

A54   A54

Winsford

A50

A34

A536

Union Canal

A41

A49

A51

Church
Minshull

A534

M6

A534

Worleston

Nantwich

A52

A53

A52

Malpas

A530

Side Trip

A41

Hack Green
Secret Nuclear
Bunker

A525

A518

Longton

A525

A495

Llangollen Canal

Adderley

A520

Longslow
Market Drayton
Longford

Shropshire Union Canal

M6

Wem

River Roden

A53

Stoke
Heath

Stroke
on Tern

Ollerton

Stafford

A528   A49

Eaton
Upon Tern

Great
Bolas

Waters Upton

Sleap

Newport

A488
A49

Longdon
on Tern

A518

A41

Wheaton
Aston

Whiston

Penkridge

Shrewsbury

Admaston

Wrockwardine

Lapley

A5

A488

A5

River Severn

Attingham

Bayston Hill

Bishop's
Wood

Brewood

Little
Wenlock

Shifnal

A49

Ironbridge Gorge

A458

Coalbrookdale

START: DAY 8

Ironbridge

Brockton Grindle

A464

Albrighton

M54

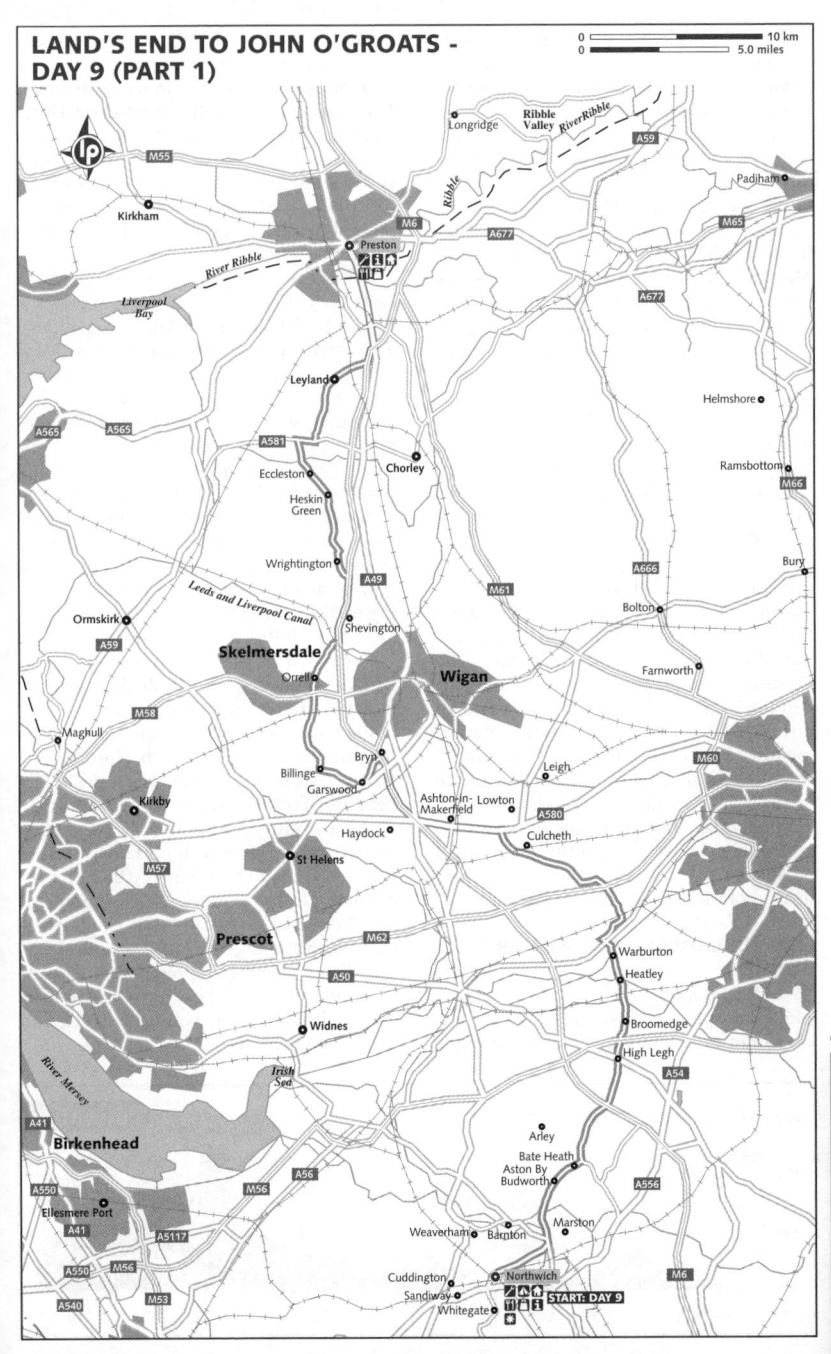

LAND'S END TO JOHN O'GROATS - DAY 9 (PART 1)

and bag it. If almost 80 miles seems a bit too much for you in one go, it's always possible to split the day into two shorter ones, stopping at Preston (49.8 miles) or Garstang (64.7 miles), but with hardly any stops on the way, you'll be surprised how far you can pedal.

It's countryside all the way from Northwich as far as Warburton, a stretch, which includes the only rural crossing of the **Manchester Ship Canal** (11.9 miles) for miles. From there continue for 17 miles from Culcheth (18 miles) to Shevington (34.3 miles). Here things go rural again until the fast A-road-approach to **Preston**, which at least has a cycle lane. Take great care on the last section into Preston, and it may be worth dismounting and walking along the verge where the A59 dual carriageway joins. Two fast lanes of traffic must be crossed to exit.

In Preston, pick up the Southport to Lancaster route at the 17.8-mile mark on that cue sheet (see Day 5, of the Marches, Cheshire & Lancashire ride in the Central England chapter p140), which becomes more bucolic again on the Lancashire plain heading towards Lancaster. A short side trip (at 74 miles) leads to **Glasson** and its historic dock and lighthouse. This interesting town had its heyday in the 18th century when the local canal from Lancaster ran to its dock basins and these remain the oldest existing tidal dock in England. Save time and a mile or two by continuing straight on to Lancaster on the A588 (72.3 miles) instead of turning left to visit Glasson.

Day 10: Lancaster to Kirkby Stephen

4½–6 hours, 53 miles

This day passes through three different counties and a variety of picturesque landscapes. The magnificent scenery encountered along **Dentdale** is particularly memorable, as is the journey through Mallerstang Dale in the **Yorkshire Dales National Park** (0300 456 0030; www.yorkshiredales.org.uk). The day's major climb is a testing 2.5-mile ascent from Cowgill (36.5 miles), which is followed by a brake-block-burning drop down to Garsdale Station.

Whichever way you choose to exit Lancaster, you'll wind up coasting along the B6354 to **Kirkby Lonsdale** (15.2 miles). This charming Cumbrian market town in the heart of the Vale of Lune is a good place to catch your breath, have a coffee and admire the surrounding landscapes that inspired the artists Turner and Constable. Stick with the River Lune, following it upstream to Sedbergh (27.5 miles) where its waters mix with the River Dee. You now enter picturesque **Dentdale**, a valley of stone houses and bridges, verdant hills and ever-changing skies. There's steady climbing up the valley to Cowgill before the final ascent to a lofty exposed summit.

For much of the remaining distance to Kirkby Stephen the road shadows the famous **Settle to Carlisle line rail line**, one of the most scenic in the country and, ergo, persistently threatened with closure. The B6259 then winds its way down the wildly beautiful dale of **Mallerstang**. The ruin of 12th-century **Pendragon Castle** (48.8 miles) was reputedly founded by Uther Pendragon, father to King Arthur. Its inhabitants today, a flock of staring sheep, aren't quite as mythical, but it is, nonetheless, an intriguing ruin in a beautiful setting. Kirkby Stephen represents a milestone on your end-to-end journey – you're halfway, at least in days, between Land's End and John O'Groats.

Elevation chart showing the route from Lancaster to Kirkby Stephen with elevation in metres (0m, 200, 400, 600) and feet (0ft, 500, 1000, 1500, 2000) on the vertical axis and distance in miles (0mi, 10, 20, 30, 40, 50) on the horizontal axis. Labelled points: Lancaster, Arkholme, Kirkby Lonsdale, Middleton, Sedbergh, Dent, Cowgill, Garsdale Station, Kirkby Stephen.

LAND'S END TO JOHN O'GROATS - DAY 9 (PART 2)

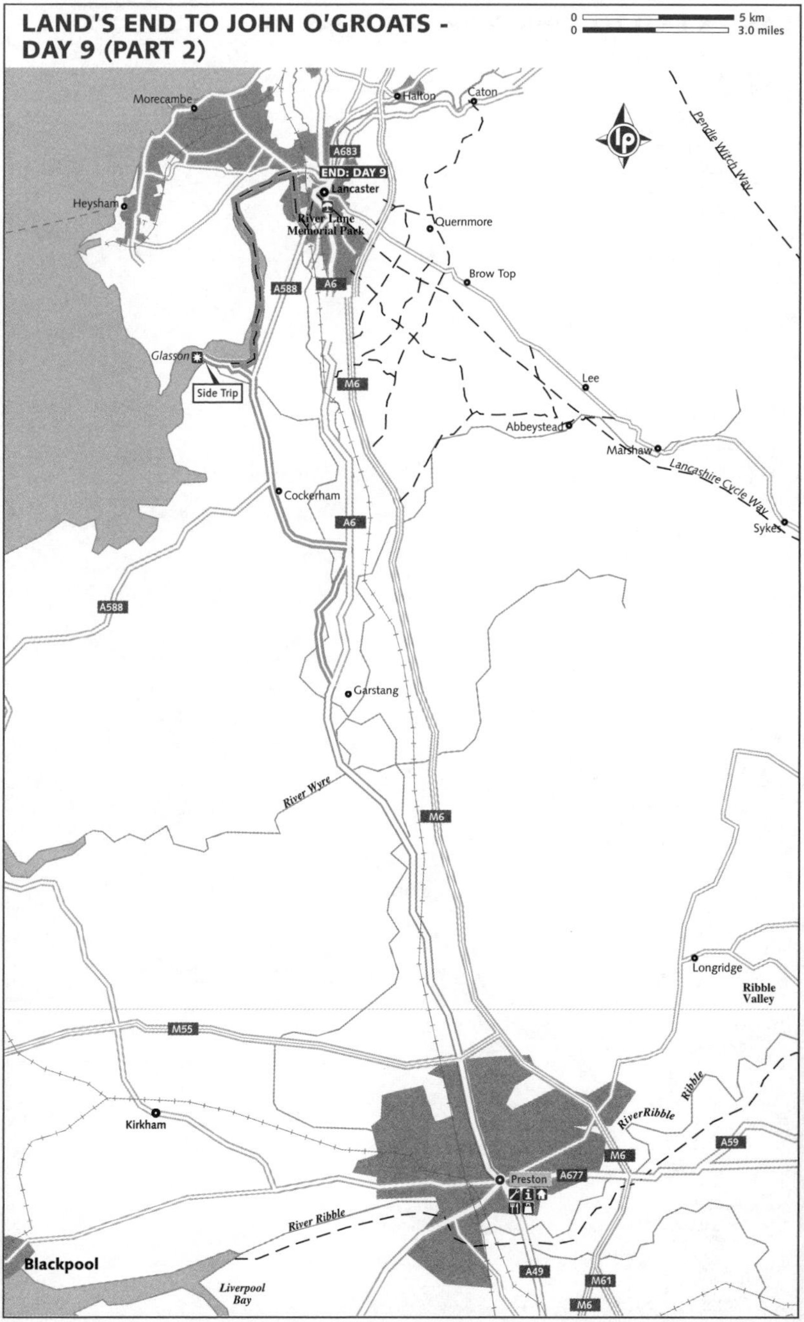

0 — 5 km
0 — 3.0 miles

Pendle Witch Way

Morecambe

Halton   Caton

A683

Heysham

END: DAY 9
Lancaster

River Lune
Memorial Park

Quernmore

A588   A6

Brow Top

M6

Lee

Glasson

Side Trip

Abbeystead

Marshaw

Lancashire Cycle Way

Cockerham

A6

Sykes

A588

Garstang

River Wyre

M6

Longridge

Ribble
Valley

M55

River Ribble

Kirkham

River Ribble

M6   A59

Preston   A677

Blackpool

Liverpool
Bay

A49   M61

M6

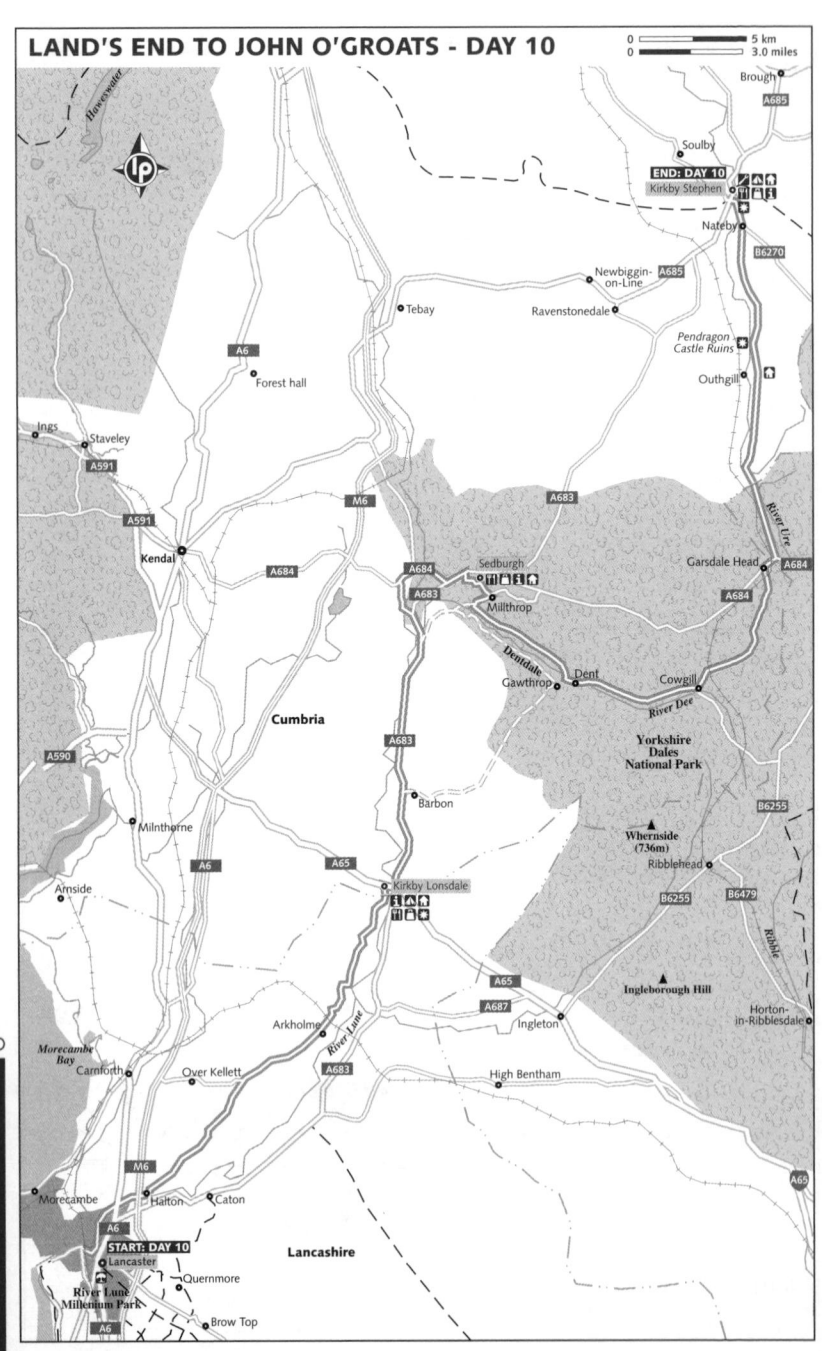

LAND'S END TO JOHN O'GROATS - DAY 10

0   5 km
0   3.0 miles

Brough
A685

Soulby

END: DAY 10
Kirkby Stephen

Nateby
B6270

Newbiggin-
on-Line
A685

Tebay   Ravenstonedale

*Pendragon
Castle Ruins*

A6

Forest hall   Outhgill

River Lune

Ings
Staveley   Garsdale Head   A684
A591

A591   M6   A683   A683

Kendal

A684
A684   Sedburgh
A684
A683
Millthrop   Garsdale Head

A683   *Dentdale*   Cowgill
Gawthrop   Dent
Cumbria   River Dee

A683   **Yorkshire
Dales
National Park**

Barbon   B6255

Whernside
(736m)
Ribblehead

Milnthorpe
A65

A590   B6255   B6479

Arnside   **Kirkby Lonsdale**

A65   Ribble

A6   A687
A65   Ingleton   *Ingleborough Hill*

Arkholme   Horton-
A683   in-Ribblesdale

River Lune
Over Kellett
*Morecambe
Bay*   Carnforth

High Bentham

M6

A66

Morecambe   Halton   Caton

A6
START: DAY 10   **Lancashire**
Lancaster   Quernmore
*River Lune
Millennium Park*
A6   Brow Top

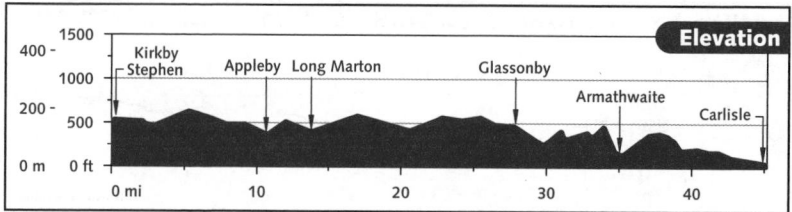

ALTERNATIVE ROUTE: VIA RIVER LUNE MILLENNIUM PARK

As you leave Lancaster you might want to take an alternative and more pleasant route through the **River Lune Millennium Park** (☎ 01524 382849), 9.3 miles of parkland studded with works of public art and with the millennium cycle bridge over the River Lune as its showpiece. Make sure you leave the park at Halton to get back onto the main route.

Day 11: Kirkby Stephen to Carlisle
4–5 hours, 45.2 miles

This enjoyable day travels along a series of quiet country lanes, through lush grazing land speckled with shaggy northern sheep. This sea of green is testimony to the region's reputation as one of England's wettest, a fact you may well experience first hand. Although the barren tops of the lofty Pennines loom close for most of the day, the ride itself is relatively flat and skirts the base of the bigger peaks along the picturesque Eden Valley.

For much of the way to Appleby-in-Westmorland (10.7 miles), the route undulates gently along part of the 280-mile Cumbria Cycleway. **Appleby**, the largest settlement encountered all day, is a picturesque bustling market town straddling the River Eden. The town's **Norman castle** (☎ 017683 53823), extensively renovated in the 17th century, is worth chaining the bike up for half an hour. It can be found at the top of Boroughgate, the principal shopping street, but isn't always open for the public to visit. Rail nerds will certainly want to get a gander at the old British Rail diesel locos plying the **Eden Valley Railway** (www.evr .org.uk) as far as Warcop 6.5 miles to the southeast. .

A CYCLIST'S TALE FROM END-TO-END

In recent years it's become increasingly easy to follow people's E2E journeys online via countless blogs and social networking sites. But some still commit their in-transit ruminations to paper – producing a more concise overview of what to expect on the trip. Before setting out to top and tail the British mainland, grab yourself a copy of one of the following rather obscure titles:

- *Follow the Yellow Gorse Road* by John Hopkins – A no-nonsense travelogue with some good photography.

- *The Middle-aged Mountaineer* by Jim Curran – Jim set out to do the route and climb as many mountains along the way as he could. He completes the route, but the climbing somewhat falls by the wayside.

- *Land's End to John O'Groats* by William B Dawson – Unemployed during the Great Depression of the 1930s, William Dawson broke the E2E record on a bike salvaged from a scrap yard, and evaded the soup kitchen by publishing an account of his journey.

- *Heading North on a By-Pass* by Ron Smith – An account of Ron's post-op cycle/walk trip.

- *Pedal Power: Land's End to John O'Groats in 26 Days* by Jenny Alexander – Aimed mainly at kids, this is the diary of a family's E2E experience.

Possibly the most interesting recent non-cycling E2E tale involves a certain Mr Richard El-loway who did the trip both ways courtesy of the British taxpayer – he used his newly-acquired old aged pensioner's (OAP) bus pass.

LAND'S END TO JOHN O'GROATS

LAND'S END TO JOHN O'GROATS - DAY 11

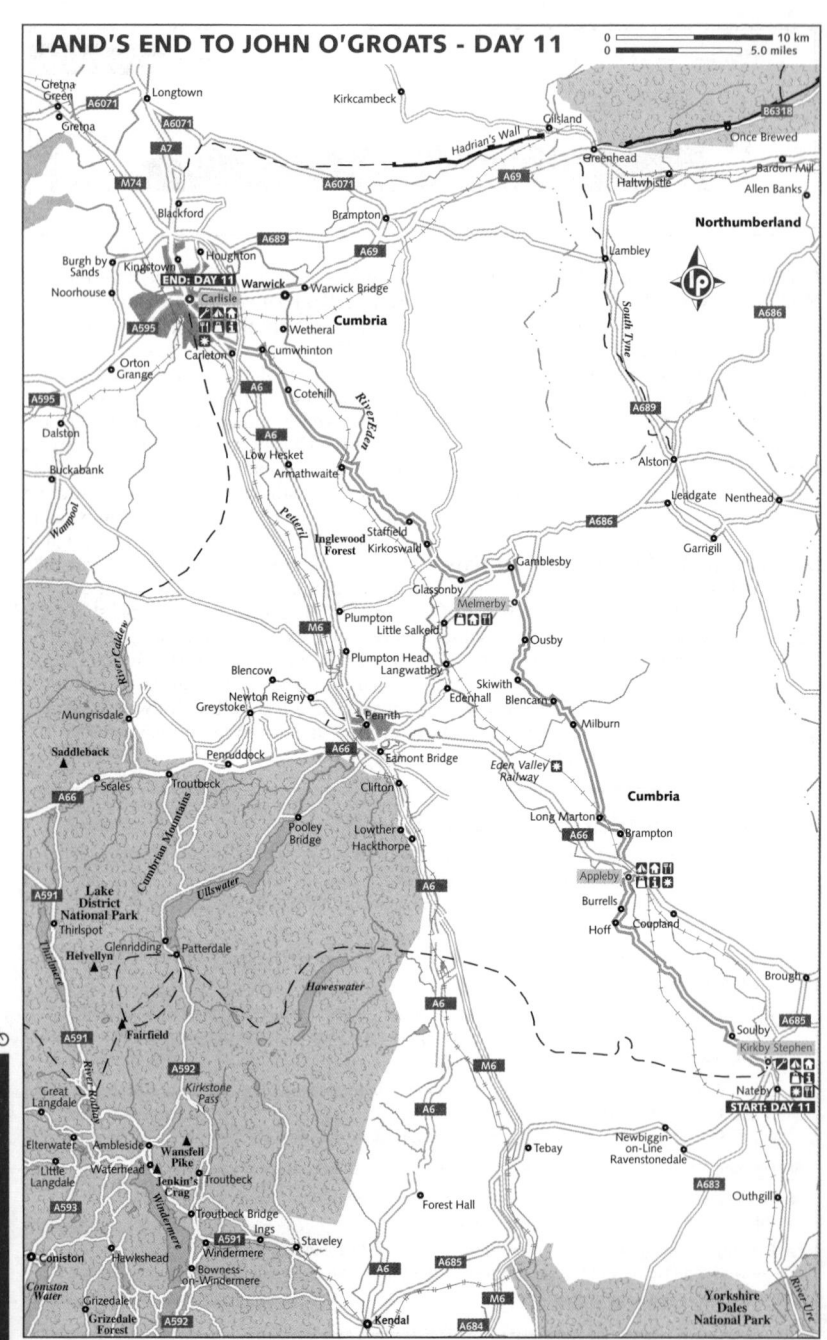

0 — 10 km
0 — 5.0 miles

Gretna
Green
Longtown
A6071
Gretna
A7
Kirkcambeck
Gilsland
Greenhead
Once Brewed
B6318
M74
Hadrian's Wall
Haltwhistle
Bardon Mill
Allen Banks
Blackford
A6071
A69
Brampton
A6071
Lambley
Northumberland
A686
Burgh by
Sands
Kingstown
A689
Houghton
A69
Noorhouse
Warwick
END: DAY 11
Warwick Bridge
South Tyne
Carlisle
Cumbria
Wetheral
Orton
Grange
Carleton
Cumwhinton
A595
A6
Cotehill
River Eden
A689
Dalston
Alston
A595
A6
Low Hesket
Leadgate
Nenthead
Buckabank
Armathwaite
Petteril
A686
Garrigill
Wampool
Inglewood
Forest
Staffield
Kirkoswald
Gamblesby
Glassonby
Melmerby
M6
Plumpton
Little Salkeld
Ousby
Blencow
Plumpton Head
Langwathby
Skirwith
Edenhall
Milburn
Newton Reigny
Greystoke
Blencarn
Mungrisdale
Penrith
Saddleback
A66
Penruddock
A66
Eamont Bridge
Eden Valley
Railway
Cumbria
Scales
Troutbeck
Clifton
Long Marton
A66
Brampton
Pooley
Bridge
Lowther
Hackthorpe
Appleby
A591
Cumbrian Mountains
Ullswater
Burrells
Hoff
Coupland
**Lake
District
National Park**
Thirlspot
A6
Brough
Glenridding
Patterdale
A685
Helvellyn
Haweswater
Soulby
A591
Kirkby Stephen
Fairfield
A6
M6
Nateby
START: DAY 11
Great
Langdale
A592
Kirkstone
Pass
Newbiggin-
on-Line
Ravenstonedale
Elterwater
Ambleside
Wansfell
Pike
Tebay
A683
Outhgill
Little
Langdale
Waterhead
Jenkin's
Crag
Troutbeck
Forest Hall
A593
Troutbeck Bridge
Ings
A591
Staveley
A6
A685
Coniston
Hawkshead
Windermere
Bowness-
on-Windermere
M6
**Yorkshire
Dales
National Park**
Coniston
Water
Grizedale
Grizedale
Forest
A592
Kendal
A684

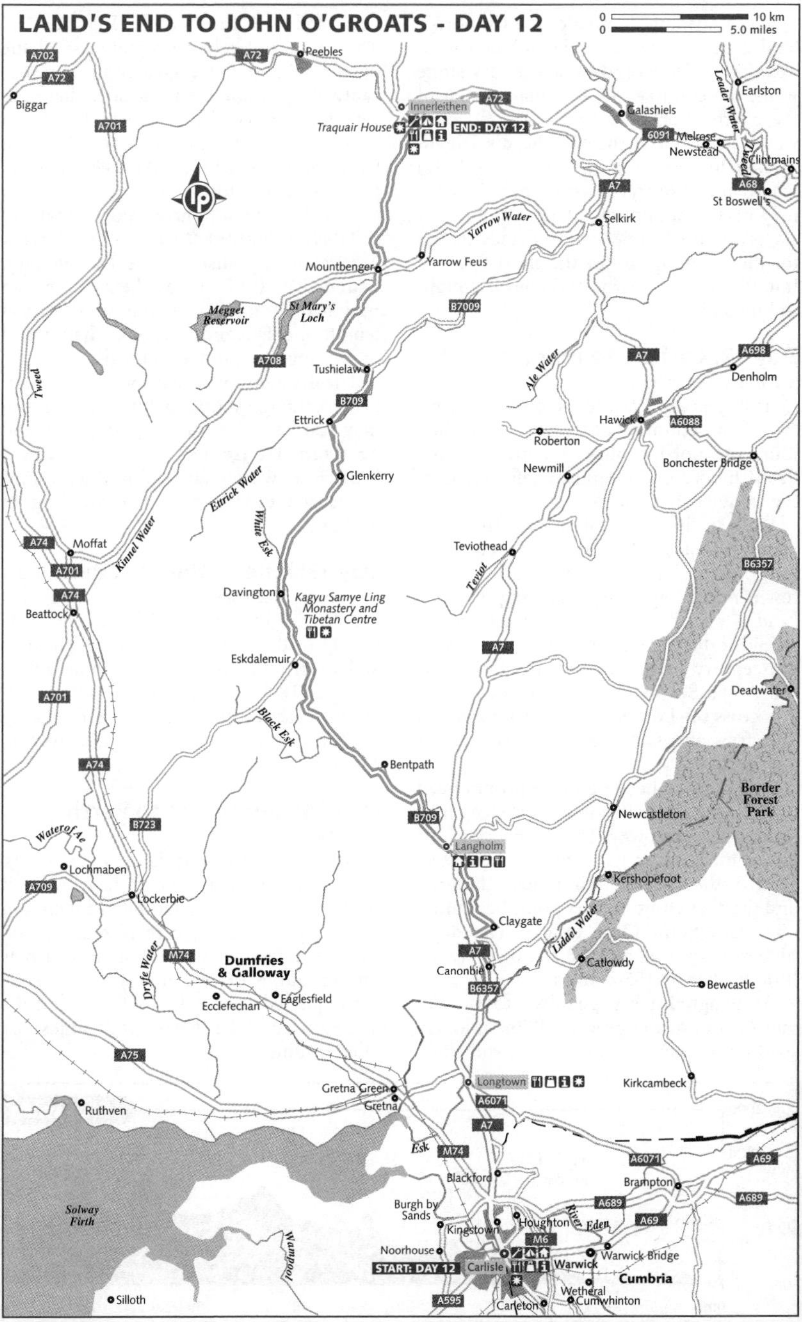

LAND'S END TO JOHN O'GROATS - DAY 12

| 0 | | 10 km |
| 0 | | 5.0 miles |

A702 A72 Peebles

Biggar

A72 Innerleithen END: DAY 12 Galashiels Earlston

A701 Traquair House 6091 Melrose Newstead

Leader Water

Clintmains

A68 St Boswell's

Yarrow Water Selkirk

Mountbenger Yarrow Feus

Megget Reservoir St Mary's Loch B7009

A698

Tweed A708 Tushielaw Ale Water A7 Denholm

B709 Ettrick Hawick A6088

Glenkerry Roberton Bonchester Bridge

Rinnel Water Ettrick Water Newmill

A74 Moffat White Esk Teviothead B6357

A701 Beattock Davington Kagyu Samye Ling Monastery and Tibetan Centre Teviot

A7

Eskdalemuir Deadwater

A701 Black Esk

A74 Bentpath Border Forest Park

Water of Ae B723 B709 Newcastleton

Lochmaben Langholm

A709 Lockerbie Kershopefoot

Dumfries & Galloway Claygate Liddel Water Catlowdy

M74 Canonbie Bewcastle

Ecclefechan Eaglesfield B6357

A75 Longtown Kirkcambeck

Ruthven Gretna Green Gretna

A6071 Esk A7

Solway Firth M74 A6071 A69

Blackford Brampton A689

Burgh by Sands Houghton A689 A69

Noorhouse Kingstown River Eden Warwick Bridge

START: DAY 12 Carlisle M6 Cumbria

Silloth A595 Warwick Wetheral Cumwhinton

Carleton

Sheep farming dominates the Cumbrian landscape, and the scenic Eden Valley is no exception. Neatly partitioned by dry stone walls, the countryside is similar to that of the nearby Yorkshire Dales. A good half-way lunch spot is the **Shepherd's Inn in Melmerby** (24.2 miles; ☎ 01768 881335) where the monster-portion pub lunches may make remounting a trial. On the outskirts of Carlisle quiet country lanes are left for the booming A6 for the short final leg into the centre of town, and your last night in England.

Day 12: Carlisle to Innerleithen
5–8 hours, 67.4 miles
Quickly leaving Carlisle's suburbs for gently rolling country lanes, this route then joins the not-too-busy A7, crossing the Scottish border (14.9 miles) before returning to quiet roads again.

Early in the day, look out for the 17th-century Gothic **Arthuret Church** (10.9 miles) on an unsigned lane entering Longtown. According to legend, King Arthur's head is buried here and the nearby wood is said to be the site of a long and bloody 6th-century battle between the Celts and the Anglo-Saxon invaders. At 14.9 miles you cross the border between Cunbria and Dumfries and Galloway – you're now in Scotland.

Undulations become more pronounced over the border with some short steep hills standing in your way. The River Esk is followed for most of its length to the watershed in the Eskdalemuir Forest, the long and gradual climb to this point beginning after Langholm (23.4 miles). The day's highest point (385m/1268ft), however, is a little further on (55.2 miles).

At Langholm say goodbye to the A7 and turn onto the peaceful B709, a lonely road if ever there was one, which will guide you safely all the way to Innerleithen. The peace and relative remoteness of the open hills and the Eskdalemuir Forest is captivating, though this means there are very few services between Langholm and Innerleithen. In this northern European landscape of trees, hills and burns (streams), perhaps the last thing you would expect to find is the **Kagyu Samye Ling Monastery & Tibetan Centre** (☎ 013873 73232; www.samyeling.org) just outside Eskdalemuir. Founded in 1967, it was the first Tibetan Buddhist monastery in the West with a temple and Tibetan tea room, a handy and interesting place to take a break.

The B709 ends its lonely journey at Innerleithen, though shortly before the town you may still have the energy to stop at grand **Traquair House** (65.9 miles; ☎ 01896 830323; www.traquair.co.uk), which claims to be the oldest inhabited dwelling in Scotland.

Day 13: Innerleithen to Edinburgh
2½–4 hours, 33.2 miles
See Day 3 of the Scottish Borders ride (p291) in the Scotland chapter for a map and description of this ride. Innerleithen starts at 18.5 miles (from the post office, go northeast on the A72 and then pick up the Scottish Borders cue 0.1 miles away at 18.6 miles).

Day 14: Edinburgh to Perth
3½–6 hours, 48.1 miles
Much of today's route is on quiet roads, and from the Firth of Forth to Kinross, it follows part of the signed Fife Millennium Cycleway. However, care is required on busy sections in central Edinburgh such as on Edinburgh Rd (6.1 miles), where bikes are requested to use the footpath, and the dogleg across the A907 (18.9 miles) by Dunfermline.

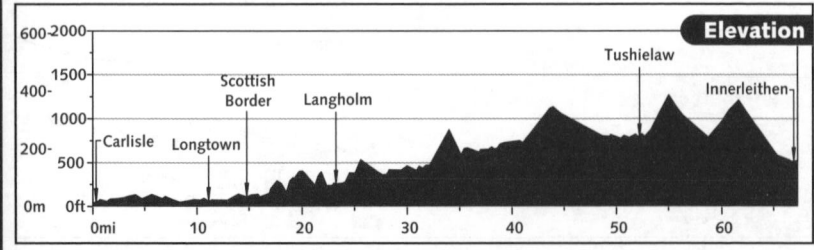

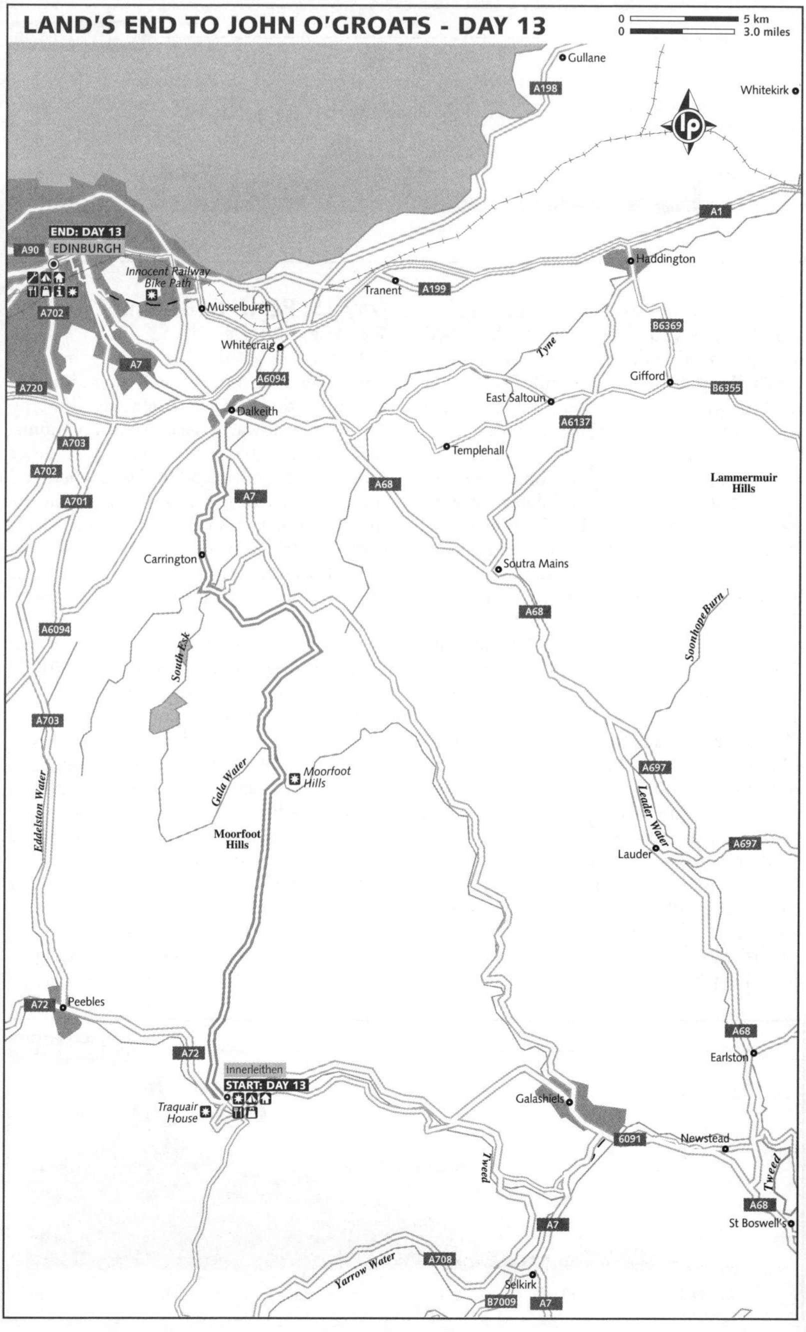

LAND'S END TO JOHN O'GROATS - DAY 13

| 0 | | 5 km |
| 0 | | 3.0 miles |

Gullane

Whitekirk

A198

A1

END: DAY 13

A90

EDINBURGH

Innocent Railway Bike Path

Haddington

A702

Tranent   A199

B6369

Musselburgh

Whitecraig

A7

A6094

Gifford   B6355

Dalkeith

East Saltoun

A703

A6137

A720

Templehall

A702

A68

Lammermuir Hills

A701

Carrington

Soutra Mains

A6094

A68

A703

Soonhope Burn

Eddelston Water

South Esk

Gala Water

Moorfoot Hills

A697

Moorfoot Hills

Leader Water

Lauder   A697

A72   Peebles

A68

Earlston

A72

Innerleithen

START: DAY 13

Galashiels

Traquair House

6091

Newstead

Tweed

A68

St Boswells

A7

Yarrow Water   A708

Selkirk

B7009   A7

LAND'S END TO JOHN O'GROATS

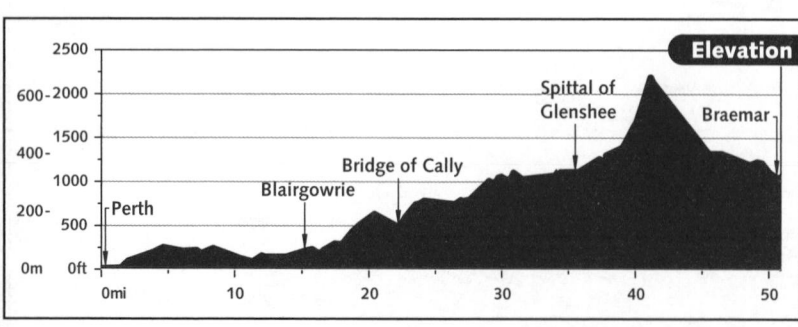

Picking your way out of Edinburgh is a trial and if you lose the route described here, just head in the direction (west) of the **Forth Road Bridge** (11.4 miles) and you can't go wrong. Suspended high above the grey cold water, the bridge provides spectacular views en route to the Kingdom of Fife and provides a very welcome shortcut.

Thereafter, the route undulates through the countryside surrounding Inverkeithing, Dunfermline and Kinross with a number of short steep hills. A fine lunch spot can be found on the banks of **Loch Leven** near Kinross, where you can munch on your lunch while admiring **Kinross House** (only the gardens are open to the public) and **Loch Leven Castle**, which stands stranded on an island in the loch. It was here that Mary Queen of Scots was imprisoned from 1567 to 1568 and where she was forced to abdicate in favour of her son James VI. The boat trip to the island is included in the castle admission charge.

After Kinross, the route continues north, undulating on quiet roads to Bridge of Earn (43.4 miles) where it joins the Old Edinburgh Rd for the final run into Perth. Superseded by the motorway, it's not especially busy but traffic is fast.

Day 15: Perth to Braemar
4–6½ hours, 50.9 miles

E2E-ites feel good when they're heading due north as this day mostly does, but this is tempered by some challenging climbing as you steer towards seriously spiky mountain country. Navigation is a no-brainer today as the entire 50 miles is spent on the A93. Any traffic you encounter in the first few miles soon dissipates to a trickle north of Bridge of Cally (22.2 miles). The busiest section leading to the twin towns of Blairgowrie and Rattray (15.2 miles) is easy riding.

Almost on the outskirts of Perth in Old Scone, **Scone Palace** (1.6 miles; ☎ 01738 552300) is generally regarded as the true home of the Stone of Scone aka the Stone of Destiny – returned to the Scots from London in 1996 (it's kept in Edinburgh). This potently Scottish place houses many a treasure including Marie Antoinette's writing table, a collection of ivory carvings and a cacophony of period clocks.

Blairgowrie (15.2 miles) is the last major population centre before Braemar, with bakeries, supermarkets and ATMs. Ailing cycles can be checked out at **Crighton's Cycles** (15.8 miles; ☎ 01250 374447;

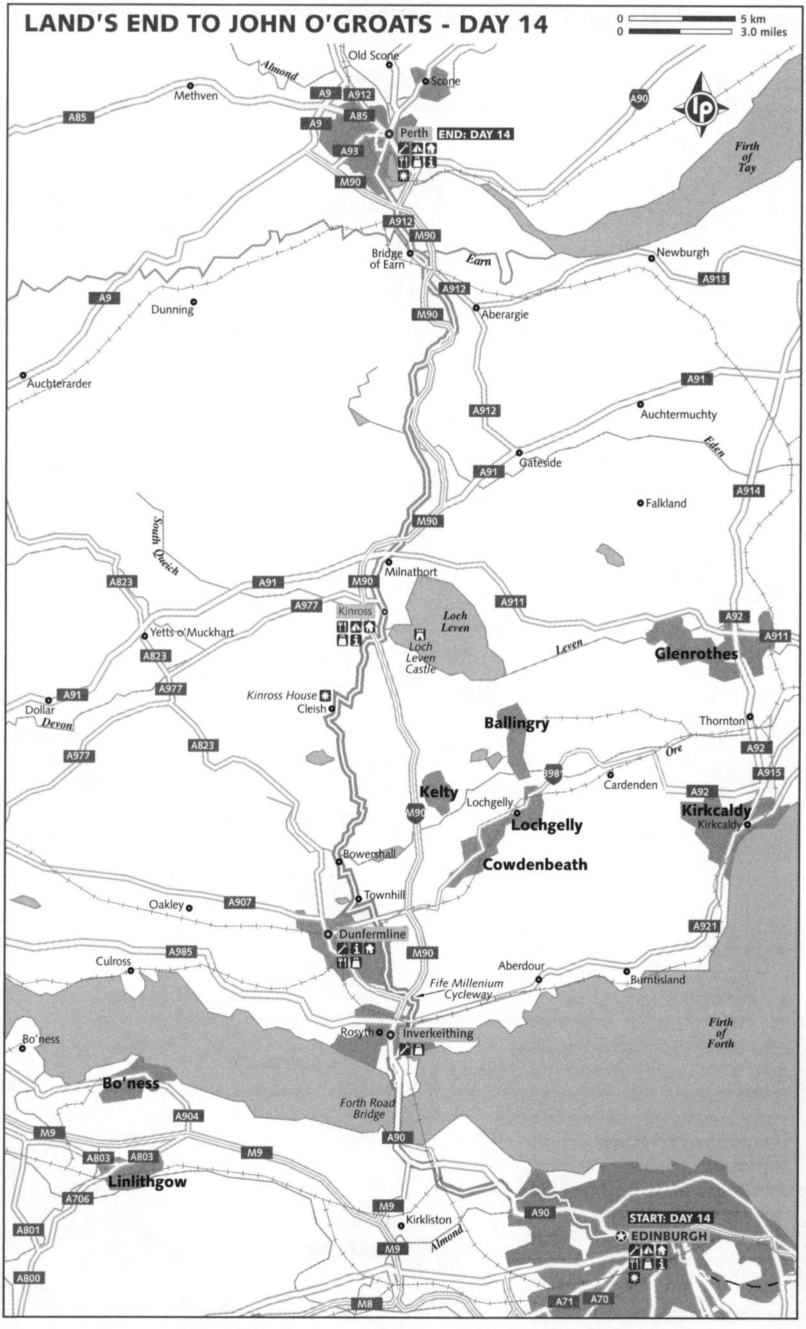

LAND'S END TO JOHN O'GROATS - DAY 14

0 ———— 5 km
0 ———— 3.0 miles

Almond

Old Scone

Scone

Methven

A85

A9   A912

A9   A85

A93   Perth   **END: DAY 14**

M90

A90

Firth of Tay

Newburgh

A912

M90

Bridge of Earn

Earn

A913

A9

Dunning

A912

M90

Aberargie

Auchterarder

A91

A912

Auchtermuchty

Eden

A91   Gateside

A914

South Quaich

A823

A91   M90   Milnathort

Falkland

A823   Yetts o'Muckhart

A977   Kinross

A823

Loch Leven

A911

A92

A911

Glenrothes

Dollar

Devon

A977

Kinross House   Cleish

Loch Leven Castle

Leven

Thornton

A92

A823

Ballingry

Ore

A915

398   Cardenden   A92

Kelty   Lochgelly

Kirkcaldy

M90   Lochgelly   Kirkcaldy

Bowershall   Cowdenbeath

Townhill

Oakley   A907

Dunfermline   M90

A921

Culross   A985   Aberdour   Burntisland

Fife Millennium Cycleway

Bo'ness   Rosyth   Inverkeithing

Firth of Forth

Bo'ness   Forth Road Bridge

M9   A904

M9   A90

A803   A803   M9

A706   Linlithgow   Almond

A801   M9   Kirkliston   A90

A800   M9   **START: DAY 14**

✪ **EDINBURGH**

M8   A71   A70

LAND'S END TO JOHN O'GROATS

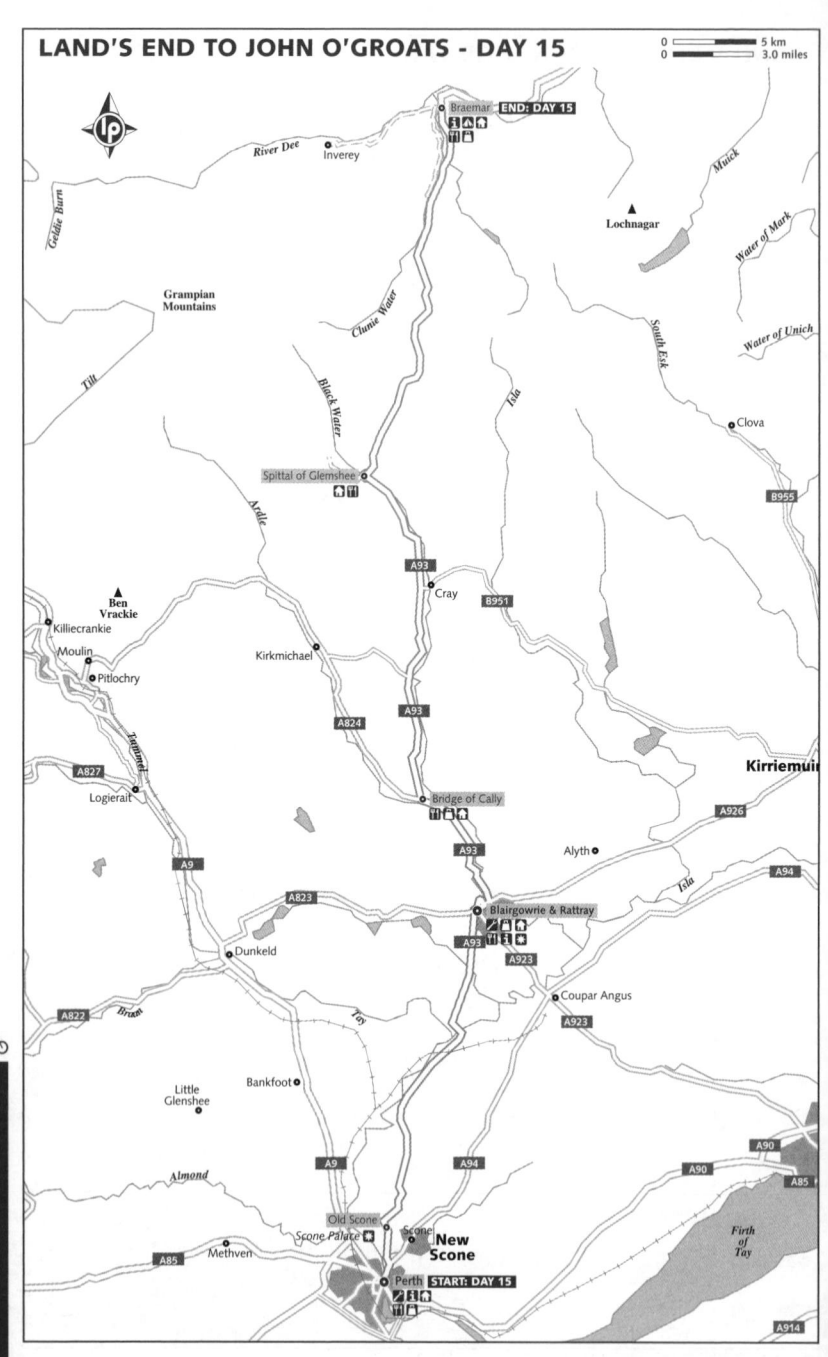

LAND'S END TO JOHN O'GROATS - DAY 15

THE BRAEMAR GATHERING

There are Highland games in many towns and villages throughout the summer, but the best known is the Braemar Gathering, which takes place on a 12-acre site on the first Saturday in September. It's a major occasion, annually organised by the Braemar Royal Highland Society since 1817, and drawing athletes from deveral countries. Events include highland dancing, tug-of-war, a hill race up Morrone, tossing the caber, hammer and stone throwing and the long jump. These types of events took place informally in the Highlands for many centuries as tests of skill and strength, but they were formalised around 1820 due to rising pseudo-Highland romanticism kicked off by individuals such as King George IV and Sir Walter Scott. Queen Victoria attended the Braemar Gathering in 1848, starting the tradition of kilted royal patronage which continues to this day.

87 Perth St) on the route. The route from Blairgowrie to the very Scottish sounding Spittal of Glenshee becomes increasingly bouncy though there's nothing too steep to worry burdened tourers. Initially wooded and then rolling farmland, the landscape transforms into rugged moorland as it creeps towards the Grampian Mountains. After a lunch stop in **Spittal of Glenshee** (a side trip at 35.5 miles) comes the showstopper, a long, demanding climb up Glen Shee (meaning 'Valley of Peace' in Gaelic), gaining almost 300m (984ft) in 6 miles and exceptionally steep for the last 3 miles. You can't have the ups without the downs and thankfully there's 10 miles of freewheeling into Braemar.

Day 16: Braemar to Grantown-on-Spey
4–6 hours, 46.6 miles
Arguably the hardest day of the lot, the ride through the heart of the gorgeous Grampians involves seven big hills, three of them monsters. The elevation chart for this section of the ride looks like a set of shark's teeth giving you some indication of

what you're in for. If you're running out of oomph halfway through, it's always feasible to break the ride at **Tomintoul** (32.5 miles), the only town en route. The **tourist office** (☎ 01807 580285; The Square) can advise on accommodation and beds or head straight to the **Tomintoul YHA** (☎ 01807 580 364) or the **Glen Avon Hotel** (☎ 01807 580218).

Climbing begins 9 miles out of Braemar where the route turns onto the single-track B976. Procrastinators can dally with a side trip to the Queen's summer residence at **Balmoral Castle** (☎ 01339 742334), the entrance to which is about 0.5 miles further on the A93. Built for Queen Victoria in 1855, its design re-launched the Scottish Baronial architectural style, which influenced architects across Scotland and beyond over the next 50 years. Only a small part of the castle is open to the public so don't expect to drop in on the Queen as she feeds the Corgies.

The up-down first climb passes from woodland to open moor, distinctively striped with scars of burnt heather (to encourage grouse), a characteristic of much

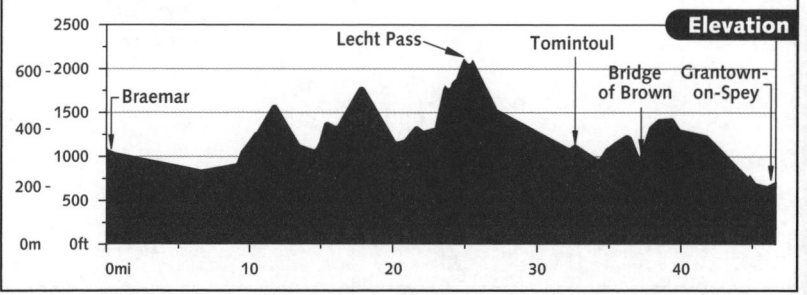

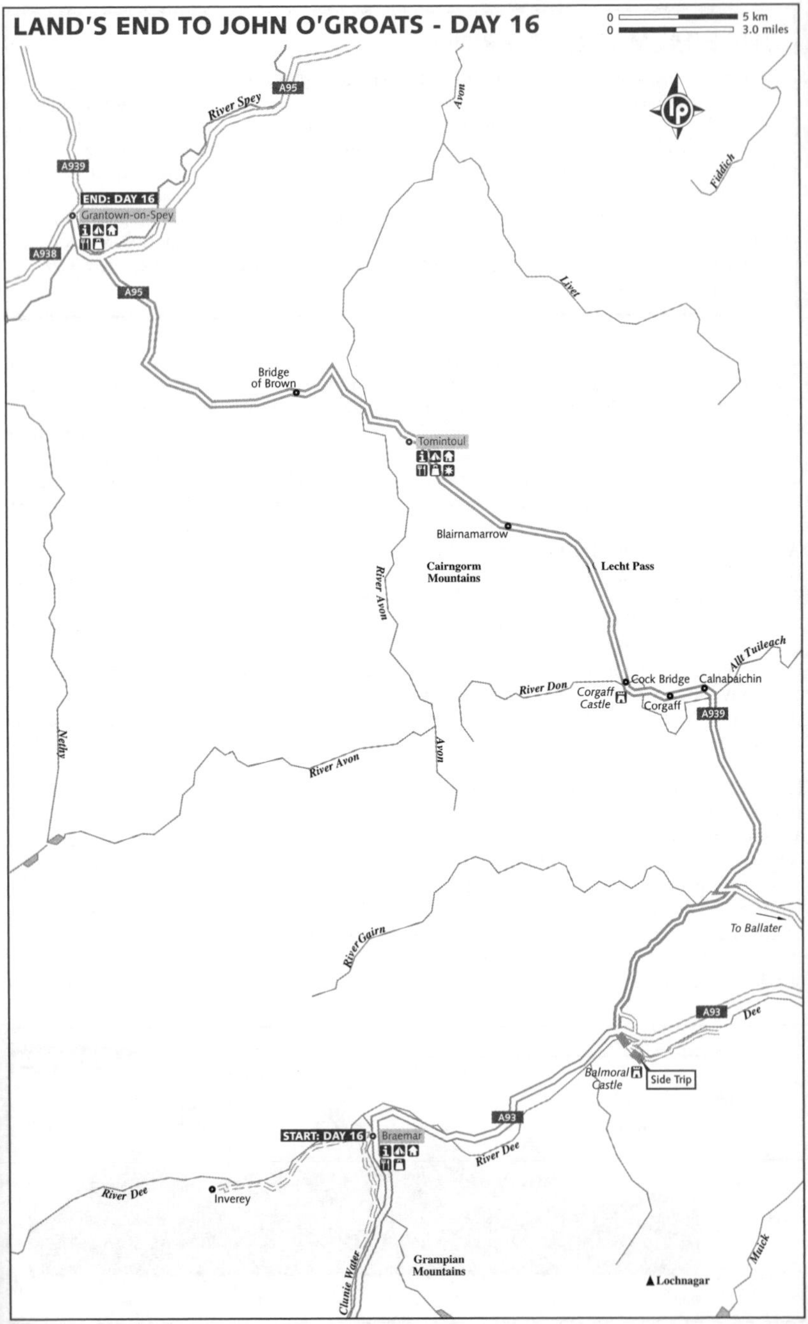

LAND'S END TO JOHN O'GROATS - DAY 16

0 _____ 5 km
0 _____ 3.0 miles

River Spey

A95

A939

END: DAY 16
Grantown-on-Spey

A938

A95

Avon

Livet

Fiddich

Bridge
of Brown

Tomintoul

Blairnamarrow

Cairngorm
Mountains

Lecht Pass

River Avon

Allt Tuileagh

Cock Bridge   Calnabaichin
River Don   Corgarff
Corgarff   A939
Castle

Nethy

Avon

River Avon

River Cairn

To Ballater

A93   Dee

Balmoral
Castle   Side Trip

START: DAY 16   Braemar
A93   River Dee

River Dee   Inverey

Clunie Water

**Grampian
Mountains**

▲ Lochnagar

Muick

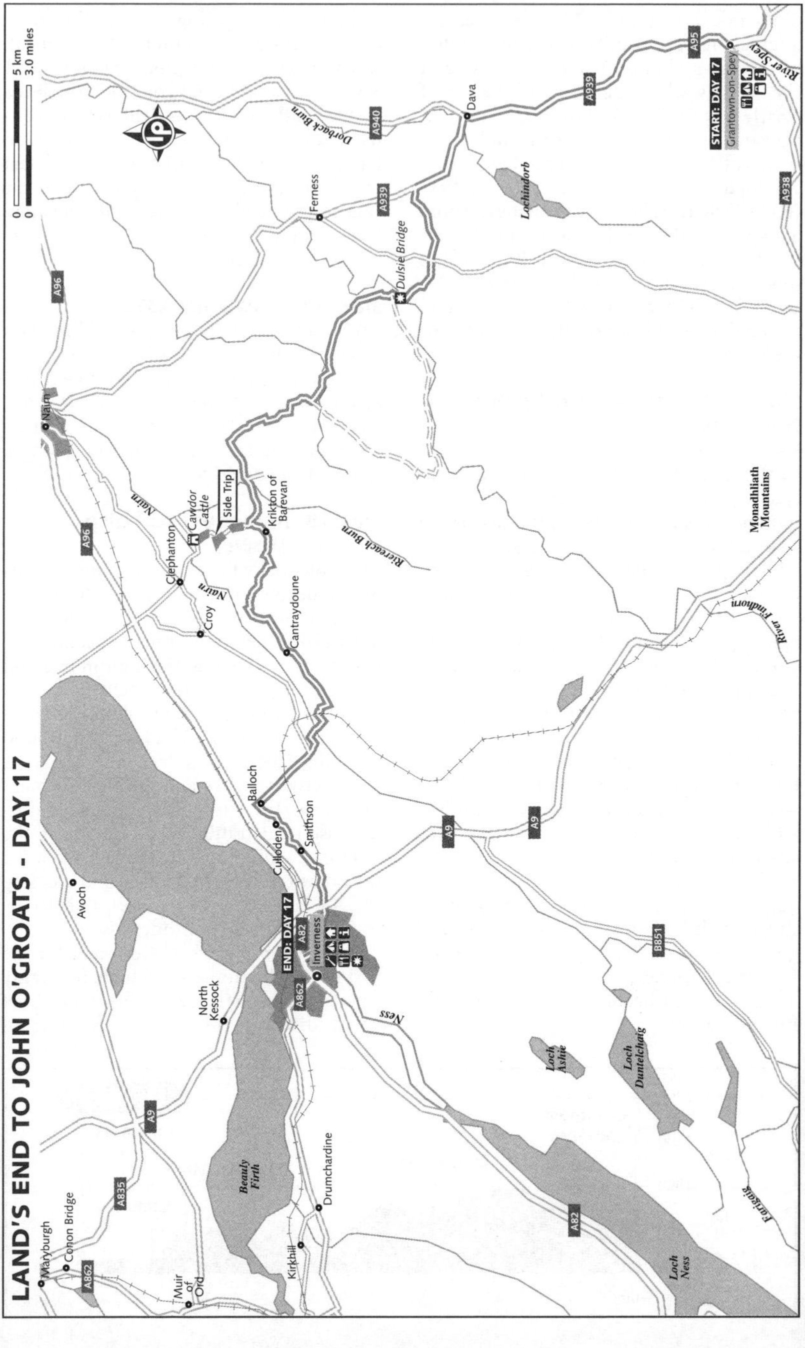

LAND'S END TO JOHN O'GROATS - DAY 17

5 km
3.0 miles

START: DAY 17
Grantown-on-Spey

River Spey

A95

A938

A939

A940

Dava

Lochindorb

Dorback Burn

Ferness

Dulsie Bridge

A96

Nairn

Nairn

Cawdor Castle

Side Trip

Clephanton

Kirkton of
Barevan

Croy

Cantraydoune

Rieroach Burn

Monadhliath
Mountains

River Findhorn

Balloch

Smithson

Culloden

A9

A9

BB851

END: DAY 17
Inverness

A82

A862

North
Kessock

Avoch

A9

A835

Maryburgh
Conon Bridge

A862

Muir
of
Ord

Kirkhill

Drumchardine

Beauly
Firth

Ness

Loch
Ashie

Loch
Duntelchaig

Loch
Ness

Farigaig

A82

LAND'S END TO JOHN O'GROATS

of the ride. A tearoom (20.8 miles) presents a refuelling opportunity before the mother of the day's climbs, 2 miles on, just past the whitewashed cuboids of **Corgarff Castle** (☎ 01975 651460). Take consolation in the roadside footprints and wheel marks of cyclists who've walked before you. A tough but rideable hill to **Lecht Pass** (637m/2089ft) follows immediately, before a long, steep descent into Tomintoul. Having crossed the River Avon (is it really that long?) there's a taxing climb after Bridge of Brown (37.1 miles) before an easy end to the day on the approach to Grantown-on-Spey.

Day 17: Grantown-on-Spey to Inverness
3–4½ hours, 38.7 miles

With the Grampian Mountains behind you (phew!), today's ride is short, sweet, townless and considerably flatter. But just as the road gets easier, the navigation gets trickier with a spider's web of unsigned roads between the 10-mile mark and Culloden, and it's easy to miss some of the insignificant-looking turns along the way (such as the one at 10.5 miles for instance). Traffic is negligible until the last 5 miles and take particular care on the B9006 coming into Inverness. Part of the ride follows Sustrans Route 7 through Culloden so look out for the standard blue signs. With virtually no sources of sustenance between Grantown and Inverness, pack your panniers with snacks and lunch.

The route sets out along the A939 to the oddly named Dava before turning off onto single-track lanes just after. It's worth lingering a while on the rare hot day at **Dulsie Bridge** (14.2 miles), a locally known swimming hole and beauty spot on the rocky River Findhorn.

Soon after cycling under the towering **Culloden viaduct** (29.5 miles), which carries the rail line over the River Nairn, a half-mile return side trip leads to the **Culloden Battlefield visitor centre** (☎ 01463 790607), site of the 1746 Battle of Culloden, which saw the defeat of Bonnie Prince Charlie and marked the catastrophic end of the Jacobite rebellion. Interestingly this was the last ever battle to be fought on British soil.

SIDE TRIP: CAWDOR CASTLE

After around two hours of riding you should reach the turn off (23.5 miles) for a short 3.6-mile return side trip to the severe Scottish facade of **Cawdor Castle** (☎ 01667 404401), made famous by Shakespeare's *Macbeth*. The sumptuous interiors can be visited on a guided tour.

Day 18: Inverness to Lairg
5–8½ hours, 71 miles

This potentially long day starts on A-roads by the Beauly Firth then passes through a series of towns on the Cromarty and Dornoch Firths, before eventually heading inland to Lairg. Despite the high mile count the terrain presents few challenges, with only two sections of light climbing when leaving Dingwall (22.3 miles), and around the Shin Falls (65.3 miles). The A862 has some busy stretches and the first 10 miles or so from Inverness are best avoided during rush hour traffic. Take care also in the last mile to Dingwall (20.3 miles), from the turn-off to Alness (28.2 miles) and crossing the A9 into Tain (44.2 miles). Otherwise, traffic is relatively non-intrusive.

Bring your two wheels to a halt for the first time today at the small town of **Beauly** where at the eastern end of the main street you'll discover the skeletal remains of

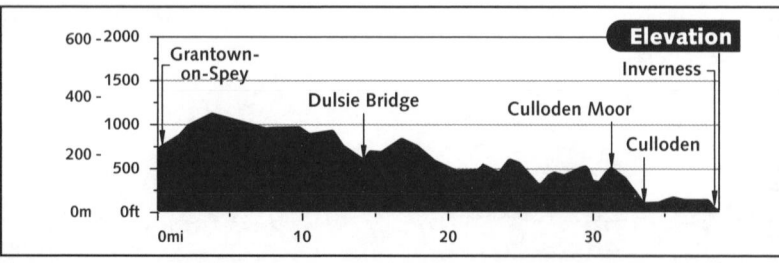

Grantown-on-Spey

Dulsie Bridge

Culloden Moor

Inverness

Culloden

Elevation

600 - 2000
1500
400 -
1000
200 -
500
0m   0ft
0mi   10   20   30

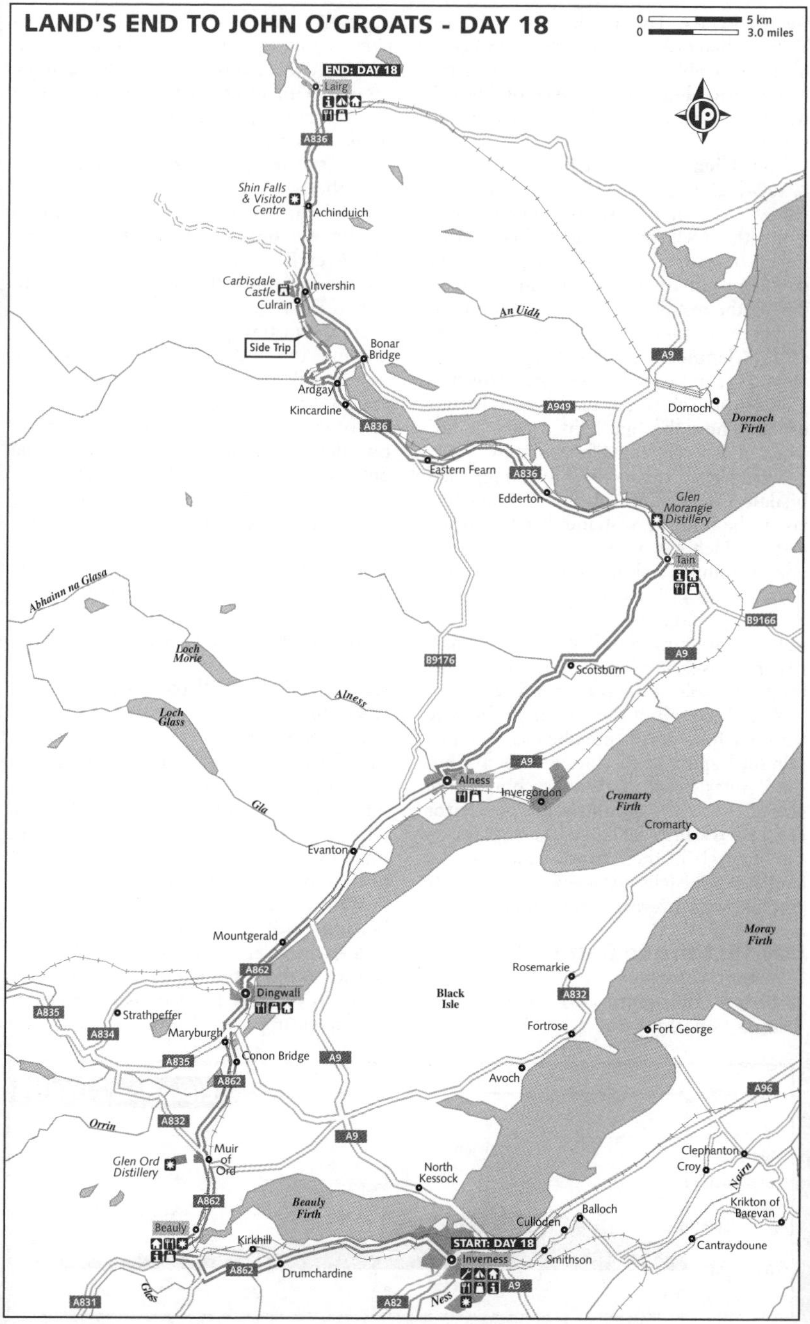

LAND'S END TO JOHN O'GROATS - DAY 18

| 0 | | 5 km |
| 0 | | 3.0 miles |

END: DAY 18
Lairg

A836

Shin Falls
& Visitor
Centre
Achinduich

An Uidh

A9

Carbisdale
Castle
Invershin
Culrain

Side Trip

Bonar
Bridge

Ardgay

Kincardine

A836

A949

Dornoch

Dornoch
Firth

Eastern Fearn

A836

Edderton

Glen
Morangie
Distillery

Abhainn na Glasa

Loch
Morie

Tain

B9166

Loch
Glass

Alness

B9176

A9

Scotsburn

Gla

Alness

A9

Invergordon

Cromarty
Firth

Cromarty

Evanton

Mountgerald

Moray
Firth

Rosemarkie

A862

A835

Dingwall

Black
Isle

A832

A834

Strathpeffer

Maryburgh

Fortrose

Fort George

A835

Conon Bridge

A9

A862

Avoch

A96

Orrin

A832

Muir
of
Ord

A9

Clephanton

Croy

Glen Ord
Distillery

North
Kessock

Nairn

Krikton of
Barevan

A862

Beauly

Beauly
Firth

Culloden

Balloch

Cantraydoune

Kirkhill

START: DAY 18
Inverness
Smithson

Drumchardine

A862

A82

A9

Ness

A831

Glass

LAND'S END TO JOHN O'GROATS

Beauly Priory. The monks of the obscure Valliscaulian order – who lived and worked here – probably gave the town its original name, Beau Lieu, meaning 'beautiful place', which has corrupted only slightly over the centuries.

The **Glen Ord Distillery** (☎ 01463 872004), the first of two on todays ride, comes at the end of a short 2-mile side trip along the A832 from Muir of Ord (15.5 miles). Tours and tastings take place every day from July to September and weekdays during the rest of the year. The second opportunity to enter single malt heaven comes at the **Glenmorangie Distillery** (☎ 01862 892477), 1 mile north of the pretty town of Tain (45 miles), where the 90-minute tour explains how the fine light whisky is finished in different casks for variation.

Turn left at Ardgay (59.3 miles) for **Carbisdale Castle**, dating from 1917 and the last to be built in Scotland. The imposing castle, which sits across the Kyle of Sutherland from Invershin is now an incredible YHA (see p344). It's also possible to reach the hostel from Invershin train station (63.6 miles) by walking your bike across the narrow railway bridge with care – check the train timetable at the platform first.

Your last stop of the day, if you're here between June and September, is to watch salmon leaping at the lovely **Falls of Shin** (66.2 miles), probably in the company of several busloads of tourists. The **visitor centre** (☎ 01549 402231) has displays on the life cycle of the Atlantic salmon and a cafe. From the falls just a few miles separate you and your overnight stop in Lairg.

Day 19: Lairg to Bettyhill
3–5½ hours, 45.3 miles

With low mileage to cover and little to distract you along the way, the penulti-mate E2E day is a short affair to compensate for yesterday's blockbuster. North of Lairg, the countryside is increasingly remote with only occasional cars along the single-track road. It's magnificently bleak country with true northern European vistas but pretty exposed, so pray for a southerly wind. There's a gentle 10-mile gradual climb from just out of Lairg into the open moors, after which it's downhill overall, albeit undulating through Strathnaver, until the final 1.2 miles into Bettyhill.

Only two tiny places of human habitation interrupt today's route. The first is the cosy **Crask Inn** (☎ 01549 411241), 13.7 miles north of Lairg, a lone landmark in a sea of green and purple and a welcoming traveller's rest. Meals are around £8. The only other services are at **Altnaharra** (20.9 miles) at the head of Loch Naver, where you'll find the **Altnaharra Hotel** (☎ 01549 411222).

Beyond Altnaharra the road traces the western shore of Loch Naver, before joining the meandering River Naver, which it follows all the way into Bettyhill.

Day 20: Bettyhill to John O'Groats
4–6½ hours, 50.3 miles

The final 50-mile stretch of this famous route begins with six tough climbs in 17 miles affording some great coastal views. After that things settle down into unremarkable farming country for the final push into John O'Groats.

With more cars than Day 19, the road becomes two-way east of Melvich (12.5 miles) – between Thurso and John O'Groats traffic on the A836 is fast and reasonably heavy. It's largely avoided (as is the Dounreay nuclear power station, east of Reay)

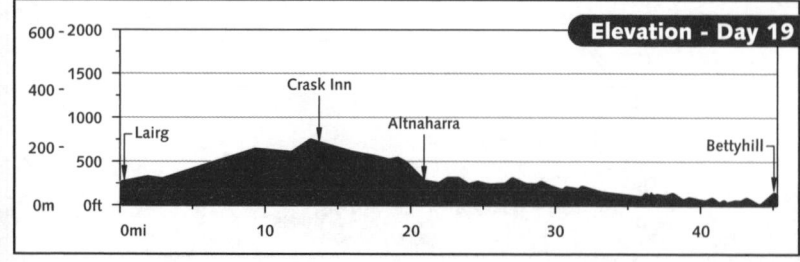

Elevation - Day 19

Lairg
Crask Inn
Altnaharra
Bettyhill

600 - 2000
400 - 1500
1000
200 - 500
0m 0ft

0mi   10   20   30   40

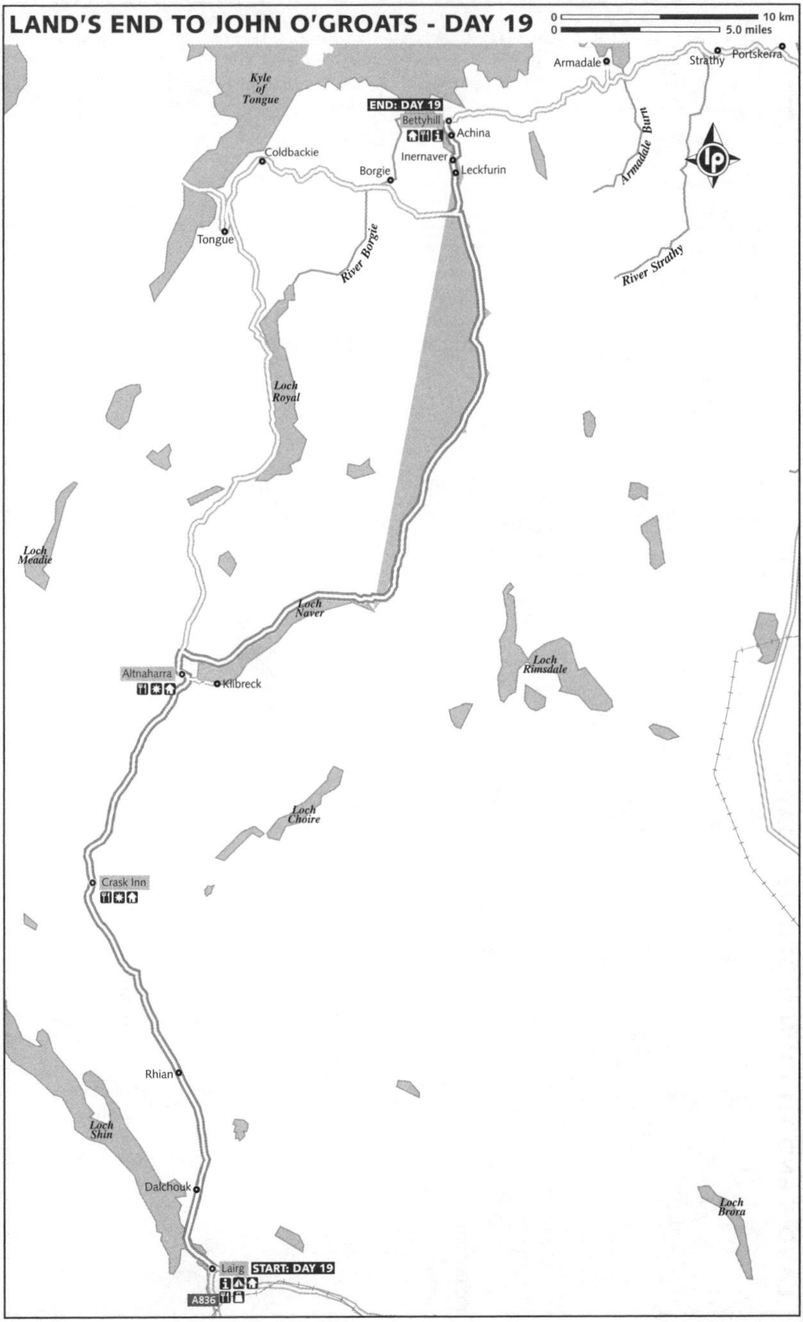

LAND'S END TO JOHN O'GROATS - DAY 19

0 _____ 10 km
0 _____ 5.0 miles

Armadale   Strathy   Portskerra

Kyle of Tongue

END: DAY 19

Bettyhill   Achina

Coldbackie

Inernaver   Leckfurin

Borgie

Tongue

River Borgie

Armadale Burn

River Strathy

Loch Royal

Loch Meadie

Loch Naver

Loch Rimsdale

Altnaharra   Klibreck

Loch Choire

Crask Inn

Rhian

Loch Shin

Dalchouk

Loch Brora

Lairg   **START: DAY 19**

A836

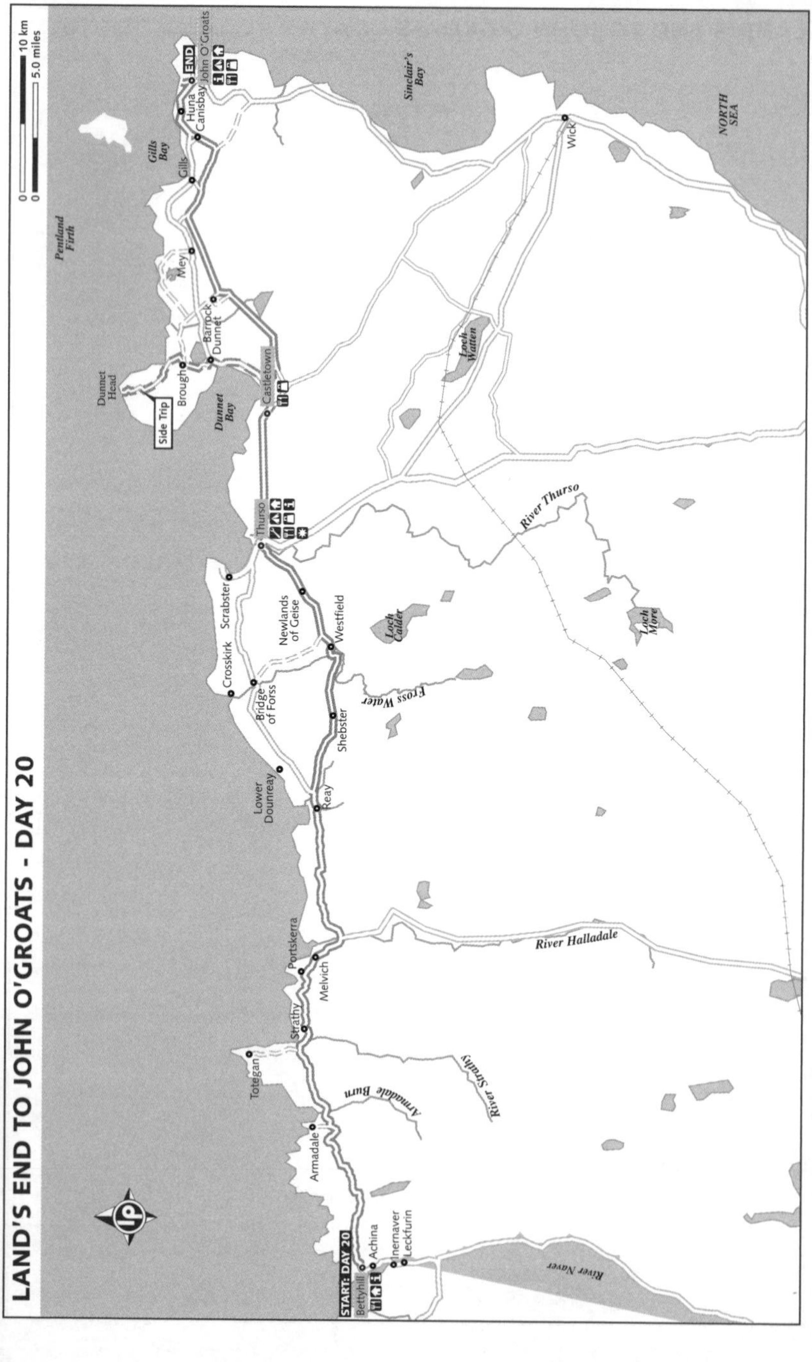

LAND'S END TO JOHN O'GROATS - DAY 20

0 — 10 km
0 — 5.0 miles

NORTH SEA

Sinclair's Bay

Gills Bay

END
Huna
Canisbay John O'Groats

Gills

Pentland Firth

Mey

Wick

Barrock
Dunnet

Loch Watten

Dunnet Head

Side Trip

Brough

Castletown

Dunnet Bay

River Thurso

Thurso

Loch More

Scrabster

Crosskirk

Newlands of Geise

Westfield

Loch Calder

Bridge of Forss

Cross Water

Shebster

Lower Dounreay

Reay

River Halladale

Portskerra

Melvich

Strathy

River Strathy

Totegan

Armadale Burn

Armadale

Invernaver
Achina
Bettyhill
Leckfurin

START: DAY 20

River Naver

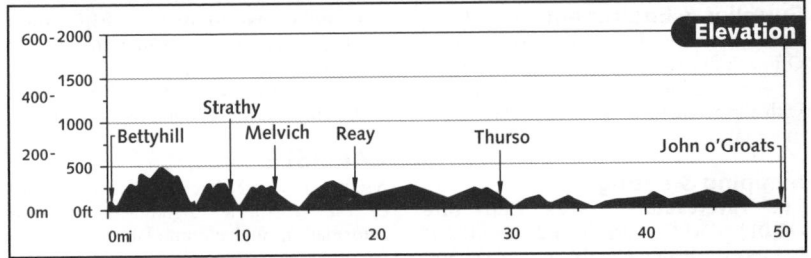

by taking country lanes between Reay and Thurso and from Castletown to Canisbay. Many, however, stick to the main road in a bid to get to John O'Groats quickly.

There are small stores at Melvich (12.5 miles) and Reay (18.4 miles), but the substantial settlement of **Thurso** (29.2 miles) is the main service town and an ideal place to stop for the last roadside lunch of the E2E.

The final 20 miles are an easy conclusion to the 20-day ride and if you've done the journey all the way from Land's End, give some time for reflection on your achievement. The John O'Groats finish line is by the turreted John O'Groats House. Air punches, high-fives and whoops all round

SIDE TRIP: DUNNET HEAD

Although John O'Groats is the farthest town from Land's End, it is not the mainland's most northerly point. That honour goes to Dunnet Head, a few miles west. To get there, stay on the A836 at 36.2 miles and turn left to Dunnet Head around 2.5 miles on.

TOWNS & FACILITIES

BETTYHILL
☎ 01641 / pop 553

Tiny Bettyhill is a crofting community (small agricultural land holds) on the north coast, named after Elizabeth, Countess of Sutherland, who resettled her tenants here after clearing them out of Strathnaver to make way for (more profitable) sheep. This is almost as remote as it gets in the UK with Bettyhill a rare outpost of civilisation in one of the country's most sparsely populated areas. The village's Gaelic name, Am Blaran Odhar, means 'The Grey Place' which doesn't do justice to this wild and beautiful place.

Information
End-to-enders can get the lowdown on Bettyhill and the surrounding area at the **tourist office** (☎ 01641 521342) at the bottom of the hill.

Sleeping & Eating
Accommodation is very limited in Bettyhill and unless you're camping, booking ahead at the **Bettyhill Hotel** (☎ 01641 521352; Bettyhill; s/d £40/70; mains £10-14) is the best way of assuring you're between sheets when night falls. Rooms without bathroom are considerably cheaper. It's worth stopping at the hotel restaurant just for the jaw-dropping gorgeous views from the large picture windows. **Dunveaden House** (☎ 01641 521273; Bettyhill; B&B £25) has six decent rooms with shared facilities, and a lockable shed for bikes. If it's full you might be able to camp in the grounds.

BRAEMAR
☎ 01339 / pop 410

Braemar, surrounded by mountains has long been a visitors' favourite. In addition to its pretty location, the village is also famous for the Braemar Gathering (see the boxed text p331), which sees tens of thousands of spectators swamp its streets in early September. If you're arriving at this time of year, book well ahead.

Information
The **tourist office** (☎ 01339 741600) stocks lots of useful information and can advise on accommodation.

Supplies & Equipment

Every morning Braemar's **Co-op** (Post Office Building, The Square) sends forth an army of hikers and cyclists equipped with replacement calories for a day in the mountains.

Sleeping & Eating

The **Invercauld Caravan Club Site** (☎ 01339 741373; Glenshee Rd; sites £18.50) is located on the edge of the village and has the usual high standards of a Caravan Club site. Despite the inflated price for a two-man tent, the slightly stony ground and many camp rules, the power showers, gorgeous Highland views and impeccably clean facilities make this a winner. Alternatively you could head for the hills and wild camp for free.

Rucksacks (☎ 01339 741517; 15 Mar Rd; dm hut/house £7/12, tw £26-30), one of the joys of Scotland is hostels like this, where the glow of happy hikers past and present is part of the fabric of the place. There's everything here you could want: a raft of comforts including barbecue, kitchen, drying-room, laundry, internet, and even a proper sauna. The well-loved Alpine hut (bring a sleeping bag) offers the simplest, cheapest berths – smarter accommodation is in the house or a new cabin out the back. Even if you're not staying, you can get online (10.30am-4.30pm, £2 per hour) or put on washing – nothing is too much trouble for the enthusiastic, welcoming owner.

Inverey SYHA (☎ 0870 004 1126; dm £12.50) is set up for walkers who want to be close to the hills not comfort – this is a cosy, basic place with tight-packed dorms and cold-water showers.

There are no showers, but you can wash in the **SYHA hostel** at Braemar (☎ 01339 741 659; Corrie Feragie, 21 Glenshee Rd) by arrangement. It's a mile past Inverey – the nearest shop is in Braemar.

Gathering Place (☎ 01339 741234; www.the-gathering-place.co.uk; 9 Invercauld Rd; mains £10-14) is one of a pair of more sophisticated Braemar dining options. This riverbank spot has an upbeat, optimistic feel, particularly when the evening sunshine bathes its conservatory dining area in light. Service is polite and efficient, and the well-presented bistro-style food satisfies without bagging any culinary awards.

Hungry Highlander Chip Shop (☎ 01339 41556; Invercauld Rd) is just what you need after a day on the road – the chips and burgers doled out hit the spot with campers, walkers and locals alike.

CARLISLE

See the Towns & Facilities section (p250) of the Northern England chapter for information on accommodation and other services.

CHEPSTOW

See Chepstow (p166) for information about accommodation and other services.

EDINBURGH

See the Towns & Facilities section (p294) of the Scotland chapter for information on accommodation and other services.

GLASTONBURY

See Glastonbury (p86) for sleeping and eating info.

GRANTOWN-ON-SPEY

☎ 01479 / pop 2239

With the Grampians behind you, Grantown (pronounced 'gran-ton'), a graceful Georgian town on the banks of the River Spey, is a welcome break after a tough day on the pedals. The main attraction here is angling and the town is well geared up to the fly fisher's needs.

Information

The town's **tourist office** (☎ 01479 872773; 54 High St) has accommodation lists and can advise on where to eat and what to see in the area.

Supplies & Equipment

As is often the case in the further-flung parts of Scotland, the **Co-op** supermarket (4 The Sq) is the best source of groceries.

Sleeping & Eating

If you're not camping, there is an ample supply of B&Bs in town and you should have no problem finding a bed. Booking ahead is, however, advisable in the summer months.

Grantown on Spey Caravan Park (☎ 01479 872474; Seafield Ave; sites £15 for tent/2 people) is conveniently located just a few hundred yards off the main thoroughfare. This Caravan Club site has a flat tent pitching area, under floor heating in the shower block and a shop.

The **Brooklynn B&B** (☎ 01479 873113; Grant Rd; s £32 d/tw £64) occupies a wonderful stone-built detached house a block north of the main road. Rooms are warm and inviting and you'll spend a lot of your time here admiring the curios, which pack the walls and corridors.

A similarly grand Victorian mansion houses the **An Cala Guesthouse** (☎ 01479 873293; Woodlands Terrace; B&B £35-37) has somewhat overfurnished rooms but is relatively bike friendly.

Sylhet Fish & Chips (☎ 01479 872711; 36 The Square) has takeaways and a restaurant, where chicken, pizza and vegie burgers start at under a fiver.

For more noble fare try the **Craggan Mill Restaurant** (☎ 01479 872288; Woodlands Tce; mains £12-20) where sublime northern European dishes such as salmon with whisky and orange sauce, or highland venison with red berries, are served in a converted mill. The owners are the authors of a fascinating and mouth-watering recipe book, *The Whisky Kitchen*, which takes the Scots' favourite tipple places it's never been before such as into soups and bakes.

INNERLEITHEN
☎ 01896 / pop 2586

Situated on the River Tweed, at the base of the Moorfoot Hills, this small former mill town provides a relaxing stop somewhat off the beaten track but still amid typical upland Borders scenery. Unless you intend to explore the surrounding country, this is most certainly a one-nighter before pressing on deeper into Scotland.

Supplies & Equipment

There's no frosty reception at **Icycles** (☎ 01896 833848; 4 Traquair Rd), the town's bike shop, where mechanics will gladly re-inflate the deflated and straighten the bent. Self-caterers should stock up at **The Village Store** (23-25 High St).

Sleeping & Eating

Tweedside Caravan Park (☎ 01896 831271; www.tweedsidecaravanparkinnerleithen .co.uk; Montgomery St; sites £8/2 people)

possesses one of the longest web addresses north of the border, grassy sites and a raft of facilities to keep campers happy. They also rent out four-berth pods, something between a tent and a garden shed, for £35.

The **Traquair Arms Hotel** (☎ 01896 830229; Innerleithen; rooms £60) has immaculate rooms and the pub-restaurant downstairs mixes Italian and Scottish cuisine to good effect. There's a generously cut beer garden where you can down a few wee drams.

The **Caddon View Guesthouse** (☎ 01896 830208; Pirn Rd; s £55, d/tw from £94) is a cut above most family-run B&Bs with plush comfortable rooms, immaculate en suite bathrooms and a sizeable breakfast.

INVERNESS
☎ 01463 / pop 44,100

Capital of the Highlands and the last large town on the route, pretty Inverness enjoys a fine location astride the River Ness between the Moray Firth and the northern end of Loch Ness. In summer it overflows with camera-toting visitors intent on getting a shot of the elusive Nessie.

Information

The **tourist office** (☎ 01463 234353; Castle Wynd) is comprehensive with currency exchange, internet access (£3 per hour), tour and accommodation booking, and a **Cal-Mac** (Caledonian MacBrayne) ferry office.

Supplies & Equipment

Tiso Outdoor (☎ 01463 716617; 41 High St) keep an army of hikers, cyclists and Nessie hunters equipped for their days in the wilds. **Bikes of Inverness** (☎ 01463 225965; 39 Grant St) is 0.8 miles along the route on Day 18.

Sleeping & Eating

The **Bught Camping Site** (☎ 01463 236920, Bught Ln; sites £12/2 people) is a level turfy site just five minutes' ride from Inverness Castle. The backpackers area has 81 sites and is rarely full. The toilets are clean enough, there's a small shop on site and the owners could not be friendlier. Midges can be a bit of a pest, but that's just Scotland in summer.

Bazpackers Backpackers Hotel (☎ 01463 717663; 4 Culduthel Rd; dm/d

£13/32) enjoys a great location near the castle and river. This cosy hostel is hard to beat with its relaxed vibe, log fire, back garden with barbecue, Nessie-view dorms and thick mattresses. There's no curfew, but the ambience is quiet sociable rather than 'pissed-up party time'. There's also a decent kitchen.

Inverness SYHA (☎ 01463 231771; Victoria Dr; dm/d £17/34) offers excellent facilities and roomy dorms, although you'll be queuing to charge your phone in some of them – this hostel is one of the SYHA's best. It has a separate kitchen and dining room to keep big groups out of the way, and offers double rooms for travelling couples. Spick-and-span with a pine feel, it has a space-age gleaming kitchen and two lounges (one with a pool table). It's 15 minutes' walk from the train station.

Bluebell House (☎ 01463 238201; www .bluebell-house.com; 31 Kenneth St; d £70-80) has guests' wellbeing on top of the agenda – there is a bubbly couple running this commodious and relaxing guesthouse, and the place exudes a comforting vibe. The two spacious front rooms – one with four-poster - command extra but worthwhile pounds, comfort throughout is excellent, and supplementaries like DVD library and homemade whisky marmalade.

Leakey's Bookshop & Cafe (☎ 01463 239947; Greyfriars Hall, Church St; snacks £3-6). This wonderful bookshop smells not of the venerable volumes lining its appealing interior but of home-baking and scrumptious soups, courtesy of the upstairs cafe, where you can keep reading as you graze.

Riva (☎ 01463 237377; 4 Ness Walk; meals £9-14) on the Ness's banks, is a so-phisticated and elegant Italian choice in a chic destination. For a great pasta combi-nation try tortellini tossed with poached chicken and artichoke hearts. The desserts, variety of breads, and warm service round out the experience.

Hootananny (☎ 01463 233651; www .hootananny.co.uk; 67 Church St) – a real mix of people patronise this huge former bank, where three floors offer something for everyone. Young Celts in love, sturdy octogenarian couples and curious back-packers dance to Scottish folk and *ceilidh* bands downstairs, cooler cats prowl the upstairs rock bar and top-floor armchair chill-out area. There's even Thai food on hand during the day.

IRONBRIDGE
☎ 01952 / pop 2457

As 'the birthplace of the industrial revolu-tion', Ironbridge on the outskirts of Tel-ford sounds a bit grim, yet the little town that grew up around the first iron bridge in the world is an appealing and fascinat-ing place. A well established fixture on the tourist trail, accommodation and eats are plentiful yet the ambience remains friendly and unhurried.

Abraham Darby I first smelted iron ore and coke in 1709 at Coalbrookdale just down the road. His grandson Abraham Darby III refined the process and erected the bridge in 1779 to demonstrate the ma-terial's potential.

Information
The Ironbridge **tourist office** (☎ 01952 884391; www.visitironbridge.co.uk; Toll-house) is by the bridge.

Supplies & Equipment
The **Bicycle Hub & Tandem Shop** (☎ 01952 883249; www.thebicyclehub.co.uk; Church Rd, Jackfield) is a cyclists Valhalla, espe-cially for those with a penchant for tan-dems. As well as selling hundreds of bikes and bike products, the expert mechanics can get any cycle back on the road in two shakes of a bike pump. Cyclists tackling the E2E route will be welcomed with open arms. For outdoor gear you'll have to ride on into Telford where the high street dou-ble-act of **Blacks** (☎ 01952 292085; Telford Forge Retail Park, Colliers Way, Old Park, Telford) and **Millets** (☎ 01952 201002; 207 Dean St, Telford) should be able to supply you with all you need.

Sleeping & Eating
Ironbridge is a tiny place with a mere hand-ful of places to chomp and kip. Some of the following options are found in neighbour-ing villages in and around the Ironbridge Gorge, and for even more choice push on to the larger town of Telford just 6 miles to the north.

Coalport YHA (☎ 0870 770 5882; ironbridge@yha.org.uk; High St, Coalport;

dm £16.95) is a historic former china factory, a big bluff industrial-looking building mere paces from the China Museum in Coalport, the canal and close to pleasant countryside walks, now houses an 83-bed hostel. The plain, modern rooms betray little of their long history, however. It has family friendly rooms.

Coalbrookdale YHA (☎ 0870 770 5882; ironbridge@yha.org.uk; Paradise Rd, Coalbrookdale; dm £16.95) is an austere former Literary and Scientific Institute – a grand blue-grey building from 1859 sitting high on the hillside behind sturdy iron gates – which now houses a newly refurbished hostel within easy walking distance of the Museum of Iron. It has a few en suite family rooms.

Library House (☎ 01952 432299; www.libraryhouse.com; 11 Severn Bank; s/d from £65/75) is a lovingly restored Georgian library building, hugged by vines, backed by a beautiful garden and elegantly decorated with light colours, deep cream sofas, rows of vintage books, and the odd African artefact. There are three charming, individually decorated rooms, with seriously comfortable beds, each named after a famous writer, and the welcome from hosts and family dog, is exceedingly friendly.

Malthouse (☎ 01952 433712; www.the malthouseironbridge.com; The Wharfage; mains £8-17) is a former malting house well worth visiting for the enormous plates of good British cooking alone, but the vibrant atmosphere, regular live jazz and riverfront terrace are an added bonus. Stylish contemporary rooms (£63) are also available.

Fat Frog (☎ 01952 432240; www.fat-frog.co.uk; Coalbrookdale; mains £10-6) – a quirky French bar-bistro cluttered with toy frogs and showbiz memorabilia, which has a rustic candle-lit basement and plays nostalgic music from the ebullient Gallic proprietor's prime. The food is excellent, and as you'd expect, there's a great wine list with plenty of half-bottles to choose from.

Restaurant Severn (☎ 01952 432233; 33 High St; two-/three-course dinner £24.95/26.95) The highly-praised food is a hybrid of British and French at this exciting fine dining waterfront restaurant. The simple decor and laid back service attests to the fact that the real star here

is the food – a delectable, locally sourced menu that changes weekly.

JOHN O'GROATS
☎ 01955 / pop 512

It may be the most northerly settlement of the British mainland, but there's nothing spectacular about tourist trap John O'Groats. The village is named after Dutchman Jan de Groot who ran ferries from here to Orkney Island in 1496. About 2 miles east is Duncansby Head, the most northeasterly point, known for its seabird colonies. Apart from its geographical location, John O'Groats is famous in Britain as the end or starting point for charity walks, cycles, runs, skateboards...you name it. For you it's the end of the line, and if you've pedalled all the way from Land's End, go you!

Information
The **tourist office** (☎ 01955 611373) sells a fine selection of local novels and books about Caithness and the Highland Clearances (see Scotland introduction p263).

Sleeping & Eating
John O'Groats Caravan & Camping Site (☎ 01955 611329; John O'Groats; www.johnogroatscampsite.co.uk; sites £12) lies right by the finish line and enjoys fine views out across the Pentland Firth.

John O'Groats YHA (☎ 01955 611424; Canisbay; dm £13-15) is actually in Canisbay, 3 miles west. Worn out cycles can get some much deserved R&R in the secure storage facility while you admire the panoramic views out across water.

The bland **Seaview Hotel** (☎ 01955 611220; www.seaviewjohnogroats.co.uk; John O'Groats; B&B from £20) is a great deal despite its austere looks, and you can celebrate your E2E triumph over a hearty meal and a few bottles of plonk in the hotel restaurant.

KIRKBY STEPHEN
☎ 017683 / pop 1832

Kirkby Stephen is a classic market town with stone Georgian-era houses fronting an attractive High St. There's nothing particularly amazing about the town though there are ample sleeping and refuelling options around to make stopping overnight straightforward enough. Unlike more illustrious tourist hotspots in the lakes and the dales it's not swamped with visitors, though you are likely to meet plenty of walkers passing through on the much tramped Coast to Coast route.

Information

For accommodation queries ask at the **tourist office** (☎ 01768 371199; Market St).

Supplies & Equipment

Kirkby Stephen's lone outdoor emporium is **Eden Outdoors** (☎ 01768 372431; Market St). The creatively named **Kirkby Stephen Cycle Centre** (☎ 01768 371658; Station Yd) handles all bicycle emergencies.

Sleeping & Eating

Pennine View Caravan Park (☎ 01768 371717; Station Rd) is five minutes' ride away on the southern fringes of town. Small and welcoming, the site has a spotlessly clean shower block (with piped music) and verdant spongy pitches, and there's a pub over the road serving grub if 'Campingaz' pasta loses its appeal.

Kirkby Stephen YHA (☎ 01768 371793; Market St; dm £17). Most redundant churches in the UK are resurrected as carpet showrooms and tat-flogging auction houses – not in Kirkby Stephen. This former Methodist Chapel on the main drag has been converted into a hostel complete with intact stained glass and pews! The main chapel contains the communal areas while dorms are out back in an adjoining building. Beds are limited so book ahead. Bikes can be stored here securely.

Black Bull Hotel (☎ 01768 371237; 38 Market St; s/d £25/50, mains £7-10) the nine newly refurbished en suite rooms at this pub-with-rooms place are a real bargain. The furniture and carpets are still fresh and unscuffed and the bathrooms, some with full-length bath, commendably pristine. In the pub dining room downstairs tuck into some northern waist bulgers such as chilli and chips, breaded scampi and Cumberland sausages in onion gravy.

Coast to Coast Chip Shop (☎ 01768 371194; 19 North Rd) serves lunch and evening sit in or takeaway at this chippy-cum-fish restaurant, well-known and deservedly popular among walkers and campers.

LAIRG

☎ 01549 / pop 904

The village of Lairg lies at the southern end of Loch Shin. In 1807, Lairg parishioners became some of the first victims of the Highland Clearances, but the village is now famous for its annual August Lamb Sale – the largest one-day sale in Europe and about the only day Lairg could be described as busy. The village's default setting is undeniably 'snooze'.

Information

Lairg's **tourist office** (☎ 01549 402160; Ferrycroft Countryside Centre) is on the west side of the River Shin, not in the main village. The staff can help you track down a bed or just advise on where to grab a bite to eat.

Sleeping & Eating

Dunroamin Caravan Park (☎ 01549 402447; www.lairgcaravanpark.co.uk; Main St; sites £6.50/2 people). You aren't done roamin' quite yet, but it's still OK to pitch up at this family run site on the edge of the village. Showers blocks are basic, there's a restaurant onsite and you won't need an alarm clock as inquisitive ducks come snuffling round your tent at sunrise. Bring buckets of midge repellent in summer.

Carbisdale Castle YHA (☎ 0870 004 1109; www.carbisdale.org; Culrain; dm £18) is, as the name suggests, housed in Carbisdale Castle in the village of Culrain (on the E2E route). As well as comfy bunks there are also hot meals served and cheap mountain bike hire for exploring the surrounding landscapes.

The immaculately furnished rooms at the **Loch View B&B** (☎ 01549 402578; www .lochviewlairg.co.uk; Lochside; B&B from £35) are a good deal and there's plenty of room to store the bike.

Park House (☎ 01549 402208; Station Rd; B&B £37) in a tranquil spot just off Main St and overlooking Loch Shin, it is a bit more luxurious.

The best place to head for a sit-down meal is the **Highland Hotel** (☎ 01549 402243; Main St; mains £7-12) or the Nip Inn as locals continue to call it.

LANCASTER

See the Towns & Facilities section (p172) of the Central England chapter for information on accommodation and other services.

LAUNCESTON
☎ 01566 / pop 7150

While not on the tourist trail, Launceston has a striking setting in hilly countryside. Its charming, old town centre near the crest of a hill is dominated by the castle ruins.

Information
For food and accommodation information, visit the **Launceston Tourist Information Centre** (☎ 01566 772321; www .visitlaunceston.co.uk; Market House Arc, Market St, Launceston)

NEWQUAY
See Newquay (p88) for info on services.

NORTHWICH
☎ 01606 / pop 19,259

Northwich lies between the Rivers Weaver and Dane and has four historic bridges and a marina. An otherwise ordinary little town, it was once part of the only large-scale salt mining operation in the country. The numerous lakes (or 'flashes') around the town are in fact collapsed mines.

Information
Northwich **tourist office** (☎ 01606 353534; www.valeroyal.gov.uk; 1 Market Arc) has a free accommodation booking service and stock info on the entire area.

Supplies & Equipment
The town's two cycle shops are **Cyclelife** (☎ 01606 781932; 12 Chester Rd, Castle), open seven days a week, and **Jack Gee Cycles** (☎ 01606 43029; 136 Witton St). Both have workshops where repairs can be carried out.

Sleeping & Eating
Forest View Inn Caravan Park (☎ 01606 882860; Gallowsclough Ln, Oakmere) is a year-round campsite around 5 miles south-east of Northwich near the village of Oakmere with an onsite pub serving meals and rurally picturesque views across to the De-lamere Forest. However the owners would do well to haul the shower blocks into the 21st century and some campers complain of noise and rowdy campervan families.

The Floatel (☎ 01606 44443; London Rd; d/tw £39) is bang in the centre on the marina. This boat hotel (or botel) has 60 en suite, cabin-style rooms. Unlike other botels, the Floatel was not converted from a decommissioned vessel but purpose-built and is the only one of its kind in the UK. The rooms may be on the small side but are perfectly maintained and the price will float anyone's boat. However, you may have to swab the decks to get staff to store more than a couple of cycles, and continental breakfast is a timber-shivering £6.95 extra.

Davenham Guesthouse (☎ 01606 43065; www.davenhamguesthouse.co.uk; Orchard House, 455 London Rd, Davenham; s/d £35/50) occupies a Victorian-era house in the pretty Cheshire village of Davenham, 2 miles south of Northwich. This small B&B has beautifully renovated rooms that evidently receive a lot of love from it's owners. It's a bit off the E2E route and you can either backtrack from Northwich or take a more direct route from Winsford via the A533, which passes through the village.

Giulios (☎ 01606-350380; 32 High St; pasta/pizza £7-8) – rest pedal-weary legs and sit down to superbly prepared and commendably affordable dishes at this simple but authentic Sicilian place in Northwich town centre. It seems some nights almost every member of the local Sicilian and Italian community squeeze themselves between the tightly packed tables where chef Giulio satisfies their discerning palette.

Cheshire Tandoori (☎ 01606 871040; 45 Chester Rd; mains £4.50-8) is found heading out of town on the Chester Rd. This relaxing Indian, a firm favourite with local curryheads, ticks all the right boxes for calorie-starved cyclists with the post-ride munchies. Open evenings and Sunday afternoon with an all-you-can-devour buffet.

PERTH
☎ 01738 / pop 43,500

Set on the River Tay, Perth is a grandly busy trading town and was once Scotland's capital. Its rise to importance derives from Scone Palace (pronounced 'scoon'), 2 miles north, to where Kenneth MacAlpin, first king of a united Scotland, brought the Stone of Destiny (on which kings and queens were crowned) in the 9th century.

Information

The town's **tourist office** (☎ 01738 450600; West Mill St) hands out maps of Perth and lots of helpful information.

Supplies & Equipment

For general outdoor kit head for **Millets** (182-186 High St) but for more specialist gear there's **Mountain Supplies** (133 South St). Between them, **JM Richards** (☎ 01738 626860; 44 George St) and **Perth City Cycles** (☎ 01738 639346; 42 Princes St) keep the city in chains (and other bike bits).

Sleeping & Eating

With no YHA or convenient campsite in or near Perth, you'll have no choice but to seek accommodation in town.

Comely Bank Cottage (☎ 01738 631118; www.comelybankcottage.co.uk; 19 Pitcullen Cres; s/d £35/56) lies on a short stretch of road bristling with upmarket, flowery B&Bs. This is our favourite on the stretch – a perfectly maintained family home offering large and commodious rooms with spacious bathrooms, and a solicitous owner who doesn't disappoint come breakfast time.

Heidl Guest House (☎ 01738 635031; www.heidl.co.uk; 43 York Pl; s/d £28/58), though a little grim from without, and on a busy street, the Heidl offers plenty of staunch hospitality allied with bright, light rooms, with cheery bedspreads in marine colours. Most rooms come with decent en-suite – those that don't have good private exterior bathroom. Free parking and proximity to the centre are further bonuses. Writer John Buchan (of *Thirty-Nine Steps* fame) was born in the house opposite.

Kinnaird Guest House (☎ 01738 628021; www.kinnaird-guesthouse.co.uk; 5 Marshall Pl; s/d £40/65) is the best of the handful of guesthouses enjoying a privileged position across the road from the lovely South Inch parkland. The elegant old house has noble original features and boasts appealing, bright rooms with big beds. The owners are engaging and extremely helpful – they are justifiably proud of what Perth has to offer.

Parklands (☎ 01738 622451; www .theparklandshotel.com; 2 St Leonard's Bnk; s/d £99/119) is tucked away near the train station – a relaxing hotel amidst a lush hillside garden overlooking the parklands of South Inch. While the rooms – which vary in size and shape – conserve the character of this beautiful building, formerly the residence of the town's mayors, they also offer modern conveniences such as flatscreen cable TV, wifi, and CD/DVD players. The restaurant has a fine reputation and a terrace to lap up the Perthshire sun.

Bread in Heaven (☎ 01738 442500; 13 High St; rolls £1.80-2.90) – with a passion for cycling and a community feel to it, this tiny cafe has a good attitude, decent espresso, and a wide range of sandwiches. Pack your panniers with panini and you won't have to stop for the rest of the day.

GlassRooms (☎ 01738 477724; Mill St; light meals £4-8) occupies part of the foyer of the ambitious, inspiring Perth Concert Hall, and this open-plan eatery has plenty to offer. The range of light daytime dishes includes several healthy and vegetarian choices as well as sandwiches and fresh juices.

Twa Tams (☎ 01738 634500; 79 Scott St) is Perth's best pub, and has a strange outdoor space with windows peering out onto the street, an ornate entrance gate, and large, cosy interior. There are regular events, including live music every Friday and Saturday night – it has a sound reputation for attracting talented young bands.

TIVERTON

☎ 01884 / pop 17,500

A flourishing mercantile centre (mainly for the wool trade) from the 17th to early 19th centuries, Tiverton dates back to pre-Saxon times and retains many historic buildings. Its setting, at the confluence of the Rivers Exe and Lowan is very attractive, and the town centre is lively.

Information

For accommodation and restaurant information, visit the **Tiverton Tourist Information Centre** (☎ 01884 255827, Phoenix Ln, Tiverton) or refer to one of these useful sites: www.visitdevon.co.uk and www.exeterandessentialdevon.com.

WORCESTER

☎ 01905 / pop 94,029

Worcester straddles the River Severn, with the city centre on the eastern bank dominated by a handsome cathedral. It has everything you need for an overnight stay but, apart from a handful of historic buildings and the famous porcelain works, little else will distract you from your epic journey north.

Information

The enthusiastic staff at the **tourist office** (☎ 01905 726311; www.visitworcester.com; Guildhall, High St) can book accommodation and field any query on Worcester you can think up.

Supplies & Equipment

Get geared up for the wilds of Worcestershire at **Blacks** (☎ 01905 611403; 24-25 The Cross) and **Yeomans Outdoors** (☎ 01905 731738; 20 The Shambles). Two of several central bike shops are the **Worcester Cycle Centre** (☎ 01905 611123; 8-9 College St) and **F Lewis Cycles** (☎ 01905 26455; Arch 50, Farrier St).

Sleeping & Eating

Mill House Caravan and Camping Site (☎ 01905 451283; Hawford) is a small campsite that lies 3 miles north of Worcester next to the A449. Only tents up to five-berth are allowed to pitch – the shower block is rudimentary but clean and there's a basic cafe and shop on site. Traffic noise can be annoying for light sleepers, so take some earplugs.

Burgage House (☎ 01905 25396; www .burgagehouse.co.uk; 4 College Precincts; s/d £36/65) is a well-camouflaged little gem, hidden on a narrow cobbled street over-

looking the cathedral. The four huge rooms (three of which are accessed up a beautiful curved stone staircase) are decked out with paintings and tapestries and are elegant yet incredibly homely – those at the front have stunning views. It's run in a warm, unobtrusive manner and is family friendly.

Ye Olde Talbot Hotel (☎ 01905 23573; www.oldenglish.co.uk; Friar St; s/d £70/90) is attached to a popular bar and bistro right in the centre of town, a pleasantly decorated inn that dates back to the 13th century and is pretty good value. Rooms sport rich fabrics, deep colours, modern gadgets and an occasional smattering of antique features. Discounted parking is available nearby.

The Quay (☎ 01905 745792; The Quay; main courses £6.95-13.75) has an informal setting right next to the river with plenty of outside tables to soak up the atmosphere. Come for light lunches, afternoon tea or more substantial dinners served in a candle lit dining room.

Mac & Jack's Deli (☎ 01905 731331; 44 Friar St) is a bright little deli and cafe serving perfect picnic fodder such as local meats, cheeses, freshly baked bread and cakes – as well as soups, sandwiches and tarts to eat in.

Old Rectifying House (☎ 01905 619622; www.theoldrec.co.uk; North Pde) has a laid-back lounge bar over a chic restaurant. There's a good selection of real ales and lagers and solid English food such as bangers-and-mash, fish and chips, and all day breakfasts. DJs play chill-out music at the weekends.

Cyclists Directory

CONTENTS

Country-wide practical information is given in this Directory. For details on specific areas, flip to the relevant regional chapter.

ACCOMMODATION

There's a huge variety of accommodation available in Britain and this guide features everything from camping and hostels to B&Bs and hotels. Listings are given in price order and are divided into budget (under £50) and mid-range (£50-120) options. Rates quoted are for high season for a double/twin room; at quieter times of the year prices drop. Single rooms are usually about 75% the double/twin rate. The exception is accommodation in London, where 'budget' means under £80 and midrange is £80-150.

Budget accommodation may be in hostels with shared dorms or private rooms in B&Bs where you may share a bathroom. Mid-range options cover B&Bs and hotels and rooms generally have a private bathroom. Finding a place to secure your bike is usually no problem; securing it undercover is sometimes more difficult.

If you arrive without accommodation head for the nearest tourist information centre, which can usually help with accommodation bookings. For last-minute online discounts try www.laterooms.com.

Camping

The opportunities for camping in Britain are numerous – ideal if you're on a tight

PRACTICALITIES

- Britain uses a bizarre mix of metric and imperial measures; for example, petrol is sold by the litre, but roadsign distances are given in miles.

- Use plugs with three flat pins to connect appliances to the 220V (50Hz AC) power supply.

- Read up on current events in (from right to left, politically) *Telegraph, Times, Independent* or *Guardian* papers or dig the dirt in the tabloids. For cycling coverage The *Guardian's* William Fotheringham is your best bet.

- To get local weather forecasts on your mobile (cell) phone text "WC TODAY + location" or "WC 5DAY+ location" to 83141. Forecasts cost 25p each, plus your normal operator text charges.

- For cycling news pick up a copy of *Cycling Weekly, Cycle Sport, Cycling Plus, Pro Cycling, Cycle Sport, MBR* (Mountain Bike Rider) or *Mountain Biking UK.*

- Turn on the TV and watch some world-class programming from the BBC, or boundary-pushing Channel 4.

- Tune into BBC radio for a wide range of shows. Its live news and sport station Radio 5Live (909 or 693 AM) offers the best cycling coverage.

budget or simply enjoy the great outdoors. In rural areas, campsites range from farmers' fields with a tap and a basic toilet, costing as little as £3 per person per night, to smarter affairs with hot showers and many other facilities charging up to £10. Free camping is rarely possible.

CAMPING BARNS & BUNKHOUSES

A step up from camping, camping barns are usually converted farm buildings, with sleeping platforms, a cooking area, and basic toilets outside. Take everything you'd need to camp except a tent. Charges are from around £5 per person

In Scotland, bothies offer simple shelter, often in remote places. They're not locked, there's no charge and you can't book. Take your own cooking equipment, sleeping bag and mat. Users should stay one night only and leave the bothy as they find it.

A bunkhouse is slightly plusher with a communal sleeping area and bathroom, heating and cooking stoves. You provide the sleeping bag and possibly cooking gear. Most charge around £10 per person per night.

Guesthouses & B&Bs

The B&B ('bed and breakfast') is a great British institution. Basically, you get a room in somebody's house, and at smaller places you'll really feel part of the family. 'Guesthouse' is sometimes just another name for a B&B, although they can be larger, with higher rates.

Facilities usually reflect price – for around £20 per person you get a simple bedroom and share the bathroom. For around £25 to £30 you get extras like TV or 'hospitality tray' (kettle, cups, tea, coffee) and a private bathroom – either down the hall or en suite. Most B&Bs serve enormous breakfasts that will set you up for the day.

B&B prices are usually quoted per person, based on two people sharing a room. Single rooms are scarce and solo travellers are at a disadvantage, paying a 20% to 50% premium and some B&Bs simply won't take single people (unless you pay the full double-room price), especially in summer. In country areas, most B&Bs cater for walkers and cyclists, but some don't, so let them know if you'll be turning up with muddy wheels.

Hostels

There are two types of hostel in Britain: those run by the **Youth Hostels Association** (YHA; ☎ 01629 592700; www.yha.org .uk) or **Scottish Youth Hostels Association** (SYHA; ☎ 0870 155 3255; www.syha .org.uk) and independent hostels.

You'll find hostels in rural areas, towns and cities, and they're aimed at all types of traveller - you don't have to be young or single to use them. The YHA also handles bookings for many bunkhouses and camping barns around the country.

YHA & SHYA HOSTELS

YHA & SYHA hostels are a great option for budget travellers. Some are purpose-built, but many are converted cottages, country houses and even castles – often in wonderful locations. Facilities include showers, drying room, lounge and equipped self-catering kitchen. Sleeping is usually in dormitories, and many hostels also have twin or four-bed rooms, some with private bathroom.

For cycle touring, hostels should be towards the top of your list of accommodation options. They're the most likely place to meet other cyclists and most have secure cycle storage.

You don't have to be a member of the YHA/SYHA (or another Hostelling International (HI) organisation) to stay at their hostels, but non-members pay £3 extra per person per night (£1.50 for u18s) in England and Wales; £1 per person per night in Scotland, so it's usually worth joining. Annual YHA membership costs £16; for the SYHA it's £9. Under-26s and families get discounts.

Small basic hostels cost from £10, larger hostels with more facilities are £14 to £19. All plus £3 if you're not a member. YHA /SYHA hostel prices vary according to demand and season. Throughout this book, we have generally quoted the cheaper rates (in line with those listed on the YHA's website); you may find yourself paying more.

YHA/SYHA hostels tend to have complicated opening times and days, especially in remote locations or out of tourist season, so check before turning up.

INDEPENDENT HOSTELS

Britain's independent hostels and backpacker hostels offer a great welcome. In rural areas, some are little more than simple bunkhouses (charging around £6), while others are almost up to B&B standard, charging £15 or more. In cities, backpacker hostels are perfect for young budget travellers. Most are open 24/7, with a lively atmosphere, good range of rooms (doubles or dorms), bar, cafe, internet, wi-fi and laundry. Prices are around £15 for a dorm bed, or £20-35 for a private room.

The *Independent Hostel Guide* (www .independenthostelguide.co.uk) covers hundreds of hostels in Britain and beyond, and is by far the best listing available. It's also available as a handy annually updated book at hostels or direct from the website. North of the border, an excellent site is www.hostel-scotland.co.uk.

Hotels

A hotel in Britain might be a small and simple place, perhaps a former farmhouse now stylishly converted or a huge country house with fancy facilities, grand staircases, acres of grounds and a row of stag-heads on the wall. On the whole hotel owners don't object to bicycles but they're not always set up to store them.

Hotel prices vary as much as the quality and ambience. At the bargain end, you can find singles/doubles costing £30/40. Move up the scale and you can easily pay to £100/150 or beyond. More money doesn't always mean a better hotel though – whatever your budget, some are excellent value, while others overcharge.

If all you want is a place to put your head down, budget chain hotels can be a good option. Most are totally lacking in style or ambience, but you'll only be there for eight hours, and six of them you'll be asleep. Most offer rooms from about £40 a night depending on season and demand but you can come across offers as low as £20 per night. **Travelodge** (www.travelodge.co.uk), **Premier Inn** (www.premierinn.com), **Etap Hotels** (www.etaphotel.com) and **Hotel Formule 1** (www.hotelformule1.com) are worth looking out for.

Pubs & Inns

As well as selling drinks, many pubs and inns offer lodging, particularly in country areas. Staying in a pub can be good fun – you're automatically at the centre of the community – although accommodation varies enormously, from stylish suites to threadbare rooms aimed at (and last used by) 1950s commercial salesmen. Expect to pay around £20 per person at the cheap end, and around £30-35 for something better. An advantage for solo tourists: pubs are more likely to have single rooms.

If a pub does B&B, it normally does evening meals, served in the bar or adjoining restaurant. Breakfast may also be served in the bar the next morning – not always enhanced by the smell of stale beer.

BUSINESS HOURS

The following are the normal opening hours in Britain. Throughout the book, opening hours are indicated only if they differ considerably from the norm.

Banks: 9.30am-5pm Monday to Friday, 9.30am to 1pm Saturday (large towns).
Shops: 9am-5.30pm Monday to Saturday, 10am-4pm Sunday
Post Offices: 9am-5pm Monday to Friday, 9am-noon Saturday.
Pubs: 11am-11pm Sunday to Thursday, to midnight or 1am Friday and Saturday
Restaurants: noon-3pm & 6-11pm.
Museums: often closed on a Monday
Offices: 9am-5pm, Monday to Friday

In smaller towns shops and post offices often close for lunch, and at weekends. In larger towns there's usually late night shopping until 8pm on Thursdays.

CHILDREN

Cycle touring with children? Yes, it really can be fun, and kids are a great excuse if you secretly yearn to visit railway museums or ride the rollercoaster. Some of Britain's traffic-free cycle paths – such as the Bristol & Bath Railway Path (p66) and the New Forest (p64) – offer great cycling opportunities for children. Other areas such as the Isle of Wight see only light traffic outside peak tourist season and make pleasant country for touring with children. It's always important to check your route carefully before leading younger riders on a road tour though. Some minor roads and lanes, even though they may see few cars, can be narrow, with vision ahead obscured by hedges.

BICYCLE TOURING WITH CHILDREN

Children can travel by bicycle from the time they can support their head and a helmet, at around eight months. There are some small, lightweight, cute-looking helmets around, such as the L'il Bell Shell. To carry an infant to toddler requires a child seat or trailer. Child seats are more common for everyday riding, and are cheaper, easier to move as a unit with the bike, and let you touch and talk to your child while moving.

Disadvantages, especially over long distances, can include exposure to weather, the tendency of a sleeping child to loll, and losing luggage capacity at the rear. The best makes, such as the Rhode Gear Limo, include extra moulding to protect the child in case of a fall, have footrests and restraints, recline to let the child sleep and fit very securely and conveniently onto a bike.

With a capacity of up to 50kg (versus around 18kg for a child seat), trailers can accommodate two bigger children and luggage. They give better, though not always total, protection from sun and rain and let children sleep comfortably. Look for a trailer that is lightweight, foldable, conspicuous (brightly coloured, with flag) and that tracks and handles well. It's also handy to be able to swap the trailer between bikes so adults can alternate towing and riding. Trailers or seats are treated as additional luggage items when flying.

Be sure that the bike to which you attach a child seat or trailer is sturdy and low-geared, to withstand – and help you withstand – the extra weight and stresses.

From the age of about four, children can move on to a 'trailer-bike' (effectively a child's bike, minus a front wheel, which hitches to an adult's bike) or to a tandem (initially as 'stoker', as the back seat is called, with 'kiddy cranks', crank extenders) – this lets them assist with the pedalling effort.

Be careful of children rushing into touring on a solo bike before they can sustain the effort and concentration required. Once they are ready and keen to ride solo, at about age 10 to 12, they will need a good quality and properly fitted touring bike. **Encycleopedia** (www.encycleope dia.com) has a good guide to quality trailers, trailer-bikes and tandems available.

Bike touring with children requires a new attitude as well as new equipment. Be sensitive to their needs – especially when they're too young to communicate them fully. In a seat or trailer, they're not expending energy and need to be dressed accordingly. Take care to keep them dry, at the right temperature and protected from the sun.

Keep their energy and interest up. When you stop, a child travelling in a seat or trailer will be ready for action, so always reserve some energy for parenting. This means more stops, including at places like playgrounds. Older children will have their own interests and should be involved in planning a tour. Try some day trips before you leave home.

Children need to be taken into account in deciding each day's route – traffic and distances need to be moderate, and facilities and points of interest adequate. Given the extra weight of children and their daily needs, you may find it easier to leave behind the camping gear and opt for indoor accommodation or day trips from a base or series of bases.

Alethea Morison

Local tourist offices are a great source of information on kid-friendly attractions. When eating out some restaurants are far friendlier than others. Those that welcome kids usually have high chairs, paper and crayons at the ready; others firmly say 'no children after 6pm'. Most pubs serving food also welcome families.

For more advice see www.babygoes2 .com – packed with tips and encouragement for parents on the move or Lonely Planet's *Travel with Children*.

CLIMATE

Britain's weather is notoriously fickle and is discussed in more detail on p352. These charts give details for specific regions with localised information available in the regional chapter climate sections.

Weather Information

The **Met Office** (www.metoffice.gov.uk /weather) is the most reliable source for weather information and provides detailed mountain area forecasts.

You can see forecasts online at www .weathercall.co.uk; use their telephone service (☎ 09068 500 400; regional numbers available online; calls cost 60p per minute); or use their SMS service (text "WC TODAY + location" or "WC 5DAY+ location" to ☎ 83141). Forecasts cost 25p each, plus your normal operator text charges.

CUSTOMS
Britain has a two-tier customs system – one for goods bought in another European Union (EU) country where taxes and duties have already been paid, and the other for goods bought duty-free outside the EU. Below is a summary of the rules; for more details go to www.hmce.gov.uk and search on 'Customs Allowances'.

Duty Free
If you bring duty-free goods from outside the EU, the limits include 200 cigarettes, 2L of still wine, plus 1L of spirits or another 2L of wine, 60cc of perfume, and other duty-free goods (including beer) to the value of £145.

Tax & Duty Paid
There is no limit to the goods you can bring from within the EU (if taxes have been paid), but customs officials use the following guidelines to distinguish personal use from commercial imports: 3200 cigarettes, 200 cigars, 10L of spirits, 20L of fortified wine, 90L of wine and 110L of beer – still enough to have one hell of a party.

DANGERS & ANNOYANCES
Britain is remarkably safe, considering the wealth disparities you'll see in many areas, but crime is certainly not unknown in London and other cities, so you should take care – especially at night. Always use licensed taxis rather than minicabs (unlicensed) – essentially a bloke with a car earning money on the side – and keep money and important documents out of sight, pickpockets operate in all major cities and towns.

In large hotels and city B&Bs, don't leave valuables lying around; put them in your bag or use the safe if there is one. In hostel dorms, especially independent/backpacker hostels in cities keep your stuff packed away and carry valuables with you. Many hostels provide lockers, bring your own padlock.

DISCOUNT CARDS
Membership of the YHA (see p349) can get you discounts in bookshops and outdoor gear shops, and on some public transport. International Student Identify Cards (ISIC) get you discounts in many shops and transport.

EMBASSIES & CONSULATES
Below is a selection of Britain's diplomatic missions overseas; for a complete list see the website of the **Foreign & Commonwealth Office** (www.fco.gov.uk) which also lists foreign embassies in the UK

British Embassies & Consulates
Australia (☎ 01902 941 555; www.britaus .net; Piccadilly Hse, 39 Brinabella Circuit, Canberra Act 2609)
Canada (☎ 0416 593 1290; www.ukin canada.gov.uk; 777 Bay St, College Pk, Toronto, M5G 2G2)
China (☎ 010 5192 4000; www.ukinchina .fco.gov.uk; 11 Guang Hua Lu, Jian Guo en Wai, Beijing 100600)
Japan (☎ 03 5211 1100; www.uknow.or.jp; No 1 Ichiban-cho, Chiyoda-ku, Tokyo 102-8381)
New Zealand (☎ 09 303 2973; www.uk tradeinvest.co.nz; Level 17, 151 Queen St, Auckland 1010)
USA (☎ 0212 745 0200; www.britainusa .com/ny; 845 Third Ave; NY 10022)

Embassies and Consulates in Britain
This selection of embassies, consulates and high commissions in London will be useful if you're from overseas and, for example, lost your passport. They won't be much help, however, if you're in trouble for committing a crime; even as a foreigner, you're bound by English laws.

Australia (☎ 020 7379 4334; www.au stralia.org.uk; Strand, WC2B 4LA)
Canada (☎ 020 7258 6600; www.canada .org.uk; 1 Grosvenor Sq, W1X 0AB)
China (☎ 020 7299 4049; www.chinese-em bassy.org.uk; 49-51 Portland Pl, London W1B 4JL)
France (☎ 020 7073 1000; www.amba france-uk.org; 58 Knightsbridge, SW1 7JT)
Germany (☎ 020 7824 1300; www.london .diplo.de; 23 Belgrave Sq, SW1X 8PX)

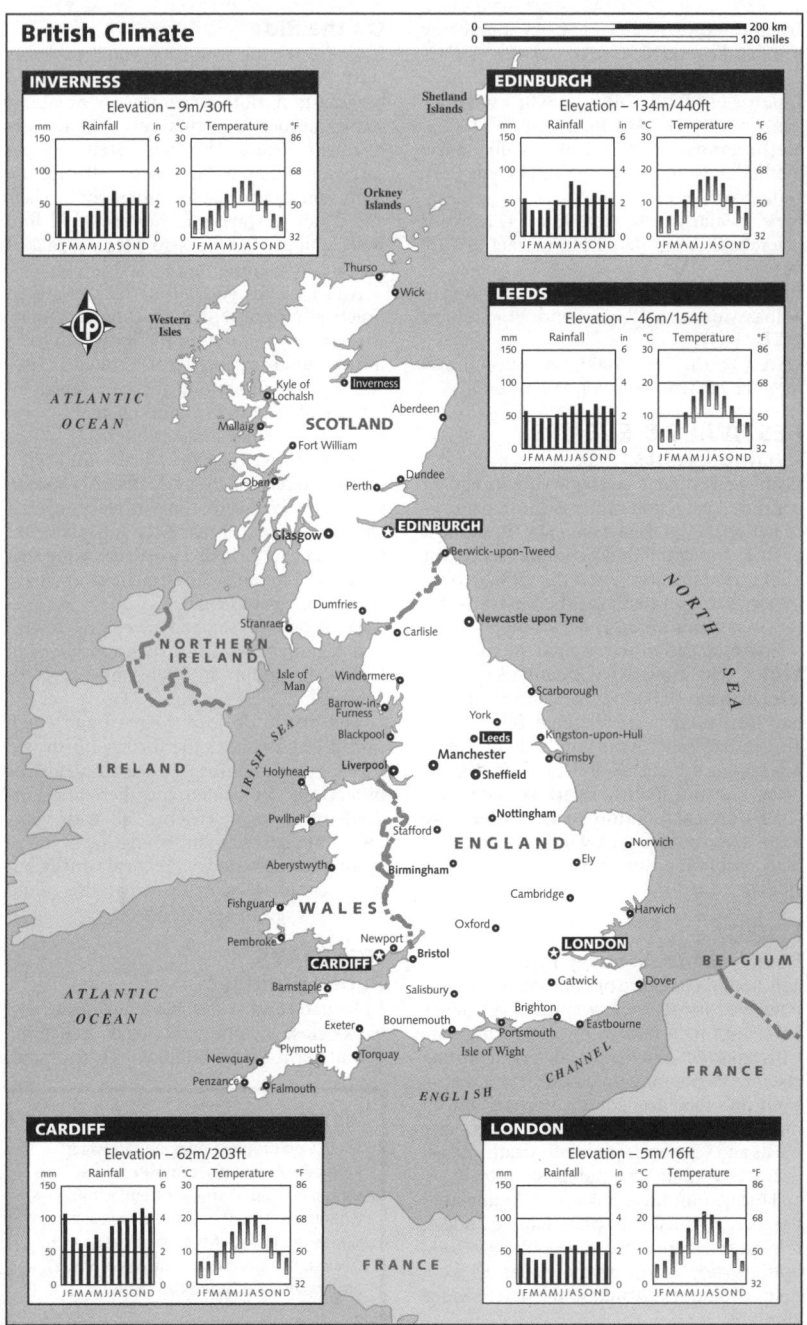

Ireland (☎ 020 7235 2171; www.embassy ofireland.co.uk;17 Grosvenor Pl, SW1X 7HR)

Japan (☎ 020 7465 6500; www.uk .emb-japan.go.jp; 101 Piccadilly, W1J 7JT)

Netherlands (☎ 020-7590 3200; www .netherlands-embassy.org.uk; 38 Hyde Park Gate, SW7 5DP)

New Zealand (☎ 020-7930 8422; www .nzembassy.com/uk; 80 Haymarket, SW1Y 4TQ)

Poland (☎ 0870 774 2700; www.polish embassy.org.uk; 47 Portland Pl, London W1B 1HQ)

USA (☎ 020 7499 9000; www.usembassy .org.uk; 24 Grosvenor Sq, W1A 1AE)

FESTIVALS & EVENTS
Cycling Events

Each year there's a staggering range of organised rides and rallies at local, regional or national level in Britain, many in support of charities. You'll find a comprehensive list of events and activities on the CTC website (www.ctc.org.uk) and on the Sustrans site (www.sustrans.org.uk).

Some of the most popular include the York Cycle Show (www.ctc.org.uk), which attracts over 10,000 visitors and is held in late June each year; National Bike Week, also in late June, with hundreds of events celebrating cycling around the United Kingdom, and the British Heart Foundation's (BHF) annual London to Brighton Bike Ride (www.bhf.org.uk/london-brighton), held each June, and host to over 27,000 riders.

FOOD

Bangers and mash, mushy peas, meat pies and stodgy Yorkshire pud: Britain never was renowned for its quality cuisine, yet things have improved immensely in recent years with gourmet kitchens and award-wining restaurants popping up all over the country. Even pub food has got an overhaul and in most places you can avoid the dreaded fatty meats and vegetables-boiled-to-death and get hearty but wholesome pub nosh instead.

Throughout this book, most 'Eating' sections are divided into price bands: budget, self-catering and mid-range. Budget food options should cost no more than £8 for a main course and drink, mid-range options about £8–16.

On the Ride

If you're staying in a B&B you'll probably start your day with a gut-busting fried breakfast; if not, stock up on breakfast staples at local supermarkets. The density of towns ensures that you rarely have to carry more than a day's food. Self-catering is the most affordable option for cyclists and if you're staying in hostels you'll find well-equipped kitchens to prepare packed lunches or evening meals.

Alternatively you'll find take-aways in practically every town in Britain. Otherwise make your way to the local pub for a hearty but affordable meal. Sooner or later you'll come across one the new breeds of 'gastropub' serving restaurant-quality food but in less formal surroundings.

In the bigger towns you'll also find cafes, usually referred to as 'caffs' or 'greasy spoons'. These seedy-looking places invariably serve cheap breakfasts and plain but filling lunches. It's also worth knowing that supermarkets and department stores have reasonably priced cafes.

Look out for seafood in coastal towns, and regional specialties such as pasties in Cornwall, rarebit in Wales or haggis in Scotland.

The British do love their tea and you'll find it gets stronger the further north you travel. For something stronger, local ales or bitters can't be beaten and there are hundreds of regional varieties, all with varying subtle flavours and strengths. If you're cycling in Scotland try the local whisky but don't ask for a 'Scotch' – what else would you be served in Scotland?

HOLIDAYS
Public Holidays

In England and Wales, most businesses and banks close on public holidays (hence the quaint term 'bank holiday'). In Scotland,

---

WATER

There's no problem drinking tap water in Britain. At country campsites water is sometimes piped straight from a spring without treatment, but there's usually a sign warning you if the water needs to be treated. If in doubt fill your water bottles at pubs or cafes along the route.

Bank Holidays are just for banks, and many other business stay open. Instead, Scottish towns normally have spring and autumn holiday, but dates vary from town to town.

Holidays for the whole of Britain (unless specified) are as follows:

New Year's Day 1 January
January 2 (Scotland only)
Good Friday March/April
Easter Monday (except Scotland) March/April
May Day First Monday in May
Spring Bank Holiday Last Monday in May
Summer Bank Holiday (Scotland) First Monday in August
Summer Bank Holiday (England & Wales) Last Monday in August
Christmas Day 25 December
Boxing Day 26 December

If a public holiday falls on a weekend, the nearest Monday is usually taken instead. On public holidays, some small museums and places of interest close, but larger attractions specifically gear up and have their busiest times, although nearly everything closes on Christmas Day. Generally speaking, if a place closes on Sunday, it'll probably be shut on bank holidays as well.

As well as attractions, virtually everything – shops, banks, offices – closes on Christmas Day, although pubs are open at lunchtime. There's usually no public transport on Christmas Day, and a very restricted service on December 26.

School Holidays

Most schools have three main terms, interspersed with three main holidays (when roads get busy and accommodation prices go up), although the exact dates vary from year to year and region to region:

Easter Holiday Week before and week after Easter
Summer Holiday Third week of July to first week of September
Christmas Holiday Mid-December to first week of January.

There are also three week-long 'half-term' school holidays – usually late February (or early March), late May and late October.

Some regions are moving towards six terms (and six holidays) of more equal length

INSURANCE

Regardless of nationality, everyone receives free emergency treatment at accident and emergency (A&E) departments of state-run National Health Service (NHS) hospitals. For other medical treatment, many countries have reciprocal health agreements with the UK, meaning visitors from overseas get the same standard of care from hospitals and doctors as any British citizen. Travel insurance, however, is still highly recommended as it offers greater flexibility over where and how you're treated. It will usually cover medical consultation and treatment at private clinics – which can be quicker than NHS places – and emergency dental care. Travel insurance will cover loss of baggage or valuable items (such as a camera) and, most importantly, the cost of any emergency flights home. Worldwide travel insurance is available at www.lonelyplanet.com/travel_services. You can buy, extend and claim online anytime – even if you're already on the road.

INTERNET ACCESS

You'll find internet cafes in most large towns and cities and all popular tourist spots. Most charge from £1 per hour, and out in the sticks you can pay up to £5 per hour. Public libraries often have computers with free internet access, but only for 30-minute slots, and demand is high. All the usual warnings apply about keystroke-capturing software and other security risks

---

TRAVEL INSURANCE

Buy a policy that generously covers you for medical expenses, theft or loss of luggage and tickets, and for cancellation of and delays in your travel arrangements. Check your policy doesn't exclude cycling or mountain biking as a dangerous activity.

Buy travel insurance as early as possible to ensure you'll be compensated for any unforeseen accidents or delays. If items are lost or stolen get a police report immediately – otherwise your insurer might not pay up.

– especially if you're using the internet to keep tabs on, say, your banking while on the move.

If you'll be using your laptop to get online, you'll find an increasing number of hotels, hostels, stations and coffeeshops (even some trains and buses) have wi-fi access, charging anything from nothing to £5 per hour.

MAPS

One of the best mapping resources for cyclists is **Sustrans'** (www.sustrans.org.uk) award-winning series of National Cycle Network Route Map & Guides (£6.99 each). These sheets break each stage of a long route into an individual panel, each including distance (traffic-free distance is indicated), an elevation cross-section, detailed inset maps for navigating through town centres, and useful contact numbers.

CTC also provides excellent maps for cyclists with route details available at www.ctc-maps.org.uk.

Britain's national mapping agency, **Ordnance Survey** (OS; www.ordnancesurvey.co.uk) produces some of Britain's finest mapping products. The **OS Landrangers** (1:50,000; £6.99) are ideal for cycling and the OS Explorer maps (1:25,000; £7.99) are even better for lowland areas, but can sometimes be hard to read in complex mountain landscapes. The OS *Great Britain Route Planner* (1:625 000, £4.99) is useful for pre-trip planning.

Specialist publishers **Harvey Maps** (www.harveymaps.co.uk) and **Goldeneye** (www.goldeneyemaps.com) produce a series of maps for hikers and cyclists that highlight route suggestions and points of interest.

Buying Maps

You can order maps online from all the mapping companies mentioned above. You'll also find a good selection of maps in most tourist information centres, local bookshops and outdoor shops, particularly in areas popular with walkers and cyclists.

MONEY

The currency of Britain is the pound sterling. Paper money comes in £5, £10, £20 and £50 denominations, although £50s can be difficult to change because fakes circulate. Prices quoted in this book are in UK pounds (£), unless otherwise stated, although other currencies are very rarely accepted if you're buying goods and services, except for some places in the ferry ports of southern England, which take Euros. A guide to exchange rates is given on the inside front cover of this book, and there are some pointers on costs on p26.

In England and Wales, notes are issued by the Bank of England, and in Scotland by Clydesdale Bank, Bank of Scotland and Royal Bank of Scotland. All are legal tender on both sides of the border, but if you have any problems ask a bank to swap them.

ATMs

Debit or credit cards are perfect companions – the best invention for travellers since the backpack. You can use them in most shops, and withdraw cash from ATMs (often called 'cash machines') which are

---

MAPS IN THIS BOOK

The maps in this book are based on the best available references, sometimes combined with GPS data collected in the field. They are intended to show the general routes of the rides we describe. They are primarily to help locate the route within the surrounding area. They are not detailed enough in themselves for route finding or navigation. You will still need a properly surveyed map at an adequate scale – specific maps are recommended in the Planning section for each hike. Most chapters also have a regional map showing the gateway towns or cities, principal transport routes and other major features. Map symbols are interpreted in the legend on the inside front cover of this book.

On the maps in this book, natural features such as river confluences and mountain peaks are in their true position, but sometimes the location of villages and routes is not always so. This may be because a village is spread over a hillside, or the size of the map does not allow for detail of the path's twists and turns. However, by using the cue sheets provided, you should have few problems following our descriptions. For more information see (p20).

easy to find in cities and even small towns. But ATMs aren't fail-safe, and it's a major headache if your only card gets swallowed, so take a back-up. And watch out for ATMs which might have been tampered with; a common ruse is to attach a card-reader to the slot; your card is canned and the number used for fraud.

Credit & Debit Cards

Visa and MasterCard credit and debit cards are widely accepted in Britain, and are good for larger hotels, restaurants, shopping, flights, long-distance travel, car hire etc. Smaller businesses, such as pubs or B&Bs, prefer debit cards (or charge a fee for credit cards), and some take cash or cheque only.

Since early 2006, nearly all credit and debit cards use the 'chip & pin' system. If your card isn't 'chip & pin' enabled, you should be able to sign in the usual way – but some places will not accept your card.

Moneychangers

Finding a place to change your money (cash or travellers cheques) into pounds is never a problem in cities, where banks and bureaus compete for business. Be careful using bureaus, however; some offer poor rates or levy outrageous commissions. You can also change money at some post offices – very handy in country areas, and exchange rates are fair (and usually commission free).

Tipping & Bargaining

In restaurants you're expected to leave around a 10% tip, but at smarter restaurants in larger cities waiters can get a bit sniffy if the tip isn't nearer 12% or even 15%. Either way, it's important to remember that you're not obliged to tip if the service or food was unsatisfactory (even if it's been added to your bill as a 'service charge'). At smarter cafes and teashops with table service around 10% is fine. If you're paying with a credit or debit card, and you want to add the tip to the bill, it's worth asking the waiting staff if they'll actually receive it. Some prefer to receive tips in cash.

Taxi drivers also expect tips (about 10%, or rounded up to the nearest pound), especially in London. It's less usual to tip minicab drivers. Toilet attendants may get tipped around 50p.

In pubs, when you order drinks at the bar, or order and pay for food at the bar, tips are not expected. If you order food at the table and your meal is brought to you, then a tip may be appropriate – if the food and service have been good, of course.

Bargaining is rare, although it's occasionally encountered at markets. It's fine to ask if there are student discounts on items such as theatre tickets, books or outdoor equipment.

Travellers Cheques

Travellers cheques (TCs) offer protection from theft, so are safer than wads of cash, but are rarely used in Britain, as credit/debit cards and ATMs have become the method of choice. If you prefer TCs, note that they are rarely accepted for purchases (except at large hotels), so for cash you'll still need to go to a bank or bureau.

PERMITS & FEES

Cyclists can use public roads, byways, designated cycle paths and cycle tracks throughout Britain. There are also 18,000 miles of bridleways, which cyclists can use, although they must give way to horse riders and walkers. Byways Open to All Traffic (also known as 'BOATs') also allow vehicle access so be prepared to meet the occasional motor cycle or 4x4.

Cycling on canal towpaths is allowed but some sections require a permit (free) from British Waterways. You can get more information and download a permit from www .waterscape.com.

Cycling is not allowed on disused railway lines unless they have been designated as cycle paths, or on open land unless special permission has been granted. Check your maps carefully and if in doubt ask locally. For information on mountain biking see p24.

TELEPHONE

Britain's iconic red phone boxes can still be seen in city streets and especially in conservation areas, although many have been replaced by soulless glass cubicles. With the advent of mobile phones (cellphones), many phone booths have been removed and not replaced at all. Either way, public phones accept coins, and usually credit/debit cards. The minimum charge is 20p.

Area codes in Britain do not have a standard format and vary in length, which can be confusing for foreigners (and locals). As well as the geographical area codes, other 'codes' include: ☎ 0500 or ☎ 0800 for free calls and ☎ 0845 for calls at local rates, wherever you're dialling from within the UK. Numbers starting with ☎ 087 are charged at national-call rate, while numbers starting with ☎ 089 or ☎ 09 are premium rate, and should be specified by the company using the number (ie in their advertising literature), so you know the cost before you call. Note that many numbers starting with 08 or 09 do not work if you're calling from outside the UK, or if they do you'll be charged for a full international call.

Codes for mobile phones usually start with ☎ 07 – more expensive than calling a land line.

International Calls

To call outside the UK dial ☎ 00, then the country code (☎ 1 for USA, ☎ 61 for Australia, etc), the area code (you usually drop the initial zero) and the number.

Direct-dialled calls to most overseas countries can be made from most public telephones, and it's usually cheaper between 8pm and 8am Monday to Friday and at weekends. You can usually save money by buying a phonecard with a PIN that you use from any phone by dialling an access number (you don't insert it into the machine). There are dozens of cards, usually available from city newsagents, with rates of the various companies often vividly displayed.

To make reverse-charge (collect) calls, dial ☎ 155 for the international operator. It's expensive, but what the hell – the person at the other end is paying.

To call Britain from abroad, dial your country's international access code, then ☎ 44 (the UK's country code), then the area code (dropping the first 0) and the phone number.

Most internet cafes now have Skype or some other sort of VOIP.

Local & National Calls

From public phones the weekday rate is about 5p per minute; evenings and weekends are cheaper – though still with a minimum charge of 20p. Local calls (within 35 miles) are cheaper than national calls. All calls are cheaper between 6pm and 8am Monday to Thursday, and from 6pm Friday to 8am Monday. From private phones, rates vary between telecom providers.

For the operator, call ☎ 100. For directory inquiries, a host of agencies compete for your business and charge from 10p to 40p; numbers include ☎ 118 192, ☎ 118 118, ☎ 118 500 and ☎ 118 811.

Mobile Phones

Around 50 million people in the UK have mobile phones. The terse medium of SMS is a national passion, with a billion text messages sent monthly.

Phones in the UK use GSM 900/1800, which is compatible with Europe and Australia but not with North America or Japan.

Even if your phone works in the UK, because it's registered overseas a call to someone just up the road will be routed internationally and charged accordingly. An option is to buy a local SIM card (around £30), which includes a UK number, and use that in your own handset (as long as your phone isn't locked by your home network).

A second option is to buy a pay-as-you-go phone (from around £50, including SIM and number); to stay in credit, you buy 'top-up' cards at newsagents.

TIME

Wherever you are in the world, time is measured in relation to Greenwich Mean Time (GMT, or Universal Time Coordinated, UTC as it's more accurately called). To give you an idea, if it is noon in London, it is 4am on the same day in San Francisco, 7am in New York and 10pm in Sydney. British summer time (BST) is Britain's daylight saving; one hour ahead of GMT from late March to late October.

For more information see the World Times Zones Map p414; www.timeanddate.com is also useful.

TOURIST INFORMATION

Before leaving home, check the informative, comprehensive and wide-ranging website VisitBritain (www.visitbritain.com) and the more specific www.enjoyengland.com, www.visitscotland.com and www.visitwales.com. Between them they cover all angles of national tourism, with links to numerous other sites. Details about local and regional websites and tourist organisations are also given at the start of each main chapter throughout this book.

Local Tourist Offices

All English cities and towns (and some villages) have a tourist information centre (TIC). Some tourist information centres are run by national parks and often have small exhibits about the area. You'll also see visitor welcome centres or visitor information centres, often run by chambers of commerce or civic trusts; for ease we've called all these places 'tourist offices' in this book. Whatever the name, these places have helpful staff, books and maps for sale, leaflets to give away and loads of advice on things to see or do. They can also assist with booking accommodation. Most tourist offices keep regular business hours; in quiet areas they close from October to March, while in popular areas they open daily year-round. For a list of all tourist offices around Britain see www.visitmap.info/tic.

Look out too for tourist information points – usually a rack of leaflets about local attractions set up in a post office or shop in a village not big enough to have its own tourist office.

VISAS

If you're a European Economic Area (EEA) national, you don't need a visa to visit (or work in) Britain or any other part of the UK. Citizens of Australia, Canada, New Zealand, South Africa and the USA are given leave to enter the UK at their point of arrival for up to six months (three months for some nationalities), but are prohibited from working.

UK immigration authorities are tough, and if they suspect you're here for more than a holiday, you may need to prove that you have funds to support yourself, details of any hotels or local tours booked, or personal letters from people you'll be visiting. Having a return ticket helps too.

Visa and entry regulations are always subject to change, so it's vital to check before leaving home. Your first stop should be www.ukvisas.gov.uk or www.ukba.home office.gov.uk and if you still have queries contact your local British embassy, high commission or consulate.

CYCLING ORGANISATIONS

The **Cyclists' Touring Club** (CTC; www.ctc.org.uk) is Britain's national cyclists' association and is without doubt the most useful contact point for touring cyclists; the £35 annual fee is well worth it. The club focuses on the social side of cycling with over 1000 events each year but also has a strong campaigning mission as well as offering members free insurance, route and touring information, and invaluable lists of cycle-friendly accommodation. UK residents must join CTC in order to access most useful information while overseas residents can buy individual information sheets without joining.

The **British Cycling Federation** (BCF; www.britishcycling.org.uk) is the governing body of cycle racing in Britain. The Welsh Cycling Union does the same job in Wales; and in Scotland it's the Scottish Cyclists' Union (SCU; www.scuonline.org).

Audax UK (www.aukweb.net) promotes non-competitive long-distance cycling and runs events from 120 miles to 370 miles; it's also the body through which British riders qualify for the 1200km Paris-Brest-Paris, held every four years.

The **International Mountain Biking Association** UK (www.imba.org.uk) promotes mountain biking in the UK, works to keep trails and public access open and offers cyclists advice on rights of way and mountain biking routes across the country.

Sustrans (www.sustrans.org.uk) is a sustainable transport charity and works on practical projects to encourage walking and cycling, so as to reduce motor traffic and its adverse effects. Its flagship project is the National Cycling Network (NCN), which covers 10,000 miles of routes on traffic-free paths and traffic-calmed and minor roads, reaching all parts of Britain.

The **Byways and Bridleways Trust** (www.thenationalbyway.org) looks after the National Byway which offers over 4000 miles of safe and easy-to-follow signposted cycle routes around the UK.

Transport

CONTENTS

GETTING THERE & AWAY

London is a global transport hub, so you can easily fly to Britain from just about anywhere in the world. In recent years, the massive growth of budget ('no-frills') airlines has increased the number of routes – and reduced the fares – between Britain and other countries in Europe.

Your other main option for travel between Britain and mainland Europe is ferry, either port-to-port or combined with a long-distance bus trip. This type of travel has less environmental impact than flying, although journeys can be long and financial savings not huge compared with budget airfares. International trains are much more comfortable, and another 'green' option; the Channel Tunnel allows direct rail serv-

THINGS CHANGE...

The information in this chapter is particularly vulnerable to change. Check directly with the airline or a travel agent to make sure you understand how a fare (and ticket you may buy) works and be aware of the security requirements for international travel. Shop carefully. The details given in this chapter should be regarded as pointers and are not a substitute for your own careful, up-to-date research.

ices between Britain, France and Belgium, with onward connections to many other European destinations.

AIR
Airports

London's main airports for international flights are Heathrow and Gatwick while Luton and Stansted deal largely with charter and budget European flights.

Some planes on European and long-haul routes go direct to major regional airports like Manchester, Glasgow or Edinburgh, while smaller regional airports such as Southampton, Cardiff and Birmingham are served by flights to/from continental Europe and Ireland.

Edinburgh (EDI; ☎ 0870 040 0007; www. edinburghairport.com) Six miles from the city centre with flights to/from European, American and other UK airports.
Gatwick (LGW; ☎ 0870 000 2468; www.gatwickairport.com) Popular with budget and charter airlines as well as big name carriers, Gatwick is 30 miles south of central London.
Glasgow (GLA; ☎ 0870 040 0008; www.glasgowairport.com) Eight miles from the city centre with flights to/from European and American airports as well as to India, the Middle East and North Africa.
Heathrow (LHR; ☎ 0870 000 0123; www.heathrowairport.com) The world's busiest airport 15 miles west of central London.
London City (LCY; ☎ 020 7646 0088; www.londoncityairport.com) A few miles east of central London, City Airport specialises in business flights.
Luton (LTN; ☎ 01582 405100; www.london-luton.co.uk) Especially well-known as a holiday flight airport, it is 35 miles north of central London.
Manchester (MAN; ☎ 08712 710 711; www.manchesterairport.co.uk) Has direct flights to/from Europe, the Gulf states, South Asia and beyond.
Stansted (STN; ☎ 0870 000 0303; www.stanstedairport.com) London's third-busiest airport, 35 miles northeast of the city.

BAGGAGE RESTRICTIONS

Airlines impose tight restrictions on carry-on baggage. No sharp implements of any kind are allowed onto the plane, so pack items such as pocket knives, camping cutlery and first-aid kits into your checked luggage.

If you're carrying a camping stove you should remember that airlines also ban liquid fuels and gas cartridges from all baggage, both check-through and carry-on. Empty all fuel bottles and buy what you need at your destination.

Airlines

Most of the world's major airlines have services to/from Britain from many parts of the world, and budget airlines fly between Britain and other European countries. Charter flights are another option; you can buy seat-only deals on the planes that carry tourists between, for example, Britain and numerous Mediterranean resorts. The best deals are usually available online, compare prices at online travel agencies such as www.expedia.com, www.travelocity.com, www.skyscanner.com, www.lowcostair lines.org, www.flightline.co.uk and www .cheapflights.co.uk.

Britain's national carrier is **British Airways** (BA; ☎ 0844 493 0787; www.ba.com) with routes worldwide.

Tickets

Because London is one of the world's main air travel hubs, there's competition between the airlines, and that means competitive fares. You can purchase your airline ticket from a travel agency (in person, by telephone or on the internet), or direct from the airline (the best deals are often available online only). However you choose, it always pays to shop around. Internet travel agencies work well if you're doing a straightforward trip, but for anything even slightly complex there's no substitute for a real-live travel agent who knows the system, the options, the special deals and so on. For short-haul flights in Europe you'll generally find the best deals online.

Australia & New Zealand

The route to Britain from the southern hemisphere is very popular, with a wide range of fares. It's also worth considering Round-the-world (RTW) tickets as they can sometimes work out cheaper than a straightforward return.

Major agencies include the following:

AUSTRALIA

Flight Centre (☎ 133 133; www.flightcentre .com.au)
STA Travel (☎ 134 782; www.statravel .com.au)

CYCLE-FRIENDLY AIRLINES

There aren't too many airlines that will carry a bike free of charge these days – at least according to the official policy. Most airlines regard the bike as part of your checked luggage. With European, Asian and Australian carriers, the usual luggage allowance is 20kg – which doesn't leave much room for your gear – and being over the limit can mean hefty excess baggage charges.

US and Canadian-based carriers work on a slightly different system: you are generally allowed two pieces of luggage, each of which must be 32kg or less. Excess baggage fees are charged for additional pieces, rather than for excess weight. On some airlines a bike may be one of your two pieces; others charge a set fee for carrying a bike which may then be carried in addition to your two other pieces.

When we looked into the policies of different carriers, we found that not only does the story sometimes change depending on who you talk to – and how familiar they are with the policy – but the official line is not necessarily adhered to at the check-in counter. If your flight is not too crowded, the check-in staff are often lenient with the excess charges, particularly for sporting equipment.

The times when you are most likely to incur excess baggage charges are on full flights – and, of course, if you inconvenience the check-in staff. If you suspect you may be over the limit, increase your chances of avoiding charges by checking in early, being well organised and being friendly and polite – a smile and a thank-you can go a long way!

NEW ZEALAND
Flight Centre (☎ 0800 24 35 44; www
.flightcentre.co.nz)
STA Travel (☎ 0800 474 400; www.sta
travel.co.nz)

Canada & the USA

There's a continuous price war on the world's
busiest transcontinental route and flights
from numerous destinations across Canada
and the USA. Major agencies include:

CANADA
Flight Centre (☎ 1877 967 5302; www
.flightcentre.ca)
Travel Cuts (☎ 1866 246 9762; www
.travelcuts.com)

USA
Flight Centre (☎ 1866 967 5351; www
.flightcentre.us)
STA Travel (☎ 1800 781 4040; www.sta
travel.com)
Travel Cuts (☎ 1800 592 2887; www
.travelcuts.com/us)

Continental Europe

You can fly between Britain and pretty
much every capital city in Europe (and
many other cities too), using national airlines such as Air France, Lufthansa and
so on, or budget airlines such as Ryanair,
easyJet and Virgin Express.

Ireland

There are numerous flights each day between the capitals Dublin and London, and
many more between other cities in Ireland
and Britain. If you book early and avoid
the busy periods (such as Friday afternoon
and evening), fares on budget airlines can
be just a few pounds or euros.

LAND
Bus

You can easily get between Britain and other
European countries via long-distance bus
or coach. The international network Eurolines (www.eurolines.com) connects a huge
number of destinations; the website is full of
information on routes and options, and you
can buy tickets online via one of the national
operators. Most Eurolines operators allow
you to take folding bikes as luggage but
check with the carrier before booking.

> **DEPARTURE TAX**
>
> Flying from Britain incurs an Air Passenger
> Duty (built into the ticket price). Those
> flying to countries in the European Union
> pay £20; those flying beyond pay £40.

Services to/from Britain are operated by
National Express (☎ 08717 818181; www
.nationalexpress.com) and some sample
journey times to/from London are: Amster-
dam 12 hours; Paris 8 or 9 hours; Dublin
12 hours; Barcelona 24 hours. If you book
early, and can be flexible with timings (ie,
travel when few other people want to) you
can get some very good deals. It's still worth
checking the budget airlines, though. You
may pay a similar fare and knock a large
chunk off the journey time.

Another option is the **European Bike
Express** (☎ 01430-422311; www.bike-ex
press.co.uk) a coach service for cyclists
picking up from 15 points in the UK and
another 30 points across France and Spain.
Buses run from May to October and bikes
are towed in a covered cycle trailer.

Train
CHANNEL TUNNEL SERVICES

The Channel Tunnel makes direct train
travel between Britain and continental
Europe a fast and enjoyable option. High-
speed **Eurostar** (☎ 08705 186 186; www
.eurostar.com) passenger services hurtle at
least 10 times daily between London and
Paris (the journey takes 2-1\2 hours) or
Brussels (two hours). You can buy tickets
from travel agencies, major train stations or
direct from the Eurostar website. You can
also buy 'through fare' tickets from many
cities in Britain - for example York to Paris,
or Manchester to Brussels. If you can fold
or dismantle your bike it can travel with
you as normal luggage. If not, you can reserve a place for it on the train (for a fee) or
use the registered baggage service (though
this does not guarantee that the bike will
travel on the same service).

If you've got a car, use **Eurotunnel**
(☎ 08705 353535; www.eurotunnel.com).
At Folkestone in England or Calais in France,
you drive onto a train, go through the tunnel,
and drive off at the other end. The trains run
about four times hourly from 6am to 10pm,

PACKING YOUR BIKE FOR AIR TRAVEL

We've all heard the horror stories about smashed/lost luggage when flying, but a more real threat to cycle tourists is arriving in a country for a two-week tour riding around on a bike that is now in little bits spread out around the baggage carousel. It could take days to fix, and they're sure to be annoying and frustrating days that could ruin your whole holiday.

How do you avoid this? Err on the side of caution (consider it an extra insurance policy) and box your bike. Trust airline baggage handlers if you want (we're told some people actually do) and give it to them 'as is' – turn the handlebars 90°, remove the pedals and deflate your tyres (partially, not all the way) – but is it worth the risk? If you want to take that sort of a risk, do it on your homeward flight, when you can get your favourite bike shop to fix any damage anytime.

Some airlines sell bike boxes, but most bike shops give them away free.

1. Loosen the stem bolt and turn the handlebars 90°.

2. Remove the wheels, seatpost and saddle (don't forget to mark its height before removing it), and the pedals.

3. Undo the rear derailleur bolt and tape it to the inside of the chainstay. There's no need to undo the derailleur cable. Some people also like to remove the chain, and while it can make things easier it isn't necessary.

4. Cut up some spare cardboard and tape it to the underside of the chainwheel, to prevent the teeth from penetrating the floor of the box and being damaged. If you forget this and several teeth are damaged chances are you'll still be able to ride on them – a professional mechanic with a European road racing team was notorious for refusing to replace chainrings damaged by riders dragging their bike bags across airport floors.

5. Deflate the tyres of your bike, otherwise they could explode inflight. Remove the quick-release skewers from the wheels and wrap a rag (or two) around the cluster so it won't get damaged or damage anything else.

6. Place the frame in the box, so it rests on the crankset and forks. You might want to place another couple of layers of cardboard underneath the forks too.

Sometimes the box will be too short to allow your front pannier racks to remain on your bike; if so, remove them. The rear ones should be fine.

7. Place the wheels beside the frame, on the side towards which the handlebars have been turned. You might want to separate the wheels from the frame by a large piece of cardboard.

8. Now add the saddle and seatpost, your helmet, tools and any other bits and pieces into the vacant areas. Wrap the skewers, chain etc in newspaper to prevent them doing damage to your bike and then add cardboard or newspaper packing to any areas where metal is resting on metal.

9. Tape the box up and write your name, address etc on several sides.

10. Strap your panniers together and take them with you as carry-on luggage.

Bike Bags

If you're planning on travelling between regions via train, plane or bus then you might want to take along a bike bag. The simplest form of bike bag has no padding built into it, is made of Cordura or nylon, and can be rolled up and put on your rear pannier rack and unfurled when you need to travel again.

The best type is not big and will require you to remove both wheels, the front pannier racks, pedals and seatpost, and then it will all fit inside the bag and make for (relatively) easy and inconspicuous train, plane or bus transfers.

then hourly. Loading and unloading is one hour; the journey takes 35 minutes. You can book in advance direct with Eurotunnel or pay on the spot (cash or credit card).

TRAIN & FERRY CONNECTIONS

As well as Eurostar, you can combine a normal train and ferry service to get to mainland Europe. You buy one ticket, but get off the train at the port, walk onto a ferry, then get another train on the other side. Routes include Amsterdam-London (via Hook of Holland and Harwich).

Travelling between Ireland and Britain, the main train-ferry-train route is Dublin to London, via Dun Laoghaire and Holyhead. Ferries also run between Rosslare and Fishguard or Pembroke (Wales), and Belfast or Larne and Stranraer (Scotland) with train connections on either side. For information on taking your bike on national train services see p362.

SEA

The main ferry routes between Britain and Ireland include Holyhead to Dun Laoghaire or Dublin Port, Rosslare to Fishguard or Pembroke, and Belfast or Larne to Stranraer. Between Britain and mainland Europe, ferry routes include Dover to Calais or Boulogne (France), Harwich to Hook of Holland (Netherlands), Hull to Zeebrugge (Belgium) and Rotterdam (Netherlands), Portsmouth to Santander or Bilbao (Spain), and Newcastle to Bergen (Norway) or Gothenberg (Sweden). There are many more.

Competition from Eurotunnel and budget airlines has forced ferry operators to discount heavily and offer flexible fares, meaning great bargains at quiet times of day or year. While most ferry companies will transport cycles, there are no hard and fast rules about charges. Some companies transport bikes for free, but others levy a charge, which is sometimes reduced in winter.

Main ferry operators include the following services:

Brittany Ferries (☎ 0871 244 0744; www .brittany-ferries.com)
DFDS Seaways (☎ 0871 522 9955; www .dfds.co.uk)
Irish Ferries (☎ 08705 171717; www.irish ferries.com)
Norfolkline (☎ 08701 450603; www .norfolkline.com)
P&O Ferries (☎ 08716 645 645; www.po ferries.com)
Speedferries (☎ 0871 222 7456; www .speedferries.com)
Stena Line (☎ 08705 707070; www.stena line.com)
Transmanche (☎ 0800 917 1201; www .transmancheferries.com)

Another very handy option is www.ferry booker.com, a single site covering all sea-ferry routes and operators, plus Eurotunnel.

GETTING AROUND

For getting around Britain your main choice is to go by car or public transport. While having your own car is time efficient and makes it easy to reach remote places, rental and fuel costs can be expensive for budget travellers – and the trials of traffic jams and parking hit everyone – so public transport is often the better way to go.

Your main public transport options are train and long-distance bus (called coach in Britain). Services between major towns and cities are generally good, although at 'peak' (busy) times you must book in advance to be sure of getting a ticket. Conversely, if you book ahead early and/or travel at 'off-peak' periods, tickets can be very cheap.

Public transport covers almost all of the country and trains, some bus (coach) services and most domestic planes and ferries will carry bikes. Although bus services are generally cheaper and cover more of the country, rail travel is generally the most convenient option for cyclists. For most travel enquiries **Traveline** (☎ 0871 200 2233; www.traveline.org.uk) is an invaluable service. It provides information on bus, coach, taxi and train services nationwide.

Getting from England to Scotland and Wales is easy. The bus and train systems are fully integrated and in most cases you won't even know you've crossed the border.

AIR

Britain's domestic air companies include British Airways, BMI, BMI Baby, easyJet and Ryanair, but flights around the country aren't necessary unless you're really pushed for time. Planes are only marginally quicker than trains if you include the time it takes to get to/from airports and to prepare your bike for travel. While you might be able to get a bargain fare on a plane, train travel can often be cheaper if you plan in advance.

British Airways (☎ 0844 493 0787; www .britishairways.com) Flies to/from London,

Southampton, Newquay, Birmingham, Manchester, Newcastle, Glasgow, Edinburgh, Inverness, Aberdeen and the Scottish Islands.

BMI (☎ 0870 6070 555; www.flybmi .com) Serves London, Norwich, Birmingham, Manchester, East Midlands, Leeds Bradford, Durham, Glasgow, Edinburgh and Aberdeen.

BMI Baby (☎ 0871 224 0224; www .bmibaby.com) Flies to/from Newquay, Cardiff, Birmingham, East Midlands, Manchester, Glasgow, Edinburgh and Aberdeen.

easyJet (☎ 0905 821 0905; www.easyjet .com) Serves London, Bristol, Newcastle, Edinburgh, Glasgow, Aberdeen and Inverness.

Ryanair (☎ 0871 246 0000; www.ryanair .com) Flies to/from London, Bournemouth, Newquay, Glasgow, East Midlands, Edinburgh and Inverness.

BUS

If you're on a tight budget, long-distance buses are nearly always the cheapest way to get around, although they're also the slowest – sometimes by a considerable margin. In Britain, long-distance express buses are called coaches, and in many towns there are separate bus and coach stations. Make sure you go to the right place!

National Express (☎ 08717 818181; www.nationalexpress.com) is the main operator, with a wide network and frequent services between main centres. North of the border, services tie in with those of Scottish Citylink (☎ 08705 505050; www.citylink .co.uk), Scotland's leading coach company. Fares vary: they're cheaper if you book in advance and travel at quieter times (special off-peak 'fun fares' are as low as £1), and more expensive if you buy your ticket on the spot and it's Friday afternoon. As a guide though, a 200-mile trip (eg London to York) will cost around £15-20 if you book a few days in advance.

Also offering fares from £1 is **Megabus** (www.megabus.com), operating a budget airline-style coach service between about 30 destinations around the country. Go at a quiet time, book early, and your ticket will be very cheap. Book later, for a busy time and…you get the picture.

The big problem with British buses is that they're not cycle friendly. National Express will only take folding bikes and Megabus will not carry bikes at all. Some regional bus companies will carry bikes but terms and conditions vary. Tourist information centres are generally the best places to ask questions about the local buses. CTC members can download an information sheet listing bus and coach operators that allow bikes on their buses from the website www .ctc.org.uk.

Bus Passes

National Express offers discount passes to full-time students and under-26s, called Young Persons Coachcards. They cost £10, and get you 30% off standard adult fares. Also available are Coachcards for people over 60, families and disabled travellers.

For touring the country, National Express also offers Brit Xplorer passes, which allow unlimited travel for seven days (£79), 14 days (£139) and 28 days (£219). You don't need to book journeys in advance with this pass; if the coach has a spare seat – you can take it.

CAR & MOTORCYCLE

You can be independent and flexible travelling by private car, and reach remote places. It is expensive for solo budget travellers, however, and in cities you'll need superhuman skills to negotiate heaving traffic, plus deep pockets for parking charges. On the other hand, if there's two of you, car travel can work out cheaper than public transport.

Motorways and main A-roads are dual carriageways and deliver you quickly from

---

HOW MUCH TO...?

When travelling long-distance by train or bus/coach in Britain, it's important to note that there's no such thing as a standard fare. Prices vary according to demand and how early you buy your ticket. Book long in advance and travel on Tuesday mid-morning, and it's cheap. Buy your ticket on the spot on Friday late afternoon, and it'll be a lot more expensive. Ferries (eg, to the Isle of Wight and Isle of Man) use similar systems. Throughout this book, to give you an idea, we have quoted sample fares but the price you pay will almost certainly be different.

one end of the country to another. Lesser A-roads, B-roads and minor roads are much more scenic and fun, as you wind through the countryside from village to village. You can't travel fast, but you won't care.

Automobile Associations

Large motoring organisations include the **Automobile Association** (www.theaa.com) and the **Royal Automobile Club** (www.rac .co.uk); annual membership starts at around £35, including 24-hour roadside breakdown assistance. A greener alternative is the **Environmental Transport Association** (www .eta.co.uk); it provides all the usual services (breakdown assistance, roadside rescue, vehicle inspections etc) but doesn't campaign for more roads.

Hire

Compared to many countries hire rates are expensive in Britain and under 25s pay a hefty supplement on top of this. As always, shop around to find the best deals. Many international websites have separate web pages for customers in different countries, and the prices for a car in Britain on, say, the UK web pages can be cheaper or more expensive than the same car on the USA or Australia web pages.

Your other option is to use an internet search engine to find small local car-hire companies who can undercut the big boys. Rental-brokers such as **UK Car Hire** (www.ukcarhire.net) or **Travel Supermarket** (www.travelsupermarket.com) can help you find the best rates.

The minimum age for renting a car is 21 and drivers must have held their licence for at least a year. Some companies will not rent to drivers over the age of 74. Your home licence should be sufficient for renting a car in Britain and most companies include insurance as standard but check the terms and conditions carefully as these, and the excess charges, can vary considerably.

Some of the main car rental companies in Britain include:

1car1 (☎ 0113 263 6675; www.1car1.com)
Avis (☎ 0844 581 0147; www.avis.co.uk)
Budget (☎ 0844 581 9998; www.budget .co.uk)
Europcar (☎ 0870 607 5000; www.euro pcar.co.uk)

Sixt (☎ 08701 567567; www.sixt.co.uk)
Thrifty (☎ 01494 751540; www.thrifty .co.uk)

Parking

Britain is small, and people love their cars, so there's often not enough parking space to go round. Many cities have short-stay and long-stay car parks; the latter are cheaper though maybe less convenient. 'Park and Ride' systems allow you to park on the edge of the city then ride to the centre on regular buses provided for an all-in-one price.

Yellow lines (single or double) along the edge of the road indicate restrictions. Find the nearby sign that spells out when you can and can't park. In London and other big cities, traffic wardens operate with efficiency; if you park on the yellow lines at the wrong time, your car will be clamped or towed away, and it'll cost you dearly to get driving again. In some cities there are also red lines, which mean no stopping at all. Ever.

For more information on road rules see p366.

TRAIN

For long-distance travel around Britain, trains are generally faster and more comfortable than coaches but can be more expensive, although with discount tickets they're competitive, and often take you through beautiful countryside. There are very few parts of Britain more than a day's ride (about 50 miles) from a train station.

About 20 different companies operate train services in Britain. For some passengers this system can be confusing at first, but information and ticket-buying services are mostly centralised. If you have to change trains, or use two or more train operators, you still buy one ticket – valid for the whole of your journey. The main railcards are also accepted by all operators.

Your first stop should be **National Rail** enquiries (☎ 08457 484950; www.national rail.co.uk), the nationwide timetable and fare information service. This site also advertises special offers, and has real-time links to station departure boards, so you can see if your train is on time. Once you've found the journey you need, links take you to the relevant train operator or to **centralised ticketing services** (www.thetrain

line.com, www.qjump.co.uk, www.raileasy
.co.uk) to buy the ticket. These websites
can be confusing at first (you always have
to state an approximate preferred time and
day of travel, even if you don't mind when
you go), but with a little delving around
they can offer some real bargains.

You can also buy train tickets on the spot
at stations, which is fine for short journeys,
but discount tickets for longer trips are usually not available and must be bought in
advance by phone or online. For planning
your trip, some very handy maps of the
UK's rail network can be downloaded from
www.nationalrail.co.uk/tocs_maps/maps
/network_rail_maps.html.

Classes
There are two classes of rail travel: first and
standard. First class costs around 50% more
than standard and, except on very crowded
trains, is not really worth it. However, at
weekends some train operators offer 'up-
grades' for an extra £10 to £15 on top of
your standard class fare, so you can enjoy
more comfort and leg-room.

Costs & Reservations
For short journeys (under about 50 miles),
it's usually best to buy tickets on the spot
at rail stations. You may get a choice of
express or stopping service – the latter is
obviously slower, but can be cheaper, and
may take you through charming countryside or grotty suburbs.

For longer journeys, on-the-spot fares
are always available, but tickets are much
cheaper if bought in advance. Essentially,
the earlier you book, the cheaper it gets.
You can also save if you travel at 'off-peak'
– ie, avoiding commuter times, Fridays and
Sundays. Advance purchase usually gets a
reserved seat too. The cheapest fares are
non-refundable though, so if you miss your
train you'll have to buy a new ticket.

If you buy by phone or website, you can
have the ticket posted to you (UK addresses
required), or collect it at the originating
station on the day of your travel, either at
the ticket desk (leave some time to spare,
as queues can be long) or via automatic
machines.

Whichever operator you travel with and
wherever you buy tickets, the three main
fare types are:

Advance – buy ticket in advance, travel
only on specific trains
Off-peak – buy ticket any time, travel off-
peak
Anytime – buy anytime, travel anytime

Advance tickets are subject to availability,
and usually available as singles only, but if
you're making a return journey (ie coming
back on the same route) you just buy two
singles.

For an idea of the price difference, an
Anytime single ticket from London to York
will cost around £100, and an Off-peak
around £80, while an Advance single can be
less than £20, and even less than £10 if you
book early enough or don't mind arriving
at midnight. Off-peak and Anytime tickets
are available as returns and the price can
vary from just under double the single fare
to just a pound more than the single fare.

Children under five travel free on trains;
those aged between five and 15 pay half price,
except on tickets already heavily discounted
– but a Family & Friends Railcard is usually
better value (see Train Passes, following).

If a train doesn't get you all the way to
your destination, a PlusBus supplement
(usually around £2) validates your train
ticket for onwards travel by bus – more
convenient, and usually cheaper, than buying a separate bus ticket. For details see
www.plusbus.info.

And finally, it's worth a look at the
Megatrain (www.megatrain.com – from
the people who brought you Megabus);
ultra-low train fares on ultra off-peak services between London and a few destinations in Southwest England and the East
Midlands.

Train Passes
Local train passes usually cover rail net-
works around a city (many include bus
travel too), and are mentioned in the individual city sections throughout this book. If
you're staying in Britain for a while, passes
known as 'railcards' are available:

16-25 Railcard – for those aged 16 to 25,
or a full-time UK student
Senior Railcard – for anyone over 60
Family & Friends Railcard – covers up
to four adults and four children travelling
together.

BIKES ON TRAINS

Bicycles can be taken on most local urban trains outside peak times, and on shorter trips in rural areas, free of charge, on a first-come-first-served basis – though there may be space limits.

Bikes can be carried on long-distance train journeys free of charge as well, but advance booking is required for most conventional bikes. (Folding bikes can be carried on pretty much any train at any time.) In theory, this shouldn't be too much trouble as most long-distance rail trips are best bought in advance anyway, but you have to go a long way down the path of booking your seat, before you start booking your bike – only to find space isn't available.

A better course of action is to buy in advance at a major rail station, where the booking clerk can help you through the options, or phone the relevant operator's Customer Service department. Have a large cup of coffee and a stress-reliever handy. And a final warning: when railways are repaired, cancelled trains are replaced by buses – and they won't take bikes.

A very useful leaflet called *Cycling by Train* is available at major stations or downloadable from www.nationalrail.co.uk/passenger_services/cyclists.html

---

These railcards cost around £25 (valid for one year, available from major stations or online) and get you a 33% discount on most train fares, except those already heavily discounted. With the Family card, adults and children get a 60% discount, so the fee is easily repaid in a couple of journeys. Proof of age and a passport photo may be required. For full details see www.railcard.co.uk.

A Disabled Person's Railcard costs £18. You can get an application from stations or from the railcard website (☎ 0191 281 8103).

If you're concentrating your travels on southeast England (eg London to Dover, Weymouth, Cambridge or Oxford) a Network Railcard covers up to four adults and up to four children travelling together outside peak times.

For country-wide travel, BritRail Passes are good value, but they're only for visitors from overseas and not available in Britain. They must be bought in your country of origin from a specialist travel agency. There are many BritRail variants, but their high cost means they will probably only suit cyclists planning to spend every second day on the train.

Below is an outline of the main options, quoting adult prices. Children's passes are usually half price (or free with some adult passes), and seniors get discounts too. For about 30% extra you can upgrade to first class. Other deals include a rail pass combined with the use of a hire car, or travel in Britain combined with one Eurostar journey. For more details see www.britrail.com.

BritRail Consecutive. Unlimited travel on all trains in England for 4, 8, 15, 22 or 30 days, for US$259/375/559/709/839. Anyone getting their money's worth out of the last pass should earn some sort of endurance award.

BritRail Flexipass. Your options are four days of unlimited travel in England within a 60-day period for US$329, 8 in 60 days for US$479, or 15 in 60 days for US$725.

If you don't (or can't) buy a BritRail pass, an All Line Rover gives virtually unlimited travel for 14 days anywhere on the national rail network. You can travel at any time, but aren't guaranteed a seat (reservations cost extra), so it's best to travel at off-peak times if you can. The pass costs £565 and can be purchased in Britain, by anyone.

Of the other international passes, Eurail cards are not accepted in Britain, and Inter-Rail cards are only valid if bought in another mainland European country.

YOUR
BICYCLE

Fundamental to any cycle tour you plan is the bicycle you choose to ride. In this chapter we look at choosing a bicycle and accessories, setting it up to best accommodate your needs and learning basic maintenance procedures. In short, everything you need to gear up and get going.

CHOOSING & SETTING UP A BICYCLE

The ideal bike for cycle touring is (strangely enough) a touring bike. These bikes look similar to road bikes but generally have relaxed frame geometry for comfort and predictable steering; fittings (eyelets and brazed-on bosses) to mount panniers and mudguards; wider rims and tyres; strong wheels (at least 36 spokes) to carry the extra load; and gearing capable of riding up a wall (triple chainrings and a wide-range freewheel to match). If you want to buy a touring bike, most tend to be custom-built these days, but Cannondale (www.cannondale.com) and Trek (www.trekbikes.com) both offer a range of models.

Of course you can tour on any bike you choose, but few will match the advantages of the workhorse touring bike.

Mountain bikes are a slight compromise by comparison, but are very popular for touring. A mountain bike already has the gearing needed for touring and offers a more upright, comfortable position on the bike. And with a change of tyres (to those with semi-slick tread) you'll be able to reduce the rolling resistance and travel at higher speeds with less effort.

Hybrid, or cross, bikes are similar to mountain bikes (and therefore offer similar advantages and disadvantages), although they typically already come equipped with semi-slick tyres.

Racing bikes are less appropriate: their tighter frame geometry is less comfortable on rough roads and long rides. It is also difficult to fit wider tyres, mudguards, racks and panniers to a road bike. Perhaps more significantly, most racing bikes have a distinct lack of low gears.

Tyres – Unless you know you'll be on good, sealed roads the whole time, it's probably safest to choose a tyre with some tread. If you have 700c or 27-inch wheels, opt for a tyre that's 28–35mm wide. If touring on a mountain bike, the first thing to do is get rid of the knobby tyres – too much rolling resistance. Instead, fit 1–1½ inch semi-slick tyres or, if riding unpaved roads or off-road occasionally, a combination pattern tyre (slick centre and knobs on the outside).

To protect your tubes, consider buying tyres reinforced with Kevlar, a tightly woven synthetic fibre very resistant to sharp objects. Although more expensive, Kevlar-belted tyres are worth it. An added benefit is that they are usually light and 'foldable' (they can literally be folded flat), which makes them very simple to pack for long-haulers wishing to carry a spare.

Pedals – Cycling efficiency is vastly improved by using toe clips, and even more so with clipless pedals and cleated shoes. Mountain-bike or touring shoes are best – the cleats are sufficiently recessed to allow comfortable walking. However, you should avoid shoes with excessive flexibility as they reduce pedalling efficiency and can create hotspots on the balls of the feet.

FOLD & GO BIKES

Another option is a folding bike. Manufacturers include: Brompton (www.bromptonbike.com), Bike Friday (www.bikefriday.com), Birdy (www.birdybike.com), Slingshot (www.slingshotbikes.com) and Moulton (www.alexmoulton.co.uk). All make high-quality touring bikes that fold up to allow hassle-free train, plane or bus transfers. The Moulton, Birdie, Brompton and Slingshot come with suspension and the Bike Friday's case doubles as a trailer for your luggage when touring.

TOURING BIKE

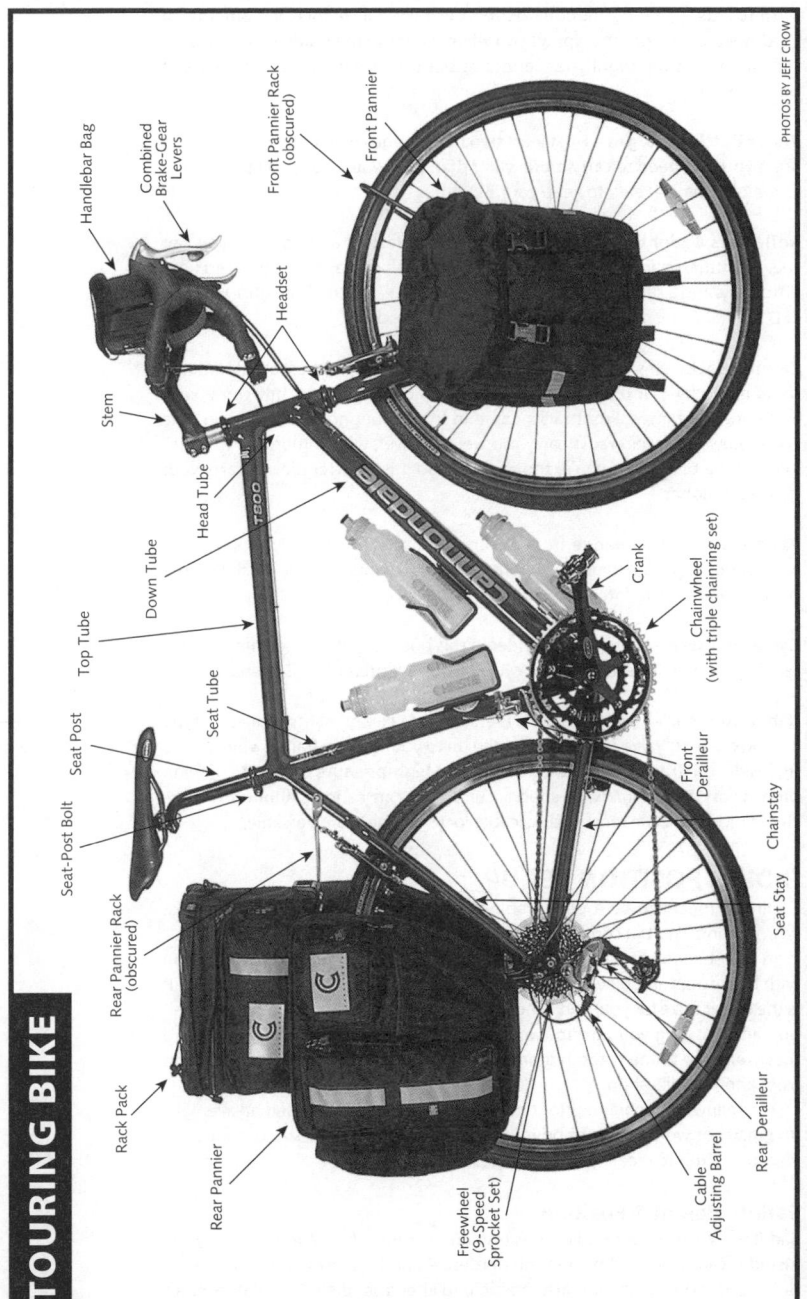

PHOTOS BY JEFF CROW

Handlebar Bag
Combined Brake-Gear Levers
Front Pannier Rack (obscured)
Front Pannier
Headset
Stem
Head Tube
Down Tube
Top Tube
Seat Tube
Seat Post
Seat-Post Bolt
Rear Pannier Rack (obscured)
Rack Pack
Rear Pannier
Freewheel (9-Speed Sprocket Set)
Cable Adjusting Barrel
Rear Derailleur
Seat Stay
Chainstay
Front Derailleur
Chainwheel (with triple chainring set)
Crank

YOUR BICYCLE

Mudguards – Adding mudguards to your bike will reduce the amount of muddy water and grit that sprays you when it rains or the roads are wet. Plastic clip-on models are slightly less effective but not as expensive, and they can be less hassle.

Water Bottles & Cages – Fit at least two bottle cages to your bike – in isolated areas you may need to carry more water than this. Water 'backpacks', such as a Camelbak, make it easy to keep your fluids up.

Reflectors & Lights – If riding at night, add reflectors and lights so you can see, and others can see you. Modern LED technology has revolutionised light efficiency, and a small headlight can also double as a torch (flashlight). Flashing LED tail-lights are cheap, compact and highly effective.

Pannier Racks – It's worth buying good pannier racks. The best are aluminium racks made by Blackburn. They're also the most expensive, but come with a lifetime guarantee. Front racks come in low-mounting and mountain bike styles. Low-mounting racks carry the weight lower, which improves the handling of the bike, but if you're touring off-road it is a better idea to carry your gear a bit higher.

Panniers – Panniers range from cheap-and-nasty to expensive top-quality waterproof bags. Get panniers that fit securely to your rack and watch that the pockets don't swing into your spokes.

Cycle Computer – Directions for rides in this book rely upon accurate distance readings, so you'll need a reliable cycle computer, preferably GPS enabled.

Other Accessories – A good pump is essential. Make sure it fits your valve type (see boxed text 'Valve Types'). Some clip on to your bicycle frame, while others fit 'inside' the frame. The stroke volume and high-pressure capability of mini-pumps vary considerably, so shop around. Also carry a lock. Although heavy, U- or D-locks are the most secure; cable locks can be more versatile.

RIDING POSITION SET UP

Cycling is meant to be a pleasurable pursuit, but that isn't likely if the bike you're riding isn't the correct size for you and isn't set up for your needs.

In this section we assume your bike shop did a good job of providing you with the correct size bike (if you're borrowing a bike get a bike shop to check it is the correct size for you) and concentrate on setting you up in your ideal position and showing you how to tweak the comfort factor. If you are concerned that your bike frame is too big or small for your needs get a second opinion from another bike shop.

The following techniques for determining correct fit are based on averages and may not work for your body type. If you are an unusual size or shape get your bike shop to create your riding position.

Saddle Height & Position

Saddles are essential to riding position and comfort. If a saddle is poorly adjusted it can be a royal pain in the derriere – and legs, arms and back. In addition to saddle height, it is also possible to alter a saddle's tilt and its fore/aft position – each affects your riding position differently.

ALL ILLUSTRATIONS BY MARTIN HARRIS

Fore/Aft Position: To check it, sit on your bike with the pedals in the three and nine o'clock positions. Check the alignment with a plumb bob (a weight on the end of a piece of string).

Saddle Tilt – Saddles are designed to be level to the ground, taking most of the weight off your arms and back. However, since triathletes started dropping the nose of their saddles in the mid-1980s many other cyclists have followed suit without knowing why. For some body types, a slight tilt of the nose might be necessary. Be aware, however, that forward tilt will place extra strain on your arms and back. If it is tilted too far forward, chances are your saddle is too high.

Fore/Aft Position – The default setting for fore/aft saddle position will allow you to run a plumb bob from the centre of your forward pedal axle to the protrusion of your knee (that bit of bone just under your knee cap).

Saddle Height – The simplest method of roughly determining the correct saddle height is the straight leg method. Sit on your bike wearing your cycling shoes. Line one crank up with the seat-tube and place your heel on the pedal. Adjust the saddle height until your leg is almost straight, but not straining. When you've fixed the height of your saddle pedal the cranks backwards (do it next to a wall so you can balance yourself). If you are rocking from side to side, lower the saddle slightly. Otherwise keep raising the saddle (slightly) until on the verge of rocking.

The most accurate way of determining saddle height is the Hodges Method. Developed by US cycling coach Mark Hodges after studying the position of dozens of racing cyclists, the method is also applicable to touring cyclists.

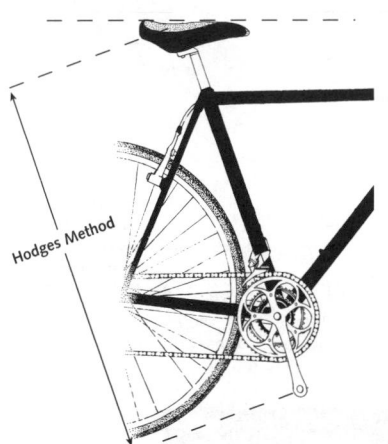

Hodges Method

Standing barefoot with your back against a wall and your feet 15cm apart, get a friend to measure from the greater trochanter (the bump of your hip) to the floor passing over your knee and ankle joints. Measure each leg (in mm) three times and average the figure. Multiply the average figure by 0.96.

Now add the thickness of your shoe sole and your cleats (if they aren't recessed). This total is the distance you need from the centre of your pedal axle to the top of your saddle. It is the optimum position for your body to pedal efficiently and should not be exceeded; however, people with small feet for their size should lower the saddle height slightly. The inverse applies for people with disproportionately large feet.

If you need to raise your saddle significantly do it over a few weeks so your muscles can adapt gradually. (Never raise your saddle above the maximum extension line marked on your seat post.)

Handlebars & Brake Levers

Racing cyclists lower their handlebars to cheat the wind and get a better aerodynamic position. While this might be tempting on windy days it doesn't make for comfortable touring. Ideally, the bars should be no higher than the saddle (even on mountain bikes) and certainly no lower than 75mm below it.

YOUR BICYCLE

Pedals

For comfort and the best transference of power, the ball of your foot should be aligned over the centre of the pedal axle (see right).

If using clipless pedals consider the amount of lateral movement available. Our feet have a natural angle that they prefer when we walk, run or cycle. If they are unable to achieve this position the knee joint's alignment will be affected and serious injury may result. Most clipless pedal systems now have some rotational freedom (called 'float') built in to allow for this, but it is still important to adjust the cleats to each foot's natural angle.

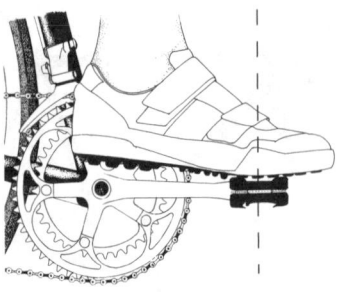

Pedal Alignment: The ball of your foot should be over the centre of the pedal axle for comfort and the best transfer of power.

COMFORT CONSIDERATIONS

Now that you have your optimum position on the bike, there are several components that you can adjust to increase the comfort factor.

Handlebars come in a variety of types and sizes. People with small hands may find shallow drop bars more comfortable. Handlebars also come in a variety of widths, so if they're too wide or narrow, change them.

With mountain bike handlebars you really only have one hand position, but 'riser' bars tend to have a more comfortable angle for touring than 'flat' bars; adding a pair of bar-ends increases hand position options. On drop bars the ends should be parallel to the ground. If they're pointed up it probably means you need a longer stem; pointed down probably means you need a shorter stem.

On mountain bikes the **brake levers** should be rotated downwards to around 45 degrees from horizontal, which ensures your wrist is straight – it's the position your hand naturally sits in. For drop bars the bottom of the lever should end on the same line as the end section.

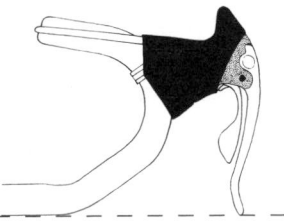

Brake Levers: Adjust your drop bars so the end section is parallel to the ground and the brake lever ends on this same line.

Getting the right **saddle** for you is one of the key considerations for enjoyable cycling. Everybody's sit bones are shaped and spaced differently, meaning a saddle that suits your best friend might be agony for you. A good bike shop will allow you to keep changing a new (undamaged) saddle until you get one that's perfect. Women's saddles tend to have a shorter nose and a wider seat, and men's are long and narrow.

If you feel too stretched out or cramped when riding, chances are you need a different length **stem** – the problem isn't solved by moving your saddle forward/aft. Get a bike shop to assess this for you. Height-adjustable stems (with a pivot) are also a versatile option, but the correct length is still required.

RECORD YOUR POSITION

When you've created your ideal position, mark each part's position (scratch a line with a sharp tool like a scribe or use tape) and record it, so you can recreate it if hiring a bike or when reassembling your bike after travel. The inside back cover of this book has a place to record all this vital data.

MAINTAINING YOUR BICYCLE

If you're new to cycling or haven't previously maintained your bike, this section is for you. It won't teach you how to be a top-notch mechanic, but it will help you maintain your bike in good working order and show you how to fix the most common touring problems.

If you go mountain biking it is crucial you carry spares and a tool kit and know how to maintain your bike, because if anything goes wrong it's likely you'll be miles from anywhere when trouble strikes.

If you want to know more about maintaining your bike there are dozens of books available (*Richard's 21st Century Bicycle Book*, by Richard Ballantine, is a classic; if you want to know absolutely everything get *Barnett's Manual: The Ultimate Technical Bicycle Repair Manual* or *Sutherland's Handbook for Bicycle Mechanics*) or inquire at your bike shop about courses in your area.

PREDEPARTURE & DAILY INSPECTIONS

Before going on tour get your bike serviced by a bike shop or do it yourself. On tour, check over your bike every day or so (see the boxed text 'Predeparture & Post-Ride Checks').

SPARES & TOOL KIT

Touring cyclists need to be self-sufficient and should carry some spares and, at least, a basic tool kit. How many spares/tools you will need depends on the country you are touring in – in countries where bike shops aren't common and the towns are further spread out you may want to add to the following.

Multi-tools (see right) are very handy and a great way to save space and weight, and there are dozens of different ones on the market. Before you buy a multi-tool though, check each of the tools is usable – a chain breaker, for example, needs to have a good handle for leverage otherwise it is useless.

Adjustable spanners are often handy, but the trade-off is that they can easily burr bolts if not used correctly – be careful when using them.

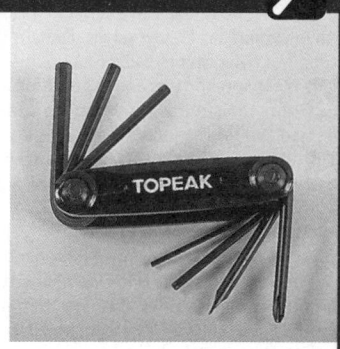

THE BARE MINIMUM:

o pump – ensure it has the correct valve fitting for your tyres (look for one that adapts to both types)
o water bottles (2)
o spare tubes (2)
o tyre levers (2)
o chain lube and a rag
o puncture repair kit (check the glue is OK)
o Allen keys to fit your bike
o small Phillips screwdriver
o small flat screwdriver
o spare brake pads
o spare screws and bolts (for pannier racks, seat post etc) and chain links (2)

FOR THOSE WHO KNOW WHAT THEY'RE DOING:

o spoke key
o spare spokes and nipples (8); can be taped to the lower rear forks
o tools to remove cassette/freewheel
o chain breaker
o pliers with side-cutters
o spare chain links; Shimano HyperGlide chains require new rivets once broken, but quick-release chain links such as the SRAM Powerlink and Wipperman Connex are an excellent alternative
o spare rear brake and rear gear cables

ALWAYS HANDY TO TAKE ALONG:

o roll of electrical/gaffer tape
o nylon cable ties (10) – various lengths/sizes
o hand cleaner (store it in a film canister)

FIXING A FLAT

Flats happen. And if you're a believer in Murphy's Law then the likely scenario is that you'll suffer a flat just as you're rushing to the next town to catch a train or beat the setting sun.

Don't worry – this isn't a big drama. If you're prepared and know what you're doing you can be up and on your way in five minutes flat.

Being prepared means carrying a spare tube, a pump and at least two tyre levers. If you're not carrying a spare tube, of course, you can stop and fix the puncture then and there, but it's unlikely you'll catch that train and you could end up doing all this in the dark. There will be days when you have the time to fix a puncture on the side of the road, but not always. If it's a wet day, be aware that patches may not glue satisfactorily. Carry at least two spare tubes; ones with holes can be patched at day's end.

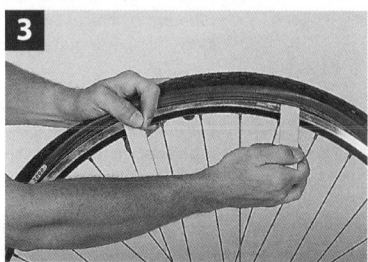

1 Note which cog the chain sits on, for reference when refitting. Take the wheel off the bike. Remove the valve cap and locknut (see 'Valve Types') on Presta valves. Deflate the tyre completely, if it isn't already.

2 Make sure the tyre and tube are loose on the rim – moisture and tube-pressure often fuse the tyre and rim.

3 Work the tyre bead as far into the central well of the rim as possible to create maximum play where the tyre is being lifted over the rim (removal and fitment). If the tyre is really loose you should be able to remove it by hand. Otherwise you'll need to lift one side of the tyre over the rim with tyre levers. Pushing the tyre away from the lever as you insert it should ensure you don't pinch the tube and puncture it again.

4 When you have one side of the tyre off, you'll be able to remove the tube. It's imperative before inserting the replacement tube that you carefully inspect the tyre (inside and out) for what caused the puncture; it's often easier to remove the tyre completely. Remove anything embedded in the tyre. Also check that the rim tape covers all spoke nipples and that none protrude through it.

VALVE TYPES

The two most common valve types are Presta (sometimes called French) and Schraeder (American or 'car'). To inflate a Presta valve, first unscrew the round nut at the top (and do it up again after you're done); depress it to deflate. The valve may need to be depressed before pumping as they can stick closed with time. To deflate Schraeder valves depress the pin (inside the top). Ensure your pump is set up for the valve type on your bike.

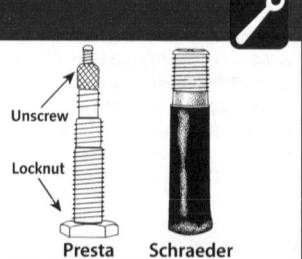

Unscrew

Locknut

Presta   Schraeder

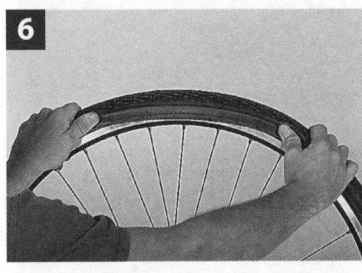

5 Time to put the new tube in. Start by partially pumping up the tube (this helps prevent it twisting or being pinched) and insert the valve in the rim-hole. Tuck the rest of the tube in under the tyre, making sure you don't twist it. Make sure the valve is straight – most Presta valves come with a locknut to help achieve this.

6 Work the tyre back onto the rim with your fingers (refer to Step 3). If this isn't possible, and again, according to Murphy's Law, it frequently isn't, you might need to release a little air and even use your tyre levers for the last 20cm to 30cm. If you need to use the levers, make sure you don't pinch the new tube, otherwise it's back to Step 1. All you need to do now is pump up the tyre and put the wheel back on the bike. Don't forget to fix the puncture that night.

FIXING THE PUNCTURE

To fix the puncture you'll need a repair kit, which usually comes with glue, patches, sandpaper and, sometimes, chalk. (Always check the glue in your puncture repair kit hasn't dried up before heading off on tour.) The only other thing you'll need is clean hands.

1. The first step is to find the puncture. Inflate the tube and hold it up to your ear. If you can hear the puncture, mark it with the chalk; otherwise immerse it in water and watch for air bubbles. Once you find the puncture, mark it, cover it with your finger and continue looking – just in case there are more.

2. Dry the tube and lightly roughen the area around the hole with the sandpaper. Sand an area larger than the patch.

3. Follow the instructions for the glue you have. Generally you spread an even layer of glue over the area of the tube to be patched and allow it to dry until it is tacky.

4. Patches also come with their own instructions – some will be just a piece of rubber and others will come lined with foil (remove the foil on the underside but don't touch the exposed area). Press the patch firmly onto the area over the hole and hold it for 2–3 minutes. If you want, remove the excess glue from around the patch or dust it with chalk or simply let it dry.

5. Leave the glue to set for 10–20 minutes. Inflate the tube and check the patch has worked.

CHAINS

Chains are dirty, greasy and all too often the most neglected piece of equipment on a bike. There are about 120 or so links in a chain and each has a simple but precise arrangement of bushes, bearings and plates. Over time all chains stretch, but if dirt gets between the bushes and bearings this 'ageing' will happen prematurely and will likely damage the teeth of your chainrings, sprockets and derailleur guide pulleys.

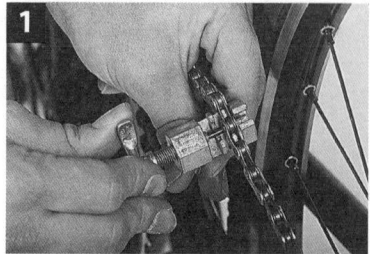

To prevent this, chains should be cleaned and lubed frequently (see your bike shop for the best products to use).

No matter how well you look after a chain it should be replaced regularly – wear depends on the quality of the chain and riding conditions, but about every 5000–8000km on average. Seek the advice of a bike shop to ensure you are buying the correct type for your drivetrain (the moving parts that combine to drive the bicycle: chain, freewheel, derailleurs, chainwheel and bottom bracket).

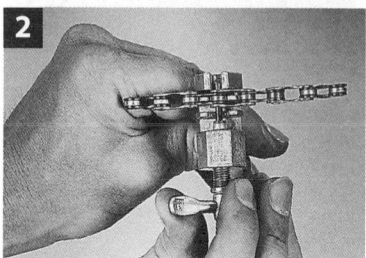

If you do enough cycling you'll need to replace a chain (or fix a broken chain), so here's how to use that funky-looking tool, the chain breaker. Of course, if you use a quick-release chain link you can avoid all of the following steps (see 'Chain Options' boxed text).

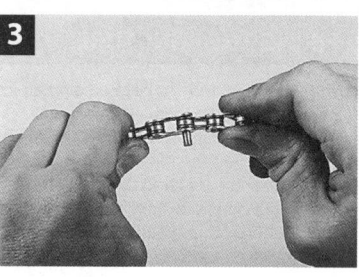

1 Remove the chain from the chainrings – it'll make the whole process easier. Place the chain in the chain breaker (on the outer slots; it braces the link plates as the rivet is driven out) and line the pin of the chain breaker up with the rivet.

2 Wind the handle until the rivet is clear of the inner link but still held by the outer link plate.

3 Flex the chain to 'break' it. If it won't, you'll need to push the rivet out some more, but not completely – if you push it all the way out, you'll have to remove two links and replace them with two spare links. If you're removing links, you'll need to remove a male and female link (ie, two links).

4 Rejoining the chain is the reverse. If you turn the chain around when putting it on you will still have the rivet facing you. Otherwise it will be facing away

CHAIN OPTIONS

Check your chain; if you have a Shimano HyperGlide chain you'll need a special HyperGlide chain rivet to rejoin the chain. This will be supplied with your new chain, but carry a spare.

A really cool alternative is to fit a two-piece joining link, such as Sachs Powerlink or Wipperman Connex Speed Connector – available for all 8-, 9- and 10-speed chains. You'll still need a chain breaker to fix a broken chain or take out excess links.

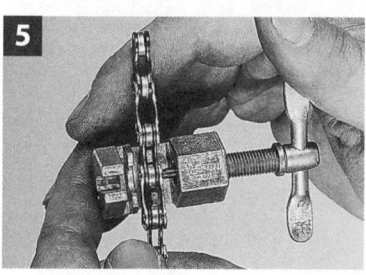

5

from you and you'll need to change to the other side of the bike and work through the spokes.

Join the chain up by hand and place it in the breaker. Now drive the rivet in firmly, making sure it is properly lined up with the hole of the outer link plate. Stop when the rivet is almost in place.

5 Move the chain to the spreaders (inner slots) of the chain breaker. Finish by winding the rivet into position carefully (check that the head of the rivet is raised the same distance above the link plate as the rivets beside it). If you've managed to get it in perfectly and the link isn't 'stiff', well done! Otherwise, move the chain to the spreaders on the chain breaker and gently work the chain laterally until the link is no longer stiff.

If this doesn't work (and with some chain breakers it won't), take the chain out of the tool and place a screwdriver or Allen key between the outer plates of the stiff link and carefully lever the plates both ways. If you're too forceful you'll really break the chain, but if you're subtle it will free the link up and you'll be on your way.

PREDEPARTURE & POST-RIDE CHECKS

Each day before you get on your bike and each evening after you've stopped riding, give your bike a quick once-over. Following these checks will ensure you're properly maintaining your bike and will help identify any problems before they become disasters. Go to the nearest bike shop if you don't know how to fix any problem.

PREDEPARTURE CHECKLIST
o **brakes** – are they stopping you? If not, adjust them.
o **chain** – if it was squeaking yesterday, it needs lube.
o **panniers** – are they all secured and fastened?
o **cycle computer** – reset your trip distance at the start.
o **gears** – are they changing properly? If not, adjust them.
o **tyres** – check your tyre pressure is correct (see the tyre's side wall for the maximum psi); inflate, if necessary.

POST-RIDE CHECKLIST
o **pannier racks** – check all bolts/screws are tightened; do a visual check of each rack (the welds, in particular) looking for small cracks.
o **headset** – when stationary, apply the front brake and rock the bike gently; if there is any movement or noise, chances are the headset is loose.
o **wheels** – visually check the tyres for sidewall cuts/wear and any embedded objects; check the wheels are still true and no spokes are broken.
o **wrench test** – pull on the saddle (if it moves, tighten the seat-post bolt or the seat-clamp bolt, underneath); pull laterally on a crank (if it moves, check the bottom bracket).

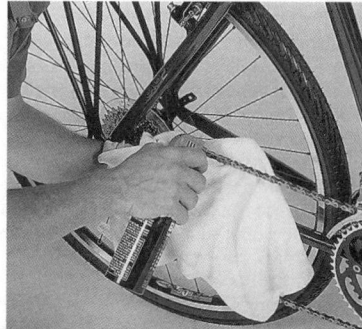

YOUR BICYCLE

BRAKES

Adjusting the brakes of your bike is not complicated and even though your bike shop will use several tools to do the job, all you really need is a pair of pliers, a spanner or Allen key, and (sometimes) a friend.

Check three things before you start: the wheels are true (not buckled), the braking surface of the rims is smooth (no dirt, dents or rough patches) and the cables are not frayed. With disc brakes the wheel should spin freely without any noticeable drag.

Begin by checking that the pads strike the rim correctly: flush on the braking surface of the rim (see right and opposite) and parallel to the ground.

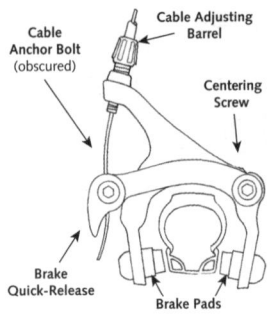

Dual-Pivot Calliper Brakes

Calliper Brakes

It's likely that you'll be able to make any minor adjustments to calliper brakes by winding the cable adjusting barrel out. If it doesn't allow enough movement you'll need to adjust the cable anchor bolt:

1 Undo the cable anchor bolt – not completely, just so the cable is free to move – and turn the cable adjusting barrel all the way in.

2 Get your friend to hold the callipers in the desired position, about 2–3mm away from the rim. Using a pair of pliers, pull the cable through until it is taut.

3 Before you tighten the cable anchor bolt again, check to see if the brake lever is in its normal position (not slack as if somebody was applying it) – sometimes they jam open. Also, ensure the brake quick-release (use it when you're removing your wheel or in an emergency to open the callipers if your wheel is badly buckled) is closed.

4 Tighten the cable anchor bolt again. Make any fine-tuning to the brakes by winding the cable adjusting barrel out.

BRAKE CABLES

If your brakes are particularly hard to apply, you may need to replace the cables. Moisture can cause the cable and housing (outer casing) to bond or stick. If this happens it's often possible to prolong the life of a cable by removing it from the housing and applying a coating of grease (or chain lube) to it.

If you do need to replace the cable, take your bike to a bike shop and get the staff to fit and/or supply the new cable. Cables come in two sizes – rear (long) and front (short) – various thicknesses and with different types of nipples.

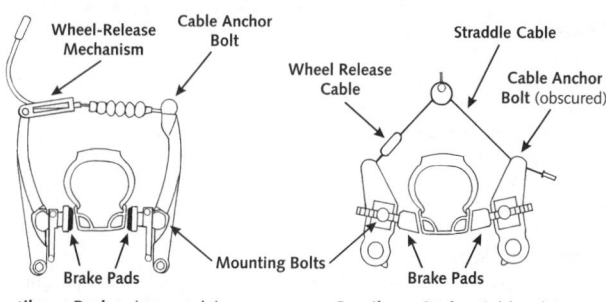

Cantilever Brakes (new style)   Cantilever Brakes (old style)

Cantilever Brakes

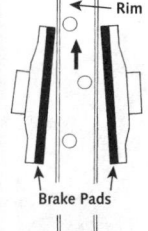

Brake Pads

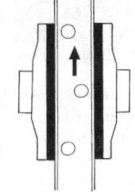

When Braking

Cantilever Brake Toe-In: This is how the brake pads should strike the rim (from above) with correct toe-in.

These days most touring bikes have cantilever rather than calliper brakes. The newest generation of cantilever brakes (V-brakes) are more powerful and better suited to stopping bikes with heavy loads.

On cantilever brakes ensure the leading edge of the brake pad hits the rim first (see left). This is called toe-in; it makes the brakes more efficient and prevents squealing. To adjust the toe-in on cantilever brakes, loosen the brake pad's mounting bolt (using a 10mm spanner and 5mm Allen key). Wiggle the brake pad into position and tighten the bolt again.

If you only need to make a minor adjustment to the distance of the pads from the rim, chances are you will be able to do it by winding the cable adjusting barrel out (located near the brake lever on mountain bikes and hybrids). If this won't do you'll need to adjust the cable anchor bolt:

1 Undo the cable anchor bolt (not completely, just so the cable is free to move) and turn the cable adjusting barrel all the way in. Depending on the style of your brakes, you may need a 10mm spanner (older bikes) or a 5mm Allen key.

2 Hold the cantilevers in the desired position (get assistance from a friend if you need to), positioning the brake pads 2–3mm away from the rim. Using a pair of pliers, pull the cable through until it is taut.

3 Before you tighten the cable anchor bolt again, check to see if the brake lever is in its normal position (not slack as if somebody was applying it) – sometimes they jam open.

4 Tighten the cable anchor bolt again. Make any fine-tuning to the brakes by winding the cable adjusting barrel out.

Disc Brakes

Disc brakes have traditionally only been used on mountain bikes, but they are starting to make an appearance in the touring bike market these days. The higher-end models offer the advantage of strong, fade-free stopping power in wet and dry conditions, plus none of the rim wear associated with all calliper and cantilever brakes. Once correctly adjusted to eliminate dragging, they are relatively trouble-free, and they are well worth considering when looking at a new bike purchase or upgrade.

Due to the many different brands and adjustment systems available for disc brakes, unless you are very familiar with your particular model, we recommend taking your bike to a reliable repairer for any maintenance or adjustment.

YOUR BICYCLE

GEARS

If the gears on your bike start playing up – the chain falls off the chainrings, it shifts slowly or not at all – it's bound to cause frustration and could damage your bike. All it takes to prevent this is a couple of simple adjustments: the first, setting the limits of travel for both derailleurs, will keep the chain on your drivetrain, and the second will ensure smooth, quick shifts from your rear derailleur. Each will take just a couple of minutes and the only tool you need is a small Phillips or flat screwdriver.

Front Derailleur

If you can't get the chain to shift onto one chainring or the chain comes off when you're shifting, you need to make some minor adjustments to the limit screws on the front derailleur. Two screws control the limits of the front derailleur's left and right movement, which governs how far the chain can shift.

When you shift gears the chain is physically pushed sideways by the plates (outer and inner) of the derailleur cage. The screws are usually side by side (see photo No 1) on the top of the front derailleur. The left-hand screw (as you sit on the bike) adjusts the inside limit and the one on the right adjusts the outside limit.

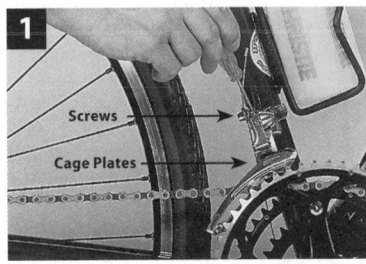

Screws

Cage Plates

After you make each of the following adjustments, pedal the drivetrain with your hand and change gears to ensure you've set the limit correctly. If you're satisfied, test it under strain by going for a short ride.

Outer Limits – Change the gears to position the chain on the largest chainring and the smallest rear sprocket. Set the outer cage plate as close to the chain as you can without it touching. Adjust the right-hand limit screw to achieve this.
Inner Limits – Position the chain on the smallest chainring and the largest rear sprocket. For chainwheels with three chainrings, position the inner cage plate between 1–2mm from the chain. If you have a chainwheel with two chainrings, position the inner cage plate as close to the chain as you can without it touching.

Front Derailleur: Before making any adjustments, remove any build up of grit from the screws (especially underneath) by wiping them with a rag and applying a quick spray (or drop) of chain lube.

Rear Derailleur

If the limit screws aren't set correctly on the rear derailleur the consequences can be dire. If the chain slips off the largest sprocket it can jam between the sprocket and the spokes and could then snap the chain, break or damage spokes or even break the frame.

The limit screws are located at the back of the derailleur (see photo No 2). The top screw (marked 'H' on the derailleur) sets the derailleur's limit of travel on the smallest sprocket's (the highest gear) side of the freewheel. The bottom screw ('L') adjusts the derailleur's travel towards the largest sprocket (lowest gear).

Outer Limits – Position the chain on the smallest sprocket and largest chainring (see photo No 3). The derailleur's top guide pulley (the one closest to the sprockets) should be in line with the smallest sprocket; adjust the top screw ('H') to ensure it is.
Inner Limits – Position the chain on the largest rear sprocket and the smallest chainring (see photo No 4). This time the guide pulley needs to be lined up with the largest sprocket; do this by adjusting the bottom screw ('L'). Make sure the chain can't move any further towards the wheel than the largest sprocket.

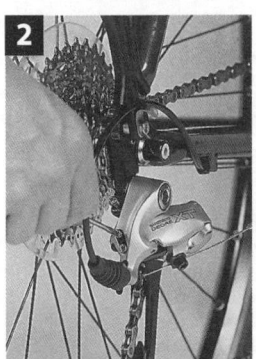
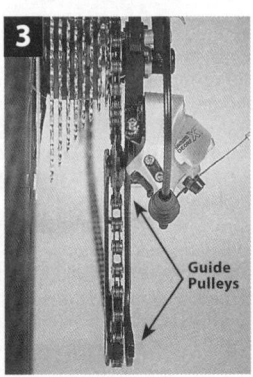

Guide
Pulleys

Cable Adjusting Barrel

If your gears are bouncing up and down your freewheel in a constant click and chatter, you need to adjust the tension of the cable to the rear derailleur. This can be achieved in a variety of ways, depending on your gear system.

The main cable adjusting barrel is on your rear derailleur (see photo No 5). Secondary cable adjusting barrels can also be found near the gear levers (newer Shimano combined brake-gear STI levers) or on the downtube of your frame (older Shimano STI levers and Campagnolo Ergopower gear systems) of some bikes. Intended for racing cyclists, they allow for fine tuning of the gears' operation while on the move.

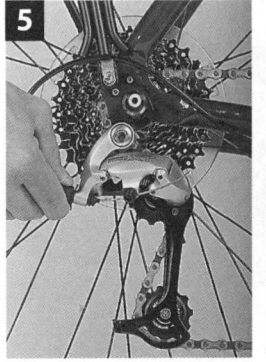

Raise the rear wheel off the ground – have a friend hold it up by the saddle, hang it from a tree or turn the bike upside down – so you can pedal the drivetrain with your hand.

To reset your derailleur, shift gears to position the chain on the second smallest sprocket and middle chainring (see photo No 6). As you turn the crank with your hand, tighten the cable by winding the rear derailleur's cable adjusting barrel anti-clockwise. Just before the chain starts to make a noise as if to shift onto the third sprocket, stop winding.

Now pedal the drivetrain and change the gears up and down the freewheel. If things still aren't right you may find that you need to tweak the cable tension slightly: turn the cable adjusting barrel anti-clockwise if shifts to larger sprockets are slow, and clockwise if shifts to smaller sprockets hesitate.

If you've made all these adjustments and gear changes are still not smooth over the entire range, it is highly likely that there is fine grit contaminating the cable housing or a minute crimp in the inner cable. Even very slight friction in the cabling can cause shifting problems, and the easiest solution is to completely replace the inner cable and outer housing. There are devices available that seal out dirt (especially useful for bikes with cables running down the rear frame stay, which allow water to run directly into the cable outer) and aid in reducing friction at the sharp bend into the rear derailleur; a good combo is the Avid Rollamajig and the SRAM Nightcrawler.

REPLACING A SPOKE

Even the best purpose-made touring wheels occasionally break spokes. When this happens the wheel, which relies on the even pull of each spoke, is likely to become buckled. When it is not buckled, it is considered true.

If you've forgotten to pack spokes or you grabbed the wrong size, you can still get yourself out of a pickle if you have a spoke key. Wheels are very flexible and you can get it roughly true – enough to take you to the next bike shop – even if two or three spokes are broken.

If you break a spoke on the front wheel it is a relatively simple thing to replace the spoke and retrue the wheel. The same applies if a broken spoke is on the nondrive side (opposite side to the rear derailleur) of the rear wheel. The complication comes when you break a spoke on the drive side of the rear wheel (the most common case). In order to replace it you need to remove the cassette, a relatively simple job in itself but one that requires a few more tools and the know-how.

If you don't have that know-how fear not, because it is possible to retrue the wheel without replacing that spoke and without damaging the wheel – see 'Truing a Wheel' (below).

1 Remove the wheel from the bike. It's probably a good idea to remove the tyre and tube as well (though not essential), just to make sure the nipple is seated properly in the rim and not likely to cause a puncture.

2 Remove the broken spoke but leave the nipple in the rim (if it's not damaged; otherwise replace it). Now you need to thread the new spoke. Start by threading it through the vacant hole on the hub flange. Next lace the new spoke through the other spokes. Spokes are offset on the rim; every second one is on the same side and, generally, every fourth is laced through the other spokes the same way.

3 With the spoke key, tighten the nipple until the spoke is about as taut as the other spokes on this side of the rim. Spoke nipples have four flat sides – to adjust them you'll need the correct size spoke key. Spoke keys come in two types: those made to fit one spoke gauge or several. If you have the latter, trial each size on a nipple until you find the perfect fit.

Truing a Wheel

Truing a wheel is an art form and, like all art forms, it is not something mastered overnight. If you can, practise with an old wheel before leaving home. If that's not possible – and you're on the side of the road as you read this – following these guidelines will get you back in the saddle until you can get to the next bike shop.

1 Start by turning the bike upside-down, so the wheels can turn freely. Check the tension of all the spokes on the wheel: do this by squeezing each pair of spokes on each side. Tighten those spokes that seem loose and loosen those that seem too tight. Note, though, the spokes on the drive side of the rear wheel (on the same side as the freewheel) are deliberately tighter than the non-drive side.

2 Rotate the wheel a couple of times to get an idea of the job at hand. If the wheel won't rotate, let the brakes off (see 'Brakes').

3 Using the chalk from your puncture repair kit, mark all the 'bumps'. Keep the chalk in the same position (brace the chalk against the pannier rack or bike's frame) and let the bumps in the wheel 'hit' the chalk.

4 In order to get the bumps out you'll need a constant point of reference – to gauge if the bumps are being removed. Often, if it is not a severe buckle, you can use a brake pad. Position the brake pad about 2–3mm from the rim (on the side with the biggest buckle).

5 With your spoke key, loosen those spokes on the same side as the bump within the longest chalked area, and tighten those on the opposite side of the rim. The spokes at the start and the finish of the chalked area should only be tightened/loosened by a quarter-turn; apply a half-turn to those in between.

6 Rotate the wheel again; if you're doing it correctly the buckle should not be as great. Continue this process of tightening and loosening spokes until the bump is as near to gone as you can get it – as the bump is removed turn the nipples less (one-eighth of a turn on the ends and a quarter-turn in between). Experienced exponents can remove buckles entirely, but if you can get it almost out (1mm here or there) you've done well.

7 If the wheel has more than one bump, move onto the second-longest chalk mark next. As each bump is removed you might find it affects the previous bump slightly. In this case, remove the previous chalk mark and repeat Steps 4–6. Continue to do this until all the buckles are removed.

Don't forget to readjust the brakes.

If you've trued the wheel without replacing the broken spokes, have them replaced at the next bike shop.

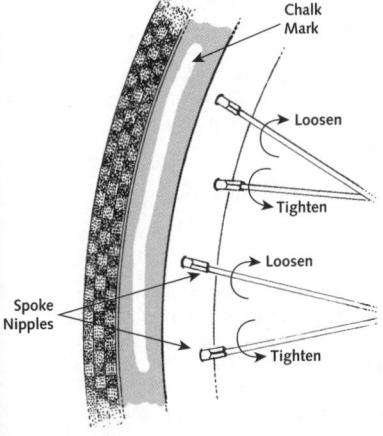

YOUR BICYCLE

LOADING YOUR BICYCLE

If you've ever been to Asia and seen a bike loaded with boxes piled 2m high or carrying four, five or six people, plus a chicken or two, you'll realise that there are more ways to carry your gear than would otherwise seem. More realistic options for you come from a combination of front and rear panniers, a handlebar bag or trailer.

'Credit-card tourists', who are intent on travelling lighter, further and faster and who are happy to stay in hotels or hostels, can get by with a handlebar bag and/or rear panniers (see top right). The downside to this configuration is poor bike-handling; the steering feels particularly 'airy'. It's possible to adopt the 'lighter, further, faster' principle and still camp, but it means frugal packing.

If you want to be more self-sufficient or you're carrying 20kg or more, you'll probably find it easier (and your bike will handle better) with front and rear panniers. The tried-and-tested configuration that works best for a touring bike is to use four panniers: two low-mounting front panniers with two high-mounting rear panniers (see bottom right). The only other thing you might want to add is a small handlebar bag for this book, snacks, sunblock, money, camera etc.

This combination, with a few light but bulky items on the rear rack (eg, tent, sleeping mat etc), allows you to carry a large load and still have predictable and manageable bike-handling.

If you're riding a mountain bike and riding off-road you'll probably want high-mounting front panniers to give you more clearance.

Pannier configurations: the four-pannier system is the best way of carrying your gear and having a bike that handles well; packing light saves weight but the compromise can be poor bike handling.

PACKING YOUR GEAR

It's frequently said that, in packing for a cycle tour, you should lay out everything you need to take and then leave half of it behind. The skill is in knowing which half to leave behind. Almost as much skill is needed in organising the gear in your panniers. Here are some tried and tested tips.

Compartmentalise Pack similar items into nylon drawstring bags (stuff sacks), to make them easier to find again (eg, underwear in one, cycling clothes in another, and even dinner food separated from breakfast food). Using different coloured stuff sacks makes choosing the right one easier.

Waterproof Even if your panniers are completely waterproof, and especially if they're not, it pays to put everything inside heavy-duty plastic bags. Check bags for holes during the trip; replace them or patch the holes with tape.

Reduce Flood Damage If your panniers are not waterproof and they pool water, you can reduce problems by putting things that are unaffected by water, say a pair of thongs, at the bottom of the bag. This keeps the other stuff above 'flood level'. Try using seam sealant on the bags' seams beforehand, too.

Load Consistently Put things in the same place each time you pack to avoid having to unpack every bag just to find one item.

Balance the Load Distribute weight evenly – generally around 60% in the rear and 40% in the front panniers – and keep it as low as possible by using low-mounting front panniers and packing heavy items first. Side-to-side balancing is just as critical.

Group Gear Pack things used at the same time in the same pannier. Night/camp things like your mat, sleeping bag and pyjamas, which you don't need during the day, could all be in the bag most difficult to access – likely to be on the same side as the side of the road you are riding on, since you will probably lean that side of the bike against a tree, pole or roadside barrier.

Put all clothing in one pannier, if possible, sorted into separate bags of cycling clothes, 'civilian' clothes, underwear, wet weather gear and dirty clothes. Keep a windproof jacket handy on top for descents.

In the Front Food and eating utensils are convenient to have in a front pannier along with a camping stove. Toiletry items, towel, first-aid kit, reading material, torch and sundry items can go in the other front bag.

In the Pockets or Bar Bag Easily accessible pockets on panniers or on your cycling shirt are useful for items likely to be needed frequently or urgently during the day, such as snacks, tool kit, sun hat or sunscreen. A handlebar bag is good for these items if your panniers don't have pockets, but remember that weight on the handlebars upsets a bike's handling.

Keep Space Spare Remember to leave some spare space for food and, if using a camping stove, for the fuel canister. Be mindful when packing foods that are squashable or sensitive to heat and protect or insulate them – unless you're working on a gourmet pasta sauce recipe that includes socks.

ANOTHER OPTION – TRAILERS

Luggage trailers are gaining in popularity and some innovative designs are now on the market. By spreading the load onto more wheels they relieve the bike and can improve rolling resistance. Their extra capacity is a boon for travelling on a tandem or with a young family. They can be combined with racks and panniers, but the hitch (point it connects with the bike) of some trailers may interfere with your panniers, so check first.

PHOTO BY PETER HINES

Two-wheeled trailers are free standing and can take very heavy loads, including babies and toddlers. Often brightly coloured, they give a strong signal to car drivers who tend to give you a wide berth. However, their relatively wide track can catch a lot of wind and makes them ungainly on rough, narrow roads or trails. Single-wheeled trailers such as the BOB Yak share the load with the bike's rear wheel.

They track well and can be used on very rough trails and may be the easiest option for full-suspension bikes. The load capacity of these units is somewhere between that of a bike with a rear rack only and a fully loaded (four panniers plus rack-top luggage) touring bike.

YOUR BICYCLE

Prevent 'Internal Bleeding' Act on the premise that anything that can spill will, and transfer it to a reliable container, preferably within a watertight bag. Take care, too, in packing hard or sharp objects (tools, utensils or anything with hooks) that could rub or puncture other items, including the panniers. Knives or tools with folding working parts are desirable.

Fragile Goods Valuables and delicate equipment such as cameras are best carried in a handlebar bag, which can be easily removed when you stop. Alternatively, carry these items in a 'bum bag', which will accompany you automatically.

Rack Top Strap your tent lengthways on top of the rear rack with elastic cord looped diagonally across from front to rear and back again, and maybe across to anchor the rear end. Be sure the cord is well tensioned and secure – deny its kamikaze impulses to plunge into the back wheel, jamming the freewheel mechanism, or worse.

WHAT TO LOOK FOR IN PANNIERS

Panniers remain the popular choice for touring luggage. They offer flexibility, in that one, two or four can be used depending on the load to be carried and they allow luggage to be arranged for easy access.

Many people initially buy just a rear rack and panniers, and it is wise to buy the best quality you can afford at this stage. These bags will accompany you on all of your tours as well as for day-to-day shopping and commuting trips for years to come. The attachment system should be secure, but simple to operate. That big bump you hit at 50km/h can launch a poorly designed pannier and your precious luggage.

The stiffness of the pannier backing is another concern – if it can flex far enough to reach the spokes of the wheel the result can be catastrophic. Good rack design can also help avoid this. The fabric of the panniers should be strong and abrasion- and water-resistant. You can now buy roll-top panniers, made from laminated fabrics, that are completely waterproof. Bear in mind that these bags are only waterproof until they develop even the smallest hole, so be prepared to check them and apply patches occasionally. Canvas bags shed water well, but should be used in conjunction with a liner bag to keep things dry. Cordura is a heavy nylon fabric with excellent abrasion resistance. The fabric itself is initially waterproof, but water tends to find the seams, so using a liner bag is a good idea once again.

Pockets and compartments can help to organise your load, but the multitude of seams increase the challenge of keeping the contents dry in the wet. A couple of exterior pockets are great for sunscreen, snacks and loose change that you need throughout the day. Carrying front panniers as well as rear ones allows more opportunities to divide and organise gear. When fitting rear panniers check for heel strike. Long feet, long cranks and short chainstays will all make it harder to get the bags and your body to fit.

Health & Safety

Britain is a pretty safe, healthy place to travel. There are no exotic diseases to worry about and the National Health Service (NHS) provides free at the point of delivery health care, which is a lot more than you'll get in most countries.

BEFORE YOU GO

HEALTH INSURANCE

European Economic Area (EEA) nationals can obtain free emergency treatment in Britain on presentation of a European Health Insurance Card (EHIC) – which has replaced the old E111 form – validated in their home country. Reciprocal agreements between the UK and some other countries (including Australia) allow their residents to receive free emergency medical treatment and subsidised dental care. For details see the Department of Health website www.doh.gov.uk. Regardless of nationality anyone will receive free emergency treatment at A&E departments of NHS hospitals. Travel insurance however, offers greater flexibility over where and how you're treated and covers emergency repatriation.

FIRST AID

It's a good idea to know what to do in the event of a major accident or illness, especially if you're intending to ride off-road in a remote area. Consider learning basic first aid, and carrying a first aid manual and small medical kit.

PHYSICAL FITNESS

Most of the rides in this book are designed for someone with a moderate degree of cycling fitness. It pays to spend time preparing yourself physically before you set out. Depending on your existing level of fitness, you should start training a couple of months before your trip. Try to ride at least three times a week, starting with easy rides (even 3 miles to work, if you're not already cycling regularly) and gradually building up to longer distances. Once you have a good base of regular riding behind you, include hills in your training and familiarise yourself with the gearing on your bike. Before you go you should have done at least one 35 miles(60km) to 45 miles (70km) ride with loaded panniers.

FIRST-AID KIT

In addition to your usual first-aid kit supplies consider taking the following for cycling trips:

- butterfly closure strips
- elastic support bandage for knees, ankles etc
- gauze swabs
- latex gloves
- non-adhesive dressings
- scissors (small pair)
- sterile alcohol wipes
- syringes & needles – for removing gravel from road-rash wounds
- tweezers
- antiseptic powder or solution (such as povidone-iodine) and antiseptic wipes for cuts and grazes

---

GETTING FIT FOR TOURING

Ideally, a training programme should be tailored to your objectives, specific needs, fitness level and health. Things to think about include:

Foundation Always start out with easy rides and give yourself plenty of time to build towards your objective.

Tailoring Once you have the general condition to start preparing for your trip, work out how to tailor your training rides to the type of tour you are planning. Consider ride length, terrain, climate and weight to be carried in panniers.

Recovery Make sure you're getting quality sleep, eating an adequate diet, doing recovery rides between hard days (using low gears to avoid pushing yourself), and stretching.

If you have no cycling background the program below will help you get fit for your cycling holiday. If you are doing an easy ride (each ride in this book is rated; see p16), aim to at least complete Week 4; for moderate rides, complete Week 6; and complete the entire program if you are doing a hard ride. Experienced cycle tourists could start at Week 3, while those who regularly ride up to four days a week could start at Week 5.

	Monday	Tuesday	Wednesday	Thursday	Friday	Saturday	Sunday
Week 1	6mi*	–	6mi*	–	6mi*	–	6mi*
Week 2	–	9mi*	–	9mi*	–	12mi*	–
Week 3	12mi*	–	12mi†	15mi*	–	15mi*	12mi†
Week 4	–	20mi*	–	22mi*	20mi†	20mi*	–
Week 5	20mi*	–	25mi†	–	22mi*	–	25mi†
Week 6	20mi*	–	25mi†	–	–	40mi*	25mi†
Week 7	20mi*	–	25mi†	–	20mi†	45mi*	20mi*
Week 8	–	40mi*	20mi†	–	25mi†	45km*	55mi*

* steady pace (allows you to carry out a conversation without losing your breath) on flat or undulating terrain

† solid pace (allows you to talk in short sentences only) on undulating roads with some longer hills

The training program shown here is only a guide. Ultimately it is important to listen to your body, slow down, take recovery days and cut back distances if you're tired. The most important thing is to ride regularly and gradually increase the length of your rides.

Kevin Tabotta

STAYING HEALTHY

The best way to have a lousy holiday (especially if you're relying on self-propulsion) is to become ill. Heed the following simple advice and the only thing you're likely to suffer from is that rewarding tiredness at the end of a full day.

HYDRATION

Don't underestimate the amount of fluid you need to replace as your ride – particularly in warmer weather. The magic figure is supposedly 0.2 gallons (1L) per hour, though many cyclists have trouble consuming this much. Sipping little and often is the key; try to drink a mouthful every 10 minutes and don't wait until you get thirsty. Keep drinking before and after the day's ride to replenish fluid.

Use the colour of your urine as a rough guide to whether you are drinking enough. Small amounts of dark urine suggest you need to increase your fluid intake. Passing reasonable quantities of light yellow urine indicates that you've got the balance about right. For more information on the effects of dehydration, see p393.

Water

Tap water is safe to drink in Britain and if you're camping in remote areas your best bet is to fill up your water bottles at cafes or pubs en route. If you do have to purify water in remote areas the simplest way is to boil it vigorously for five minutes.

Sports Drinks

Commercial sports drinks such as Gatorade and PowerAde are an excellent way to satisfy your hydration needs, electrolyte replacement and energy demands in one but make sure you drink plenty of water as well.

NUTRITION

Cycle touring puts great demands on your body, so it's important to eat well. The main part of your diet should be carbohydrates rather than proteins or fats. While some protein (for tissue maintenance and repair) and fat (for vitamins, long-term energy and warmth) is essential, carbohydrates provide the most efficient fuel. They are easily digested into simple sugars, which are then used in energy production. Less-refined foods like pasta, rice, bread, fruits and vegetables are all high in carbohydrates.

AVOIDING CYCLING AILMENTS

Many cycling ailments stem from an incorrectly adjusted bike. For more information on adjusting your bike for greater comfort see p370.

Saddle Sores & Blisters

While you're more likely to get a sore butt if you're out of condition, riding long distances does take its toll on your behind. To minimise the impact, always wear padded bike shorts, shower as soon as you stop and put on clean, preferably non-synthetic, clothes. Guard against chafing by liberally applying moisturising or baby nappy rash cream around the crotch area before riding. If you do suffer from chafing, wash and dry the area and carefully apply a barrier (moisturising) cream.

Knee Pain

Knee pain is common among cyclists who pedal in too high a gear. It's more efficient (and better for your knees) to use a low

---

AVOIDING THE BONK

The bonk, in a cycling context, is not a pleasant experience; it's that light-headed, can't-put-power-to-the-pedals, weak feeling that engulfs you when your body runs out of fuel.

If you experience it the best move is to stop and refuel immediately. It can be quite serious if it's not addressed as soon as symptoms occur. To avoid the bonk base your meals around carbohydrates and maintain your fuel intake while riding.

Good on-bike cycling foods include:

- bananas (in particular) and other fruits
- bread with jam or honey
- breakfast and muesli bars
- rice-based snacks
- pre-packaged high-carbohydrate sports bars (eg, PowerBar)
- sports drinks.

---

enough gear so you can pedal quickly with little resistance. For touring, the ideal cadence (the number of pedal strokes per minute) ranges from 70 to 90. Try to maintain this cadence even when you're climbing. You can also get sore knees if your saddle is too low, or if your shoe cleats are incorrectly positioned.

Numbness & Backache

Pain in the hands, neck and shoulders is a common complaint, generally caused by leaning too much on your hands. Apart from discomfort, you can temporarily damage the nerves and experience numbness or mild paralysis of the hands. Prevent it by wearing padded gloves, cycling with less weight on your hands and changing your hand position frequently. If you're carrying too much weight on your hands either raise the height of your handlebars or, if you are stretched out too much, fit a smaller stem.

Fungal Infections

Warm, sweaty bodies are ideal environments for fungal growth. To prevent fungal infections, wash frequently and dry yourself carefully. Change out of sweaty bike clothes as soon as possible. The most common infections are athlete's foot (tinea) between

STRETCHING

Stretching is important when stepping up your exercise levels: it improves muscle flexibility, which allows freer movement in the joints; and prevents the rigidity developing in muscles that occurs through prolonged cycling activity.

Ideally, you should stretch for 10 minutes before and after riding and for longer periods (15 to 30 minutes) every second day.

You should follow a few basic guidelines:

- before stretching, warm up for 5 to 10 minutes by going for a gentle bike ride, jog or brisk walk
- ensure you follow correct technique
- hold a stretch for 15 to 30 seconds
- stretch to the point of discomfort, not pain
- breathe freely and try to relax your body
- don't 'bounce' the stretch
- repeat each stretch three times
- do not stretch when you have an injury to that area.

The main muscle groups for the cyclist to stretch are: quadriceps, calves, hamstrings, lower back and neck.

QUADRICEPS

Facing a wall with your feet slightly apart, grip one foot with your hand and pull it towards the buttocks. Ensure the back and hips are square. To get a better stretch, push the hip forward. You should never feel pain at the knee joint. Hold the stretch, before lowering the leg and repeating the stretch with the other leg.

CALF

Stand facing a wall, placing one foot about 30cm in front of the other. Keep the heels flat on the ground and bend the front leg slowly toward the wall – the stretch should be in the upper-calf area of the back leg. Keep the back straight and bend your elbows to allow your body to move forward during the stretch. Hold the stretch; relax and repeat the stretch with the other leg.

HAMSTRINGS

Sit with one leg extended and the other leg bent with the bottom of the foot against the inside of the extended leg. Slide your arms down the extended leg – bending from the waist – until you feel a pull in the hamstring area. Hold it for 15 seconds, before returning to the start position. Keep the toes pointed up; avoid hunching the back.

LOWER-BACK ROLL

Lie on your back (on a towel or sleeping mat) and bring both knees up until you feel a stretch in the lower back. Hold the stretch for 30 seconds; relax.

'CAT STRETCH' HUNCH

Another stretch for the lower back. Move to the ground on all fours (hands shoulder-width apart; legs slightly apart), lift the hips and lower back towards the sky until you feel a stretch. Hold it for 15 seconds; return to start position.

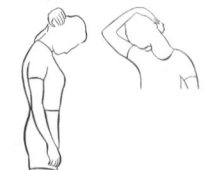

NECK

Gently and smoothly stretch your neck each of the four ways: forward, back and side to side. Do each stretch separately. (Do not rotate the head in a full circle.) For the side stretches, use your hand to pull the head very gently in the direction of the stretch.

the toes or fingers, and infections on the scalp, in the groin or on the body.

If you do get an infection, wash the infected area at least daily with a disinfectant or medicated soap and water, and rinse and dry well. Apply an antifungal cream or powder like tolnaftate. Expose the infected area to air or sunlight as much as possible, avoid artificial fibres and wash all towels and underwear in hot water, change them often and let them dry in the sun.

Staying Warm
Except on extremely hot days, put on another layer of clothing when you stop cycling – even if it's just for a quick break. Your body cools down quickly after you stop working, particularly in wet or sweaty clothing. Muscle strains occur more easily when your body is chilled. Always be prepared for Britain's unpredictable weather with warm clothing and a waterproof layer.

MEDICAL PROBLEMS & TREATMENT

ENVIRONMENTAL HAZARDS
Sun
Despite Britain's unreliable weather you can get sunburnt quite quickly, even on cool or cloudy days, especially during spring and summer and at higher altitudes. Take sun protection seriously: cover up, use high protection sunscreen, wear good sunglasses and sit in the shade during rest breaks.

Heat
DEHYDRATION & HEAT EXHAUSTION
Dehydration is a potentially dangerous and easily preventable condition caused by excessive fluid loss. The first symptoms are weakness, thirst and passing small amounts of very concentrated urine. This may progress to drowsiness, dizziness or fainting when standing up and, finally, coma.

It's easy to forget how much fluid you are losing via perspiration while you are cycling. Make sure you drink sufficient liquids and avoid caffeinated drinks such as coffee, tea and some soft drinks.

Dehydration and salt deficiency can cause heat exhaustion. Salt deficiency is characterised by fatigue, lethargy, headaches, giddiness and muscle cramps; salt tablets may help, but adding extra salt to your food is probably sufficient.

If one of your party suffers from heat exhaustion, lie the casualty down in a shady spot and encourage them to drink slowly but frequently.

HEATSTROKE
Heatstroke can occur if the body's heat-regulating mechanism breaks down and the body temperature rises to dangerous levels. Symptoms include feeling unwell, not sweating very much and a high body temperature (39°C to 41°C or 102°F to 106°F). Severe, throbbing headaches and lack of coordination will also occur, and the sufferer may be confused or aggressive. Hospitalisation is essential, but in the interim get the casualty out of the sun, remove their clothing, cover them with a wet sheet or towel and then fan continuously. Give them plenty of cool water, if conscious.

Cold
HYPOTHERMIA
Hypothermia occurs when the body loses heat faster than it can produce it and the core temperature of the body falls. Symptoms include exhaustion, numb skin, shivering, slurred speech, irrational or violent behaviour, lethargy, stumbling, dizzy spells, muscle cramps and powerful bursts of energy.

To prevent hypothermia, dress in layers, protect yourself against wind, particularly for long descents, eat plenty of high-energy food and keep drinking.

To treat mild hypothermia, find shelter, remove wet clothing and replace it with dry, warm clothing. Give the victim hot liquids – not alcohol – and some high-kilojoule, easily digestible food. Do not rub victims. Early recognition and treatment of mild hypothermia is the only way to prevent severe hypothermia, a critical condition.

INFECTIOUS DISEASES
Diarrhoea
Serious diarrhoea is caused by infectious agents transmitted by faecal contamination. Paying particular attention to personal hy-

giene, drinking purified water and taking care of what you eat are important measures to take to avoid getting diarrhoea while touring.

Dehydration is the main danger with any diarrhoea, particularly in children or the elderly, as it can occur quickly. Under all circumstances, the most important thing is to replace fluids (at least equal to the volume being lost). If you have small amounts of dark-coloured urine, you need to drink more. With severe diarrhoea use a rehydrating solution to replace lost minerals and salts. In an emergency, make a solution of six teaspoons of sugar and a half teaspoon of salt in a litre of boiled or bottled water. Keep drinking small amounts often. Seek medical advice if you pass blood or mucus, are feverish or suffer persistent or severe diarrhoea.

Another cause of persistent diarrhoea in travellers is giardiasis.

Giardiasis

This intestinal disorder is contracted by drinking water contaminated with the giardia parasite. The symptoms are stomach cramps, nausea, a bloated stomach, watery and foul-smelling diarrhoea, and frequent gas. Giardiasis can appear several weeks after you have been exposed to the parasite. The symptoms may disappear for a few days and then return; this can go on for several weeks. Seek medical advice if you think you have giardiasis.

Tetanus

Breaks in the skin leave you vulnerable to a tetanus infection. Symptoms include discomfort in swallowing, or stiffening of the jaw and neck; followed by painful convulsions of the jaw and whole body. The disease can be fatal but can be prevented by vaccination.

TRAUMATIC INJURIES

Unless you're an experienced first-aider it's possible to do more harm than good when treating injuries. Always seek medical help if it is available, but if you are far from any help, follow these guidelines.

Cuts & Other Wounds

Small wounds can be cleaned with an antiseptic wipe (only wipe across the wound once with each). Deep or dirty wounds need to be cleaned thoroughly:

- Clean your hands.
- Wear gloves if you are cleaning somebody else's wound.
- Use bottled or cooled boiled water or an antiseptic solution like povidone-iodine.
- Flush the wound with plenty of water.
- Embedded dirt or gravel can be removed with tweezers or flushed out using a syringe.
- Dry wounds heal best: avoid using antiseptic creams; instead apply antiseptic powder or spray.
- Dry the wound with clean gauze before applying a dressing.
- Change the dressing each day and watch for signs of infection.
- Raise the affected limb to reduce swelling.
- Get a tetanus injection if yours is not up to date.
- Seek medical advice for any wound that fails to heal after a week.

Major Accident

If a major accident does occur you need to be prepared to do at least an initial assessment and to ensure that the casualty comes to no further harm. First of all, check for danger to yourself. If the casualty is on the

---

BLEEDING WOUNDS

To stop bleeding from a wound:

- Wear gloves if you are dealing with a wound on another person.
- Lie the casualty down if possible.
- Raise the injured limb above the level of the casualty's heart.
- Use your fingers or the palm of your hand to apply direct pressure to the wound, preferably over a sterile dressing or clean pad.
- Apply steady pressure for at least five minutes before looking to see if the bleeding has stopped.
- Put a sterile dressing over the original pad (don't move this) and bandage it in place.
- Check the bandage regularly in case bleeding restarts.

TIPS FOR BETTER CYCLING

The following tips on riding technique are designed to help you ride more safely, comfortably and efficiently.

- Ride in bike lanes if they exist.
- Ride about 3ft from the kerb or from parked cars.
- Stay alert; constantly scan ahead and anticipate the movements of others.
- Keep your upper body relaxed.
- Don't weave across the road.
- To negotiate rough surfaces, take your weight off the saddle.

At Night

- Use a front and rear light and a reflective vest.

Braking

- Apply front and rear brakes evenly.

Climbing

- When climbing out of the saddle, keep the bike steady.
- Use your gears to keep your legs 'spinning'.

Cornering

- Loaded bikes are prone to sliding out in corners: approach slowly.
- If traffic permits, hit the corner wide, cut across the apex and ride out of it wide – but never cross the dividing line on the road.
- Apply the brakes before the corner.

Descending

- Stay relaxed, let your body go with the bike.
- Be aware that a loaded bike is harder to control at speed.
- Pump the brakes to shed speed.

Gravel Roads

- Avoid patches of deep gravel.
- Avoid sudden turning and take it slowly on descents.
- Brake in a straight line using your rear brake.
- On loose gravel, loosen your toe-clip straps or clipless pedals so you can put your foot down quickly.

Group Riding

- Keep your actions predictable and let others know before you brake, turn, dodge potholes etc.
- Don't overlap the wheels of fellow cyclists.
- Ride in single file on busy, narrow or winding roads.

In Traffic

- Obey the rules of the road
- Scan for trouble: look inside the back windows of parked cars for movement – that person may open the door on you.
- Look drivers in the eye; make sure they've seen you.

In the Wet

- Be aware that you'll take longer to slow down with wet rims.
- On descents apply the brakes lightly to keep the rims free of grit/water etc and encourage quicker stopping.
- Don't climb out of the saddle; shift down a gear or two and climb seated.

HEALTH & SAFETY

road ensure oncoming traffic is stopped or diverted around you. A basic plan of action is:

○ Keep calm.
○ Get medical help urgently; phone ☎ 999/911.
○ Carefully look over the casualty in the position in which you found them.
○ Check for a response from the casualty.
○ Check for pulse, breathing and major blood loss.
○ If necessary, and you know how, start resuscitation.
○ Check the casualty for injuries, moving them as little as possible; ask them where they have pain if they are conscious.
○ Don't move the casualty if a spinal injury is possible.
○ Control any obvious bleeding by applying direct pressure to the wound.
○ Make the casualty as comfortable as possible and reassure them.
○ Keep the casualty warm.

SAFETY ON THE BIKE

ROAD RULES

A foreign driving licence is valid in Britain for up to 12 months. If you plan to bring a car from Europe, it's illegal to drive without (at least) third-party insurance. Some other important rules:

○ drive on the left (!)
○ wear fitted seat belts in cars
○ give way to your right at junctions and roundabouts
○ always use the left-side lane on motorways and dual-carriageways, unless overtaking
○ don't use a mobile phone while driving unless it's fully hands-free.

Additionally cyclists should:

○ use a white front and red rear light at night
○ ensure a red rear reflector is fitted to their bike
○ not cycle more than two abreast
○ ride in single file on narrow or winding roads.

Speed limits are 30mph (48km/h) in built-up areas, 60mph (96km/h) on main roads and 70mph (112km/h) on motorways and most (but not all) dual carriageways. Drinking and driving is taken very seriously; you're allowed a blood-alcohol level of 80mg/100mL and campaigners want it reduced to 50mg/100mL.

All drivers should read the Highway Code (www.direct.gov.uk/en/TravelAndTransport/Highwaycode).

EMERGENCY PROCEDURES

Use the following basic guidelines in case of emergency:

○ Use your first aid knowledge and experience to make a medical assessment of the situation.
○ If possible leave one person with the casualty while others go for help.
○ If you leave someone, mark their position carefully on your map and mark their position on the ground with something conspicuous.
○ Attract attention with a whistle or torch, a smoky fire or by waving bright clothing; shouting is tiring and not very effective.

EMERGENCY NUMBERS

In the case of an emergency call ☎ 999

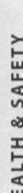

Glossary

A

afon – river (Wales)
almshouse – accommodation for the aged or needy
AONB – Area of Outstanding Natural Beauty
ATM – automatic teller machine
AUK – Audax UK, body that promotes non-competitive long distance cycling
auld – old (Scotland)
aye – yes; always (Scotland)

B

B&BRP – Bristol and Bath Railway Path
BABA – Book-A-Bed-Ahead scheme
bag – reach the top of (as in 'to bag a couple of peaks')
bailey – outermost wall of a castle
bairn – baby (Newcastle & Scotland)
banger – old, cheap car
bangers – sausages
bap – bun (northern England)
barrow – see tumulus
BCF – British Cycling Federation
ben – mountain (Scotland)
bent – not altogether legal
bevvy – a drink (originally northern England)
billion – a million million (not a thousand million)
biscuit – cookie
bitter – beer
black pudding – a type of sausage made from dried blood
bloke – man (colloquial)
BOATS – Byways Open to All Traffic, legal for cycling
bodge job – poor-quality repairs
bothy – hut or mountain shelter (Scotland)
bridleway – path that can be used by walkers, horse riders and cyclists
Brummie – native of Birmingham
BTA – British Tourist Authority
bus – local bus; see also coach

C

C2C – Sea to Sea ride
Cadw – Welsh Historic Monuments agency
caff – cheap cafe
capel – chapel (Wales)
car bonnet – hood
car boot – trunk
carry-out – takeaway (Scotland)
cashpoint – automatic teller machine; ATM
CCW – Countryside Council for Wales
ceilidh – (pronounced 'kaylee') informal evening entertainment and dance (Scotland)
cheers – goodbye
chemist – pharmacist
chips – French fries
clogwyn – cliff (Wales)
clun – meadow (Wales)
coach – long-distance bus; see also bus
couchette – sleeping berth in a train or ferry
crack – good conversation, good times (anglicised version of Gaelic 'craic')
crannog – artificial island settlement
cream tea – afternoon tea typically including scones with jam and cream
crisps – potato chips
croft – plot of land with adjoining house worked by the occupiers
crofting – subsistence farming
cromlech – burial chamber (Wales)
CTC – Cyclists' Touring Club

D

dear – expensive
din (dinas) – fort (Wales)
dolmen – chartered tomb
dosh/dough – money
downs – rolling upland, characterised by lack of trees
dram – measure of whisky
duvet – quilt replacing sheets and blankets ('doona' to Australians)

E

EH – English Heritage (organisation)
eisteddfod – festival in which competitions are held in music, poetry, drama and the fine arts (Wales)
EN – English Nature
ESA – Environmentally Sensitive Area

Essex – derogatory adjective, as in 'Essex girl', meaning 'tarty'
EU – European Union
evensong – daily evening service (Church of England)

F

fag – cigarette; also a boring task (colloquial)
fagged – exhausted
fanny – female genitals (not backside; offensive slang)
FC – Forestry Commission
fell – hill or section of upland moor (northern England and Scotland)
fen – drained or marshy low-lying flat land
firth – estuary (Scotland)
fiver – five-pound note
flat – apartment
FNR – Forest Nature Reserve
footpath – sidewalk on which cycling is not permitted

G

gaffer – boss or foreman
glen – valley (Scotland)
glyn – valley (Wales)
grand – one thousand (colloquial)
greasy spoon – cheap cafe
gutted – very disappointed
guv, guvner – from governor, a respectful term of address for owner or boss, can be used ironically

H

haar – fog off the North Sea (Scotland)
hammered – drunk (northern England)
HI – Hostelling International
High Street – British term for main street
Highland Clearances – Period in the 19th century where Highlanders were forced off their land by the English government to make way for sheep farming
Hogmanay – New Year's Eve (Scotland)
HS – Historic Scotland
Huguenots – French Protestants

I

inn – pub with accommodation

J

jam – fruit conserve often spread on bread
jelly – sweet desert of flavoured gelatine
jumper – sweater

K

karst – landscape usually featuring limestone rock, caves, sinkholes and a lack of surface water
keep – main tower within the walls of a medieval castle or fortress
kippers – salted and smoked fish, traditionally herring
ken – know (Scotland)
kirk – church (Scotland)
kyle – narrow strait

L

lager lout – see yob
laird – estate owner (Scotland)
lands – multistorey apartment buildings (Scotland)
lift – elevator
links – golf course (Scotland)
llyn – lake (Wales)
loch – lake (Scotland)
lock – part of a canal or river that can be closed off and the water levels changed to raise or lower boats
lolly – money; also boiled sweet, toffee or candy on a stick (possibly frozen)
lorry – truck

M

mad – insane, not angry
Martello tower – small, circular tower used for coastal defence
mate – a friend of any sex; also a term of address for males
mere – marsh, lake
midge – a mosquito-like insect
moor – exposed upland, usually heath-covered
moss – marsh, peat bog (northern England and Scotland)
motorway – freeway
motte – mound on which a castle was built
MTB – mountain bike
Munro – mountain of 3000ft or higher (Scotland)

N

nappies – diapers
NCN – National Cycle Network
neeps – turnips (Scotland)
NNR – National Nature Reserve
NSA – National Scenic Area (Scotland)
NT – National Trust, see Useful Organisations in the Facts for the Cyclist chapter
NTS – National Trust for Scotland

O

oast house – building containing a kiln for drying hops
off-licence (offie) – carry-out alcoholic drinks shop
OS – Ordnance Survey

P

pete – fortified houses
Pict – early Celtic inhabitants (from the Latin 'pictus', meaning painted, after their body paint decorations)
pint – beer
pissed – drunk (not angry)
pissed off – angry
pitch – playing field; also campsite
plas – hall/mansion (Wales)
ponce – ostentatious or effeminate male; also to borrow (usually permanently)
pop – fizzy drink (northern England)
postbuses – minibuses that follow postal delivery routes
pub – short for 'public house'; a bar usually with food, sometimes with accommodation
punter – customer

Q

quid – pound (colloquial)

R

rail trail – disused railway line converted for walking and cycling
ramble – to go for a short walk
roll-up – roll-your-own cigarette
rood – alternative word for crucifix, especially one at the entrance to a church
RSA – Royal Scottish Academy
RSPB – Royal Society for the Protection of Birds
rubber – eraser
rubbish bin – garbage can
rugger – rugby
RUPPS – Roads Used as Public Paths, legal for cycling

S

sacked – fired
Sassenach – an English person or a lowland Scot (Scotland)
sett – tartan pattern
shag – have sex (slang); also a tough or tiring task (colloquial)
shagged – tired (colloquial)
shout – to buy a group of people drinks, usually reciprocated

SNH – Scottish National Heritage
snogging – kissing
spondoolicks – money
sporran – purse (Scotland)
SSSI – Site of Special Scientific Interest
STB – Scottish Tourist Board
subway – underpass
sweet – candy
SYHA – Scottish Youth Hostel Association

T

ta – thanks
takeaway – takeout or carry-out food
TIC – Tourist Information Centre
toastie – toasted sandwich (Scotland)
TOC – train operating company
ton – one hundred
tor – Celtic word describing a high hill (often shaped like a wedge)
torch – flashlight
towpath – a path running beside a river or canal
traveller – nomadic person (traditional and New Age hippy types)
tube – the London Underground railway (subway)
tumulus – a heap of earth placed over one or more prehistoric tombs; also barrow
twitchers – bird-watchers

U

UCR – unclassified country road; legal for cycling
uisge-bha – the water of life: whisky (Scotland)
Underground, the – London's underground railway system

V

VAT – value-added tax, levied on most goods and services, currently 17.5%
verderer – officer upholding law and order in the royal forests

W

way – a long-distance trail
wide boy – ostentatious go-getter, usually chasing women
wold – open, rolling country
WTB – Wales Tourist Board

Y

YHA – Youth Hostel Association (England and Wales)
yob – hooligan; also lager lout

Behind the Scenes

THIS BOOK

This guidebook was commissioned in Lonely Planet's Melbourne office, and produced by the following:

Publisher Chris Rennie
Associate Publisher Ben Handicott
Commissioning Editor Bridget Blair, Janine Eberle
Coordinating Cartographer Peter Shields
Managing Cartographer David Connolly
Cover Designer Mary Nelson Parker
Cover Layout Designer Indra Kilfoyle
Project Manager Jane Atkin
Thanks to Lucy Birchley, Rebecca Dandens, Wayne Murphy, Darren O'Connell, Julie Sheridan, Simon Tillema
Production [recapture]

ACKNOWLEDGMENTS

Internal photographs by Rey Rojo/iStockphoto p4 (#2); Jonathan Ling/iStockphoto p4 (#3). All other photographs by Lonely Planet Images, and by Doug McKinlay p2 (#1), p12; Judy Bellah p2 (#2); Dennis Johnson p3 (#1); Anders Blomqvist p3 (#3); Wayne Walton p4 (#4); David Tomlinson p5 (#1); David Else p6 (#1), p8 (#2); Chris Mellor p6 (#2), p9 (#1, #2); Glenn Beanland p6 (#3); Barbara Van Zanten p7 (#4); Nicholas Reuss p8 (#3); Trevor Creighton p10 (#4); Martin Moos p10 (#3); Izzet Keribar p10 (#1); Gareth McCormack p11 (#2).

All images are the copyright of the photographers unless otherwise indicated. Many of the images in this guide are available for licensing from Lonely Planet Images: www.lonelyplanetimages.com.

THANKS
Marc Di Duca

Many thanks to Bridget Blair for entrusting me with Cycling Britain, and to Janine Eberle for her expert guidance and support throughout. I am also indebted to my fellow authors for their advice and wisdom in all matters bike.

Big thanks also go to Gemma and Dave Allerton for their invaluable assistance in Norfolk; to staff at tourist offices around the UK, specifically in Bedford, Bellingham, Wooler, Edinburgh, Stamford and Oundle; to Evo Bikes of Oban; to everyone at Sustrans and the CTC for their hard work and expert advice (what would we do without you guys?); to all at the End to End Club; to Scott Kennedy for his expertise; to Cycles UK of Canterbury for kitting me out; to the Greystoke Cycle Cafe' for just being

---

THE LONELY PLANET STORY

Fresh from an epic journey across Europe, Asia and Australia in 1972, Tony and Maureen Wheeler sat at their kitchen table stapling together notes. The first Lonely Planet guidebook, *Across Asia on the Cheap*, was born.

Travellers snapped up the guides. Inspired by their success, the Wheelers began publishing books to Southeast Asia, India and beyond. Demand was prodigious, and the Wheelers expanded the business rapidly to keep up. Over the years, Lonely Planet extended its coverage to every country and into the virtual world via lonelyplanet.com and the Thorn Tree message board.

As Lonely Planet became a globally loved brand, Tony and Maureen received several offers for the company. But it wasn't until 2007 that they found a partner whom they trusted to remain true to the company's principles of travelling widely, treading lightly and giving sustainably. In October of that year, BBC Worldwide acquired a 75% share in the company, pledging to uphold Lonely Planet's commitment to independent travel, trustworthy advice and editorial independence.

Today, Lonely Planet has offices in Melbourne, London and Oakland, with over 500 staff members and 300 authors. Tony and Maureen are still actively involved with Lonely Planet. They're travelling more often than ever, and they're devoting their spare time to charitable projects. And the company is still driven by the philosophy of *Across Asia on the Cheap*: 'All you've got to do is decide to go and the hardest part is over. So go!'

there for C2Cers; to my parents Paul and Jacqueline and to the British weather for holding good throughout the weeks of research. Finally a huge thanks to my wife Tanya for her support throughout the write-up and for all the days we spend apart.

Aaron Anderson

Big thanks to my Zimbabwean in-laws, Christian and Bernice Maenzanasie for all their on the ground help in England and their unwavering hospitality. To my wife, Becca, thank you for all the support and help. I'd also like to thank my boys: Eric Hoerske, Brian DeFouw, Jon van Spriell and Mike McClain for being a party of my wedding. To my Grandma Pauline and Uncle Joe, I love you and thank you for the support all these years, I couldn't have done it without either of you. And to my new family: David, Patricia, Jessica, Dennis, Regina, Vera, Lillie, Joe, Janette, Steve, Eric, Matt, Jenn and Denise, Spanky & Brittany, I love you guys, thank you for the warm welcome and wonderful wedding. Also props to all 18 tbs. At Lonely Planet: thanks to Janine Eberle for your patience and all the editors and cartos working on this project.

SEND US YOUR FEEDBACK

We love to hear from travellers – your comments keep us on our toes and help make our books better. Our well-travelled team reads every word on what you loved or loathed about this book. Although we cannot reply individually to postal submissions, we always guarantee that your feedback goes straight to the appropriate authors, in time for the next edition. Each person who sends us information is thanked in the next edition – and the most useful submissions are rewarded with a free book.

To send us your updates – and find out about Lonely Planet events, newsletters and travel news – visit our award-winning web-site: **lonelyplanet.com/contact.**

Note: we may edit, reproduce and incorporate your comments in Lonely Planet products such as guidebooks, websites and digital products, so let us know if you don't want your comments reproduced or your name acknowledged. For a copy of our privacy policy visit www.lonelyplanet.com/privacy.

Index

000 Map pages
000 Photograph pages

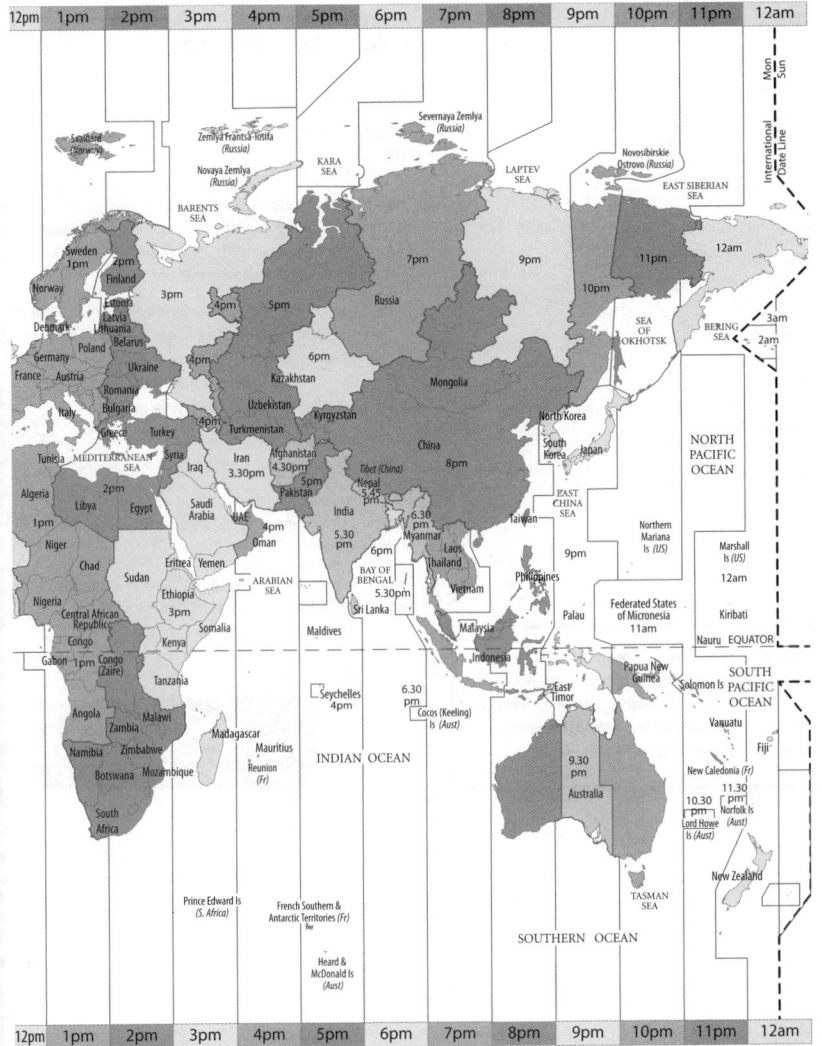

LONELY PLANET OFFICES

Australia
Head Office
Locked Bag 1, Footscray, Victoria 3011
☎ 03 8379 8000, fax 03 8379 8111
talk2us@lonelyplanet.com.au

USA
150 Linden St, Oakland, CA 94607
☎ 510 893 8556, toll free 800 275 8555
fax 510 893 8572
info@lonelyplanet.com

UK
2nd fl, 186 City Rd,
London EC1V 2NT
☎ 020 7106 2100, fax 020 7106 2101
go@lonelyplanet.co.uk

Although the authors and Lonely Planet have taken all reasonable care in preparing this book, we make no warranty about the accuracy or completeness of its content and, to the maximum extent permitted, disclaim all liability arising from its use.

PUBLISHED BY LONELY PLANET PUBLICATIONS PTY LTD

ABN 36 005 607 983

© Lonely Planet Publications Pty Ltd 2009

© photographers as indicated 2009

Cover photograph: Cover photograph: England, Cumbria, Lake District, stone wall in foreground, autumn, Chris Simpson/Getty Images. Many of the images in this guide are available for licensing from Lonely Planet Images: www.lonelyplanetimages.com

Printed through Colorcraft Ltd, Hong Kong.
Printed in China

Lonely Planet and the Lonely Planet logo are trademarks of Lonely Planet and are registered in the US Patent and Trademark Office and in other countries.

Lonely Planet does not allow its name or logo to be appropriated by commercial establishments, such as retailers, restaurants or hotels. Please let us know of any misuses: www.lonelyplanet.com/ip.

Mixed Sources
Product group from well-managed forests and other controlled sources
www.fsc.org Cert no. SGS-COC-005002
© 1996 Forest Stewardship Council
FSC